LIBERTY, JUSTICE, and MORALS

Contemporary Value Conflicts

LIBERTY, JUSTICE, and MORALS

Contemporary Value Conflicts

SECOND EDITION

Burton M. Leiser

MACMILLAN PUBLISHING CO., INC.
NEW YORK
COLLIER MACMILLAN PUBLISHERS
LONDON

Macmillan Publishing Co., Inc.
866 Third Avenue, New York, New York 10022

Collier-Macmillan Canada, Ltd.

Library of Congress Cataloging in Publication Data

Leiser, Burton M.
    Liberty, justice, and morals.

    Bibliography: p.
    Includes index.
    1. Law and ethics.   I. Title.
BJ55.L44   1979   340.1'12   78-9663
ISBN 0-02-369510-2

Printing: 2 3 4 5 6 7 8   Year: 9 0 1 2 3 4 5

To My Parents

Preface

The idea for this book originated in an experimental course, "Controversy," that I taught while I was a member of the Department of Philosophy at the State University of New York College at Buffalo. Without the constant encouragement of Professor Nicholas Fotion, who was then chairman of the department, and his defense of me and the course when it became the most controversial issue on campus, neither the course nor the book to which it has given rise would have seen the light of day.

I am deeply indebted to so many persons for their assistance, both direct and indirect, and for their comments, criticisms, and resources, that it is difficult to single out any for specific mention without running the danger of omitting some who might have made important contributions. But among those to whom I feel I have a special obligation are the following:

Professor Thomas T. Love, who read the first draft of the manuscript of the first edition with great care and offered hundreds of detailed criticisms and suggestions that were most helpful, both in terms of content and in matters of style.

Professors William Smith, George Sessions, James M. Smith, Victor Grassian, Guilbert DuMont, and John P. Clark, whose comments on the first edition were of invaluable assistance as I prepared the second.

Charles E. Smith, who first urged me to write this book, and Kenneth E. Scott, Ronald C. Harris, and Marge Flynn, whose careful editing has been enormously helpful.

My colleagues at Drake University, but especially Professors Francis M. Wilhoit, Donald R. Keyworth, Dale Miller, Kenneth E. Miller, David Robinson, William B. Bjornstad, Philip S. Riggs, Theodore A. Stroud, Joe D. Woods, Maurice La Belle, Peter Conrad, Joseph W. Schneider, Henry Borzo, Janet Johnson, and Jon Torgerson.

Colleagues at other institutions who have shared their thoughts and their still-unpublished articles with me, especially the late Professor William Blackstone, many of the members of Amintaphil, and Professors Richard Wasserstrom, Carl Cohen, Carl Wellman, Paul Edwards, Norman Bowie, Richard T. De George, Robert Friedlander, and Richard Van Iten.

My research assistants, Linda Johnson Hunter, Kenneth Grady, and Ralph

J. Schindler, who located materials that might otherwise have escaped my notice.

Mr. William Verberne of Wassenaar, The Netherlands, for his valuable assistance in my research on terrorism.

Mr. Kenneth MacQueen, who prepared the bibliography for the first edition, and Miss Susan Tabor and Mrs. Herman Hurowitz, who helped to bring it up to date for this edition.

The extraordinarily devoted and skillful staff at the Drake University libraries, but especially Dr. William A. Stoppel, Kaye Stoppel, J. Elias Jones, Patricia Dawson, Liga Briedis, and Ronni Begleiter.

Mrs. Rachel Buckles, who somehow managed to keep both her sanity and her sense of humor as she typed portions of this manuscript while meeting the needs of two very demanding departments.

Most of all, I owe a special debt of gratitude to my long-suffering children, Ellen, Shoshana, David, Susan, Illana, and Phillip, who have patiently foregone the attention I might otherwise have given them as I pursued my research; and my wife Barbara, whose commitment, dedication, solace, and advice were indispensable.

A word about gender: In deference to the sensitivity of some persons to gender distinctions in language, I hereby stipulate that unless the context clearly requires some other interpretation, the word "man" and masculine pronouns shall not have the slightest sexual connotation, but shall refer indifferently both to males and to females. In keeping with long-established English usage, and to avoid an endless and tiresome succession of such constructions as *he/she, he or she*, or others of more recent invention, I have employed masculine pronouns in a purely neutral sense. Because the suffix *-man* has no sexual connotations whatever, I have not replaced it with the colorless, overworked, and jarring barbarism, *-person*.

Contents

Introduction

The law is often thought of as being the guardian of our liberties, and rightly so. When it imposes a duty upon my neighbor to refrain from taking my life, it enables me to live in relative security, free from the fear that I may be murdered. When it imposes a duty upon me to refrain from interfering with my neighbor's business, or to refrain from discharging my employees because of their hair styles, my neighbor and my employees are assured of a degree of freedom that otherwise they might not have.

But law and liberty are opposites, in a sense, for where the law governs a given kind of behavior, people are no longer free to decide for themselves whether or not to engage in that form of behavior without the risk of possibly serious sanctions.

Nevertheless, imposing duties upon some men and restricting their liberties are the only ways to guarantee the freedom of others. So long as Lester Maddox was permitted to give axe handles to his customers to prevent blacks from entering his restaurant, black citizens were denied the liberty of eating at Lester Maddox's restaurant. If all the restaurant owners along the highway enjoyed the same liberty and exercised it as Lester Maddox did, all black citizens would have been denied the right to eat anywhere along the highway. Liberty for the restaurant owners was incompatible with liberty for black travelers. The latter could acquire the liberty to eat along the highway in Georgia only if Lester Maddox and other restaurant owners were deprived of their liberty to refuse to serve them. Indeed, without the sanction of law, even the liberties of some restaurant owners might not have been assured, for if a restaurant owner had wanted to serve black customers, he might have been unable to do so, prior to the enactment of the

1

Civil Rights Act, because informal community pressures might have been exerted to prevent him from deviating from the norm. Passing a law that obliges everyone to adhere to a given standard may enable some who were anxious to adhere to the standard but were unable to do so to act according to their will and be relieved of an undesirable restriction. For example, a manufacturer of paper may want to clean up his operation so as to reduce the pollution of the streams in the neighborhood but be unable to do so because of the economic advantage his competitors would derive if they were less concerned about the purity of the streams. By imposing the same standards upon all, the conservation-minded manufacturer acquires the freedom to do what he wants to do, though the others are deprived of the freedom they previously enjoyed to pollute the rivers without hindrance.

From these examples it is evident that justice may require restrictions upon the liberties of some persons, or of all persons, whereas extensions of liberty may entail a certain degree of injustice. It is not always clear, though, what injustice is. It is sometimes said that injustice consists of treating persons unequally, but what constitutes unequal treatment? Among all the applicants for a position as captain of an airliner, the employer ought to distinguish between those who know how to fly and those who do not, between those who are mentally stable and sober and those who give evidence of being unstable or alcoholic. Such positions certainly ought not to be handed out to applicants by drawing lots or by some other method that would give each applicant an "equal" status with every other. But justice may require that certain benefits be made available to all citizens, the only "qualification" being the fact that the individual is a human being.

It is sometimes thought that injustice is any act that deprives any person of his personal liberty, his property, or any other thing to which he is legally entitled. But as the case of Maddox's restaurant illustrates, the law may entitle one man to the right to deprive another of something that is very important to him, and that deprivation, though sanctioned by law, may nevertheless be unjust. It follows, therefore, that some lawful acts may be unjust, and that some forms of just behavior may be unlawful. Law, it seems, is not the final determinant of justice, though law and justice are clearly bound up with one another. When a law is unjust, we say that it violates human rights, or moral rights, the rights that we believe ought to be guaranteed to all persons, though in practice, they often are not.

Some laws prescribe sanctions—usually punishments—for forms of behavior of which the lawmakers disapprove. When a person is judged to have committed some wrong, or to have violated some duty or obligation, that judgment is often expressed as a desire or a wish that he be punished for his wrongful behavior. If his behavior is thought to be particularly reprehensible but is not legally punishable, people will often say, "There ought to be a law," meaning that they wish it would be possible to punish him for behaving in such a manner. Duty is a thing that can be, or that people think ought to be, exacted from the members of society. When there is a law, the duty it imposes usually can *be exacted by bringing the power of the state to bear upon the law violator.* When there is no law and people believe that a person is violating his moral duties or obligations, then they say that those duties or obligations ought to be enforceable, *that men ought to be* compelled *to behave in one way rather than in the other, and that they should* not be free *to behave wrongfully.*

On the other hand, those who believe that society's business should be to secure as much liberty for all as is possible, consistent with a reasonable degree of order and security, argue that the law should be limited in its scope and that the state should not be permitted to interfere in the private affairs of its citizens. They contend that morals are a private matter and are no affair of the state, that state interference in private affairs is in itself unjust, and that any laws that attempt to impose moral standards upon all citizens ought to be abolished so as to increase the scope of each citizen's personal liberties. They sometimes appeal to. the old cliché, "You can't legislate morality," by which they appear to mean either that such legislation is bound to prove ineffective, or that lawmakers should not attempt to impose moral restraints upon people through the power of legislation. It is obviously possible to legislate morality, since so much legislation is based upon ancient moral principles. The laws prohibiting murder, rape, fraud, theft, and robbery are clearly based upon ancient moral codes and religious beliefs, as are the rules providing for compensation for victims of accidental, negligent, or deliberate acts that result in damage to themselves or to their property. The laws governing marriage, divorce, and other family matters are clearly inspired by moral principles. Such elementary business transactions as the making of a contract, the honest weighing of a commodity, and the timely payment of a laborer for his services were all embodied in the moral-religious-legal codes of the Bible and the peoples of the ancient Middle East thousands of years ago. If the slogan, "You can't legislate morality," means that such legislation is bound to be ineffective, then it would be appropriate to demand some meaningful criterion by which one might determine whether a law was effective or not. Although no law is observed by all of the people all of the time, it is not unreasonable to suppose that many laws, at least, are observed more often than not, and that their existence tends, on the whole, to make life a little better and a little easier for most of the people most of the time. And if that is the case, then legislation inspired by or incorporating moral principles may well be justified on pragmatic, utilitarian, or other grounds. Laws are often passed because of the prevalence of practices that the people believe are intolerable abuses. The imposition of legal restraints upon persons who tend, in their absence, to cheat or defraud their customers or to harm innocent persons can be effective and help to make for a better society for all.

But there may be a sense in which the cliché is true—if it is interpreted to mean. that private acts between consenting adults that harm no one, or no one but themselves, and are regarded by many people as immoral should *not be restrained by criminal sanctions. Homosexual relations, prostitution, gambling, and the smoking of pot are considered by many thoughtful persons to be victimless crimes, for everyone involved in them participates voluntarily. By way of contrast, the victims of murder, rape, and fraud do not consent to be murdered, raped, or defrauded. This analysis may not be completely satisfactory, for there may be indirect victims of so-called victimless crimes, such as the children of the pathological gambler who are deprived of the amenities of life because their father gambles away his paycheck, or the taxpayers of a community who must support the family with welfare assistance. But if such subtleties are laid aside, at least provisionally, the distinction is an important one. In general, victimless crimes are* not *thought to be evil because of the harm they do to others, but because of the harm they do to their perpetrators or because they are thought to be* intrinsically *evil or vicious. The state becomes an agent in the enforcement of morals, pure and simple. It goes beyond its function of guarding the physical safety of its citizens and seeing that justice is done, and assumes in addition the paternalistic role of guardian of its citizens' moral and spiritual well-being. Those who advocate or support this role for the state sometimes argue by analogy: If we grant the state the power to control the food we eat in order to protect our physical health, we should give it the power to protect our moral or spiritual health, which is (so they say) far more important than mere physical well-being. If a state is founded upon certain moral principles, it may claim the right to prevent persons who do not accept those principles from destroying the moral qualities of the state through the expression of their own preferences and the development of a life-style that is inconsistent with the state's principles. In denying to its citizens the right to develop new life-styles, or to carry out ideas or fulfill desires that are new or different, the state may render itself incapable of carrying out its other functions. In its zeal to suppress immorality, the state and its agents may perpetrate grave injustices. When moral principles come into conflict with the principles of justice, all the elements of tragedy are present. The suppression of individual freedom goes hand in hand with the denial of equal rights and equal protection of the laws to all citizens. Some classes of citizens are singled out for special treatment. They are either accorded special favors or are subjected to harsher restrictions than others. From a zeal for morality arises a restriction of liberties, and such restrictions bring injustices in their train. The disappointment of what the oppressed consider to be their legitimate expectations through the enforcement of moral principles that are not universally accepted leads to resentment, anger, defiance, and in the end, to rebellion and revolution.*

Considering the practical consequences of the enforcement of morals and the punishment of those who commit victimless crimes, one man conclude that the evil effects of the laws outweigh the good that they are supposed to do. But other considerations may be sufficient to justify maintaining penal sanctions against those who violate moral rules that are considered to be fundamental. Where is the proper balance? Under what conditions is a state justified in interfering with its citizens' freedom of choice and of life-style in order to maintain certain moral standards? This is the problem posed in Part I of this book—the problem of the enforcement of morals, the wisdom of passing laws whose chief goal is the maintenance of the community's moral standards, at the expense of individual freedom, when violation of the norm itself causes no demonstrable harm to others.

If the enforcement of morals is problematic, it might be supposed that the enforcement of laws designed to protect citizens against harm that might be done to them by others would not be problematic at all. But this is not so. Some persons argue that punishment is an outmoded concept and that criminal penalties ought to be abolished in favor of some other form of treatment. Some writers have suggested that those who violate the law are unable to do otherwise and that to punish them is barbarous. Others are inclined to place the responsibility upon society as a whole. Because of its manifest injustices, they say, men and women who might otherwise be completely law-abiding are driven to criminal behavior and, because the fault is not theirs but society's, they should not bear the entire burden of responsibility by being punished for their acts. On the other hand, if justice is dependent upon the existence of sanctions, it is difficult to see how a just society can exist without some form of of social control embodying rewards or penalties. Even if enforcement of the criminal law by the imposition of penalties is accepted, the practical problem of the kind of penalty to be exacted of those who violate the law remains. From the harsh penalties of earlier days, many of which involved maiming or mutilating the convicted criminal, to modern prisons and such devices as parole, the indefinite sentence, and probation, it seems that no completely satisfactory treatment for those who are guilty of antisocial, destructive, or dangerous behavior has been found. Most difficult of all perhaps are the problems posed by the death penalty, which is unique in its severity and which many people feel should be maintained or reinstated because of its supposed deterrent effect, and those presented by the special case of the juvenile offender, who is thought to deserve some special considerations and methods of treatment. Part II is devoted to the general question of criminal punishment. In addition to chapters on the concept of punishment and the death penalty, the reader will find an extended discussion of the ultility and the morality of the penitentiary as a form of punishment.

The conflict between liberty and law, and between liberty and morals, goes beyond the criminal law. It extends into many other areas of our personal and communal lives and affects us in ways that go beyond the reach of the criminal law. Men and women hurt one another in many ways, not all of them amenable to rectification by legal means. One such area is illustrated in Part III, which is devoted to the morality of telling the truth and business ethics. The adman's freedom to distort the truth often results in a loss to the consumer when he or she buys the product. The physician's freedom to exercise his judgment as to whether to tell a dying patient the truth about his malady may deprive the latter of his right to die in dignity. But rigid adherence to the doctrine that the physician must always tell the truth might result in the untimely death of sensitive patients and unnecessary suffering for them and for their families. Should good or noble intentions excuse or justify distortions of the truth? The problems raised by the power of giant corporations are illustrated in the chapter on competition and corporate responsibility.

Finally, there exist some areas that have not yet been resolved by the institutional machinery of organized society, though they are very much concerned with the fundamental questions that law has always attempted to resolve. What is to be done when the law is evil, or seems to be so, or when the state commands its citizens to commit immoral or barbarous acts? The personal consequences of disobedience can be disastrous, but morality is not always predicted only upon the consequences to oneself. In Part IV the troublesome issues raised by those who advocate civil disobedience are discussed. If personal autonomy can be carried so far as to permit individuals to disobey the laws laid down by the representatives of the people, what justification can there be for punishing criminals for their allegedly antisocial behavior? And if the state is to be the final authority for determining the rightness and wrongness of its citizens' behavior, then what is to prevent national leaders from committing the gravest atrocities under the cloak of sovereignty, while those who assist them enjoy an immunity conferred upon them by the fact that they were acting in strict accordance with the laws of their own states, and that they should not be held liable by any other standard? Under what conditions, if ever, may a person properly violate the dictates of law? And under what conditions, if ever, should some higher law be invoked to punish those who have obeyed the laws of their own nations but have nevertheless violated fundamental moral precepts of mankind? The phenomenon of international terrorism has placed an extraordinary burden upon the legal apparatus of the state and the moral conscience of the people, for the terrorists themselves make moral claims in justification of their acts, which by any ordinary standard violate both legal and moral norms. And certain relatively new programs sponsored by the federal government in order to rectify old injustices are accused by some of perpetrating new ones. How can the requirements of social justice and morality be met in these areas?

The principles of liberty and law have always been in conflict, for, as we observed earlier, whenever one is permitted to expand, the other must necessarily contract. The fundamental dilemmas in our time are to be found in the search for means of accommodating the demand of freedom-loving people for greater liberties without at the same time dissolving the protections that law gives to all of us; of maintaining decent standards of public morals without at the same time working grave injustices or depriving people of their fundamental rights. In this book some of the major areas of conflict in the contemporary world are examined in an attempt to determine how they might be resolved while preserving personal liberties, without giving up our society's moral standards, and without abandoning either our legal system or the principles of justice upon which it is founded.

I have not hesitated to express my opinions about the questions and issues discussed in this book. Where I have done so it has always been with a good deal of trepidation and with the expectation that the reader will formulate his own judgments in accordance with his assessment of such facts as may be available to him, as well as his assessment of the arguments that I have set forth in support of my views. In a dynamic world such as the one we inhabit, Heraclitus's aphorism that no one can ever step into the same river twice, for the river is changing at every moment with new waters flowing in and old flowing out, seems singularly appropriate. Not only the rivers and the world change every moment, but so do we. The attitude of those philosophers of the Middle Ages and the eighteenth and nineteenth centuries who supposed that they had possession of the last word in science, or philosophy, or morals seems today to be born of arrogance. Perhaps there are some eternal verities, but in this time of rapid change, of revolutions in politics, in cultures, and in moral attitudes, it is at least the better part of prudence, if not of humility, to offer such a book as this to the reading public as a contribution to a continuing discussion rather than as the last word. Many will no doubt disagree with much of what I have had to say. Most will disagree with at least some of what I have had to say. If Heraclitus is correct, I will probably change my mind about some, at least, of the things that I have said here. I trust, however, that my exposition of the issues themselves and the arguments I have offered in support of my own views will make some contribution to the reader's thinking about them and will stimulate him to respond in some way—at least to inquire further about those issues about whose solution he entertains some continuing doubts. It was, after all, because of their abiding faith in man's capacity to arrive at reasonable and just solutions to such issues as these that our ancestors fought for the liberties we now enjoy.

Part One
The Enforcement
of Morals

1

Lord Devlin and the Enforcement of Morals

It has long been taken for granted that law was the servant of morals, that law was designed, among other things, to protect and enhance the moral tone of society. Recently this theory has fallen out of favor, at least in some circles. But it is still held by many influential thinkers, and has been ably defended by some. One of the most widely discussed statements of the theory that the law not only may but ought to enforce morals was made in 1959 by Sir Patrick Devlin, who served for many years as a judge of the Queen's Bench and was made a Lord of Appeal in 1961.

Lord Devlin had been asked to testify before the Wolfenden Committee, which recommended, in 1957, that England's laws on homosexuality should be liberalized, so that homosexuality between consenting adults would no longer be a crime. The committee based its recommendation upon its members' conclusion that there is a realm of private morality that is none of the law's business, and that there is a significant distinction between crime and sin that must be maintained. As the authors of the report put it, the function of the law is "to preserve public order and decency, to protect the citizen from what is offensive or injurious, and to provide sufficient safeguards against exploitation and corruption of others, particularly those who are specially vulnerable because they are young, weak in body or mind, inexperienced, or in a state of special physical, official or economic dependence." [1] They went on to say that they did not consider it the function of the law "to intervene in the private lives of citizens, or to seek to enforce any particular pattern of behavior, further than is necessary to carry out the purposes we have outlined." [2] They added that they did not intend, in saying that, to encourage private immorality. [3]

There had already been some precedent for their action, taken by a committee that had looked into the question of the law on prostitution. That committee had defined private immorality as immorality that is not offensive or injurious to the public [4] and had concluded that such conduct should not be considered criminal unless it was accompanied by indecency, corruption, or exploitation. "It is not the duty of the law to concern itself with immorality as such," the committee on prostitution said. The Wolfenden Committee concurred, saying: "It should confine itself to those activities which offend against public order and decency or expose the ordinary citizen to what is offensive or injurious." [5]

In considering these assumptions, Devlin recalled that the criminal law never permits the consent of the victim to be used as a defense.[*] For example, consent of the victim is no defense against the charge of murder or assault. Further, the victim of assault or any similar crime may not forgive the offender and demand that the state cease to prosecute. This principle, which is followed quite consistently throughout the criminal law, is inconsistent with the Wolfenden Committee's assumption, for if the law were designed solely for the protection of the individual, there would be no reason why the individual should not forego such protection if he did not want it. From the fact that the law does not permit the victim to forego such protection, it would seem to follow that the law is *not* designed solely for his protection, but that some other purpose must be involved. That purpose, Devlin says, is the protection of society. Murder, assault, and other crimes for which consent is no defense are crimes against society, and it is for that reason that society permits neither the defense of consent nor the withdrawal of charges if the victim so desires. Devlin points out that where such offenses are concerned, it matters not whether anyone has been shocked, corrupted, or exploited, or whether the offenses have been committed in public or in private. He adds that they are not punished on the pragmatic ground that the punishment of violent men will protect other members of society, for a murderer who acts only with the consent or on the request of his victims is no menace to others who may not desire his services. Persons who commit such offenses are punished, in Devlin's view, because they "threaten one of the great moral principles upon which society is based, that is, the sanctity of human life." There are certain standards of behavior or moral principles, he observes, that society insists upon, and their violation is an offense against society as a whole as well as against the injured person.[6]

A number of examples may be offered of acts that can be done in private without giving offense to anyone and that do not involve the corruption or exploitation of other persons: euthanasia, the killing of another at his request, suicide, dueling, abortion, incest—all of these are of such a nature. Although some advocate reform of the law on some of these matters, Devlin observes, no one has advocated the abolition of all restraints on all of them. But if they adhered faithfully to the principle that the law should not inter-

---

[*] Rape is not an exception, because consent changes the nature of the offense.

fere in matters of private morality, they should be prepared to accept the lifting of all legal sanctions against all such behavior.

Devlin presents a number of arguments in support of his view that morals are not merely a matter of private judgment, that society has the right to enforce moral standards, and that there are ways of distinguishing those moral standards that society should enforce from those that it may refrain from enforcing.

1. There is a difference between private morality and private behavior in matters of morals. Society, he says, is a community of ideas. It has, as part of its basic structure, a moral foundation, which determines, to a large degree, the manner in which its members are supposed to conduct their lives. The institution of marriage is an important example of an area in which morals and law intersect. The institution is itself based upon certain fundamental conceptions, which all societies have enforced in one way or another. Adultery is not merely a private matter, according to Devlin; it is a public matter, because the institution of marriage—which is a fundamental social institution—depends for its survival upon the observance of certain norms with regard to marital chastity. People in predominantly Christian nations consider monogamy to be "something that is good in itself and offering a good way of life." For that reason, Devlin says, our society has adopted it as a norm for marriage. Although two people may commit adultery in private, the question of the morality of adulterous relationships is not a matter of private morality, for society has a deep and abiding interest in the preservation of that form of marriage which it has sanctioned; adultery, therefore, is a matter of public morality. Similarly, even though three people decide to enter into a polygamous relationship, they may not do so if they choose to remain in England, Canada, the United States, or any other Christian nation (or in any nation whose laws are derived from Christian norms), for such relations threaten the institution of marriage as it exists in those nations. "Without shared ideas on politics, morals, and ethics," Devlin says, "no society can exist. . . . Society is not something that is kept together physically; it is held by the invisible bonds of common thought. If the bonds were too far relaxed, the members would drift apart. A common morality is part of the bondage. The bondage is part of the price of society; and mankind, which needs society, must pay its price." [7]

2. Once it is established that society has the right to preserve itself through the enforcement of those moral standards that are so important a part of its basic structure, the question of the extent to which society should use the law to enforce those standards is answered relatively easily. Society is entitled to protect itself from any dangers, whether those dangers threaten its existence from without or from within. Societies disintegrate more often from internal causes—particularly from "the loosening of moral bonds," according to Devlin—than from outside attack. Because this is the case, he concludes, "the suppression of vice is as much the law's business as the

suppression of subversive activities; it is no more possible to define a sphere of private morality than it is to define one of private subversive activity." [8] Consequently, there are no theoretical limits to the extent to which the law may move against immorality. If a man chooses to get drunk every night in the privacy of his living room, this *is* society's business, and not merely his own, for society would not long survive if large numbers of people got drunk every night in the privacy of their homes.

3. The measure of society's morals is, according to Devlin, the standards of "the reasonable man, . . . the man on the street," who may also be characterized as "the right-minded man" or "the man in the jury box." "Immorality," according to Devlin, "is what every right-minded person is presumed to consider immoral." [9]

4. Nevertheless, the individual cannot be expected to give up to society all rights to freedom of action. There are private interests as well as public ones, and the former must be given due consideration, together with the latter. Devlin supports the principle that individual freedom should be tolerated as far as possible, so long as it is consistent with the integrity of society.[10] The measure of the limit of tolerance, he says, is the ordinary man's feelings about a given practice. If the ordinary man has a "real feeling of reprobation," a deeply felt sense of disgust, then this is a pretty good indication that we have reached the outer bounds of toleration.[11] Reasoning alone is not sufficient, because it is possible, on logical grounds, to come to more than one conclusion with regard to a given matter on the basis of evidence and arguments that may be presented. This sense of disgust, indignation, and reprobation must, according to Devlin, be very strong indeed to justify invoking the sanctions of the law. Strong disapproval of a practice is not sufficient, in itself, to justify the invocation of such sanctions.[12] In addition, even when there is a general feeling of indignation and disgust, there must be a "deliberate judgment that the practice is injurious to society." [13]

Devlin recognizes the fact that there are shifts in the levels of tolerance and departures from the moral standards of one generation by the generations that follow. But he believes that in all such matters, the law should be slow to act, for if it acts too hastily, it may undermine very important principles or institutions that will be sorely missed later on, once the passionate cry for reform has passed.[14]

5. To be sure, privacy must be respected. But if one person has injured another, he has forfeited some of the rights that he might otherwise have enjoyed against any intrusions by the state's agents upon his privacy. By the same token, Devlin argues, where consenting adults have engaged in acts that society deems to be damaging to itself, they may also forfeit some of their right of privacy. Still, the detection of such crimes, committed in private between consenting adults, is likely to be rather haphazard, and the law must balance its own interests against those of individuals whose right

to privacy should, in general, be respected. When the enforcement of a moral prohibition would intrude too greatly upon the right of privacy, which must also be respected, the law must be moderated.[15]

6. The law is not completely consistent in its application of moral standards. Some very harmful kinds of behavior, such as adultery of the sort that tends to break up marriages, have been left outside the criminal law in England because, according to Devlin, it would be too hard to enforce a legal prohibition against it. It is too generally regarded, he says, as a human weakness of such a nature that punishment would not serve to deter those who are tempted to engage in it. "There is no logic to be found in this," he declares, but from the fact that adultery, fornication, and other immoral acts are not punished by the law, it does not follow that homosexuality should not be so punished.

7. The logical inconsistencies and the strange operations of legal reasoning become particularly evident when one considers the old abortion laws. Abortionists were subject to severe punishment because their crime was considered a particularly harmful one. Their ministrations often led to serious injury or death. But abortions were dangerous because legislators outlawed them. Once abortion became lawful, skilled practitioners were able to perform them and there was no need for anyone to turn to an unskilled amateur. The law punished those who did what they did only because the law left no other outlet for those who wanted or needed such services. The law itself was at least partially responsible for the creation of the dangerous situation in which women seeking abortions found themselves. This anomolous situation illustrates Devlin's contention that law and sin are not identical and cannot be made so by legislation. The community must be imbued with a sense of sin in other ways—principally by education. If the law is unassisted by the educational organs of the state, and those other instrumentalities that are in a position to influence human thought and conduct, it cannot bear the burden alone and is bound to be warped, as it has in abortion and in other cases. Without the help of strong moral training, Devlin concludes, the law is bound to fail.

LORD DEVLIN'S CRITICS

H. L. A. HART
Devlin's theory has been the subject of intense discussion and widespread criticism since its publication. One of the most important critiques of Devlin and of others who hold similar views was published by H. L. A. Hart in a little book entitled *Law, Liberty, and Morality*.[16] Hart noted that the Wolfenden Committee's report was based upon John Stuart Mill's principle, enunciated in his essay *On Liberty*, that "the only purpose for which power can rightfully be exercised over any member of a civilized community

against his will is to prevent harm to others." [17] Mill went on to specify that the law must not interfere with an individual's behavior for his own good, whether that be physical or moral. "He cannot rightfully be compelled to do or forbear because it will be better for him to do so, because it will make him happier, because in the opinions of others, to do so would be wise or even right." [18]

Hart proceeds under the assumption, with which one may suppose Devlin would agree, that one needs some special justification for depriving individuals of the liberties that may be taken from them if they are punished by the law. He also assumes that when there is a law forbidding a certain form of conduct, the existence of that law coerces people into conformance and restricts the freedom they might otherwise enjoy to experiment in those areas of conduct; but freedom of choice is a valuable thing, and any interference with it requires some rather strong justification. Finally, he assumes that laws designed to enforce sexual morality, to the extent that they interfere with certain forms of sexual expression and restrict the sexual outlets that may be available, impose an acute form of suffering upon those who are thus deprived of the only outlets that may be available to them. Such laws, and the coercive measures that may be used to enforce them, "may create misery of a quite special degree," according to Hart.[19] All these restrictions, then, must be justified by rather strong reasons. The principal reason offered by Devlin is the danger to the fabric of society posed by moral breakdown and degeneracy. We shall see how Hart replies to this.

First, he argues that Devlin's appeal to the laws that exist is not convincing. By appealing to the existence of such laws as those forbidding incest, homosexuality, euthanasia, and the like, as supporting evidence for his argument that morals may be enforced, Devlin merely invokes "the innocuous conservative principle that there is a presumption that common and long established institutions are likely to have merits not apparent to the rationalist philosopher." [20] In doing so, Devlin argues from what *is* to what *ought to be*. But the whole point of those who support Mill's principle is that laws that presently restrict the freedom of the individual because such restrictions are supposed, by those in positions of authority, to be in his best interests ought to be changed. Their present existence and their long history prove nothing to the point.

Hart also points out that Devlin's assertions that the function of the criminal law is only to enforce moral principles is not completely true. The appeal to laws that allow of no defense on the ground that the victim consented does not prove, of itself, that the sole purpose of such laws is the enforcement of morals. Hart points out that there may be an element of paternalism, designed to protect people against themselves. Pure food and drug laws, which are designed to protect the consumer against his own ignorance, and the law that certain drugs may be sold only on prescription are clearly paternalistic. "It would seem very dogmatic," Hart says, "to say of the law creating this offense that there is only one explanation, namely.

that the law was concerned not with the protection of the would-be purchasers against themselves, but only with the punishment of the seller for his immorality." [21] Devlin's assumption that laws were either designed to protect people from one another or to punish moral wickedness turns out to be insufficient, for there may be, and in fact there are, laws that endeavor to reduce suffering—not only human suffering, but even (as in the cases of laws against cruelty to animals) the suffering of animals.

The bigamy example is used by Devlin to show how the law is used to enforce morals. But Hart points out that the law will not interfere if a man lives with one woman, or even with several women, in adulterous relationships. He may even go through all the ceremony associated with weddings to celebrate the union, so long as he does not in fact marry her. When he marries, the law intervenes, not only to nullify the bigamous marriage but also to punish the offender. This is a strange way for the law to treat offenses against morality—or at least, an inconsistent way for it to treat them. Hart cites a number of attempts to justify the law's severe sanctions against bigamy and its hands-off attitude toward adultery. Some people say that bigamy is punished because it may lead to confusion of public records or to attempts to misrepresent illegitimate children as legitimate. Others say that it is "a public affront and provocation to the first spouse," and because cohabitation under color of matrimony is especially likely to lead to desertion, nonsupport, and divorce.[22] Still others have argued that a bigamous marriage ceremony performed in a country where there is a strong religious and moral tradition of monogamy will offend people's feelings and be regarded by many as a publicly sanctioned desecration. Some of these attempts to reconcile the inconsistencies in the laws on this point are, according to Hart, "more ingenious than convincing." But the last, he suggests, would, if correct, support the view that the bigamist is punished, not because he is morally wicked but because he is, in some sense, a public nuisance. This is not the only case in which public behavior may be punished because it is deemed to be a nuisance. Some forms of behavior, legitimate in themselves, are punishable if they are committed in public. A husband may quite properly have sexual intercourse with his wife, but not on the public streets, where it is an affront to public decency. The distinction between prostitution as such and street-walking is based upon this concept, for, though prostitution may be immoral, it may be legalized without legalizing street-walking on the ground that the latter offends the sensibilities of those who may be unwillingly exposed to its manifestations. A case may be made for the view that people have a right not to be offended by sights that are imposed upon them in public places, just as they have a right not to be made an unwilling audience to loud noises emanating from bars, record shops, and transistor radios in public streets, parks, buses, and beaches.

Devlin's principal thesis that society has the right to enforce morality because immorality may weaken it or lead to its collapse has, as an unexpressed underlying assumption, the theory that "sexual morality together

with the morality that forbids acts injurious to others such as killing, stealing, and dishonesty—forms a single seamless web, so that those who deviate
from any part are likely or perhaps bound to deviate from the whole." [23]
Though Hart is prepared to admit that society would not long endure if it
were not reinforced by a morality that proscribed conduct that was injurious
to others, he is not convinced that those who deviate from the norms of
sexual morality are a general threat to society. Hart goes on to say that to
the extent that Devlin holds that every society depends upon some degree
of shared morality, he may be correct, but his move to the proposition that
a society is virtually identical with its morality is absurd. According to Hart,
the adoption of the latter position would require us to assume that the
slightest change in a society's moral or legal code would be tantamount to
the disappearance of that society and its replacement by a new one.[24] This
latter assumption, labeled "absurd" by Hart, underlies Devlin's comparison
of immorality and treason. Conventional morality, according to Hart, could
change without destroying or subverting a society. Such change, he suggests,
could be more aptly compared to peaceful constitutional change in a society,
and is consistent, as he puts it, "not only with the preservation of a society
but with its advance." [25]

LADY WOOTTON

Lord Devlin's thesis was also subjected to systematic attack in a series
of lectures by Lady Wootton, who observed that his definition of a crime
as an act about which the good citizen would feel guilty is circular,
because one would presumably be able to identify a "good citizen"—or as
Devlin put it, the "right-minded man," or the "man in the jury box"—only
by determining whether he would feel guilty about the commission of such
acts.

Further, Lady Wootton notes that some acts, though bad in some contexts,
are proper or even beneficial in others, and that as a result, one must conclude that no act is bad in itself. Cutting open a man's chest and slicing into
his heart is clearly wrong and is illegal in some circumstances, but if such
an act is performed by a surgeon attempting to save a man's life, it is neither
morally nor legally wrong. The moral law changes because of new conditions, and the criminal law tends to adapt itself as well. The tendency to
regard wrongs that were condemned by ancient authors as being somehow
more wrong than those that were not condemned by them because they
could not have foreseen them is a mistake. "The fact that there is nothing
in the Ten Commandments about the iniquity of driving a motor vehicle
under the influence of drink cannot be read as evidence that the ancient
Israelites regarded this offense more leniently than the contemporary British." [26] Of course not, for they did not regard them at all! But there is a
tendency to suppose that because there is no Mosaic prohibition against
drunken driving, whereas there is one against homosexual relations, the

former is somehow less evil than the latter, or the latter is more deserving of severe punishment than the former.

There is no logic in the criminal law, Lady Wootton says. "For administering a drug to a female with a view to carnal knowledge a maximum of two years is provided, but for damage to cattle you are liable to fourteen years' imprisonment. For using unlawful oaths the maximum is seven years, but for keeping a child in a brothel it is a mere six months." [27] How the "good citizen" feels about such matters is a matter of speculation, perhaps, but Lady Wootton is convinced that most people will find these facts "quite fantastic." The point is that the good citizen will feel rather different degrees of guilt over stabbing his wife, having homosexual relations, and parking overtime. All of these are crimes, but not all of them are sins. "Whether or not they are also sins is a purely theological matter," she asserts, "with which the law has no concern. If the function of the criminal law is to punish the wicked, then everything which the law forbids must in the circumstances in which it is forbidden be regarded as in its appropriate measure wicked." [28] But obviously, not everything in the criminal law does correspond to anyone's view of wickedness, and there are some kinds of "criminal" behavior that everyone would presumably agree are not morally wicked in themselves.

If moral wickedness is indeed involved, she argues, then the law's former insistence on *mens rea*—voluntariness and intent—makes sense. But the law's present tendency to assign strict liability to some kinds of offenses cannot be squared with the view that the criminal law's function is to punish wickedness, for under strict liability, one may be held liable for an act even when he can establish that he had no knowledge of its possible effects and no intention to cause the harm that he caused, and even when he can show that he exercised due care to avoid causing any harm to anyone and to avoid violating any legal prohibition. Lady Wootton suggests that the recent tendency to hold people strictly liable for certain kinds of offenses reveals that the law is being thought of, to an ever larger degree, as a means of *preventing* certain kinds of behavior, rather than as a means of *punishing* them. The gravity of an offense under strict liability, such as a traffic offense in which a pedestrian has been injured or killed, is measured more by the consequences of the offense than by the state of mind of the offender. Thus, a driver who had knocked down a pedestrian was booked on a charge of careless driving, but the charge was raised a month later—after the death of the injured party—to causing death by dangerous driving. Offenses of strict liability reveal, according to Lady Wootton, that "in the modern world in one way or another, as much and more damage is done by negligence, or by indifference to the welfare or safety of others, as by deliberate wickedness." [29] She recalls that there was a time when animals, and even inanimate objects, such as trees and stones, could be held legally responsible for harm that they did to people.[30] Now, she suggests, perhaps the time has come "for the concept of legal guilt to be dissolved into a wider concept of responsibility or at least accountability, in which there is room for negligence as well as purposeful wrongdoing, and for the signifiance of a conviction to be reinterpreted merely as evidence that a prohibited act has been committed, questions of motivation being relevant only insofar as they bear upon the probability of such acts being repeated." [31]

THE ROLE OF MORALS IN THE LAW

There can be no doubt that, historically at least, the law and morals were very closely related and that in many areas the law continues to look upon its function as the enforcement of morals, the reinforcement of moral standards in society, and the punishment of moral depravity. Moral principles are appealed to in determining not only what laws will or will not be enacted by legislators, but also what sentences will be imposed upon violators. In some areas of the law—and not only in the criminal law—moral standards are implicitly or explicitly made an inherent part of the criteria for making certain important judgments.

This is not so say that there is no distinction between law and morals. Clearly, important distinctions exist, not the least of which is the fact that in law there are formal sanctions and formal means for determining guilt or responsibility that are lacking in morals. Also, though the law is not always concerned with motives or with the subject's attitudes, morals—at least according to many moral theorists—always are. And finally, even the most fastidious legal moralist agrees that the scope of morals is far broader than that of law. Nevertheless, the two norms—legal and moral—often intersect, as the following examples will illustrate.

CASE 1. MORALS AS A TEST FOR CITIZENSHIP

On September 22, 1944, a Mr. Repouille applied for naturalization as a United States citizen. The naturalization law requires that any applicant, prior to being approved, must show himself to have been a person of "good moral character" for the five years preceding the filing of his petition. On October 12, 1939, Repouille had deliberately put his thirteen-year-old son to death. His reason for this tragic deed was that the child had suffered certain injuries at birth that rendered him an idiot and left all his limbs grotesquely malformed. He was blind, mute, and deformed; he had to be fed; he had no control over his bowels or his bladder; and he had spent his entire life in a small crib.

Repouille had four other children to whom he was a loving and dutiful father. He concluded that he would not be able to give them the support that they needed and were entitled to if the deformed child were permitted to live. He therefore used chloroform to dispatch him. Although he was indicted for manslaughter in the first degree, the jury brought in a verdict of manslaughter in the second degree with a

recommendation of the "utmost clemency." The trial judge, moved by
the circumstances and by the jury's recommendation, imposed a sentence of five to ten years, but suspended the sentence and put the
defendant on probation. He was discharged from probation in December, 1945. Aside from this one illegal act and his conviction for it,
Repouille conducted himself in such a way that the court conceded
that he demonstrated "good moral character," but because he had filed
his petition September 22, three weeks short of the five-year period, his
petition for naturalization was denied, and, on appeal, the denial of
his application was upheld. Judge Hand, in his majority opinion, said:

> Very recently we had to pass upon the phrase "good moral character"
> in the Nationality Act, and we said that it set as a test, not those
> standards which we might ourselves approve, but whether "the moral
> feelings, now prevalent generally in this country" would "be outraged" by
> the conduct in question: that is, whether it conformed to "the generally
> accepted moral conventions current at the time." In the absence of some
> national inquisition, like a Gallup poll, that is indeed a difficult test to
> apply; often questions will arise to which the answer is not
> ascertainable, and where the petitioner must fail only because he has
> the affirmative. Indeed, in [this case], the answer is not wholly certain;
> for we all know that there are great numbers of people of the most
> unimpeachable virtue, who think it morally justifiable to put an end to a
> life so inexorably destined to be a burden to others,—and—so far as
> any possible interest of its own is concerned—condemned to a brutish
> existence, lower indeed than all but the lowest forms of sentient
> life. Nor is it inevitably an answer to say that it must be immoral to do
> this, until the law provides security against the abuses which would
> inevitably follow, unless the practice were regulated. Many people—
> probably most people—do not make it a final ethical test of conduct that
> it shall not violate law; few of us exact of ourselves or of others the
> unflinching obedience of a Socrates. . . . There have always been
> conscientious persons who feel no scruple in acting in defiance of a
> law which is repugnant to their personal convictions, and who even regard
> as martyrs those who suffer by doing so. . . . It is reasonably clear
> that the jury which tried Repouille did not feel any moral repulsion at his
> crime. Although it was inescapably murder in the first degree, not
> only did they bring in a verdict that was flatly in the face of the
> facts and utterly absurd—for manslaughter in the second degree
> presupposes that killing has not been deliberate—but they coupled even
> that with a recommendation which showed that in substance they
> wished to exculpate the offender. Moreover, it is also plain, from the
> sentence which he imposed, that the judge could not have seriously
> disagreed with their recommendation.
> One might be tempted to seize upon all this as a reliable measure of
> current morals, and no doubt it should have its place in the scale; but
> we should hesitate to accept it as decisive, when, for example, we
> compare it with the fate of a similar offender in Massachusetts, who,

although he was not executed, was imprisoned for life. Left at large, as we are, without means of verifying our conclusion, and without authority to substitute our individual beliefs, the outcome must needs be tentative; and not much is gained by discussion. We can say no more than that, quite independently of what may be the current moral feeling as to legally administered euthanasia, we feel reasonably secure in holding that only a minority of virtuous persons would deem the practice morally justifiable, while it remains in private hands, even when the provocation is as overwhelming as it was in this instance.[32]

Judge Hand went on to explain that he believed that the ultimate test of moral character would be the attitude of "our ethical leaders," but that because of precedents, he would have to rely upon the moral feelings of the public at large—a matter which it was impossible for him to determine. He therefore ordered the case sent back to the court from which it originated, with instructions to the judge to have both parties present evidence on "contemporary moral standards" in the matter at issue. In the meantime, Repouille was entitled to file a new petition for naturalization, for the five-year period had clearly elapsed.

The practical problem faced by Judge Hand and his colleagues in the United States District Court—that is, the problem of ascertaining the moral sense of the community—will be discussed later. Meanwhile, it is abundantly clear from this case that morals enters very intimately into the operation of the law, at least in this area. In fact, it is an integral part of the law itself, for the law stipulates that moral character is a condition for the enjoyment of certain fundamental rights and privileges, including (in this case) citizenship.

This is by no means the only law to contain such moral standards in so integral a fashion. The Constitution of the United States contains a number of provisions embodying moral judgments, including, among others, the Eighth Amendment's prohibition against "cruel and unusual punishments." One could make a case for the view that a punishment's being unusual is not, in itself, a moral objection to such a punishment's being employed, and for the view that the assertion that a given form of punishment is unusual is not a moral judgment. But to assert that a punishment is cruel is to pass moral judgment on it; it is to say that that punishment is "inhuman" or "barbarous" or "uncivilized," all emotionally charged, evaluative terms.[33] Justice Frankfurter held that the Fourteenth Amendment was intended "to withdraw from the States the right to act in ways that are offensive to a decent respect for the dignity of man, and heedless of his freedom," and he asserted that "taking human life by unnecessarily cruel means shocks the most fundamental instincts of civilized man." [34]

Similarly, the due process clause has been interpreted to bar the execution of an insane man, for, as Justice Frankfurter put it, that clause "embodies a system of rights based on moral principles so deeply embedded in the traditions and feelings of our people as to be deemed fundamental to a civilized society as conceived by our whole history. Due process is that which comports with the deepest notions of what is fair and right and just." [35]

The concept of "good moral character" that is written into the Immigration and Naturalization statutes, which caused so many problems for Repouille, is quite broad and covers many aspects of behavior, but it has also been undergoing rather significant modification in recent years, possibly because the changes in public morals have come to be recognized by the courts. "Good moral character" is also significant in many other areas of the law, including divorce law and the right to be admitted to the bar. A few examples may be of interest:

A seaman who openly cohabited with another seaman's wife was denied naturalization on the ground that he lacked good moral character,[36] but an unmarried alien who occasionally had sexual relations with single women was *not* denied naturalization.[37] More recently, an alien was granted naturalization despite the fact that he had committed adultery with a single woman on a number of occasions and made her pregnant. His wife had left him two years earlier, and as soon as he learned that his girl friend was pregnant, he took steps to have his marriage dissolved, married her, and cared for her and their child. The court held that

such conduct, while not to be condoned, should not be viewed as so reprehensible, or of such evil and meretricious character as to compel this court to conclude that Mr. Edgar is, by reason thereof, a man of bad character. . . . We do not believe that the present sentiment of the community views as morally reprehensible such faithful and long continued relationships under the conditions here disclosed.[38]

A man who failed to contribute to the support and maintenance of his institutionalized, mentally deficient daughter, and had not inquired about her welfare for over three years, was held not to be of good moral character, and his petition for naturalization was therefore denied.[39]

One who engaged in homosexual relations was deemed to be unfit, on moral grounds, for naturalization,[40] but a few years later, another homosexual's petition for United States citizenship was granted. In the latter case, the person involved had led a quiet, peaceful, law-abiding life as an immigrant in the United States and had had purely private relationships with consenting adults. He did not engage in public or offensive displays and was not guilty of corrupting the morals of minors. He was gainfully employed, was highly regarded by his employer and his associates, and had previously submitted to therapy, which had not been successful. The court held that the principal issue was whether his conduct was public or private. If public, then the court held that it might pose a threat to the community. But if it was purely private, then there was minimal danger of harm to others, and any attempt to regulate such conduct might result in unjustified invasions of the individual's constitutional rights, particularly his right to privacy. The court concluded,

> In short, private conduct which is not harmful to others, even though it may violate the personal moral code of most of us, does not violate public morality, which is the only proper concern of [the Immigration and Naturalization Act].[41]

Thus, it would appear that a relatively new element has been introduced—public as opposed to private morality—and that only public immorality will count in cases of this sort, at least where that particular court is concerned.

A narcotic addict was held on that account not to be a person of good moral character and was denied naturalization.[42]

A conscientious objector, who was ordered to report to a wartime work camp in lieu of military service, refused to do so, was convicted of violation of the Selective Service Act, and was sentenced to a three-year term in prison. After serving 22 months of his term, he was paroled. He served for a number of years as an attorney specializing in civil rights and civil liberties cases. Upon moving to the state of Washington, he applied for admission to the bar, but his application was denied, and that denial was upheld by the State's Supreme Court on the ground that his violation of the law nearly 20 years previously and his present insistence that he would do the same if confronted with the same circumstances were sufficient to establish that he lacked the good moral character necessary for admission to practice law in that state.[43]

When morals are not explicitly written into the law, they are often insinuated into it in other ways. The extent of a penalty may be determined by the gravity of the offense, which may in turn be measured by the moral offensiveness of the crime or its perpetrator. The majority of the Pennsylvania Supreme Court quoted with approval the decision rendered by a trial court in a case involving murder:

> In turning to the individual who committed this crime, we are concerned with his *depravity*. The facts of this murder convince us that he is an individual who is dangerous to society and undoubtedly of *savage nature*. There was no reason to mow this victim down in *cold blood*, no occasion to fire so precipitously except as a manifestation of a *savage and depraved nature*.
> . . . We have searched his history carefully for some justifiable explanation. We have found none, only *a depraved, cruel, ruthless and brutal individual*. There can be but one choice.
> The court therefore adjudges the defendant, Theodore Elliott, to be guilty of murder in the first degree and fixes the penalty at death.[44]

The words emphasized clearly reveal their moral character, and illustrate how the trial judge was influenced by his assessment of the moral character of the crime or of the criminal (or both) in fixing the penalty. The highest court in the state approved of this approach.

Justice Musmanno dissented, partly on the ground that the imposed penalty was "directed to the offense," which he conceded was a "terrible crime," and "not to the offender." As he put it, "There is no punishment in the scale of justice heavy enough to make atonement for what Theodore Elliott did, but for what Theodore Elliott is, a different scale, it seems to me, must be used. Punishment is to be applied according to the capacity of the individual, as well as the enormity of the delinquent act." Justice Musmanno dissented because in his opinion, Elliott was a mental defective who did not have a meaningful choice when he committed his crime. In Justice Musmanno's view, then, Elliott should not be executed, but, being a "dangerous creature, he must be restrained, as the tiger is restrained." According to this opinion, then, the controlling factor is not the destructiveness of the crime, but the moral capacities of the criminal. In Justice Musmanno's opinion, when the defendant was incapable of having the intentions that are necessary for the commission of an immoral act, he should not be "punished" in the conventional sense at all—any more than one would punish a bull that had gored a man or a tiger that had slashed a person with its claws. Rather, one should lock him up as a menace to society—as one might pen a bull or cage a dangerous tiger—not as punishment, and not as a consequence of an "immoral deed" (for one can hardly think of a bull's goring as immoral), but as a simple prudential measure of self-protection. But Justice Musmanno did not rule out, in his opinion, the possibility that another man, committing a similar offense, but not so mentally incapacitated as Elliott allegedly was, might properly be punished for the savagery of his act and for his own moral depravity.

THE COMMUNITY'S MORAL STANDARDS

That moral standards enter into the law, both intrinsically (as in morals offenses and in rules against cruel punishment) and extrinsically (as in cases where penalties or levels of compensation are determined, at least in part, by the moral opprobrium of the act or of the actor) is now well established. Where moral standards are involved, though, there is often some disagreement over the exact nature of the moral norm that ought to apply. Lord Devlin appealed, as lawyers often do, to the "man in the jury box" or the ordinary "reasonable" man for some judgment as to what constitutes moral behavior and what is immoral, and for an authoritative pronouncement on what is and what is not beyond the limits of toleration. There are some problems, though, about ascertaining just what the ordinary man thinks, or what the current "community attitude" might be on any given moral issue.

Not the least of the problems is the definition of *community*. If a man in a small town commits an act that offends the citizens of his town but is generally tolerated as a minor aberration by the citizens of nearby communities, or the state as a whole, should he be judged on the consensus in the small town in which he happened to commit his "offense," or should the "community" be given a broader base, and consist of the entire state in which he lives? Or should the "community" be considered to be the entire nation in which he lives—particularly today, when communications are so rapid, and the entire nation is exposed to the same radio and television programming, the same magazines, and the same press service releases?

Even supposing that one has resolved the question of the definition of *community*, there may be some problem in determining just what the "community's" standards are. Letters to the editor won't serve adequately as a test, for, in the first place, they are edited. It would be very difficult to determine the extent to which the editors themselves permit an expression of the "community's views"—whatever those might be—to be reproduced in their letter columns. Further, there is no evidence that the people who write letters to the editor are truly representative of the community as a whole, or even of those who are informed about the issues on which they choose to write. And in this connection, it must not be forgotten that a substantial proportion of the community may not be at all informed about a particular issue. Should the community be defined in such a way as to exclude those who do not read newspapers carefully, or to include only the best-informed citizens? This would be a long way from Lord Devlin's man in the jury box.

Questionnaires won't do, either—no matter how scientific they may be. For those who reply to questionnaires tend, on the whole, to be more interested in the subject matter, to have a higher socioeconomic status, and to be better educated than those who do not respond.[45]

Judge Frank, in discussing a proposed test for "cruel and unusual punishments"—that "it shocks the conscience and sense of justice of the people of the United States"—concluded that such a test was impossible of application, for it relies on "common conscience." But, he said, "such a standard—the community's attitude—is usually an unknowable. It resembles a slithery shadow, since one can seldom learn, at all accurately, what the community, or a majority, actually feels." Even a carefully taken "public opinion poll" would be inconclusive in a case like this.[46]

It has been suggested that large-scale scientific studies, patterned after those of Dr. Alfred C. Kinsey,[47] might provide some measure of contemporary community attitudes. But there may be a significant difference between what people *do* and what they think they and others *ought* to do; and proof that they behave, on the whole, in one way is no necessary indication that legal obstacles in the way of such behavior ought to be removed. Kinsey did suggest that sex laws should be repealed because, as his studies revealed, so many people violate them. One might argue, though, that such promiscuous violation of the law and of moral standards should encourage legislators to strengthen the laws, that police should enforce them more strictly, and that judges should impose stiffer sentences on those who violate them. The Kinsey reports themselves demonstrated that the very groups that engaged in forbidden practices most strongly disapproved of those practices.[48]

A scientific study of false swearing and perjury might reveal that vast numbers of citizens testified falsely in court and deliberately misrepresented themselves in such instruments as income tax returns. But this would hardly be treated as good reason for repealing the laws prohibiting perjury.[49] Though such widespread disobedience of the laws against perjury might lend some credence to the view that they were "unrealistic" and "barbarous" and inconsistent with "normal" human behavior, most people would go on believing that the laws should be retained, both because of the supposed utility of the threat of punishment in deterring at least some of this behavior and because of the damage that removal of the legal sanctions might do to the overall moral climate of the community.

Finally, the Kinsey reports themselves have been subjected to searching criticism. There is serious doubt in the scientific community, not only about the accuracy with which they reflect community attitudes at the time that the studies were conducted, but even whether they accurately report the facts about sexual conduct at the time. Doubts about sampling techniques, populations, and statistical analyses, among others, have all been raised—serious enough, in many scholars' opinion, to compromise the value of the reports for making policy decisions.[50] It would seem, then, that the Kinsey reports, or any other report of a similar nature, would not serve well as a basis for making either moral or legal judgments.

SOME ADDITIONAL CRITICISMS
OF DEVLIN'S THEORY

1. Devlin maintains that society is a community of ideas having a certain moral foundation. This premise is fundamental to all that follows in his argument, for his defense of society's right to enforce morals rests upon his assumption that a breakdown in that moral foundation threatens the very existence of society itself. But as we have seen, it is no easy matter to find the "community of ideas" to which Lord Devlin refers, at least in such a diverse society as the United States; one would venture to guess that a "community of ideas" could not be identified in Great Britain or in any large modern society. In any nation composed of distinct and diverse racial, ethnic, and religious groups, spread over vast territories, and exposed to different historical and geographical influences, cultural diversity is almost inevitable. One might suppose that the "community of ideas" to which Lord

Devlin refers might have existed in earlier times, when life was simpler, when people all had much the same education (or lack of education), and when the swift and free flow of information and opinions did not exist and so could not interfere with time-honored customs and ways of thinking. So one might suppose. But it is doubtful whether such a "community of ideas" has ever existed in the pristine form that Lord Devlin seems to imagine it may be found even today. Societies have never been simple. They have always been subject to radical and revolutionary winds of doctrine. Populations have always been diverse, with exchanges taking place in times of war and as a result of commerce. It is quite possible, however, that they were more easily governed in earlier times and that a "community of ideas" could readily be found among those who governed. For those who governed constituted a rather small class of people, and, so far as they found it desirable or convenient to do so, they imposed their ideas, their moral and even their religious beliefs and practices, upon the people who fell under their dominion. With the rise of democracy, that small group of rulers, who might well have held certain fundamental beliefs in common, was replaced by a vast number of rulers—an entire adult population—whose diverse backgrounds and interests would inevitably be reflected in a wide diversity of opinions on many matters, including questions of morality. Such a society could be called a community of ideas only in the loosest sense. More accurately, it should be considered a collectivity of ideas and attitudes, an assemblage or gathering of people who live together and work together and govern themselves collectively in spite of the great differences that divide them. Plato was right when he described a democracy, more than two millennia ago, as a regime in which "liberty and free speech are rife everywhere," where "every man will arrange his own manner of life to suit his pleasure," where there will be "a greater variety of individuals than under any other constitution," and where a man might rise to eminence even if he lacked the specialized education of the aristocratic elite.[51] Lacking the specialized education of the aristocratic elite, the rulers in a democracy—that is, every man—may not share the moral views of those who would, like Plato, impose their own moral standards upon everyone if they could. They may not approve of those standards or of the standards of many of their compatriots. And in that respect they would not constitute a community of ideas. But Plato was wrong in supposing that democracy was doomed to failure because of its lack of central moral authority and its tolerance of moral diversity. The great experiments in democracy have demonstrated that such political systems can survive and flourish and that multitudes of men can be self-governing without imposing moral or religious uniformity upon one another in the process. Devlin's community of ideas does not exist, and it is doubtful that it would be a good thing for it to exist if it could be brought about. To be sure, mankind needs some form of government, but "the price of society," as Devlin puts it, need *not* be the "bondage of a common morality."

2. Devlin is correct in saying that it is society's business if a man chooses to get drunk every night in the privacy of his home, but for the wrong reasons. And the sense in which he says that it is society's business is not totally acceptable. It is society's business, he says, because society would not long survive if large numbers of people got drunk every night in the privacy of their homes. Of course not. But until society is in imminent danger because of such widespread private drunkenness, does it have the right to interfere with the private behavior of individual citizens? Because some activity might lead to disaster if it were carried out on a large scale, it does not follow that that activity ought to be outlawed if it is carried out on a small and relatively harmless scale. When vast numbers of people use detergents, there is danger of eutrophication of lakes, and such use can therefore properly be outlawed. But if only a few people had been using detergents, there would be no such danger and there would be no justification for the law's interfering with their washing habits. The rights of privacy and of freedom of action deserve to be protected and should be interfered with only when private behavior ceases to be private and becomes a menace to the public or to some part of the public.

3. We have already seen how difficult it is to identify the "reasonable man" or the "ordinary man on the street" or the "right-minded man" upon whom Devlin pins his hopes for enlightenment on the moral standards of the community. We have seen how public opinion polls, surveys, and even scientific studies fail to give the kind of guidance Devlin looks for. But even if they did, even if it were possible to find out what the community's moral standards were, or what the majority of the citizens considered to be moral and immoral, it is not clear that such a judgment would constitute a justification for applying the sanctions of the criminal law against that minority of persons who believe otherwise, or those members of the majority who slip from time to time and fail to live up to the principles they espouse when poll takers are in their living rooms.

4. Devlin's approach has a clear conservative bias, for, though the community's moral sense is to be the guide for legislation on morals, it turns out that the *present* community's moral sense is of less importance than is that of the *former* community. Why the community of bygone years should be permitted to govern the present community is not at all clear. If it is true, as Devlin says, that hasty legislation may do away with institutions that will later be sorely missed, it is equally true that slow legislation will preserve institutions that are presently deeply resented.

5. Devlin notes that the law has long refused to sanction acts of certain sorts committed in private, even when the so-called victim gives his consent. Therefore, he argues, private homosexual acts between consenting adults may properly be forbidden by the criminal law. But those who adopt Mill's libertarian principle might well maintain that *all* acts of the same sort should be permitted, including not only homosexuality, adultery, and fornication, but suicide, euthanasia, abortion, and any others that Devlin might care to

name. They are not impressed by Devlin's list of laws that are presently on the books forbidding consensual "immoral" acts done in private. They say that the list only shows how widely the law is abusing its powers. The issue, after all, is not what the law *does* forbid, but what the law *ought* to forbid, and no list of acts presently forbidden or permitted gives us the answer to that question.

The criminal law, like law in general, is limited in its capacity to rectify all the wrongs that may be perpetrated in society. Any society, no matter how primitive or how advanced it might be, must rely upon the voluntary acquiescence and cooperation of its members in most areas of conduct in order for the business of the society to go on. Every society has developed an elaborate set of informal and unwritten rules that are learned at an early age and are generally accepted without question by its members. Through those rules, and the habits and manners which they engender, life proceeds in a relatively regular, dependable, and consistent way. Breach of those rules may be surprising, shocking, and highly provocative. Where the rules are deemed to be so important that their breach will likely provoke severe retaliatory measures, civilized societies have provided the formal procedures and remedies of the law as a substitute for the private retaliation that might otherwise ensue. No society, however, can successfully enforce every rule that governs the behavior of its members. There could not possibly be enough policemen, lawyers, and judges to handle such an enormous burden. Nor is it possible for every kind of complaint to be remedied by law, for the formal procedures of law require proof before a remedy can be granted, and some matters are simply not amenable to objective proof.* When the law tries to do too much, it is likely to fail to do anything well. If the courts and other law enforcement officials are overburdened with trivial cases, or with the enforcement of rules that might be handled more effectively or more efficiently in some other way, they are likely to find themselves unable to perform their primary function of keeping the peace and protecting the persons, the liberties, and the property of the citizens who come under their jurisdiction. Swamped by great numbers of cases, they will be forced to delay consideration of each case and thus to risk denying justice to those who must wait to recover their money or their liberty, or to be relieved of the anxiety that inevitably accompanies an anticipated appearance in court. Denial of justice leads to contempt for the entire judicial process and for the law as a whole. Such contempt can lead more directly to the destruction of a social or political system than most, or any, of the allegedly moral offenses that we are about to consider. On pragmatic grounds, then—that is, on the same kinds of grounds appealed to by Lord Devlin when he compared moral

---

* How would one prove, for example, that he had suffered great emotional distress when there was no overt physical manifestation of such distress? A claim for damages for fright occasioned at the sight of a street action is rightly disallowed on the ground that it is too hard to prove that such a condition did occur as a result of the cause in question, and on the further ground that it is too easy to fake such claims to warrant permitting them and taking the risk.

offenses to subversion—one may maintain that private consensual moral offenses should not be legally prohibited because of the difficulty of enforcing such laws, the near impossibility of detecting most offenses without an unconscionable invasion of privacy, and the danger of flooding the courts with cases and imposing impossible burdens upon the police when they might spend their time more profitably solving crimes of violence, bringing those who have harmed others to book, and settling domestic and civil grievances.

Still, there are those who feel that some of these moral offenses involve such fundamental principles that they cannot be ignored by the criminal law.

2

Homosexuality

THE ROOTS OF THE PROBLEM

Severe condemnation of homosexual activity is not new. In the Hebrew Bible, copulation of one man with another is categorically condemned, and in one passage, the death penalty is prescribed for those who engage in such practices.[1] Temple prostitutes, both male and female, were common among the ancients, but were specifically forbidden in the Hebrew Bible.[2] According to one Jewish tradition, Sodom and Gomorrah were destroyed because of the "sodomy" that was committed within their borders. An ancient legend tells how Lot's house was surrounded by hordes of men demanding that his guests be produced so that they could engage in sexual relations with them, as was their right according to a law of their city.[3] The flood in Noah's time was also said to have been brought about, at least in part, because of the homosexuality and bestiality practiced by the people of that generation.[4] According to one tradition, the people of Israel were exiled because of their sins, one of which was sodomy.[5] But though homosexual activity was denounced, adultery, fornication, and other forms of sexual misbehavior were severely condemned with far greater frequency, and in later Jewish law, there is little evidence that the harsh penalties for homosexuality were actually enforced.

In the Epistle to the Romans, St. Paul wrote that the Gentiles were punished because their women engaged in lesbianism and men, "leaving the natural use of the women, burned in their lust one toward another; men with men working that which is unseemly." [6] Elsewhere, he warned that neither effeminate men nor those who "abuse themselves" with other men would inherit the kingdom of God.[7] St. Augustine, like most of the early Fathers of the Church, condemned homosexuality, remarking that such sins are "in all times and places to be detested and punished." He declared that even if all nations engaged in such conduct, they would still be held guilty by God, and warned his readers that man's friendship with God is endangered when man pollutes his nature with "so perverted a lust." [8] When the Roman Empire became Christian, sodomists were ordered to be burned. Justinian offered an intriguing argument in justification of the application of harsh measures against homosexuals:

> Because some persons, instigated by the devil, abandon themselves to the most serious forms of lewdness, and commit crimes against nature, we enjoin them to fear God and his future judgment, and to abstain from these diabolical and illicit lewdnesses, so that their acts might not provoke the just wrath of God, nor serve as the occasion for the destruction of cities and their inhabitants. . . . Crimes against nature are responsible for famines, earthquakes, and plagues. To avert such evils, and to save men from losing their souls, we therefore want them not to give themselves up to such impieties.[9]

Sodomy and other forms of "unnatural" sexual behavior have been countenanced in some societies, encouraged in others, and subjected to the most severe penalties in still others. In ancient Greece, in Rome, and elsewhere, the ideals of masculine love were praised. Plato's famous dialogue on love is in fact an encomium to homosexual love.[10] The writings of Juvenal, Petronius, and Suetonius describe the debaucheries of the Roman rulers in great detail. It is said that Nero had his favorite male consort castrated and then went through a marriage ceremony with him. Julius Caesar was described by a senator of the time as being "every woman's man and every man's woman." Those who disapproved of such practices were amused by them or contemptuous of those who engaged in them, but there seems to have been no serious effort to deter people through criminal sanctions from engaging in them.

Nevertheless, some sexual practices were punished, and those that were punished carried severe penalties. A slave who had relations with a free-born youth was liable to be subjected to a public whipping. An Athenian citizen who became a male prostitute was liable to lose all his civil rights. And for pederasty (homosexual relations with a child) a man could be sentenced to death.[11]

A survey of anthropological literature reveals that in a rather high percentage of societies that have been the subject of anthropological research, some form of homosexuality is considered normal and acceptable, and in some it is actively encouraged. In some tribes, for example, all men and boys are expected to engage in homosexual sodomy, and if any man fails to have relations with both male and female partners, he is considered peculiar. In others, older men introduce young men to anal intercourse at puberty, and the latter are expected to do the same to their friends as they reach puberty and to continue to engage in such activities until they are sufficiently mature, in the eyes of their elders, to have relations with women. Some peoples have rigid rules against any form of heterosexual behavior up to a certain age, or hedge heterosexual relations around with a multitude of moral and legal restrictions; but they are completely indifferent to homosexual relations between men or between women.[12]

In our own society, however, homosexual relations, as well as certain other forms of sexual behavior that are considered to be unnatural, sinful, abominable, or otherwise deplorable, have been subjected to severe restrictions for many centuries; and these restrictions are still reflected in our laws and in the attitude of public officials and private persons toward those who engage in such behavior. In seventeenth-century England—a period often described as the Age of Reason—people were hanged for having homosexual relations. People were hanged and pilloried for the same offenses through the eighteenth and into the nineteenth centuries. Oscar Wilde was sent to prison after three sensational trials on homosexual charges.[13]

Though other times and other peoples have been tolerant of what we would call deviant sexual behavior, we are living in our time among our own people. It is instructive, of course, to be informed that other peoples have had attitudes different from those that are prevalent or dominant among us. But, as we have seen earlier, such information does not in itself provide a justification for supposing that our own values or practices are unimportant, foolish, backward, irrational, or unscientific; nor does such information provide a justification for the view that our own practices and attitudes are more advanced, more scientific, more rational, more sensible than those others. If there is some way of judging our practices, of determining whether they are right or wrong, just or unjust, it must be other than by comparing our system with others.

It is widely believed that married couples may legally practice any form of sexual gratification with one another in the privacy of their bedrooms. But this is not necessarily the case. In many states a number of forms of "unnatural" intercourse are legally prohibited even when they are performed by a married couple in private. In the state of Georgia, for example, sodomy is legally defined as "the carnal knowledge and connection against the order of nature, by man with man, or in the same unnatural manner with woman," and is punishable by life imprisonment. The law is similar in almost every other state in the Union. Such laws are not often enforced, but prosecution of cases under their provisions are not unknown; and so long as such laws exist, those who violate them are subject to prosecution and to heavy penalties.

In addition to statutes prohibiting sex perversions or unnatural sex acts, sex crimes are prosecuted under other acts, including public indecency, lewdness, indecent exposure, vagrancy, and disorderly conduct. Such statutes are often construed very broadly by police, prosecutors, and judges, so that a multitude of sins or alleged sins may be covered by them.

Donald W. Cory has observed that the existence of such legal prohibitions on the statute books is not so harmless as one might suppose. These laws "transform the majority of our adult population into felons. We have become a nation . . . of law-abiding criminals. If our laws covering sex crimes were to be enforced, we should have to transform entire states into huge concentration camps, and there would hardly be enough people remaining free to act as jailors." [14] If more people were aware of the existence of laws condemning what they do in private, Cory says, the result would be either constant awareness that they have committed punishable felonies with the psychological toll that is likely to flow from such guilty awareness, or a growing contempt for a system of laws that brands as criminal what so many otherwise law-abiding citizens do.[15] Nevertheless, the laws remain on the statute books, unenforced for the most part, but available whenever prosecutors and police feel the need or the desire to bring them to bear against the citizens who fall within their jurisdiction.

It is impossible here to attempt to discuss thoroughly all the legislation that governs sexual relations, or even all the legislation that governs so-called unnatural sexual behavior. This chapter will concentrate, therefore, on homosexuality alone, under the assumption that many of the lessons to be learned from this paradigm may be applied to related areas as well.

THE HOMOSEXUAL AND THE LAW

Early English common law defined sodomy as anal intercourse, but American law has expanded the meaning of that term and of the phrase that is used in many state statutes, "the infamous crime against nature," to include any sexual relations between two persons other than purely genital contact between a man and a woman. The prohibition against sodomy has been construed (and was no doubt intended) to be applicable to so-called unnatural acts between husband and wife as well as between unmarried persons. However, as a result of a United States Supreme Court ruling in a contraception case (to be discussed in the next chapter), in which the Court held that sexual relations between husband and wife were protected by a constitutional right of privacy, a number of courts have recently held that such prohibitions, as applied to married couples, are unconstitutional.[16] Some courts have gone even farther, ruling that the application of such laws

to unmarried heterosexual couples who have engaged in anal or oral intercourse without compulsion denies those couples the equal protection of the
laws that is guaranteed them by the Constitution.[17] However, others have
refused to go along with this and have upheld convictions of unmarried
heterosexual couples under the sodomy statutes.[18]

No court has found a constitutional bar to the application of criminal
sodomy proscriptions to homosexual relations. In a recent case, two homosexuals brought suit against the State of Virginia, seeking to have its
sodomy statute declared unconstitutional. They relied on the privacy argument and on numerous others, including a claim that by prohibiting homosexual relations between consenting adults, the state was inflicting cruel and
unusual punishment upon homosexuals. They also argued that they were
being deprived of the right of free expression. The lower federal court held
that none of these constitutional protections was being denied the petitioners, insisting that the right of privacy upheld by the Supreme Court
in the contraception case involved marriage, the sanctity of the home, and
family life, none of which was applicable to homosexuals. The third judge
dissented vigorously. When the case reached the United States Supreme
Court, the decision of the lower court was upheld without comment. At
the same time, the Supreme Court declined to review a case from North
Carolina in which a man who had committed a homosexual act with a
seventeen-year-old boy (who had been cooperating with a local detective)
was convicted of sodomy and sentenced to one year in prison.[19]

Some homosexuals have attempted to get around the prohibition against
homosexual intercourse by going through the motions of a marriage ceremony and then claiming that they were entitled to the constitutional right
of marital privacy that is accorded to heterosexual couples. This tactic has
not succeeded anywhere. Most courts have held that even where marriage
between two persons of the same sex was not specifically prohibited by
statute, the word *marriage* refers exclusively to a relationship between two
persons of opposite sex. This conclusion, the courts say, is justified by long
and universal usage. In trying to determine the intent of the legislature, the
courts have analyzed the statutes dealing with marriage. These statutes,
they say, are full of words and phrases that clearly indicate that the legislature had in mind persons of opposite sex. They have therefore concluded
that the legislature never intended to sanction homosexual marriage, and
have accordingly ruled that marriage license bureaus were not obliged to
issue licenses to persons desiring to enter into homosexual marriages, and
that the marital right of privacy does not apply to homosexuals who are
living together.[20]

Homosexuals who desire to marry argue that by being deprived of the
right to marry, they are also being denied all the benefits that accrue to
married couples in our society, including the right to file joint income tax
returns, to enjoy the savings to which spouses are entitled under provisions

of the federal and most state estate tax laws, certain gift tax benefits, and the social and business or professional benefits that accrue to married couples.[21]

Divorced parents who have active homosexual relationships have considerable difficulty in getting and keeping custody of their children.

The armed forces of the United States have a firm policy against the employment of homosexuals in any capacity. The army considers homosexuals to be unfit for military service because their presence allegedly impairs the morale and discipline of the army and because homosexuality is allegedly a manifestation of a severe personality defect "which appreciably limits the ability of such individuals to function in society." [22]

Some laws have been modified. A number of states have repealed sodomy statutes. Numerous cities and towns have dropped homosexual offenses from their books and others have quietly stopped enforcing such laws. Some communities have gone so far as to ban discrimination against homosexuals. The United States Civil Service Commission issued new guidelines, under which persons may not be disqualified for federal employment solely on the basis of homosexual conduct. In Colorado, one or two communities issued marriage licenses to homosexuals. California passed a law that legalized all sex acts in private between consenting adults. But in most parts of the country, laws against homosexuality continue to be enforced.

Homosexuals have been designated as sexual psychopaths under some state laws that provide for an indefinite term of treatment. Since such a hearing is regarded as a civil matter, it is fraught with danger for the accused, for the rules of evidence and the protections accorded to defendants in criminal trials need not be followed. A person who is hospitalized as a sexual psychopath can be confined indefinitely—until several psychiatrists are willing to testify that he has been "cured." The question of the psychiatric treatment of homosexuals will be discussed later.

REASONS FOR CONDEMNING HOMOSEXUAL BEHAVIOR

Many reasons have been advanced by those who favor the retention of legislation forbidding homosexual behavior. As we shall see, some of these reasons have considerable foundation in fact, whereas others do not. Some of these claims follow.

1. Homosexuals tend to molest children. Even the most liberal advocates of legal reform in this area agree that children and teenagers should not be fair game for homosexuals; but the effect of liberalized legislation would be to bring the homosexuals out into the open, to increase their numbers, and to encourage them to prey upon the young boys whom they find most attractive.

2. When homosexuals do seduce youngsters, they often initiate them

irreversibly into their way of life. These young people are then prevented from having a normal sex life, and often end up either unable or unwilling to be married and to make their contribution to society in a normal way; or, if they do marry, they find that they are irresistibly drawn back into the perverted forms of sexual activity that they learned when they were younger, thus causing irreparable harm to their wives and to any children that they may have had, and to society as a whole.

3. Homosexuality is a promiscuous way of life. Few homosexual relations are more than one-night stands, and fewer still have any semblance of permanence. Aside from the blatant immorality of such a life, it encourages the spread of venereal disease, and it leads to loneliness, misery, and unhappiness for those who become entangled in it. It is virtually impossible for homosexuals to enjoy warm and satisfactory personal relationships such as are often found in heterosexual marriage.

4. Those who become entangled in the homosexual life are afflicted by serious psychological problems—by feelings of guilt, by insecurity, and by constant fear of disgrace and ruin.

5. Homosexuals are unreliable and are poor risks. They should not be given sensitive jobs, either in government or in industry, for they have proved themselves to be more likely than others to reveal secrets for sexual favors, or to submit to blackmail attempts that play upon their sexual weaknesses. And they should particularly be kept from jobs that may bring them into close contact with youngsters, such as teaching, camp counseling, and the like, because they are more likely than others to use their positions to corrupt the morals of their young charges.

6. Homosexual activity is offensive. It is a source of disgust to those who must witness public displays of behavior that offend ordinary moral, religious, and even aesthetic feelings. Public lavatories, parks, and theaters become the gathering places of homosexuals who are looking for sexual contacts. The general public has a right to be spared such scenes. Not only children, but adults too, should be able to visit public facilities without being exposed to them. The impersonation of women by men, too, is unnatural, indecent, and offensive, and should be forbidden in public places, particularly where children may be exposed to it.

7. Homosexual activity is unnatural.

8. Homosexual activity is dangerous. Its practice by some people encourages others to do the same, and, if everyone or even if large numbers of persons were to become homosexuals, there would be no future for the human race. Furthermore, homosexuality may lead, as Lord Devlin pointed out, to a general moral breakdown and to the destruction of vital social institutions.

For all these reasons, then, homosexuality is condemned and legal sanctions against it are maintained. If the legal barriers are lowered, it is said, those who practice homosexuality will come out into the open, those who do not practice it may be encouraged to do so, and the evil consequences of a general lowering of moral standards, of family breakdown, of a spread of venereal disease, of psychological harm to those who are inducted into the homosexual life, and the rest, are sure to follow.

AN ANALYSIS OF THE ARGUMENTS

Now let us examine the facts, as far as they are known.

PEDOPHILIA AND PROMISCUITY

Point 1, on the tendency of homosexuals to molest children, is based upon a confusion between homosexuality and pedophilia. The latter, a tendency on the part of an adult to find sexual satisfaction in relations with children, is not peculiar to homosexuals, for there are many heterosexuals who molest little girls; and homosexuals have no particular inclination, as a group, to seek out young boys—no more, at any rate, than their heterosexual counterparts.[23]

Most heterosexual men confine their sexual activities to women who are approximately their own age. As men grow older, they tend to prefer sex partners of their own age and station in life, unless they are interested in a very temporary sort of affair. Even then, however, they will seldom consider entering into a sexual relationship with a girl who is underage, either because of fear of the possible consequences—legal and social—that may follow upon such an encounter or because they find the contemplation of such a relationship distasteful. The attitudes of homosexual men seem to run along parallel lines. The scientific studies that have been made of homosexuals tend, almost universally, to reveal that homosexuals are no more prone to molest children than are heterosexuals. Scholars in the field now distinguish carefully between homosexuality and pedophilia, recognizing that there is no demonstrable connection between one and the other.[24] To be sure, liberalized legislation, doing away with criminal penalties for homosexual behavior between consenting adults in private, would "bring the homosexuals into the open"—or some of them, at least; but there is no convincing evidence that it would encourage homosexuals to engage in widespread pedophilia, and it would not reduce the penalties for pedophilia in any case.

Point 2, on the long-term results of pedophilia, thus becomes somewhat academic, for once a clear distinction is drawn between homosexuality and pedophilia, and between liberalization of the laws governing homosexual behavior, on the one hand, and laws penalizing pedophilia, on the other, it becomes clear that the one is not necessarily related to the other.

Point 3, that homosexuality is a promiscuous way of life, that it encourages the spread of venereal disease, and that it leads to loneliness and an absence of warm and permanent relationships seems to be borne out by the available evidence. Few homosexual relationships last very long. On rare occasions they may last for many years. But they lack the stabilizing protections offered by the laws of marriage and the birth of children. They are easily dissolved; one partner merely packs his bags and moves out. There are no social sanctions—formal or informal—against the breakup of a homosexual union. On the contrary, the majority culture encourages such breakups. Most homosexual relationships are anonymous, lasting no more than a single night. Descriptions of a "typical" homosexual's life reveal that very few homosexuals are able to establish lasting relationships with one another, and many of them are not interested in doing so. Many homosexual gathering places are specifically designed to encourage promiscuity. It is not uncommon for a given individual to have sexual relations with a number of individuals in a single night.[25] This promiscuity has led to an alarming increase in the incidence of venereal disease among homosexuals. In New York City, for example, half of all new cases of syphilis involved homosexual men, while the incidence of venereal disease among heterosexuals was declining.[26]

"The most serious problem for those who live in the gay world," according to Martin Hoffman, "is the great difficulty they have in establishing stable paired relationships with one another." [27] He reports this not as his own personal judgment, but as the opinion of homosexuals themselves. "In general," he says, "they are very unhappy about the grave difficulties which inhibit the formation of stable relationships. They are continually looking for more permanence in their socio-sexual lives and are all too often unable to find it." [28] Hoffman, in attempting to find the reasons for this, reduces them to the general male penchant for variety, one not shared by females, which leads, therefore, to a significant difference in the stability of lesbian relationships as opposed to those of male homosexuals. In his report on female sexual behavior, Kinsey noted that

> among all peoples, everywhere in the world, it is understood that the male is more likely than the female to desire sexual relations with a variety of partners. . . . The female has a greater capacity for being faithful to a single partner. . . . [She] is more likely to consider that she has a greater responsibility than the male has in maintaining the home and in caring for the offspring of any sexual relationship, and she is generally more inclined to consider the moral implications of her sexual behavior.[29]

Kinsey attributes this difference in behavior to the male's tendency to be more easily aroused than the female.

A recent scientific study concluded that "the majority of urban male homosexuals are promiscuous during most of their adolescent and adult life." However, the same study concluded that promiscuity "did not preclude long-lasting relationships."[30] That is, although some male homosexuals were able to establish and maintain long-lasting affairs with one another, these affairs were characterized by infidelity, one or both partners freely entering into brief sexual encounters with third parties. One of the most eloquent defenders of the homosexual recently argued that the admitted promiscuity of the male homosexual may be no greater than the heterosexual male's rate of promiscuity might be if the latter had the same opportunities as the former.[31] He suggests that the promiscuity that characterizes even the long-lasting relationships may be accounted for by the fact that males are generally easily aroused, that male homosexuals recognize this fact, and that they are often willing to reach an accommodation with one another that is more difficult to establish when a woman is involved.

By contrast, homosexual women have a far higher ratio of long-lasting relations than do men, and their relations tend to be accompanied by strong emotional feelings in a higher proportion than do those of men. Moreover, homosexual women tend to be more faithful to one another than are homosexual men, and more jealous of one another. Even among women, most affairs break up within three years, infidelity being one of the chief causes of such breakups. Among men, infidelity is more readily tolerated.[32]

In addition to the lack of legal sanctions noted earlier, Hoffman notes how difficult it would be for a homosexual couple to live the kind of life that a heterosexual couple might lead. Homosexual couples are not likely to be invited to dinner parties, picnics, and family outings, for example. A business executive would ordinarily be ill-advised to bring his male "wife" to the company's annual dinner dance at the country club. The social barriers, the legal barriers, the lack of legal sanction for a gay marriage, the natural male propensity for sexual variety, if there is one, all contribute to the unstable nature of homosexual relations. In addition, there may be one further factor that could outweigh them all, though if it exists (as it clearly does in at least some cases), it may be conditioned by the existence of some of the others. That is the desire on the part of many homosexuals *not* to form lasting partnerships, but to keep their relations on a strictly temporary, anonymous, physical basis. Many homosexuals do not want a permanent relationship, possibly because of guilt feelings that make it undesirable, from their point of view, to attempt to develop the warm and intimate relationship that heterosexual couples strive to achieve and preserve, and that some lesbians seem to be able to maintain.

PSYCHOLOGICAL PROBLEMS

Point 4, on the psychological problems of homosexuals, and their fears of disgrace and ruin if they are found out, have already been touched on. Many of these problems are undoubtedly conditioned by the attitude taken by society toward homosexuals and toward homosexual relationships. There would be no fear of disgrace and ruin if society accepted homosexuality with equanimity; the strong likelihood of disgrace and ruin if a homosexual is found out constitutes excellent justification for his fears.

A detailed inquiry into the psychology of homosexuals is beyond the scope of this chapter. The results of those scientific studies that have been made are mixed. Some of them are rather startling, suggesting either that something is wrong with the tests or that certain preconceptions about homosexuals are not justified. For example, one test administered to a group of active homosexuals revealed that they were more masculine, in terms defined by the test, than is the average soldier.[33] According to some authorities, certain psychological tests will successfully distinguish homosexual males from heterosexual males three times out of four, but others maintain that at least some kinds of homosexuals cannot be identified by these tests.[34] In one test that has a reputation for a fairly high degree of accuracy in picking out persons suffering from mental illness, or liable to suffer from some form of neurotic breakdown, no substantial difference was noted between the scores of overt homosexuals and those of persons with a heterosexual bent. And in another investigation, based on a study of volunteers from American homosexual organizations, it was found that homosexuals were as well adjusted as their heterosexual counterparts. In fact, according to the experts who examined the tests, two thirds of those examined seemed to be average or above average insofar as psychological adjustment was concerned.[35]

There is room for some doubt as to the soundness of the arguments that have been offered in support of the view that homosexuality is a psychological disease, or that it is symptomatic of some form of mental illness. No doubt many homosexuals suffer from neurotic symptoms, as do many heterosexuals. Indeed, it would be surprising if they did not, in view of the persecution to which they may be subjected if they are found out and the anxiety to which such potential persecution is likely to give rise. Psychiatrists and psychoanalysts who generalize about the neuroses of homosexuals, based upon their experiences with their patients, tend too often to forget that their experiences are confined to those homosexuals who come to them for help. There may be many homosexuals suffer from neurotic symptoms, as do many heterosexuals. because they feel quite secure, having made what they consider to be a satisfactory adjustment to their deviant mode of living. Of course, if the criterion for mental health is that the subject be living a "normal" or non-deviant life, then all homosexuals would be psychologically ill by definition; but such a conclusion would reveal less about homosexuals than it would about the predilections of those who had chosen to define their terms in that way. As Freud once wrote, "Inversion [i.e., homosexuality] is found in people who exhibit no other serious deviations from the normal. It is similarly found in people whose efficiency is unimpaired, and who are indeed distinguished by specially high intellectual development and ethical culture."[36] Many persons who engage in homosexual behavior seem to lead normal lives in every other respect. Whether they are more neurotic, on the whole, than those who prefer to engage in heterosexual behavior should remain, for the time being at least, an open question.

Certain psychiatrists and some defenders of homosexuals have attempted to pass judgment on the psychological health of homosexuals without taking the precaution of subjecting their determinations to careful scientific analysis and without adhering scrupulously to accepted standards of scholarly objectivity. Some supposedly scientific pronouncements on the subject are marred by bias and emotionalism that borders on bigotry.

Dr. Edmund Bergler, for example, claims to have had nearly 30 years' experience dealing with homosexual patients, some of whom he says he has treated successfully. In his view, homosexuality is a serious neurosis. Every homosexual is a "psychic masochist" who constantly "creates . . . situations in which he finds himself 'behind the eight-ball.'" [37] He is a "frantic fugitive from women, . . . mortally afraid of them," [38] "perpetually on the prowl," [39] possessing a constant "masochistic craving for danger." [40] "The sometimes visible flippant hilarity of the 'gay,'" he says, "is a very thin pseudo-euphoric camouflage, . . . a technique for warding off masochistic depression; another such technique is the homosexual's exaggerated and free-flowing malice, which is ready for use at any time." [41] He then goes on to say:

> Homosexuals are essentially disagreeable people, regardless of their pleasant or unpleasant outward manner. True, they are not responsible for their unconscious conflicts. However, these conflicts sap so much of their inner energy that the shell is a mixture of superciliousness, fake aggression, and whimpering. Like all psychic masochists, they are subservient when confronted with a stronger person, merciless when in power, unscrupulous about trampling on a weaker person. The only language their unconscious understands is brute force. What is most discouraging, you seldom find an intact ego among them. [42]

Dr. Bergler deplores the fact that homosexuals have some influence in certain professions. The fact (if it is a fact) that homosexuals are prominent in the fashion industry is a "fantastic state of affairs" in his view, for it results in women being "dressed by their worst enemies!" [43] He theorizes that women's clothes are a masculine invention forced upon women "as an unconscious reassurance against man's own repressed fears of woman's body." The "punitive" fashions in women's clothing and the frequent shifts of fashion are, according to him, the homosexual's way of showing his superiority to women: he can force them to follow his dictates in order to demonstrate to himself that he needn't be afraid of them. By forcing them to wear uncomfortable clothes, the homosexual takes out his hatred upon them. [44]

Not a scintilla of scientific proof is offered for any of these assertions. Indeed, it is difficult to imagine what kind of evidence could be offered for them. Without so much as a hint of an attempt to perform controlled experiments or to obtain representative samples, Dr. Bergler draws broad and all-encompassing generalizations, based upon selected excerpts from interviews with patients that may or may not be reported verbatim. And how can one possibly know that a homosexual who has all the outward signs of being happy (what Bergler calls "flippant hilarity," in obviously emotive terms), how can one know that this is all a "pseudo-euphoric camouflage" designed to ward off "masochistic depression"? It would seem that whatever a homosexual does, it can't be right. His "hilarity" is a cover-up for depression, and if he reveals his depression, he is "whimpering." If he obeys higher authorities, he is "subservient," and if he exercises authority, he is "merciless" and "unscrupulous." In short, homosexuals are utter failures, according to Bergler—even when they succeed.

Pointing out the flaws in Bergler's analysis is not meant to suggest that homosexual behavior may not be a symptom of a serious psychological problem. The purpose is to demonstrate that the subject has been obscured by fuzzy thinking, pseudoscientific jargon, and exceedingly emotional judgments made by persons whose credentials lend an air of authority. That homosexuals may suffer from psychological problems is a possibility that cannot be discounted.

Some homosexuals are inclined to believe that homosexuality either is a form of psychological illness or is a symptom of some deep-seated psychological problem. For example, D. W. Cory, himself a homosexual, has written two highly regarded books on homosexuality under a pseudonym. In the first edition of his book *The Homosexual in America*, Cory defended the life of the homosexual and mounted one of the most widely hailed defenses of the rights of the homosexual in recent decades. Ten years later, in the preface to the second edition of his book, he wrote regretfully about his failure to emphasize the abnormality, the sordidness, of many aspects of the homosexual's life. Reflecting on attempts of some defenders of the homosexual life to portray it as essentially normal but nonconformist, different from that of most people but every bit as healthy, Cory concluded that such attempts to defend the homosexual were misguided because the premises upon which they were founded were false. The homosexual's behavior, or his desire for homosexual behavior, he said, "is a symptom of an emotional maladjustment." He argued that the psychological disturbances of homosexuals should not be glossed over in order to win points in the fight for civil rights for them. "If I may be permitted a few analogies, the alcoholic is disturbed, but is not expelled from the society of man. The woman who engages in prostitution is likewise suffering from unhealthy motivations, as is the narcotic addict. To emphasize the disturbance of these individuals is not to betray them to some mortal enemy; in fact, when this is done by friends who would defend their rights, it could be the greatest aid they can be given." [45]

If sickness is defined as a pathological condition that interferes with a person's daily life or functions so as to render him incapable of functioning effectively, then it would seem on the surface that homosexuality is not a sickness. Few, if any, homosexuals are disabled by their sexual preferences. Moral indignation is not a sufficient ground for labeling a condition a form of illness. The mere fact that an individual has sexual preferences that differ from those of other persons in his society is not in itself sufficient to establish a right in those other persons to treat him by psychological means so as to change his preferences, particularly if the individual is not seeking treatment and is content with his preferences. Despite some claims to the contrary, the "success" rate in the treatment of homosexuals—that is, the number of homosexuals who have successfully been transformed into heterosexuals—is very small indeed. "There is no known treatment of homosexuality, and success in treating homosexuals depends to a large extent on the nature of the associated or related disorders." [46] That is, if a person who happens to be a homosexual seeks psychiatric treatment for acute depression or alcoholism, he may be successfully treated for his depression or for his alcoholism, but treatment of his homosexuality as such is much more problematic.

The notion that homosexuals are necessarily suffering from a severe psychopathic disorder may arise from the fact that the homosexuals who seek psychiatric advice are usually suffering from some such disorder. Some psychiatrists have improperly generalized from the small sample of homosexuals who come to see them, assuming—contrary to every canon of scientific procedure—that all homosexuals resemble those who consult psychiatrists. The same method would undoubtedly lead to an interesting corollary: that all heterosexuals are suffering from psychological maladjustments or from pathological conditions. Only a study of homosexuals who have adjusted satisfactorily to their lives, as have many doctors, lawyers, judges, police officers, clergymen, government officials, teachers, university professors, athletes, and social workers, could possibly yield the desired information, and these are the people who feel no need to see a psychiatrist.[47]

On December 15, 1973, the trustees of the American Psychiatric Association (APA) decided to discontinue listing homosexuality as a mental disorder. Four months later, a majority vote of the members of the association ratified that decision. (The vote was 5854 to 3810.) [48] The very notion that an association can determine a supposedly objective question by majority vote (and at that, the majority was only 60% of those voting) is in itself revealing. It is rather comparable to a vote on the question whether the earth is round or flat. The vote can do no more than reveal the prevailing opinions or sentiments of those voting; it is incapable of deciding the truth or falsity of the proposition. Ordinarily, people don't vote on matters of fact. They vote on questions of *policy*. And this is what the American Psychiatric Association was doing. It could not decide, as a matter of objective, scientific fact, whether homosexual behavior is or is not a mental disorder, by polling its members. But it could and did decide that as a matter of policy, the association would no longer advocate or support the proposition that homosexuals *ought* to be given psychiatric treatment against their will.

For some purposes, at least, the determination that a given condition is pathological and that persons having that condition are ill is a *value* judgment and not a purely factual determination. Once a person is judged to be ill, one automatically makes certain judgments as to how he ought to be treated and how he ought to behave, and most particularly, one concludes that he ought to do whatever is reasonably necessary to rid himself of his diseased condition. On the other hand, the judgment that a given set of objective facts is not to be regarded as evidence of disease or malfunction is equivalent to saying that these value judgments and imperatives are not warranted. The APA made the matter perfectly clear by declaring that those "who are either bothered by, in conflict with, or wish to change their sexual orientation" could be diagnosed as suffering from a "sexual orientation disturbance." That is, psychiatrists shouldn't attempt to treat patients who happen to be homosexual unless the patient happens also to be disturbed by his irregular sexual preferences, and, presumably, seeks professional help because of them.

The relatively close vote of the APA members indicates that the dispute over whether homosexuality is an illness is far from over. Some members of that association have been attempting—so far without success—to have the matter reconsidered. The association's decision is not binding on its members in their professional capacity as psychiatrists, and it does not have the effect of law. Those psychiatrists who continue to believe that homosexuals are mentally ill may still subject them to compulsory psychiatric treatment, which may involve deprivations of individual liberty. Not the least of those is the right of an individual to maintain his personality intact, not to have it interfered with by other persons, no matter how well-intentioned their efforts might be. Another, scarcely less important, perhaps, is the indeterminate nature of such treatment. Instead of a judge or a jury setting a certain time for an offender to serve out his sentence, the ultimate judgment is placed in the hands of a psychiatrist or a group of medical men, who will decide, in accordance with their own criteria, when the so-called patient is ready to be released.

In a number of American states persons may be designated sexual psychopaths even if no crime has been shown to have been committed. In New Hampshire, for example, a sexual psychopath is "any person suffering from such conditions of emotional instability or impulsiveness of behavior, or lack of customary standards of good judgment, or failure to appreciate the consequences of his acts, or a combination of any such conditions as to render such person irresponsible with respect to sexual matters and thereby dangerous to himself or to other persons." [49] A person may be sent to a mental hospital under such a statute, even if he has committed no crime, or he may be committed for an indefinite term for a minor offense whose penalty might have been no more than a few months in jail. And worst of all, such a law places into the hands of certain medical practitioners the power to deprive men of their liberty in accordance with their own standards, whatever those may be, and to return to society men who may well be highly dangerous, in spite of the fact that the latter may have committed grave offenses for which they might otherwise have had to remain in prison. Recent reports from the Soviet Union reveal how pernicious the use of psychiatric wards and mental hospitals may be when they are converted into compulsory treatment centers for those who are accused of criminal behavior. The czars who sent political prisoners to Siberia were guilty of monstrous injustices. They condemned men to live miserable existences in the wastes of the Russian wilderness. But they did not mount direct attacks upon the minds of their victims. In the Soviet Union today, men and women who are accused of anti-Soviet activities, of publishing subversive literature, or of wanting to emigrate to Israel or to any other free society, are condemned to mental hospitals where they will presumably be purged of their mental diseases and return to normalcy—to the value systems of the regime under which they live. For the courts of a free society to send men or women to mental hospitals against their will in order to "cure" them of their sexual predilections is very nearly a contradiction in terms. If a man chooses to engage in what most persons in a given society consider to be immoral behavior—particularly if that behavior is such as to harm no one but himself and those who consent to participate with him in those activities—then *at most* the authorities of that society should be authorized to punish him; but they should not be permitted to use drugs, electric shock, insulin shock, or the other methods of modern psychiatric medicine to change his personality to conform to the value system of the society as a whole or of the doctors who will treat him. Society has a right to protect its members, but not at the expense of their minds and their personalities when they violate its norms. Without the offender's consent, no one should be permitted to tamper with his personality. The homosexual who wants to be a homosexual, who chooses to remain a homosexual, and who is not at all interested in becoming a heterosexual may have chosen a way of life that is repugnant to many, or even to most of us, but his personality should remain inviolate. To turn him over to a psychiatrist for therapy when he has no desire to be altered is an invasion of a man's very soul, an invasion that only the most totalitarian regime could countenance.

HOMOSEXUALS IN POSITIONS OF TRUST

Point 5, on the unreliability of homosexuals, their susceptibility to blackmail attempts, and the dangers of putting them into positions of trust with youngsters, is a mixed bag. From what has already been said on the distinction that must be drawn between homosexuality and pedophilia, it should be apparent that there is no justification for keeping homosexuals out of positions of trust where young boys are concerned. It should be as sensible to say that heterosexuals should not be permitted to serve as teachers or counselors where girls are concerned. In either case, the issue is not so much the homosexual or heterosexual propensities of the individual concerned as his proclivity to engage in sexual relations with underage persons. Certainly, if there is reasonable evidence that a given individual has such inclinations, whether he is homosexual or heterosexual, a responsible administrator will refrain from entrusting the care of youngsters to him. But there is considerable evidence that some homosexuals, who are not inclined to pedophilia, have made excellent teachers, counselors, and advisers to young people. Their talents should not be lost because of their personal sexual habits when the latter do not affect their conduct vis-à-vis their young charges.

On the problem of blackmail, there is general agreement among the authorities in the field that homosexuals are peculiarly susceptible to blackmail attempts. In a report submitted to the Committee on Expenditures in the Executive Departments (the committee having to do with civil service employment policies) of the Eighty-first Congress, homosexuals were declared to be unsuitable for government employment because of their frequent victimization by blackmailers who threaten to expose their sexual deviations.

> Law enforcement officers have informed the subcommittee that there are gangs of blackmailers who make a regular practice of preying upon the homosexual. The modus operandi in these homosexual blackmail cases usually follow[s] the same general pattern. The victim, who is a homosexual, has managed to conceal his perverted activities and usually enjoys a good reputation in the community. The blackmailers, by one means or another, discover that the victim is addicted to homosexuality and under the threat of disclosure they extort money from him. These blackmailers often impersonate police officers in carrying out their blackmail schemes. Many cases have come to the attention of the police where highly respected individuals have paid out substantial sums of money to blackmailers over a long period of time rather than risk the disclosure of their homosexual activities. The police believe that this type of blackmail racket is much more extensive than is generally known, because they have found that most of the victims are very hesitant to bring the matter to the attention of the authorities.[50]

It should be remembered, though, that homosexuals are not unique in their vulnerability to blackmail and extortion. Heterosexuals, particularly those who are married, are at least as vulnerable as homosexuals are. More than one man has been ruined by a well-endowed prostitute, working for an intelligence organization, who has seduced him and then, after gathering incriminating evidence, threatened to expose him. The Profumo-Keeler-Davies scandal involved no homosexuality but shook the government of Great Britain to its foundations. In the United States, men with the most robust heterosexual instincts have gotten into deep trouble because of their perfectly healthy preferences. A powerful member of Congress, Representative Wayne Hays, was driven out of office when Elizabeth Ray, piqued at his failure to meet her demands, revealed that she was on his payroll as secretary despite the fact she had no secretarial skills, and alleged that her employment consisted of satisfying the congressman's libido.* Another powerful congressman, Representative Wilbur Mills, lost his seat in Congress after his affair with Fannie Foxe, a stripper, was given sensational treatment

---

* Congressman Hays subsequently sought treatment for his alcoholism and devoted himself to helping other alcoholics.

in the press. It is not homosexuality alone that renders a person vulnerable to blackmail or to being compromised, no matter how powerful his position may be.

It has been argued that if society were less stringent in its application of sanctions against homosexuals, they would be less likely to succumb to blackmail, and the risks in hiring them in any position would be minimal. But there is some reason to doubt whether this is entirely accurate. Italian psychiatrists have been quoted as saying that the threat of social exposure is often used quite effectively for purposes of blackmail in Italy, where homosexual practices are not subject to formal legal sanctions.[51] This would indicate that where there is considerable public repugnance to such behavior, even when it is not the subject of legal penalties, the opportunity for blackmail always exists. The law itself has recognized the vulnerability of the homosexual to blackmail in a number of ways, not all of them to the detriment of the homosexual. William Blackstone, who took a dim view of homosexuality, argued that it was "a crime which ought to be strictly and impartially proved, and then as strictly and impartially punished. But it is an offense of so dark a nature, so easily charged, and the negative so difficult to be proved, that the accusation should be clearly made out: for, if false, it deserves a punishment inferior only to that of the crime itself." [52] Modern courts have held that a threat to accuse a person of sodomy is "sufficiently equivalent to force and violence to constitute robbery if the threatened person parts with money because of the threat." American courts have held that the crime of sodomy is "so abominable, . . . and so destructive is even the accusation of it, of all social right and privilege, that the law considers that the accusation is a coercion which men cannot resist." Another court held that although the offense of solicitation for sodomy is a relatively minor one, where the law is concerned, rated less serious than reckless driving, "in the practical world of every day living it is a major accusation." "It follows," the court said, "that threatened accusation of this offense is the easiest of blackmail methods. The horror of the ordinary citizen at the thought of such an accusation may impel him to comply with a demand for money under such a threat." [53] The court therefore concluded that the victims of such threats were entitled to special protections in order to prevent unwarranted, irreparable destruction of their reputations.

The Wolfenden Commission concluded, on the question of blackmail, that there may be some truth to the charge that homosexuals are especially susceptible, though other persons with certain "weaknesses" are liable to be compromised to about the same degree—people who are prone to become drunk, for example, as well as gamblers and persons who may get into compromising heterosexual situations. "While it may be a valid ground for excluding from certain forms of employment men who indulge in homosexual behavior," the Commission concluded, "it does not, in our view, constitute a sufficient reason for making their private sexual behavior an offense in itself." [54] This question, more fundamental than the question of the kinds of employment from which homosexuals might properly be excluded because of special problems they might have to face, will be considered later.

THE OFFENSIVENESS ARGUMENT
AND FREEDOM OF EXPRESSION

Point 6 concerns the offensiveness of homosexual conduct and remarks that public displays of homosexual behavior, because they are disgusting and offensive to the ordinary person, should be outlawed, for the general public has a right to use public facilities without being assailed by such offensive scenes.

Most of those who advocate reform of the laws on homosexuality would agree with at least a part of these observations. Not only homosexual relations, but also heterosexual relations are offensive when they are acted out in public, at least to a sufficiently large number of people to justify some control over such public manifestations. A husband and wife have every right to engage in sexual intercourse with one another, but not in full view of the public on a beach, in a park, or in an airliner, as one couple is alleged to have done recently. The public has a right not to be assailed by offensive smells and noises, as the law has recognized for many centuries. Loud music emanating from transistor radios in public places is an outrageous interference with the rights of those who go to those places to enjoy their leisure in peace and quiet. The public has the right to zone certain areas in such a way as to keep factories, pig farms, and chicken coops, with their noise, their smells, and their filth, at a distance from places where people reside. By extension, it is not unreasonable to require those who would perform acts that may in themselves be harmless or even desirable but are offensive to substantial numbers of people when they are performed in public to confine such behavior to the privacy of their homes, their private clubs, or such other private places as they may establish for such purposes. Whether the behavior is heterosexual, then, or homosexual, or even if it is neither (for example, nudity), the public has a right not to be exposed to its manifestations if there is a general consensus that such manifestations are offensive. To be sure, there must be limitations on the public's right to prohibit public manifestations of what it finds "disgusting" or "offensive." The public may be offended by a demonstration for women's rights, for example, or for civil rights for black citizens; it may find beards disgusting; it may object to the display of a Star of David on the outside walls of a synagogue. Or—as in the Soviet Union or in some Moslem nations—the public may be offended by the display of a crucifix outside a church. Where does one draw the line between what the public may properly prohibit on the ground that it is offended by its display and what the public may not prohibit on such grounds?

The answer to this question depends, to a large extent, upon the extent of one's commitment to freedom of expression. When freedom of expression comes into conflict with the public's sensibilities, a choice must be made between upholding the former and protecting the latter. In a free society the public must suffer more frequent ruffled feelings than it would in a more rigidly controlled society. Or it must learn to overlook some displays that it might otherwise consider offensive. In Nazi Germany those who were offended by the sight of a bearded Jew were able to demonstrate their disgust and to relieve it somewhat by pulling the beard that offended them, by slapping the face behind the beard, and, if they were sorely offended, they could kill the man who dared to display himself in public, and be congratulated for having rid the city of such an obscene person. Where the public is thoroughly committed to freedom of expression, it will learn to overlook displays of books that cater to the lowest and most sensation-seeking elements of the reading public; it will look the other way when girlie shows are advertised, concluding that such shows may be patronized by those who find their pleasures there and that their proprietors have as much right to advertise their existence as producers of Shakespeare have to advertise theirs for the benefit of those who find their pleasures in watching performances of *Hamlet* and *Macbeth*. It is dangerous to use the public sense of outrage and disgust as a measure of the propriety of a given public display, for nothing is more fickle than the public's standards of taste. Those who set themselves up as the guardians of public morality are always ready, if given the power, to outlaw what offends them rather than to give it an opportunity to win acceptance or rejection in the free market.

No easy criterion exists for distinguishing public displays that should be permitted from those that may properly be forbidden. Clearly, the fact that a given form of display disgusts some citizens, or even a majority of the citizens of a given community, is not enough, because such a criterion can lead to the banning of modes of personal behavior, ways of life, and expressions of religious, political, or other beliefs that should be permitted in a society of free men. It would be very neat if some general rule or principle could be found that would apply to every case enabling us to determine, in some logical fashion, what forms of behavior should be permitted and what should be forbidden. The infinite variety of conditions to which human beings are subject and their manifold desires, interests, and practices, as well as the constantly changing texture of human society make it impossible to arrive at such a rule. Nevertheless, reasonable restrictions on free expression may be necessary in some circumstances. Not only sexual freedom, but even such carefully guarded liberties as freedom of speech and the free exercise of religion may occasionally have to give way when substantial state interests are at stake, or are perceived by the courts to be at stake. In this connection, the United States Supreme Court has tried to distinguish carefully between belief and action, arguing that although the law may not interfere with mere beliefs and opinions, it may interfere with actions.[55] The court has held that freedom of belief is absolute but that the freedom to act is not. "Conduct remains subject to regulation for the protection of society." [56] "Legislative power over mere opinion is forbidden but it may reach people's actions when they are found to be in violation of important social duties or subversive of good order, even when the actions are demanded by one's religion." [57]

Thus, for example, the Court has upheld laws that prohibit polygamy, though under the tenets of the Mormon faith at that time, every man had a solemn religious duty to marry more than one woman.[58] On the ground that the state had an interest in assuring all its citizens at least one day of rest each week, it has upheld state laws requiring the closing of businesses on Sunday, despite the fact that such laws placed serious economic burdens on observant Jews and Seventh-Day Adventists, who faced the option of violating the practices of their faiths or suffering grave economic losses.[59]

In the 1940s, Massachusetts, like most states, had child labor laws that were strictly construed to prevent minors from engaging in many kinds of work that were deemed likely to be harmful to them. Among activities in which children were not permitted to engage was the selling of newspapers, magazines, or other merchandise on the streets or in other public places. The police therefore arrested the guardian of a nine-year-old girl who had been selling *Watchtower* and other publications of the Jehovah's Witnesses on the streets of Brockton. Sarah Prince, the defendant, claimed that she was acting in accordance with her religious convictions, which placed upon her and the little girl a religious duty to spread God's word. The United States Supreme Court ruled that "neither rights of religion nor rights of parenthood are beyond limitation. Acting to guard the general interest in youth's well-being, the state . . . may restrict the parent's control by requiring school attendance, regulating or prohibiting the child's labor, and in many other ways." [60] Hence, after concluding that selling on busy streets does pose a threat to the well-being of a child, the Court ruled that Sarah Prince's conviction for violating the Child Labor law should be upheld. Similar rulings have upheld compulsory vaccinations, compulsory blood transfusions, and a ban on the use of poisonous snakes in religious ceremonies, all on the ground that public safety and welfare can override the general right to the free exercise of religion where practices (as opposed to beliefs) are concerned.[61]

Similar limitations have been imposed by the United States Supreme Court, or have been advocated in the dissenting opinions of some of its most distinguished justices, with regard to free speech. In 1969, for example, the Court ruled in favor of some Des Moines high school students who had challenged their principal's action in suspending them after they came to school wearing black armbands as a mark of protest against the American involvement in the Vietnam War. The majority held that the students were being punished for "a silent, passive expression of opinion, unaccompanied by any disorder or disturbance on [their] part." Justice Hugo Black, one of the Court's greatest champions of freedom of expression, dissented, partly on the ground that schools ought to have broad powers to control student behavior. The students involved had "crisply and summarily refused to obey a school order" that the administration believed was necessary to keep the minds of students on the work they had come to school to do. "Of course students, like other people, cannot concentrate on lesser issues when black armbands are being ostentatiously displayed in their presence to call attention to the wounded and dead of the war, some of the wounded and the dead being their friends and neighbors. It was, of course, to distract the attention of other students that some students insisted up to the very point of their own suspension from school that they were determined to sit in school with their symbolic armbands." [62] Later that year, the Court dealt with a case in which the defendant had been convicted of burning an American flag as a symbol of protest against racial injustice and in defiance of a statute prohibiting desecration of the flag. In this case, too, the Court's majority overturned the conviction. But this time, Justice Black was joined in his dissent by Chief Justice Earl Warren and Justice Abe Fortas, both consistent defenders of First Amendment freedoms, and by Justice Byron White. Justice Fortas was the author of the majority opinion in the armband case. Justice Black said that he "would not balance away the First Amendment mandate that speech not be abridged in any fashion whatsoever," but he would have sustained the conviction on the ground that burning a flag is not speech. Justice Fortas argued that the state surely has a right to prohibit burning one's shirt or other garments on the public sidewalk and that the burning of a flag should be regarded in the same light. Moreover, "the fact that the law is violated for purposes of protest does not immunize the violator." In addition, Justice Fortas declared that there is something special about the flag which distinguishes it from other property, and that one who owns a flag has "peculiar obligations and restrictions," which are not necessarily arbitrary or unconstitutional. Although protest is broadly protected by the Constitution, he said, "protest does not exonerate lawlessness." [63]

One might well argue that such abridgements of free speech and the free exercise of religion are unjustifiable. Also, whatever dangers there may be to society as a whole or to given individuals by permitting parents to interfere with the administering of vaccinations or blood transfusions to their children, by allowing small children to roam the streets to sell religious literature, by giving license to religious sects to practice snake handling and polygamy, by permitting students to violate rules laid down by school administrations when they are interested in demonstrating their political convictions in school buildings, and by allowing the burning of flags in public places—all of these dangers, one might argue, ought to be risked for the sake of the vital principles of free speech and freedom of religion. But one must ask whether there are *no limits?* Can *anything* be justified on such grounds? If a religious sect decides that human sacrifice is an essential practice, that God wants the faithful to eat human flesh, and that when a man dies, his wife should be burned on his funeral pyre, should the members of that sect be permitted to engage in such practices? It is doubtful whether a very strong case could be made for the proposition that religious freedom is so sacred a principle that it ought to take priority over such other values as the sanctity of human life that also deserve to be protected.

The Wolfenden Report was uncompromising in its attitude toward public manifestations of homosexuality, which it believed should be forbidden, just as street solicitation by prostitutes for heterosexual relations would be forbidden if prostitution were legalized. Advocates of liberalized laws on homosexuality have generally confined their advocacy to a demand that prohibitions of *private* relations between consenting adults be relaxed. They might well argue, as opponents of all liberalization of such prohibitions might, that the freedom to engage in acts of public sexual activity has never been regarded as a liberty that is fundamental to the existence of a free and democratic society. If it is reasonable to limit such fundamental liberties as free speech and the free exercise of religion, then how much more should it be permissible to impose limitations upon public sexual displays.

On the other hand, certain distinctions should be drawn for public policy purposes. Solicitation, mutual masturbation, and homosexual intercourse might be forbidden in public places and distinguished carefully from certain mannerisms and clothing styles that are supposedly common to some homosexuals. If any person is so sensitive as to be offended by the sight of a transvestite, perhaps it would be best for him to look the other way. Although it is certainly difficult to draw a firm line between displays that only the most ultrasensitive person would find offensive and those that would almost universally be regarded as indecent, it may be necessary to make such distinctions if the rights of all are to be protected.

HOMOSEXUALITY AND NATURAL LAW

Point 7, on the "unnaturalness" of homosexuality, raises the question of the meaning of *nature, natural,* and similar terms. Theologians and other moralists have said homosexual acts violate the "natural law," and that they are therefore immoral and ought to be prohibited by the state.

The word *nature* has a built-in ambiguity that can lead to serious misunderstandings. When something is said to be "natural" or in confirmity with "natural law" or the "law of nature," this may mean either (1) that it is in conformity with the descriptive laws of nature, or (2) that it is not artificial, that man has not imposed his will or his devices upon events or conditions as they exist or would have existed without such interference.

1. *The descriptive laws of nature.* The laws of nature, as these are understood by the scientist, differ from the laws of man. The former are purely descriptive, where the latter are prescriptive. When a scientist says that water boils at 212° Fahrenheit or that the volume of a gas varies directly with the heat that is applied to it and inversely with the pressure, he means

merely that as a matter of recorded and observable fact, pure water under standard conditions always boils at precisely 212° Fahrenheit and that as a matter of observed fact, the volume of a gas rises as it is heated and falls as pressure is applied to it. These "laws" merely *describe* the manner in which physical substances *actually behave*. They differ from municipal and federal laws in that they *do not prescribe behavior*. Unlike man-made laws, natural laws are not passed by any legislator or group of legislators; they are not proclaimed or announced; they impose no obligation upon anyone or anything; their violation entails no penalty, and there is no reward for following them or abiding by them. When a scientist says that the air in a tire obeys the laws of nature that govern gases, he does *not* mean that the air, having been informed that it *ought* to behave in a certain way, behaves appropriately under the right conditions. He means, rather, that as a matter of fact, the air in a tire *will* behave like all other gases. In saying that Boyle's law governs the behavior of gases, he means merely that gases do, as a matter of fact, behave in accordance with Boyle's law, and that Boyle's law enables one to predict accurately what will happen to a given quantity of a gas as its pressure is raised; he does *not* mean to suggest that some heavenly voice has proclaimed that all gases should henceforth behave in accordance with the terms of Boyle's law and that a ghostly policeman patrols the world, ready to mete out punishments to any gases that violate the heavenly decree. In fact, according to the scientist, it does not make sense to speak of a natural law being violated. For if there were a true exception to a so-called law of nature, the exception would require a change in the description of those phenomena, and the law would have been shown to be no law at all. The laws of nature are revised as scientists discover new phenomena that require new refinements in their descriptions of the way things actually happen. In this respect they differ fundamentally from human laws, which are revised periodically by legislators who are not so interested in *describing* human behavior as they are in *prescribing* what human behavior *should* be.

2. *The artificial as a form of the unnatural.* On occasion when we say that something is not natural, we mean that it is a product of human artifice. A typewriter is not a natural object, in this sense, for the substances of which it is composed have been removed from their natural state—the state in which they existed before men came along—and have been transformed by a series of chemical and physical and mechanical processes into other substances. They have been rearranged into a whole that is quite different from anything found in nature. In short, a typewriter is an artificial object. In this sense, clothing is not natural, for it has been transformed considerably from the state in which it was found in nature; and wearing clothing is also not natural, in this sense, for in one's natural state, before the application of anything artificial, before any human interference with things as they are, one is quite naked. Human laws, being artificial conventions designed to exercise a degree of control over the natural inclinations and propensities of men, may in this sense be considered to be unnatural.

When theologians and moralists speak of homosexuality, contraception, abortion, and other forms of human behavior as being unnatural and say that for that reason such behavior must be considered to be wrong, in what sense are they using the word *unnatural?* Are they saying that homosexual behavior and the use of contraceptives are contrary to the scientific laws of nature, are they saying that they are artificial forms of behavior, or are they using the terms *natural* and *unnatural* in some third sense?

They cannot mean that homosexual behavior (to stick to the subject presently under discussion) violates the laws of nature in the first sense, for, as has been pointed out, in *that* sense it is impossible to violate the laws of nature. Those laws, being merely descriptive of what actually does happen, would have to *include* homosexual behavior if such behavior does actually take place. Even if the defenders of the theological view that homosexuality is unnatural were to appeal to a statistical analysis by pointing out that such behavior is not normal from a statistical point of view, and therefore not what the laws of nature require, it would be open to their critics to reply that any descriptive law of nature must account for and incorporate all statistical deviations, and that the laws of nature, in this sense, do not *require* anything. These critics might also note that the best statistics available reveal that about half of all American males engage in homosexual activity at some time in their lives, and that a very large percentage of American males have exclusively homosexual relations for a fairly extensive period of time; from which it would follow that such behavior is natural, for them, at any rate, in this sense of the word *natural.*

If those who say that homosexual behavior is unnatural are using the term *unnatural* in the second sense as artificial, it is difficult to understand their objection. That which is artificial is often far better than what is natural. Artificial homes seem, at any rate, to be more suited to human habitation and more conducive to longer life and better health than are caves and other natural shelters. There are distinct advantages to the use of such unnatural (artificial) amenities as clothes, furniture, and books. Although we may dream of an idyllic return to nature in our more wistful moments, we would soon discover, as Thoreau did in his attempt to escape from the artificiality of civilization, that needles and thread, knives and matches, ploughs and nails, and countless other products of human artifice are essential to human life. We would discover, as Plato pointed out in the *Republic*, that no man can be truly self-sufficient. Some of the by-products of industry are less than desirable, but neither industry nor the products of industry are intrinsically evil, even though both are unnatural in this sense of the word.

Interference with nature is not evil in itself. Nature, as some writers have put it, must be tamed. In some respects man must look upon it as an enemy to be conquered. If nature were left to its own devices, without the intervention of human artifice, men would be consumed by disease, they would be plagued by insects, they would be chained to the places where they were born with no means of swift communication or transport, and they would suffer the discomforts and the torments of wind and weather and flood and fire with no practical means of combating any of them. Interfering with nature, doing battle with nature, using human will and reason and skill to thwart what might otherwise follow from the conditions that prevail in the world is a peculiarly human enterprise, one that can hardly be condemned merely because it does what is not natural.

Homosexual behavior can hardly be considered to be unnatural in this sense. There is nothing artificial about such behavior. On the contrary, it is quite natural, in this sense, to those who enage in it. And even if it were not, even if it were quite artificial, this is not in itself a ground for condemning it.

It would seem, then, that those who condemn homosexuality as an unnatural form of behavior must mean something else by the word *unnatural,* something not covered by either of the preceding definitions. A third possibility is this:

3. *Anything uncommon or abnormal is unnatural.* If this is what is meant by those who condemn homosexuality on the ground that it is unnatural, it is quite obvious that their condemnation cannot be accepted without further argument. The fact that a given form of behavior is uncommon provides no justification for condemning it. Playing viola in a string quartet may be an uncommon form of human behavior. Yet there is no reason to suppose that such uncommon behavior is, by virtue of its uncommonness, deserving of condemnation or ethically or morally wrong. On the contrary, many forms of behavior are praised precisely because they are so uncommon. Great artists, poets, musicians, and scientists are uncommon in this sense; but clearly the world is better off for having them, and it would be absurd to condemn them or their activities for their failure to be common and normal. If homosexual behavior is wrong, then, it must be for some reason other than its unnaturalness in this sense of the word.

4. *Any use of an organ or an instrument that is contrary to its principal purpose or function is unnatural.* Every organ and every instrument—perhaps even every creature—has a function to perform, one for which it is particularly designed. Any use of those instruments and organs that is consonant with their purposes is natural and proper, but any use that is inconsistent with their principal functions is unnatural and improper, and to that extent, evil or harmful. Human teeth, for example, are admirably designed for their principal functions—biting and chewing the kinds of food suitable for human consumption. But they are not particularly well suited for prying the caps from beer bottles. If they are used for that purpose, which is not natural to them, they are likely to crack or break under the strain. The abuse of one's teeth leads to their destruction and to a consequent deterioration in one's overall health. If they are used only for their proper function, however, they may continue to serve well for many years. Similarly, a given drug may have a proper function. If used in the furtherance of that end, it can preserve life and restore health. But if it is abused and employed for

purposes for which it was never intended, it may cause serious harm and even death. The natural uses of things are good and proper, but their unnatural uses are bad and harmful.

What we must do, then, is to find the proper use, or the true purpose, of each organ in our bodies. Once we have discovered that, we will know what constitutes the natural use of each organ and what constitutes an unnatural, abusive, and potentially harmful employment of the various parts of our bodies. If we are rational, we will be careful to confine behavior to the proper functions and to refrain from unnatural behavior. According to those philosophers who follow this line of reasoning, the way to discover the proper use of any organ is to determine what it is peculiarly suited to do. The eye is suited for seeing, the ear for hearing, the nerves for transmitting impulses from one part of the body to another, and so on.

What are the sex organs peculiarly suited to do? Obviously, they are peculiarly suited to enable men and women to reproduce their own kind. No other organ in the body is capable of fulfilling that function. It follows, according to those who follow the natural-law line, that the proper or natural function of the sex organs is reproduction, and that strictly speaking, any use of those organs for other purposes is unnatural, abusive, potentially harmful, and therefore wrong. The sex organs have been given to us in order to enable us to maintain the continued existence of mankind on this earth. All perversions—including masturbation, homosexual behavior, and heterosexual intercourse that deliberately frustrates the design of the sexual organs—are unnatural and bad. As Pope Pius XI once said, "Private individuals have no other power over the members of their bodies than that which pertains to their natural ends." [64]

But the problem is not so easily resolved. Is it true that every organ has one and only one proper function? A hammer may have been designed to pound nails, and it may perform that particular job best. But it is not sinful to employ a hammer to crack nuts if you have no other more suitable tool immediately available. The hammer, being a relatively versatile tool, may be employed in a number of ways. It has no one proper or natural function. A woman's eyes are well adapted to seeing, it is true. But they seem also to be well adapted to flirting. Is a woman's use of her eyes for the latter purpose sinful merely because she is not using them, at that moment, for their "primary" purpose of seeing? Our sexual organs are uniquely adapted for procreation, but that is obviously not the only function for which they are adapted. Human beings may—and do—use those organs for a great many other purposes, and it is difficult to see why any *one* use should be considered to be the only proper one. The sex organs seem to be particularly well adapted to give their owners and others intense sensations of pleasure. Unless one believes that pleasure itself is bad, there seems to be little reason to believe that the use of the sex organs for the production of pleasure in oneself or in others is evil. In view of the peculiar design of these organs, with their great concentration of nerve endings, it would seem that they were designed (if they *were* designed) with that very goal in mind, and that their use for such purposes would be no more unnatural than their use for the purpose of procreation.

Nor should we overlook the fact that human sex organs may be and are used to express, in the deepest and must intimate way open to man, the love of one person for another. Even the most ardent opponents of "unfruitful" intercourse admit that sex does serve this function. They have accordingly conceded that a man and his wife may have intercourse even though she is pregnant, or past the age of child bearing, or in the infertile period of her menstrual cycle.

Human beings are remarkably complex and adaptable creatures. Neither they nor their organs can properly be compared to hammers or to other tools. The analogy quickly breaks down. The generalization that a given organ or instrument has one and only one proper function does not hold up, even with regard to the simplest manufactured tools, for, as we have seen, a tool may be used for more than one purpose—less effectively than one especially designed for a given task, perhaps, but properly and certainly not *sinfully*. A woman may use her eyes not only to see and to flirt, but also to earn money—if she is, for example, an actress or a model. Though neither of the latter functions seems to have been a part of the original design, if one may speak sensibly of *design* in this context, of the eye, it is difficult to see why such a use of the eyes of a woman should be considered sinful, perverse, or unnatural. Her sex organs have the unique capacity of producing ova and nurturing human embryos, under the right conditions; but why should any other use of those organs, including their use to bring pleasure to their owner or to someone else, or to manifest love to another person, or even, perhaps, to earn money, be regarded as perverse, sinful, or unnatural? Similarly, a man's sexual organs possess the unique capacity of causing the generation of another human being, but if a man chooses to use them for pleasure, or for the expression of love, or for some other purpose—so long as he does not interfere with the rights of some other person—the fact that his sex organs do have their unique capabilities does not constitute a convincing justification for condemning their other uses as being perverse, sinful, unnatural, or criminal. If a man "perverts" himself by wiggling his ears for the entertainment of his neighbors instead of using them exclusively for their "natural" function of hearing, no one thinks of consigning him to prison. If he abuses his teeth by using them to pull staples from memos—a function for which teeth were clearly not designed—he is not accused of being immoral, degraded, and degenerate. The fact that people *are* condemned for using their sex organs for their own pleasure or profit, or for that of others, may be more revealing about the prejudices and taboos of our society than it is about our perception of the true nature or purpose of our bodies.

In this connection, it may be worthwhile to note that with the development of artificial means of reproduction (that is, test tube babies), the sex organs may become obsolete for reproductive purposes but would still contribute greatly to human pleasure. In addition, studies of animal behavior and anthropological reports indicate that such nonreproductive sex acts as masturbation, homosexual intercourse, and mutual fondling of genital organs are widespread, both among human beings and among lower animals. Under suitable circumstances, many animals reverse their sex roles, males assuming the posture of females and presenting themselves to others for intercourse, and females mounting other females and going through all the actions of a male engaged in intercourse. Many peoples all around the world have sanctioned and even ritualized homosexual relations. It would seem that an excessive readiness to insist that human sex organs are designed only for reproductive purposes and therefore ought to be used only for such purposes must be based upon a very narrow conception that is conditioned by our own society's peculiar history and taboos.[65]

To sum up, then, the proposition that any use of an organ that is contrary to its principal purpose or function is unnatural assumes that organs *have* a principal purpose or function, but this may be denied on the ground that the purpose or function of a given organ may vary according to the needs or desires of its owner. It may be denied on the ground that a given organ may have more than one principal purpose or function, and any attempt to call one use or another the only natural one seems to be arbitrary, if not question-begging. Also, the proposition suggests that what is unnatural is evil or depraved. This goes beyond the pure description of things, and enters into the problem of the evaluation of human behavior, which leads us to the fifth meaning of *natural*.

5. *That which is natural is good, and whatever is unnatural is bad.* When one condemns homosexuality or masturbation or the use of contraceptives on the ground that it is unnatural, one implies that whatever is unnatural is bad, wrongful, or perverse. But as we have seen, in some senses of the word, the unnatural (the artificial) is often very good, whereas that which is natural (that which has not been subjected to human artifice or improvement) may be very bad indeed. Of course, interference with nature may be bad. Ecologists have made us more aware than we have ever been of the dangers of unplanned and uninformed interference with nature. But this is not to say that *all* interference with nature is bad. Every time a man cuts down a tree to make room for a home for himself, or catches a fish to feed himself or his family, he is interfering with nature. If men did not interfere with nature, they would have no homes, they could eat no fish, and, in fact, they could not survive. What, then, can be meant by those who say that whatever is natural is good and whatever is unnatural is bad? Clearly, they cannot have intended merely to reduce the word *natural* to a synonym of *good, right,* and *proper,* and *unnatural* to a synonym of *evil, wrong, improper, corrupt,* and *depraved.* If that were all they had intended to do, there would be very little to discuss as to whether a given form of behavior might be proper even though it is not in strict conformity with someone's views of

what is natural; for *good* and *natural* being synonyms, it would follow inevitably that whatever is good must be natural, and vice versa, by definition. This is certainly not what the opponents of homosexuality have been saying when they claim that homosexuality, being unnatural, is evil. For if it were, their claim would be quite empty. They would be saying merely that homosexuality, being evil, is evil—a redundancy that could as easily be reduced to the simpler assertion that homosexuality is evil. This assertion, however, is not an argument. Those who oppose homosexuality and other sexual "perversions" on the ground that they are "unnatural" are saying that there is some objectively identifiable quality in such behavior that is unnatural; and that that quality, once it has been identified by some kind of scientific observation, can be seen to be detrimental to those who engage in such behavior, or to those around them; and that *because* of the harm (physical, mental, moral, or spiritual) that results from engaging in any behavior possessing the attribute of unnaturalness, such behavior must be considered to be wrongful, and should be discouraged by society. "Unnaturalness" and "wrongfulness" are not synonyms, then, but different concepts. The problem with which we are wrestling is that we are unable to find a meaning for *unnatural* that enables us to arrive at the conclusion that homosexuality is unnatural or that if homosexuality is unnatural, it is therefore wrongful behavior. We have examined four common meanings of *natural* and *unnatural,* and have seen that none of them performs the task that it must perform if the advocates of this argument are to prevail. Without some more satisfactory explanation of the connection between the wrongfulness of homosexuality and its alleged unnaturalness, the argument of point 7 must be rejected.

HOMOSEXUALITY AND THE BREAKDOWN OF PUBLIC MORALITY

Point 8, the last of the points in defense of legislation designed to punish homosexual behavior, is based upon the alleged social dangers of homosexuality. By permitting homosexuals to engage in their immoral behavior, it is said, others may be encouraged to do the same, leading to a general moral breakdown, to the destruction of the family—one of society's most fundamental institutions—and possibly to the destruction of the human race through a reduction in the number of fertile sexual unions.

In a time of overpopulation and a continuing population explosion, it would not be difficult to make a case in favor of *encouraging* sexual outlets that would not lead to an increase in population. Homosexuality might be one of them. It is unrealistic to suppose that homosexuality will become so popular, if it is permitted to flourish without restriction by the law, that the human species will be in danger of becoming extinct. At the moment, at any rate, it would seem that the world's governments should be less concerned with the control of homosexual behavior and more concerned with the control of heterosexual behavior. Even those countries that have made great efforts to educate their people in the techniques of birth control have thus far been unable to control their rising birth rates. The continuing rise in population, without a comparable rise in the production of food and other goods necessary for the maintenance of a decent standard of living, cannot but lead one to the conclusion that the suggestion that homosexuality could lead to extinction of the human species is, if not completely preposterous, at least so remote as to be unworthy of serious consideration for the remainder of this century. In some other age, perhaps, if human habits become quite different from what they are today, and if there is a serious shortage of manpower, the argument might have more plausibility.

Nevertheless, one may reasonably conclude that if homosexuality becomes more widely accepted, if the legal sanctions against it are abolished, and especially if the social consequences of homosexuality cease to be as serious as they are in most circles today, more people are likely to come out into the open as practicing homosexuals than there are at the present time. There can be no doubt that the risks associated with the so-called gay life make that life anything but attractive to most persons. The elimination of those risks may cause some persons who were deterred from sampling it, though they might have been curious enough to want to do so, to engage in some explorations that might lead some of them to adopt a way of life that most persons consider to be immoral or at least undesirable. The letters that authors of books and articles on homosexuality receive would indicate that many people who are homosexual, or are at least inclined to be homosexual, are deterred from following their inclinations by the obstacles placed in their way by society.[66] Removal of the obstacles would undoubtedly enable these people to come out into the open, to live as they choose without engaging in subterfuge, and to seek partners without fear of legal or social reprisals. This in turn could lead to the enticement into the homosexual life of many people who might otherwise have remained "straight." This effect, which may be regarded as undesirable from one point of view, may be seen as salutary from another. People who are now forced into hiding and ridden with feelings of guilt and persecution would be able to come out into the open, to admit to being what they are without shame and without fear. Surely this is a goal ardently to be desired in a society that prides itself on its tradition of freedom for all, including dissenters and members of minority groups.

As for the destruction of the family, the case seems to be very weak indeed. There is no evidence to support the suggestion that legitimation of homosexuality would lead to widespread breakdown in family life or to a failure on the part of many people to establish marriages and families. The argument is almost perverse, resting on the assumption, as it seems to do, that tens of thousands of people are eagerly awaiting the passage of legislation that would enable them to break away from the shackles of their heterosexuality so that they could do what they *really* want to do, namely, enter into homosexual relations. It is doubtful whether a substantial number of men would be seriously interested in giving up their relations with women for the gay life, even if all the laws on sodomy were repealed and all the social stigma disappeared. Nevertheless, there is a certain plausibility to the argument that *some* families might be hurt by a legalization of homosexuality. Some men whose strongest inclinations are toward homosexual relations have married because of social or business pressures, but might be prepared to give up their families for a male lover if the sanctions against doing so were lifted. Here one must weigh the harm that is being done to many homosexuals because of the existence of these sanctions against the hurt that might come to some people as a result of the elimination of sanctions. Not enough is known about the number of homosexually inclined persons who are married to enable one to make informed estimates of the number of families that could potentially be affected by such a change in the law; but because other factors would undoubtedly enter into any person's decision to break up his family and because some of these marriages are probably very unhappy anyway, the potential damage should not be exaggerated.

The possibility of a general moral breakdown has been dealt with in the preceding chapter. It may be appropriate to observe here that Lord Devlin, the most articulate modern spokesman for the theory that society has the right to impose criminal sanctions upon those whose practices lead to moral breakdown, signed a joint letter to the editor of the London *Times* in 1965 in which he conceded that homosexuality does not constitute a threat to the moral foundations of the community, and argued in favor of the proposals of the Wolfenden Committee.[67] The problem of moral breakdown has more than one facet, as evidenced by the methods employed by the police in tracking down homosexuals and effecting their arrest. These methods are so demoralizing and so corrupting that one could well argue that the legalization of homosexuality would be a boon to the community, for it would remove from the shoulders of the police department one of its most sordid and oppressive burdens and would eliminate one pretext for the use of corrupt practices by the police against the citizens of their communities.

The argument against the legalization of homosexuality on the ground of its danger to the community, then, is not convincing, for there is no evidence that open homosexuality would lead to a general breakdown in family life or even that it would seriously disrupt any large number of families presently existing; the chances of open homosexuality causing a general corruption in the morals of the community seem not to be very great; and the benefits that the community would reap from the new freedoms given to homosexuals, both in terms of the homosexuals' own relief from oppressive sanctions and in terms of the removal of a particularly sordid job from the shoulders of the police, would probably outweigh any harm that might ensue through the enlistment of new recruits into the gay life.

THE CASE AGAINST CRIMINAL SANCTIONS

We have seen how weak the case for criminal sanctions is. Whenever there is considerable doubt about the propriety of employing criminal sanctions against a given form of behavior, the most prudent path is the most conservative one—that is, the one that refrains from imposing sanctions or using the ponderous machinery of the criminal law and opts in favor of freedom of action. When freedom is limited in doubtful cases, there is good reason to believe that the decision is not a good one and that society would be better off in the long run if the opposite course had been adopted. It goes without saying that those who find themselves hounded by the law for forms of behavior that harm neither society as a whole nor any of their neighbors feel that they are the victims of the gravest form of injustice. But society itself, far from being protected or improved by such legislation, may actually suffer because of it.

Consider the following case.

CASE 2. THE DOWN-AND-OUT SAILOR

A few years ago, Officer Arscott of the District of Columbia police force made a telephone call to a gentleman named Rittenour at the latter's home. Arscott represented himself to Rittenour as being "down and out," claimed that he did not have much money, and asked Rittenour if he could stay at the latter's home until he "could catch a bus out of town." On receiving Rittenour's permission to come to his home, Arscott and his companion, Officer Fochett, went to Rittenour's home, arriving there at about 9:30 in the evening. Fochett stationed himself outside the door and Arscott was admitted inside by Rittenour.

Arscott told Rittenour that he had just been discharged from the Navy and that he was "down and out." Rittenour asked Arscott where he had learned of his "place of business," and Arscott explained that he had heard about it from someone he had met at the bus station. Later in the conversation, Rittenour touched Arscott's genitals and made what Arscott considered to be a suggestion that they have homosexual relations together. Arscott called Fochett, who joined him in arresting Rittenour, and Rittenour then admitted that he had had homosexual relations with some of the men who came to his home.

In the penal code of the District of Columbia, there is a provision making it unlawful for any person "to make any obscene or indecent exposure of his or her person, or to make any lewd, obscene, or indecent sexual proposal, or to commit any other lewd, obscene, or indecent act in the District of Columbia, under penalty of not more than $300.00

fine or imprisonment of not more than ninety days, or both, for each and every such offense." [68] The court refused to convict Rittenour under this statute on a number of grounds: (1) The common-law conception of a lewd, obscene, or indecent act referred only to behavior that was open or public, but not to behavior that was done privately or in the presence of only one other person who solicited or consented to the act. (2) Officer Arscott led Rittenour to believe that he would consent, or at least not object, to the latter's homosexual advances. (3) Arscott's description of his own behavior—particularly his telephone call to Rittenour and his subsequent conversation with him while in his home—reveals clearly that Arscott suspected that Rittenour was a homosexual and embarked upon an investigation designed to confirm his suspicions. But that investigation involved entrapment, a procedure whereby Arscott trapped Rittenour into making a homosexual proposal so that Arscott could then arrest him. The court suggested that such entrapment invalidates an arrest. (4) Finally, the court held that Rittenour was arrested, tried, and convicted on a charge of being a homosexual, although homosexuality as such is not a crime. The court here distinguished carefully between homosexual behavior (especially homosexual behavior that is public and open) and homosexuality— that is, the tendency or inclination to engage in homosexual behavior. While homosexual behavior is a crime, the inclination to engage in such behavior is not.[69]

Because homosexuality almost invariably involves consent on the part of the persons involved, there is seldom a complainant against a homosexual. The exceptions are when force has been used—a rare occurrence with homosexuals—or when there has been an indecent assault on a nonhomosexual, or when someone has been offended by a public display. Ordinarily, though, the police find it very difficult to enforce the laws against homosexual behavior, because they receive so few complaints from the general public. They are therefore forced, by the pressure of public opinion, which sometimes noisily demands that "something be done about the fags and the fairies," to resort to such tactics as those employed by Officer Arscott and his partner. In large cities, where the haunts of homosexuals are known to the police, patrols are regularly assigned to those places. Ordinarily, members of the vice squad, dressed in plain clothes, are assigned to such tasks. They sometimes dress in such a manner as to attract the attention of homosexuals who are cruising around, looking for a contact. They may also behave in a provocative manner. A British police expert has said, concerning such practices:

The term *agents provocateurs* is a justly pejorative name for young police decoys, whose squalid hunting ground is the public urinal. . . . I should have thought it apparent that the time had now come to discontinue this

miserable stratagem in importuning cases, rather than go on denying that it
exists. If the importuning is as difficult to detect as all that, it can't matter
much to "public decency." [70]

A typical example of such entrapment procedures is illustrated by the
Kelly case, which has served as one of the leading cases in the development
of the legal doctrine on entrapment in the United States.

CASE 3. THE FRIENDLY STRANGER

Officer Manthos, a member of the vice squad, was in Franklin Park,
dressed in plain clothes, for the purpose of making arrests of homosexuals. He was accompanied by Officer Winemiller, who stationed
himself on a bench not far from the bench on which Officer Manthos
seated himself. Shortly after midnight, Kelly walked through the park,
and seated himself on an unoccupied bench between the benches occupied by the two officers. A conversation developed between Kelly and
Manthos, about the time, the weather, their mutual interest in plastics;
about Atlanta, Georgia, where both of them had lived; and about other
matters. At the end of the conversation, which will be related shortly,
the two men walked to Kelly's car. Manthos then placed Kelly under
arrest and called to his partner, who had heard none of the preceding
conversation.

According to Manthos, at the culmination of their conversation, Kelly
proposed that they go to his (Kelly's) apartment for an act of perversion. Kelly, however, claimed that Manthos had suggested that they
get a drink, and that Kelly then invited Manthos to his apartment,
where he said that he had a bottle which they could share.

A number of facts are relevant here. First, Kelly shared his apartment with a roommate, and he knew that his roommate was at home
at that time. Further, Manthos claimed that he could not recall how
many such arrests he had made that night, but Winemiller informed
the court that he had made six. Ten character witnesses, most of them
fellow workers in the Public Health Service, testified in Kelly's behalf.
And Kelly had had a date with a young lady before the incident in the
park. Kelly was convicted and sentenced to a prison term.

The appeal court held that the uncorroborated testimony of a single
witness could not support a conviction. The nature of the alleged
offense is such, the judge said, that it must be proved beyond dispute.
As he put it:

> The public has a peculiar interest in the problem before us. The alleged
> offense, consisting of a few spoken words, may be alleged to have
> occurred in any public place, where any citizen is likely to be. They may
> be alleged to have been whispered, or to have occurred in the course of
> a most casual conversation. Any citizen who answers a stranger's inquiry
> as to direction, or time, or a request for a dime or a match is liable
> to be threatened with an accusation of this sort. There is virtually no

protection, except one's reputation and appearance of credibility, against an uncorroborated charge of this sort. At the same time, the results of the accusation itself are devastating to the accused.

The threatened accusation of this offense is the easiest of blackmail methods. . . . The public has a great interest in the prevention of any such criminal operation.

So, as in all acute conflicts between public and private interests, the law must be exceedingly careful in its processes. While enforcement of this particular statute must seek the prevention of the offense, it must also seek to prevent unwarranted irreparable destruction of reputations, and it must seek to prevent the equally criminal offense of blackmail; it must not foster conditions or practices which make easy and encourage that offense.

As a result of these considerations, the court counselled the lower courts to receive the testimony of a single witness to a verbal invitation to sodomy only with great caution and issued a number of other cautions as well. Kelly's conviction was reversed.[71]

The Kelly case illustrates the dangers inherent in entrapment procedures, but it offers only one part of the rationale behind the courts' refusal to admit evidence gained through such procedures. In a later case,[72] the court noted that when flirtation between one man and another is encouraged and mutual, and leads to an overt act that is neither discouraged nor repelled, such an act may not be considered to be a criminal assault. The court observed that "an officer of the law . . . has the duty of preventing, not encouraging crime. . . . An officer should not be permitted to 'torment and tease weak men beyond their power to resist' and then attempt to make out a case of assault."

Entrapment is one of the chief means of enforcing laws regarding morals offenses. When such techniques are employed, they prey upon those who are so entrapped, they create crime where none might otherwise exist, and they constitute in themselves an unlawful and immoral abuse of governmental authority and power. If the enforcement of such laws can be carried out only through the use of such means, then society might be better off if it were to tolerate the moral evil (if it is that) of homosexual behavior rather than to subject its citizens to such abuses at the hands of the police or to run the risk of the public becoming contemptuous of the law and its enforcers.

More than once Socrates is reported to have observed that although it is bad to be the victim of injustice, it is even worse to be the perpetrator of injustice, for the victim of an injustice suffers physical harm, or loss of liberty, or loss of property, but he is not made a worse person for his experience. Morally, at least, he maintains his personal integrity. But the perpetrator of an injustice loses his personal integrity; he becomes a dishonest man, a corrupt and perverse personality. In Socrates's view, no man could suffer a greater loss than this. We may have some reservations about this doctrine, but there is good reason to believe that sordid, immoral, and unjust behavior tends to make a man sordid, immoral, and unjust. When a police officer works on the vice squad, his own character may suffer, to some extent, from his contacts. When his work involves the use of such techniques as those described, he may lose something himself in the process.* Society, too, if it permits its own agents to behave lawlessly, suffers from spiritual and moral impoverishment as a result.

Besides the corruption entailed in such practices as entrapment, the policeman who is assigned to the vice detail may be subjected to the temptation of giving in to bribery. In some cities it has been established that no gay bar operates for very long without the police becoming aware of its existence. It is only a matter of time, then, before the police are in a position to close it down, relying on liquor laws, public nuisance statutes, or other legal devices to justify their actions. In most large cities, however, the police tend to have a relatively tolerant attitude toward such operations. In many instances, their tolerance is rewarded by small favors that pass from the proprietors of the bars to the law enforcement officers. Many reporters have testified that they have seen police stop at gay bars nightly for a drink. Some bars are equipped with special lights or bells that are activated whenever a policeman enters, warning the men inside to keep their distance from one another until after the danger is past. Others, however, continue to operate normally when the police are present, secure in the knowledge that the police have been paid off. However, whenever the city administration is about to change, or when the public outcry against corruption grows too loud, a few bars must be raided and closed down. They spring up again, in another location, with the same bartender, the same clientele, and often the same cop raking in his payoff.

Police corruption is not the same as the exercise of police discretion, though the results may be similar. Officially, the police are seldom empowered to exercise any discretion in determining whether a particular offender should or should not be arrested. The statutes usually require the police officer to arrest "all" violators or "all persons committing an offense in his presence," or impose a duty to enforce "all" the criminal laws.[73] Nevertheless, studies reveal that the police exercise a considerable degree of discretion in carrying out their duties. The problem must inevitably arise: How

---

* David Senak, a Detroit policeman whose work was concentrated primarily in the morals squad, illustrates this point. In an interview with John Hersey after the Algiers Motel incident, in which Senak was involved, he explained that he had arrested close to 200 girls and had succeeded in getting convictions on them for prostitution. "I think not so much being a police officer," he said, "as doing vice duties has on the whole given me a bad outlook on women in general." He explained that since he had joined the police department, he had had trouble relating to the women he dated. When Hersey asked him whether his experiences on the vice squad had made him think of women as essentially evil, or more apt to be criminal than men, he responded by asking, "Who gave who the apple?" See John Hersey, The Algiers Motel Incident (New York: Bantam Books), 1968, pp. 75ff.

fair are the police in deciding who should be arrested for a given offense and who should not? Indeed, can a reasonable standard of fairness be developed for such situations, in which the policeman is, in a sense, acting not only in his own official capacity but also as judge and jury by deciding in advance that some offenders should not be punished, regardless of what the law requires? To what extent will the policeman's own prejudices and personal tastes be permitted to influence these decisions? Will he base his decisions on such variables as the attractiveness of a particular offender, or his or her personal offensiveness, as measured by the policeman's personal standards? If such criteria are in fact employed, there is some question whether justice is being done. The problem of unfair and unjust exercise of discretion, whether such discretion is authorized by the law or not, undoubtedly pervades every aspect of a policeman's work. But there may be a special danger where morals statutes are concerned, for the temptation to prey upon those who exhibit special weaknesses may be more than some officers are able to resist. If homosexuals are particularly liable to be subjected to special discretionary treatment by the police—and I would assume that they, along with other offenders against the morals statutes, are more likely to be subjected to such discretionary treatment than are other classes of offenders—this would be one more argument for repealing the present laws against homosexual behavior between consenting adults.

The problem of the efficacy of the criminal law as a means of deterring homosexuality inevitably arises. Although some people have suggested that the criminal law is not at all effective in this area, it is doubtful that that is the case. On the contrary, much of the evidence points to its effectiveness in a great many cases. The stories of homosexuals who suffer lonely and unhappy lives because of their fear of entering into the only kind of love affair that they feel able to participate in illustrate as well as anything can the effectiveness of the legal and the social sanctions in reducing the incidence of homosexual behavior. This is not to say that the threat of criminal sanctions is totally effective. Obviously, it is not. The threat of criminal sanctions is not totally effective in *any* field, whether it be gambling, prostitution, embezzlement, robbery, or murder. Some persons are willing to take their chances, hoping that they will not be caught. Others, however, afraid of the possible consequences, choose to stay on the right side of the law, even though it means giving up a form of conduct in which they might otherwise have wanted to engage.

Some of the most consistent opponents of homosexuality have advocated repeal of laws whose effect is to punish homosexual behavior between consenting adults in private. A Roman Catholic Advisory Committee formed to study the problems of homosexuality and prostitution in relation to the existing laws in England restated the Church's opposition to "all directly voluntary sexual pleasure outside marriage" on the ground that such pleasure is sinful. The committee's report distinguished carefully between sin and crime, defining the latter as a social concept and not a moral one. "Sin," it said, "is not the concern of the State but affects the relations between the soul and God." The committee also upheld the traditional justifications for criminal punishment on grounds of deterrence and reform and suggested that retribution, too, might be a legitimate reason for punishing certain kinds of behavior. However, the committee maintained that "the State should not go beyond its proper limits in this connexion," that is, in its effort to restrain individuals from committing the "more detestable offences." "Attempts by the State to enlarge its authority and invade the individual conscience, however high-minded, always fail and frequently do positive harm. . . . It should accordingly be clearly stated that penal sanctions are not justified for the purpose of attempting to restrain sins against sexual morality committed in private by responsible adults." The committee then advocated the abolition of all criminal sanctions for such behavior on the grounds that:

   (a) they are ineffectual;
   (b) they are inequitable in their incidence;
   (c) they involve severities disproportionate to the offense committed;
   (d) they undoubtedly give scope for blackmail and other forms of corruption.[74]

The committee noted that existing criminal procedures resulted in the burden of penalties falling upon a small minority of actual offenders, and often upon those least deserving of punishment. It noted also that imprisonment was ineffectual in helping to reorient persons with homosexual tendencies, and stated that incarceration often had deleterious effects upon them. This was one factor in its decision.

At a time when the public is rightly concerned over rising crime rates—that is, with the rising rates of such serious crimes of violence as muggings, rapes, robberies, and murders—another argument commends itself for serious consideration. When police manpower is diverted from the prevention and detection of such crimes to the tracking down of homosexuals, one must wonder whether society's resources are being used in the most effective manner. Is the punishment of homosexuals so important as to deserve *any* attention from undermanned police forces in cities where there is only one arrest for every ten crimes of violence? Would the meager resources available in such cities not be expended more wisely if first priority were given to the protection of life and property, with the pursuit of homosexuals and other "immoral" persons being relegated to the bottom of the list, or removed from the list entirely?

It is sometimes said that if the penalties against homosexual relations were removed, that action would be tantamount to society's putting its stamp of approval upon behavior that our long tradition and some of our most respected theologians and moralists consider to be immoral. On such grounds, much progress in the reform of the law is thwarted. But the argument is not convincing. If society declares that it will not punish persons for certain kinds of behavior, that declaration does not constitute, in itself, a stamp of approval for such behavior. Parents have been known to declare to their children that they do not approve of those with whom the latter associate, though they may not penalize them for continuing to associate with those persons. A wise parent knows that some forms of behavior, though they may not be such as he approves of, are nevertheless not so bad as to warrant the expenditure of energy and emotion that are involved in the infliction of punishment. He reserves punishment for those offenses that he considers to be most destructive to the good order and welfare of the family, or of society, or—most importantly, perhaps—of the child himself. He relies instead upon education and persuasion and reason as means of inducing his children to adopt the norms that he considers to be good and to reject those forms of behavior that he considers to be bad. A society is not essentially different in this respect. Its lawmakers and others who are in a position to set social policy may consider the expenditure of wealth and human resources required for the enforcement of rules on sexual conduct to be too great for the benefits that might accrue from such enforcement. They may wish to rely instead upon education and other means of persuasion to convince the public that such behavior is not desirable. Instead of enacting a multitude of laws to enforce every petty offense, they may find, in the long run, that there is considerable benefit in relying upon the good will and the common sense of the people. Following such a course, the police would be free to fight dangerous criminals and to maintain order in the community, the courts would be relieved of a part of their crushing burden, jails and prisons would be emptied of those whose offenses are basically petty and of no great or immediate social consequence, and, most important of all, a great many people would be relieved of the constant fear that they might be arrested for forms of behavior that they consider to be completely harmless—if not to themselves, at least to society at large. The abolition of penal sanctions could be accompanied by wide publicity, if the legislature felt so disposed, in which its collective disapproval of homosexual behavior could be expressed, with appropriate reasons. At the same time, it could explain why it had concluded that the forces of the law were not appropriate for the control of that particular moral problem. And it would naturally want to inform the public, carefully and clearly, about the restrictions that would continue to exist—restrictions on offensive public behavior, on homosexual relations with children, and the like.

The laws in various countries, and in various states within the United States, vary considerably. Nearly one-quarter of the states have repealed statutes providing for criminal punishment of homosexual acts committed in private by consenting adults. The Model Penal Code of the American Law Institute proposed that private sexual acts, whether heterosexual or homosexual, should be criminal only when minors are involved or some force or coercion was employed, but only Illinois has adopted the proposed reform. Other states have harsh penalties on the books, ranging from three months in prison or one year's probation in New York to life imprisonment in one state of every seven. In some states, the *minimum* punishment can be quite harsh, as in South Carolina, for example, where a man must be sent to prison for not less than five years for such an act.

In England, the latest legislation (1967) generally followed the recommendations of the Wolfenden Committee. For private acts committed by consenting adults there are no penalties, but an adult who commits any homosexual act with a youth between sixteen and twenty-one years of age can be sent to prison for five years, and if the boy is under sixteen, the adult may be imprisoned for life.

In Europe the picture is mixed. For consensual relations between adults, Denmark, Belgium, France, Holland, Italy, and Sweden impose no penalties. In Finland, Norway, and Germany both parties are punishable; and in Austria, both parties are punishable, even if the offense is lesbianism.

The reader may have wondered why this discussion of homosexuality has concentrated almost exclusively on the male variety. The answer is that except for Austria, lesbians are seldom prosecuted, even where lesbianism is illegal; and in most places, including those that have strict penalties against male homosexuality, there are no laws forbidding lesbianism. More than a decade ago, Kinsey observed that although there had been tens of thousands of prosecutions and convictions for male homosexuality in New York during the period covered by his study, only three women had been arrested for lesbianism, and all three of those cases were dismissed. Even in social relations, lesbianism—as long as it is not too open or blatant—is more readily accepted than male homosexuality. Women may room together without occasioning any comment from their neighbors. They may walk arm in arm down the street. They may dance together. They may even kiss one another warmly when they meet. For reasons into which we need not enter here, such forms of behavior between women are accepted quite readily in the Western world, but are not acceptable when engaged in by men. Austria seems to be the only country in the world that actively enforces its laws against lesbianism.[75]

Sending homosexuals to prison is scarcely likely to effect a cure, if that is what is desired. In order to "cure" a man of his desire for men, we send him to a place where women are never seen, where his only companions are other men who are deprived of every sexual outlet but masturbation and homosexuality, and where other homosexuals are to be found in great abundance. It would make more sense to send him to a place where he was surrounded by dancing girls, specially trained in the art of arousing men who tend not to be particularly interested in women. But this is scarcely likely to commend itself to the authorities as a feasible or suitable penalty for homosexuality.

In any event, most efforts to "cure" homosexuals have ended in utter failure. A few homosexuals who undertake one form of therapy or another are effectively "cured," in that they become heterosexual. But a very high proportion of those who seek to become heterosexual, particularly when they have been homosexual for a very long period of time, do not succeed.[76]

CONCLUSION

If Justinian were right, and sodomy caused earthquakes, plagues, and famines, harsh penalties for sodomy would certainly be in order, for it would be a serious crime against society, and it would cause much needless suffering to many innocent persons. But all the available evidence indicates that Justinian was wrong and that if homosexuality is harmful to anyone at all, it is harmful only to those who engage in it. At that, most of the harm that comes to homosexuals is the result of society's attitude toward their peculiar form of erotic behavior rather than a direct result of that behavior itself. If society would reduce its condemnation of homosexual behavior, at least by removing the penalties that it imposes upon those who are caught, the condition of homosexuals would be greatly ameliorated. The dire predictions that Lord Devlin made, about the moral decay of society if such proposals as those of the Wolfenden Committee were adopted, seem not to be realistic, and Lord Devlin finally came out in support of those proposals. Society has better things to do with its resources than to enforce private morality, particularly in a time of such great social disruption as the present.

Certain societies of homosexuals and their sympathizers have expressed a desire not only for the removal of criminal penalties for their behavior, but also for the introduction of legislation that would enable them to enjoy many of the privileges and rights that have heretofore been enjoyed only by married heterosexual couples. They have complained, for example, about what they consider to be the unfair tax laws, which offer considerable advantages to married couples. Homosexual couples are deprived of those advantages and must file individual returns, even though they may have very stable relationships—even more stable than those of some male-female marriages. Again, some homosexuals have asked why they should not be permitted to adopt children. Like many heterosexual couples, they find themselves unable to have children of their own, but they feel that they might be able to offer a child a warm and loving home with two parents. Because of the laws of most states and provinces, they are unable to do so. And finally, if they were permitted to marry, their relationships might be given a degree of stability that they lack today without the safeguards and protections to family stability offered by the laws of marriage and divorce. By bringing homosexuals within those laws, they would not only receive the tax and inheritance advantages that heterosexual couples enjoy, but they would be able to achieve a degree of stability in their relationships with one another that has eluded most such couples in the past. If the homosexual marriage could be "sealed" with one or more children, as most heterosexual marriages are, it is hoped that they would become even more stable and achieve a higher degree of permanence.

Our society is obviously a long way from accepting such proposals as these. The institution of marriage has such a long history and is encrusted with so many emotional, historical, and literary associations, all of them heterosexual, that it is not likely that anything called homosexual *marriage*, in the true legal sense, will come into existence in our time. But it is not beyond the realm of possibility that some of these proposals might be given effect in some form that does not embody the concept of marriage. Homosexuals might be permitted to form partnerships, for example, and the laws might be rewritten to permit persons living in special kinds of partnerships to enjoy the tax benefits and the inheritance advantages that have heretofore been reserved to married couples.

Recently there have been reports of homosexuals adopting one another, thus achieving some of these goals. It is of course quite unusual for one grown man to adopt another, but it can be done. When it is, the adoption is permanent—far more permanent even than a marriage might be—and the benefits that the adoptive son receives from his adoptive father cannot be taken from him by a later act of the adoptive father. In those states, for example, where a son is automatically entitled to a certain proportion of his father's estate even if the latter has cut him out of his will, the adoptive father in such a relationship may find himself with an unwanted son of whom he is unable to rid himself, and he may be unable to dispose of his estate as he would like to do.

Whether one agrees with the legislative proposals of the Mattachine Society and other organizations of homosexuals or not, one may sympathize with the members of this persecuted minority who are struggling for the recognition of rights that are granted to other citizens as a matter of course: for equal treatment before the law; for freedom from police harassment; for the right to pursue their way of life without fear of arrest, imprisonment, or compulsory psychiatric treatment; and for the right to be judged in their professions or trades on the quality of their work rather than on their private conduct when they are not on the job.

There are hopeful signs. Clergymen have a reputation for being among society's more conservative members. But more and more churches are becoming open to the ordination of homosexuals. A bishop of the Episcopal church has openly presided at the ordination of a professed lesbian. Some homosexual clergymen are "coming out," revealing publicly the fact of their sexual preferences. A Jesuit priest who admits to having homosexual inclinations has written a book in which he asserts that homosexual clergy can bring special sensitivities and gifts to ministering to all their constituents, heterosexual as well as homosexual. On the other hand, an annual convention of the Southern Baptists declared that homosexuality is a sin and vowed to keep homosexuals out of the clergy and church employment. And at least one candidate for priesthood in the Roman Catholic church has been denied ordination on the ground that this would represent tacit approval of unrepentant homosexuality.[77]

Perhaps even more important, the business community has discovered that it is profitable to do business with the homosexual market. According to the *Wall Street Journal,* more products are being geared specifically to that market, and many consumer products are being advertised in publications directed toward the homosexual segment of the population.[78]

On the other hand, there are signs that some of the more serious problems confronting the homosexual are not likely to go away. The rate of venereal disease among homosexuals is increasing dramatically. Also, homosexuals continue to be vulnerable to attack as they "cruise," looking for pickups; young boys often lure older men into soliciting sex from them, and then beat or rob them.[79]

One might conclude that the life of the typical homosexual is squalid and immoral. The promiscuity, the furtive pickups, the cruising, the gay bars, the whole scene may strike some persons as being most unsavory. One should not forget, however, that this is not the whole scene. From accounts that are beginning to emerge, as wealthy and prominent homosexuals reveal themselves as such to the public, there is another homosexual scene, hidden from the public gaze, that is quiet, relatively stable (perhaps not much less stable than the typical American marriage today), and—in its own way— quite respectable. Stereotypes of the "typical" homosexual may have been derived from atypical situations, or at least from situations that represent a certain class in society whose heterosexual activities may be no more tasteful than their homosexual activities are.

An American serviceman runs the risk of being arrested by the military police, however successful he might be as a military man, if he enters a homosexual bar or any establishment that is known to be frequented by homosexuals. He may then be discharged on no other grounds than that he is a homosexual. But innumerable servicemen have picked up foreign women overseas, had sexual relations with them, caused them to become pregnant, and then abandoned them to shift as best they could with their illegitimate children. In some societies, including Vietnam, where thousands of children fathered by American military personnel now live, both the mother and the child are shunned by the members of their communities and bear a stigma that may attach to them for the rest of their lives. No GI has ever been subject to significant sanctions for having brought such disgrace and hardship upon a woman and his own child. However wicked one might assume homosexuality to be, it would seem that there is something very wrong about a system that apparently condones the fathering and subsequent abandonment of illegitimate children and at the same time imposes such harsh sanctions upon men whose sexual activities are unlikely ever to have such ruinous effects upon others.

In the United States, a number of communities have enacted gay rights ordinances, granting immunity against prosecution for their private sexual activities to persons whose sexual preferences differ from those of the majority, and also the right not to be discriminated against in jobs, housing, and other areas. There recently has arisen, however, a powerful movement dedicated to bringing about the abrogation of those ordinances. Members of that movement evidently base their activities upon the assumption that homosexuality is wicked, having been forbidden by Scripture and frowned upon by religious and moral authorities of the past. They seem to assume that homosexuals exert a dangerous, corrupting influence upon the youth and the general moral quality of the communities in which they live. And they appear to be unconcerned about the suffering engendered by invoking the harsh sanction of the criminal law against persons whose activities, by all available evidence, are unlikely to harm anyone, and also to be unconcerned about the needless suffering their actions and attitudes are promoting, as individuals and groups continue to harass and persecute a relatively harmless minority within their communities.

3

Contraception and Abortion

THE PROBLEM

In most parts of the world contraceptives may now be legally sold, and physicians or other persons may offer advice to those who wish to plan their families or to limit the number of children they bring into the world by taking deliberate steps to avoid conception. Some countries are afflicted with massive overpopulation and with all that that entails—serious overcrowding, food shortages, desperate conditions of poverty, misery, squalor, and disease, and, with all that, a continuing increase of the population in geometrical proportions. The governments of some of these nations have organized campaigns designed to introduce family planning to their people and to provide them with the means to carry out the program. Some, such as India, Jamaica, and Japan, have spent vast sums of money to educate their people on the desirability of family planning and the use of contraceptives and have provided financial and other incentives for those who use government-supplied devices and services.

However, there are still places where the use or sale of contraceptive devices is illegal and the offering of advice on their use, even by physicians, is prohibited. Substantial segments of some communities oppose the use of artificial means of birth control on moral or religious grounds. When possible, they use their influence to prevent the liberalization of laws governing such matters; and when that is impracticable, some of them use their powers of moral suasion to convince their followers not to employ such means in their own lives.

On the other hand, some nations have gone to great lengths to encourage or even to impose birth control upon their people. For a number of years, India has pursued a vigorous family-planning program because its population (620 million at the end of 1976, with 35,000 births every day) is growing far too rapidly for its backward economy. The poverty of India's people and the periodic famines that sweep over its territory seem to leave its rulers with no alternative.

In addition to advertising, educational campaigns, and free clinics, which distribute contraceptive devices and perform free vasectomies (a relatively simple operation that sterilizes men), India moved, during Indira Gandhi's reign as Prime Minister, to methods of coercion. The government called these programs "incentives and disincentives." Official vasectomy quotas were set throughout the nation. Teachers and low-ranking government officials were expected to bring a certain number of vasectomy candidates to the clinics each month, and civil servants were informed that their jobs might depend upon their success in limiting their families to no more than three children.

In 1976 about 7 million persons (mostly men) submitted to sterilization operations. But in some areas, bloody riots broke out in protest against what the people construed to be compulsory measures that were being enforced against them when they refused to submit to such operations. One state, Maharashtra, introduced legislation that would forbid any family from having more than three children without the government's approval. In addition to the threat of loss of government employment, people who failed to comply with the family-planning program could be denied loans or new housing plots. Women were given maternity benefits only if they agreed to tubal ligations that rendered them sterile. As Prime Minister Gandhi has put it, "We should not hesitate to take steps which might be described as drastic. Some personal rights have to be kept in abeyance for the human right of the nation, the right to live, the right to progress." [1]

In Pakistan, another extremely poor and overcrowded nation, the expenditure of millions of dollars in an effort to solve the population problem has thus far been a dismal failure. The birth rate is estimated at three times that of the United States. Some 75 million people live in a territory twice the size of California, and the combined effects of a huge birth rate and a lower death rate (the result of better sanitation and health care) will double that population within 23 years. Prime Minister Ali Bhutto has said that "the shadow of overpopulation darkens the prospect of our economic advance; it nullifies our efforts toward social progress." [2] Ignorance, poverty, superstition, fear, and traditional religious and social values have all undoubtedly contributed to the failure of this program. With every passing year, as the populations burgeon in these and other impoverished nations, they and the world as a whole come closer to a calamity of the first magnitude. A few years of drought in the major food-producing nations could set off a world-wide famine that could breed riots, rebellions, revolutions, and a series of wars that could engulf the entire world.

Some influential Americans are now advocating measures similar to those adopted in India. For example, The Environmental Fund has run full-page newspaper advertisements advocating a moratorium on all American food aid and technical assistance to any country whose population growth rate is above the world average, "unless it officially acknowledges that its national birth rate must be lowered and unless it adopts stringent measures to control population growth, which measures must be judged adequate by the United States as the donor nation." Anticipating the response of those who would feel that such measures would be immoral when the alternative is starvation of millions of innocent persons, the ads continue:

> Those who feel this way must weigh the morality of the moratorium against the morality of any action which contributes to overpopulation. Overpopulation today makes it impossible for half of those within the hungry nations to have the diet necessary to protect them against debilitating diseases that bring early death. Overpopulation makes whole nations dependent upon the vagaries of the weather to prevent famine in their lands. Overpopulation leads to more suffering and more deaths, to war, and to chaos. . . .
>
> Who, then, are the moral—those who advocate steps that will decelerate population growth, or those who advocate steps that will encourage population growth. [3]

In addition, the Fund advocates the enactment of a "national population stabilization program" and the "encouragement" of smaller families. Although it does not spell out what such a program would consist of, or how people would be "encouraged" to have smaller families, it is at least possible that compulsory measures such as those adopted by the Indian government might be considered as appropriate by some of the Fund's directors. Less drastic measures might include elimination of the income tax exemption for each dependent over a certain number, or tax penalties for "excess" children.

With the emphasis in Western societies upon individual liberty and the powerful commitment to each person's right to determine the size of his own family, it is difficult to accept the propriety of such coercive measures. But on the principle that a person may do whatever he pleases so long as he harms no one else, it is possible to make a case for the proposition that compulsory limitation of the size of a person's family may be morally permissible. For as Prime Minister Gandhi said, an individual's choice to have more than his "quota" can result in irreversible damage to innumerable others and to the nation as a whole.

Up to 1965, certain American states had laws on their books forbidding the distribution of advice and information on contraception by physicians, pharmacists, and other professionals. The sale or use of contraceptive devices was prohibited. Connecticut had such a law. The Planned Parenthood League of Connecticut opened a family-planning center in New Haven in defiance of that law, and its executive director and medical director (a licensed physician and professor at Yale University's Medical School) were arrested for having given information, instruction, and medical advice to married persons on means of preventing conception, and for prescribing contraceptive devices. They were found guilty and appealed to the United States Supreme Court.

The Court held that "the First Amendment has a penumbra where privacy is protected from governmental intrusion." That is, although the right of privacy is nowhere mentioned in the Constitution, the exercise of certain rights that *are* protected in the Constitution would be impossible without a corresponding right to privacy. Thus, for example, freedom of association would be meaningless if groups and organizations could be forced to reveal their membership lists and thus subject their members to harassment. In this case, the Court (through Justice William O. Douglas) asked:

> Would we allow the police to search the sacred precincts of marital bedrooms for telltale signs of the use of contraceptives? The very idea is repulsive to the notions of privacy surrounding the marriage relationship.
>
> We deal with a right of privacy older than the Bill of Rights—older than our political parties, older than our school system. Marriage is a coming together for better or for worse, hopefully enduring, and intimate to the degree of being sacred.[4]

Justice Arthur Goldberg, concurring with the majority decision, cited an earlier case in which Justice Harlan had written:

> The integrity of [family] life is something so fundamental that it has been found to draw to its protection the principles of more than one explicitly granted Constitutional right. . . . Of this whole 'private realm of family life' it is difficult to imagine what is more private or more intimate than a husband and wife's marital relations. . . .
>
> The intimacy of husband and wife is necessarily an essential and accepted feature of the institution of marriage, an institution which the State not only must allow, but which always and in every age it has fostered and protected. It is one thing when the State exerts its power either to forbid extra-marital sexuality . . . or to say who may marry, but it is quite another when, having acknowledged a marriage and the intimacies inherent in it, it undertakes to regulate by means of the criminal law the details of that intimacy.[5]

In responding to some of his colleagues on the Court, who had dissented on the ground that no right of privacy could be found in the Constitution, Justice Goldberg wrote:

Surely the Government, absent a showing of a compelling subordinating state interest, could not decree that all husbands and wives must be sterilized after two children have been born to them. Yet, by their reasoning [that is, the reasoning of the dissenters], such an invasion of marital privacy would not be subject to constitutional challenge because . . . no provision of the Constitution specifically prevents the Government from curtailing the marital right to bear children and raise a family. . . . In my view it is . . . shocking to believe that the personal liberty guaranteed by the Constitution does not include protection against such totalitarian limitation of family size, which is at complete variance with our constitutional concepts. Yet, if upon a showing of a slender basis of rationality, a law outlawing voluntary birth control by married persons is valid, then, by the same reasoning, a law requiring compulsory birth control also would seem to be valid. In my view, however, both types of law would unjustifiably intrude upon rights of marital privacy which are constitutionally protected.[6]

Two diametrically opposite views on contraception, both appealing to important moral considerations, are thus in evidence: one (that which prevails among government officials in India) that the government has the right to interfere with the growth of families by imposing regulations that require sterilization or the use of artificial methods of contraception, and the other (represented by the United States Supreme Court's decision) that the government has no right whatever to interfere in this private matter. There is yet a third position: that the government *does* have a right to interfere, but on the side opposite to that of the Indian government's stand— that is, that the government may (or ought to) take measures designed to discourage the use of artificial means of birth control, and that people generally have an obligation to refrain from the use of contraceptives. This last view has been most forcefully articulated by the Roman Catholic Church, whose views will be outlined in some detail in the next section.

Some of the most popular and effective methods of birth control are also likely to be abortifacients. That is, instead of preventing a human sperm from uniting with an ovum to produce a zygote that could, if allowed to develop normally, become a fully formed human being, these birth control methods act *after* the zygote is formed and prevent the implantation of the zygote in the woman's uterus. In a sense, then, they cause an abortion to occur. The pill and intrauterine devices (IUD's) seem to operate in this fashion. It follows, then, that any arguments against abortion would also be arguments against at least some kinds of contraception. (Strictly speaking, from this point of view, the pill and the IUD are not measures of preventing conception, but measures of assuring very early abortions.) The intimate connection between the problem of abortion and the problem of contraception has been pointed out by Germain Grisez:

> If one recognizes that human life is at stake if these methods [the pill and the IUD] do indeed work in an abortifacient manner, then it is clear that the willingness to use them is a willingness to kill human beings directly.

The effect of killing the already conceived individual, if it occurs, is no accident, but the precise thing sought in committing oneself to birth prevention. *If one is willing to get a desired result by killing, and does not know whether he is killing or not, he might as well know that he is killing,* for he is willing to accept that as the meaning of his act: Everyone who knows the facts and who prescribes or uses birth control methods that might be abortifacient is an abortionist at heart.[7]

Few subjects are as intimately entwined with religious tradition as this. Different religious traditions approach the problem differently. Although it is certainly possible to discuss the issues without reference to the religious background against which they have developed, some appreciation of the history of legal, moral, and religious attitudes toward contraception and abortion in the Western world will be helpful to anyone who is interested in understanding the depth of the feeling surrounding this highly emotional controversy.

A SHORT HISTORY OF RELIGIOUS AND MORAL THINKING ON CONTRACEPTION AND ABORTION

HELLENISM

In ancient Greece and Rome, contraception, abortion, and infanticide were not at all uncommon. According to Plato's calculations, men and women passed their prime child-bearing and child-begetting years after the ages of fifty-five and forty, respectively. Once they had passed those ages, he said, they should be permitted to have relations freely, so long as they were not incestuous. But they would be warned that "no child, if any be conceived, shall be brought to light, or, if they cannot prevent its birth, [they are] to dispose of it on the understanding that no such child can be reared."[8] The citizens were to be encouraged, then, to take precautions against conception, and, if those precautions failed, they were either to secure an abortion or to commit infanticide, on eugenic grounds. Even defective children born to parents in their prime were to be "hidden away, in some appropriate manner that must be kept secret."[9] According to Aristotle, "if no restriction is imposed on the rate of reproduction, . . . poverty is the inevitable result; and poverty produces, in its turn, civic dissension and wrong doing." In order to reduce the chances for civil strife, then, and to eliminate poverty, Aristotle advocates a limitation on the population, and therefore, the imposition of limits on family size. Such limits, he suggests, should be fixed to allow for infant mortality and the amount of infertility among married couples.[10] Elsewhere, he takes up the question of infanticide and abortion:

> The question arises whether children should always be reared or may sometimes be exposed to die. There should certainly be a law to prevent the rearing of deformed children. On the other hand, there should also be a law,

in all states where the system of social habits is opposed to unrestricted increase, to prevent the exposure of children to death *merely* in order to keep the population down. The proper thing to do is to limit the size of each family, and if children are then conceived in excess of the limit so fixed, to have miscarriage induced before sense and life have begun in the embryo.[11]

From these quotations, it is evident that far more is involved here than the code of Sparta, which gave every father the right to dispose of his children by slaying them, but imposed upon all parents the duty of bringing their children before state inspectors, who would examine them for physical or mental defects. Any children who were found to be defective were thrown from a cliff and smashed on the rocks below.[12] In the Hellenistic period, abortion was freely permitted throughout Greece and Macedonia. Wives who had abortions would be punished only if they had done so without the permission of their husbands. Families were kept small, either by abortion or by exposure of infants, particularly girls. Few wealthy Greek families in the third pre-Christian century had more than one or two children. As a result, the population of some important cities began to decline drastically. Philip V of Macedon brought about a 50% increase in the population of his country by forbidding such methods of family planning, and Polybius, in the second pre-Christian century, complained of houses and of entire districts becoming desolate because of the refusal of luxury-loving men and women to burden themselves with children.[13] At about the time Christianity arose, the Romans were engaging in profligate and luxurious living. Women thought nothing of having numerous divorces and even more numerous extramarital affairs. They avoided the burdens of motherhood by emulating the practices of their Greek mentors, by resorting to abortions and to contraceptives. They sometimes sought abortions in order to avoid ruining their figures by carrying to term. Men found that children were a burden in the city, though they might have been an asset if they were still on the farm. And they found, also, that if they were childless, they were more attractive to young and beautiful women as they grew older, for the women would be interested in the prospect of inheriting an estate that they would not have to share with others. Therefore, the men, too, avoided marital entanglements, finding sexual outlets in other ways—by patronizing prostitutes or by living with concubines. It was because of this widespread moral decay and the steady decline in population that Augustus passed the laws mentioned previously, and others as well, designed to restore some of the older moral virtues about which he had read.[14] But his laws failed of their purpose. Marriage came to be a loose contract, entered into merely for convenience. Some women married eunuchs in order to be spared the trouble of contraception and abortions, whereas others entered into marriage agreements that specified in advance that they were not to be required to bear children and could have relations with other men at will.[15]

It is small wonder that there was such a strong reaction against these practices by the early Christians, as there must have been among some non-

Christian Romans. But the development of church doctrine included new elements that exerted a profound influence upon later attitudes, practices, and laws.

THE DEVELOPMENT OF CHURCH DOCTRINE

Biblical Sources. According to the Biblical tradition, after God created man, he blessed him, saying, "Be fruitful and multiply; fill up the earth and subdue it." The same blessing was repeated after most of mankind was destroyed by the flood in Noah's time, and other versions of the same thought appear elsewhere throughout the Bible.[16] There is a positive emphasis on the value of having children and, where possible, of having many of them. Being barren, unable to conceive, is considered a source of great sorrow. There is a clear implication that having children is more than a mere blessing. It assumes the force of a positive duty.

One of the key texts to the understanding of the Church's attitude toward contraception is Genesis 38:8–10. Judah's son, Er, married Tamar, but died an untimely death. Tamar was left childless. According to ancient Jewish law, whenever a man died without leaving children to carry on his name and his estate, his nearest relative was obliged to marry his widow—unless he deliberately refused to do so—and to treat the first child born of their union as if it were the child of the deceased. Er's brother, Onan, married Tamar in accordance with this rule. The narrative then goes on to relate what happened: "Onan knew that the child [that would be born of his union with Tamar] would not be [considered] his own. So when he had relations with his brother's wife, he let his seed be wasted on the ground rather than providing an heir for his brother. God disapproved of his action, and took his life as well."

It is possible to read this passage as a condemnation of contraception—specifically, of "wasting one's seed" or of permitting one's seed to be spilled upon the ground. In the narrowest terms, it might be seen as a condemnation of coitus interruptus, but the principle may be broadened to include any "wasting" of sperm by not permitting it to enter the female at the climax of sexual intercourse. As we shall see, such interpretations of this text were given considerable importance throughout the Middle Ages and have assumed enormous significance for the question of the legitimacy of contraception down to our own time. Not all of them, however, reached the same conclusion, as will become apparent later.

The New Testament made a radical break with Old Testament teachings on sex and marriage in a number of important respects. The most important of these was probably the New Testament's emphasis on the value of virginity, exalting virginity above marriage to such a degree that abstinence from marriage is regarded as a virtue and as a means of bringing on the second coming. As Luke puts it, "The children of this world marry and are given in marriage. But those who shall be accounted worthy of that world and of the resurrection from the dead neither marry nor take wives. For neither shall they be able to die any more, for they are equal to the angels, and are sons of God, being sons of the resurrection." [17] In other passages, Jesus is represented as having urged his disciples to make themselves eunuchs,[18] and as assuring them that "at the resurrection, they will neither marry nor be given in marriage, but will be like the angels in heaven." [19] Paul compares the unmarried virgin, who dwells upon the Lord and is holy in body and spirit, to the married person, who concerns himself with the things of this world.[20] According to this view, the only marriage worth consummating is the marriage of the individual with God or with Jesus.

However, in the New Testament there are also passages commending marriage, particularly monogamous, nonadulterous, and permanent marriage.[21] But the emphasis remains that of Paul, who maintained that marriage was acceptable as an alternative for those who were "unable to control themselves," suggesting that it is "better to marry than to burn." [22] Marital intercourse is lawful and permitted, but, in contrast to the Hebrew Bible's stress on the positive value of such relationships, it is rather considered in the New Testament to be a concession to human weakness.

We need not dwell on questions concerning the original intentions of the authors of these texts, because it was the later interpretations of theologians and religious scholars that affected our ancestors' attitudes toward the issues that concern us now.

One final observation must be made at this point. The New Testament attitude toward marriage reflects an attitude that was common in the Roman world of the time. As the Stoics and others were saying, sexual intercourse was never right unless it served a procreative purpose; if it was indulged in for pleasure alone, it was morally reprehensible.[23]

The Church Fathers Through the Middle Ages. The early Church Fathers taught that the ideal of continence required a constant battle against desire. "Our ideal is not to experience desire at all," Clement declared in the second century; and in the following century, Origen said that the only proper justification for intercourse with one's wife was for the sake of children. They argued against intercourse with pregnant women on the ground that such intercourse could not be fruitful and served only to satisfy animal lusts. John T. Noonan, whose study of the history of doctrines on contraception is probably the most thorough of modern times, was able to find only one statement prior to the sixteenth century countenancing intercourse for pleasure's sake, and even that was equivocal.[24] The same source insisted, however, that the sex organs had only one "proper" purpose, and that was procreation. To others, contraception was so unnatural as to be worse than homicide.

Early Christians reacted strongly against the prevailing Roman indifference to infanticide. Around the beginning of the fourth century, a council at Elvira enjoined excommunication until death for any woman who had an abortion, and another, at Ancyra, provided ten years of penance for such women. Later councils followed suit. They thus extended the Roman law on parricide, which originally applied to any intentional, unlawful killing of a relative, to the destruction of a fetus, which had not been included before. But they went even further, calling homosexuals parricides, thus suggesting that the semen emitted by a man contains children within it, and that the intentional waste or destruction of the semen causes the death of those human beings. From this it is a very short step indeed to the assertion that anyone using contraceptives is committing homicide.

Throughout the Middle Ages these doctrines were repeated and expanded. Augustine, for example, declared that marital intercourse for the sake of pleasure was a venial sin, but only if "no evil prayer or evil deed" was employed to obstruct procreation. "Those who do this," he said, "although they are called husband and wife, are not; nor do they retain the marital state in reality. Instead, they cover their shameful deed with a respectable name." He went on to denounce oral contraceptives: "Sometimes this lustful cruelty, or cruel lust, comes to this: they even procure poisons of sterility, and if these do not work, they destroy the fetus in some way in the womb, . . . killing their baby before it is born." He condemned those who used such methods of contraception or feticide in the harshest terms, declaring that they were not joined in genuine matrimony, but in fornication. If husband and wife conspire to engage in sexual relations for pleasure while employing contraceptive measures, the wife must stand condemned, he said, as a harlot, and the husband is guilty of committing adultery with his own wife.[25]

A study of sanctions imposed for various sins during the Middle Ages reveals that anal and oral intercourse were generally regarded as more serious crimes than intentional homicide, and were universally considered to be more serious than the abortion of a fetus prior to the fortieth day of gestation. Drinking contraceptive potions was treated by some authorities as more serious than premeditated murder, whereas other experts disagreed, maintaining that each conception that was prevented was just another homicide, and should be punished accordingly. Thus, for example, the eighth-century Canons of Gregory prescribe seven penances for a layman who commits intentional homicide, fifteen for one who engages in anal intercourse. St. Hubert prescribes ten for homicide or for contraception.[26]

Throughout the centuries that followed, Augustine's words were repeated, with insistent emphasis on the sinfulness of sexual intercourse—including intercourse of married couples—"for delight, the satisfaction of lust" or as a result of "concupiscence."[27] In the later Middle Ages, sanctions for improper sexual behavior extended beyond the penances that were prescribed earlier. St. Thomas Aquinas ranked the "sin against nature" as the greatest of all sexual vices, even worse than fornication, seduction, rape, incest, or sacrilege.[28] Bernardine followed the same line, saying that it would be better for a woman to permit herself to have relations with her own father than it would be for her to engage in "unnatural" relations with her husband. The woman who consents to her husband's commission of onanism was condemned as a mortal sinner in the thirteenth century by Alexander of Hales, and in the following century, women were advised to permit themselves to be killed before submitting to such indecencies. Contraceptive behavior was discouraged by enforced separation of spouses who engaged in it. A priest who learned from his confessant that she was engaging in intercourse in such a way that conception was impossible was told to go immediately to his bishop, who would enforce a separation decree against the sinning couple.[29]

Toward the end of the sixteenth century, Pope Sixtus V decreed that any person offering contraceptive potions to women, or participating in abortions, or counseling women on matters of contraception or abortion, as well as the women themselves who resorted to such measures, were to be excommunicated and turned over to the secular authorities. They were to be treated in all respects like murderers. Abortion, contraception, murder, and adultery, among other crimes, became capital offenses. After his death, his successor, Gregory XIV, annulled the penalties for most of these crimes, but kept those for abortion of forty-day fetuses.

With the passage of time some authorities took a more relaxed approach to these problems. In 1816 the Penitentiary gave permission to a woman whose husband practiced coitus interruptus to continue to have relations with him if refusal would result in harm to her. However, less than forty years later, the Holy Office of the Inquisition ruled that women could not participate in intercourse if the man used a condom, since "it would be participation in what is intrinsically unlawful." [30] But the Penitentiary continued to be more lenient, suggesting that confessors remain silent about such matters unless asked.[31]

St. Thomas Aquinas departed from the strict condemnation that had been the rule by appealing to a distinction Aristotle drew between an act and the pleasure associated with the act. "The pleasure proper to a worthy activity," Aristotle had said, "is good, and that proper to an unworthy activity bad." [32] It would follow, then, that if intercourse performed within marriage is good, the pleasure the couple derives from such intercourse is not bad. Nevertheless, the act itself determines whether the pleasure that accompanies it is legitimate, and not the converse. Therefore, if the purpose of the act is the pleasure it brings, according to Thomas, the act must be sinful. In other words, pleasure is legitimate if it is derived from legitimate intercourse, that is, from intercourse whose purpose is procreative. But if the sex acts are indulged in for the sake of pleasure, the acts themselves are sinful, and so is the pleasure derived from them.[33] Marriage, in fact, is a state that requires an "excuse," and is not good for its own sake.[34]

In the fifteenth century, Martin Le Maistre, a Parisian divine, introduced a new approach. Marriage, he said, was originally permitted as a means of preventing fornication. (This is reminiscent of some current arguments on the drug problem: If you can't stop people from doing it, legalize it so that they're not violating the law.) He concludes, therefore, that if a man is going to visit a woman with whom he had been accustomed to commit fornication before his marriage, and he fears that his old desires will come upon him, "his priest or any wise man would counsel him" to extinguish his desires through prudently having relations with his wife before setting out for his visit. Further, he said, one may take pleasure, either for the love of the pleasure itself, or "to avoid tedium and the ache of melancholy caused by the lack of pleasure." In either case, he says, the pleasure-seeking is not sinful, because deprivation leads to melancholy, and that in turn leads to illness, which is not good, for "the healthy are more fit for generation." [35] He argued that the view that copulation for the sake of pleasure is a mortal sin was dangerous for human morals, for it would then be no more sinful to have relations with another woman, under the impulse, than it would be to have them with one's wife.

Thomas Sanchez, in the seventeenth century, conceded that married couples could have intercourse without sin, even though they knew that the relationship would not be a fertile one; but he maintained that intercourse for the purpose of pleasure alone was sinful. This seems to have been the normative position for many centuries. If a spouse had an "urgent cause" to "show and foster mutual love," he was permitted to do so, even if it would result in unintentional semination.[36] Thus, the doctrine was maintained; the pleasure derived by spouses from their sexual behavior is not good in itself, but is tolerated only as a necessary evil—or, at best, as an unavoidable, or nearly unavoidable, by-product.

This emphasis on the undesirability of pleasure associated with sex is closely tied in with the concept of original sin, which assumes particular importance in the abortion controversy. According to St. Augustine, procreation was accomplished, before the Fall, by a virtuous act of the will, without the slightest hint of lust. After their sin, however, Adam and Eve "knew they were naked," that is, they became aware of a new and uncontrollable lust (concupiscence). Their genitals were no longer obedient to their will, but acted, as it were, of their own accord. Their sexual impulses could be satisfied only by an orgasm, a "shameful state" that completely engulfs the rational faculties. Every child, then, was literally conceived in the shameful, sinful heat of his parents' lust, and thus was transmitted to each child the original sin of his primordial ancestors, Adam and Eve. Some later theologians held that original sin was merely transmitted from father to son through the act of begetting, not as a part of the sex act itself, but as a part of the heritage of all mankind, suffered because "we were all present in his [Adam's] loins" when he committed his great offense.[37] Origen thought that baptism was designed to cleanse the soul of the stain of original sin, and that anyone who had not been so cleansed was doomed to a terrible fate in the next world. St. Fulgentius, in the sixth century, expressed the theory well when he wrote, "Even little children who have begun to live in their mother's womb and have there died, or who, having just been born, have passed away from the world without the sacrament of holy baptism, must be punished by the eternal torture of undying fire." [38] This doctrine has left its impress on later practice. It explains, at least partially, why abortion would be regarded as worse than murder, for the fate awaiting the unbaptized child is far worse than that which awaits the baptized victim of murder. Catholic physicians are supposed to remove the fetus from a deceased mother's womb for emergency baptism. To take care of those cases in which the fetus seems unlikely to survive birth, a special syringe has been invented that enables the physician to baptize the fetus while it is still in its mother's womb —with sterile holy water that is kept on hand for such emergencies. If a diseased organ containing a living fetus is excised, canon law requires that "the fetus should be extracted and baptized before the excised organ is sent to the pathologist." [39]

Modern Developments.   In the middle of the nineteenth century, the Inquisition under Pope Pius IX declared that onanism (by which they meant coitus interruptus or other means of avoiding conception that resulted in "wasting" semen) was "scandalous, erroneous, and contrary to the natural law of marriage." [40]

The birth control movement became formally organized in the 1860s. Books and pamphlets advocating birth control were banned, and their authors and publishers were tried in England and elsewhere. But the movement caught on and hundreds of thousands of copies of the banned books and pamphlets were sold. Organizations for the dissemination of birth control information were formed in England, Germany, Spain, Brazil, Switzerland, Sweden, Italy, and elsewhere, and in the early twentieth century, a number of international congresses were held. The diaphragm was developed in 1880, and hundreds of other devices followed. As the movement gained momentum, efforts to check its effects became better organized, too. In France, a law was passed in 1920 forbidding the dissemination of "contraceptive propaganda" under pain of six months imprisonment. In the following decade the French government resorted to the ancient system of providing an inducement through cash bonuses or allowances that were increased as the size of the family increased. In the United States, the Comstock laws imposed penalties of up to ten years' imprisonment for anyone importing contraceptives, advertising them through the mails, or manufacturing, selling, or possessing them in the District of Columbia or other federal territories. As the years passed, however, the courts and Congress, as well as some of the state legislatures, whittled the laws down.

Modern arguments against contraception, in addition to those employed in earlier times, have included the argument that society ultimately will be brought to ruin and destruction if men are permitted to enjoy the pleasures of sex without the consequent burden of feeding and educating children. They will avoid bringing children into the world in order to be free of the burden of raising them, and will have lost nothing, because they will not be deprived of fulfillment of their sexual desires. Father John A. Ryan of the Catholic University of America argued that marriage is "the divinely appointed plan for cooperating with the Creator in perpetuating the race," and that true idealism of the highest sort "accepts the responsibility of bringing children into the world," where they may prove to be "either a blessing or a curse to society at large." Selfishness, however, leads to "race suicide," and is a "detestable thing." Further, through children, "the bond of love is strengthened, fresh stimulus is given to thrift and industrious effort, and the very sacrifices which are called for become sources of blessing." [41]

The Anglicans, after condemning contraception at the Lambeth conferences of 1908 and 1920, declared, in 1930, that a "clearly felt moral obligation to limit or avoid parenthood" could lead to measures to do so, based upon "Christian principles," of which the primary ones were complete abstinence from intercourse and a life of discipline and self-control. While strongly condemning the use of alternative methods from motives of "selfishness, luxury, or mere convenience," the bishops declared that they might be used, "provided that this is done in the light of the same Christian principles." [42] In December of the same year, Pope Pius XI issued the encyclical *Casti connubii*, which remained the principal Roman Catholic document on birth control for the next 40 years. The Pope upheld the Church's traditional teaching that "any use whatever of marriage, in the exercise of which the act by human effort is deprived of its natural power of procreating life, violates the law of God and nature, and those who do such a thing are stained by a grave and mortal flaw." [43] Some people have suggested that this encyclical was not authoritative, that it did not carry with it the claim of papal infallibility. But according to Noonan, "it had immense doctrinal authority as a solemn declaration by the Pope." [44]

> By the ordinary tests used by the theologians to determine whether a doctrine is infallibly proclaimed, it may be argued that the specific condemnation of contraceptive interruption of the procreative act is infallibly set out. The encyclical is addressed to the universal Church. The Pope speaks in fulfillment of his apostolic office. He speaks for the Church. He speaks on moral doctrine that he says "has been transmitted from the beginning." He "promulgates" the teaching. If the Pope did not mean to use the full authority to speak *ex cathedra* on morals, which Vatican I recognized as his, what further language could he have used? [45]

The encyclical, for all practical purposes, was accepted as authoritative by the church's officialdom. It condemned coitus interruptus; the use of condoms, diaphragms, and other contraceptive devices; the use of postcoital douches; and any form of sterilization. The use of the sterile period (that is, the "rhythm" method) received cautious approval, and was accepted without reservation by Pope Pius XII in 1951. The use of *amplexus reservatus* seems to have more theoretical than practical interest, but theoretically at least it is sanctioned as a legitimate form of contraception by the Church.

The male partner may bring his wife to climax, withdraw, take a cold shower, and go about his business, all with the sanction of the Church, so long as he does nothing "unnatural" either during or after intercourse.

In addition to the older arguments, a number of novel approaches were developed during recent years to answer critics of the Catholic doctrine. It was held, for example, that children in small families grow up spoiled and selfish; that contraception was a factor leading to family breakdown and divorce, as evidenced by the high proportion of divorces in families with one or no children; that it led to extramarital relations; that it caused physical or psychological harm to one or the other of the spouses (such as pelvic disorders in women, or cancers of various sorts, as well as nervous disorders); that it led to a "loss of reverence" for the wife, who was treated like a harlot by her contraceptive-using husband; that the use of contraceptives was selfish, exploitative, and destructive of meaningful relationships between husband and wife; that children born to parents who used contraceptives would die prematurely; that by increasing the number of children, those singing God's praises, both on earth and in heaven, are multiplied; and, of course, that any use of contraceptives was against nature.[46]

After extensive discussion, both in its inner councils and in various public forums, the Roman Catholic Church, through Pope Paul VI's encyclical *Humanae Vitae*, issued in 1968, reaffirmed its long-standing opposition to all forms of birth control except those traditionally found acceptable: abstinence and the rhythm method. The encyclical recognized the crisis posed by the world population explosion and acknowledged the problems faced by individual families who were sometimes taxed beyond their means to support themselves. It also noted the problems of the developing countries, whose economic, political, and educational development was threatened by overwhelming population growth. And it conceded that due consideration must be given to the role of women in modern society and the value of sexual love in marriage.

However, the encyclical adhered to traditional doctrines by insisting that proper sexual relations must be "fecund," for, as the Pope put it, "marriage and conjugal love are by their nature ordained toward the begetting and educating of children." [47] It follows, therefore, that husband and wife "are not free to proceed completely at will," but that they "must conform their activity to the creative intention of God," which is "that each and every marriage act must remain open to the transmission of life." Any behavior inconsistent with this rule contradicts the nature, "both of man and of woman and of their most intimate relationship," and is therefore contrary to God's plan and to God's will.[48]

On abortion, the Pope declared that "the direct interruption of the generative process already begun, and above all, directly willed and procured abortion, *even if for therapeutic reasons*, are to be absolutely excluded as licit means of regulating birth." [49] Similarly, direct sterilization, whether temporary or permanent, is specifically prohibited—thus eliminating the use of the pill—as is every other action which is intended to render procreation impossible, whether such action precedes intercourse, accompanies it, or follows it.[50] This effectively eliminates every known method of contraception, except the rhythm method, which the Pope considers to be acceptable on the ground that it "make[s] legitimate use of a natural disposition," whereas other methods "impede the development of natural processes." Any act of marital intercourse that violates these rules "is intrinsically dishonest." [51]

In addition to the traditional arguments against contraception, the encyclical contains several that we did not notice earlier. (1) Young men, who are particularly vulnerable and weak, need special encouragement to abide by the moral rules governing marriage. The availability of contraceptives constitutes an incentive to violate those rules. (2) A man who uses contraceptives in his relations with his wife may come to lose respect for her, finally coming to think of her, and to treat her, as "a mere instrument for selfish enjoyment, and no longer as his respected and beloved companion." (3) Immoral public authorities may impose upon their communities a duty to use contraceptives favored by the authorities for the solution of social problems. If the use of such methods is legitimate for married couples in the solution of family problems, they will argue, it would be legitimate for the solution of community problems. Thus, "the most personal and most reserved sector of conjugal intimacy" would be placed "at the mercy of the intervention of public Authorities." [52]

The reaction of the Roman Catholic community to this encyclical is well known. Throughout the world influential Catholics, both lay and clergy, protested the Pope's decision and his reasoning. Others, more conservative in their approach, hailed the decision as an important landmark in the Church's battle against a "materialistic, permissive, humanist society," and called for unwavering, loving obedience.[53] There was a spate of resignations from the Church by clergymen and by nuns who were disappointed by the failure of the leadership in Rome to take the opportunity to liberalize the law and to relieve the anguish of those who had wanted to remain loyal to the Church but were finding increasingly difficult to live within the framework of its policy on contraception.[54]

Despite the outcry and the uproar, the official position of the Church remains what it has been for centuries, with a few minor modifications.

The Church's only major departure from the medieval stand on abortion has been toward a stricter definition of the time when abortion becomes a criminal act. During the Middle Ages, it was widely assumed that "ensoulment"—that is, the moment when a fetus received its soul and thus became a human being in the true sense of the word—occurred on the fortieth day for males and on the eightieth day for females.[55] Therefore, the abortion of a fetus prior to the fortieth or the eightieth day would not be as serious as the abortion of a fetus that had passed those landmarks, because an earlier abortion would be an abortion of a *potential* human being, but not of an *actual* one. Because no soul had entered the fetus, no one would suffer an eternity of torment in hell for having died unbaptized and therefore tainted with original sin. In 1869 Pope Pius IX eliminated the distinction between an animated and an unanimated fetus, decreeing that all fetuses should be considered to be ensouled from conception. Thus, *any* abortion would now be considered equivalent to murder.[56] In the United States, abortion before quickening (that is, before the mother could perceive fetal movements) was not punishable until about 1860, and even after that the distinction between a "quick" child and one that had not yet "quickened" remained in most states.[57]

Prior to the 1973 Supreme Court decision, destruction of a fetus that had not quickened was no crime in Mississippi, for example, whereas in other states, it was less severely punished than abortion after quickening. A judge in Wisconsin justified the distinction between "quick" fetuses and those that are not "quickened" as follows:

> In a strictly scientific and psychological sense there is life in an embryo from the time of conception, and in such sense there is also life in the male and female elements that unite to form the embryo. But law for obvious reasons cannot in its classifications follow the latest or ultimate declarations of science. It must for purposes of practical efficiency proceed upon more everyday and popular conceptions, especially as to definitions of crimes that are *malum in se*. These must be of such a nature that the ordinary normal adult knows it is morally wrong to commit them. That it should be less of an offense to destroy an embryo in a stage where human life in its common acceptance has not yet begun than to destroy a quick child is a conclusion that commends itself to most men.[58]

"Quickening" is thus defined here in its "common acceptance" as the time when human life begins, that is, as the time when ordinary people would conceive of the fetus as something more than a mere cluster of cells or a relatively undifferentiated mass of human tissue. Exactly when one state is transformed to the other is presumably dependent upon the possession by the embryo of such features as independent movement, an operative circulatory system, and more or less well-developed human facial and bodily characteristics. It would be difficult to pinpoint the moment at which such a transformation might occur, but the prescientific forty- and eighty-day criterion of Aristotle and the medievals need not be adopted; nor is it necessary to adhere rigidly to the rather indefinite and subjective criterion of the mother's feeling of fetal movements. If the court should wish to have some clear and definite criterion, it might have to be disappointed; but it would seem that in this area, as in so many others, the existence of borderline cases should be no hindrance to rendering decisions in those that evidently fall on one side or the other of the fuzzy area that lies between.

THE DEVELOPMENT OF JEWISH DOCTRINE

Judaism knows nothing of the doctine of original sin. Pious Jews recite a prayer each morning thanking God for having given them a soul that is pure, and throughout rabbinic literature, the emphasis is upon man's capacity to maintain himself in a state of "purity" through good works and the avoidance of sinful behavior. Sin is viewed not so much as a state, but as a form of behavior. An ancient commentary on the Bible says, "Even as the soul is pure upon entering upon its earthly career, so let man return it pure to his Maker." [59] Sin, according to the ancient rabbis, was universal, but not because of a hereditary blemish. Rather, human weakness and the multitude of wrongful acts that one may perform, intentionally or unintentionally, cause damage or harm to persons or to the order of the state or the universe. [60]

The problem of interpretation posed by the Biblical story of Er and Onan is a difficult one, too complex to be discussed in detail here. In Jewish tradition there has been considerable disagreement over the true intent of the passage and over its legal and moral implications. Some authorities have accepted an interpretation similar to that which was adopted by Christian commentators—that the sin for which Er and Onan were killed was coitus interruptus. They have accordingly concluded that any "wasting" of seed is sinful and is prohibited. But most of them, including Maimonides, ruled that because there is no explicit condemnation of the practice in the Bible, nothing more can be inferred than that it is undesirable and that it may be punished by divine wrath, but that it is beyond the jurisdiction of human courts. [61] From about the thirteenth century, after the publication of the Zohar, a mystical work that had enormous influence on some persons but was totally rejected by others, a tendency to be more severe, along the lines of Catholicism, developed, comparing the wasting of seed to homicide. But for the most part, the authorities clung to the older assumption that the story of Er and Onan offered no justification for judicial condemnation of coitus interruptus or of other contraceptive acts. [62]

Some Talmudic passages suggest that Er's sin consisted in selfishly preventing his wife from conceiving in order to preserve her physical charms, whereas later commentators thought that he didn't want to be burdened by the responsibilities of raising children. In either case, the sin consisted of a violation of the commandment (as it is interpreted by these commentators) given to Adam and to Noah—to be fruitful and multiply. But Onan's transgression, which is the only one actually mentioned in the Biblical text, was not understood by most rabbinical authorities as the Church understood it. The rabbis connected it with Onan's duty as a levirate, that is, his duty, as Tamar's deceased husband's closest relative, to bring a child into the world to carry on his late brother's name and estate. The death penalty inflicted by God may be understood if we recall that elsewhere in the Bible a man is forbidden to marry his deceased brother's wife on pain of an untimely death, that is, early death through natural (or divine) causes.[63] Strictly speaking, then, Onan had no right to marry Tamar. But he had a duty to marry her as a consequence of his being the levirate after his brother's death. The prohibition against his having relations with Tamar was lifted so that he could fulfill his obligation under the duty of levirate marriage, namely, to provide an heir for his deceased brother. When he frustrated that purpose by using contraceptive methods—whatever those methods may have been— he violated the condition upon which the original prohibition was lifted. Therefore, the prohibition returned in full force, and he suffered the penalty for violating it.[64] The rabbis of the Talmud clearly understood the implications of these passages, for they declared that one might take a wife for beauty, for money, or for other qualities, but "he who has relations with his levirate wife because of her beauty or for similar reasons has engaged in illicit intercourse."[65] Because of the special circumstances in Onan's case, it is impossible to apply the rule to ordinary marital relations.

On the question of virginity as opposed to marriage, there was no equivocation among Jewish authorities. Of course virginity was desirable, but only up to the time of marriage. Marriage was not a state that was merely tolerated because of human weakness and lust, but rather a divine commandment. "It is not good for man to be alone," the Bible had said, and the rabbis of the Talmud and of later generations reaffirmed the principle by urging their followers to marry early and to fulfill the sacred task of bringing children into the world. But a wife was more than a mere breeding machine; she was a "helpmate for him." "He who has no wife," said one authority, "lives without good, or help, or joy, or blessing, or atonement." And another added, "He is not really a complete man; he diminishes the image of God."[66] Still another said, "If a man marries a goodly wife, it is as though he had fulfilled the whole Torah from beginning to end," that is, he has fulfilled every divine commandment.[67] Although men were encouraged to marry young in order to avoid falling into evil behavior through temptation, marriage was not considered an escape valve for persons having a disposition to sinful thoughts or behavior, but as a state that was desirable in itself.

The rabbis were not hedonists. They reserved some of their most vituperative remarks for "Epicureans," that is, materialists who denied the existence of spiritual beings and followed a hedonistic ethic. But being antihedonistic does not necessarily require the adoption of an ascetic ideal. Pleasure may not be the ultimate end of all action, but that is not to deny that it might be the legitimate end of some actions. Pleasure may not be the only good, but that does not entail the denial that pleasure is good at all. The rabbis of the Talmud and most of the rabbis of later generations could see nothing wrong with the pleasure that accompanied sexual intercourse. There was nothing wrong with pleasure, though the intercourse itself, and therefore the pleasure that accompanied it, might be illegitimate for any of a number of reasons, such as adultery, incest, and the like.

If sexual pleasure is not evil, then perhaps intercourse for the sake of pleasure alone, including intercourse that one knows cannot result in impregnation, is legitimate. In fact, the rabbis were remarkably liberal in their attitudes toward unions in which procreation was impossible. Because marriage was valuable in itself, regardless of its possible procreative outcome, they permitted men and women who were childless to remain together, even though it was evident that no children would ever result from the marriage. A fourteenth-century decision by Isaac ben Sheshet held that a childless couple who did not want a divorce was to be left undisturbed, for the marriage involved "nothing immoral or forbidden or even offensive to holiness." [68]

The rabbis of the Talmud found justification in a Biblical text for their view that marital intercourse is a duty, a positive obligation, regardless of its possible outcome.[69] In their view this entailed a number of consequences. One was the nullification of any premarital agreement entered into by husband and wife that relieved either of his or her duty to give sexual satisfaction to the other. Another had to do with vows of abstinence. Pious men would occasionally vow to abstain from one kind of pleasure or another (such as drinking wine) as a form of penance or as a means of approaching a state of oneness with God. If anyone vowed to deny his wife the pleasure of marital intercourse, however, the Talmudists declared that his vow—even though it might have been made in accordance with all the religious forms—was null and void. And if he took a vow to deny such pleasure to *himself*, a time limit of one week was imposed upon him because, after all, his wife was involved too.[70] A woman was obliged to fulfill her husband's desire. Sex was considered a beautiful and a holy thing, as well as a pleasurable one. With such attitudes as these, "spiritual marriage," in which husband and wife live together as brother and sister in the name of sexual asceticism—a practice that was not uncommon in early Christianity and is still practiced from time to time—is virtually unthinkable.[71] When a man has relations with his wife, he is said, by rabbinic authorities in all ages, to be fulfilling the divine command of "giving his wife pleasure," recalling the Biblical draft law: If a man had been married recently, he was to be granted a year's deferment from military service so that he might "rejoice with the wife whom he had married." [72] In the thirteenth century, Maimonides summed up Judaism's attitude toward asceticism as follows.

> Some people suppose that since jealousy, lust, pride, and the like are considered to be vices, it would be best to avoid them by going to the opposite extreme, by not eating meat, or drinking wine, or marrying, or dwelling in a nice home, or wearing beautiful garments. . . . But this too is wrong, and one is forbidden to behave in such a way. One who lives an ascetic life is considered sinful. . . . Our sages have decreed that no man should deprive himself of anything unless it is specifically forbidden by law . . . for they asked, "Has the law not prohibited enough for you? Must you impose additional deprivations upon yourself?" [73]

Even the most pietistic sects among the Jews of the Middle Ages rejected asceticism, particularly sexual asceticism. Sexual abstinence was never considered an appropriate vehicle for penitence, and sexual asceticism was never considered to have any religious value.[74] One of the most important works of medieval Jewish piety assigned a prominent place to the establishment and maintenance of normal and reasonable sexual life within marriage.[75]

If pleasure is not only legitimate but desirable, then many restrictions, though certainly not all of them, may begin to fall away. The purpose of intercourse is not only procreation, but also pleasure. Again, Maimonides, who was by no means in favor of overindulgence in sex, either from a moral point of view or on medical grounds, expressed the traditional law, which was reiterated throughout the centuries:

> A man and his wife have the right to have relations with one another. Therefore, he may do what he wishes. He may have intercourse with her at any time [except during her menstrual period], he may kiss her wherever he pleases, and he may have relations with her either in the usual fashion or in some other way. . . .[76]

In the eighteenth century, Jacob Emden, in his commentary on the traditional prayer book, observed that the Sabbath was a particularly appropriate day for marital relations, because it was a day that was both sacred and joyous. Then he continued:

> To us the sexual act is worthy, good, and beneficial even to the soul. No other human activity compares with it; when performed with pure and clean intention it is certainly holy. There is nothing impure or defective about it, rather it is most exalted.[77]

Judaism is not monolithic. It has no central organization, comparable to the Roman hierarchy, empowered to pass final judgment on faith and morals for all Jews everywhere. Each community has its own spiritual leader, whose judgment sets the tone for that community. He will naturally consult other authorities, particularly if he respects them for their wisdom and their learning, and he will base his judgments, as far as practicable, upon precedents recorded in the literature. But because of the lack of central authority, considerable differences in practice may be observed from one community to another, and there is no lack of disagreement among the authorities on many issues. Nevertheless, certain trends are distinguishable, and in this area, the consensus seems to be that the first five foundations upon which the Catholic condemnation of contraception and abortion rests were not acceptable to traditional authorities from early times onward; they were even more explicitly rejected by the more liberal movements in modern Judaism. Original sin is unknown; the story of Er and Onan is interpreted in such a way as to deny that they were put to death for what has come to be known as onanism; marriage is not a concession to human weakness, but a positive divine commandment, a duty that every person is expected to fulfill; even the most ascetic sects, who were always a tiny minority, refused to deny the legitimacy of sexual pleasure; and most authorities, for the past 2,000 years at least, have maintained that marital intercourse *for pleasure alone* is not only legitimate, but may, in certain circumstances, be a positive obligation. *Pleasurable* sex, and not only procreative sex, is *natural*. It should not be surprising, therefore, if we find that contraception and abortion are not looked upon with the abhorrence that is so common within the Christian tradition. From Talmudic times, dating back at least to the second century, we find references to the use of contraceptive devices and practices, and most such references do not condemn the practice. Indeed, some references prior to the second century that remain authoritative to this day in traditional circles impose an obligation upon women to use contraceptive tampons when pregnancy may cause physical harm to them or to their children, as it might, for example, if the woman were too young or too weak to bear children, or if she were still nursing and a pregnancy would cut off her baby's supply of milk.[78]

Although there was considerable disagreement over the use of mechanical devices to prevent conception, there was near unanimity, even in ancient times, over the use of oral contraceptives. The latter are mentioned as early as the Mishnah and the Tosephta (prior to about the second century), where women are explicitly granted permission to use them.[79] Though the authorities had some reservations about mechanical contraceptives, their only major concern about oral contraceptives had to do with the safety of the product. Even the most conservative authorities on the question of mechanical contraceptives agreed that oral contraceptives may be used, for "it is agreed, without dissent, that this is the best of all measures to take." [80] Early in the nineteenth century, the renowned and highly respected Hatam Sofer (Moses Schreiber Sofer of Pressburg) was confronted with a case in which a woman suffered unusual pain in childbirth. He ruled that she should use contraceptives, for, as he put it, "she need not build the world by destroying herself." He added that if her husband refused to grant her permission to use oral contraceptives, she could either obtain a divorce or refuse to engage in sexual relations with him. She had no duty to endure such pain for his sake.[81]

In recent years, as new methods of contraception have been developed, the literature has been full of opinions; and here, again, the most orthodox rabbis are surprisingly lenient. They welcomed the invention of the diaphragm because, as Hayyim Sofer, a disciple of the Hatam Sofer, wrote in the 1860s, it does nothing to impede contact, and thus does not diminish the natural gratifications of the sex act or the "full physical pleasure and . . . the flaming ardor of passion." [82] Spermicides were accepted quite readily, and intrauterine devices were received by some with mixed feelings only because of the possibility that some form of abortion might be involved. Thus far, however, there has not been much reaction, either to the IUD's or to the pill. The legitimacy of the pill seems to be taken for granted in the literature that has appeared so far, based upon analogies with oral contraceptives permitted through the centuries. The only major reservations have been based on medical grounds, on fears that some unforeseen harm may come to the mother as a result of resorting to these relatively new and untested methods. As for the so-called safe period, the consensus seems to be that although there are times when a woman may not conceive, it is too difficult to know just when those times may occur with any degree of accuracy. Abstinence is of course permitted, under proper conditions (namely, when neither the husband nor the wife is unreasonably deprived of marital rights); but when pregnancy must be avoided on medical grounds, it is deemed to be an inadequate safeguard.[83]

So far as contraception is concerned, then, the Jewish tradition, because of its rejection of the major principles upon which the Catholic rejection of artificial means of birth control is based, is quite lenient. With some exceptions, even the most orthodox authorities throughout the past two millennia have permitted some forms of birth control. Where a hazard to the woman's health is concerned, they are unanimous: she is not only permitted to resort to artificial methods of contraception, but she may have a religious duty to do so.

We turn now to the question of abortion.

The principal issue here is whether feticide is a form of homicide. The answer was given in the Talmud in the early Middle Ages, during the course of a discussion of a passage in the Book of Exodus. "He who causes the death of a man must be put to death." [84] By comparing this passage with another in the Book of Leviticus, which contains the same legal principle but an important variation in wording, the authorities arrived at an answer to the question of the status of abortion. In Leviticus, the text reads, "If a man causes the death of any living human being, he must be put to death." The qualification introduced by the word *living*, they said, indicates that the rule on homicide applies only to a human being who has already been born.[85] The Biblical text offers further support for this view, for in Exodus 21:22, a person who negligently causes a woman to miscarry is held liable for payment of damages, but there is no suggestion that he is guilty of homicide.[86] Until the moment of birth, then, there was no criminal liability for the destruction of a fetus; but from the moment of birth, the fetus assumed a status different from that which it had had the moment before, and it acquired rights—including the right of inheritance, for example—that it had not enjoyed while it was still in its mother's womb.[87] Because the fetus is considered to be merely a part of its mother's body, like her appendix, prior to its actual birth, there is no legal prohibition whatever against causing its death or destroying it, though one would not ordinarily encourage people to do so unless there were some special justification for such an action. But when there are special justifications, as when the mother's life is threatened, there is no question whatever in the rabbis' minds that the fetus may be destroyed. As they put it, if the mother's life is threatened, the fetus may be cut out limb by limb, if that is necessary to save her.[88]

The time of animation or ensoulment, it would appear, would not be particularly important if, as we have seen, a child may be sacrificed right up to the moment of its birth. (From that moment on, the rabbis are in unanimous agreement that it may not be destroyed, no matter what the reason.) This opinion is borne out in many sources, including one that dates back to the thirteenth century. Meir Abulafia concludes that the soul enters the fetus at the moment of conception, but that this has nothing whatever to do with the question of feticide, because the fetus is not a "living person" until it is born. Most of the Jewish religious and legal thinkers who considered the question seem to have concluded that the precise moment when a child becomes a person in a sufficiently "complete" sense to warrant admission to heaven is one of the secrets of God which no amount of speculation will ever reveal.[89] Because they were untroubled by the doctrine of original sin, they had no need to concern themselves over the possibility of an eternity of torment for the soul, or even a period in limbo, if the fetus died without baptism.

Therapeutic abortion is accepted in most of the sources. But what of abortion for other causes? As we have seen, the prevailing view is that if any person causes the death or destruction of a fetus prior to its birth, he is not criminally liable, though he may be liable for damages. However, though one may not be *liable* for causing a nontherapeutic abortion, in that no penalty attaches to such an act in Jewish law, it seems clear that one may have a *prima facie* duty not to participate in such an abortion, unless there is some justification for doing so. The question remains, then, as to what other justifications there might be.

Among the justifications that Jewish legal thinkers have found for abortion —both in previous generations and in recent and contemporary literature on the subject—are the following:

1. When the woman's continuing pregnancy or her giving birth to the fetus will result in her death or constitute a serious threat to her physical well-being.
2. When the pregnancy poses a danger of extreme mental anguish to the mother. The most conservative authorities limit this to cases where the mother shows suicidal tendencies, but others maintain that a risk to mental health is as serious as a risk to physical health and that abortion is indicated even when the woman shows no suicidal tendencies.
3. When the pregnancy poses a danger to the health of an existing child, as when the infant depends upon its mother's milk and cannot be put on a formula, and the new pregnancy threatens to shut off the flow of milk.[90]
4. When the woman has become pregnant as a result of rape. As Yeruham Perilman put it in 1891, though a woman may be a vehicle for reproduc-

tion, she must not be compared to Mother Earth, for she need not nurture seed implanted within her against her will. On the contrary, he said, she has the right to uproot seed that was sown illegally.[91]

5. When carrying the child or bearing it will cause serious mental suffering to the mother—even though such suffering may be short of mental illness. Included under this rule would be thalidomide babies, fetuses whose mothers have been exposed to German measles (rubella), and even illegitimate babies whose birth would cause great anguish to their mothers.[92]

All the authorities cited in this discussion are extremely conservative. In modern terms they would all be considered orthodox. No authority from the more liberal branches of modern Judaism has been discussed here. Many of the latter advocate abortion on demand and would eliminate all legal sanctions against abortions performed for any purpose. The authors whose views have been discussed here, representing some of the most respected thinkers in Jewish jurisprudence and religious thought of the past 2,000 years, do not go that far. With a few notable exceptions, they would not allow abortion on demand. But they would clearly not favor criminal prosecution of persons who had participated in abortions, and they recognized most, if not all, of the grounds for abortion that are being advocated today by those who would reform our laws.[93] Clearly, they were able to develop positions such as these because they were unfettered by the ideological presuppositions that have done so much to determine the Catholic Church's stand on this issue.

THE LAW ON ABORTION

Until January 22, 1973, nearly every state in the United States had laws on the books prescribing criminal penalties for procuring an abortion, or for causing or attempting to cause a woman to give birth prematurely, or for destroying the life of a fetus or embryo in a woman's womb.[94] On that date, the United States Supreme Court ruled on the question in *Roe* v. *Wade*, a decision that has completely changed the situation in the United States and has given rise to bitter controversy and to movements to amend the Constitution so as to nullify the Court's decision.

The written opinion is a long one and includes considerations of the statistical evidence, constitutional questions, religious and philosophical positions, and other aspects of the problem. The following discussion considers only some of the conceptual and moral principles that underlie the Court's decision.

Justice Blackmun, delivering the opinion of the Court, began by acknowledging the sensitive and emotional nature of the abortion controversy, and went on to say that one's philosophy, one's experiences, one's exposure to the raw edges of human existence, one's religious training, one's attitudes toward life and family and their values, and the moral standards one establishes and seeks to observe are all likely to influence and to color one's thinking and conclusions about abortion.

In addition, population growth, pollution, poverty, and racial overtones tend to complicate and not to simplify the problem.[95]

As it did in the Connecticut contraception case,[96] the Court relied in part upon the concept of privacy in support of its decision. As the Court put it:

The detriment that the State would impose upon the pregnant woman by denying this choice [of whether or not to terminate her pregnancy] altogether is apparent. Specific and direct harm, medically diagnosable even in early pregnancy, may be involved. Maternity, or additional offspring, may force upon the woman a distressful life and future. Psychological harm may be imminent. Mental and physical health may be taxed by child care. There is also the distress, for all concerned, associated with the unwanted child. . . . In other cases . . . the additional difficulties and continuing stigma of unwed motherhood may be involved.[97]

With this recognition of the woman's right to have something to say about whether her pregnancy should be continued or brought to an end, however, the Court went on to say that hers are not the only interests involved, and that she did not have an *absolute* right to terminate her pregnancy whenever and however she pleased, and for whatever reason she alone might choose. The Court disagreed with those who claimed that a person has, or ought to have, an unlimited right to do whatever he or she pleased with his or her body.

The second major ground for the Court's decision was its determination of the meaning of the term *person* in relation to the abortion controversy. In the Fourteenth Amendment and elsewhere, the Constitution says that no state shall "deprive any person of life, liberty, or property, without due process of law; nor deny to any person within its jurisdiction the equal protection of the laws." If a fetus is a person, it would follow that it would be entitled to the same protection, under state and federal laws, that any adult receives, and that any person taking the life of a fetus would be guilty of murder or manslaughter, according to the circumstances.

Up to the time of the abortion decision, no case had ever decided the question of whether a fetus is a person within the meaning of the Fourteenth Amendment. The Court therefore scrutinized every usage of the word *person* in the Constitution and found that almost every instance clearly referred to human beings who had already been born. For example, Article I, Section 2 states that "No Person shall be a Representative who shall not have attained to the age of twenty five Years." Obviously, every such person must have been born. In fact, Section 1 of the Fourteenth Amendment defines citizens as "persons born or naturalized in the United States." The Court was unable to find a single instance in which the term clearly applied to human fetuses.

Moreover, the Court wondered about the states' application of the concept of personhood to fetuses. With regard to the state of Texas, which was one of the states involved in the appeal that led to the abortion decision, the Court observed that like all other states, it had provided for an exception to the general prohibition against abortions. When the purpose of an abortion was to save the mother's life, Texas permitted the operation to be performed. But, the Court asked, "if the fetus is a person who is not to be deprived of life without due process of law, and if the mother's condition is the sole determinant, does not the Texas exception appear to be out of line with the Amendment's command?" Further, the Court observed that in Texas (as in most states), the woman who has an abortion is not regarded as a principal or an accomplice to the crime, but if the fetus is a person, she should be. And finally, the penalties for committing an abortion are far less than those for murder. If the fetus is a person, a lower penalty for abortion than for murder would be indefensible.[98]

Regarding the claim that "life begins at conception," the Court observed that medicine, philosophy, and theology had been unable to arrive at a consensus on the matter and concluded that the judiciary would be best advised to refrain from attempting to resolve the matter. However, the Court did rehearse the long history of the question, noting along the way that "in areas other than criminal abortion, the law has been reluctant to endorse any theory that life, as we recognize it, begins before live birth or to accord legal rights to the unborn except in narrowly defined situations and except when the rights are contingent upon live birth." [99] The Court concluded:

> In view of all this, we do not agree that, by adopting one theory of life, Texas may override the rights of the pregnant woman that are at stake. We repeat, however, that the State does have an important and legitimate interest in preserving and protecting the health of the pregnant woman . . . and that it has still *another* important and legitimate interest in protecting the potentiality of human life. Each grows in substantiality as the woman approaches term and, at a point during pregnancy, each becomes "compelling." [100]

The Court's final prescriptions were based upon its assessments of the dangers to the mother at various stages of pregnancy. Dividing pregnancy into three "trimesters" of approximately three months each, the Court concluded that:

> (a) any state law that prohibits abortions except where they are intended to save the life of the mother without regard to the stage of pregnancy and other interests involved violates the Due Process Clause of the Fourteenth Amendment and is therefore unconstitutional.
> (b) During the first trimester, the decision of the woman's physician should be controlling as to whether she should or should not have an abortion.
> (c) During the second trimester, the State might regulate abortion procedure in ways reasonably related to the mother's health.

(d) For the stage subsequent to viability [that is, from the beginning of the third trimester], the State in promoting its interest in the potentiality of human life may, if it chooses, regulate, and even proscribe, abortion except where it is necessary, in appropriate medical judgment, for the preservation of the life or health of the mother." [101]

In a companion case, *Doe* v. *Bolton,* the Court also struck down state requirements that the abortion be performed in an accredited hospital (for it might reasonably and safely be performed in a clinic or in a physician's office), that it be deferred until approved by a hospital committee (the Court holding that a single physician's judgment is enough), and that two other physicians acquiesce in the procedure (on the ground that this requirement unduly infringes on the physician's right to practice and that it has no rational connection with the patient's needs).[102]

Since the Supreme Court's 1973 decision overturning state laws that prohibited abortions, numerous attempts have been made to circumvent the Court's action. Among them are the following:

1. Legislation requiring a woman to secure the written consent of her husband before she could have an abortion, unless a licensed physician certified that the abortion was necessary to preserve her life. Such legislation was declared unconstitutional [103] on the ground that the state cannot delegate a power that it does not possess. Of course, a husband has a deep and proper concern and interest in his wife's pregnancy and in the growth and development of the fetus she carries. Moreover, a decision to have an abortion that is not consented to by a woman's husband can have profound effects on the future of the marriage. But it is difficult to see how mutuality of decision would be furthered by giving a husband veto power over his wife's decision to have an abortion. The Court concluded that where there was a disagreement, only one of the parties could prevail, and that since the woman was the one who was most directly and immediately affected by the pregnancy, her decision should be decisive.

2. Legislation requiring an unmarried woman under 18 years of age to secure the written consent of at least one of her parents before she could have an abortion, unless a licensed physician certified that the abortion was necessary to preserve her life. This too was declared unconstitutional on similar grounds. The Court held that although the state has an interest in safeguarding the authority of the family relationship, that interest has definite limits. One could not seriously argue, the court said, that a minor would have to submit to an abortion upon her parents' insistence. Why, then, should she not be entitled to the same right of self-determination, provided she is sufficiently mature to understand the procedure and to make an intelligent assessment of her circumstances with the advice of her physician, as an adult woman would have? Furthermore, the state does not have the right to give anyone an absolute and possibly arbitrary veto over an abortion decision.

3. Legislation prohibiting the use of saline amniocentesis (the injection of salt solutions into the sac surrounding the fetus) as a means of inducing abortions after the first 12 weeks is unconstitutional, the court ruled, noting that this is the most commonly used, and one of the safest, methods of inducing abortions.

4. Legislation that requires a physician to exercise professional care to preserve the fetus's life and health during and after an abortion is unconstitutional, because it "does not specify that such care need be taken only after the stage of viability has been reached." The clear implication is that such a statute might be acceptable if it specified that the physician was required to take reasonable precautions to preserve the life of a viable fetus that was being aborted.

5. Some public hospitals have refused to permit or to perform elective abortions. In some instances, refusal has been based on allegedly overcrowded facilities and unwillingness of the staff to participate in such procedures. Thus far, no court has permitted a public hospital to refuse to use its facilities to perform abortions. However, private hospitals—including those that receive public funds—have been successful in refusing to permit use of their facilities to perform abortions.[104]

6. In order to limit the opportunities for women to obtain abortions, some states have prohibited the advertising of abortion clinics. The Supreme Court has ruled that such restrictions are unconstitutional.[105]

7. In some states, Medicaid payments for abortions have been denied. In Utah, the state Department of Social Services ruled that indigent, pregnant women who were entitled to medical services and care for pregnancy under the Medicaid program were not entitled to abortions under that program unless their applications were certified as therapeutic, that is, as necessary to save the pregnant woman's life or to prevent serious and permanent damage to her physical health. On the ground that such policies constitute "invidious discrimination," most courts overruled such measures, but the United States Supreme Court upheld their constitutionality in 1977.[106]

Since shortly after the *Roe* v. *Wade* decision, there has been a movement to overrule it by passing a Constitutional Amendment. The best known of these efforts is the Buckley Amendment, which defined the word *person* as used in the Fifth and Fourteenth Amendments to apply to "all human beings, including their unborn offspring at every stage of their biological development, irrespective of age, health, function, or condition of dependency," except in an emergency in which "a reasonable medical certainty exists that continuation of the pregnancy will cause the death of the mother." The Helms Amendment was similar, except that it did not provide for the exception in case of danger to the mother.[107] Passage of either proposed amendment would have outlawed, or enabled the state and federal governments to outlaw, all or most abortions. Both amendments died in committee, but the so-called right-to-life movement is likely to revive them and push for their ratification at an opportune moment.

SOME ESSENTIAL FACTS ABOUT ABORTION

Prior to the Supreme Court's decision overturning state laws that made abortion a criminal offense, most states had such laws and enforced them. It was almost impossible to obtain a legal abortion anywhere in the United States until a few states liberalized their laws, despite great pressure against such liberalization. The following cases illustrate the problems that occasionally arose:

CASE 4. THE THALIDOMIDE TRAGEDY

In 1962 Mrs. Sherri Finkbine learned about the terrible effects a supposedly harmless sleeping pill was having upon children born to mothers who had been using it. An extremely large number of children had been born in Europe, where the drug was being sold over the counter, with the most grotesque deformities. Mrs. Finkbine, a mother of four healthy children, had innocently taken a pill that her husband had brought home from a trip to Europe. After reading the article, she checked with her doctor, who wired the pharmacy that had filled her husband's prescription in England. Upon receiving the response, he told her, "Sherri, if you were my own wife I'd tell you the exact same thing. The odds for a normal baby are so against you that I am recommending termination of pregnancy." He assured her that it was a very simple matter, that a number of abortions were performed every year in Phoenix, and that she merely had to write a note to a three-doctor medical board explaining her reasons for wanting the operation.

After all the arrangements had been made, she began to think of all the other women who might have taken thalidomide and remained unaware of the tragedy that might be awaiting them. Out of concern for them, she called the local newspaper and suggested to the editor that a suitable warning should be published. Of course, she asked the editor not to use her name. He kept his word, but the next day's paper bore a sensational front-page article, bordered in black, with the headline, "Baby-Deforming Drug May Cost Woman Her Child Here." The wire services picked up the story, and, because of the national publicity the case had received, the doctors canceled her operation. Concerned over the possibility that someone might bring a court challenge to their right to perform the abortion, in view of the state's rather vague law, which permitted abortion only to save the life of the mother, they sought a declaratory judgment in court, but were turned down by an unsympathetic judge.

The official Vatican newspaper did pronounce judgment, however, and condemned Mrs. Finkbine and her husband as murderers. She received thousands of letters, many of them sympathetic, but some of them seething with religious hatred: "I hope someone takes the other four and strangles them, because it is all the same thing," one said, and another expressed the hope that God would punish her for her "murderous sin." Many letters were written by well-meaning persons who put themselves in the position of Mrs. Finkbine's unborn child: "Mommy, please dear Mommy, let me live. Please, please, I want to live. Let me love you, let me see the light of day, let me smell a rose, let me sing a song, let me look into your face, let me say Mommy." And there were many, many more.

Unable to obtain a legal abortion anywhere in the United States, she decided to go overseas. Japan, which had a lenient abortion law, refused to issue a visa out of fear of anti-American demonstrations. Finally, she went to Sweden, and, after going through the rigorous Swedish screening process, she was given the medical board's approval for an abortion. After the abortion, she asked her doctor whether the baby was a boy or a girl. He replied that it was not a baby, but an abnormal growth that would never have been a normal child.[108]

CASE 5. CHILD OF VIOLENCE

In 1955 a twenty-seven-year-old mother returned to her home after visiting her husband at the hospital. A 220-pound guard from a nearby Air Force base forced his way into her home, gagged her, tied her hands, and attacked her. In spite of medical treatment that she received, both at a hospital and from her own physician, she became pregnant as a result of the episode. No hospital in her state was willing to permit her to have a therapeutic abortion, although that state's law was at that time one of the most liberal in the nation.

She and her husband could not afford to travel abroad for a legal abortion. They were accordingly left with two alternatives: a clandestine, illegal abortion or bringing the baby to term. Because they were deeply religious people, and deeply committed to respect for the law, they chose the latter alternative. She carried the fetus in her womb, hating it—as she said many times—every minute, waiting for the moment when she would at last be rid of it. Thus the child, conceived in violence and born in hatred, came into the world.

At Johns Hopkins hospital some years ago, the Children's Aid Society was unable to procure an abortion for a fourteen-year-old girl who had become pregnant as a result of an attack upon her by her drunken father.[109] The potential damage to this young child, both physically and psychologically, was judged by the state's legal authorities to be insufficient to warrant an abortion.

Women who suffered from serious diseases, such as heart disease, tuberculosis, and leukemia, received sympathetic understanding, though usually they could expect very little more from those to whom they turned for help.

But women who had become pregnant by accident and felt that they were past the child-raising stage of life, having sent all their children through school; women who believed that a pregnancy would destroy their careers or their marriages; and women who conceived out of wedlock—all of these women received little sympathy or understanding for their problems in many hospitals and doctors' offices, and even less in their state capitols.

The problem was aggravated by other factors, not the least of which were the grave risk that every woman who sought an illegal abortion took and the danger to her life and her health. Because there are no accurate figures on the number of illegal abortions performed each year, it is impossible to determine what percentage of such abortions led to serious injury to the patient. But the cases that came to the attention of the police were numerous and shocking enough. One case, authoritatively reported, concerned a quack doctor who displayed a counterfeit diploma in his office. He had no medical training, but "practiced" for a number of years in Harlem's black ghetto. Among other gimmicks, he used a machine that he designed himself. This machine, the "electrohelomat," consisted of a large cabinet with numerous switches and flashing lights. During the treatment the patient was instructed to press certain switches. Meanwhile, the so-called doctor operated an impressive array of buzzers, relays, and sparking devices. He was arrested following the death of one of his patients, a young waitress. The autopsy revealed "that the defendant had punctured the uterus in five places with a sharp loop-type currette and had also pulled down sixteen inches of intestine before he became panic stricken and deposited the dying girl in Central Park." According to the autopsy report, he also managed to rupture the girl's bladder.[110] Not only quacks who knew nothing of medicine or female anatomy, but also some licensed physicians treated their desperate victims brutally and sadistically. More than one woman discovered that part of the price of her abortion consisted of satisfying the sexual appetites of her abortionist, with or without her consent. The literature abounds in many well-documented horror stories.

Many women attempted to induce their own abortions. Most such attempts were unsuccessful. Desperate women employed every device imaginable, from hat pins, clothes hangers, and knitting needles, to injections of soap solutions, lye, and other poisons. Some attempted to abort themselves by jumping from high places, by falling down stairs, or by resorting to other means of bringing on physical trauma. When an abortion followed such attempts, it was not necessarily a result of the woman's efforts to induce it, for it might have occurred spontaneously anyway. In the meantime she exposed herself to serious danger of permanent injury or death.

Opponents of abortion reform have their own chamber of horrors. They sometimes project slides showing fetuses at a fairly mature stage of development. They relate tales of aborted infants crying for twenty minutes or more after the operation before expiring in the pans or trays or cans into which they have been consigned. Occasionally they produce real human fetuses in jars or bottles, which may be examined by those who are sufficiently curious in order to produce in them an appropriate sense of revulsion. The president of the Catholic Physicians Guild of Colorado brought four such pickled fetuses to a hearing that the State Senate was holding prior to passage of that state's liberalized abortion law. After he was graveled down, he told a reporter, "I got mad. They said a fetus wasn't a human being. I wanted to show them they were dealing with babies, not blobs of protoplasm." [111]

Such emotion-packed stories and displays are not entirely inappropriate in discussions of this issue, though they are surely not conducive to dispassionate consideration of the arguments on either side. The issue is, after all, at least partly an emotional one. Strong feelings are evident on all sides. The existence of such feelings must not be overlooked, for it is indicative of the depth of the moral concerns involved.

According to the Federal Center for Disease Control, an analysis of the records of nearly two million legal abortions performed between 1972 and 1974 reveals that there were 3.9 deaths for every 100,000 legal abortions, leading to the conclusion that "in terms of risk of death, legal abortion is a relatively safe surgical procedure." By comparison, 15 of every 100,000 women who gave birth during that period died, as well as five of every 100,000 persons who had tonsillectomies, and 352 of every 100,000 persons who had appendectomies. Prior to 1970, 20% of the deaths among pregnant women were caused by illegal abortions. The study concluded that legal abortions were saving the lives of many women who probably would have terminated their pregnancies illegally.[112] These figures corroborate others that had been released earlier, indicating that during the first two years after California liberalized its abortion laws, there was a significant decline in abortion-related deaths. Much the same experience was reported in New York after its abortion reform act was passed. In one San Francisco hospital, postabortion cases decreased by 68% during the first two years, and in a Los Angeles hospital, by 88%. Ten New York hospitals reported a 52% decline in cases caused by complications following abortion during the first three years of legalized abortion in that state. Cook County Hospital in Chicago admitted about 4,000 women annually for medical care following criminal abortions between 1962 and 1968. In April and May, 1973, a few months after the Supreme Court's decision, there were no more than five cases per month at that hospital.[113]

Certain hereditary diseases can now be diagnosed quite accurately by a method known as amniocentesis. This involves drawing a small amount of amniotic fluid from the sac that surrounds the fetus and subjecting it to microscopic examination. It is now possible to determine whether a fetus will suffer from Down's syndrome (mongolism), microcephaly, cystic fibrosis of the pancreas, Turner's syndrome (in which the female genitalia remain infantile after puberty, growth is stunted, and kidneys are abnormal), Klinefelter syndrome (characterized by retarded development of male genitalia, absence of sperm in testes, mental retardation, enlarged breasts, and other symptoms), and Tay-Sachs disease (amauratic idiocy), among others.

Tay-Sachs may serve as a good example for detailed study. A child afflicted with this genetic disorder suffers a degeneration of the nerve cells in the central nervous system, including the retina, the spinal cord, and the brain. Symptoms, which may commence between early infancy and early to late childhood, include loss of vision, convulsive seizures, paralysis, dementia, and finally, death. These symptoms are irreversible and progressive. There is no known cure. The emotional cost to those whose children are afflicted with this dreadful malady is incalculable, and the financial burden upon them and upon the communities in which they live is enormous. A simple examination could reassure a young couple who are known to be carriers (this can be determined by simple tests that they should have had before they were married or at least before the woman became pregnant) that the child is normal; or, if the child is not normal, the couple can, under the law as presently interpreted by the Supreme Court, choose to have an abortion, thus sparing themselves and the growing fetus the agony of the certain death that would otherwise await their child. Those who would change the law by amending the Constitution would force such couples to seek illegal abortions or to have their defective babies, with all the suffering that that would entail.

PHILOSOPHICAL ARGUMENTS AGAINST ABORTION

The principal argument against abortion can be summarized rather briefly. For convenience, each statement is numbered:

1. Human life is sacred; that is, every human being has the fundamental right to live.

2. Everyone has a moral duty to respect the sanctity of human life, that is, to refrain from any act that can reasonably be expected to cause another human being's death.

3. Hence, no one has the right to impose conditions upon any other human being that are likely to cause the latter's death. (Such conditions may assume many different forms, including the deprivation of such vital necessities as air, water, or food, the infliction of such grave physical injury to the individual that he is likely to perish as a result of his wounds, exposing him to conditions such as extreme cold or heat, dangerous drugs, toxic chemicals, or lethal bacteria, a concentration camp or the front line of a raging battle that are almost certain to cause death, and so on.)

4. A fetus is a human being.

5. Hence, no one has the right to impose conditions upon a fetus that are likely to result in that fetus' death.

6. Every abortion deprives the aborted fetus of conditions necessary for its survival and either directly causes such grave physical injury that it is almost certain to die, or places it in such a hostile environment that it is not likely to survive.

7. Every abortion therefore violates the fetus' right to live.

8. Therefore, no person has the right to commit an abortion.

Notice that in this reformulation of the antiabortionist's argument, the fetus is not referred to as a person. Instead, the term, *human being*, or male pronouns, are used throughout.* The United States Supreme Court has established to its satisfaction that in the Constitution the term *person* has reference only to human beings who have been born. This does not resolve the moral question (or perhaps the factual question) whether a fetus is a person entitled to the same moral rights as a postnatal infant, a ten-year-old child, or an adult. *Human being* and *person* will be used interchangeably in the remainder of this discussion.

The assertion in premise 1 is a moral judgment to which few persons are likely to take exception. Almost everyone would agree that all things being equal, no one ought to take another's life. Premise 2 is a restatement of premise 1, or a statement of the corollary of premise 1. Ordinarily, there is a logical connection between rights and duties. If one person has a right to something, it follows that at least one other person has a duty to him with respect to that thing. For example, if you have a right to be paid for your services, it follows that others have a duty to pay you for your services. If you have a right to publish your opinions, it follows that others have a duty not to interfere with your publishing activities. Similarly, if a person has the right to live, it follows that others have a duty not to do anything that would cause his death.

But this is true only when all things are equal, or under ordinary circumstances. Most people recognize that the principles enunciated in statements 1 and 2 are not absolute but are subject to some qualifications. In time of war, for example, the enemy soldier's right to life is tenuous at best, at least so far as his enemy is concerned. The situation is such that the duty the combatants would ordinarily have to avoid doing anything that might cause the death of other persons they encounter is suspended with regard to the enemy on the battlefield. The soldier's duty is to injure and kill. Similarly, a felon who is in the act of committing a violent and destructive crime, such as rape, murder, or arson, has thereby transformed the moral as well as the legal situation from one in which all other persons, but especially the police, have a duty to refrain from harming him into one in which the police have a positive duty to harm him—if necessary, to kill him—to bring an end to his violent behavior. Under appropriate circumstances, a duty to refrain from killing can be transformed into a duty to kill.

Some people might argue, however, that the principle in statements 1 and 2 is absolute, based on the principle that life, liberty, and the pursuit

---

* Male pronouns are used to avoid the question-begging impersonal *it* and are to be understood generically as referring to females as well as males.

of happiness are inalienable rights. They believe that even brute creatures have rights—the right not to be subjected to cruel treatment, for example. Some people believe that animals as well as human beings have a right to life and therefore those persons refuse to eat meat. In India, some people are so sensitive to the right of all creatures to live that they walk with great care so as not to step on an unwary insect, and they wear surgical masks to avoid inhaling and thereby causing the death of some flying organism. The underlying assumption is that life is of absolute value and should never be extinguished if that can possibly be avoided.

When the authors of the Bill of Rights laid down the rule that no one could be deprived of the right to life without the process of law, they implicitly recognized that under certain circumstances even that most precious of rights, together with the fundamental right to liberty, could be taken away with due process of law. They were aware that the right of each person to live may, on rare occasions, come into conflict with other fundamental rights, and that when such conflicts arise, it may be necessary for one or more persons to give up their lives. Thus, they recognized the right of self-defense. They held that human life was sacred and deserving of the most intensive protective measures on the part of the state, but the right to life could be forfeited under certain circumstances. A dangerous criminal could be deprived of liberty and thrown behind bars. Citizens could be deprived of portions of their property through taxation or exercise of the right of eminent domain for the sake of the general welfare. As the political philosophers of the seventeenth and eighteenth centuries understood the term, an inalienable right was not necessarily absolute. It was one that a person could not give away to anyone else, one that he was always entitled to defend, but one that another could deny under appropriate circumstances.[114] Thus, the conclusion in statement 3 cannot be regarded as being absolute and unconditional.

Statement 4, that a fetus is a human being, is the real crux of the issue. A good part of the proof that proponents of this proposition offer consists of well-accepted biological facts of human conception and the growth of a fetus. There is virtually no dispute about the following facts.

A sperm penetrates the wall of an ovum, a barrier surrounds the outer layer of the ovum's covering, thus preventing any other sperm from entering, and the nuclei of sperm and ovum unite. This brings the chromosomes of both parents together, with their genetic material, and results in a unique combination. Mitosis begins and new cells are formed, each with the same genetic package. In a very short time, cells are undergoing differentiation, some destined to become parts of the developing embryo (its various organs and limbs), and others, parts of the placenta through which wastes will be absorbed into the future mother's bloodstream and essential nutrients and oxygen transferred from her system into that of the growing fetus.* A

---

* Technically speaking, some biologists distinguish between the embryo, the fetus, and other stages of human development, along more or less arbitrary lines. These distinctions have not been standardized and are irrelevant to this discussion.

few days after the union of sperm and ovum, the rapidly changing clump of cells attaches itself to the uterus and embeds itself within the uterine wall, where it will continue to develop, if nothing intervenes to interrupt the process, into a full-term baby. The basic pattern of its development is set at the moment of conception—the moment of the initial union of sperm and egg. The fetal heartbeat can be perceived relatively early in the fetus' development. The brain, which develops quite rapidly, begins to function, and in a matter of weeks the fetus looks like a human baby. As it floats in amniotic fluid, it sucks its thumb, it moves its arms and legs, and it reacts to such stimuli as bright light by moving its head and arms as if to shield its eyes.[115]

According to some authorities, the fetus is a human being from the moment of conception. A typical statement of that position follows:

> The sperm and the ovum, prior to fertiliation, can be considered as belonging to those from whom they derive. But once conception occurs, a cell exists which cannot be identified with either parent. The fertilized ovum is something *one* derived from two sources. As the facts of genetics . . . make clear, the unity of the fertilized ovum is continuous with that which develops from it, while the duality of the sperm and ovum are continuous with the duality of the two parents. Thus, the proper demarcation between parents and offspring is conception, and so the new individual begins with conception. From this point of view, then, it is certain that the embryo from conception until birth is a living, human individual.[116]

Similarly, a physician who specializes in neonatology has said:

> Science admits to only one point of beginning of human life. This occurs when the sperm carrying the father's 23 chromosomes, and the ovum, carrying the mother's 23 chromosomes, unite at fertilization. From this moment on a new, unique individual is present.
>
> Although in the beginning the fertilized ovum does not look like a baby, from moment to moment following that union each increase in development is a barely perceptible and very gradual one. At no point is there a sudden change when he becomes a "baby." Each day is characterized by gradual maturation and growth. Genetically the baby is the same at birth as he is at fertilization.[117]

It is not at all uncommon for informed persons to insist that the question of the precise moment when human life begins is not a matter of opinion "but a matter of scientific findings." "Scientific evidence," they say, "verifies fertilization as the beginning of human life." [118] Does it follow from the scientific evidence that the moment of fertilization, or the moment of conception, is the time at which the right to life and the correlative duty not to cause death begins, or ought to begin? Is the moral issue solved by the scientific proof that there is a continuity—physical and developmental—from fertilized egg to adult? Must one confer upon a fertilized egg the rights possessed by an adult person? Is it in fact proper, in all contexts, to think of the fertilized egg, or the fetus in its later stages of development, as a *person?*

A number of arguments have been offered in support of the proposition that a fertilized egg is *not* a person (or a human being). In the discussion that follows, I shall give a brief summary of some of these arguments, a response by a critic of those arguments, and my own reply to the critic.

The Acorn Analogy. A squirrel that eats 15 acorns has not thereby eaten 15 oak trees—though the acorns would develop into oak trees under appropriate conditions, one of which would be that they not be eaten by the squirrel. An acorn is a *potential* oak tree, not an oak tree. Similarly, the zygote is a *potential* person, not a person.

The Critic's Response. An acorn is an inactive phase in the life cycle of the plant from which it comes. But the human embryo does not go through such an inactive phase. It is constantly growing and developing, unlike the acorn. A more fitting analogy would be to the seedling, which *is* an oak tree, though a small one.

Reply to the Critic. The crucial point made by those who argue from the scientific fact that the fertilized ovum is continuous with the mature individual is the uniqueness of its hereditary makeup, its completeness insofar as its ultimate structure is concerned. In this respect, at least, the analogy is complete. The acorn bears within it all the genetic materials the full-grown oak will ever possess. From this point of view, then, the acorn's dormancy would seem to be irrelevant. If a human zygote could be rendered dormant by some cooling process, would the critic then be prepared to concede that the analogy is a good one? Perhaps another analogy would be more fitting. Compare the freshly fertilized human ovum to a freshly laid fertile hen's egg. Would the critic contend that a person eats scrambled chicken for breakfast? Does the gourmet who applies a thick covering of caviar to a cracker devour a school of sturgeon at one gulp? Surely the answer to each of these questions must be in the negative. Everyone recognizes that a fertilized hen's egg will eventually develop into a chicken and a sturgeon's into a fish, but what an egg might potentially *become* is not identical with what it *is*. The same is true in many areas: the small child who possesses great musical talent is not a great singer or violinist, though he may *become* one. This simple distinction between what a thing is *potentially* and what it is *in actuality* dates back at least to the time of Aristotle. One would expect modern thinkers to be able to use it with some facility. The fertilized egg of a human being has the potential to *become* a human being, but it is not yet a human being, and will not become one unless proper conditions are present for it to do so. In any case, analogies are often misleading and should not be taken too seriously. Whether the human zygote is more like an oak seedling than it is like an acorn can be left to the reader's imagination, but it would seem that if any comparison is to be used at all, it would be more appropriate to think of the seedling rather than the acorn as most like the newborn infant.

The Blueprint Analogy.   The genetic information contained in a newly fertilized ovum resembles a set of blueprints for a house, or a program manual for a computer. Destruction of the blueprints for a $50,000 house is not the same as destroying the house; nor is destruction of the program manual the same as destroying the program or the computer. Analogously, destruction of the zygote is not the destruction of a human being.

The Critic's Response.   The zygote and the blueprints cannot be compared, for the zygote is *alive*, but the blueprint is not. More importantly, the blueprint does not *become* the house, it merely serves as a *plan* for the house; the zygote *becomes* the human being into which it grows. The analogy fails.

Reply to the Critic.   It is indeed a poor analogy. But we may be making progress. At least you're willing to admit that the zygote *becomes* a human being. In any case, shooting down this argument on the ground that it makes use of a weak analogy is not the same as proving your own point, that the zygote is entitled to all the rights due to a person who has been born.

The Socialization Argument.   A human embryo or fetus "does not become functionally human until humanized in the human socialization process. Humanity is an achievement, not an endowment." [119] In other words, a human being is not merely a blob of biological material that has the capacity to be organized into the shape which human beings ordinarily have; nor is a human being a mere living organism that happens to belong to the biological species *homo sapiens*. Rather, the concept *human being* is narrower than that. A human being is a living creature who acts and responds in certain ways that are peculiar to the human species. Until it has developed the capacity to act and respond in those ways, no organism can properly be considered to be a human being, whatever its potentialities might be.

The Critic's Response.   This criterion is dangerously elastic. It would certainly allow for the abortion of unborn fetuses. But it would also allow infanticide. Even more, it could be invoked in justification of the extermination of such unsocialized persons as Helen Keller prior to her training by a dedicated teacher and nurse and of others who are so gravely handicapped as to be unable to reach the standard of achievement set by some judge of humanization who would have the power of life or death over them. This is too reminiscent of Adolf Hitler's programs of racial purification, which included the killing of mentally ill and mentally retarded persons.

Reply to the Critics.   This reply must be divided into several parts: (a) the infanticide question; (b) the Helen Keller case; and (c) the Hitler argument.
  (a) *The infanticide question.* The socialization theory is one of several theories, all of which have the same general outcome: that a biologically human organism does not become human for some purposes until it reaches

a certain point of development. Such theories also allow for a corollary at the other extreme of life's passage: that in the absence of certain signs of humanity, the person is no longer regarded as being alive. Thus, a person whose brain has ceased to function, who is no longer able to communicate or (so far as can be determined) to perceive what is going on in the world around him may be considered as if he were dead despite the fact that such physiological processes as heartbeat and respiration continue to function. Although this outcome might have been shocking at one time, it is now widely accepted among physicians, philosophers, theologians, and members of the legal profession. Nor is infanticide necessarily considered to be criminal or immoral in all circumstances. An infant born with such gross deformities as to be incapable of living anything remotely resembling a normal life may be better off if it is allowed to die by withholding heroic measures to preserve its life. In extreme cases, when the infants born resemble monsters more than human beings and when it is obvious that as long as they live they and their parents may suffer the most extreme pain and anguish, some physicians have chosen to withhold relatively simple treatments that would have kept them alive so as to spare everyone concerned. This is a difficult choice but not necessarily an immoral one. Those who advocate the socialization theory and others like it do not conclude from the theory that the wanton killing of those who have not yet reached full socialization, or who have passed their prime and are slipping into senility, is permissible. But they do say that because becoming human is a process, under certain conditions (particularly those that involve the potential for great suffering), acts whose purpose is to remove or avoid such suffering are not immoral and should not be illegal, even when they necessarily entail the death of fetuses, infants, or persons who have reached advanced stages of senility or other forms of mental incapacity. It is important to notice that the closer a person comes to being socialized, the more carefully his right to live is to be guarded. By the time an infant reaches the age of one month, it may already have become sufficiently well socialized that no one could claim the right to deny it the necessities of life. (The concept of socialization is too complicated to be discussed in detail here, but it would include the effects that an infant has upon its parents and others, and their attitudes toward it. These develop very rapidly after the infant's birth. As a result, the death of the infant after it has been born is likely to cause far more grief than would the death of a fetus, however advanced its stage of development.)

(b) *The Helen Keller case.* Antiabortionists frequently cite such examples as Helen Keller, the remarkable woman who overcame total deafness and total blindness and managed to inspire millions with her courage and her beautiful writings.* Another case that is sometimes cited is that of Charles P. Steinmetz, an electronic genius whose contributions to electrical

---

* Helen Keller was not born with her handicaps, but developed them later. We may assume, however, that she—or someone just like her—was born with them.

technology helped to make the Westinghouse Corporation the giant that it is and who made great strides toward the understanding of lightning. Steinmetz was badly deformed and was a hopeless cripple all his life. Under the criteria ordinarily applied by those who favor abortion of deformed or seriously defective fetuses, such people as Helen Keller and Charles Steinmetz might never have seen the light of day and the world would have been poorer without them. When a bill to liberalize New York's abortion law was being debated in the state legislature, a deformed legislator rose and gave an impassioned speech in which he reminded his colleagues that if such a liberal law had been in existence while his mother was carrying him, he might never have been born.

Such arguments are appealing because they have powerful emotional impact. But on cool, unemotional analysis, they carry little weight. No objective participant in this discussion can deny that some of the fetuses that have been aborted and that will be aborted might have become beautiful human beings who might have made important contributions to those closest to them or to all of mankind. This is not only true of fetuses. It is also true of the billions of children who might have been born if men and women were not employing various contraceptive devices. Every potential child, including those who might have been conceived but weren't, might make important contributions. On the other hand, many of these children might have become oppressive burdens upon their families and society at large. For every congenitally deformed genius the antiabortionists can name, the proabortionists can point to a hundred pitiful and tragic cases. Whatever the world may have lost because of the practice of abortion can at least be matched by a comparable gain. The argument leads to a standoff.

(c) *The Hitler argument.* Hitler is deservedly popular among moral philosophers, for he was the incarnation of everything evil, and he conducted his vicious and malevolent business during the lifetime of many of us. Hitler is unlike most villains of the past, because many living people remember him and the horrors he inflicted upon the world. Some of his victims are still living, bearing witness to one of the blackest, bloodiest, and vilest epochs of human history. The invocation of his name inevitably raises powerful feelings of disgust and revulsion. The warped minds of Hitler and his followers found ways to employ the latest discoveries of science and technology to further evil plans, one of which was to exterminate what he considered *inferior races* (Jews, gypsies, Slavs, and blacks) and to purify and improve what he termed the *master race* (the Aryans). Part of this program involved the systematic murder of inmates of mental hospitals and homes for the mentally retarded. Other "inferior" persons were exterminated en masse. Jews and other allegedly inferior groups were forced to undergo massive x-ray treatments and surgical operations, the purpose of which was to sterilize them so they could not bring more of their kind into being. Pregnant women were often the first to be shoved into the gas chambers and the ovens in the notorious death camps to which they were shipped. Abortion and infanticide became commonplace when they offered the only hope, slim as that hope was, that a woman might live a little longer.

That such a madman as Hitler would pervert a principle to his own evil ends does not constitute proof that the principle is false. Nor does the existence of possibly evil uses of a new technology constitute an argument against its development. New discoveries in physics, chemistry, biology, and medicine can be turned to evil purposes. The solution does not lie in hindering the process of discovery, suppressing scientists, or outlawing new methods for curing ancient ills or resolving complex human problems, but in being ever watchful against the rise of totalitarian and dictatorial powers. Sterilization is of course an almost foolproof method of contraception. The fact that Hitler sterilized thousands of his victims does not mean that physicians must not sterilize their patients upon the request of the patients. The operation is not evil in itself. It was the compulsion, the genocidal purpose of the operation under Nazi tyranny, that made the sterilization of Jews evil.

A similar argument follows:

> Those who intend to kill often find it helpful to define their intended victims as nonhuman. Such conceptual juggling . . . could verify the general practice of the device by a study of the history of the treatment of Negro slaves or American Indians. We would find examples of argument that such victims were not human, did not have souls, were not full persons.[120]

There is a world of difference between those whose purpose is the enslavement or extermination of a group of human beings and those who support a public policy as a result of a compassionate response to human suffering. Similar comparisons are often made by persons who disapprove of the policies of a given nation or community. The armed forces of the United States have often been compared to Hitler's storm troopers, and the FBI and the local police forces of certain American cities have been likened to the Gestapo. The American system has been called fascistic, and other democratic states, such as Israel, France, and West Germany, have been condemned for their allegedly Nazi-like policies. Such fatuous comparisons ignore fundamental moral differences. They contribute nothing toward the clarification of issues. They merely confuse and obscure the real questions. In the abortion controversy, the comparison is based upon a false impression of the motives of those who favor the right of women to make their own choices in this area—choices which American Indians, American Negroes during the days of slavery, and the Jews of Nazi Europe were never permitted to make.

Members of groups marked for extermination or slavery have been labeled nonhuman by their enemies as a supposed justification for their evil designs. But it does not follow that everyone who employs the claim that x is nonhuman as part of his justification for killing x has embarked upon an immoral campaign of the enslavement or extermination of human beings or that that claim is being used to cover up an immoral practice.

It seems, then, that the premises upon which the conclusion in proposition 5 is based do not hold up under critical analysis. The argument must therefore be rejected as unsound. The second argument (Propositions 6, 7, and 8) rests upon the assumption that a fetus has a right to live—an assumption that presupposes the answer to the very question at issue. The argument is therefore question-begging and hence of no value.

FURTHER ARGUMENTS AGAINST ABORTION

The following arguments may be summarized briefly, with appropriate responses from a liberal point of view.

The Right to Life. "*It is a basic principle . . . that every man possesses his right to life from God—not from man or society. . . . There is thus no man, no human authority, no science, no indication (whether medical, eugenic, social, economic, or moral) that can justify deliberate and direct destruction of innocent human life. The life of an innocent human being is simply inviolable, altogether immune from direct acts of suppression.*" [121] The author of this statement, Father Richard A. McCormick, notes that it contains an important qualification: *innocent* human life; for capital punishment and defense against unjust aggression constitute exceptions to the rule. A further qualification is the word *direct,* which is meant to exclude acts that result in death of the fetus but are not intended to do so —such as removal of a cancerous uterus when the uterus contains a fetus. Aside from these points the principle is unqualified: there is no price on human life.

However, one may accept this principle without accepting the conclusion that all (or any) abortions are wrong; for one may insist that the life of a fetus is not the life of a human being, because a fetus is a potential, and not an actual, human being. Certainly there can be no objection to the destruction of human cells and tissues; such destruction takes place every day in the operating rooms of hospitals, and no one thinks that it is immoral. Under proper conditions, and with sufficient technical advances, it is now believed that *any* cell taken from any part of a person's body can be developed into a human being, complete and sound in every respect, and identical in its genetic makeup with the person from whom the first cell was taken.[122] One could carry the antiabortionist argument to absurd lengths and argue that *any* cell, being a potential human being, deserves the protection of the law and ought not to be destroyed. Certainly any sperm should fall under the ban. (Is this where the ban on onanism comes from?) If a line can be drawn at one point, it can as easily be drawn at another—say, birth, or the fifth month of pregnancy.

The rejoinder is this:

> The presence of a rational soul is attributable to a creative act of God. Since it is a creative act, the time of its occurrence ultimately escapes the tools of direct human inquiry. . . . And secondly, the spiritual and material interests of the child are not sufficiently protected if we are allowed to act on non-conclusive estimates (by embryologists and physiologists) of the time of animation. If there is a human being, in the fullest sense, present from the moment of conception, directly destructive actions based on an opposite assumption will be in violation of his inviolable rights. The practical conclusion, therefore, is that there *is* a human being—because no other conclusion protects sufficiently the most voiceless, voteless, helpless, unorganized minority imaginable.[123]

We shall leave aside the obvious emotionalism of the last sentence in order to examine the argument. First, it assumes that there is a rational soul—a dubious assumption that we shall not attempt to challenge here. Second, it assumes that the soul enters the embryo through a creative (miraculous) act of God. If not for the miraculous intervention of God, the fetus would develop into something nonhuman. The mere biological process with which we are all familiar is not sufficient to produce human beings. But these assumptions are not merely assumptions; they are articles of faith, unprovable by any empirical test, as Father McCormick himself concedes. Without evidence, those who are untouched by the faith have the right—both the moral right and the intellectual right—to reject these assumptions. If the assumptions are not granted, the rest of the argument falls to the ground. Many embryologists and physiologists are not at all interested in the moment of animation, for they do not believe that such a moment exists. They are quite satisfied that they can, at least in principle, explain all the phenomena of human life without such an otiose assumption. Applying Occam's Razor,* they slice off the "rational soul," and with it the "moment of animation," and work with what is empirically observable.

But there is more: "Sufficient" protection of the right to life turns out to be an absolute ban on abortion, right from the moment of conception, because of our lack of certainty about the moment of animation. Even though we do not *know* when the fetus is animated, we must *act as if* it were animated at conception in order to protect what *we will assume* is human life, though we cannot be sure that it is. How does this compare to those cases in which the mother's life is in danger? About the mother's life there is no doubt. We *know* that she is a human being, and there is no dispute over the fact that

---

* A principle enunciated by the fourteenth-century philosopher, William of Occam (or Ockham). Sometimes called the Law of Parsimony, it says that entities are not to be multiplied beyond necessity. It has been employed to defend the Copernican hypothesis. Some modern philosophers of science (e.g., Ernst Mach) maintain that science should present the facts of nature in the simplest, most economical conceptual formulations.

to kill her would be morally wrong. Yet Father McCormick maintains that if the choice is between the life of the mother and the life of the fetus, the mother must lose. Even if the choice were between aborting the fetus and losing both mother *and* fetus, he opts for the latter; for as he puts it, "the choice was never between one death and two deaths, but rather between two unavoidable deaths and one murder." [124] He fails to see that the abortion is murder only if the fetus is a human being, only if it *is in fact animated* (to use his own terminology). Because he does not know when animation takes place, it would be reasonable to assume that the fetus is only a *possible* human being, whereas the mother is *certainly* a human being. Permitting the mother and the fetus to die by doing nothing may not be murder, technically speaking, but for the mother and her family the end result is the same. The refusal to save the life of a living human being, who is loved and needed by others, on such technical grounds, strikes me as being indefensible.

The argument is sometimes extended in other ways. If abortion is allowed on medical, social, economic, psychiatric, or eugenic grounds, it is said, then why not permit the deliberate elimination of adolescents, the elderly, and others who become a burden upon others? Because we know that it would be wrong to kill an adolescent or an old man for the sake of some other person's health or economic well-being, it must therefore be equally wrong to take the life of a fetus.[125] The answer is that the analogy simply does not hold. A fetus is not comparable to an adolescent or an old man. It has established no relations with other persons, it has no personality, it has contributed nothing to anyone; it has not participated in the life of its family or of the community in any way. Though it has done no wrong to anyone, it need not be regarded as entitled to the absolute protection of its right to life, because it may be regarded as a nonperson, as a being that lacks the protection of the law.

The proponent of legal abortions may not be saying that the fetus has *no* right to life. He may merely be saying that that right should not carry with it the sanctions that the law brings to bear against those who wrongfully cause the death of an adolescent or of an old man, or of a day-old baby. Your right to speak freely may be violated by someone; if it is, the wrongdoer will not be sent to prison for life, and he will not be prevented from practicing his profession. Though we might say that he *ought* to respect your right to express yourself, we do not ordinarily think it appropriate to bring the penal force of the law into play to protect that right. The proponent of abortion law reform is not altogether denying that the fetus has a right to live. He says, merely, that that right should not carry with it the penal sanctions that most states presently enforce.

Legal Abortion Leads to Increased Promiscuity. *It is said that the ready availability of abortions leads to a general moral breakdown, with wide-*

spread promiscuity becoming the rule, because the fear of becoming pregnant is one of the most important deterrents to promiscuity.

There is no statistical evidence to support this assertion. No significant rise in rates of premarital or extramarital coitus has been verified as having resulted from legalized abortion, though, as one might expect, there has been a great increase in the number of legal abortions.

If the argument were valid, it would follow, by the same reasoning, that contraceptives should be banned. Some people *do* use this argument. If a woman insists on having her pleasure, they say, let her—and, one must assume, her baby—suffer. The same reasoning would lead to the conclusion that if a girl contracts venereal disease, she should be denied treatment for it. If people can avoid the evil consequences of sex (pregnancy, carrying a fetus to term, or venereal disease), they will become promiscuous. Therefore, to prevent promiscuity, keep the evil consequences.

So goes the argument, when broken down to its essentials. It completely ignores the evils of bringing motherless children into the world, the scandal and shame of an illegitimate birth, and the harm that may result to young women who are forced to go through pregnancy against their will. All these evils, it is assumed, are as nought when compared to the evil of illegitimate sex. However, without advocating indulgence in illicit sex, one can quite properly argue that some of its possible consequences may be still worse, and that failure to remedy the latter when remedies are available is no cure for the former. Besides, most women who seek abortions—more than 80%, according to some statistics—are married mothers of two or more children and have not become pregnant because of illicit intercourse.

The "Tacit Promise" Argument. "*Whenever a woman willingly engages in coitus,*" it has been said, "*she, in so doing, makes an implicit promise that in the event of conception she will bear and give life to the fruit of her act. This promise exists even in the case of the woman who responsibly uses contraception in an attempt to avoid pregnancy.*" [126]

Every promise entails the existence of at least two persons—one who makes the promise and one to whom the promise is made. Also, genuine promises exist only when the person who promises knows that he is promising and intends to promise. But when a woman has intercourse, she may have no intention to promise; her intention may be only to have sexual relations. If contraceptives are employed, it would seem that there is a deliberate withholding of any commitment. And further, to whom is the promise made? To the child who might be born of the union, in spite of all precautions that are taken? What a strange promise! "I promise you, whoever you may be, that, although you do not now exist, *if* you ever do come into existence. . . ." A promise to a nonexistent but possible person. This is stretching the meaning of the word *promise* beyond all recognizable limits. [127]

Legalization May Lead to Governmental Abuses. As noted earlier, Aristotle alluded to the possibility of the state's compelling certain persons to undergo abortions or to permit their children to be slaughtered on eugenic or other grounds. Humanae Vitae *makes the same point, in a slightly different way, by alleging that loosening the restrictions on abortion laws and on laws restricting the sale and use of contraceptives could lead to a loss of respect for human life and could give the officers of a state an excuse for instituting compulsory abortions or infanticide.*

This objection is unsound because of its failure to deal with political realities. Any government that is so tyrannical as to want to order the institution of such laws, as Hitler did, does not need to base its policy upon such humanitarian measures as liberalized abortion laws. It *might* do so as a public relations gimmick, but certainly the liberal abortion law would not have *led* to the repressive measures. There is a world of difference between a law that gives women the freedom to determine how their bodies shall be used (such as a liberal abortion law) and one that takes that freedom away from them. Notice that both *restrictive* abortion laws, which do not permit *any* abortion or which permit the state to interfere with a woman's right to determine whether she shall have a child or not, and *compulsory* abortion laws have in common a very important feature: state interference in the use of a woman's body and in the determination of whether she *must* or *must not* have a baby. A tyrant could well seize upon the Church's advocacy of such interference as justification for his own, if he were interested in offering rationalizations for his repressive legislation.

ARGUMENTS FOR LIBERAL ABORTION LAWS

Restrictive Abortion Laws Assume That Women Are Chattel. Women are treated as if they were property, the property of the state, perhaps—as if the control of their bodies did not belong to them but belonged to someone else—the legislature, the courts, the doctors, or whoever presumes to make the decisions for them. This is a demeaning and degrading state of affairs, hardly consistent with the professed goal of freedom in a democratic society. A woman should be the master of her own body, and should not be forced, against her will, to serve as the soil for the growth of seed that she does not want to be there. As Baroness Summerskill said, in the debate on the British bill,

> Today, literate people of the space age . . . are not prepared to accept taboos unquestioning, and in the matter of abortion the human rights of the individual mother . . . with her own fully developed personality and her responsibilities to her family, must take precedence over the survival of a few weeks old foetus without sense or sensibility. . . . A girl who has been the victim of rape . . . [has had] her human rights . . . totally disregarded,

and when pregnancy results it violates her maternal functions. Can it be argued that it is socially desirable and reconcilable with human rights that she should be compelled to bear and rear a child criminally begotten? [128]

Concern for the Fetus.   Where abortion is illegal, women are driven to seek illegal abortions in abominable conditions, and sometimes to attempt to abort themselves. Aside from the terrible danger that they are in when they resort to such measures, they endanger the well-being of the fetuses they bear within them, if the attempt should fail and no subsequent abortion attempt succeeds. Many children have been born to women who had attempted to induce an abortion; the children have been seriously malformed in a significant number of cases as a result of trauma to them or to the womb. It would be better to permit the fetus to be aborted in sanitary conditions by an expert than to risk its being born with defects that could destroy its chances for a happy life. Even if the fetus is brought to term and is normal in every way, if its mother was desperate enough to try to destroy it while it was in her womb, its chances for a happy childhood and a normal upbringing would seem to be considerably reduced. The social cost, as well as the cost to the child and its family, is incalculable. The problem is compounded when the child is given up by its natural parents, and is made still worse if the child is a victim of its mother's German measles or some other deforming disease or drug.

Psychological Effects May Be Beneficial.   Opponents of legalized abortion sometimes argue that women who have abortions are more likely than others to suffer from acute anxiety and from severe guilt feelings. However, no convincing statistics on this matter are available. In addition, three further possibilities must be considered. First, some women who have had abortions seem to have a positive sense of relief, a feeling that they are rid of an unendurable burden. Second, the psychological trauma of bringing an unwanted child into the world, or of bearing a child whom one knows is bound to be severely handicapped, must be enormous. It is difficult to see how the continuing suffering—lifelong, perhaps, particularly in the latter case—can be compared to any postpartum depression that the mother might suffer from an abortion. And finally, some thought should be given to the remote causes of such depressions and guilt feelings as do occur. If theologians would change their attitudes and their preachings, perhaps some women who now feel guilty over what they have done out of an instinct for self-preservation would instead rejoice over their good fortune in having averted a nearly certain tragedy.

The Drop in Maternal Death Rates.   As we have already seen, a significant decline in the number of maternal deaths occurred after legal abortions became readily available. A further dividend, at least from some points of view, is the decline in the number of illegitimate births.

Discrimination Against the Poor and the Black. Until legal abortions became available, those who were moderately well-to-do were able to obtain safe abortions, either by traveling to one of the abortion havens or by paying a private physician. But the poor were shut out, because they were unable to travel and did not have access to private physicians. (Those physicians who would perform abortions would do so only when the patient was willing to pay a very high fee, in view of the risks of detection, prosecution, and conviction.) Virtually no therapeutic abortions were performed on ward patients, but a significant number of private patients in the same hospitals did have abortions. Ward doctors were unwilling to take the risks that private doctors took for their patients, for they had no financial incentive to do so.

Political pressures upon the United States Congress and a number of state legislatures have led to restrictions upon the use of Medicaid funds for elective abortions. Although one of the benefits that resulted from the legalization of abortion was the extension of the right to have an abortion to those who were too poor to afford the costs of illegal abortions by competent physicians, it is important to distinguish carefully between the legalization of abortion (that is, the removal of criminal penalties for the performance of an abortion) and welfare payments, or the use of tax money, to pay for abortions. There is a difference between the right to have an abortion without interference by the state and the right to have an abortion paid for by the state. A person may quite consistently support the one and oppose the other. Naturally, those who oppose abortions as such will also oppose the use of tax funds for abortion procedures. But just as the right to publish one's views does not necessarily include the right to demand tax subsidies for one's publications, the right to an abortion does not necessarily include the right to demand a tax subsidy for one's abortions—though one might make a case for the wisdom of such payments on other grounds.

A MODIFIED DEFENSE OF THE RIGHT
TO HAVE AN ABORTION

In one of the most widely discussed treatments of the abortion issue, Judith Jarvis Thomson defended the view that under certain circumstances, but possibly not under others, it is not morally wrong for a woman to have an abortion, and that in any case, it ought not to be legally forbidden for women to have abortions.[129]

She begins by granting the assumption made by those who oppose all abortions that the fetus is a person from the moment of conception. The argument, she says, is usually something like this: Every person has a right to life, so the fetus (being a person) has a right to life. A person's right to life is stronger and more stringent than the mother's right to decide what happens in and to her body. Hence, the fetus may not be killed by being aborted. But according to Thomson, this argument does not validly demonstrate the truth of its conclusion.

She asks the reader to suppose that he wakes up one morning to find himself back to back in bed with an unconscious violinist who has a fatal kidney ailment. After discovering that you alone have the right blood type to help, the Society of Music Lovers has kidnapped you and plugged his circulatory system into yours. The director of the hospital, although not approving of what the Society of Music Lovers has done, argues that you must remain in bed, plugged in to the violinist, for nine months, nine years, or life (depending upon how long it takes him to regain the use of his own kidneys) because all persons, including violinists, have a right to life, a right that outweighs your right to decide what happens in and to your body. Because unplugging you would result in his death, you cannot be unplugged.

What is wrong with the hospital director's argument is this, according to Thomson: A given person's right to life does not carry with it a right or claim against any particular person that he or she provide the conditions that may be essential for his life to continue. Thus, the violinist's right to life does not carry with it a claim on the continued use of your kidneys, even though that may be essential for him to continue living. And by the same token, he has no claim against the hospital director's authorizing someone to assist you in getting yourself unplugged from him so that you might not have to spend the next nine months, or nine years, or the rest of your life in bed with him. Because you have given him no right to the use of your kidneys, and because no one else has the right to confer such a right upon him, you do him no injustice when you unplug yourself from him. Even though the violinist has the right not to be killed, your killing him would appear to be no injustice to him, for he has no claim against you, no right to demand that you not unplug yourself from him. The application of this reasoning to the abortion controversy is obvious: "It is by no means enough to show that the fetus is a person, and to remind us that all persons have a right to life—we need to be shown also that killing the fetus violates its right to life, i.e., that abortion is unjust killing." [130]

A woman who has become pregnant as a result of rape has become "plugged in" to a fetus against her will and may argue that the fetus has no right to the use of her body without her consent. Although the fetus may have a right to life, she would do it no injustice if she "unplugged herself" from it by having an abortion. But what of a woman who has become pregnant as a result of voluntarily engaging in sexual intercourse, knowing that she might become pregnant? It would seem that her partial responsibility for the fetus' presence in her womb, and indeed for its very existence, would give it a right to the use of her body. If so, then unplugging herself from the fetus by having an abortion would violate the fetus' claim against her and would be an unjust deprivation of its right to life.

But even this will not do, at least for all cases. Thomson proposes yet another analogy: If a woman opens a window to let air into a stuffy room, it would be absurd to proclaim that a burglar who climbed in had a right to use her house since she is partially responsible for his presence there, having voluntarily made it easier for him to get in, knowing that burglars take advantage of such opportunities. If she had installed bars outside her windows precisely in order to keep burglars out, but one had gotten in because of a defect in the bars, it would be still more absurd to insist that he had a right to be there. By the same token, it would seem that a woman who has employed all available means to avoid pregnancy would have a very limited (if any) obligation to a fetus that results from a defect or failure of those measures.

In response to the suggestion that her analogies may be weak because, after all, mothers have special relationships and responsibilities to their children and fetuses are neither violinists who are complete strangers nor invading burglars, Thomson asserts that there may be *no* special responsibility of a woman toward the fetus that happens to be in her body.

> Surely we do not have any such "special responsibility" for a person unless we have assumed it, explicitly or implicitly. If a set of parents do not try to prevent pregnancy, do not obtain an abortion, and then at the time of birth of the child do not put it out for adoption, but rather take it home with them, then they have assumed responsibility for it, they have given it rights, and they cannot *now* withdraw support from it at the cost of its life because they now find it difficult to go on providing for it. But if they have taken all reasonable precautions against having a child, they do not simply by virtue of their biological relationship to the child who comes into existence have a special responsibility for it.[131]

This is not to say, of course, that they may not want to assume such responsibilities toward the child. A Good Samaritan would undoubtedly do so. A Splendid Samaritan, as Thomson puts it, would even make enormous sacrifices in order to assure the child its right to life. They would probably do the same for the violinist. But we have no right to demand of a woman that she adhere to a standard above that of the Minimally Decent Samaritan. "It would be indecent," she says, for a woman to request an abortion, and for a doctor to perform it, "if she is in her seventh month, and wants the abortion to avoid the nuisance of postponing a trip abroad." But "a sick and desperately frightened fourteen-year-old schoolgirl, pregnant due to rape, may *of course* choose abortion, and . . . any law which rules this out is an insane law." [132]

Thomson notes that arguing for the permissibility of abortion in some cases is not the same as arguing for the right to secure the death of the unborn child. A woman's distress at the thought of her aborted child continuing to live is not a sufficient reason for taking its life. She may have a right to have the fetus detached from her, but she has no right to demand that once the procedure is completed, a fetus that survives be put to death.

And finally, she concludes by reminding us that she has assumed that a fetus is a human being only for the sake of the argument. Her own opinion, though, is that a very early abortion is "surely not the killing of a person" and is therefore immune to any of the restrictions she might permit to be placed upon later abortions.

The tenacity with which both sides in this controversy adhere to their positions makes it exceedingly difficult to argue dispassionately about it. As a liberal, one is naturally tempted to ask the conservatives (those who oppose abortion on religious or moral grounds) to be tolerant of the wishes of others, to refrain from interfering with what they perceive to be their right to be let alone. But the conservative is surely justified in responding that if abortion is indeed the unjustified murder of innocent and defenseless human beings, he has no right to stand idly by while the wholesale slaughter goes on.

But because the conservative claims the right to interfere in the private decisions of others and to impose restrictions upon them that can drastically alter their entire lives, surely the burden of proof is upon him: He must convince us of the truth of each element in the antecedent of that last sentence: that abortion is in fact unjustified, that it is murder, and that human fetuses are indeed human beings. Thus far, the proofs of these propositions have amounted to nothing more than a repetition of the claim that abortion is wrong. Something more than circular, question-begging arguments is needed before the intense and widespread suffering that would follow from restrictive abortion legislation (and did exist prior to the Supreme Court's 1973 decision) can be condoned.

4

Freedom of the Press and Censorship

The present chapter is concerned principally with the conflict between the principles of free speech and free press, on the one hand, and other values that seem on occasion to conflict with them, on the other. The focus here is upon communication that is principally concerned with facts and political or religious opinions, and with artistic expression that is not sexually explicit, but which certain individuals and governments believe should, never-theless, be repressed for the furtherance of what they consider to be overriding principles of public policy. The questions raised by legislation designed to suppress allegedly obscene or pornographic materials or displays are treated separately in the next chapter.

CENSORSHIP IN THE WORLD COMMUNITY

In some parts of the world, censorship has been a normal practice for centuries. In eastern Europe, in Yugoslavia, in the Union of South Africa, and in most of what is called the Third World, rigid censorship regulations have been enforced for many years. In many parts of the world, including those countries, such as the United States, that have strong safeguards against most forms of interference with freedom of speech and press, some thoughtful persons advocate some degree of censorship. The problem is not confined to any specific part of the world, but certain forms of government impose far more stringent controls than others upon what their citizens may say and publish, and certain parts of the world suffer far more than others from thought control and rigid restrictions upon what may be said and written.

The Soviet Union and the nations of the Eastern bloc that are subject to its control constitute the most massive single system of systematic censor-ship ever established, with the possible exception of the Roman Catholic Church from the beginning of the Middle Ages to the present century. De-spite their endorsement of a statement expressing the hope that there would be increased dissemination of information by radio,[1] the Soviet bloc has waged a propaganda barrage against broadcasts by Radio Liberty and Radio Free Europe, which beam news in 19 languages to those nations. Soviet writers, artists, and scientists who have been exiled or expelled from their native lands claim that those broadcasts play an important role in keeping people in that part of the world informed of what is happening, because the state-controlled newspapers and broadcast media in their own countries either fail to report certain important events or confine reports to specific "lines" designed to foster the government's own views. In order to thwart reception of information from abroad, the Soviet bloc maintains more than 3,000 transmitters whose sole function is to jam broadcasts of these and other Western radio stations.[2]

Not only news broadcasts and print media dealing with current events, but all forms of artistic expression are censored in these and other countries, and artists who either fail to conform to the government's standards of artis-tic performance or behave in what the officials deem to be politically im-proper ways are banished or reduced to the status of nonpersons, as the following case demonstrates:

CASE 6. THE COMPASSIONATE CELLIST

Mstislav Rostropovich is widely considered to be one of the world's greatest cellists. His wife, Galina Vishnevskaya, is a renowned opera singer. Rostropovich refused to participate in officially organized campaigns of persecution against composers, writers, artists, and scientists who had fallen out of favor with the Soviet government. When his friend, the great novelist Alexander Solzhenitsyn, was banned by the government, Rostropovich gave him refuge. As a result, Rostropovich and his wife were "artistically buried," as he put it. Galina's performance at the premiere of Prokofiev's opera *The Gambler* at the Bolshoi was ignored by the press for six months, and when it was finally mentioned, her name, as leading performer, was omitted. When their recordings were played on the air, announcers would not mention their names. Rostropovich's concerts were cancelled on the ground that all the halls were booked. When he was sent to play in small provincial towns, he discovered that posters announcing his concerts and recitals had been pasted over on orders from Communist party leaders. Even those who heard about the concerts were afraid to attend. "We had no one to complain to," Rostropovich said. "Our government was systematically corroding and stifling our artistic life. They wanted to prove that we did not exist. We were treated like lepers. We lost our identity. It was like looking into a mirror and not finding your reflection. In Russia, if one little blade of grass grows higher than another, they send in bulldozers to trim it down."

Rostropovich and his family received a two-year exit permit and moved to the West, where they and their art are flourishing. As Rostropovich put it after his American conducting debut, "I am so happy! I am so happy! Only *here* can I speak from the heart! Only here can I fulfill my life as an artist! Vishnevskaya and I have suffered too much. Now we can live! Now we can work!"

Rostropovich has been officially informed that his Russian citizenship has been revoked.[3]

After Valery and Galina Panov, renowned ballet dancers, requested emigration permits, they were confined to their home, where they were unable to practice their art or keep their bodies in shape. They were finally permitted to leave for Israel in 1974, and appeared on the ballet stage there and in other countries.

A deputy minister of culture raised an objection to a painting, entitled *The Mystery of the 20th Century*, that was to be displayed in Moscow's House of the Artist as part of a one-man show by Ilya Glazunov. The painting, which depicted many of the twentieth century's most important personalities, was removed from the exhibit, Glazunov disassociated himself from the exhibition, and the entire show was cancelled by the Ministry of Culture.[4]

Several years earlier, a more informal exhibit came to a more dramatic end. A group of nonconformist artists set up an outdoor exhibit of their works in a vacant lot in Moscow. Several hundred artists, western diplomats, correspondents, and neighborhood residents were viewing the exhibit when dump trucks, water-spraying trucks, and bulldozers converged on the site and charged into the crowds. As uniformed police looked on, a group of young men ripped up, trampled, and threw the paintings into a truck, where they were covered with mud. Protesting artists were beaten and arrested. The confiscated art works were burned. Western correspondents and photographers who were at the scene were punched and beaten.[5]

A renowned cinematographer was sent to a forced labor camp for a six-year term for producing a film on the destruction of religious frescoes in the cathedrals of Kiev under the regimes of Lenin and Stalin.[6] And a popular folk singer was stripped of his East German citizenship after the authorities concluded that his songs were too critical of the regime and its methods.[7]

In an official news release circulated by the Soviet Embassy in Washington, the government announced that the homes of a number of human rights activists had been searched because they had been guilty of the "distribution of slanderous materials biasedly selected and compiled, denigrating the Soviet social system and the foreign and domestic policies of the Soviet Union." It went on to explain that when measures "aimed at exerting moral influence" had failed to stop them, "stronger actions" were necessary.[8] Their crime consisted of disseminating allegedly anti-Soviet literature, composing satires, and "slandering" the Soviet system and life in the USSR and other Communist countries, all of which are prohibited by the criminal code.[9] One of the dissidents, Vladimir Bukovsky, was found guilty of "anti-state acts, instigative propaganda, collecting and smuggling abroad deliberately false, slanderous materials and information about the Soviet Union," and was sentenced to seven years of imprisonment. Part of his alleged crimes consisted of passing information to foreign correspondents. According to the Moscow press bureau, "under their official status, newsmen are expected to give unbiased information about life in the Soviet Union."[10]

Soviet censorship has even been extended to the United Nations. Two Swiss bookshops, which had been licensed to sell books on the premises of the United Nations in the Palais des Nations in Geneva, were displaying French, Russian, and English versions of Solzhenitsyn's *Gulag Archipelago*, which depicts the horrors of Soviet prison camps. The shops were forced to remove the books from their shelves, and soon thereafter, one of the stores was closed. The Director-General of the Geneva office of the U.N. explained that it was his duty to inform the managers of the bookshops of the displeasure felt by certain delegates toward the sale of "publications that are insulting to a member state."[11]

Fernando Gasparian, editor of a Brazilian newspaper, closed the publication rather than continue under the intolerable censorship that authorities imposed upon him. On some occasions, as much as half of the paper's copy was suppressed by the censors, whole issues were confiscated from vendors, and staff members were arrested. Among the items the paper was prevented by the censors from publishing were the United Nations Declaration on Human Rights, protests against South African apartheid, and protests against violations of human rights in the Soviet Union. One censor refused to permit a chess problem to be published on the ground that "the blacks were in an inferior position." And a censor named Leonardo deleted a psychoanalytical commentary on Leonardo da Vinci inspired by Freud's suggestion that the artist might have had homosexual leanings.[12]

A good summary of the situation in some countries is contained in a manifesto issued by an informal association of Czech citizens in January, 1977. "The right of free expression," they said, "is quite illusory." Tens of thousands of people have been deprived of the right to work, they charged, simply because their views differed from official dogmas. The children of dissidents were prevented from continuing their education, while others "live in constant peril of losing their jobs or other benefits if they express their opinions." The manifesto continued:

> Freedom of speech is suppressed by the government's management of all mass media, including the publishing and cultural institutions. No political, philosophical, scientific, or artistic work that deviates in the slightest from the narrow framework of official ideology or esthetics is permitted to be produced. Public criticism of social conditions is prohibited. Public defense against false and defamatory charges by official propaganda organs is impossible. . . . Open discussion of intellectual and cultural matters is out of the question. Many scientific and cultural workers, as well as other citizens, have been discriminated against simply because some years ago they legally published or openly articulated views condemned by the current political power.[13]

In addition, the manifesto charged that priests and other religious functionaries were subjected to severe limitations and that religious expression was either prohibited or discouraged by the imposition of official or informal sanctions.

Among the nations that signed the 1975 Helsinki Accords, which contained a commitment to facilitate "the freer and wider dissemination of all kinds, to encourage cooperation in the field of information and the exchange of information with other countries, and to improve the conditions under which journalists from one participating State exercise their profession in another participating State," the following were *some* of the violations recorded two years later:

• The homes of journalists were searched by state police or military intelligence agents, and journalists were either arrested or placed under some other form of detention. Foreign journalists were arrested, expelled, or denied entry.

- Broadcasts of foreign radio services were jammed.
- Western periodicals are not on sale in some countries, whose citizens are not permitted to subscribe to them; those that are ordered never reach their destinations; and books and magazines are confiscated from foreign visitors.
- The works of some authors are blacklisted and removed from library shelves. Those that remain are under lock and key and are available only to persons who receive special permits.
- Certain topics were placed off-limits to journalists, and those who defied the bans were arrested and sentenced to long prison terms.
- Journals containing articles or photographs deemed insulting to the Catholic Church or the pope were seized.
- Western movies are censored. In Rumania, only films that show human tragedies in Western countries (such as drug victims, the world of crime, and so on) may be shown, and in these scenes are cut and dialogue translated to serve Marxist goals.
- In the United States, judges issued "gag" orders and the right of journalists to protect the confidentiality of their sources was not upheld by the courts.[14]

A free press does not exist in most of the developing nations of Africa, Asia, and Latin America. In Africa, for example, about 84% of the 45 governments own and operate daily newspapers, radio, and television, which serve the interests of the governments that control them. Of 25 national news agencies in Africa, only three—those of Morocco, Rhodesia, and South Africa—gather news independently of their governments. The national news agencies have exclusive contracts with foreign news services and are thus able to screen all incoming news before it is published or broadcast. Several African states—The Congo, Equatorial Guinea, Malawi, Guinea, and Uganda—either ban newsmen as a class and thus keep their internal affairs out of the foreign press, or admit foreign newsmen on a selective basis, allowing only friendly correspondents to report news of their affairs to the outside world. Although the Union of South Africa is rightly criticized for its racism and its dictatorial form of government, it probably has greater press freedom than any other country on the continent, with competing dailies that maintain an adversary relationship with the government.[15]

Such behavior is not confined to totalitarian regimes. Shortly before the opening of the 1976 summer Olympics in Montreal, the city spent $385,000 erecting steel scaffolding along one of the city's main thoroughfares. The scaffolding was to support a vast display of photographs, paintings, and sculpture by some of the leading talents in the Province of Quebec. Under orders from Mayor Jean Drapeau, the entire display was torn down in a single night on the pretext that the scaffolding represented a hazard to children. According to sources within the city government, however, the exhibit was removed because it included a series of photographs of graceful, old Montreal homes that had been razed to make room for high-rise office buildings, conveying a political message that the mayor and the city's executive council found intolerable.[16]

CENSORSHIP IN THE UNITED STATES

Although the suppression of printed materials in the United States is generally not a serious problem, except in the case of sexually explicit materials, problems do occasionally arise in a variety of contexts.

For example, Victor L. Marchetti, co-author of *The C.I.A. and the Cult of Intelligence,* was ordered by a court to submit all his future writing about the CIA to the agency for prepublication censorship. The courts held that he had waived his right to invoke the First Amendment's guarantee of freedom of the press when he signed contracts with the Central Intelligence Agency promising not to reveal information he had received as its employee. On May 27, 1975, the Supreme Court upheld the order. The CIA originally deleted about 170 passages, or 10% of the book.[17]

The National Security Agency (NSA) was accused by a number of scientists, who happened to be working on codes, of harassing and threatening them with sanctions or with prosecution for publishing articles about their work. The situation came to a head when a group of scientists at Stanford University received a letter from the NSA warning them not to publish or distribute scientific papers dealing with their work on a certain problem that was of interest to the agency. They were told that failure to heed the warning could result in prosecution under the Arms Export Control Act. (The problem on which they were working had potential application as a device for "locking" data into computer memory banks as protection against theft, and also in the development of codes that would be immune to eavesdropping.) [18]

Another example involved Walter and Miriam Schneir, authors of *Invitation to an Inquest,* a book critical of the FBI's role in the Rosenberg-Sobell case. The Rosenbergs were convicted of passing atomic secrets to the Russians, a crime for which they were executed. According to Schneir, the FBI harassed him and his wife while the book was being written and became involved in a nationwide campaign to keep him from being interviewed about the book on television talk shows so that the book's publicity would be kept to a minimum. A memorandum, written by one of the FBI's top agents in Washington and initialed by J. Edgar Hoover, the Bureau's director at the time, reported that certain television personalities were being told not to permit the Schneirs to appear on their programs. The memorandum stated, "The first thing we should do in this matter is to take careful steps to secure the cooperation of friendly television stations and prevent this subversive effort [the effort to publicize the Schneirs' book] from being successful. It should be kept off television programs and smothered and forced out of the public eye thereby." [19]

The American Library Association has passed a resolution inspired by the Council on Interracial Books for Children that urges librarians to become more aware of racism and sexism in books and to pass that awareness on to readers. The council argues that books that blatantly offend persons because of some human condition such as sex, race, or age ought to be removed from open shelves and be placed in a section of the library where adult researchers can make use of them. Among such offensive books would be *Little Black Sambo* and *Doctor Doolittle*. According to the council, literary quality should not save a book's place on the open shelves, for the more well-written a racist book is, the more dangerous it becomes. Among the librarians who oppose such a plan, one noted that members of a police department were outraged when a librarian refused to remove a children's book that portrayed police as pigs. Others have observed that librarians should not presume to determine what people—including children—may or may not read. The librarian's job, they say, is to provide a great many books that represent a multitude of views so people can choose what they wish to read for themselves. [20]

In addition to official censorship, various groups attempt to use economic or political pressure to prevent the airing of views or programs of which they disapprove. A number of groups banded together to threaten boycott of the products of advertisers whose messages were aired in conjunction with the television series "Soap," which was condemned by some as being obscene. General Motors dropped its sponsorship of a miniseries, "Jesus of Nazareth," when evangelical groups threatened a boycott after they heard that Jesus would be portrayed as a mere mortal. The National Rifle Association and other opponents of gun-control legislation coerced advertisers into cancelling spots on a CBS documentary, "The Guns of Autumn," which they presumed to be contrary to their interests. Other advertisers were threatened with boycotts by viewers who were incensed by the high fee paid Richard Nixon for his broadcast interviews with David Frost several years after he resigned the presidency, and a union, on strike against ABC, successfully induced advertisers to withdraw their spots from the network's programs. [21]

The *New York Times* editorially supported such boycotts and threats, claiming that entertainment programs, as opposed to news shows and documentaries, have no claim to immunity from pressure groups. "What serious alternative is there," the *Times* asked, "for those who feel that their beliefs are being assaulted, their values mocked? Do their civil liberties consist of being permitted to write a letter to their local newspaper after the offending show has been screened?"

The editorial went on to observe that the medium responds to the demands of the marketplace, and asked rhetorically why networks and stations should be protected against the workings of the market when public objections to violence, sex, or anything else drove advertisers away. GM's decision to drop its sponsorship of "Jesus of Nazareth" was "a reasonable commercial decision," the *Times* said. "When organizations opposed to violence on children's shows distribute lists of sponsors of the most objectionable programs, they are behaving in accord with the mores of the medium." The heads of a network have the right to "take flak, accept the risk, and see what happens" if they feel that the program can succeed financially despite the boycott threats. "That is their right, just as it is the right of all citizens to object as strenuously and effectively as they can to whatever they deem offensive on the public airwaves." [22]

On the other hand, the executive director of the American Civil Liberties Union and others objected, saying that such pressure was "pernicious" and "reprehensible," for it was an attempt by one group of citizens to deny another group the right to see or hear what they want. They objected to the manufacturers of detergents or deodorants deciding what they and their families could see on television. [23]

And the Federal Communications Commission (FCC) was urged by the United States Commission on Civil Rights to "undertake an inquiry and proposed rule making regarding the portrayal of minorities and women on network television," suggesting, in effect, that the FCC lay down rules governing the kinds of roles that certain minorities and women might play on television shows. [24]

THE CASE FOR CENSORSHIP

Behind these repressive actions lies a rationale. In the Third World, there is a feeling that the dissemination of news about peoples, their governments, and their activities is dominated by Western news agencies that are guilty of cultural bias. Some governments resent stories that call attention to national problems or shortcomings of national leadership, or that seem to them to offend the dignity of their people. They often complain that reporting is one-sided or tendentious. In much of the Third World, there is a sense that the libertarian theory has no reasonable applicability, for where there is such massive illiteracy and extreme poverty, the notion that the press should serve as a watchdog over the government seems quite irrelevant.

The prevailing philosophy appears to be based upon the assumption that the press should be used to further national development, to encourage economic survival, and to help mold disparate ethnic, linguistic, and tribal groups into a single national entity. The government, under this approach, has a right to regulate the press in behalf of the national interest. Freedom of the press is a luxury that must wait until economic stability and national unity have been achieved. As one Nigerian publisher has put it, "A news item or editorial concerning government that would merely raise eyebrows in London can incite intertribal riot or violent antigovernment demonstrations in an African country. It may bring down the government, and where there is no organized opposition party, or where it is not ready to be an alternative government, there will be anarchy." [25] The job of the press, according to some Third World spokesmen, is to "mobilize the masses around precise objectives, improve the quality of education in the country, help educate the masses and rally support for the government, and promote and disseminate the socialist way of nation-building."

The United Nations Educational, Scientific and Cultural Organization (UNESCO) has been considering a resolution which would recognize that "States are responsible for the activities in the international sphere of all mass media under their jurisdiction." [26] Although no definitive action has yet been taken on that resolution, other UNESCO programs indicate what the inclinations of the Communist bloc and the Third World nations are. On the assumption that the "new international economic and social order" will be best served by a "balanced flow of messages" between nations, UNESCO proposes that there be "new national policies for the sovereign determination" by governments of the nature of news and information that flows across international borders. Governments must have "an equal footing in the control over and use of international channels of dissemination." For this purpose, the United Nations agency proposes to establish "supplementary," "noncommercial" communications systems, to strengthen "state-owned mass communications media," to encourage "overall development planning," and to "hasten the process of national and regional integration of communication between countries."

Former Prime Minister Indira Gandhi of India, whose government imposed dictatorial rule upon India for a period of time prior to her defeat in 1977 and subjected the Indian press to severe censorship, said, "We should be able to get an Indian explanation of events in India." Her information minister explained:

> The theme of "free" flow of information, which was chanted in a chorus, was aimed to enable all countries in name only but the powerful countries in reality, to pump their information into all regions of the world without let or hindrance. . . . In fact, the idea of a "free" flow of information fits insidiously into the package of other kinds of "freedom" still championed by the adherents of nineteenth-century liberalism.[27]

In Sri Lanka, where dictatorial control of the press has included the padlocking of newspapers that were deemed too offensive to be tolerated by the government, arguments in support of the policy of repression included the following:

- The press is guilty of disrupting national unity by promoting civil commotion and conflict.
- The press's "wholesale imitation of Western standards" is a danger to the nation's economic well-being.

• Because a large proportion of the editorial staffs were educated in Roman Catholic missionary schools, they have been conditioned to "accept the Graeco-Roman-Christian tradition as something superior," and therefore readily accept management's campaign "to fight for the preservation of the undue privileges that a certain class had obtained from foreign rulers." As a result, the press was responsible for "the prevailing disunity of the various racial and religious groups."

• Newsprint is expensive and foreign exchange is scarce. They should not be used for such "selfish ends" as the publishing of nude and seminude pictures "with the ulterior motive of diverting the attention of the country's youth from solving national problems." The country's development should take precedence over all talk about freedom.[28]

CENSORSHIP ON THE CAMPUS

In recent years certain groups have attempted—often successfully—to prevent the expression of views that they regard as offensive or false. During the Vietnam War, such personalities as General William Westmoreland, Chief of Staff of the United States Army, and Secretary of State William Rogers were denied access to university audiences or were driven from lecture platforms by violent harassment and heckling. Professor William Shockley, a Stanford University physicist, and Professor Richard Herrnstein of Harvard University, who propound theories concerning the genetic transmission of human intelligence that many persons consider to be both false and racist, have been hounded from classrooms and lecture halls at universities all over the country.

The Committee on Freedom of Expression at Yale University has compiled a detailed report [29] of a series of events at that university that included administration intervention, the withdrawal of an invitation to Governor George Wallace of Alabama, threats of violence by student groups, and the use of shouts, chants, and obscenities that made it impossible for Professor Shockley to be heard in a debate arranged by a student organization.

The Shockley incident is particularly instructive, for the ideological justifications for censorship were well articulated. The Progressive Labor party dismissed freedom of speech as "a nice abstract idea to enable people like Shockley to spread racism," and an organization of Puerto Rican students called the debate "an insult to the Third World community." Other students declared that the debate "must not be tolerated" and warned that Shockley would not be given the opportunity to speak. The university administration condemned the organization that had extended the invitation to Shockley for having made "use of free speech as a game" and for having shown "lack of sensitivity to others, . . . and lack of responsible concern for the university as an institution." The president of the university recommended a boycott of the event as "the best way to show one's scorn and distaste." One group after another extended new invitations to Shockley after earlier ones were withdrawn under pressure. At last, a conservative student organization, Young Americans for Freedom (YAF), organized a debate between

Shockley and the publisher of *National Review*. Henry Chauncey, Jr., the university secretary, warned that "severe discipline" would be imposed against students who used "violent or coercive action."

> As the debate was about to get underway, YAF officers could not make them-selves heard. Secretary Chauncey took the platform to repeat his warning and was shouted down. The speakers were not permitted to say an audible word. They were drowned out by derisive applause, insults chanted at Shockley, and shouted obscenities. . . . Chauncey sought to quiet the dis-rupters and to warn them of disciplinary penalties, but without effect. "Racist Chauncey, go home!" became part of the chanting. After an hour and fifteen minutes, Chauncey closed the meeting. The disruption of the speakers had been a complete success. . . .[30]

Twelve students were found guilty of participating in the disruption but were granted leniency because (among other things) the subject of the debate was "both insulting and provocative," and because they felt "frustra-tion" at having been unable to prevent Shockley from appearing on campus in the first place. They were suspended for the fall term but were read-mitted at the beginning of that term under no penalty by disciplinary pro-bation for one semester.

The committee that investigated the matter concluded, with one dissent-ing opinion, that the university was committed to the principles of free speech and that there were therefore clear limits to the type of protest that would be permissible. Among its conclusions were the following:

1. Individuals who oppose a speaker's views may protest "in a wide-open and robust fashion" and may seek to dissuade inviters from proceeding. "But it is a punishable offense against the principles of the university for the objectors to coerce others physically or to threaten violence."

2. All forms of peaceful speech, including counterspeeches "in appropriate locations" and peaceful picketing that does not interfere with entrance to or exit from a building, are permissible, but picketing is "entitled to no protection" if it is coercive.

3. Within university buildings, forms of protest that disrupt university activities are not permissible.

4. Members of an audience may register their protest in a silent, symbolic fashion, or by briefly booing, clapping hands, or heckling, but they may not materially interfere with a speaker's right to proceed.

> Nor does the content of the speech, even parts deemed defamatory or insulting, entitle any member of the audience to engage in disruption. While untruthful and defamatory speech may give rise to civil liability, it is neither a justifica-tion nor an excuse for disruption, and it may not be considered in any subsequent proceeding against offenders as a mitigating factor. Nor are racial insults or other "fighting words" a valid ground for disruption or physical attack—certainly not from a voluntary audience invited but in no way compelled to be present. Only if a speech advocates immediate and serious illegal action, such as burning down a library, and there is danger that the

audience will proceed to follow such an exhortation, may it be stopped, and then only by an authorized university official or law enforcement officer.

The banning or obstruction of lawful speech can never be justified on such grounds as that the speech or the speaker is deemed irresponsible, offensive, unscholarly, or untrue.[31]

Among the arguments *against* this position and in favor of censorship or the disruption of speeches by persons who hold views such as those of Shockley are the following:

1. We tolerate free speech because it furthers truth. But under certain circumstances, *limitations* upon free speech further truth and the pursuit of truth. It is true, for example, that oppressed peoples should be liberated and that true equality among all men and women should be one of the principal goals of every freedom-loving society. Any speech, like that of Shockley, that sets back the liberation of the oppressed peoples of the earth and impedes the movement for the equality of all ought to be censored, for it is not in the interests of truth or of justice.

2. Free speech is not the only, and perhaps not even the principal, value of this society. When it is used—or better still, *abused*—in a malicious way so as to further racism or imperialism and the perpetuation of the oppression of minorities, then those other values should have priority, and such malicious speech should be suppressed.

3. One of the principal functions of a university is the moral and ethical instruction of its students, for it is the university's business to turn out good and moral citizens, not merely well-trained scientists, scholars, and technicians. Permitting such persons as Shockley to speak under the auspices of a campus organization lends a degree of respectability and credence to him and to his ideas, which are not deserved and which might, in the short run, at least, lead to their acceptance by ill-informed students. As the Yale committee's dissenter put it, "If, for example, Hitler was invited to Yale to discuss his research into the area of Aryan racial superiority, and his policy prescription of extermination of all non-Aryans, I would have a hard time justifying allowing him to speak. Even if I were confident that his theories would, if wrong, eventually be disproved in the 'long run,' I have learned from history that the 'short-run' costs would be overwhelming." [32]

4. If the university's mission is the quest for knowledge through scholarship and the dissemination of this knowledge through teaching, then speeches such as those of Shockley simply do not qualify: His doctrines are false, and therefore they do not qualify as *knowledge*, but merely as false opinions or dogmas. Such speeches do not constitute research, but are merely designed to disseminate his opinions. There are plenty of other forums, such as TV talk shows, admirably designed for such purposes.

5. The First Amendment only protects against *governmental* interference with free expression; it does not impose upon any *private* organization, such as a university, an obligation to provide a forum and a polite reception to all ideas, however repugnant they might be.

6. Extending an invitation to speak at a university goes beyond mere *speech,* and into the realm of *action,* which is *not* protected by the First Amendment. Moreover, speeches such as those of Shockley either do or can lead to action which is contrary to the express ideals of both the university and the United States. A person who advocates such racist *policies* as the sterilization of allegedly inferior genetic types goes beyond mere speech into political action, the advocacy of a pernicious racial doctrine and of action suited to that doctrine. As the world has seen in the case of Hitler, the costs of such a political campaign are prohibitive, and it therefore ought to be resisted by appropriate political means.

7. Affording a public forum at a prestigious academic institution for a person who lectures on the alleged genetic inferiority of blacks constitutes an implicit acknowledgment that the question of the inherent inferiority of blacks is an unresolved, debatable topic. Such an acknowledgment is in itself both false and dangerous.

8. The remedy of civil damages does not exist in the United States for group libels. Anyone can utter the most outrageous lies about racial or religious minorities and be immune from any prosecution for libel or slander, however great the emotional, economic, or physical harm those he slanders may suffer as a result of the dissemination of his lies.

9. If the speaker has rights, surely the audience does too. Among the rights of an audience are the right of free assembly, the right to protest, and the right to dissent. These entail the right to express emotions and outrage. An audience's expression of its views is one method for the propagation and dissemination of new, minority, and unconventional ideas, and should therefore be given free rein.[33]

Similar arguments have been employed in other contexts by those who have been gravely offended by statements uttered or published by university faculty members. A typical example is that of Arthur R. Butz, a professor of electrical engineering at Northwestern University, who published a book in which he claimed the Nazi program for the extermination of the Jews was a gigantic hoax and that it is not true that millions of Jews were deliberately slain in Nazi death camps. In addition to the denunciations and shocked reactions that followed publication of the book, there were demands for Butz's dismissal. As one academician put it:

> Tenure in a university faculty implies certain stipulated responsibilities, not the least of which are academic integrity and moral rectitude. It appears that Professor Butz falls far short on both. In our university, . . . a faculty member who demonstrates academic incompetence or moral turpitude shall be brought before a panel of his peers to answer these charges and, if found guilty, shall be stripped of his tenure and employment.
> To defend a professor's right to advocate "whatever he pleases" is academically dishonest. Should he therefore have the right to promote the

seduction of children, the "invalidity" of Newton's laws or Charles Manson's right to depopulate California?[34]

No one who is at all familiar with the facts can doubt that Professor Butz's book reveals his utter incompetence in the field of history. There are mountains of incontrovertible evidence, including the Nazis' own photographs and films, tons of meticulous documents, their anti-Jewish propaganda, their legislation and court records, the written and oral testimony of thousands of eyewitnesses to their atrocities, and the testimony of the perpetrators of those hideous crimes, who made no secret of the fact, as the commandant of Auschwitz testified in 1946, that "the final solution of the Jewish problem meant the complete extermination of all Jews in Europe." Butz's book may reveal something more than mere incompetence: its publication may indicate that Butz suffers from some grave moral defect. But such a defect, whatever it may be, is rather different from what is usually meant by the term *moral turpitude* as applied to academics. The academic liberal who subscribes to the principle of academic freedom would undoubtedly conclude in this case that Butz's competence as an electrical engineer—which is, after all, his field—cannot be measured by his amateur ventures into history. Moreover, even if he were a professor of history, the academic liberal would insist that he ought to enjoy the right to publish whatever he chooses, however absurd it might be. His colleagues will no doubt pour an appropriate amount of scorn, ridicule, and condemnation upon him and his work, and publish well-reasoned and thoroughly documented responses and refutations that would set the record straight. But even in such a clear-cut case of bad judgment as this, the academic liberal would insist that the remedy should not lie in breaking the deviant scholar's tenure and ousting him from the university.

Still other forms of censorship exist, and each of them has its defenders—men and women who can appeal to high principle to justify the forms of censorship they favor, but who condemn censorship in general.

For example, Professor Michael Selzer of Brooklyn College's Department of Political Science was doing research into the psychology of terrorists. After contacting the CIA to determine whether the intelligence agency might have any information that would assist him, he travelled to Europe to pursue his research. Upon his return, he was contacted by the CIA and asked over the telephone whether he had learned anything that might be useful. His colleagues promptly charged him with having engaged in "covert intelligence-gathering" for the CIA and thereby having violated academic standards. They alleged that his activities cast doubt on his "credibility as a teacher, scholar, and professional colleague," for they maintained that the secret gathering of intelligence for the government "impedes the free flow of ideas and information among colleagues" and "violates the faculty member's responsibility to students, who must not be in doubt about their teachers' commitment to scholarship and to free and open discussion in the classroom." [35]

OTHER JUSTIFICATIONS FOR CENSORSHIP

In the United States, Justices of the Supreme Court have frequently cited various justifications for government censorship or other forms of restraint on speech and the press. Justice Felix Frankfurter once put the case as follows:

> The right of a government to maintain its existence—self preservation—is the most pervasive aspect of sovereignty. "Security against foreign danger," wrote Madison, "is one of the primitive objects [the original purposes] of civil society." The constitutional power to act upon this basic principle has been recognized by this Court at different periods and under diverse circumstances. "To preserve its independence, and give security against foreign aggression and encroachment, is the highest duty of every nation, and to attain these ends nearly all other considerations are to be subordinated. It matters not in what form such aggressions and encroachment come. . . ." The most tragic experience in our history [the Civil War] is a poignant reminder that the Nation's continued existence may be threatened from within. To protect itself from such threats, the Federal Government "is invested with all those inherent and implied powers which, at the time of adopting the Constitution, were generally considered to belong to every government as such, and as being essential to the exercise of its function." [36]

Justice Frankfurter then went on to explain that even the power of self-protection is subject to constitutional limitations, one of which is imposed by the First Amendment's guarantees of free speech and the free press. However, he said, free speech, too, has its limits. For example, persons who circulated printed matter opposing the draft during World War I, or who published newspaper articles describing the sufferings of American troops and alleging the futility of America's war aims, were convicted of criminal offenses for those acts. The justification for those limitations was the fact that their acts posed a "clear and present danger" to the nation and its people. He went on:

> Not every type of speech occupies the same position on the scale of values. There is no substantial public interest in permitting certain kinds of utterances: "the lewd and obscene, the profane, the libelous, and the insulting or 'fighting' words—those which by their very utterance inflict injury or tend to incite an immediate breach of the peace." [37]

Justice Frankfurter proceeded then to apply these premises to a case in which a number of defendants had been convicted of violating a federal law that prohibited advocating the overthrow of the Government of the United States by force and violence. They had appealed their conviction on the ground that the law violated their right of free speech under the First Amendment. Frankfurter found that there is a difference between advocacy and the mere interchange of ideas. As Justice Jackson observed, there is no immunity for speech or writing used as an integral part of conduct in violation of a valid criminal statute. Illegal wagers are made by speech, fraud and combinations in restraint of trade may be committed through speech or the written word, and so may threats that amount to assault or extortion. Freedom of speech has never been thought to grant immunity against prosecutions for perjury. To interpret the First Amendment so expansively as to permit speech and written words that are integrally bound up with criminal acts "would make it practically impossible ever to enforce laws against agreements in restraint of trade as well as many other agreements and conspiracies deemed injurious to society."

In the same case, Chief Justice Vinson, writing for the majority, observed that the defendants were not engaged in the pursuit of "peaceful studies and discussions or preaching and advocacy in the realm of ideas," or conducting courses "explaining the philosophical theories set forth in the books which have been placed in evidence," but in active preparations for and advocacy of the overthrow of the government by force and violence. Their actions constituted a clear and present danger, he said, even though it was not likely that they would succeed against the overwhelming power of the American military and government. The government need not wait, he said, "until the *Putsch* is about to be executed, the plans have been laid and the signal is awaited." Even if such a plan is doomed to failure, "the damage which such attempts create both physically and politically to a nation makes it impossible to measure the validity in terms of the probability of success, or the immediacy of a successful attempt." [38]

Even Justice Douglas, who dissented, agreed that:

> if this were a case where those who claimed protection under the First Amendment were teaching the techniques of sabotage, the assassination of the President, the filching of documents from public files, the planting of bombs, the art of street warfare, and the like, I would have no doubts. The freedom to speak is not absolute; the teaching of methods of terror and other seditious conduct should be beyond the pale along with obscenity and immorality. [39]

He contended, however, that the defendants in this case were not guilty of such conduct, but merely of forming a political party and teaching and advocating overthrow of the government. Although the First Amendment provides that "Congress shall make no law . . . abridging the freedom of speech," Justice Douglas concluded that

> this does not mean . . . that the Nation need hold its hand until it is in such weakened condition that there is no time to protect itself from incitement to revolution. . . . We should not allow Congress to call a halt to free speech except in the extreme case of peril from the speech itself. [40]

More recently, the United States Supreme Court upheld the right of newspapers to publish the *Pentagon Papers,* a large quantity of highly secret documents that had been obtained unlawfully by Daniel Ellsberg, who had surreptitiously copied them and turned them over to the *New York Times* for publication. The federal administration had argued not only that they were classified and had been obtained through unlawful means, but also that their publication would be damaging to vital interests of the United States. In a dissenting opinion, Justice Harry Blackmun argued in favor of the administration's position:

> The First Amendment, after all, is only one part of an entire Constitution. Article II of the great document vests in the Executive Branch primary power over the conduct of foreign affairs. . . . Each provision of the Constitution is important, and I cannot subscribe to a doctrine of unlimited absolutism for the First Amendment at the cost of downgrading other provisions.[41]

Because the majority of the Court did not concur with him, Justice Blackmun urged the publishers of newspapers to exercise great care, for he believed that publication of some of the documents "could clearly result in great harm to the nation," namely, "the death of soldiers, the destruction of alliances, the greatly increased difficulty of negotiation with our enemies, the inability of our diplomats to negotiate."

This reasoning is not too far from that of Thomas Hobbes, who wrote:

> It is annexed to the sovereignty to be judge of what opinions and doctrines are averse and what conducing to peace, and consequently on what occasions, how far, and what men are to be trusted withal in speaking to multitudes of people, and who shall examine the doctrines of all books before they be published. For the actions of men proceed from their opinions, and in the well-governing of opinions consists the well-governing of men's actions, in order to their peace and concord. And though in matter of doctrine nothing ought to be regarded but the truth, yet this is not repugnant to regulating the same by peace. For doctrine repugnant to peace can no more be true than peace and concord can be against the law of nature.[42]

Censorship rests upon the assumption that the sovereign or some person or committee appointed by him possesses the truth and is the final judge of right and good, and that the ruler is charged with the responsibility of seeing that false or harmful doctrines are not spread abroad. During long periods of history certain propositions have been considered, by virtually all authorities, to be self-evidently true. Anyone who expressed doubts about those propositions was branded a heretic or a madman. Yet those same propositions are now known—or believed, at any rate—to be false.

CASE 7. THE PERSECUTION OF GALILEO

When Galileo announced that he had discovered four satellites revolving around Jupiter, he concluded that this was a decisive argument in favor of the Copernican (heliocentric) hypothesis. Until this discovery, opponents of the Copernican theory had argued that the earth could not revolve around the sun, for if it were moving along an orbit around the sun, the moon would be left behind. Now he could show that there was a planet moving through an orbit carrying four moons along with it. The objections offered to his book *The Starry Messenger*

(*Siderius Nuncius*), in which he announced his discoveries and his conclusions, boiled down to the following: (1) His theory contradicted common sense and everyday experience, for everyone could see the sun rising in the east and setting in the west. (2) The theory of earth moving through space was contrary to the laws of physics. (3) If the earth moved, astronomers on earth should be able to detect parallax in their observations of the stars, but no such observations had ever been recorded. (4) The Copernican theory contradicted Scripture, for Joshua would scarcely have commanded the sun to stand still if it did not move,[43] the Psalmist declared explicitly that God had established the earth on its foundation, not to be moved forever,[44] and Ecclesiastes stated that the sun rises and sets and hastens to the place where it will rise again.[45] Galileo responded by observing that the Bible was not intended to be a source of scientific information and that its authors used ordinary language and figures of speech in order not to confuse their readers. Nevertheless, he conceded that any scientific propositions that were not rigorously demonstrated and that were contrary to Scripture should be considered to be false.

In 1616 eleven theologians were assigned the task of judging Galileo's work. After five days of deliberation, they announced their verdict: The heliocentric theory, they said, "is philosophically foolish and absurd, and formally heretical, inasmuch as it expressly contradicts the doctrines of holy scripture in many places both according to their literal meaning and according to the common exposition and interpretation of the holy fathers and learned theologians." Copernicus's works were put on the Index until they could be purged of any suggestion that the theory presented in them was anything more than a very tentative hypothesis, and all books (including those of Galileo) that attempted to reconcile the Copernican theory with the Bible were condemned.

Nevertheless, in 1632 Galileo managed to publish another important work, *A Dialogue Concerning the Two Chief World-Systems*, with a license from the Holy Office and a dedication to Pope Urban VIII. The Jesuits, after examining the book, concluded that it treated the Copernican system not as a hypothesis but as an established fact, and they denounced it as being more dangerous than all the heresies of Luther and Calvin. The Inquisition forbade all further sales of the book and ordered the confiscation of all outstanding copies. Galileo, sixty-eight years old and very ill, was summoned to the Inquisition to answer the charges of heresy. In its hearings, which dragged on for several months, the Inquisition produced a document that had allegedly been discovered in the files of the 1616 case. In it, Bellarmine, the chief hearing officer, was reported to have ordered Galileo in absolute terms not to hold, teach, or defend the Copernican hypothesis in any way. Galileo, according to the document, expressed his consent to that order. In the new hearings, Galileo denied that any such injunction had been issued, and he denied further that he had ever agreed to comply with such a decree. He insisted throughout his trial that he had no memory of such an injunction. The Inquisition decided that Galileo had obtained the license to publish his book fraudulently, that it had been "extorted" under false pretenses, because he was under orders not to publish his opinions on the Copernican theory. On the strength of the Bellarmine document they were able to prosecute Galileo for "vehement suspicion of heresy," and were successful, at last, in forcing the sick and aged philosopher to recite a formula in which he "abjured, cursed, and detested" his past errors and heresies, swore that he would never again say or assert anything that would give anyone cause to suspect him of harboring heretical thoughts, and promised to denounce any heretic or anyone suspected of heresy to the Holy Office. He was sentenced to life imprisonment and spent the remainder of his life under house arrest in Florence.

There is a general consensus (not universally accepted) among historians, based upon evidence uncovered when the file on Galileo's trial was published in 1877, that the Bellarmine document was a forgery, planted in the 1616 file to give the Holy Office the ammunition it needed to convict Galileo. Without it they had no case, because Galileo's book had the *imprimatur*. It was necessary to prove that the *imprimatur* had been obtained fraudulently in order to nullify it.

In the course of time, refined instruments enabled astronomers to observe the parallax that was not perceptible with the instruments of Galileo's time, and the laws of physics were revised to account for the phenomena that had been newly discovered. Common sense was shown to be fallible, as were Aristotelian and Biblical doctrines that had been accepted throughout the scholarly world for many centuries.[46]

The persecution of such men as Galileo illustrates how the disregard of civil liberties and official refusal to allow opinions contrary to established dogmas to be expressed openly and freely can retard the progress of science and the expansion of human knowledge. Countless other men in every field have been subjected to similar persecutions by state churches and totalitarian regimes. They have been deprived of the opportunity to pursue their researches and to publish their findings, and, what is more important, the rest of the world has been deprived of the opportunity to hear what they have had to say and to pass judgment upon their opinions.

THE LIBERTARIAN RESPONSE

More than 100 years ago John Stuart Mill published his essay *On Liberty*, part of which was devoted to establishing the proposition that there should be no restraints on the voicing of opinions, no matter how radical or heretical they might seem to be, no matter how wrong they might be in the light of the "truths" allegedly "known" and "held sacred" by the community.

Mill argued, first of all, that "we can never be sure that the opinion we are endeavouring to stifle is a false opinion." And he argued that even if we were sure that it was false, "stifling it would be an evil still." [47]

No one is infallible, he said. Even the most superficial study of history reveals the grave errors that men have made in the past—men who were invested with great power and authority and were thought by their contemporaries to be very wise—in the conduct of their personal affairs and in their conduct of the affairs of the communities or organizations over which they held sway.

Mill's advocacy of complete freedom from censorship was based upon the principle that the state has no right to legislate on any matter that restricts the citizens' freedoms except in those areas where such restriction is necessary to protect the persons or property of others. Legislation restricting the individual's freedom in order to protect him from harming himself was, in Mill's opinion, insupportable. If censorship was intended to protect people against hurting themselves, it was unjustifiable on the grounds of this basic principle. And if it was intended to protect other persons against harm that might arise because of the spread of false or vicious doctrines or beliefs, then Mill replied that the evil and the harm arising from censorship itself far outweighed any harm that might come from the spread of supposedly evil or false opinions. The harm that resulted from the persecution of Galileo is a case in point. It is impossible to estimate how far the advance of science was set back by the intolerant attitude taken by the Church to the Copernican hypothesis and to those who advocated it. As it happened, the Copernican theory eventually won out, in spite of all the effort that went into extirpating it. On the basis of this example, and others that might be adduced, some people maintain that truth cannot be permanently lost by persecution; rather, they say, if it survives persecution and intolerance, it is established ever the more firmly. Truth, according to this view, may be subjected to trial by ordeal. But such a trial is no more rational when applied to doctrines than it is when applied to persons. Mill noted that persecution is a strange reward to bestow upon those who have endeavored to enlighten mankind. More importantly, there is no guarantee that the truth will survive the persecution and martyrdom of its defenders. Because the losers seldom write the history books, it is impossible to estimate how many people have endured needless suffering because of the suppression of discoveries and theories that might have contributed to human happiness, if they had been given a free forum.

We may flatter ourselves into believing that we no longer persecute heretics or burn those who express unpopular opinions. But we would do well to look at the question more closely. There are among us those who maintain that our society exhibits grave weaknesses, that it is sick unto death, that it ought to be replaced by a new and better social order. These dissidents sometimes express their opinions in a manner that is quite offensive to many of their fellow citizens, who are incensed at any suggestion that their country is not the greatest country in the world or that certain laws and social norms are oppressive and evil. The latter may conclude that those who express such opinions are part of an international conspiracy to take over the world and impose a totalitarian form of government over free people everywhere. When the expression of such unpopular views is accompanied by a life-style that is deemed to be undesirable or improper (for example, by living in communes, wearing beards or long hair, wearing garments that are not in keeping with the fashions of the day, engaging in interracial dating or marriage), the members of the community express their intolerance and disapproval by refusing employment to the dissidents, by harassing them legally and in other ways, and in the last resort, by running them out of town.

Mill argued that such official and unofficial intolerance of persons and groups whose views differ from those of the majority is itself a kind of tyranny that ought not to be tolerated, for it tends to stifle discussion, and no one can be so certain that his views are correct that he should prevent those with other opinions, on even the most vital issues, from having their say. Not the greatest evil attendant upon such intolerance is the harm done to those who are not heretics, for their mental development is cramped and their characters are robbed of that healthy skepticism and robust spirit of inquiry that is never welcome where oppression reigns. They are intimidated by fear of being exposed to public scorn and ridicule if any of their views should turn out to be unacceptable, and their intellects are thus deprived of the stimulation that disagreement and a rich diversity of opinions engender.

This brings us to another possibility—that the opinions being suppressed are in fact false. Even then, in Mill's opinion, they should be permitted free expression, for they encourage everyone who encounters them to search once again for the roots of his beliefs, for the grounds upon which they are based. Nothing is so destructive to meaningful belief, even in religion, than lack of genuine discussion and blind adherence to orthodox or received opinions. In the course of time unexamined beliefs become empty and meaningless slogans, platitudes, and clichés that have no more impact upon those who utter them than do the babblings of a parrot.

More often than not, however, the full truth is found neither in the received opinion nor in that of the dissenters, but in some combination of the two. Only by permitting free expression of both opinions, then, and by encouraging reasoned argument to proceed between opposing factions can the truth be found.

All of this leads to the conclusion that there should be no restraints on freedom of information, that the community as a whole, and its individual members benefit from free and open communication and free expression of all opinions.

Those who live in a free society choose to govern themselves, even though self-government entails certain dangers against which the subjects of totalitarian regimes are protected. One of these dangers, if it can be called that, is the danger of slipping into error. Those who live in a free society choose not to be protected against error; they must therefore assume the responsibility of searching for the truth. As another great libertarian, Alexander Meiklejohn, put it:

> We have adopted it [the search for truth] as our "way of life," our method of doing the work of governing for which, as citizens, we are responsible. Shall we, then, as practitioners of freedom, listen to ideas which, being opposed to our own, might destroy confidence in our form of government? Shall we give a hearing to those who hate and despise freedom, to those who, if they had the power, would destroy our institutions? Certainly, yes! Our action must be guided, not by their principles, but by ours. We listen, not because they desire to speak, but because we need to hear. If there are arguments against our theory of government, our policies in war or in peace, we the citizens, the rulers, must hear and consider them for ourselves. That is the way of public safety. It is the program of self-government.[48]

A self-governing nation is one that is prepared to take the risks that Plato and Hobbes and the other defenders of totalitarianism would concentrate in the hands of a few. It has not yet been shown how the few—whether they be called philosopher–kings, sovereigns, or commissars—are to be chosen in such a way as to avoid error on their own part and assure those who live under their dominion that their best interests will be served if they are kept in ignorance about matters that the few decide may be harmful to them, and if they permit the few to make decisions for them.

In his opinion in the *Pentagon Papers* case, Justice Black wrote:

> The press was to serve the governed, not the governors. The Government's power to censor the press was abolished so that the press would remain forever free to censure the Government. The press was protected so that it could bare the secrets of government and inform the people. Only a free and unrestrained press can effectively expose deception in government. And para-·mount among the responsibilities of a free press is the duty to prevent any part of the government from deceiving the people and sending them off to distant lands to die of foreign fevers and foreign shot and shell. . . . [The newspapers that revealed the contents of the Pentagon Papers] should be commended for serving the purpose that the Founding Fathers saw so clearly. In revealing the workings of government that led to the Vietnam war, the newspapers nobly did precisely that which the Founders hoped and trusted they would do.[49]

Justice Douglas, in the same case, condemned governmental secrecy as "fundamentally antidemocratic, perpetuating bureaucratic errors." He conceded that there is a very narrow class of cases in which the First Amendment's ban on prior restraint might be overridden, but such cases exist only when the nation is at war—suggesting that since the war in Vietnam had never been authorized as such by Congress, the nation was not at war, and therefore the only conditions on which prior restraint might constitutionally apply did not hold.

And Justice Stewart, agreeing that the successful conduct of international diplomacy and the maintenance of an effective national defense depend upon both confidentiality and secrecy, argued that "the responsibility must be where the power is." The Executive branch must take care that its secrets are kept, he said, and advised the Executive not to overclassify, because "the hallmark of a truly effective internal security system would be the maximum possible disclosure, recognizing that secrecy can best be preserved only when credibility is truly maintained."

In a libel suit brought against the *New York Times* for having published an allegedly defamatory advertisement, Justice Black said:

> The theory of our Constitution is that every citizen may speak his mind and every newspaper express its view on matters of public concern and may not be barred from speaking or publishing because those in control of government think that what is said or written is unwise, unfair, false, or malicious. In a democratic society, one who assumes to act for the citizens . . . must expect that his official acts will be commented upon and criticized. Such criticism cannot, in my opinion, be muzzled or deterred by the courts at the instance of public officials under the label of libel.[50]

In an older case, Justice Brandeis put the argument for free expression as well as anyone ever has:

> Those who won our independence believed . . . that public discussion is a political duty; and that this should be a fundamental principle of the American government. They recognized the risks to which all human institutions are subject. But they knew that order cannot be secured merely through fear of punishment for its infraction; that it is hazardous to discourage thought, hope and imagination; that fear breeds repression; that repression breeds hate; that hate menaces stable government; that the path of safety lies in the opportunity to discuss freely supposed grievances and proposed remedies; and that the fitting remedy for evil counsels is good ones. Believing in the power of reason as applied through public discussion, they eschewed silence coerced by law—the argument of force in its worst form. Recognizing the occasional tyrannies of governing majorities, they amended the Constitution so that free speech and assembly should be guaranteed.[51]

In responding to the arguments made by those who attempt to justify censorship, either in the United States or elsewhere, it is appropriate to begin by noting that even the most liberal exponents of free expression agree that there are reasonable limits, and that when there is in fact a "clear and present danger" either to the society as a whole or to innocent persons, certain forms of speech may be at least temporarily forbidden. In many parts of the world, where huge proportions of the people are still illiterate, where the climate is tense, and free institutions have not yet had a chance to take root, some control of the press and of speech may be justified—but only so much as is absolutely necessary to avoid domestic violence. It appears that many regimes have used the primitive conditions under which their people live and the instability of their governments and their economies as an excuse for repressive measures that are greatly in excess of what is necessary to maintain order. The use of government censorship in order to maintain the power of the government or to keep it in office, tempting though it may be, seems almost inevitably to lead to abuses and ultimately to corruption, which cannot be corrected without violence when there is no free press to expose scandals as they arise. The governments of Sri Lanka and of India under Indira Gandhi argued that the proper function of the press is the furtherance of their own goals—goals that might or might not correspond with the true interests of the people whom they had been empowered to govern. If a given segment of the press is not filling needs felt by the people, the solution is not the forcible closing of that medium, but the opening of a new one, allowing it to compete in a free market with the others.

The arguments of the Yale dissenter are particularly instructive, and deserve a response:

1. It is true that one of the reasons free speech is so jealously guarded is the fact that it furthers the truth. Those who would limit it when others wish to express different opinions concerning the truth are presuming that they already have the truth, that they are infallible, and that no other opinion is worthy of expression or of being heard by those who wish to listen. But however firmly one may believe in and be committed to a given opinion, it is always *possible*, however unlikely that may seem, that some other opinion may contain at least a grain of truth.

2. It is also true that free speech is not the only value of a democratic society. Speech may indeed be used to subvert the very foundations upon which such a society is based. When that happens, the solution advocated by believers in free speech is the use of free speech, not its suppression. As the demise of the late Senator Joseph McCarthy demonstrated, it was his exposure to the nation on television during the Army-McCarthy hearings that brought about his downfall. As someone once observed, the best disinfectant is sunlight.

3. The assumption that students are incapable of distinguishing true from false doctrines and that they should therefore be protected from diverse ideas and opinions is both paternalistic and presumptuous, as well as an insult to the emotional and intellectual maturity of a university community. Believers in the value of free speech might hesitate to invite an enemy of freedom—such as Adolf Hitler—to speak before a university forum, but most of them would defend his right to do so if he were in fact invited. Those who have had an opportunity to enjoy the benefits of a truly free society are unlikely to be swayed by the arguments of such a totalitarian demagogue as Hitler, particularly if they continue to enjoy the freedom that he would deny them if he were in power.

4. Again, there is an assumption of infallibility in the statement that

Shockley's research is not research because he has arrived at conclusions that one believes, sincerely and profoundly, to be false.

5. Although the First Amendment does impose restraints upon governments, universities, as institutions dedicated to free and open inquiry, are obligated, by their own principles, to permit the expression of diverse views, however absurd they may be, however horrifying some people may find them, with an equal opportunity for opponents of those views to express their opinions as well.

6. The extending of an invitation to speak is not an action, but a part of the business of intellectual inquiry in which universities are engaged. The advocacy of allegedly racist policies *is* a form of speech, however repugnant and erroneous those policies may be.

7. The extending of an invitation to a public forum at an academic institution constitutes no acknowledgment whatever of the soundness of the speaker's views or of the reasonableness of the assumptions upon which he predicates his discussion. It may represent nothing more than a desire on the part of some members of the university community to satisfy their curiosity about a matter in which they have some interest.

8. It is true that there are no provisions for group libel in the laws of the United States. This policy has been adopted deliberately so as not to squelch free discussion of matters that are of great concern to all, however painful such discussion may be to some persons on some occasions.

9. An audience's rights are limited. An audience may applaud, cheer, or express its disapproval, so long as such demonstrations do not interfere with the rights of those who have come to hear the speaker. Freedom of speech would be meaningless if opponents of a given viewpoint were permitted to prevent the advocates of that point of view from expressing themselves in public.

THE LIMITS OF LIBERTY

Any society must have rules governing its members' behavior, including their oral behavior. No deliberative body, whether it is a court, a legislature, a professional society, a faculty meeting, or a committee meeting, can grant unlimited rights of free expression to anyone—even its own members— without being reduced to chaos and utter frustration of its efforts to achieve its professed aims. Rules of order have been established because without them it would be impossible to carry any meeting to a reasonable, effective conclusion. The chairman of a meeting must have some means of controlling the members so that those who wish to be heard may have an opportunity to speak, and so that those who wish to listen to the proceedings may be able to hear what the speakers are saying. During such a meeting, those who have not been recognized by the chair do not have the right to speak, no matter how important they may conceive their statements to be, no matter how urgent they may believe it is that the group hear what they have to say. If they feel that they have the right to disrupt the orderly procedures of the meeting in order to have their say, they must acknowledge the right of those who are conducting the meeting to expel them or to prevent them from gaining access to the hall so as to avoid such disruption. For unless one can demonstrate that the meeting is illegal or so dangerous to the well-being of society that it cannot be permitted to go on, one is on very dangerous ground by claiming to have a right to disrupt it. It is very difficult to maintain that I have the right to disrupt your meetings and to deny that you have the right to disrupt mine.

Of course, there are people who behave in such a manner. When Hitler was getting organized, he had groups of bullies stationed at meetings of democratic parties and societies who heckled, shouted, and rioted in an effort (successful, in the end) to destroy them. At his own meetings, though, these same bullies were posted with strict orders to bash in the heads of any who were so bold as to attempt to interfere with the orderly progress of the agenda. Stalinists, Maoists, and fascists of all stripes have had the same double standard wherever they have attempted to assume power. Not by the orderly process of parliamentary debate, not by an attempt to arrive at the truth through the free expression and exchange of ideas and opinions, but by theatrical role playing, by provocative harassment, by violence, and by playing on emotions, they have attempted to destroy the workings of democratic deliberative bodies and to impose their own iron-disciplined machines upon those who were unable or unwilling to fend off their attacks.

It is sometimes forgotten that the purpose of a meeting, any meeting, is not unregulated talk, but the conduct of some kind of business. A meeting of any deliberative body is not for the purpose of everyone saying whatever comes to mind, but to hear everything that is pertinent to the subject under discussion so that an informed decision may be reached. Freedom of speech does not mean that speech is totally immune to regulation, but that *no expression of opinion ought to be suppressed because the opinion is considered to be false, heretical, harmful, or subversive.* Even the expression of opinions that are generally acknowledged to be true, saintly, beneficial, and patriotic is out of order when the speaker does not have the floor or when his opinions are irrelevant to the goals of the meeting. Opinions as such ought not to be regulated, and there should be public forums for the expression of all opinions, but there are places and occasions when the expression of any opinion, or the expression of opinions on certain subjects, is out of place and may be declared out of order.

Some forms of verbal expression are not expressions of opinion at all and therefore do not come under the protection of the First Amendment or of the liberal theory of freedom of speech and press. Suppose, for example, that someone has concluded that the president of the Chase Manhattan Bank, as a symbol of capitalism and of the military–industrial complex, should be assassinated. Suppose he expresses this opinion before a mob of angry demonstrators in front of the home of that bank official. And suppose that his words tend to inflame the passions of the mob to such a degree that they storm the house and cause serious injury to its occupants. Certainly such speech ought not to be protected.

Suppose that a group of pranksters decides to play a "joke" on the audience assembled in an old theater whose exits are narrow and not easily accessible from the center aisles. During a tense moment in the performance, the pranksters shout "Fire!" and create a panic in the crowd. That single word, uttered in the proper circumstances, can be as damaging as a match lit in an explosive atmosphere. The pain and suffering that might be caused to members of the audience as they rush toward the exits cannot be excused or justified on the ground that free speech is at stake. No legal protection has ever been granted to anyone to use words as weapons to harm others. Just as matches and knives may be used freely and legitimately for certain purposes but not for others, so also may words be used for some purposes but not for others. The use of words as a means of communicating information and opinion is relatively (but not absolutely) unrestricted in free societies, but their use as weapons of destruction and harm to others has always been limited.

Some statements are so damaging to individual citizens that their utterance or publication may subject those who are responsible for them to civil or criminal actions under the laws of defamation of character, slander, or libel. A well-known basketball coach was once accused by a leading national magazine of having accepted bribes to throw important games. Such an accusation, unsubstantiated but widely read, could have destroyed his professional career, and certainly must have caused him and his family months of anguish. A rumor that a certain physician was mentally unbalanced and that he had started to molest his female patients began to circulate in the small town in which he lived. His practice dried up overnight, though there was not a scintilla of truth to the rumor. A high school teacher was accused by a local newspaper of being a communist, though she had never had the slightest interest in politics. In none of these cases could the protection of the right of free speech or freedom of the press be invoked, because according to the laws of slander and libel, the false statements defame the private, professional, or business reputation of the individuals. The law provides the opportunity for persons damaged by such false charges to seek compensation through damage suits in the courts. For certain kinds of slander and libel there are criminal penalties as well.

In the common-law countries truth is a defense against a charge of libel or slander. That is, if a person accused of libel can prove that he has published the truth, then no damages can be assessed against him. But in some states truth is not always a defense, for it is believed that some matters should not be afforded the protection of the law when they are widely published, even if they are true. Unless some matter of public welfare is at stake, for example, no one has the right to publish the fact that a particular individual is an alcoholic, that he suffers from severe depressions, or that he has frequent arguments with his wife. Though such reports may be true, no public interest is served by publishing them, and public reports of such facts may cause grievous harm, acute embarrassment, or great anguish to the parties involved. Therefore, on such private matters, laws of slander and libel can be brought to bear to protect persons against their public exposure.

Where private rights, including the right to privacy, come into conflict with the right to speak and to publish freely, the latter may have to give way to the former, particularly when no public interest is served by publication of such material. The courts have held, for example, that exposés of the private lives of public figures are relatively immune to the libel laws, because such exposés may be relevant to public decisions on matters of public policy. Defamatory statements directed against the private conduct of a public official or of a private citizen are not protected by the Constitution of the United States, for purely private defamation has little to do with the political ends of a self-governing society. But where public officials or public matters are concerned, the balance is shifted in favor of freedom of expression rather than against it.[52] Newspapers cannot be required, either, to adhere to a standard that provides that *only* the truth shall be a defense against libel action, particularly where criticism of public officials is at issue; for if critics of public officials and their actions had to guarantee the truth of all their statements under threat of criminal or civil liability, there would be a stifling effect upon them, amounting to a kind of self-censorship. Some libel laws require, therefore, that the person pressing the complaint must demonstrate not only that the report was false, but also that it was made maliciously, with actual knowledge of its falsity, and with reckless disregard of whether it was false or not.[53]

Another area in which the law places restrictions upon the publication of statements, even though they may be true, is in the divulging of the contents of private communications without the permission of the sender or receiver. If a telephone lineman overhears a conversation while repairing a cable, he does not have the right to divulge the contents of that conversation to any other person, and in many states he may be held criminally liable if he does. On the other hand, however, if a telephone employee discovers that the company's lines are being used for unlawful purposes, he may be *required* to furnish such information to the appropriate law enforcement officers or agencies and may be punished if he fails to do so. Thus, there are times when one must remain silent, and there are other times when silence is forbidden. One is not always justified in divulging the truth, nor is one always justified in respecting other persons' privacy.

If truth is not always protected, it is evident that falsehoods should not be. The utterance of some falsehoods is prohibited by criminal law, because they cause so much mischief and are potentially so destructive and so costly that they cannot be justified on the usual grounds reserved for free speech.

A person who initiates or circulates a false report or warning of a fire, explosion, crime, or other emergency under circumstances in which it is likely that public alarm or inconvenience will result cannot plead that he was justified in doing so because of his rights to speak freely. The public inconvenience caused by such false reports is so great that the freedom to make them is not protected by the law and does not deserve to be protected. On the contrary, legislators are perfectly justified in imposing penalties upon persons who deliberately engage in such public mischief.

Similarly, some kinds of statements may be prohibited, whether they are true or false. The rights of freedom of expression do not extend to the protection of persons who reveal secrets with which they have been entrusted. Ideas, like material goods, can be stolen or misappropriated. A man working for a chemical company or a pharmaceutical firm might learn the formulas of valuable compounds that had recently been discovered or the methods for producing certain compounds inexpensively. Freedom of speech does not extend to permission for him to reveal these secrets to competing companies that might then use them to take business away from the company for which he had been working. Similarly, attorneys, accountants, and physicians do not have the right to reveal facts about their clients that they have learned in confidential conversations with them, or through their examination of documents relating to their clients' personal lives or businesses. Freedom of the press does not grant a professor the right to publish his students' grades or the contents of letters of recommendation that might have been written to the university at the time of their admission to the institution. To allow such breaches of confidence would undermine the trust that persons put in one another in a number of sensitive areas. For certain kinds of assistance to be given to people, complete trust must prevail. In recognition of this, governments have foregone their customary right to compel people to testify about one another when the relation between them is of such a nature that breach of confidence would not be in the public interest. Thus, lawyers, doctors, ministers, and others are generally immune from the state's power to require that people reveal what they know about one another when called upon to do so in court or in other legitimate governmental inquiries. However, public interest sometimes requires that the right to silence and respect for the confidentiality of the doctor–patient relationship be superseded. Physicians may be *required to volunteer* information, even though no official of the state has requested it; and they may be held criminally liable if they fail to make certain reports. If a given patient is discovered to have the plague, for example, it would clearly be in the public interest for the doctor to be compelled to report the fact to the appropriate officials so that the patient might be quarantined, others inoculated, and other steps taken to prevent the spread of the disease. Similarly, if a physician discovers that a child is being beaten, severely maltreated, or neglected in such a way as to endanger its life or its physical or psychological well-being, he may be required by law to report these facts to the proper agencies, so that they may take appropriate action to protect the child against further abuse. The public interest is better served in such cases as these by breaking the trust ordinarily existing between doctor and patient.

There are other areas where the line is not so easily drawn and where there is considerable room for disagreement. One is illustrated by a case that made the headlines in 1971. A physician in England was asked by the minor daughter of a friend of his for a prescription for contraceptives. He reported the request to her father, under the assumption that his duty to look after the welfare of his patient (the young lady) would be best served by informing her father of her sexual activities. Not all of his colleagues in the medical profession agreed, for they considered it to be a gross violation of the doctor–patient relationship and a breach of professional ethics. Other medical men, however, concluded that it was quite appropriate for him to involve the girl's parents, because they were, after all, her legal guardians and had a responsibility to look after her conduct and her well-being. Whatever one may think of this physician's motives, one must ask what the consequences would be if young people had no assurance that their communications with their doctors would be held in the strictest confidence, particularly where such sensitive problems as contraception, pregnancy, venereal disease, and drug abuse are concerned. There is reason to believe that there would soon cease to be any doctor–patient relationship in such cases, for the young people concerned would stop seeking medical advice from competent physicians. Where there is fear of breach of confidence, many young people have taken their chances on home remedies or black market medicine rather than risk exposure.

These are only some examples of types of speech and publication that are not permitted, even in the most liberal society. The advertiser cannot claim the right to publish what he will about his product, whether it is true or false, under the First Amendment guarantee of freedom of the press, for that guarantee does not apply to commercial advertisements. It applies to expressions of opinion, to the expression of ideas, and to artistic expressions, but publications offering things for sale do not come under the same protection. They *are* protected, though, under the due process clause of the Fifth Amendment, which says that no one "may be deprived of life, liberty, or property without due process of law." The vendor may circulate his advertisements freely, unless he is enjoined against doing so by due process of law. But it is quite clear that his liberty to publish statements about his products is *not* the same as that referred to in the First Amendment's absolute prohibition against restraints upon freedom of the press.

The liberty to speak is not absolute. Nor is the liberty to publish what one pleases completely unrestricted. There are subjects, such as those about which one has been given confidential or secret information, about which one may not be at liberty to speak. And there are facts, such as those whose publication may harm persons who have a right to be protected against such injury, that one ought not to publish, even if they have been verified. There are occasions when one has no right to speak at all, and others when, if one speaks, one must confine oneself to a particular topic. In his own living room, a person may wander from topic to topic at will and hold forth at length on his favorite subject if he so chooses. But he may be restrained from doing this at a meeting or at a rally or in a courtroom where such musings are not on the agenda. A salesman may not (or should not) make false claims for his merchandise, and if he does, there should be sanctions that can be applied against him.

Yet the libertarian claims that freedom of speech and freedom of the press are, or should be, absolute. If it is proper to restrict the freedom of the salesman, to restrain him from disseminating false information whose worst effect may be to deprive his customer of a few dollars, how can it be improper to forbid political, moral, and religious hucksters from spreading false doctrines that may weaken our morals and destroy our society? The libertarian replies by pointing out that the salesman is peddling merchandise, whereas the others are dealing with ideas. There are standard tests for determining whether the claims the salesman makes for his merchandise are true—tests that everyone, including the salesman himself, will acknowledge to be valid. But there are no standard tests for determining whether the clergyman's claims are true; no scales to weigh the capitalist's views against those of the communist; no test to provide an infallible, or even a highly probable, judgment as to whether one economic theory is to be preferred over another.

And finally, the libertarian replies by observing, as Alexander Meiklejohn did, that the free man is prepared to take the risks of living in a society that offers the liberty to speak, to publish, and to think false or incorrect or even harmful thoughts; for the risks of living in a society where those liberties do not exist are so much greater.

5

Obscenity and Pornography

The Congress of the United States, in establishing a National Commission on Obscenity and Pornography, whose members were to be appointed by the president, declared that the traffic in obscene and pornographic materials was "a matter of national concern." Estimates of the trade in such materials in the United States alone range from $500 million to $2.5 billion per year.

At the most conservative estimate, then, there is considerable demand for pornographic magazines, books, photographs, films, sound recordings, slides, and other devices. The Supreme Court has been involved in many controversial cases involving pornography and has had to pass on the constitutionality of many state and local statutes designed to limit the sale and distribution of erotic materials, as well as upon administrative actions (such as actions by the Post Office and by Customs officials in seizing or destroying these books and magazines) directed against allegedly obscene matter.

For these reasons, the questions that the commission was directed to answer are clearly of wide concern. Once the fundamental liberties guaranteed by the Bill of Rights—the First Amendment right of free expression, both in speech and in the press—is involved in these disputes. Some defenders of the right of purveyors of allegedly pornographic materials to publish, display, distribute, and sell their wares maintain that the right of free expression is itself under attack whenever any attempt is made to interfere with the traffic in obscene materials. They compare antipornography statutes to the proverbial camel, who managed to get his nose into the Arab's tent, only to take over the tent and destroy it. Allow the censor to get his nose in the door, they say, by permitting him to put the ban on the most offensive books, films, and magazines, and he will soon be passing judgment on serious works of art, political tracts, and treatises that he considers to be damaging to the public welfare, and social documents that he (or those whose opinions he respects) deems to be dangerous or offensive. There is ample evidence from the past, these libertarians say, that works of art and literature that are today considered to be great classics were once banned by censors: works by Chaucer, Montaigne, Shakespeare, Ovid, Boccaccio, Aristophanes, Fielding, Balzac, Jonathan Swift, and Mark Twain, to mention only a few. So have the ideas of great iconoclasts, inventors, innovators, and dissenters from the predominant views on science, religion, and politics been condemned, including those of Galileo, Giordano Bruno, Maimonides, Spinoza, Socrates, and Jesus of Nazareth. More recently, works by William Faulkner, Ernest Hemingway, James Joyce, Erskine Caldwell, James T. Farrell, and Theodore Dreiser have fallen under the ban.*

The recital of the names of authors whose works are held in high esteem by scholars and critics should not blind one to the fact that there is a strong tendency for persons who become involved in discussions of public policy concerning the censorship of literature to assume an elitist stance. They often condemn as trash or garbage popular literature that does not appeal to members of their own social class or to their own literary tastes. It is tempting to assume that censors will ban only those publications and films that have no redeeming social value, but that assumption is not borne out by the historical facts. A few instances of film censorship in the not-so-distant past, together with the justifications offered, may be of interest:

---

* For a list of recent legal cases of censorship involving works that are widely regarded as having literary value, see the appendix to this chapter.

- In some cities Walt Disney's nature film *The Vanishing Prairie* was censored. The officials deleted a sequence showing the birth of a buffalo.
- Before World War II, the Chicago censor denied licenses to a number of films portraying and criticizing life in Nazi Germany, including the *March of Time* documentary *Inside Nazi Germany* and Charlie Chaplin's satire on Hitler, *The Great Dictator*. This censorship was apparently out of deference to Chicago's large German population.
- In 1959 the Chicago censor refused to license *Anatomy of a Murder* because the words *rape* and *contraceptive*, which were essential to the story, were objectionable.
- In Memphis, censors banned *The Southerner*, which dealt with poverty among tenant farmers, "because it reflects on the South," and *Curley* because it contained scenes of white and Negro children in school together.
- In 1950 Atlanta's censors banned *Lost Boundaries*, a film that told the story of a black physician and his family who "passed" for white, on the ground that it "will adversely affect the peace, morals, and good order" of the city.
- A Russian film, *Professor Mamlock*, portraying the persecution of Jews by the Nazis, was banned by the Ohio censors on the ground that it was "harmful" and would tend to "stir up hatred and ill will and gain nothing." The police in Providence, Rhode Island, did not permit it to be shown because it was, in their opinion, "Communist propaganda."
- Ohio and Kansas banned newsreels considered pro labor; and Kansas ordered a speech by Senator Wheeler opposing the bill for enlarging the Supreme Court (during Roosevelt's second term) to be cut from the *March of Time* because it was "partisan and biased."
- *Carmen* was rejected by censors in a number of states: in one, because cigarette-girls smoked cigarettes in public; in another, because a kiss lasted too long.
- In New York, censors forbade the discussion in films of pregnancy, venereal disease, eugenics, birth control, abortion, illegitimacy, prostitution, miscegenation, and divorce.
- The police sergeant in charge of censorship for the city of Chicago was quoted by the Chicago *Tribune* as saying, "Children should be allowed to see any movie that plays in Chicago. If a picture is objectionable for a child, it is objectionable period." [1]
- In an important censorship case in New Jersey, a psychiatrist called as an expert witness by the state testified that portrayal of any sex abnormality or perversion was necessarily obscene. She also testified that if sex is used for excitement and as an end in itself, it becomes obscene. "When sex isn't just for the propagation of the race and of the species," she said, "or the intent isn't, then it is abnormal or perverted." [2]

Censors exert power not only to prevent the public from seeing or reading what has already been produced, but also to inhibit artistic expression. The great Russian novelist Leo Tolstoy once wrote: "You would not believe how, from the very commencement of my activity, that horrible censor question has tormented me! I wanted to write what I felt; but at the same time it occurred to me that what I wrote would not be permitted, and involuntarily I had to abandon the work. I abandoned, and went on abandoning, and meanwhile the years passed away."[3] In 1974 Alexander Solzhenitsyn revealed that he had "shuffled around, cut, and reorganized" his books in a vain attempt to make them palatable in Moscow. He warned Western readers that *any* book by a Soviet author has been self-censored, that anything that might offend the official censors is left out or toned down.[4] Countless potential creations of artistic genius have undoubtedly been lost because of the artists' conviction that they would be banned by the censors.

THE CASE FOR CENSORSHIP

One may argue that the threat to freedom by censorship might be justified by the improvement that might result from the suppression of genuine pornography—books, magazines, films, and recordings that are contributing to a breakdown of morals among adults as well as young people and are encouraging experimentation with perverse forms of sexual behavior not acceptable in a civilized society. It has also been suggested that the authors of the First Amendment to the Constitution did not intend it to protect the sort of pornography that is sold in adult bookstores, because such materials have no redeeming social importance and do not deserve the protection of the laws. And some experts claim that pornography is sometimes the trigger that leads some persons to commit acts of violence against others. These critics point to such cases as an unstable young man who raped a young girl after he had been aroused by the lurid scenes in an obscene comic book, and the gruesome "Moors" murders of young children in England by self-styled disciples of the Marquis de Sade, whose books figured prominently in their collection.[5] If good literature can have desirable effects upon those who read it, they say, then it is reasonable to assume that bad literature may have undesirable effects. Such critics deny that literature has no influence upon those who read it. It is therefore impossible, in their opinion, to defend pornography on the ground that it has no evil effects.

According to Ernest Van den Haag, pornography almost always leads to sadistic pornography, because "it deindividualizes and dehumanizes sexual acts; by eliminating all contexts, it reduces people simply to bearers of impersonal sensations of pleasure and pain. This dehumanization eliminates the empathy that restrains us ultimately from sadism and nonconsensual acts." [6]

In the end, it is claimed, pornography is "antihuman." If it were directed against blacks or against Jews, those who now oppose censorship would be in the forefront of its supporters, according to Van den Haag. "But why should humanity as such be less protected than any of the specific groups that compose it? That the hate articulated is directed against people in general rather than against only Jews or Negroes makes it no less dangerous; on the contrary, it makes it dangerous to more people." [7]

In another defense of the censorship of pornography, Raymond D. Gastil drew an analogy to a small square in a large city. The square was surrounded by apartments, most of whose residents were clean, neat, and orderly. Only a few people dropped trash in the square, so even the most fastidious residents were satisfied with the city's weekly cleaning. But one year, a small number of the square's users started to drop their trash into the square. By the time the cleanup crews made their weekly rounds, the trash was piled high as others had begun to dump their trash onto the heaps. Finally, the messy apartment dwellers were all fouling the square, the more fastidious began to stay away, and cleanup crews were unable to keep up with the accumulations. As time went on, even the once-fastidious apartment dwellers became litterers and permitted their own apartments to deteriorate.

> I see no reason why in the name of individual freedom the courts should not . . . do away with such laws against littering. Why is the filling of the public area with pornography and obscenity to be regarded as different from the delict of littering? When the movie marquee, newstands, and popular songs all blare out *Deep Throat* and its equivalents, the city becomes a different place to walk in just as it does when everyone carelessly drops his lunch sack, candy wrapper, or pop bottle. [8]

Zoning regulations have been employed for many years to keep legitimate enterprises out of areas that were not compatible with the activities in which they were engaged. Chemical plants, rendering plants, and rubber manufacturers, for example, are not permitted to establish operations in residential areas, and even such relatively inoffensive businesses as hamburger stands and ice cream shops may be confined to particular strips within a city so as to avoid undesirable concentrations of automobiles and unsightly signs in residential areas. Such zoning laws have been tried in a number of cities that have been disturbed by an overabundance of sex-related businesses, the Supreme Court has upheld their constitutionality, and they have been working successfully. [9] One of the reasons such an approach has succeeded in the courts is that it removes or reduces the threat to neighborhoods without at the same time depriving persons who may wish to patronize such establishments of their right to do so. The purpose of such regulation is not, then, to impose a total ban on the sale, distribution, or display of such materials, but to confine it within reasonable limits in order to prevent the spread of "the squalor and crime which results from concentrations of commercial sex and which destroy other citizens' rights of residence, commerce, and entertainment." [10]

Willing masochists are not permitted to commit suicide on stage or to submit to physical torture. Bearbaiting, cockfighting, and bullfighting are not permitted, both out of compassion for animals and because such spectacles tend to debase and brutalize those who participate in and watch them. If euthanasia were legalized, suppose physicians brought their patients (assuming that they would give their consent) to theaters, where they would be interviewed so long as they were conscious, for the amusement or enlightenment of the audience. Following the fatal injection, critics might write accounts of the performance for the morning papers, comparing the drama and the efficiency of one physician against that of another.[11] If democracy is more than a collection of personal liberties, if it entails a certain vision of the quality of human life and the preservation of fundamental values other than those embodied in the concept of liberty, then it is obvious why such displays would be prohibited, even if all concerned were willing, either for personal gain or as a contribution to public enlightenment, to consent to such public spectacles.

Certain kinds of spectacles have an almost irresistible attraction. In the *Republic*, Plato remarks upon the difficulty he experienced when he passed by the scene of a public execution: He could not resist the temptation to go out of his way to gape at the bodies of the victims, even though he felt that it was a ghastly sight, one that he should not have gone to see. It seems that dead bodies, the process of dying, and certain other scenes, including nudity, buggery, bestiality, and other kinds of sexual behavior, possess both an attractiveness and a powerful repellent quality that may account for a reluctance to permit them to be displayed in public. As Joel Feinberg has noted, "The conflict between these attracting and repressing forces, between allure and disgust, is exciting, upsetting, and anxiety-producing." When confronted with an actual display or with a replica of such a scene, many people react with a sense of shame, receiving "a kind of psychic jolt that can be a painful wound." [12] Under some circumstances, Feinberg concludes, people have the right to be protected against such shocks. For an offensive display (one that induces repugnance, embarrassment, shame, and the like) to be outlawed, Feinberg says, the reaction it induces should be one "that could reasonably be expected from any person chosen at random, taking the nation as a whole, and not because the individual selected belongs to some faction, clique, or party." But he adds that public cross burnings, the display of swastikas, and cruel utterances that are extremely offensive to the racial, religious, or ethnic groups that are insulted ought also to be included. He therefore adds a further qualification: that "the flaunting of abusive, mocking, insulting behavior of a sort bound to upset, alarm, anger, or irritate those it insults" ought also to be banned. And finally, he suggests that the principle should be limited by what he calls the "standards of reasonable avoidability." "No one has a right to protection from the state against offensive experiences," he says, "if he can easily and effectively avoid those experiences with no unreasonable effort or inconvenience." Hence, it is permissible to ban nude passengers from buses and airliners, loudspeakers blaring obscene remarks, and billboards that excite the reactions he has described. But on these grounds, books cannot be suppressed. For they are easily avoided. All one need do is not read them, not open them. Unlike the smell of rancid garbage, which cannot easily be avoided, "when an 'obscene' book sits on a shelf, who is there to be offended? Those who want to read it for the sake of erotic stimulation presumably will not be offended (else they wouldn't read it), and those who choose not to read it will have no experience of it to be offended by." Whereas Feinberg advocates some form of regulation of public displays, then, he sees no justification for the censorship of books. But there are others, arguing from similar principles, who go further.

Harry M. Clor contends that no society can be so libertarian as to blind itself to its avowed enemies when confronted by them. He contends also that it is a mistake to suppose that anything any person who calls himself an author or an artist does must necessarily benefit society. Some so-called authors and artists, he says, are actually enemies of civilized society and their works can do a great deal of harm. He concludes that society has the right to censor their works in order to protect itself against their pernicious influences.

What kind of harm does he envision as flowing from obscene works? He concedes that there is no conclusive scientific evidence that obscene works in themselves are the cause of criminal or immoral behavior, but English and American law have always recognized the right of the state to preserve the moral welfare of the state. In 1890 the Supreme Court upheld laws against the teaching of polygamy as "legislation for the punishment of acts inimical to the peace, good order and morals of society." [13] And in an earlier case, the Court said, "The foundation of a republic is the virtue of its citizens. They are at once sovereigns and subjects. As the foundation is undermined the structure is weakened. When it is destroyed the fabric must fall. Such is the voice of universal history." [14] Aristotle held that the aim of legislation was to make citizens good by training them in habits of right action. Men come together in political communities not merely for mutual protection against aggression that might lead to the destruction of their lives or their liberties or the deprivation of their property, but for the cultivation of those qualities in man that are distinctively human, as distinguished from those that he shares with the brute creation. Law performs a civilizing and humanizing function, he said, and is *not* (contrary to Mill's view) intended merely to protect the citizen against physical harms that his neighbor might be tempted to inflict upon him.

Thus, under this view of society and the law, censorship may serve a very important function: it may protect the citizen against those influences that would tend to dehumanize or brutalize men and the societies in which they live.

As Lord Devlin wrote:

> A sense of right and wrong is necessary for the life of a community. It is
> not necessary that their appreciation of right and wrong, tested in the light

of one set or another of those abstract propositions about which men forever dispute, should be correct. . . . What the lawmaker has to ascertain is not the true belief but the common belief.[15]

Government, then, has the right to search out those common values that all men in a given society cherish and to reinforce them through legislation. It need not remain indifferent to the moral standards of its citizens. And it may utilize censorship to restrict "such forms of sensualism as are contrary to our deepest values."

Finally, those who favor this view maintain that the government may have the duty to prevent those vices that are incompatible with the well-being of society and the security of the government. If a man fails to observe reasonable standards of health and morality, he does less than his share toward the welfare of all. Society is harmed when its members are weakened by sickness, by poverty, or by vice. This is not paternalism, for paternalism is concerned to benefit the individual, even against his will. This is not so much concern for the well-being of the individual as for the well-being of society, which may be damaged by the corruption or sickness of the individual.

Men and women who become overly concerned with the gratification of their own desires, whatever they may be, cannot make their full contribution to society. Certain vices cannot be tolerated, even in the most liberal society, according to the advocates of censorship, for their spread can lead to the destruction of that society, or to the deterioration of the very conditions under which liberty can thrive. Thus, even a liberal society may have to suppress certain kinds of publications on the ground that their distribution tends to undermine the moral foundations of that society.

Every society exercises control over "standards of decency," particularly with respect to sex, because of the powerful nature of sexual passions. Men need guidance, either from the law or from the more informal sanctions of custom, as to the manner in which these emotions may be expressed. The law, in a civilized society, provides such guidance. It sets the tone for the moral community; it maintains the standards of the civilization when temporary fads and fashions may veer off in other directions. As Clor puts it, "there is a more stable and more continuous 'underlying' public opinion" that has, among its more important sources, the tradition and customs that are supported by the laws of the country. The home, the church, and the school do a great deal to maintain public morality, but they are incapable of doing the job alone, because they are molded by the law themselves, and the law provides the context and the framework in which they must operate.

Censorship, then, can serve to support and promote public morality—that morality upon which a good society depends—in two ways: "(1) by preventing or reducing some of the most corrupt influences and (2) by holding up an authoritative standard for the guidance of opinions and judgment." [16]

Clor advocates censorship "primarily" of the "most vicious materials." Among the more significant effects of such censorship, he says, would be the deterrent effect: "Publishers are deterred from publishing, and authors from writing, materials which cannot legally be circulated. Thus the results of legal censorship consist not in the confiscation of the relatively few obscene publications which the censor catches, but in the general reduction in the circulation of materials of that kind." [17]

Even more important, however, is the educative effect of legal censorship of obscene publications. Censorship laws "announce a moral decision of the community. . . . They assert, in effect, that the organized community draws a line between the decent and the indecent, the permissible and the impermissible. . . . Individuals . . . are made aware that the community is committed to a distinction between what is right and what is not. In the long run this awareness must have an effect upon the moral attitudes and values of most people." The community, by taking a stand, shows to one and all that it is serious about morality, according to Clor's view.

Before turning to the arguments of those who oppose censorship of allegedly obscene materials, it would be well to examine in some detail the attempts of psychologists, philosophers, and the courts to define the terms most crucial to this discussion: *obscenity* and *pornography*, and to determine, as far as the evidence permits, what effects allegedly pornographic literature, films, and related materials have upon individuals and upon society as a whole.

THE PROBLEM OF DEFINING OBSCENITY

The word *obscene* is said, by most experts, to be derived from the Latin *obscenum*, which they claim to be related to *caenum*—"dirt," or "filth." Others have suggested that it may refer to that which is "out of the scene," that which ought not to be depicted on stage because of its lewd or lascivious character.

Whatever the derivation of the word may be, it is evident that in ordinary English usage, it has a pejorative effect: anything that is said to be obscene is disapproved of by the speaker. In calling any word, book, or picture obscene, one expresses one's disgust with it or one's revulsion at it. Obscenity is not a property or quality as is weight or magnitude. It is the propensity of certain kinds of things to induce in people belonging to a particular culture feelings of disgust, revulsion, shock, horror, and outrage. Naturally, people differ from place to place, and even from one time to another in the same place, in the extent to which they will react to given forms of human display (for example) with feelings of disgust or outrage. Some years ago any woman's neighbors would have been scandalized if she had walked down the street with her skirts above her ankles. Today very few people are scandalized by a considerable exposure of female flesh. A significant proportion of younger people is not at all scandalized by complete nudity in public. At some of the rock festivals and at other large gatherings of youth in recent years, some participants have disrobed without provoking any noticeable feelings of outrage on the part of other participants. But in the wider community, there are still limits to what will be tolerated.

Because of the constant changes in public attitudes, some authorities have concluded that it is impossible to assign an operationally meaningful definition to such terms as *obscenity* and *pornography*, and have accordingly inferred that any legislation in which such terms are used must be unconstitutionally vague.

Judge Bok of Pennsylvania put the problem as well as anyone has in his classic decision in *Commonwealth* v. *Gordon*. Commenting on the modern rule that obscenity "is measured by the erotic allurement of a book upon the average modern reader," he said:

> Current standards of what is obscene can swing to extremes if the entire question is left open. . . . What is pure dirt to some may be another's sincere effort to make clear a point. . . .
>
> I can find no universally valid restriction on free expression to be drawn from the behavior of "l'homme moyen sensuel," who is the average modern reader. It is impossible to say just what his reactions to a book actually are. Moyen means, generally, average, and average means a median between extremes. If he reads an obscene book when his sensuality is low, he will yawn over it or find that its suggestibility leads him off on quite different paths. If he reads the Mechanics' Lien Act while his sensuality is high, things will stand between him and the page that have no business there. How can anyone say that he will infallibly be affected one way or another by one book or another? When, where, how, and why are questions that cannot be answered clearly in this field. The professional answer that is suggested is the one general compromise—that the appetite of sex is old, universal, and unpredictable, and that the best we can do to keep it within reasonable bounds is to be our brother's keeper and censor, because we never know when his sensuality may be high. This does not satisfy me, for in a field where even reasonable precision is utterly impossible, I trust people more than I do the law.[18]

In reference to the definition of *obscenity* as "sexual impurity" and its allegedly dangerous qualities, so dangerous as to constitute a "clear and present danger," Judge Bok observed:

> A book, however sexually impure and pornographic, . . . cannot be a present danger unless its reader closes it, lays it aside, and transmutes its erotic allurement into overt action. That such action must inevitably follow as a direct consequence of reading the book does not bear analysis, nor is it borne out by general human experience; too much can intervene and too many diversions take place. . . . [The law] only proscribes what *is* obscene, and that term is meaningless unless activated by precise dangers within legal limits. [But] the law provides no standard. . . .
>
> The public does not read a book and simultaneously rush by the hundreds

into the streets to engage in orgiastic riots. . . . How can it be said that there is a "clear and present danger"—granted that anyone can say what it is—when there is both time and means for ample discussion? . . .

Who can define the clear and present danger to the community that arises from reading a book? If we say it is that the reader is young and inexperienced and incapable of resisting the sexual temptations that the book may present to him, we put the entire reading public at the mercy of the adolescent mind and of those adolescents who do not have the expected advantages of home influence, school training, or religious teaching. . . . If the argument be applied to the general public, the situation becomes absurd, for then no publication is safe. How is it possible to say that reading a certain book is bound to make people behave in a way that is socially undesirable? And beyond a reasonable doubt, since we are dealing with a penal statute?

We might remember the words of Macaulay:

"We find it difficult to believe that in a world so full of temptations as this, any gentleman, whose life would have been virtuous if he had not read Aristophanes and Juvenal, will be made vicious by reading them." [19]

Hugo Black, late Associate Justice of the United States Supreme Court, in a dissenting opinion in the case of *Ginzburg* v. *United States* (1966), argued along similar lines—as he did consistently through many years on the Supreme Court—that obscenity is indefinable. Wise and good governments, he said, hedge the great power given to them by confining it within "easily identifiable boundaries." Written laws came into being in order to enable men to know in advance what areas of conduct were proscribed and what kinds of conduct were likely to bring the power of the criminal sanction to bear. In contrast, he noted, evil governments have written no laws at all, or have written them in unknown tongues, or have made it so difficult for the public to get access to them that no one could know what conduct might later be considered criminal by the government. He concluded that the criteria employed by the Court in upholding the conviction of Ginzburg for publishing or circulating obscene materials were "so vague and meaningless that they practically leave the fate of a person charged with violating censorship statutes to the unbridled discretion, whim and caprice of the judge or jury which tries him." He went on, then, to discuss these criteria in detail:

(a) The first element considered necessary for determining obscenity is that the dominant theme of the material taken as a whole must appeal to the prurient interest in sex. It seems quite apparent to me that human beings, serving either as judges or jurors, could not be expected to give any sort of decision on this element which would even remotely promise any kind of uniformity in the enforcement of this law. What conclusion an individual, be he judge or juror, would reach about whether the material appeals to "prurient interest in sex" would depend largely in the long run not upon testimony of witnesses such as can be given in ordinary criminal cases where conduct is under scrutiny, but would depend to a large extent upon the judge's or juror's personality, habits, inclinations, attitudes and other individual characteristics. In one community or in one courthouse a matter would be condemned as obscene under this so-called criterion but in another community, maybe only a few miles away, or in another courthouse in the same community, the material could be given a clean bill of health. In the final analysis the submission of such an issue as this to a judge or jury amounts to practically nothing more than a request for the judge or juror to assert his own personal beliefs about whether the matter should be allowed to be legally distributed. Upon this subjective determination the law becomes certain for the first and last time.

(b) The second element for determining obscenity . . . is [supposedly] that the material must be "patently offensive because it affronts contemporary community standards relating to the description or representation of sexual matters. . . ." Nothing . . . that has been said . . . leaves me with any kind of certainty as to whether the "community standards" referred to are world-wide, nation-wide, section-wide, state-wide, country-wide, precinct-wide, or township-wide. But even if some definite areas were mentioned, who is capable of assessing "community standards" on such a subject? Could one expect the same application of standards by jurors in Mississippi as in New York City, in Vermont as in California? So here again the guilt or innocence of a defendant charged with obscenity must depend in the final analysis upon the personal judgment and attitude of particular individuals and the place where the trial is held. . . .

(c) A third element which [is supposedly] required to establish obscenity is that the material must be "utterly without redeeming social value." This element seems to me to be as uncertain, if not even more uncertain, than is the unknown substance of the Milky Way. If we are to have a free society as contemplated by the Bill of Rights, then I can find little defense for leaving the liberty of American individuals subject to the judgment of a judge or jury as to whether material that provokes thought or stimulates desire is "utterly without redeeming social value. . . ." Whether a particular treatment of a particular subject is with or without social value in this evolving, dynamic society of ours is a question upon which no uniform agreement could possibly be reached among politicians, statesmen, professors, philosophers, scientists, religious groups or any other type of group. A case-by-case assessment of social values by individual judges and jurors is, I think, a dangerous technique for government to utilize in determining whether a man stays in or out of the penitentiary.

My conclusion is that . . . no person, not even the most learned judge, much less a layman, is capable of knowing in advance of an ultimate decision in his particular case by this Court whether certain material comes within the area of "obscenity" as that term is confused by the Court today." [20]

Note that Justice Black, in accordance with his long-held view that "obscenity" is indefinable, stated that the Court had *confused* the term, not that it had *defined* it.

According to Justice Black and Judge Bok, then, no meaningful definition of *obscene* is possible because: (1) Each man will tend to look upon the offensiveness of a given book or photograph or film from his own individual viewpoint, and even that, as Judge Bok pointed out, may differ from time to time with the same individual. (2) There are no objective criteria by which to judge the effects that a given book will have upon the public, for the effects that any book may have upon any particular individual depend very much upon many variables that are completely unpredictable. (3) There is no "average" man to whom the question can be addressed. (4) Any attempt to ban a book by the effects it allegedly has upon adolescents restricts the reading matter of mature adults to what will presumably be acceptable for consumption by adolescents. (5) It is impossible to define the "community" by whose standards publications are supposed to be judged. And (6) there is no way to determine objectively whether any particular work has "redeeming social value" or not.

Many eminent authorities, including the majority of Justice Black's colleagues on the Supreme Court, do not agree with this point of view.

For about 100 years the standard legal definition of *obscene*, known as the Hicklin definition, was that "the test of obscenity is this, whether the tendency of the matter charged as obscenity is to deprave and corrupt those whose minds are open to such immoral influences, and into whose hands a publication of this sort may fall." As long ago as 1913, Judge Learned Hand objected to this definition on the ground that instead of leaving the test of obscenity to the average adult, it fettered it to the lowest and least capable, "those whose minds are open to such immoral influences." He questioned the wisdom of reducing the permissible treatment of sex in literature to the standard of a child's library in the interest of a salacious few. The word *obscene*, he suggested, being incapable of exact abstract definition, should not be tied to the standards of a bygone age, but should be allowed to indicate "the present critical point in the compromise between candor and shame at which the community may have arrived here and now." Others attacked the Hicklin definition on the ground that it permitted undue concentration on parts of the work without giving sufficient attention to the effects or purposes of the work as a whole. Thus, in an appeal against an order of postal and customs officials that imported copies of James Joyce's *Ulysses* be destroyed on the ground that the book was obscene, Judge Augustus N. Hand held that even if some passages in the book might be objectionable, the book, taken as a whole, did not tend to promote lust. "We believe," he wrote, "that the proper test of whether a given book is obscene is its dominant effect." But Judge Manton, in a vigorous dissent, enumerated the pages on which objectionable passages appeared, and said, "Who can doubt the obscenity of this book after a reading of the pages referred to, which are too indecent to add as a footnote to this opinion?" He quoted with approval the charge of the judge in an earlier obscenity case: "The test of obscenity is whether the tendency of the matter is to deprave and corrupt the morals of those whose minds are open to such influence, and into whose hands a publication of this sort may fall. . . . Would it suggest or convey lewd thoughts and lascivious thoughts to the young and inexperienced?" But another judge observed that under the Hicklin test, the Bible could be banned, for it contains numerous passages that could lead immature minds to lascivious thoughts. The story of Lot's daughters, who conspired to put their father into an alcoholic stupor, after which they both had incestuous relations with him, is one of the milder examples.

The Hicklin definition, then, did not fare well, and was replaced, for a time, by another in connection with the attempt to burn *Ulysses*. Judge Learned Hand, in his opinion in the case, wrote:

> That numerous long passages in Ulysses contain matter that is obscene under any fair definition of the word cannot be gainsaid; yet they are relevant to the purpose of depicting the thoughts of the characters and are introduced to give meaning to the whole, rather than to promote lust or portray filth for its own sake. . . . The book as a whole is not pornographic, and, while in not a few spots it is coarse, blasphemous, and obscene, it does not, in our opinion, tend to promote lust. The erotic passages are submerged in the book as a whole and have little resultant effect.[21]

The new rule, then, rested upon the *dominant effect* of the book, rather than upon the effect that any given passages, taken in isolation, might have. Other decisions broadened the base of the public upon whose morals the book might be judged from the weakest among them to the average. In the late 1950s the American Law Institute drafted a model penal code, in which the following definition of "obscenity" was enunciated:

> A thing is obscene if, considered as a whole, its predominant appeal is to prurient interest, i.e., a shameful or morbid interest in nudity, sex or excretion, and if it goes substantially beyond customary limits of candor in description or representation of such matters.[22]

There is some problem about the meaning of "prurient interest." Some people say that it refers to physical sexual arousal. Others maintain that it may refer to curiosity alone. Compare, for example, Justice Brennan's definition of prurience as material having a tendency to incite lustful thoughts, or to arouse morbid or lascivious longings, with that of Justice Harlan, who said that "appeal to prurient interest" refers to "the capacity to attract individuals eager for a forbidden look." [23]

In his history-making opinion in *Roth* v. *United States,* Justice Brennan contended that obscenity, unlike even the most hateful ideas, is "utterly without redeeming social importance," for obscene utterances "are no essential part of any exposition of ideas." He concluded, therefore, that obscenity does not fall within the constitutional protections afforded to speech or press, which are offered because of the social value of permitting untrammeled expression of *ideas*. Obscenity may be distinguished from discussions about sex, then, by determining whether ideas or opinions are being expressed. If the material deals with sex in a manner appealing to prurient interest—i.e., in such a way as to excite lustful thoughts—then it is obscene, and if not, then it is not obscene. It should be noted, however, that though this seems, on the surface, to be a definition of *obscenity*, it does not really tell us what obscenity is. Relying upon the ill-defined term *prurient*, it tells us what obscene material presumably *does* to the reader or viewer.

Justice Harlan added yet another element: Regardless of its effect on the beholder, he said, obscene works must consist of "debasing portrayals of sex" and be patently offensive. Without such an additional criterion, he maintained, the public might be denied access to many worthwhile works of art and literature; for many such works might tend, on the whole, to appeal to the prurient interest but nevertheless not be "patently offensive." What it is to be "patently offensive" is never defined. But perhaps Justice Stewart's answer to the question, "What is hard-core pornography?" will provide a clue: "I shall not today attempt further to define the kinds of material I understand to be embraced within that short-hand definition; and perhaps I could never succeed in intelligibly doing so. But I know it when I see it." [24] As one critic has observed, this approach is no help whatever to book publishers and distributors, theater managers, and trial judges who do not "know it when they see it" or who "see it" differently from Justice Stewart. This definition, if it can be called that, is subjective, and if adopted in law, would be subject to Justice Black's criticism of any society that does not offer its citizens clear and well-defined rules for their conduct.

But the most recent cases have completely altered the situation. Chief Justice Burger, speaking for the majority of the Court, held in a 1973 case that the requirement that a work be *utterly* without redeeming social value is too restrictive, placing an impossible burden of proof upon the prosecution. The criterion for obscenity was therefore broadened to include those works which, "taken as a whole, appeal to the prurient interest," depicting or describing, "in a patently offensive way, sexual conduct specifically defined by the applicable state law," and which "taken as a whole, lack serious literary, artistic, political, or scientific value." [25] The word *utterly* was thus eliminated. On the ground that the United States is simply "too big and too diverse" for a single national standard to apply to all, the Court permitted each state to apply its own "contemporary community standards" to the determination of "customary limits of candor" and decency. "People in different States vary in their tastes and attitudes," Chief Justice Burger said, "and this diversity is not to be strangled by the absolutism of imposed uniformity."

Justice Burger insisted that equating "the free and robust exchange of ideas and political debate with commercial exploitation of the First Amendment demeans the grand conception of the First Amendment," and is a "misuse of the great guarantees of free speech and free press." The public portrayal of hard-core sexual conduct for its own sake or for commercial gain, he said, has no relationship to the exchange of ideas that the First Amendment was designed to protect.

In a companion case, the Court rejected the theory that "obscene, pornographic films" are immune from state regulation if they are exhibited to consenting adults only. The individual's alleged right to view such films is overridden by other interests that have higher priority: the public's interest in the quality of life and its community environment, the tone of commerce in urban centers, and public safety. He compared the regulation of pornography to state regulation of sewage and garbage removal, which are not left to individual discretion, but are subject to stringent rules designed to protect public health and the appearance of public places. Moreover, he said, there is no right of privacy in such public places as theaters and bars.[26]

The Court has since held that "community standards" may be local or statewide,[27] and that in a federal prosecution in a state that has no obscenity laws applicable to adults, the jury may rely on national standards or on their own views of their community's standards, despite the fact that their legislature has demonstrated its belief that the citizens of their state hold a standard under which no regulation of sexually explicit materials is considered to be justified.[28]

Justice Douglas dissented in the *Miller* case, arguing that the question was essentially one of personal taste. "What shocks me may be sustenance for my neighbor," he said. "What causes one person to boil up in rage . . . may reflect only his neuroses, not shared by others." Moreover, he said, no one can know in advance of a new court decision whether the books or pamphlets he publishes or sells are obscene, for there is no objective test. "Obscenity—which even we cannot define with precision—is a hodgepodge. To send men to jail for violating standards they cannot understand, construe, and apply is a monstrous thing to do in a Nation dedicated to fair trials and due process." The First Amendment was not intended to serve as a method for dispensing tranquilizers to the people, he argued. Its prime function was to enable "offensive" as well as "staid" people to enjoy the right to express themselves freely. Even if the material is garbage, he argued, so is much of what is said in political campaigns, on television, and on the radio.

In his dissenting opinion in the *Miller* case, Justice Brennan reversed his earlier contention that obscene publications were not protected by the First Amendment. He argued that there is little empirical basis for the assertion that exposure to obscene materials may lead to deviant sexual behavior or to crimes of sexual violence. Even if it could be shown that it might lead to such forbidden conduct, he insisted that the proper deterrent to such behavior in a free society would lie in the fields of education and punishment of the forbidden behavior.

Moreover, he said, under the American system of government, the state has no legitimate concern with the content of an individual's thoughts. But under the Court's decision, based as it was upon the assumption that the state may regulate commerce in obscene books or public exhibitions that exert a corrupting or debasing impact upon individuals who are exposed to them, it would seem to follow that for the same reasons—that is, in order to maintain a certain moral tone in the community—the state might have the right to decree that its citizens *must* read certain books or view certain films. However desirable the end might be, Justice Brennan said, it cannot be obtained by means that are prohibited under the Constitution. He recalled that for the welfare of his ideal commonwealth, Plato advocated infanticide and compulsory abortions, and Sparta took all control over children's education from their parents. Quoting an earlier decision, Justice Brennan said, "Although such measures have been deliberately approved by men of great genius, their ideas touching the relation between individual and State were wholly different from those upon which our institutions rest; and it hardly will be affirmed that any legislature could impose such restrictions upon the people of a State without doing violence to both letter and spirit of the Constitution." Therefore, he concluded, even a "legitimate, sharply focused state concern for the morality of the community cannot . . . justify an assault on the protections of the First Amendment."

The difficulty encountered by the highest court in the United States in defining *obscenity* is merely a reflection of the problems others have encountered in attempting the same task, although at least one thoughtful writer has asserted that its meaning is so clear that everyone really knows what it means. Ernest Van den Haag has suggested that literary critics who testify in court that they cannot distinguish pornography from literature have no business being critics, for if anyone can tell the difference, surely critics can.[29] In order to show how simple it is, Van den Haag offers the following formula for making this critical distinction:

1. If pornographic intention is admitted, or proved by testimony and circumstances, there is no problem. If doubtful, intention must be tested by the intrinsic qualities of the work.
2. Regardless of the author's intent, his work may be advertised or sold by stressing its [actual or putative] prurient appeal. By itself this justifies action against the seller only. Yet, although sales tactics are neither sufficient nor necessary to establish the prurient appeal of what is sold, they can be relevant: the image created by the seller may well fuse with the object of which it is an image and have effects on the consumer. . . .
3. The actual effect on the consumer—whether "prurient interest" is or is not aroused—depends on the work, its presentation, and the character of the consumer. A work not intended to be pornographic may nonetheless awaken lust, or have lewd effects; and one intended to do so may fail. Censors must not only consult their own reactions but rely on testimony about probable and prevailing reactions and standards. Pornography, to be such, must be likely to have a prurient or lewd effect. But this effect alone, though necessary, is not sufficient. However, together the three extrinsic qualities certainly are. Any two of them seem quite enough.[30]

But there are also intrinsic qualities to pornography, and in doubtful cases, these must be considered. This is how Van den Haag describes them:

Characteristically, pornography, while dreary and repulsive to one part of the normal [most usual] personality, is also seductive to another: it severs sex from its human context [the Id from Ego and Superego], reduces the world to orifices and organs, the action to their combinations. Sex rages in an empty world as people use each other as its anonymous bearers or vessels, bereft of love and hate, thought and feeling, reduced to bare sensations of pain and pleasure, existing only in (and for) incessant copulations without apprehension, conflict, or relationship.

[It] is but the spinning out of preadolescent fantasies which reject the burdens of reality and individuation, of conflict, commitment, thought, consideration and love, of regarding others as more than objects. . . .[31]

Pornography, he says, has only one aim: "to arouse the reader's lust so that by sharing the fantasy manufactured for him, he may attain a vicarious sexual experience." In this respect it is unlike literature, "which aims at the contemplation of experience, at the revelation of its significance."

Van den Haag's "definition" is far from simple, and its application would be exceedingly difficult. But it suffers from more serious defects than that of complexity. The following are only a few of its more important deficiencies.

1. Van den Haag gives no clear idea as to how one might prove "by testimony and circumstances" that an author's intention was pornographic. What objective facts would reveal this?

2. The merchandising of a product is *not*, and should *not* be, an element in determining whether its maker intended it to be what it is represented as being. If a storekeeper pastes a misleading label on a can of grapefruit sections, representing them as olives, the cannery should not be liable for the customer's disappointment. One might argue that if a book is clothed in a jacket that misleads its purchaser into believing that it contains explicit sex when in fact it does not, the publisher might well be liable to Federal Trade Commission action on misleading advertising. The purchaser ought to get what he pays for.

3. "Purient appeal" is a notoriously ambiguous term.

4. Van den Haag admits that the consumer may be sexually aroused by the most innocent work. Some people are aroused by women's stockings, others by the color red, and some may be stimulated by nothing at all. This is not to deny that some books and films are more likely than others to produce sexual excitement in those who read or view them. But Van den Haag admits that even this propensity is not sufficient to establish that a work is pornographic.

Suppose that a work is advertised in a sexually suggestive way and also has a tendency to stimulate its readers sexually. Is this enough to establish that it is in fact pornographic? The report of the Federal Commission on Obscenity might have such an effect on some people, and it might be clothed in suggestive covers and sold as a titillating piece, but that would surely not render it pornographic. Parts of *Gulliver's Travels* are quite explicit and might easily be sexually stimulating to some persons—perhaps even to most. Promotion of the book as a sex thriller would not make it one, despite the presence of such passages.

5. The psychological assumptions made by Van den Haag (about the existence of the Id, the Ego, and the Superego, for example) are open to serious question and are too ill-defined to serve as objective means of determining whether a man ought to go to jail or remain free.

6. The rejection of "the burdens of reality and individuation" and the rest might well be the subject of an excellent dissertation, a superb and enlightening novel, or the inspiration for a very moving poem. It has in fact been the foundation for more than one school of philosophy and for certain important religious movements. It scarcely counts as a sufficient condition for literature that ought, on that account, to be banned.

Other attempts to define obscenity abound. Here are a few of them:

Harold Gardiner, S.J., says that an obscene work is one that "must, of its nature, be such as actually to arouse or [be] calculated to arouse in the viewer or reader such venereal pleasure." Venereal pleasure is sexual passion, or, more concretely, "the motions of the genital apparatus which are preparatory to the complete act of sexual union." Any voluntary stimulation of the sex organs outside of marital sex is sinful and any literary work that provides such stimulation is obscene. This definition is precise enough, but is so broad as to be unacceptable to any large percentage of the general public outside the Catholic Church, and even, perhaps, to many of the members of that Church. It goes much farther than Justice Brennan went in the Roth decision, for it brands as obscene anything whatever that arouses sexual interest, and not merely those that lead to "lustful desires" or "prurience." [32]

Eberhard and Phyllis Kronhausen, who have devoted much of their career as psychologists to the study of pornography and obscenity, assert that "the main purpose [of hard-core pornography] is to *stimulate erotic response* in the reader. And that is all." They contrast this to writing that may be classed as "erotic realism." The latter, they say, is a "*truthful description* of the basic realities of life, as the individual experiences it," and may move the reader, through humor or revulsion, to decidedly antierotic responses; or it may move him to erotic responses, just as the sensitive reader may respond to a sad scene by crying, or to a humorous one by laughing. [33] The distinguishing features of pornographic works include a succession of increasingly stimulating scenes, heavy emphasis on the physiological sexual responses of the participants, and on deviant forms of sexuality, extremely sadistic scenes in which the victims respond passively or with positive enjoyment to the pain inflicted upon them (sadomasochism), gross exaggeration of the sexual powers and desires of the participants, and complete lack of realism in the portrayal of the characters.

This elaborate definition may be useful to psychologists, but is unlikely to be helpful to anyone concerned with the formulation of public policy or the enforcement of laws designed to prevent the spread of pornographic literature. To distinguish pornography from erotic realism on the basis of the "truthfulness" of the latter, for example, is to suppose that judges have a special insight into the truth and that in such matters as sex, there is a meaningful criterion by means of which truth can be distinguished from fantasy. In any case, much literature does not clearly fall into either of these categories, but lies somewhere in between.

Another psychologist, George Elliott, says that pornography "offends the sense of separateness, of individuality, of privacy; it intrudes upon the rights of others." [34] Certain barriers that people have around themselves are broken down by pornographic works. Such barriers serve an important function, and intruding upon them may not be in the interest of those who are affected. Beyond being an intrusion upon one's privacy, obscenity degrades and debases the subjects of which it treats and those who partake of it.

In one of the most thoughtful analyses of recent years, Harry M. Clor observes that "art is not primarily concerned with making us *want* something; it is primarily concerned with making us *see* something." He goes on to say that if a work promotes lust or disgust to a high degree, then it is not a work of art; for "art teaches by promoting an experience of some aspect of life and presenting that experience for contemplation and interpretation. The predominance of lust or disgust is incompatible with that detachment which is a prerequisite for the interpretation of experience. Therefore good literature cannot literally invade man's private affairs and it does not promote an obscene experience of life." Obscene literature, then, is "that literature which presents, graphically and in detail, a degrading picture of human life and invites the reader or viewer, not to contemplate that picture, but to wallow in it. . . . Obscenity is a depreciating view of intimate or physical things which is accompanied by desire or loathing." The difference between a scientific study of sadomasochism and an obscene novel that centers around sadomasochism consists in the fact that the readers of the latter would not be invited "to reflect upon the nature of degrading human experiences, but, simply, to have such experiences." It does not maintain the intellectual or artistic "distance" that is necessary to enable the reader to maintain his identity, to keep himself separate from the action of the novel.

"Art" is here being used in an evaluative sense. Clor does not analyze the difference between "contemplative" art and graphic and detailed pictures that lead to "wallowing" rather than to contemplation. There are experiences that may be provoked by the plastic arts or by literature that may "invade one's private affairs" and lead to a kind of "wallowing" rather than to "contemplation," but which no one would call obscene. Consider a deeply moving description of a mystical religious experience, one that describes the experience in great detail, and is so powerful and magnetic in its effect that it closes the gap between the reader and itself, engulfing him in the experience portrayed in the book, transporting him outside himself, and conveying a feeling of contempt or loathing for physical things. Such a work would not invite the reader to reflect upon the nature of mystical religious experiences, but would induce such experiences in him.

Yet it is doubtful whether it would be called obscene on that account, and it is not clear that such a work would for these reasons alone be classed as nonart. Some of the best art (or works that are widely regarded as superb art) was originally designed for just such purposes: to induce certain feelings and passions in those who were exposed to them, and not necessarily to lead them to contemplation. It is likely that Clor would not regard them as obscene, even though they correspond in every respect to the conditions laid down in his definition of "obscenity."

Clor concedes that his definition is "not wholly free of vagueness or ambiguity," and that it is incapable of serving alone as a means of distinguishing works of art that deal with the obscene from obscene works. But its most distinguishing feature is its emphasis upon the *dehumanization*, the *depersonalization* that takes place in the obscene work. Pornography is "sexual obscenity in which the debasement of the human element is heavily accentuated, is depicted in great physiological detail, and is carried very far toward its utmost logical conclusion." [35]

Clor claims that his definition does a great deal to clarify what previous definitions had left unclear. Whereas earlier definitions relied upon "prurient interest," which might be anything from mild curiosity to overwhelming sexual arousal, Clor's definition makes it clear that the obscene is that which is characterized by "sexual passion in the absence of love or affection, . . . *depersonalized* sexual desire." This, he says, is what the ordinary man means when he speaks of prurience or lust—not sexual relations in marriage, or in a relationship that can be broadly defined as love, or in a situation in which the participants are concerned with one another as human beings. What the law denounces (or should denounce), he says, is not mere sexual arousal or desire as such, but "impersonal lust," in which human qualities are "stripped away and a person becomes an instrument existing solely for the pleasure or manipulation of others." [36] Clor's assumption that sexual relations between persons who are married to one another may not be lustful and deficient in the quality of love is false. Some women's groups, aware of this fact, have recently been demanding legal protection against sexual assaults by their husbands that they consider to be lustful, immoral, and unwanted.

Clor claims that earlier definitions, such as that of the American Law Institute, have confined their attention to "a shameful or morbid interest in nudity, sex, or excretion." But there are other kinds of obscenity as well, including a morbid interest in brutality, death, and the human body. A more elaborate definition, then, is the following:

> An obscene book, story, magazine, motion picture, or play is one that tends predominantly to:
>
> 1. Arouse lust or appeal to prurient interest.
> 2. Arouse sexual passion in connection with scenes of extreme violence, cruelty, or brutality.
> 3. Visually portray in detail, or graphically describe in lurid detail, the violent physical destruction, torture, or dismemberment of a human

being, provided this is done to exploit morbid or shameful interest in these matters and not for genuine scientific, educational, or artistic purposes.

4. Visually portray, or graphically describe, in lurid physical detail, the death or the dead body of a human being, provided this is done to exploit morbid or shameful interest in these matters and not for genuine scientific, educational, or artistic purposes.[37]

Though this is one of the clearest definitions of obscenity to have been produced thus far, it suffers from a number of serious difficulties. How, for example, is one to determine whether a given book, story, or other article tends to do any of these things *predominantly?* Is a work to be judged by the subject matter of most of its pages? By two thirds, or three quarters of them? Or is it to be judged by the effect it has in society as a whole? Does *predominant* refer to the book or to the people who read it? If it is the latter, how is one to make such a judgment in a particular case?

How is one to distinguish those works that are designed to exploit persons who have a morbid and shameful interest in sex, violence, death, and the human body from those who have a "genuine" scientific, educational, or artistic purpose? Who shall judge whether a given work's purpose is genuinely artistic? Shall the judges be drawn from the art community, from among those who are presumably conversant with the deeper purposes of artists and writers? Will rival schools of art be represented on the jury, including the school of the defendant himself (assuming he belongs to one)? Or shall the judges be drawn from the general community, a community that may have little or no knowledge or appreciation of the kind of work on which judgment is to be rendered? Scientists would presumably be in a better position to determine whether a given work had "genuine" scientific interest or not, because a certain degree of expertise might be helpful in making such a determination. By the same token, artists, critics, and perhaps collectors and students of art might be in a better position than the ordinary layman to judge whether a work has "genuine artistic purpose." But there is always the danger that by submitting works to a jury, whether the jury be chosen from laymen or from professionals, one may perpetuate established and conventional values and techniques and stifle daring innovativeness. For a group of scientists might well conclude that a work that proceeds along radically novel lines has no genuine scientific interest. The word *genuine* is the villain here. Before Clor's definition becomes embodied in the law, some clear and precise guidelines must be developed on the manner in which *genuine* scientific, educational, and artistic works are to be distinguished from those that are *not* genuine.

Finally, how can one distinguish those works that are predominantly devoted to "impersonal" or "degrading" or "dehumanizing" lust from those that are not? Even if such a distinction can be made, on what grounds does society presume to prevent those who get their thrills from reading such materials from doing so? It is said that works that fall within this definition of obscene have evil consequences, either for the individual who reads them or for society as a whole. But this is at least in part a statement of fact that must be proved by scientific means before it may be used to restrict the right of parts of the public to have access to works from which they derive much pleasure.

Some people maintain that everyone should have only the best pleasures. But the best pleasures turn out to be those pleasures that the people with the best taste enjoy. And to most people, those who have the best taste always turn out to be those who agree with *them*. But it is not clear why any one person or any one group in society should impose his or its preferences upon any other group. Some people like scotch, and others prefer beer. Some people like Mickey Spillane and others prefer Jane Austen. It is not clear that there is any principle, moral or otherwise, that would give the lovers of one beverage or one kind of literature the right to deprive lovers of the other of that which they enjoy. If fans of Mickey Spillane were to write treatises on the merits of various types of literature, they could undoubtedly come up with some excellent reasons for banning Jane Austen.

THE EFFECTS OF OBSCENITY

If no satisfactory definition of *obscenity* has thus far been developed, it cannot be for lack of effort. When the nine justices on a single court cannot arrive at a single definition that they can work with, but consistently come up with as many as seven or eight separate views on the meaning of the term in a given case, it is obvious that the problem is not only a difficult one, but that it has serious practical consequences. For the student who is interested in studying the effects of obscene materials, such a state of affairs must be most disconcerting; for if no definition of the key term can be found, then it is impossible to inquire meaningfully into the effects of obscene materials, because there is no way to distinguish such materials from those that are not obscene.

Until quite recently no sustained scientific research had been done in this area. But the Commission on Obscenity and Pornography, armed with a $2 million appropriation from Congress, was able to initiate a number of studies that have started to provide some answers to some of the most troublesome questions.

Instead of attempting to define *obscenity*, the commission chose to discuss "erotic materials," without passing moral or legal judgment on them. The problem, then, was to determine what effects erotic materials of various sorts have upon people in a variety of contexts.

Some of the research findings can be dismissed as trivial. Surveys, for example, revealed that at least half the population believes that explicit sexual materials provide information about sex, and that more than half of all police chiefs believe that obscene materials contribute to juvenile delinquency. They have also found that erotic materials cause sexual arousal in many males and females and that females are not as aroused by material designed to arouse male homosexuals as they are by material depicting heterosexual conduct.

Other findings, however, are more important for our purposes. The commission's studies concluded that a significant number of persons increased their masturbatory activity after exposure to erotic materials. Persons who reported increased rates of intercourse were generally those who were already experienced and had established sexual partners. In general, the commission concluded, any such increase in sexual activity tended to be temporary and was not significantly different from the kind of sexual behavior in which the individual had engaged prior to his or her exposure to the erotic materials. Erotic dreams, sexual fantasies, and conversation about sexual matters all tended to increase after exposure to such materials. Some married couples reported more agreeable relations and greater willingness to discuss sexual matters after such exposure than before.

One might have expected delinquent youth to have more and earlier exposure to erotic materials than nondelinquent youth. Both of these expectations turn out to be ill founded, according to the commission. Both delinquent and nondelinquent youth have wide exposure to such materials.

According to the commission's report, there is no statistical correlation between sex crimes and exposure to erotic materials. Although the United States has experienced a significant increase in arrests for rape during the past decade of relaxed restrictions on erotic material, arrests for juvenile sex crimes decreased during the same period. In Denmark there was a notable decrease in sex crimes after Danish law was changed to permit virtually unrestricted access to erotic materials.

The commission's overall conclusion was that "empirical research designed to clarify the question has found no evidence to date that exposure to explicit sexual materials plays a significant role in the causation of delinquent or criminal behavior among youth or adults. The commission cannot conclude that exposure to erotic materials is a factor in the causation of sex crime or sex delinquency." [38]

Other authorities had earlier come to much the same conclusion, but without the benefit of the extensive studies sponsored by the commission.

This is not the place for a detailed summary or evaluation of the commission's report or the data on which it based its findings. It is appropriate to note, however, that several members of the commission protested its findings, and wrote a minority report that contained the following major disagreements with it: A number of studies available to the commission were ignored or underrated by it in its final report. Thus, one research team found that there was a definite correlation between juvenile exposure to pornography and precocious heterosexual and deviant sexual behavior. Another study found that there was a direct relation between the frequency with which adolescents saw movies depicting sexual intercourse and the extent to which the adolescents themselves engaged in premarital sexual intercourse. In a third study it was found that "the rapists were the group reporting the highest 'excitation to masturbation' rates by pornography both in the adult (80%) as well as teen (90%) years." The dissenters add, "Considering the crime they were imprisoned for, this suggests that pornography (with accompanying masturbation) did not serve adequately as a catharsis [as some researchers have suggested it might], prevent a sex crime, or 'keep them off the streets.'" The same study reported that 80% of prisoners who had had experience with erotica reported that they "wished to try the act" they had witnessed in the erotic films they had seen, and when asked whether they *had* followed through, between 30 and 38% replied that they had. In still another study, 39% of sex offenders reported that "pornography had something to do with their committing the offense" of which they were convicted.[39]

In addition, the minority accused the majority of being biased, of suppressing evidence, of misinterpreting statistics and conclusions of researchers, and of misrepresentation.

No attempt will be made here to analyze these findings. However, a number of venerable fallacies may have been perpetrated in them. One, known by its Latin description, *post hoc ergo propter hoc*, consists of supposing that because one phenomenon follows another, the later phenomenon must be caused by the earlier one. But this is not necessarily the case. Nor is the fact that one phenomenon regularly accompanies another evidence that the one is necessarily the cause of, or caused by, the other. They may both be caused by some unknown third factor. Thus, in the cases before us, both the delinquent behavior and the reading of erotica may have been caused by some other factors in the lives of the adolescents who were surveyed; there is no way, with the information presently available, to show that the erotic material caused the delinquent behavior. Nor is the fact that some sex criminals report that they read pornographic books or saw pornographic films prior to the commission of their crimes an unequivocal indication that the pornography contributed to their criminal behavior. For one thing, they may have been seeking some excuse for their behavior or a scapegoat on whom to fasten the guilt. It would be useful if a rapist could claim that he is really not to blame for his crime. The man who should be in jail, he might claim, is the one who published the obscene book he read just before he raped his victim, or the governor who signed the liberalized censorship law, or the Supreme Court Justice who removed the ban on it. But this will not do at all, because so many persons read the same pornographic works and do not commit sex crimes.

This is not to say that there is *no* causal connection between erotic literature and sexual behavior. It is to suggest merely that the answers are not in yet, and that even such research as is presently available must be approached with considerable caution.

Thus far, one must conclude that available evidence does not support the thesis that erotic materials have socially undesirable effects upon the people who are exposed to them, but it does not support the thesis that such materials do *not* have such effects either.

THE CASE AGAINST CENSORSHIP

The extreme difficulty—some would say the impossibility—of defining *obscenity* and related terms, and the lack of reliable evidence for the harmful effects that some people believe follow from the free distribution of sexually explicit materials, together with liberal principles that support freedom of expression and the right of individuals to choose their own lifestyles and their own forms of entertainment, so long as they harm no one else in the process, have led many persons to oppose any form of censorship, even of materials that they personally find most offensive.

Many Americans have an innate distrust of government. Since the Revolution, they have hedged government about with manifold restrictions, with "checks and balances," that restrain its power and jealously guard the liberties of the people. In this respect, it has been said, they differ from Canadians and British subjects, who generally trust and respect their governments and who are not as particular as Americans about securing written guarantees against governmental interference in 'their affairs. The long experience of mankind with censorship has convinced many people of the danger of permitting government agents to sit in judgment over what the people may or may not be permitted to read. Though Clor's comments on the social importance of certain moral standards, and on the vital need of every society to protect itself against the moral depravity into which its people may fall, are true, censorship may not be the best way of assuring a society of the maintenance of high moral standards. The libertarians have proceeded under the generally optimistic assumption that most men are fairly sensible, and given the choice, will usually choose what is best for them in the long run. They have also proceeded under the generally pessimistic assumption that given sufficient power, most governments will misuse it to perpetuate themselves and to constrict the liberties available to the citizenry. It may be more desirable, therefore, to rely upon education and upon positive measures to inform the public with a sense of responsibility, rather than upon the police power of the state.

Clor's prediction that censorship would have inhibiting effects upon publishers and writers is borne out by the complaints of Tolstoy and Solzhenitsyn, but there is a notable difference in emphasis. Clor looks upon this inhibiting effect as a positive contribution to public morality. Tolstoy and Solzhenitsyn, as well as many other writers, have argued that it is an oppressive force that stops up their energies and wastes away their most creative years. What is no loss at all to one man is an irretrievable loss of something that might have been of great value to another.

Nor is it any help to permit the legislatures or the courts to pronounce on the "moral decision of the community," for even if they can assess what that vague and ill-defined decision might be, there is some reason to wonder whether it ought to be imposed upon *all* members of the community, whether they share the community's standards or not. No tyranny is more oppressive than that of the majority upon the minority. It was recognition of that fact, and of the right of the minority to live by its lights, that impelled the framers of the United States Constitution to incorporate the Bill of Rights into it, and to write the First Amendment in the categorical and absolute terms emphasized by Justice Black.

When Clor pronounces his readiness to permit "classics" and "recognized" works of art and literature to be exempt from the general censorship regulations that he advocates, he forgets that there is seldom any unanimity, even in the academic community, as to whether a given work is a "classic" or not. The censor would thus be burdened not only with weighing the proportions of obscene and redeeming materials in a given work, but also with determining whether it is a classic or not. Because many new works are not recognized as "classics" until some years after their publication, Clor's censor would be obliged to predict which works might be considered classics in the future—an impossible task—in order to avoid depriving the world of them.

It is altogether possible that some persons are triggered into the performance of unlawful acts by the materials they read and the films they see. Those who claim that some literature is socially beneficial because it inspires people to do what is good and right and just and because it helps to create in them those qualities that are most salutory for the social good appear to be right. It would be absurd, then, to deny that other forms of literature might have precisely the opposite effects, at least upon some people, particularly if they expose themselves to a steady diet of such publications and films. But libertarians have always contended, with considerable cogency, that those who are "normal and strong" should not be denied their rights and liberties because of potential harm to those who are "abnormal and weak." Nor should adults be denied the right to select their own forms of entertainment on the ground that such entertainments are likely to harm young and immature persons. Most telling of all, perhaps, is the argument that once they are given the power to determine what people may read and what they may not, censors tend to apply principles and standards that impinge upon the rights of all, and to destroy or inhibit the creation of potentially important and beneficial works, as demonstrated by the lists of books and films that have been censored in the United States, with its liberal traditions.

Van den Haag's claim that those who defend the right of "pornographers" to write and publish their materials and of the public to purchase and read them would change their tune if the materials in question were anti-black or anti-Semitic is false. Mill's argument that even false claims ought to be heard, because they too may be helpful in establishing the truth or in helping to remind people of important truths that they might otherwise tend to overlook or take for granted is one to which many opponents of censorship subscribe.

Gastil's comparison of the community that is inundated with obscene literature to the town square the beauty of which is destroyed by trash and garbage is attractive but fallacious, for however offensive obscene literature and films may be to some members of a community, they are not in themselves destructive of the community. As Feinberg pointed out, no one has to open a book that he considers to be offensive, and if he does open it and, upon commencing to read it, finds it offensive, he has the option of laying it aside. If he owns the book, he may burn it if he so desires. He may turn away from theaters showing sexually explicit films, or films that depict violence, and if he enters such theaters and finds the film offensive, he may leave. In short, he may avoid being offended by simply not opening the books or entering the theaters. This is not true of the residents around the littered square.

It is true, however, that adult bookstores and triple-X theaters attract concentrations of persons, and sometimes other sex-oriented businesses, that may destroy the character of a neighborhood. The proliferation of such establishments in a given area *can* be extremely offensive to those who live within it or who work or shop there, and who cannot avoid them without great inconvenience. In this respect, the problem can become analogous to that of the littered town square. And the solutions may be comparable. First, people in the area might be informed about the problem and its solutions. (In the one case, they may be urged to avoid littering the square, and in the other, to boycott the offending establishments.) Also, appropriate zoning ordinances may be passed, limiting such establishments to certain areas or limiting the number that may be concentrated in a given area.

Freedom of speech and the press does not necessarily include the freedom to do whatever one chooses before an audience composed of random members of the public. Bearbaiting, cockfighting, and the like are unlawful for good reasons. Whether the public display of the dying is contrary to any statute, it undoubtedly would be made so if anyone exploited the public taste for such a gruesome spectacle. The libertarian position on freedom of speech and press does not entail the mindless assumption that *any* form of expression or *any* public display must be regarded as legitimate.

The recent surge in the production and sale of kiddie porn, exploiting children, has raised new concerns. No libertarian has come out in defense of the exploitation of children for such purposes. But it must be remembered that it is not and never has been a criminal offense to publish accounts of, or photographs of, unlawful behavior. One need not be an advocate of the murder of criminal suspects to defend the right of magazines and television stations to display photographs of Jack Ruby's shooting of Lee Harvey

Oswald in Dallas a few days after President Kennedy's assassination. Similarly, although the publication and sale of kiddie porn is morally reprehensible, particularly since the publications could not exist were it not for the unlawful and immoral corruption and exploitation of the children whose photographs appear in those publications, the right of persons to purchase those publications should not be subject to governmental interference. However, those publications might be used as evidence in the prosecution of those responsible for the corruption of the minors whose photographs appear in them.

SOLUTIONS TO THE PROBLEM

Proposed solutions to the problem of obscenity and pornography are many and varied. Some groups, particularly some church groups, favor strict censorship laws. Some of these groups advocate the removal of all "obscene" books from bookstores, drugstores, and all other places where they might be sold; from libraries; and in some instances even from private collections. They urge legislatures to impose harsh penalties upon the publishers and purveyors of what they consider to be obscene materials. When they have the power to do so, they drive men out of business in order to demonstrate the wickedness of pandering to the public taste for the sensational and to show how risky it can be for a businessman not to accept *their* guidelines and *their* judgment in determining what he may sell or exhibit. A theater owner in upper New York State, during the summer resort season, exhibited a film of which some townspeople disapproved. He refused to bow to a local clergyman's insistence that he stop displaying the offending film, because there was great box office demand for it and because he was in principle opposed to permitting any group to become unofficial censors for his community. When the summer season was over, the protectors of public morals organized a boycott of the theater (though it was then displaying innocuous films) and eventually forced its owner to close its doors and to move out of town.

While they were on the Court, Justices Douglas and Black opposed *any* interference with the right of free speech or free press. Justice Black put his position succinctly as follows:

> Certainly the First Amendment's language leaves no room for inference that abridgements of speech and press can be made just because they are slight. That Amendment provides, in simple words, that "Congress shall make no law . . . abridging the freedom of speech, or of the press." I read "no law . . . abridging" to mean *no law abridging*. The First Amendment, which is the supreme law of the land, has thus fixed its own value on freedom of speech and press by putting these freedoms wholly "beyond the reach" of *federal* power to abridge.[40]

He went on to explain that under the court's interpretation of the Four-teenth Amendment, the protections of the First Amendment extend to the states as well, so that *no* governmental power in the United States might abridge the rights to free speech and free press in any way whatever—except, presumably, where there is a "clear and present danger."

Since the *Miller* decision, the Court has opened the way to a multitude of prosecutions under previously existing laws, and state legislatures have been encouraged to enact new legislation designed to protect the public against the harm that pornographic literature, films, and other displays presumably might cause. The *Miller* decision represented the personal feel-ings of repugnance of the Justices who made up the majority and *was* inconsistent with the clear and unambiguous language of the First Amend-ment. Although there may be no immediate danger of the hands of the censors reaching out to proscribe what many would consider to be good literature, the historical evidence indicates quite clearly that as censors become more secure, their views of what is bad become ever broader. However revolting the "porn" may be to those who do not purchase or peruse it, it is presumptuous, in a free society, for those in power to prevent others from indulging their own tastes, so long as they harm no one else in the process.

If one supposes that such books and films are indeed harmful to those who read or view them, it may be appropriate to ask whether members of the vice squads in cities that have been afflicted with adult bookstores and triple-X movie theaters have been gravely injured by the books they have read and the films they have had to view in order to determine whether they *were* pornographic and therefore subject to seizure and prosecution. Because the judges who try obscenity cases must read the books and view the films that are on trial, it is reasonable to inquire whether, and to what degree, they have been harmed by those experiences. The assumption seems to be that police and judges are immune to any baleful influences such materials might exert upon those who pay to read or view them.

It is also worth noting that there are few, if any, reports of anyone being molested during the showing of sexually explicit films in theaters, and that although the policemen, the judges, and the jurors who must view such films are as likely to be sexually aroused as paying patrons, they are not induced by their arousal to harm anyone.

The only people in the United States who are *compelled* to watch triple-X films are the judges and jurors who must pass upon their obscenity. All the others are free either to see them or to refrain from doing so. The assumption that persons who view such films are likely to be harmed by them must not be accepted by the courts, for if it was, they would surely not permit jurors to view them, any more than they are permitted to shoot heroin during a drug trial.

When a jury determines that a particular item is obscene, based upon its judgment of the standards of the community from which it is drawn, that jury sets the standard for the rest of the nation as well, because the effect is to deter its distribution, display, and sale in other parts of the country for fear of prosecution there. In that respect, obscenity trials differ from almost any other. In the others, the jury is empowered to do no more than to determine the guilt or innocence of only one person, whereas in obscenity cases, it sets a standard for an entire nation.

That a jury in Cincinatti or in Omaha should be empowered to dictate what the people of New York or San Francisco or Des Moines should be permitted to read is repugnant to the spirit and the letter of the First Amendment. It is bound to have a chilling effect upon the production and dissemination of the kinds of products that district attorneys are likely to prosecute and juries are likely to condemn. The immediate victims of such prosecutions are likely to be the Larry Flynts and the Harry Rheems's, but the process will inexorably lead to the prosecution of future James Joyces, Erskine Caldwells, and Walt Whitmans.

The most reasonable solution, in practical terms, is that which was proposed by the Obscenity Commission. It has the virtue of protecting freedom of expression but offering those who choose to avoid exposure to erotic materials protection against such exposure.

THE RECOMMENDATIONS OF THE COMMISSION ON OBSCENITY

The Commission on Obscenity and Pornography made the following recommendations:

1. *All statutes prohibiting the sale, exhibition, or distribution of erotic materials to consenting adults should be repealed.* This recommendation was based upon the commission's conviction that there is no evidence that exposure to such materials plays a significant role in the causation of social or individual harms; that they are a source of entertainment for many adults; that they sometimes have a salutary effect on married couples; that key terms (*obscenity, salacious, prurient, community standards, patently offensive*) are indefinable; that laws against erotic materials are largely unenforceable and are not consistent with the spirit or the letter of the Constitution's prohibition on interference with free speech and free press; that the trade in such materials is relatively small in any event; that there is no evidence to support the view that such literature has a deleterious effect upon the moral climate of the nation as a whole or upon the morality of individual citizens.

2. *The commercial distribution of explicit sexual material to young persons should be regulated by law.* This includes the sale, lease, commercial exhibition, or display of such materials in places to which young persons have

access. Prohibited materials are defined as those which are "made up in whole or in dominant part of depictions of human sexual intercourse, masturbation, sodomy . . . [etc.]; provided, however, that works of art or of anthropological significance shall not be deemed to be within the foregoing definition."

The commission justified this recommendation on the following grounds: There is even less information available on the effects of erotic materials upon children than there is on their effects upon adults, for there are strong ethical reasons for not subjecting children to experimentation in these areas. Further, there is widespread agreement that children should not be exposed to such materials, and the commission felt that parents should be free to make their own conclusions regarding the propriety of exposing their children to them. In drawing up its recommendations, the commission defined the forbidden materials as explicitly as possible. But the commission concluded that such definition is impossible insofar as textual materials are concerned. The commission therefore confined its recommendations to pictorial representations only, for without a clear definition, there was some concern that booksellers and others would be put in needless jeopardy and that the distribution of books and magazines would be endangered.

3. *State and local legislation prohibiting public displays of sexually explicit pictorial materials should be enacted, and the post office should be authorized to compile and keep lists of persons who do not wish to receive certain materials and to prohibit mailers of unsolicited advertisements of such materials from sending their advertisements to persons on those lists.* Persons who do not wish to be subjected to such displays and who do not want to receive through the mails unsolicited materials that they consider to be offensive should be protected against them. The right of free speech and free press does not include the right to subject unwilling persons to such utterances, displays, or publications.[41]

These proposals (not accepted by a dissenting minority of the commission) recognize some of the problems considered throughout this discussion: the problem of defining obscenity, the conflict between the alleged right of the individual to set his own moral and literary standards and the supposed right of the government to regulate public morals; the important difference between the mature adult and the immature child or adolescent, so far as the law is concerned (that is, the law's duty—or right, if you will—to protect the parent's control over his child's environment and his moral, intellectual, and social development); and the right of the public to be protected from offensive public displays and from the intrusion of what they may consider to be offensive materials into the privacy of their homes.

In keeping with their commitment to make recommendations on the basis of scientific findings, they proposed what seem to many observers to be excessively permissive legislation. Because, in the commission's view, there is no convincing evidence that erotic materials harm either individuals or society, there is no justification for restricting their distribution, except to minors, particularly very young minors, whose rights in this area, as in others, ought to be subordinated to the right of their parents to determine what they will and will not be exposed to during their formative years.

The tension that has developed between those who have adopted a libertarian stance on this issue and those who favor the imposition of more rigid regulation of erotic or violent materials is not likely to slacken in the near future, for even when there is agreement on the facts, there remains a persistent disagreement in attitude. Such attitudinal disagreements are not ordinarily dispelled by any amount of research or by any scientific findings, no matter how thorough they may be. But in the end it seems to come down to a fundamental question of principle: whether the principle of free choice, even for those who appear to be misguided, or the principle of paternalism, under which those in power will attempt to protect the general population, will prevail. In essence, the question resolves itself as follows: Will adult citizens of a democratic state be treated as children who are considered by their guardians to be too immature, too lacking in judgment, to make their own decisions; or will they be treated as free men and women, sovereigns in their own country and over their own lives, capable of making their own choices, for good or for ill.

APPENDIX

It would be futile to attempt to list all of the books that have been the subject of obscenity litigation in the United States. The following is merely intended to offer a sampling of those that have been banned by the Post Office or by Customs agents, or brought before the courts on obscenity charges, and have also received some critical and scholarly acclaim.

Aristophanes, *Lysistrata.*
Apuleius, *The Golden Ass.*
Ovid, *The Art of Love.*
Boccaccio, *The Decameron.*
Balzac, *Droll Stories.*
Defoe, *Moll Flanders* and *Roxana.*
Flaubert, *The Temptation of St. Anthony.*
The Arabian Nights.
Rabelais, *Works.*
Rousseau, *Confessions.*
Tolstoy, *Kreutzer Sonata.*
George Bernard Shaw, *Mrs. Warren's Profession.*
James Joyce, *Ulysses.*
D. H. Lawrence, *Lady Chatterley's Lover.*

Theodore Dreiser, *An American Tragedy.*
Erskine Caldwell, *God's Little Acre* and *Tobacco Road.*
Henry Miller, *Tropic of Cancer* and *Tropic of Capricorn.*
Eugene O'Neill, *The Hairy Ape* and *Desire Under the Elms.*
William Faulkner, *Sanctuary.*
James T. Farrell, *Young Lonigan.*
Sinclair Lewis, *Elmer Gantry.*
John Dos Passos, *Manhattan Transfer.*
Sherwood Anderson, *Dark Laughter.*
Ernest Hemingway, *The Sun Also Rises.*
Walt Whitman, *Leaves of Grass.*

Part Two
Criminal Punishment

Part One examined society's attitudes toward those whose behavior is not socially acceptable but does not demonstrably result in harm to anyone except the person or persons who participate in such activities. The thrust of the argument was that it is reasonable to expect the law to maintain a hands-off attitude concerning such behavior. For a great many reasons, criminal sanctions are out of place. In some instances, the law applies a kind of civil penalty and maintains a punitive approach that is both archaic and incompatible with the ideas of a free and democratic society. In general, the conclusion was that in the area of private morality, the machinery of the state ought not to be permitted to interfere.

To suppose that the same conclusion would follow from application of the principles discussed in Part One to criminal behavior that is demonstrably harmful to others would be fallacious. Nothing in the preceding chapters would justify the conclusion that in a free society all things must be permitted. Nor has there been the slightest hint of any principle that would warrant the conclusion that the punishment of criminals, as such, is wrong, or evil, or repressive, or that it is somehow inconsistent with the ideals of democracy and freedom. When the law condemns a form of behavior just because many people consider it to be evil, such legal condemnation and the penalties that follow upon it constitute an unnecessary and improper invasion of the liberties of the citizen who chooses to deviate from the norm. Punishing such persons is unjust because the law ought not to interfere with the citizen's right to choose whether to behave in a manner that is considered respectable, proper, or moral by the community as a whole, or to follow his own "unrespectable," "improper," or "immoral" desires. But if an individual's behavior is both immoral by community standards and harmful to others, the question as to whether he ought to be subjected to criminal sanctions is on an altogether different footing. We turn now to the question of whether penalties ought to be exacted of such persons, and, if the answer to that question is affirmative, to the problem of deciding what penalties are appropriate and ought to be enforced.

6

The Concept of Punishment

THE RIGHTS OF THE ACCUSED

When a man is brought into court and is accused of having committed a grave offense against society, all the machinery of the state is set into motion to bring him to justice. The public prosecutor or the district attorney often has a veritable army at his disposal, all trained to ferret out information that may be relevant to the crime, all paid by the state to spend their working hours questioning witnesses, examining evidence, and building a case that will presumably lead to conviction of the accused. The latter, on the other hand, usually has very limited means at his disposal. More often than not, a defendant is fortunate if he has enough assets to pay the fees of an attorney. Few men can hire teams of private investigators who can devote their time, skills, and resources exclusively to the search for evidence and the building of a defense. No private citizen can match the modern state when the latter brings all its forces into play after he has been accused of having violated the law.

It is because of the inherent inequality of the contest that common-law countries have built into their laws special protections for the citizen who is accused of a criminal offense. The accused is legally presumed to be innocent, placing the entire burden of proof upon the state. To overcome this presumption of innocence, it is not sufficient that the prosecution provide a preponderance of evidence that the accused is guilty. The prosecution must prove "beyond a reasonable doubt" that the accused is guilty. Nor is it sufficient if a majority of the jurors are convinced of the defendant's guilt. Nothing less than unanimity will do. If even one juror is not convinced of the guilt of the defendant, the court is obliged to continue to presume that he is innocent.*

As a further protection for the accused against the power of the state, the agents of the government are forbidden to exort confessions. Some countries have moved a long way from the days when the most fiendish tortures were employed to extract confessions from men and women who were suspected of wrongdoing. There is little doubt that virtually anyone can be forced, through ceaseless physical and mental torture, to confess to almost anything if he is promised relief from his agonies. Unfortunately, there is ample evidence that some totalitarian regimes, including those of most of the nations of the Communist world, nearly all of the Arab states, many Asian and African nations, and numerous Latin American regimes, are still resorting to this barbaric means of dealing with their opponents. Interested in convictions rather than in truth or justice, they use any device that will further their aims. By contrast, in the United States, the Supreme Court has in recent years extended the Fifth Amendment's protection against self-incrimination to many areas where it had traditionally been considered to be nonoperative. In the controversial case of *Escobedo* v. *Illinois* (1964), the Court broke new ground in this area and in the Sixth Amendment's guarantee of the right to counsel. The latter had originally been construed as an absolute right only in the federal courts. It was later extended to state courts, but only in capital cases. Finally, in 1963 the distinction between capital and noncapital cases was abandoned. Again, at first the right applied only to the trial. It was later extended to the arraignment and then to the preliminary hearing. At last, in *Escobedo*, it was carried to the very beginning of the police interrogation of a suspect, for, as Justice Goldberg pointed out, if confessions could be wrung from suspects at an early stage in the investigation, the formal trial would be a "very hollow thing." Quoting an earlier decision, he added, "One can imagine a cynical prosecutor saying: 'Let them have the most illustrious counsel, now. They can't escape the noose. There is nothing that counsel can do for them at trial.'" †

Thus, although the defendant in a criminal trial faces severe disabilities because of the great machinery the state may bring to bear in carrying out its investigation and prosecution, the balances are tipped in the defendant's favor by the guarantees and protections that are built into the system.

---

* A recent decision by the United States Supreme Court permits convictions by less than unanimous decisions in state courts. A similar rule has prevailed in Great Britain for some years. This trend marks an important departure from common-law tradition.

† Another landmark decision was the 1966 *Miranda* case. The decisions of the Warren court provoked a great public outcry and are now being modified by the Burger court, though the changes are not as radical as some critics of the Burger court contend.

Some people are prepared to argue that for the sake of individual security and "law and order," citizens must be prepared to sacrifice certain liberties that they had previously taken for granted. So long as you obey the law, they say, you have nothing to fear. These so-called guarantees are merely guarantees for the criminal; they protect the lawless elements in society and leave law-abiding citizens open to victimization by them.

Some of the world's most orderly societies and some of its safest streets and parks are to be found in precisely those totalitarian countries where guarantees of individual liberties are the weakest. Safety in the streets and security at home can be bought, for a time, by a citizenry that is prepared to forfeit certain rights and liberties that were considered to be fundamental during the development of the Western democracies. That price, however, is too high. The insidious process by which governments take unto themselves the liberties of their people on the ground that only thus can the security of the population be assured ultimately leads to tyranny, whose absolute power is far more fearsome than the evils that engender it. Such regimes are seldom replaced by less oppressive ones without great social upheavals and much death and destruction. In the meantime, the innocent have been deprived of their liberties because of the behavior of the guilty. In case of emergency, it is not inappropriate for government to ask the citizens of a state to give up some of their liberties. But a state of affairs that lasts for many years is not an emergency, and a people that gives up its liberties to fight crime ceases to be a free people.

Crime can be combatted in other ways. When its causes are known and are curable, their elimination will result in a diminution of the crime rate. And when it is possible to apprehend and convict the lawbreaker, punishing him may help to reduce the dangers that criminal behavior poses to the society that brings him to justice.

Although the theories propounded here have some applicability in any society, we are concerned principally with the existing social order in the United States, Great Britain, Canada, and other liberal democratic societies where it is not only possible, but in fact highly probable that any person accused of criminal activity will receive a fair trial.

At one time it was almost impossible for members of certain minority groups to receive a fair trial in certain parts of the United States. Judges and juries acted upon irrational fears and prejudices and brought about serious miscarriages of justice. But changes in the law, both by legislation and by judicial interpretation, as well as widespread changes in attitude, seem to have resulted in a significant increase in the chances of any defendant in a criminal trial receiving a hearing by a fair and impartial judge and jury who will make a conscientious effort to convict the guilty and acquit the innocent. One of the most important developments in this connection is the requirement that juries be representative of the community and that the deliberate exclusion of members of any minority group from a grand jury or a petty jury is enough to nullify such a jury's actions—that is, to warrant dismissal of a grand jury's indictment or reversal of a petty jury's conviction of a criminal defendant. Such discrimination can be established merely by demonstrating that the number of blacks, for example, who have served on juries over a period of years is grossly disproportionate to the number of blacks in the population who are eligible for jury service. The nullification of numerous jury trials was sufficient to bring about a vast increase in the number of minority group members serving on juries in all parts of the country, thus eliminating one important cause of suspicion of discrimination against defendants.[1]

In the United States, the accused has a constitutional right against self-incrimination, as well as a right to counsel. These rights have been broadly construed in recent years, so that the state's burden of proof and the protection afforded the accused make it all but impossible for prosecutors to win convictions that will stand up under appeal of anyone whose crime is not manifest—and, in some cases, even when the accused's guilt of the crime is manifest to all. Consider the following case, for example:

CASE 8. THE CHRISTIAN BURIAL SPEECH

Pamela Powers, a 10-year-old girl, went with her family to the YMCA in Des Moines to watch a wrestling tournament in which her brother was participating. When she failed to return from a trip to the washroom, an unsuccessful search was made for her and her disappearance was reported to the police.

Robert Williams, a black escapee from a mental hospital, was residing at the YMCA. Soon after the girl's disappearance, he was seen carrying some clothing and a bundle through the lobby of the building. A 14-year-old boy helped Williams open the door of the building and of Williams' car, and as Williams placed the bundle in the front seat of his car, the boy saw "two legs in it and they were skinny and white." Two days later, Williams surrendered to the police at Davenport, about 160 miles east of Des Moines. In the meantime, he had talked to an attorney in Des Moines who had advised him to surrender to the police but not to talk to anyone about the case. He was advised by the police of his rights, including his right to remain silent and his right to counsel. In the presence of police officers, he was advised by his Des Moines attorney that a police detective named Leaming would be picking him up in Davenport and returning him to Des Moines. He was also advised that he would not be mistreated or interrogated and was told not to talk to the police about Pamela Powers. He was arraigned before a judge in Davenport and again advised of his right to remain silent and of his right to be represented by an attorney. There too he conferred with an attorney who once again advised him not to say anything until he had conferred with his attorney in Des Moines.

When Detective Leaming and another officer arrived, they advised

Williams yet again of his rights. The officers were told by the Davenport attorney that they were not to interrogate Williams during the trip
to Des Moines.

Soon after they left Davenport, Leaming addressed Williams:

"I want to give you something to think about while we're traveling
down the road," he said. He then pointed out that it was the day after
Christmas, that it would be dark early, and that the weather forecasters
were predicting snow. He then went on to say, "I feel that you yourself
are the only person that knows where this little girl's body is, that you
yourself have only been there once, and if you get a snow on top of it,
you yourself may be unable to find it. And, since we will be going right
past the area on the way into Des Moines, I feel that we could stop
and locate the body, that the parents of this little girl should be entitled
to a Christian burial for the little girl who was snatched away from
them on Christmas Eve and murdered. And I feel we should stop and
locate it on the way in rather than waiting until morning and trying
to come back out after a snowstorm and possibly not being able to
find it at all."

Leaming later told Williams that he didn't want to discuss the
matter further. He simply wanted Williams to think about it. About
a hundred miles down the road, Williams asked whether the police
had found the child's shoes. He then directed them to a service station
where he said he had left her shoes, but a search for them was unsuccessful. Still later he directed them to a rest stop where he said he
had deposited the blanket. Finally, he took them to Pamela Powers'
body.

At his first-degree murder trial, Williams' attorney moved for the
suppression of all the evidence elicited from Williams during that trip,
but the judge ruled that by his actions, Williams had waived his right
to have an attorney present as he gave that information to the officers.
Williams was convicted.

The Supreme Court of the United States held that Williams' right
to counsel had been violated by Leaming's "Christian burial" speech.
"There can be no serious doubt," the Court said, "that Detective
Leaming deliberately and designedly set out to elicit information from
Williams just as surely as—and perhaps more effectively than—if he
had formally interrogated him." The Court held that Leaming's "use of
psychology" on Williams was evidence enough to refute the contention
that Williams had freely waived his right to counsel. Williams, the
Court held, had not made a "knowing and intelligent" waiver of his
rights.

Concluding that "the crime of which Williams was convicted was
senseless and brutal," the Court nevertheless determined that he was
convicted on evidence that should have been excluded because it

was obtained in violation of Williams' rights. It therefore ordered the conviction to be overturned.

In a concurring opinion, Justice Marshall cited a dissent by Justice Brandeis 50 years earlier:

> In a government of laws, existence of the government will be imperilled if it fails to observe the law scrupulously. Our Government is the potent, omnipresent teacher. For good or for ill, it teaches the whole people by its example. Crime is contagious. If the Government becomes a lawbreaker, it breeds contempt for law; it invites every man to become a law unto himself; it invites anarchy. To declare that in the administration of the criminal law the end justifies the means—to declare that the Government may commit crimes in order to secure the conviction of a private criminal—would bring terrible retribution. Against that pernicious doctrine this Court should resolutely set its face.[2]

In his dissent, Chief Justice Burger wrote:

> The result in this case ought to be intolerable in any society which purports to call itself an organized society. It continues the Court . . . on the much-criticized course of punishing the public for the mistakes and misdeeds of law enforcement officers, instead of punishing the officer directly, if in fact he is guilty of wrongdoing. It mechanically and blindly keeps reliable evidence from juries whether the claimed constitutional violation involves gross police misconduct or honest human error.[3]

He went on to suggest that the basis for the majority's ruling had to be the assumption that once a suspect has asserted his right not to talk without the assistance of an attorney, it becomes legally impossible for him to waive that right until his attorney is present. "It denigrates an individual," he said, "to a nonperson whose free will has become hostage to a lawyer so that until the lawyer consents, the suspect is deprived of any legal right or power to decide for himself that he wishes to make a disclosure."

Moreover, he went on, the purpose of the rule excluding evidence obtained through unlawful or unconstitutional conduct is precisely to deter such conduct. But in this case the police conduct was not so flagrantly objectionable as to justify the uncritical application of the rule. Williams' statements and actions were not involuntarily wrung from him by threats, brutality, or any other form of coercion. If he had confessed under threat of bodily harm or under torture, his confession would have been tainted, for it would have been unreliable as a guide to the truth. But Williams was not coerced and the child's body was an unmistakable guide to the truth of what happened. Chief Justice Burger concluded by quoting the late Justice Hugo Black, who said, in a similar case, that "it is becoming more and more difficult to gain acceptance for the proposition that punishment of the guilty is desirable, other things being equal."

Other dissenters noted that as a consequence of the decision in the case, "a mentally disturbed killer whose guilt is not in question may be released." [4]

After a new trial at which the evidence supplied by Anthony Williams was suppressed but new evidence was admitted, Williams was once again convicted of first-degree murder.

The Williams case illustrates the lengths to which courts will go to protect criminal suspects against unfair trial procedures or coercive police measures. Among other things, the defendant in a criminal trial has the right to examine the prosecution's evidence before trial; he is fully protected against self-incrimination; he possesses the right to cross-examine witnesses, to be tried before a jury, to stand innocent in the eyes of the law until proved guilty; to be represented by an attorney at every stage in the process; and to a multitude of other rights, collectively known as *due process,* that have been spelled out in court rulings over the years. This is not to say that police and courts do not occasionally violate the rights of suspects. But under the Constitution and the laws of state and federal governments, defendants in criminal trials possess a remarkable array of rights, which guarantee them a fair hearing and, for all practical purposes, assure them an opportunity to be heard once again if any of those rights is violated. The accused's initial disadvantage as against the state's formidable power and resources is outweighed by these rights and by the burden of proof beyond a reasonable doubt imposed upon the prosecutions. [5]

Carrington [6] cites numerous cases to illustrate the extraordinary lengths to which the Court has gone in favor of the accused. Some recent cases, however, have been moving in the opposite direction. For example, on February 18, 1968, Lloyd Powell was arrested for vagrancy in Henderson, Nevada. A search incident to his arrest revealed that Powell possessed a .38-caliber revolver that implicated him in a murder committed in California the previous night. The gun was introduced into evidence during his trial, and Powell was convicted of murder. His defense attorney objected that the gun should not be introduced into evidence, because it was obtained without warrant, and the statute on which Powell was arrested was unconstitutionally vague. On its way through the various appeals courts, this contention was alternately accepted and rejected.

When it reached the Supreme Court of the United States, it was considered along with a similar case, in which materials for the construction of explosive devices were discovered in a search of the home of a suspect who was accused of causing the bombing death of an Omaha police officer. Here too the defense argued that the evidence should have been excluded since the search was illegal. In these cases, the Supreme Court upheld the admissibility of the evidence. The Court's majority argued that the primary justification for the rule excluding improperly acquired evidence was the deterrence of police transgressions that violate an individual's rights under the Fourth Amendment's protection against unlawful search and seizure. The right to have such evidence excluded was *not* a constitutional right of individuals, but a court-created remedy for unlawful police behavior. The courts concerned have the right, the Court said, to determine in each case whether use of the exclusionary rule in a given case will further the goal of deterring such unlawful behavior on the part of the police.[7]

Although no one would presume to insist that any government or any legal system is so perfect that it always avoids miscarriages of justice, it is not altogether unreasonable to conclude that ample precautions are taken to prevent such incidents from occurring in the United States and in many other Western democracies. There is some justification for the conclusion adumbrated in the dissenting opinion of Chief Justice Burger that the rights of defendants are often given so much weight as to deprive the victims and the general public of their due and of the protection that the law is at least partly designed to afford them. Justice, after all, is always double-edged; it is possible for either side to be denied its just deserts. We may refer once again to Justice Brandeis' declarations on the importance of the government abiding by the law. It is true that the government should not break the law in order to secure the conviction of a criminal, for such official lawlessness would breed contempt for the law and invite anarchy. But the government is charged to uphold *all* the laws and to enforce them against private individuals who are contemptuous of them and of the values that they were designed to preserve. To permit lawless individuals to act as they will, preying upon the innocent and acting as if the laws did not apply to them, and spreading over them an almost impenetrable barrier of legal protections that renders successful prosecution of their crimes nearly impossible is to invite anarchy from another direction. In the long run, competing interests must be placed in balance and a decision made: Is Detective Leaming's offense against Anthony Williams' right (assuming that he *did* violate that right) so substantial that the public should be deprived of protection against the murderer of Pamela Powers? Or should the public's right to protection against murderers be paramount, so that even evidence obtained in violation of the rights of the accused may be used to establish the truth of the incident that is before the jury during his trial? Is it right to "punish the public" by excluding such evidence obtained improperly by its servants so as to deter law enforcement officials from engaging in such improper behavior in the future? Or might there be some other method of dealing with overzealous officials—one that would not jeopardize the public's right to a fair trial in which all the facts are brought forth?

Let us assume that the accused has been found guilty by a fair and conscientious jury, that the judge has been scrupulous in his insistence that the rights of the accused be respected, and that the attorneys for both the prosecution and the defense are competent, ethical men who have put forth their best efforts. (No one, after all, wants to argue for the punishment of innocent men.)

Even under these conditions, certain problems inevitably arise:

1. What is the nature of punishment, and how does it differ from other kinds of events that may happen to people, and from other kinds of things that people can do to one another?
2. What are the aims, goals, purposes, or ends of punishment?
3. What justifications can be offered for a private person, or an agent of society, deliberately inflicting harm upon another person?
4. If a man has violated one of the rules of society whose infringement ordinarily calls for punishment, what conditions, if any, ought to serve to excuse his behavior and so to free him from the odium of being punished?
5. Are there any conditions so general that they supply every person accused of a criminal violation with an excuse, the recognition of which would require of society that it abandon all programs of punishment in favor of some other form of treatment for such offenders? For example, would the theory of determinism, if it were true, be such a universal excuse for antisocial behavior? Are there grounds for saying that every person who deliberately violates a criminal statute does so because of some illness, so that he cannot be held responsible for his acts?
6. How can modern penal institutions—particularly prisons or penitentiaries—be evaluated, and how do they stand up under critical scrutiny as a means of punishing persons convicted of violating the criminal law?
7. What are the arguments in favor of the abolition of the death penalty, and what may be said against its abolition? How do these arguments stand up under critical examination?

THE NATURE OF PUNISHMENT

Every punishment may be analyzed into the following elements:

1. There are at least two persons, one who inflicts the punishment and one who is punished.
2. The person who inflicts the punishment causes a certain harm, or unwanted treatment, to occur to the person who is being punished.
3. The person who inflicts the punishment has been authorized, under a system of rules or laws, to harm the person who is punished in the particular way in which he does harm him.
4. The person who is being punished has been judged by a representative of that authority to have done what he is forbidden to do or to have failed to do what he is required to do by some rule or law to which he is subject.

5. The harm that is inflicted upon the person who is being punished is *for* the act or omission mentioned in item 4.

This analysis may be better understood if it is illustrated by an example, which may serve also to demonstrate how the analysis may be used to distinguish punishments from other kinds of undesirable events that may take place in a person's life.

Suppose that Burger takes $1,000 from Deckelbaum. The loss of $1,000 is a harm, or an unwanted event, in the life of Deckelbaum. Deckelbaum undoubtedly would agree that he would have preferred to have kept the money in his own account.

Burger's taking this money from Deckelbaum is not a *punishment* unless all the other conditions are met. If condition 3, for example, were not met, then Burger would be guilty of a crime. If Burger were a holdup man, a con man, or an extortionist, he might relieve Deckelbaum of his money but this loss would not be a punishment for Deckelbaum. But meeting condition 3 alone is not sufficient. Burger might have a perfect right to take Deckelbaum's money from him, and still not be punishing him. Burger might be a tax collector, for example. If the harm inflicted upon Deckelbaum is to count as punishment, conditions 4 and 5 must also be met. If Burger had had the right to confine Deckelbaum but Deckelbaum had not violated a rule, Burger's action against Deckelbaum would not count as punishment. Consider quarantine, for example.

Condition 4 requires that Deckelbaum be judged to have violated a rule, and 5 stipulates that the harm he suffers be *for* that violation. Neither of these alone is sufficient. If Deckelbaum is "punished" for a crime of which he has not been convicted, he is clearly not being *punished* at all. The state may decide to use him as an example to potential violators of a given regulation by pretending that he has been convicted of violating it; but this is not punishment. It is rather a form of brutality. One cannot properly *punish* a man for a crime unless one has first determined that he has in fact committed the crime for which he is being punished.

Though this is essentially a legal definition of punishment, it may be usefully applied to other forms of punishment as well. When a mother spanks her child, she ordinarily does so because she believes that he has violated some rule of the household. She first satisfies herself that he has violated the rule, and then applies the penalty she deems appropriate to the violation. Being his mother, she has a right to spank him—a right that the neighbors do not have* If she spanks the child merely to vent her anger or to assuage her personal frustrations, then her behavior is not properly punishment at all. In its most extreme forms it becomes transformed into an all too common form of aggression and brutality.

A subtle distinction must be drawn between the infliction of a harm

---

* The mother's right is legal, moral, and customary. The neighbors lack the right, in all of these senses, to punish another person's child.

and the withholding of a benefit. Withholding a benefit or a privilege is
not a punishment, though the two bear remarkable resemblances to one
another. The hurt of a boy who is not accepted on his school's football
team because he is not as well qualified as others who have applied is
very real, but his rejection is not a penalty for his failure to have the
physical prowess of his classmates. To harm a man is to take away what
he has or to deprive him of what he otherwise has a right to have or to do
or to enjoy. A fine involves depriving a man of money that he would otherwise have every right to keep. Imprisonment involves depriving him of
liberties that he would otherwise have the right to expect to enjoy. In
short, failing to qualify for a benefit is not to be confused with breaking a
rule, and depriving a person of a benefit to which he does not have a
pre-existing right is not to be confused with punishment.

When a professor or a teacher records an F for a student, one might be
tempted to suppose that this is a kind of punishment—for the student's
failure to study, perhaps, or for his failure to provide enough correct answers
to the questions on the final exam. This, too, is a false comparison, but for
significantly different reasons. To say that a professor "gives" a student his
grade is misleading. It would be more correct to say that a professor *records*
the grade that the student has earned. The student who fails to do passing
work in a course and finds an F on his record is not being punished any
more than the worker who fails to show up at his job for a week and
discovers that his pay envelope is empty.

To sum up: *A punishment is a harm inflicted by a person in a position
of authority upon another person who is judged to have violated a rule
or a law.*

THE AIMS OF PUNISHMENT

Some philosophers have confused the aims of punishment with its nature,
or have defined punishment at least partially in terms of its supposed aims.
This can be misleading, for by packing into its definition those aims of
which one approves, one can refuse to allow any behavior that has some
other aim to be called punishment, even though such behavior is quite
generally considered to be a form of punishment. Such question-begging
techniques and attempts at "persuasive definition" do not resolve questions.
They merely add to the confusion that already exists. It is best, therefore,
to consider the aims of punishment separately from its nature.

The aims or goals of punishment have traditionally fallen into the following categories:

1. Incapacitation, depriving the offender of the capacity to harm others.
2. Reform of the offender, deterring the offender from future violations, or

improving his character so that he no longer gives in to the temptation to commit such violations.
3. Deterring persons other than the offender.
4. Retribution.

PROTECTION OF SOCIETY

The ultimate justification for any punishment is the protection of innocent members of society from the depredations of dangerous persons. One of the major purposes for the establishment and maintenance of governments is the need of all persons to band together to protect one another from all forms of danger. The skin of man is soft and easily pierced. Whether the danger is from tooth or claw or from the knives, bullets, or bombs of members of his own species, man is susceptible to attack. He lacks the instincts and the built-in capacities of some of the lower animals that provide them with protection against predators that would feed upon them. Men have therefore learned to work together with other members of their own kind for their mutual protection.

The enjoyment of the earth's bounties is impossible, then, to men who live in a state of anarchy, where all men are in perpetual terror that their lives may be brought to a sudden end. In such a state, there is no true freedom, for there is no security. As Hobbes said long ago, in a state of anarchy

> there is no place for industry, because the fruit thereof is uncertain: and consequently no culture of the earth; no navigation nor use of the commodities that may be imported by sea; no commodious building; no instruments of moving and removing such things as require much force; no knowledge of the face of the earth; no account of time; no arts, no letters; no society; and, which is worst of all, continual fear and danger of violent death; and the life of man solitary, poor, nasty, brutish, and short.[8]

Some philosophers have theorized that in ages far more remote than historical records go, our ancestors must have organized themselves into bands or troops or tribes, at least partly because of their instinctive drive for self-preservation. And this same instinctual drive undoubtedly brought them to the conclusion that when a man became a threat to the community or to the individuals within it, the community or its members had the right to use all means necessary to protect themselves from him, including banishment or death, where other means failed. For by violating the primary purposes for which the group had constituted itself, he literally made himself an outlaw—that is, one who is outside the law. By repudiating the discipline of the group, either through his words or through his actions, he placed himself outside the group, and thus lost the immunities that membership in the group conferred upon him, including immunity from physical harm by other members of the group.

It is not necessary, however, to assume that a "state of nature" ever existed as a matter of historical fact. As Hobbes pointed out, the "state of nature" may be thought of as a theoretical construct: If we imagine what life would be like without the discipline imposed by law and government, we inevitably (or so he thought) find ourselves driven to the state of anarchy, or the state of nature, in which, as he described it, life is "poor, solitary, nasty, brutish, and short." Because of man's competitive nature, his desire to hold what he has successfully acquired, and his desire for honor, violence is inevitable, Hobbes said, unless people are willing to give up their right to all things in the lawless but fearsome state of nature, and to take on certain duties toward one another—duties that are spelled out in a code of laws and enforced by some form of government. Hobbes maintained that any rational person would be prepared to give up some of his rights and take on some obligations toward others in order to assure himself of the safety and security—and therefore the likelihood of enjoying a longer and happier life—of a life under a system of laws.

Various philosophers have differed with Hobbes on the details of the state of nature and on his assumptions about human nature and the impulses that govern human conduct. But there is little doubt that one of the chief justifications for legal sanctions against wrongdoers has been the assumption that people accept the discipline and the authority of government because of the protection they believe it is able to afford them against others who would deprive them of their property, their liberty, and their very lives were it not for fear of some form of reprisal by an authority powerful enough to exact some form of punishment upon them if they violated the laws promulgated by that authority.

Theories of punishment have traditionally been divided into two general categories: utilitarian and retributive. *Utilitarian* theories are so called because they find the justification for punishment primarily in the institution's supposed usefulness as a means for preventing crime * or, more generally, contributing to the sum of human happiness and reducing the amount of pain and suffering in the world. Such theories may in turn be divided into several subcategories.

1. *Incapacitation,* which holds that the function of punishment is to make it impossible for a person who is likely to commit a crime to do so.
2. *Reform or rehabilitation,* which holds that the function of punishment is to improve the character of the offender, to make him a better person, so that he will no longer commit offenses of the sort of which he was convicted, or perhaps any offenses at all, and to enable him to become a useful, contributing member of society.

---

* This discussion concentrates upon the punishment of criminals. However, similar considerations apply to most, if not all, other forms of punishment or penalties.

3. *Deterrence*, which holds that the punishment of one person tends to deter others from committing similar crimes.

The *retributive* theory, on the other hand, holds that the principal justification for punishing a man is that he *deserves* to be punished, that his past behavior renders him liable to be treated in a way that would be unacceptable, regardless of future benefits that might flow from such treatment, if he had not behaved as he did.

We will discuss each of these theories in turn. It should be remembered, however, that most theories of punishment actually incorporate one or more of the subtheories in some combination.

Incapacitation. Incapacitation, or the direct prevention of a person's committing a forbidden act, is often cited as a reason or justification for imposing punishments upon offenders. By putting a convicted felon behind bars, he is prevented from committing any more felonies—at least those he might have committed if he were out on the street. By whacking off a thief's hand, he is effectively prevented from stealing again. The murderer's electrocution or hanging provides the community with a firm guarantee that he will never again commit murder or, for that matter, any other crime. But, in fact, incapacitation is not a very good justification for punishment, and it is certainly not a necessary part of any punishment. Moreover, people can deliberately incapacitate others without intending to punish them.

If a suspect is jailed prior to his trial, the effect is to incapacitate him, that is, to make it quite impossible for him to commit any crimes against the general population. But his jailing is in no sense a part of his punishment, for he has not yet been adjudged to be guilty of the offense with which he is charged. The principal purpose of his jailing is, in fact, to assure his presence at his trial. Innocent witnesses to a crime can be jailed in order to assure their appearance in court, though there is no doubt that they have committed no offense for which they deserve to be punished. The restraint on the one is no less than that on the other. Similarly, a madman may be restrained by shackles or confinement, though such restraint is not a penalty. The physician who amputates a gangrenous arm is as effective in preventing its owner from employing it to pick pockets as the Saudi Arabian executioner is with his axe; in the one case, no penalty is involved, whereas in the other, it is. The important point to note, however, is that neither the physician nor the executioner intends by his action to incapacitate the amputee. The physician intends to heal him; the executioner, to punish him. The incapacitation is in each case an important consequence of the act performed, but it is not necessarily the reason for it. The physician is justified in amputating the arm because it is necessary to do so to save his patient's life. The executioner is justified in amputating the thief's arm (assuming for the moment that he is) because that is the penalty prescribed by Saudi law for the crime of theft.

Incapacitation is not a necessary condition for punishment, for many penalties—indeed, most, including fines, the stocks, and flogging—do not incapacitate and are not intended to do so.

If incapacitation were a justification for imposing penalties upon wrong-doers, then, unless other considerations intervened, one could justify such harsh penalties as amputations, long prison terms, and death for a great many offenses. But it is difficult to see how, from a moral point of view, that *could* be justified. The fact that a person has committed an offense, however wicked it might have been, is no guarantee that he will commit a similar offense in the future. Moreover, there may be less damaging ways of protecting society from future criminal outrages by the defendant than those that result in incapacitation. Furthermore, if a man is mutilated, placed behind bars, or executed, he is also prevented from performing acts of charity and kindness as well as any useful things he might have done if he had not been incapacitated.

About 50 years ago, Justice Oliver Wendell Holmes, Jr., wrote a Supreme Court opinion upholding the right of authorities at the Virginia State Colony for Epileptics and Feeble Minded to order the sexual sterilization of patients afflicted with hereditary forms of insanity, imbecility, and other serious mental conditions. Holmes wrote:

> We have seen more than once that the public welfare may call upon the best citizens for their lives. It would be strange if it could not call upon those who already sap the strength of the State for these lesser sacrifices, often not felt to be such by those concerned, in order to prevent our being swamped with incompetence. It is better for all the world, if instead of waiting to execute the degenerate offspring for crime, or to let them starve for their imbecility, society can prevent those who are manifestly unfit from continuing their kind. The principle that sustains compulsory vaccination is broad enough to cover cutting the Fallopian tubes. Three generations of imbeciles are enough.[9]

The woman to whom Justice Holmes referred was not being punished for anything, but her capacity to bear children was being taken from her. Compare this with a law requiring castration of a man convicted of rape. To the extent that the castration is in fact a punishment, it is *not* designed purely for the protection of other potential victims of the convicted rapist, but is for what he has already done. At the same time, however, it may render him incapable of perpetrating similar crimes in the future.

Though the end result is at least partially the same, the sterilized imbecile, the quarantined victim of smallpox, and the draftee who dies on the field of battle are significantly different from the castrated rapist, the incarcerated embezzler, and the executed murderer. In each case the subject is required to make a great sacrifice for the common good. But in the first three cases, the justification for demanding that the sacrifice be made is purely forward-looking and has nothing whatever to do with any fault on the subject's part. In the last, the justification is at least partially backward-looking: the deprivation the offender is compelled to undergo is principally justified by *what he has done*. The law that empowers the state's officials to impose these penalties upon him is forward-looking and is designed to prevent such behavior from taking place. Finally, there attaches to the punishment something that is not at all relevant to any of the other cases—namely, blame and reproof. We shall return to this subject later.

Reform and Rehabilitation. The term *reform* has at least two principal uses in the context of discussions of punishment. The first is sometimes called special deterrence, and has to do with the anticipated or hoped-for effects of punishment: by undergoing punishment for his offenses, it is hoped that the criminal (or other offender) will be deterred from committing similar offenses in the future. The criterion of success would be easily observable: the offender's adherence to the rules he had previously broken. The second application has more to do with introducing a significant change in the offender's character or personality: it is hoped that by undergoing punishment, the offender will become a more moral human being and that he will no longer commit the offenses for which he was being punished—not so much because of his fear of the pain of future punishments as because of newly acquired appreciation of the wickedness of such behavior and his determination not to indulge in immoral actions.

Some ethical thinkers have been content with the special deterrent theory, but others have insisted that punishment ought to aim at the higher goal of making over the characters of persons who have been unable to restrain themselves from giving in to the temptation to behave wrongly, or who have not learned how to distinguish right from wrong.

In defense of the special deterrent theory, it has been argued that even if a person abstains from evil actions for the "wrong" (i.e., selfish) motives, that may be the beginning of a new habit, which can pave the way for a more laudable reason for behaving rightly. Aristotle assumed that the way to develop a moral character was to establish habits that conformed to moral forms of behavior; on the other hand, corrupt behavior leads to evil habits and eventually to a corrupt mind and character. So doing the right thing for the wrong motives may not be altogether bad.

Not only the pain of the punishment, but the condemnation that accompanies it helps to impress upon the offender's mind the fact that he has done wrong, or at least what society considers to be wrong. Unfortunately, however, many wrongdoers are not particularly impressed by either the pain they are forced to endure or the ceremoniousness with which they are condemned. They believe they are martyrs whose rights are being trampled by a vicious system or by individuals whose power far exceeds their virtue. In such cases, punishment alone is likely to result either in mere deterrence of future offenses because of fear of still greater penalties or in bitterness and resentment that will lead to still greater acts of defiance, with a renewed determination to escape detection, capture, and further punishment.

Reform by punishment often goes hand in hand with efforts at rehabilitation, but the two should not be confused. Out of humane considerations, and a desire to offer the convict the opportunity to find a useful place in society once he has "paid his debt to society," modern penal institutions commonly provide educational and vocational services, as well as facilities for religious services, recreation, and so on. But, though these services may serve the same long-term goal as the penalty that is inflicted upon him, and though they may be administered by the same persons who administer the "penal" institution of which they are a part, they are not part of the penalty itself. If a prisoner had been sentenced to forty lashes, and if, after the penalty was inflicted, the authorities provided him with bandages and soothing ointments, no one would suppose that the bandages and ointments were any part of his punishment. The recreational and educational programs of penal institutions should not be considered a part of the punishment of their inmates (as indeed they are not), but a separate enterprise that may be intended to achieve the same overall results.

Of course, the incarceration of criminal offenders offers an opportunity to rehabilitate them. Those whose education has been defective may be offered an opportunity to take courses or to learn skills that they somehow missed before they entered prison. Those who are mentally disturbed or otherwise maladjusted may be given therapy appropriate to their condition. Most modern penologists have argued that the purpose of incarceration either was or ought to be the extension of such remedial efforts to those confined. As a result, many institutions have coerced their inmates, either directly or indirectly (by holding out the possibility of an earlier release), into participating in rehabilitative programs.

Although the intention was undoubtedly a good one, and although some prisoners have undoubtedly benefited from those programs, students of the subject are becoming convinced in ever-growing numbers that the programs as a whole have failed. For example, Sweden's liberal jail system was long regarded as the model for experimental prison reform. Facilities for persons serving terms of less than a year offer individual rooms similar to those in university dormitories. Inmates earn wages comparable to those of people outside. They have sauna baths, swimming pools, golf driving ranges, and skiing areas, as well as educational, psychiatric, and job-training facilities. Closed prisons (those for inmates serving longer sentences) provide for conjugal visits at least once a week and three-day furloughs every other month for all except a few inmates who are regarded as high risks. Guards are unarmed, violence is rare, and homosexual rape is almost unheard of. With all this, one would suppose that the rate of recidivism (those who return to prison after release because of renewed criminal activity) would be low. The fact is, however, that more than 70% of released prisoners return with new convictions. According to Lasse Bjorklund, who is serving his eighth or ninth term as head of the Central Organization for Prisoners, "the living conditions in our prisons are quite acceptable and certainly no deterrent to crime. You get used to institutional life. I don't think prisons can rehabilitate most people." [10] Bjorklund may have a profound insight into prison conditions and their effects upon those who are supposed to be affected by them. He appears to be saying that comfortable and pleasant prisons will not deter potential offenders. On the other hand, he is observing that as people become accustomed to institutionalization and dependent upon the institution for their physical and psychological support, they are less likely to be rehabilitated, that is, prepared to accept life outside the institution, however extensive the counselling, vocational, and recreational programs of the institution may be. In a study of asylum life, the sociologist Erving Goffman arrived at much the same conclusion. [11]

Whether prisons do or do not have the capacity to rehabilitate their inmates is, of course, a question that can best be answered by sociologists and others trained to make appropriate observations and to compile the necessary statistics. For our purposes, it is sufficient to notice that the rehabilitative function of prisons, if they do have such a function, is different from their punitive function. Although any penal system that succeeds in turning out men and women who no longer engage in criminal activities is surely superior to one that fails to do so, the *purpose* of punishment as such is *not* the rehabilitation of those who are punished. Rehabilitation is a concept that is quite distinct from punishment. Rehabilitative efforts are conceptually different from those involved in punishment and may also be different in practice. It is possible, at least, that the justifications for rehabilitation by force differ from those for punishment. That is, one may be justified in *punishing* a person who has committed an offense but *not* in compelling him to undergo such treatments as are deemed necessary for his rehabilitation, whether psychiatric or educational in nature. For committing armed robbery or forgery, a man may be sentenced to a term in prison. To sentence him to a stint of psychiatric treatments is an altogether different matter, however, and must be based upon completely different assumptions about the nature of crime and, more importantly, the rights of society over those who offend against its laws. We will discuss this later. At this point, it is sufficient to suggest merely that from a purely punitive point of view, once a guilty person has served the sentence imposed upon him, he is— and ought to be—free to go about his business, regardless of the success or failure of any rehabilitative measures that might have been applied to him, and regardless of his cooperation or lack of cooperation in efforts to rehabilitate him.

Deterrence. People learn from the experiences of others as well as from their own. Reading reports of one or two tragic automobile accidents that have resulted from heavy drinking is sufficient to persuade some people not to drive after they have been drinking, or not to drink if they intend to be driving. It is not necessary for them to go through such a tragic experience themselves. Similarly, reading a few reports of the penalties inflicted upon persons who have broken the law is enough to persuade many people not to risk incurring similar penalties for themselves.

As a general rule, as the penalty becomes more severe, people become less likely to engage in the proscribed conduct. If the fine for overtime parking is $1, many people will feel that it is worth the risk, because in the long run, it may turn out to be less expensive than utilizing private parking lots. If the fine is raised to $5, fewer people are likely to take the risk. It it is raised to $15, violators will be fewer still. As the fines go up, the propensity to risk having to pay them goes down. And as other penalties, such as jail terms, corporal punishment, and death are imposed, one may assume that people will become even more reluctant to subject themselves to the suffering and deprivation that they entail. Punishments, then, may serve not only to reform those who have violated the rules, but also to deter those who might otherwise be tempted to violate them.

Although some people are inclined to doubt the common-sense assumption that penalties deter crime, some evidence is becoming available to support the thesis. A study of drunken driving in Great Britain, for example, revealed that after the adoption of a highway safety act that empowered the police to demand a breath test of anyone they had reason to believe had been drinking, with automatic revocation of his driver's license for a year, a heavy fine, and a possible prison sentence of up to four months if his blood alcohol level exceeded a certain limit, there was a significant decline in automobile fatalities and injuries. During the first twelve months after the effective date of the act, there were 1,152 fewer fatalities, more than 11,000 fewer serious injuries, and more than 28,000 fewer slight injuries than there had been during the comparable period a year earlier. Certain variables may have affected the total picture, but there is ample evidence that the principal factor was the deterrent effect of the new law and its vigorous enforcement.[12]

On the other hand, there is ample evidence that when all fear of punishment is removed, men and women who are ordinarily law-abiding citizens may become lawless and violent. One of the best examples of the extent to which such a situation can go occurred in Montreal in the fall of 1969, when the police went on strike. The most elementary traffic regulations were violated by persons who seemed to enjoy driving through red lights, secure in the knowledge that there was no policeman to write a ticket for the violation. Bank robbers, who ordinarily work swiftly and efficiently, took their time—in at least one instance stopping at the bank's water fountain for a drink on the way out. The Montreal police strike forced all the banks in the city to close for lack of security. Aggrieved taxi drivers converged on the headquarters of a limousine service that had a monopoly on airport service, set fire to the garage, and threw gasoline bombs at vehicles owned by the company. In the gunfights that ensued, many people were shot, one of them fatally. Looters and holdup men roamed the streets at will, smashing windows and removing merchandise. Along a stretch of 21 blocks, shops on one street alone suffered the loss of $300,000 worth of plate glass windows.

Bombs were tossed into shops, residences, and restaurants owned by people the bombers disliked. An immigrant psychologist who had lived through Hitler's death camps heard someone attempting to jimmy his bedroom door. He fired at the door three times, opened the door, and found the body of a man who was later revealed to be a habitual burglar. The psychologist said, "I looked at the man lying there, and I cursed him. I thought, how does he dare? Who does he think he is to threaten me, to come into my home this way?" And he then went on to cite a nineteenth-century study of crowd psychology: "The crowd—the mob—is amoral, and if the law relaxes, the people in the crowd act out their impulses. Morals and ethics are externalized by the presence of the police; if the police are not there, the mob does as it pleases." The events in Montreal—ordinarily one of the world's most civilized cities—seemed to add weight to those words.[13] Even when the police are present, if other conditions prevail that make it unlikely that their intervention will be effective, chaos can ensue. A particularly striking example took place in New York City during a massive power failure in July, 1977. Under cover of the total darkness that resulted, thousands of persons poured into the streets, smashing windows, looting, and setting fire to entire blocks of buildings.

The fear of punishment does seem to help prevent some crimes that might otherwise be committed. When fear of detection, arrest, or punishment is removed, as it was during the Montreal police strike and the New York City blackout, persons who would ordinarily have gone peacefully about their business may succumb to temptation or act out deep-rooted resentments and participate in violent crimes.

Some problems with utilitarian theories of punishment can best be discussed with reference to the deterrent theory. As the founder of utilitarianism, Jeremy Bentham, once put it:

> In point of utility, apparent justice is everything; real justice, abstractedly from apparent justice, is a useless abstraction, not worth pursuing, and, supposing it contrary to apparent justice, such as ought not to be pursued. . . . From apparent justice flow all the good effects of real justice—from real justice, if different from apparent, none.[14]

From a utilitarian point of view, all that counts is what the public *thinks*, not what *actually* happened. If the purpose of punishment is merely to deter potential criminals from committing crimes they might otherwise commit by demonstrating to them the suffering that is inflicted upon people who are convicted of such offenses, the frameup, conviction, and punishment of an innocent man would do as well as the conviction and punishment of a guilty one. All that matters is that the potential criminal *thinks* that guilty persons are treated in that fashion. The punishment of the innocent would be every bit as effective as punishment of the guilty; and from a purely utilitarian point of view, that is all that matters.

Moreover, on purely deterrent principles, one could argue that the stronger the temptation to commit an offense, the more disagreeable the punishment ought to be, for it would presumably take a threat of greater harm to overcome the more powerful temptation than it would to overcome a weaker one. Extenuating circumstances are often supposed to make it more rather than less likely that a person might commit an offense, and for that reason are regarded as justifying less rather than more severe punishment.

If it could be proved that certain psychological tests were capable of selecting those most likely to commit crimes and that such persons could be deterred by being punished in advance, utilitarianism would seem to permit such punishment to go forward, despite the fact that those being punished were up to that time completely innocent of any wrongdoing.

The utilitarians have responded to these arguments in various ways. The most important involves a significant variation in the utilitarian theory.

The simplest form of utilitarianism, now usually referred to as *act utilitarianism*, maintains that in order to determine what is right in a particular situation, it is necessary to determine what the long-term consequences of a given act in that situation are likely to be; that act which is most likely to produce the greatest happiness for the greatest number would be the right act for the individual concerned to do. If that act involved breaking a promise previously made to someone else, or punishing an innocent person, it would *still* be right, according to this theory, if it could be shown that the long-term consequences were likely to produce the greatest happiness for the greatest number.

The *rule utilitarians*, however, argue that experience has shown that certain social and legal rules, such as those that require the keeping of promises, the punishment of only those who are proved guilty, and strict adherence to fair and equitable judicial procedures are in themselves powerful forces for human happiness. The violation of such rules tends to erode their effectiveness and their credibility. As the people at large begin to violate them, or as public officials are perceived to violate them, their good effects are diminished and the general well-being of the people suffers. Therefore, they conclude, in the long run, one can seldom, if ever, justify punishing an innocent man, at least not on utilitarian grounds.

As for the innocent man who has been diagnosed as an imminent threat, a utilitarian might well argue that although the institution of *punishment* would be inappropriate, because he has not yet violated any law, some other form of treatment might be called for. After all, those who are afflicted with dangerous infectious diseases can be quarantined against their will so as to protect the rest of the population from contamination. No one would suggest that their enforced confinement is a penalty for wrongdoing or that the slightest moral reprobation attaches to it. It is simply a measure for the protection of others. In a similar fashion, a person who is diagnosed as potentially violent can be confined and given such treatment as is necessary, both to protect others against harm he might cause to them and to protect him against harm he might do to himself. Such measures would not be punitive at all, though they might include treatment that is quite similar to that accorded to persons who have already committed criminal offenses. Surely, the utilitarian might insist, no moral code can possibly insist that society wait until a dangerous lunatic has caused irreparable harm before it disarms him and locks him up. Preventive measures should not be confused with punishments.

Although the rule utilitarian need not be saddled with advocacy of the punishment of innocent persons, it is not difficult to imagine situations in which the punishment of an innocent person might be justified on utilitarian or perhaps on other moral grounds. If the choice lies between death or cruel suffering for many people and the punishment of a man or woman who is known by the authorities to be innocent, the punishment of the innocent might well be morally permissible. Such situations have evidently occurred from time to time. Cities under siege have been given the choice of perishing by slow starvation or by overwhelming military assault, or turning over certain military, political, or religious leaders for exemplary punishment by the enemy. It is at least an open question whether it would be wrong to comply with such a demand in order to save the rest of the city's inhabitants.

As for the increased severity that might be justified on utilitarian grounds for offenses that were a result of greater temptation or more irresistible impulses, the utilitarian is concerned not only with the protection of society in general, but also with the protection of the offender against excessive pain and suffering. His happiness also enters into the calculation of appropriate penalties. The utilitarian is concerned to devise a system that will entail no more suffering than is necessary to produce maximal pleasure for all. As legislators wrestle with the problem of fixing penalties for various offenses, they must consider (from a utilitarian point of view) both the costs to society and the costs to the individual offender. No doubt the threat of 20 years in prison for an act of fornication, or the death penalty for drunken driving would reduce the incidence of those crimes. But the harm to the individuals concerned, and to their families, must also be placed into the balance. No utilitarian is likely to go along with a system of harsh punishments for relatively minor offenses, even though the incidence of such offenses would be diminished by harsher penalties.

VENGEANCE OR RETRIBUTION

There is a widespread feeling that justice requires that no man should be allowed the advantage that accrues to him from his misdeeds, that any man who has committed a crime should somehow "pay his debt to society," regardless of whether he is reformed by having to do so and regardless of the deterrent effects such "payment" may have upon others. By his wrongful act, it is said, the offender has "tipped the scales of justice out of balance," and it is necessary to rectify the imbalance by taking from him what he has taken from others.

Some thinkers have said that when an injustice has been committed in the world, there is a stain that must somehow be washed away. The Hebrew Bible and the tragedies of ancient Greece are full of incidents that seem designed to illustrate this concept. Once Oedipus had violated the moral law by committing patricide and incest, misfortune came to his kingdom and remained until his guilt had been expiated. In the Hebrew Bible many passages clearly presume that the earth itself is stained by the guilt of the murderer, and that nothing can cleanse it of this stain but punishment of the guilty or some form of expiation. Thus, after Cain has murdered his brother, Abel, God says to him, "What have you done? The blood of your brother is crying out to me from the ground! Now you are cursed by the earth that has opened its mouth to swallow the blood of your brother that you have spelled." [15] And again, in connection with the need to punish the murderer, God commands the children of Israel by saying, "You must not defile the land in which you reside, but blood defiles the earth; and there is no way to cleanse the earth of the blood that has been spilled upon it but by the blood of him who has spilled it." [16]

In modern times, the popular demand for retribution is often expressed when the public, informed of a particularly brutal crime, demands revenge, feeling that justice is served only when the guilty party has been punished. Many of those who advocate the return of the death penalty argue that murderers should be put to death "because they deserve to die for their crimes." The popular demand for punishment is often unaccompanied by any thought of reform or deterrence; rather, it seems to be activated by the thought that the criminal ought to "get what is coming to him" or "get what he deserves." There is little evidence of any popular feeling that the earth has been defiled by spilt blood. But some expressions, such as, "The victim of this crime will not rest easy until her killer has been caught and justice has been done," reveal an underlying sentiment that derives from the same source. There seems to be a feeling, too, that one who commits a crime owes a "debt" that he must pay, and that so long as that debt remains unpaid, there is an imbalance in the community or in the universe, a kind of state of being—injustice—that can be rectified only with the punishment of the wrongdoer.

One of the most respected moral thinkers of modern times, Immanuel Kant, maintained that from a moral point of view, punishment is primarily retributive. In discussing the problem he went so far as to say that if the world were about to come to an end, and it was therefore evident that no one would benefit from the punishment of prisoners who have been sentenced to death, those prisoners should be executed nevertheless, in the interest of righting the balance of justice.[17]

Kant believed that the punishment of the guilty is good in itself, regardless of any benefits that may flow from it. In his view, the only reason for punishing a person was that he had in fact committed a crime, and it was the nature of the crime committed that determined the type and severity of punishment that was to be imposed. He adopted the *lex talionis* literally: a life for a life and an eye for an eye. When the harm done to the victim could not be duplicated (for example, in sexual offenses), then the punishment should be as similar as possible, or at least as appropriate as possible. For example, it might involve the permanent deprivation of all human rights.

Unfortunately, Kant offered no proof for this theory. Instead, like so many other pronouncements that he made, he seems to have based it upon some kind of intuition, a special insight into the nature of things, which Kant evidently felt he had. The theory may be related to Kant's view that no man should ever be used as a means to any other person's end, but should always be treated as an end in himself. Under this theory, it is easy to see why Kant would reject the deterrent approach to punishment: punishing one man in order to deter another potential offender from committing a similar crime in the future would be to *use* the person who is being punished. Even punishment for the sake of reform might be inconsistent with the Kantian view of human autonomy, for it would have to rest upon the assumption that the punishing authority knows more about what is in the best moral and spiritual interests of the person being punished than he does himself. The authority would be presuming to transform the criminal offender into an image that *he* would impose upon him, denying the offender the right to his own moral choices.

The problem with such intuitive theories is that too many others do not share the intuitions upon which they rest. To some people the retributive theory seems (perhaps on intuitive grounds) to be clearly wrong, for it seems to require the infliction of pain for its own sake, and that, they feel, is a useless cruelty. How, they ask, is an evil situation, the wickedness of the criminal, and the harm done by his crime reduced by adding still another evil—the infliction of pain? The only possible moral justification for inflicting pain upon the criminal, they say, is if it produces some good results, either by helping to change the criminal's character or by reducing the likelihood of other persons committing similar crimes. In some respects, in fact, retributive punishment may be more evil than the crime that brought it about, for as one philosopher put it, "the infliction of pain for pain's sake is just the definition of the worst type of cruelty." [18]

Moreover, some rationalists (persons who believe that certain *a priori* or intuitive insights are necessary to morality) maintain that according to their intuitions, it is important that crime be diminished, that criminals be reformed, and that these goals be taken into account when punishment is inflicted. As one of them put it, "Retributive justice may be a very good thing, but the saving of souls is a much better thing, and to seek to achieve the first at all costs, even where it will probably involve the sacrifice of the second, seems to me not a moral duty but positively, and in a serious degree, wrong." [19] Thus, if the retributive principle would demand the infliction of a severe penalty that would have bad social consequences and contribute nothing toward the reform of the criminal (by increasing his anger and resentment against the system that caused him so much suffering), whereas a lighter penalty might help to bring about his reform and avoid the undesirable social consequences, these philosophers would unhesitatingly advocate the lighter punishment.

In finally disposing of the retributive theory, A. C. Ewing wrote:

> Nowhere else is it right deliberately to inflict evil as such. Yet here we are asked to inflict pain for pain's sake. It seems strange that a kind of action which under ordinary conditions is regarded as the very extreme of moral depravity should become a virtue in the case of punishment.[20]

Under the retributive theory, the type and degree of the penalty is determined by the offender's guilt: the more serious the offense, the harsher the penalty should be. But there are some difficulties with this:

1. The degree of an offender's wickedness can be determined only by knowing the exact state of his mind at the moment when he committed the crime, and that is impossible to do, for it is not possible to determine just what his thoughts were at any given time.

2. One can never know what events in the offender's life led him to commit his offense, and therefore one can never know just how guilty he really is; there may be factors beyond his control that determined what he would do and these ought therefore to be regarded as excusing conditions that would lighten or perhaps eliminate any punishment he might receive.

3. A man should not be judged only by his worst acts. If we are to judge his moral character, we ought to consider the entire tapestry of his personality, not just that facet that is revealed by the crime he committed.

4. We never know just what punishment will cause the proper amount of pain in a criminal because we don't know how sensitive he is. It is therefore impossible to fix a punishment that will cause the offender an amount of pain equal to that which he caused his victim.

5. On the retributive theory, everyone ought to be punished, because everyone has sinned in some way and no one is truly innocent. It is wrong, according to the retributivist, to allow the guilty to go unpunished, and it is especially wrong to allow some of the guilty to go free while others are singled out for punishment.[21]

A retributivist might respond to these last arguments in the following way:

1. We do not argue that people ought to be punished for their moral wickedness. To attribute this doctine to us (at least to most of us) is to misrepresent our position completely. We insist, however, that when a person is punished, it ought to be because he *deserves* to be punished, and not for some other reason, commendable as such reasons might be in other respects. However wicked a person might be from a purely moral point of view, he ought to be punished only if he has violated a particular law

proscribing an act that he performed. Now, we would not say, any more than any utilitarian might, that it is possible to know precisely what is in any given individual's mind at a particular time. But like most legal philosophers and, in fact, like most persons who practice law and sit in judgment on others, we do say that the best evidence of what goes on in a man's head is the action he performs. If a person purchases a quantity of potassium cyanide and spikes his wife's tea with it, it is perfectly reasonable to infer that he *intended* to kill his wife. To be sure, we might be mistaken. He *might* (logically) have imagined that the blue cyanide crystals were sugar, and his intention *might* have been merely to sweeten the brew for his beloved spouse. But really, that is quite far-fetched. Even if he did not intend to kill his wife, but merely to sweeten her tea, he is *still* culpable, for he has a legal as well as a moral obligation to take reasonable care not to substitute cyanide for sugar. The retributive theory poses no special difficulty for the law in this regard. We can easily say, with the most authoritative legal scholars, that a man may be presumed to intend the natural and ordinary consequences of his actions.

2. The problem of excusing conditions is not unique to the retributivist. When a person acts as a result of factors that are totally beyond his control, no theory would hold him legally responsible or subject him to punishment, with rare exceptions. Other excusing conditions can and do mitigate penalties.

3. The retributivist is not interested in punishing every wicked act or every person who has ever violated some moral standard or other. Moreover, the retributive theory is not based upon the principle that people ought to be punished because of their moral characters. It says merely that people ought to be punished if and only if they have committed certain immoral *acts*.

4. It is true, of course, that some people are more sensitive to pain than others. It is also true that some will respond more to the threat of punishment than will others. So utilitarians have the same problem. The retributivist may appeal to general rules, as the utilitarian does. Although we may not know just what this offender's threshold of pain may be, we know what most people find painful, and we can make fairly accurate judgments as to the relative pain and suffering that a given type of punishment will impose upon most persons.

5. Again, the criticism is founded upon a misunderstanding of what the retributivist is advocating. He is not urging the punishment of every person who carries a burden of moral guilt; he does believe that it is proper to distinguish between those who deserve to be punished and those who do not, being fully cognizant of the fact that everyone occasionally offends against the code of morals. Although we might say of a given person, "He deserves to be punished for what he has done," it does not follow that we, or anyone, either possesses the right or has the obligation to give him what he deserves. Whereas, from a cosmic view of things, certain people deserve

to be punished, from a human point of view, only those who commit certain types of violations, who are caught, tried, and convicted ought to be punished by those who possess the right to inflict penalties upon their fellow men. It would certainly be wrong to let some of those who are guilty of offenses forbidden by law to go free while others are punished; but according to a retributivist's view, the authorities do no wrong in permitting those who are guilty of certain moral offenses (say, cursing their parents) to go unpunished while they deal severely with those who are guilty of other offenses (such as assaulting young women).

Herbert Fingarette recently defended the retributive theory in his presidential address to the Pacific division of the American Philosophical Association.[22] Law, he said, exercises power to require people to do certain things. The power law exercises manifests itself in many ways, even when the law is not actually using physical force or violence, though the eventual use of such force lies behind the law's power to make people do its bidding. Those subject to the law also have power—the power to act contrary to the law's bidding if they so choose. The point of laying down a legal obligation, Fingarette says, is that the person subject to a particular law is "required to *will* what complies with that law," though, of course, he retains the power to will otherwise. The law's power, then, is essentially over the will and not over the body or over a person's behavior. But the law's requirement is no mere request. It forbids people to go against its requirements and threatens them with pursuit and punishment if they fail to comply. If the law failed to apply some sanction against those who violated its provisions, then it would become nothing more than an empty formality, a ceremonial act.

Fingarette points out that the law employs means other than punishment under certain circumstances. Marriages and business contracts entered into by fraud, for example, can be *annulled*. A person who has stolen property or negligently caused damage to another may be forced to make *restitution*. Either of these may be painful, but neither is a form of punishment. Restitution, in fact, may be taken care of by some government agency or by an insurance company and need involve no special loss to the person who initially caused the loss. But such measures are not the real heart of the law, for if *post hoc* enforcement becomes the rule, rather than the exception, then the law has lost its distinctive power, which is to assure initial compliance with its requirements.

What does it mean, then, to say that the law has power over your will? It means, first, that you usually do of your own free will whatever the law requires, and that you do so for no other reason than that the law says you must—that is, because you respect the law. Also, it means that if you don't do what the law requires, then the law constrains your will, directly as a consequence of your failure to abide by its provisions.

The purpose of punishment is not reparation or restitution, but simply "that the will be subject to law, that is, either conform or in consequence be constrained." Punishing, Fingarette says, is "the humbling of the defiant—or at least the disrespectful—will." It is pure suffering, the imposition of an experience that is *against* the violator's will. In this respect, punishment is retributive, for its aim is not to reform the offender or to prevent future violations, but to impose "pure suffering" upon him *because of what he has done*—for no other reason than that he has violated the law. This retributive notion is carried through to the amount and kind of punishment to be imposed. The gravity of the wrong has to do with the gravity of the requirement that has been violated, and this in turn will determine the kind and amount of punishment to be exacted. "The graver the legislators mean their requirement to be, the graver the punishment. Or, to put it another way, the graver the requirement laid upon the subject's will, the graver must be the humbling of the defiant will."

Fingarette recognizes that punishment may also have deterrent or reformative effects. But he notes that it might also have precisely the opposite effects. The criminal who is punished often feels that he is a victim of an unjust system and is more determined than ever to succeed in his life of crime. The terrorist's penalty may transform him from a common criminal into a hero or a martyr and may serve as the pretext or the occasion for even more dangerous and widespread offenses against the law, peace, and public order. Thus, particular punishments may be challenged if their principal purpose is to reform or to deter. But the essence of punishment is in fact nothing more than the suffering of those who disobey the requirements of the law. Although the deliberate infliction of suffering upon a human being is an evil, which merely adds yet another evil to that which was done by the wrongdoer, retributivists are right in insisting that offenders be punished for their offenses. For if law is morally justified, then whatever it takes to make law meaningful is also morally justified; and the punishment of lawbreakers is absolutely essential to the existence of any meaningful system of laws.

EXCUSES

"ALL CRIMINALS ARE SICK"

One often hears that all criminals are sick and that instead of subjecting them to the brutal treatment that is entailed in punishment, whatever form that might take, a civilized society ought to provide some form of *treatment* for them as it does for all its sick and disabled members. The criminal, it is said, is unable to do other than he does. He is the unfortunate victim of the heredity with which he was endowed and the environment into which he was thrust. He chose neither. Yet both his heredity and his environment have made him what he is. If only he had been raised in other circumstances, he would not have become what he did in fact become. If only he had been born to parents other than his own, or if only the chromosomes that made up the germ plasm from which he came had had slightly different genetic coding, he would have been a very different kind of person from the one that he is today. He is as much the master of his own actions as the epileptic is of his when he thrashes about in a *grand mal* seizure. It makes as much sense to punish the murderer as it does to punish the epileptic or the insane; and, indeed, it was not so very long ago that the latter were treated much as the criminal is treated today. Samuel Butler, in his remarkable novel *Erehwon*, pictured a society where criminals were provided with special hospitals where they might be treated, but persons suffering from various forms of illness were hauled into court and subjected to increasingly severe penalties, according to the severity of their illnesses. Thus, for a common cold, a man might be required to pay only a moderate fine, but for pneumonia he might be sentenced to several years in prison. The burglar, the rapist, and the arsonist, however, were given the benefit of the latest medical advances, and once their treatments were completed they were sent on their way, because they were cured.

Butler's point is obvious. He is suggesting that there is no significant difference between the kinds of conditions that we call illness and the kinds that we call criminal behavior, and that the form of treatment accorded to each ought to be similar. He suggests that it is no more sensible to subject a burglar to fines or prison sentences than it would be to subject persons suffering from gout to such treatment. Thus, for example, John Hospers, after describing an incident in which a woman refused to do what was necessary to save the life of her child until it was too late, concludes:

> Was she responsible for her deed? In ordinary life, after making a mistake, we say, 'Chalk it up to experience.' Here we would say, 'Chalk it up to the neurosis.' *She* could not help it if her neurosis forced her to act this way— she didn't even know what was going on behind the scenes, her conscious self merely acted out its assigned part. This is far more true than is generally realized: criminal actions in general are not actions for which their agents are responsible; the agents are passive, not active—they are victims of a neurotic conflict. Their very hyperactivity is unconsciously determined.[23]

Hospers goes on to explain that this "is not to say that we should not punish criminals." He explains that "for our own protection, we must remove them for our midst so that they can no longer molest and endanger organized society." But such means of self-defense are not quite what is meant by punishment. They are a form of preventive detention. The "criminal" is not punished for his crime, under this scheme, but for the danger he imposes to society. In this respect, his treatment does not differ at all from the detention enforced upon the epileptic in our earlier example, or from the victim of tuberculosis, who can legally be required to be hospitalized and quarantined until all danger of infection has been eliminated.

This theory, that all criminals are sick, sounds suspiciously as though it might be guilty of begging the question. What definition of *sickness* entitles one to claim that criminal behavior is necessarily symptomatic of some form of illness? Is it not possible that some criminals are actually quite in possession of all their faculties, but that, unlike most persons, they have chosen to achieve their ends by illegal means rather than by the conventional, legal means that most persons use?

CASE 9. THE MAN WHO BLEW UP HIS MOTHER

A young man once purchased a large insurance policy on his mother's life just before she boarded an airliner that was about to depart from Denver's airport. He had previously placed a bomb in one of her suitcases. The bomb exploded, causing the plane to crash, killing its entire crew and all its passengers, including the young man's mother. He collected the insurance money, but as a result of a careful investigation, he was finally apprehended. Many people are inclined to believe that no one who is in full possession of his faculties, and who is not seriously deranged, would be capable of such a monstrous crime. But the psychiatrist who was assigned to the case concluded that the defendant knew perfectly well what he was doing, that he planned and executed his scheme as carefully as any merchant might have done if he were embarked on a major business enterprise, and that it was impossible to diagnose any particular mental illness as being responsible for his bizarre behavior. The defendant was accordingly found guilty and was executed in Colorado's gas chamber.

Those who say that all criminals are sick often have in mind those offenders who have engaged in the most brutal forms of crime—rape, armed robbery, murder, and the like. There is little reason to doubt that some people who commit such crimes *are* sick. Some of them are subject to uncontrollable fits of rage and passion, others are known to be subject to delusions and hallucinations. Whether the usual procedures of the criminal law should be brought to bear upon such persons, and whether they should be subject to punishment in the usual sense, will be discussed in the next section. But the proponents of the theory now under discussion tend to forget another very important class of criminals—those who clearly do not act in fits of passion, but with due deliberation, carefully and methodically working out their plans of action, sometimes alone, but often in concert with others. Their motives are frequently the same as those of perfectly normal persons. They want the better things in life; they want the leisure to enjoy the benefits of their prosperity; they want to provide their families with nice homes, nice clothes, and the little amenities that our society provides and that most of us consider to be good and desirable. The manner in which they attempt to achieve those goals, however, is not legal. Ordinarily, those who engage in such illegal activities do so with the hope that they will not be caught. They are often quite clear-headed about the entire business. They seldom become involved because of paranoid delusions or schizophrenic flights from reality. And interestingly enough, they seldom receive the attention of the press or become the objects of campaigns of citizens demanding that they be considered the unfortunate victims of circumstances. Consider the embezzler, the businessman who is convicted of income tax evasion, the corporation executive who engages in illegal restraint of trade or monopolistic practices, the food processor who allows his products to become contaminated, the logger who deliberately encroaches upon national park land, felling trees that will not be replaced for generations, and the operator of a chemical plant who knows that his smokestacks and the sewer lines of his plant are pouring out effluents that are poisoning the atmosphere and the water supplies of the towns down-river. Consider the executives of major electrical supply companies who defrauded public utilities and communities out of millions of dollars by engaging in illegal conspiracies to fix prices of generators and other electrical equipment; the chief executives of giant oil companies who knowingly misused corporate funds to make illegal political contributions; and the managers of General Motors who authorized the substitution of Chevrolet engines in Oldsmobiles while praising the virtues of the Olds engine in their ads and concealing from their customers the fact that the substitution had been made. In none of these cases can a plausible argument be devised to prove that the persons involved were mentally ill. Each of them held a position of enormous responsibility and performed his tasks efficiently and competently. The only possible argument for their being sick is circular: that only sick people commit criminal acts and that they were criminals, so they must have been sick. But this proves nothing.

In this connection, it is worth noting that some commentators insist that the real causes of crime are poverty, poor medical and dental care, crowded housing conditions, inadequate schooling, hunger, and victimization because of racial prejudice. Ramsey Clark once explained a young boy's violent crimes by the fact that the child had never seen a dentist and had such rotten teeth that he was ashamed to smile. But the presidents of General Electric, General Motors, Allied Chemical, and Gulf Oil had adequate housing. John Mitchell and the other Watergate conspirators were well educated—most of them had law degrees—and showed no signs of malnutrition. Nor were they victims of racial or religious discrimination. The theory falls flat, for it fails to account for white collar crime, the crimes most often committed by members of the middle and upper classes. Someone has calculated that the total financial loss in the entire history of the United States from robberies, burglaries, property damage caused by vandalism, and protection payments to racketeers is less than the losses suffered in a single year from illegal stock manipulations, embezzlement, shortweighting and misgrading of commodities, fraudulent insurance claims, and other forms of white collar crime.[24] Those who engage in such criminal behavior are usually clever and sophisticated and show no signs of any known form of pathology; nor are they victims of any of the conditions that are alleged to be the "real reasons" for criminal behavior.

Advocates of the theory that all criminals are sick tend to cite dramatic cases of psychotic criminal behavior as proof of their thesis. Such cases do exist, but it is fallacious (the "fallacy of dramatic instance," as Sidney Gendin calls it) to generalize from a few extreme cases that may involve psychopathology to the conclusion that all criminals suffer from some form of mental disease.

INSANITY

Around the year 1840 a British gentleman by the name of Daniel M'Naghten, suffering from paranoid delusions, imagined that the Tories were plotting to destroy him. He set out to assassinate the Tory leader, Prime Minister Pitt, by shooting him as he drove by in his carriage, believing he was doing so in self-defense. Unknown to M'Naghten, however, the prime minister's secretary was riding in the prime minister's carriage, and it was he who was shot and killed by M'Naghten's bullet.

The court in M'Naghten's case held that to establish a defense on the ground of insanity, "it must be clearly proved that, at the time of the committing of the act, the party accused was labouring under such a defect of reason, from disease of the mind, as not to know the nature and quality of the act he was doing; or, if he did know it, that he did not know he was doing what was wrong." [25] The court further distinguished the kind of delusion that would provide exemption from punishment and that which would not: If his delusion led him to imagine that someone was attempting to take his life so that it was necessary for him to kill in self-defense, he would be exempt; but if the delusion had to do with the other's spreading malicious gossip about him that damaged his reputation and if he then killed him in revenge for this imagined injury, he would be liable for punishment. In more general terms, he is exempt from punishment if he acts under a delusion that, if true, would have provided an excuse or a justification for his act; but he is not exempt if the truth of his false beliefs would not have excused his actions.

A later American version of the insanity rule, known as the Durham rule, provided that an "accused is not criminally responsible if his unlawful act was the product of mental disease or mental defect." [26] By *disease* the court meant any condition that was capable of improving or deteriorating, whereas a defect was a nonchanging condition resulting either from some congenital disorder or from some injury or physical or mental disease. This was not especially helpful, because neither courts nor juries knew what mental disease was or whether it was a medical term whose definition was to be established by psychiatrists, a legal term that was to be defined by lawyers or judges, or a question of fact for juries to decide. One court held that the term *mental disease* might have a certain meaning for clinical purposes but that that might be quite different from its meaning in a trial held to identify criminal responsibility. "For the jury's purpose . . . a mental disease or de-fect includes any abnormal condition of the mind which substantially affects mental or emotional processes and substantially impairs behavior con-trols." [27] But this "clarification" leaves much to be clarified, for it employs terms and concepts—*emotional processes, mental processes, behavior con-trols, abnormality, impair, affect,* and *substantially*—that are equally unclear and are in any case essentially included in the M'Naghten rule, which this rule was supposed to have supplanted.

According to Herbert Fingarette,[28] *mental disease* is like *inadequate vision:* What is adequate vision for a driver may not be for a diamond cutter. The oculist is not an expert in what constitutes adequate vision, though he can measure a person's vision along a standard scale and give advice on methods by which one might make it more adequate for one purpose or another. As to what is adequate, even for driving, that is a policy decision that depends upon the community's balancing of such factors as safety, the availability of public transportation, economics, and others. Much the same is true of mental disease or mental health. One way to effect a policy de-cision to withdraw certain classes of persons from the sanctions of the criminal law is to declare that they are suffering from mental disease. Once an individual has been judged to be suffering from a mental disease, he is held not to be criminally responsible for actions of a given type. This has been done in various communities with drug addicts, alcoholics, homo-sexuals, and others. The important point to note is that there is no "objec-tive" criterion by which such persons are assigned to the class of individuals who are mentally diseased. Rather, it is a policy judgment that is expressed in the language of psychiatry.

The M'Naghten test refers to the accused's knowledge of right and wrong, making such knowledge the chief measure of his responsibility for his ac-tions. Now it might seem that the demand that a person *know* what is right and wrong is in itself a kind of prejudgment of some of the most crucial issues; for one of the chief questions at issue, at least among moral philoso-phers, is whether it is at all possible to *know* what is right and what is wrong —whether there is any objective criterion by which anyone can distinguish the one from the other. If a psychiatrist testifies that a patient-defendant *knew* that what he was doing was wrong, the psychiatrist is assuming that he, the psychiatrist, knows what is wrong, and thus is passing judgment on the conduct of the patient-defendant. On the other hand, if he testifies that he "knew that it is generally considered to be wrong, that it is contrary to the law," he avoids making any moral commitments of his own. One might reasonably ask, however, whether a psychiatrist who is ignorant of the general condemnation of rape, murder, and robbery and of their criminal character is qualified to testify in cases that involve defendants accused of having committed such offenses.

One of the chief criteria of mental health is the ability to perceive reality, to adapt to it, and to be able to distinguish it from fantasy. It would appear that certain facts about society and the behavior and expectations of one's fellow citizens are as much a part of reality as the color and location of one's home or the number of fingers on one's hand. A person may not subscribe to the principle that taking another person's life for trivial reasons is wrong; but if in addition he is not aware of the fact that such behavior is strongly condemned by society, he is simply not in contact with a very important part of reality. One way of pointing out the difference between an insane person and a perfectly sane one is to show that the one is unaware of the fact that people condemn random slayings whereas the other is fully aware of that fact and takes it into account in order to avoid detection and capture.

The M'Naghten rule has been criticized on the ground that it is slanted toward the intellectual side of man's nature, placing too much emphasis upon what the defendant *knows,* as opposed to what he has *done.* It is argued that a person may be insane and still know that what he has done (say, under an irresistible impulse) was wrong. Such a person, it is argued, should not be held responsible for his actions even though he was fully aware of the fact that it was wrong.

In fact, however, it appears that the M'Naghten rule merely sets the conditions for assigning responsibility to a person and that knowledge in the usual sense is not the crucial issue.

It is important to distinguish between (a) being a responsible agent but not being held responsible for a particular act because there was no *mens rea* on that particular occasion and (b) not being a responsible agent at all, and therefore not being held responsible for any act.

A small child is not a responsible agent. Whatever he knows, however deliberately he may have set fire to the hotel room or discharged the shotgun, he cannot be held responsible, because as a matter of public policy, small children are held not to be liable for their misdeeds, however horrendous they may be. By the same token, those who are judged to be insane are not responsible for what they do, not because they lack the necessary *mens rea* for liability in that particular case (although they do lack the *mens rea*), but because as a matter of public policy persons who are found to be out of touch with reality are held to be free of responsibility for their offenses and to be subject to some form of treatment and control other than that provided by the criminal law. When a person is found "not guilty by reason of insanity," he has not been found innocent, and he is not entitled to full freedom. He is "innocent" only in the sense in which one who cannot possibly be guilty is innocent: He is found to be incapable of having the capacity to act as a free and responsible citizen.

The "knowledge" to which the M'Naghten test refers cannot possibly be knowledge of the fact that society generally condemns murder; for if that were the test, M'Naghten himself would have been hanged, for he surely knew that in general it was regarded as wrong to kill the British prime minister. Nor will it do to suppose that a person's subjective views on morality should determine whether he is insane; for under that criterion, anyone could get away with anything, so long as he did it in good conscience. Consider the following case:

A schizophrenic mother drowns her child in the bathtub under the delusion that the child is suffering excruciating pains caused by an incurable illness. She is convinced that she has a duty to relieve the child of its (imaginary) agony and feels gratified that she has succeeded in doing so. She clearly meets the M'Naghten test, because she was incapable of distinguishing wrong from right. Now suppose that in a similar case the mother believes it is a great sin to kill the child, but does so just the same, while suffering delusions, hallucinations, and other symptoms of schizophrenia. She feels deep remorse and regret and repeatedly assures all who examine her that she fully realizes how sinful her action was and how guilty she is. It should be clear that the slight differences between these two cases are not sufficient to establish that the woman in the second case is criminally responsible for her baby's death. In fact, whether she believed that what she was doing was wrong is beside the point. What really counts is how she came to do what she did, just as in the first case what really counts is how she came to believe what she believed.

The plain fact is that most insane conduct is purposive. It is initiated and carried out with skill and care with a specific goal in view. No outside agency forces an insane person to do what he does, nor are his actions involuntary, though they may appear to the outside observer to be so.

If M'Naghten himself should have been judged sane under the M'Naghten test; if some clearly insane behavior is nevertheless purposive; if some insane persons know that what they are doing is wrong—then what is it that distinguishes sane from insane behavior?

Fingarette responds by observing that there are various senses of the terms *rational* and *irrational*. A person is said to be irrational not only if he thinks illogically, unreasonably, or unintelligently but also if he lacks certain emotional capacities and if he responds to certain situations in a grossly inappropriate fashion. It is irrational, for example, to chuckle with glee at the sight of a mangled human body or to feel pleasure at the death of a loved one.

If Jones picks up a stone in the woods and thoughtlessly tosses it into the greenery, it would be inappropriate to call his action irrational, though it might be called mindless or meaningless. This amounts to a denial that his behavior is crazy, mad, or insane.

If Smith suddenly appears in the line of fire and Jones, seeing Smith, refrains from throwing the rock or tosses it in another direction, his conduct is clearly rational, for he has responded to important facts in an appropriate fashion—that is, the potential impact of the rock, the possible pain, suffering, and moral and legal implications of carrying out his original intention of throwing the rock in Smith's direction. Indeed, Jones's behavior strengthens the conclusion in the first instance that he was not irrational, for he has demonstrated that he would react appropriately to relevant changes in circumstances.

If Smith appeared, as before, and Jones recognized him as an old enemy, completed the throw, and then apologized profusely but insincerely for having seen Smith too late to avoid throwing the rock, we would say that he was not behaving irrationally. On the contrary, his behavior is quite rational, though it is also malicious. Such a response, in a sense, is as relevant and appropriate as it was in the preceding case for Jones to toss the rock in another direction.

Now suppose that Jones fails to see how throwing the rock at Smith would result in injury to him, or in suffering, or in any moral or legal consequences: In short, he fails to see that throwing the rock at Smith would be wrong. As Smith crumples to the ground, Jones shrugs his shoulders and walks away. This would constitute a paradigm case of irrational behavior. Jones was incapable of responding appropriately. His response ability was impaired. Whether because of a toxic reaction to alcohol or to drugs or because of schizophrenia or some other mental illness, Jones's reactions are inappropriate to the situation, bizarre, crazy, evidencing an incapacity to attend to and act upon essentially relevant factors. Even if Jones is aware of the fact that his behavior is likely to result in punishment, and thus takes appropriate measures to hide from the authorities and to cover up his crime, his incapacity to appreciate the wrongness of his act is a sign of insanity, of irrationality.

This helps to disentangle some of the problems surrounding the issue of criminal insanity, according to Fingarette, for

> criminal law is in some fundamental sense an expression of community moral conscience, and . . . one who is genuinely incapable of responding at least to rudimentary moral issues cannot be a fit agent under that law. The professional criminal who is not insane can respond to human-moral issues and to the law viewed as rooted in moral meaning. His relevant but criminal response is an income-oriented flouting of the law. But a person like Jones is incapable of flouting the law, if we think of law as rooted in moral meaning, since he is blind to the morally relevant dimension of law, blind to what law really means. But he can disobey what to him must remain inherently arbitrary social rules. He may be restrained or deterred by threats of sanctions or by physical control, but this is neither responsiveness to law nor responsibility under law. It is mere control by fear or actual force—sheer power, to his mind.[29]

Finally, if Jones violently throws the rock at Smith under the delusion that Smith is involved in a plot to kill him, we conclude that Jones is insane (or irrational) for much the same reason: While he responds appropriately, consistently with his deluded beliefs, those beliefs are false, having been arrived at and tenaciously clung to by him despite evidence to the contrary.

This is the essence of the distinction between a stubborn man and one who is incapable of responding meaningfully to reality.

An insane person is one who lacks the capacity to think or behave rationally as a result of some grave defect in his nature. The judgment that a particular person is insane is arrived at purely through observation of his behavior in the context of relevant information about his life. This is just what was meant by the authors of the M'Naghten test: a "defect of reason" from "disease of the mind" is a "substantial defect in capacity for rational conduct" as an "endogenous (pathological) condition of the mind." [30] Thus the paradox that Daniel M'Naghten would seem not to have been insane under this test is answered: Though he knew that he was attempting to kill and laid elaborate plans to carry out his plot, he lacked an essential element of what is necessary if his conduct is to be judged rational. Because he was incapable of responding appropriately to available evidence, he clung to his delusional belief that the Tories were attempting to destroy him. The mistake made by those who imagine that M'Naghten knew what he was doing is that they define his act too narrowly. If his act is the shooting itself, or the preparation for the shooting, then he knew what he was doing. But the act was shooting the prime minister in order to save himself from destruction. And he was incapable of rationally assessing that act—of knowing what he was doing—because of the paranoid delusions from which he was suffering. His mistake was more than a mere error and it did not result from misinformation or sheer stupidity. It was the direct consequence of his irrational mind. As such it was, and ought to have been, excused, so far as criminal punishment is concerned.

The recognition of insanity as a defense against criminal responsibility is not the same as extending blanket immunity to criminal prosecution to everyone who commits any crime. On the contrary, the presumption is that every person is sufficiently rational to distinguish right from wrong and to foresee the natural consequences of his actions. Exceptional cases justify exceptional treatment, but such cases require special proof and ought to be very rare indeed. It is unlikely that many persons would be able to establish that they suffer from conditions that would render them liable to criminal prosecution if they should commit serious violations of the criminal law. And there is no reason, either in science or in philosophy, why this should not be so.

7
Imprisonment

From the early Middle Ages until relatively modern times, punishment was as much for the salvation of the sinner's soul as it was for the protection of the innocent and the deterrence of crime. If nothing else would bring the sinner to cry out to his Lord for mercy, the lash, the rack, the gallows, or the flames could be counted upon to convince him to do so.

Some groups of Puritans concluded that a long stretch of absolute silence, combined with isolation, the stench of human excreta, vermin, and a starvation diet would encourage those who did the work of Satan to repent. Thus, for the greater glory of God, they built sanctuaries of penitence which were called, appropriately, penitentiaries.

In the late eighteenth century, and on into the nineteenth and twentieth centuries, movements for prison reform have been a constant feature of the social and political scene in England and in North America. The argument has generally centered upon the wisdom of "coddling" criminals by allowing them to live in quarters that had at least minimal standards of hygiene and comfort. At times, too, the debate has been devoted to the question of the kind of treatment that ought to be accorded prisoners in the penitentiaries. Should they be forced to engage in hard labor, labor that was basically useless, serving no function other than its supposed "softening" effect upon the criminals themselves? The inmates of some prisons have been forced to work at splitting rocks, forever having to start a new pile when the old one was depleted. Others have had to walk treadmills or turn cranks that merely plowed through piles of sand—backbreaking, degrading, dehumanizing labor.

In some prisons, inmates were confined in long rows of steel cages. They were cut off, not only from the rest of humanity, but even from the world of nature.

In some prisons the sanitation was so primitive that disease was rampant, sometimes spreading to the general community through delivery men, visitors, and released prisoners. The sanitation system consisted of buckets that were left in each cell. These were emptied by the prisoners once a day into open holes or trenches that carried the waste out, whenever they were not blocked.

"In prisons which are really meant to keep the multitude in order," an English divine wrote in 1816, "and to be a terror to evil-doers, there must be no sharing of profits—no visiting of friends—no education but religious education—no freedom of diet, no weavers' looms or carpenters' benches. There must be a great deal of solitude; coarse food; a dress of shame; hard, incessant, irksome, eternal labour; a planned and regulated and unrelenting exclusion of happiness and comfort."

Over the years, reformers have managed to overcome some of these "Christian" sentiments, and have brought some measure of humanity to the administration of a few prisons. The addition of medical treatment for the sick, wholesome (if unappetizing) food, opportunities for education, libraries, meaningful work, and counseling services have done much to alleviate the suffering of hundreds of thousands of men and women who are consigned to spend years in penal institutions.

Nevertheless, there remain many vestiges of the primitive and barbaric prisons of the eighteenth century. In the United States a third of all prisons in use were built in the last century, more than seventy years ago. Those that are in use sometimes house two, three, or even four times as many prisoners as they were built to accommodate. Small cells become crowded dormitories. Experiments have repeatedly demonstrated that rats forced to live in overcrowded conditions go mad, becoming vicious and destructive and exhibiting the symptoms of schizophrenia. The same thing happens to men, but the lesson seems to have made no difference in prison architecture or in the budgets allotted by state legislatures to the penal system. Nor has knowledge of this fact had much effect upon the thought of those who continue to believe that prison sentences are suitable penalties to inflict upon men who have committed crimes against society.

When a man is sent to prison, what is the penalty that is being imposed upon him? Clearly, it must be the·deprivation of the liberties that he would otherwise have enjoyed. But consider the liberties that are taken away from him. He is taken away from his wife, from his parents, from his children. He is deprived of every opportunity to engage in useful work. He is cruelly deprived of virtually every outlet for his sexual impulses. He cannot choose his own associates, but must live in close quarters with every manner of derelict. His conversation may be confined to talk about sex, crime, and money, for lack of anyone with whom to discuss other topics. He may be subjected to sexual assaults by fellow inmates, to physical assaults by inmates or guards, and to a constant psychological conditioning that renders him outwardly subservient and dependent while he rages inside. After several years of such torment, he is supposed to emerge from his cell a grateful member of the society that condemned him to it. It is hardly surprising that of every thousand persons in maximum security prisons in Canada, five either commit suicide or attempt to do so. This is nearly five times the rate for all Canadians.

When he comes out, his job is gone, his wife may be gone, his family life is destroyed. He must learn to be independent again, to find his own way, to make his own meals, to find gainful employment, and to stay out of trouble. But his criminal record follows him everywhere, making it impossible in most instances to find a decent job. Try as he may, he may not be *able* to find an employer who is willing to hire an ex-con, to trust him with his goods, or to give him access to his money. How, then, is it possible that people are surprised when they read the sorry statistics that reveal that more than half of all the men and women released from prison are back again within five years? These are the ex-prisoners who are caught and convicted. No one knows how many are not, though they too may have returned to a life of crime because nothing else was open to them.

In spite of the efforts of some foresighted penologists, too many institutions today are still too small, too crowded, and too backward in their treatment of the criminal offender. Though they claim to be principally interested in reform, they still function as if they were primarily interested in vengeance. Clearly, when a man is condemned to a prison sentence, his punishment is the deprivation of liberty itself. The prison is not a place that is supposed to add to this most fundamental deprivation by degrading him and dehumanizing him and taking away every vestige of human dignity that is left to him. To pile punishment upon punishment day after day is neither humane nor civilized. Many prisons are no better than the old slave ships, though if anyone were to propose that the latter be returned to service, an outraged howl of protest would immediately—and rightly—be raised.

No one who has ever read an account of a Siberian prison camp written by a former inmate would suppose that it is a civilized form of penal institution. It is cruel and inhuman. But in some respects, it is superior to the American prison. For one thing, convicts sent to Siberia are frequently allowed to bring their wives along, so that they are able to maintain some degree of sexual normalcy in their lives and are not completely separated from their families.

In a few parts of the United States, arrangements are made for prison inmates to spend some time alone with their wives. Parchman Prison in Mississippi, for example, has cottages on the prison grounds that married men may occupy on weekends with their wives. In this way, the men are able to maintain some semblance of a normal sex life, and their wives are able to do so as well, without resorting to adultery or divorce. But such facilities are available to a very small percentage of all the prison inmates in the United States.

In a few institutions, weekend passes are available; in others, it is possible for inmates who are nearing the end of their terms to work on the outside, returning to the institution at night and on weekends. Thus, the men begin their rehabilitation before they leave their prison cells for good. Elsewhere, there are halfway houses or other rehabilitation centers that devote their efforts to making the transition from prison life to life outside the prison walls a little easier.

It must be pointed out once again that one ought not to confuse rehabilitation with punishment, at least from a purely philosophical point of view. Nevertheless, if one is concerned about the long-run results of the penal system and its moral justifications, then one must consider both the effects that imprisonment has upon the prison population and the extent to which prison conditions are degrading and dehumanizing to those persons who are subjected to them.

Vocational training, an important aspect of the rehabilitative work of any modern prison, is often handicapped by lack of skilled instructors and even more by opposition from unions and industries who object to competition from prison laborers. More than one farsighted project has been scuttled by just such opposition on the part of powerful forces within the community.

Mental health services, so obviously important to any meaningful rehabilitation of that very large proportion of prison inmates who are mentally ill, are quite minimal. It is not likely that they will be improved significantly, in view of the extreme shortage of trained personnel and the general unwillingness of lawmakers to allocate large sums of money to such programs.

Most of the personnel in these systems (some 80% in the United States) are concerned solely with custodial duties. In short, they are the guards and maintenance personnel who supervise the prisoners while they are in custody. The remainder perform the many other tasks that make up the penal system, including the so-called rehabilitative tasks, parole supervision, and the like. Because there are so few of them, and because they must service such large numbers of prisoners or paroleees, it is impossible for them to give meaningful attention to any of the convicts who come under their jurisdiction. When they are saddled with a myriad other tasks in addition, it becomes all but impossible for them to do more than give token attention to the rehabilitation of the men and women whom they are supposed to help.

The so-called rehabilitative function of the prison system is, for the most part, purely fictitious. Prisons breed contempt for the entire legal system in the minds of those who must serve time in them. When a man is sent to jail he knows as well as anyone can that he is being sent there not because society is genuinely interested in making him a better man, in giving him a new opportunity to remake his life, but because society wants to punish him for a crime that he has been found guilty of having committed. He knows as well as anyone that his punishment is to consist of a multitude of deprivations. But no one can ever anticipate the genuine reality of prison life unless he has had to live through it himself. Far from being the "hotel" that so many conservative critics say it is, even the most modern prison facility is still a penitentiary—a place where men are supposed to repent but where instead (with few exceptions) they learn more about the techniques of crime as they are brutalized and degraded by the institution. If education consists at least partially of character building, then prisons must be considered antieducational institutions, because they serve so often to destroy character and to instill hatred, anger, and brutality in those who enter them.

Because no one is very clear about the real purpose of prison (is it penal, rehabilitative, or custodial?), there is no clear policy on the sentencing of offenders. A man convicted of a certain crime in a certain city may be fined $100. Another man, in the same city, convicted of the same crime, may be sentenced to five years in prison. One judge may think principally of rehabilitation and thus sentence the offender who stands before him to a period of probation. The other may be more concerned with the protection of society or with the punitive aspects of criminal punishment and will sentence the offender who stands before him to a long stretch in prison. Or, to make the entire business even more tragic, the same judge, with the same motives, may sometimes do the one and sometimes the other.

Some contemporary reformers argue in favor of the indeterminate sentence. By setting an upper limit ("Not more than ten years," for example), they believe that the judge is able to permit the introduction of a degree of flexibility into the penal system that ultimately will result in better administration of justice and better treatment of the offender who will be able to win his release much earlier by cooperation with the authorities. There is some reason to doubt, however, whether placing such power in the hands of prison officials or parole boards is necessarily beneficial. How is the system improved if the sentencing is done, in effect, by a prison official or a parole board, rather than by a judge? Will these officials possess a kind of wisdom that judges do not possess? Will they have meaningful information on the chances of a particular prisoner's returning to a life of crime that the judge does not possess? Are they more or less likely to be influenced in their decisions by such considerations as the administrative burden of maintaining an overcrowded prison facility, or by personal whims and prejudices? How meaningful can such a proposal be when one of the strongest advocates of the indeterminate sentence admits that the cunning of some prisoners is such that even the most skilled profesional prison officials can be fooled by them? In the next breath he admits that "we know most prisoners who are released will commit more crimes."

The prison, as it exists in the modern democracies, is an archaic relic of an outmoded and cruel religious and social ethic. The thesis that life in prison is somehow a more desirable fate than death in the gas chamber is dubious at best. Most penal institutions are inhumane places where men are deprived not only of their liberties but even of such elementary rights as will enable them to preserve their human dignity. Prisoners may be stripped of their rights as citizens, including the right to return to the practice of their occupations, once they have "paid their debts to society." How, then, have they been helped along the way to "repentance" or "atonement"?

One common rejoinder is this: "No one is to blame but the criminal himself. He knew the price of his misbehavior before he misbehaved. It was his own mischief that brought this fate down upon him. Now let him suffer the consequences."

But this answer is too facile. It will not do under the reformative theory, under the rehabilitative theory, or for that matter, even under the deterrent theory. If the aim of punishment is reform or (as some people incorrectly suppose) rehabilitation, then clearly a form of treatment that demonstrably fails to perform either function can hardly be appropriate for such functions. As for deterrence, one would hope not only that other potential criminals would be deterred by a given convict's punishment, but that he would himself be deterred from further offenses. Any treatment that actually increases both the number and the "quality" of offenses (as the "school for criminals" manifestly does) can hardly serve as a model of deterrence. When even the men who have been to prison are not deterred by the fear of being returned there from committing further crimes, one may suspect that the deterrent effects on others may be quite minimal.

As for the retributive theory, there is nothing in the theory itself that would justify such cruel and unrelenting forms of punishment. A retributivist can quite properly advocate the death penalty but insist that prison is too cruel and inhuman to be tolerated in a civilized society. He might add the observation that under his theory, if a man has been punished for his crime once, there is no justification for punishing him further. If a man has been deprived of all his liberties for a period of time, it is unjust to deprive him of anything, including any of the rights he might have enjoyed in society if he had never been convicted of a crime, once he has been punished. Having paid his debt, he should not be asked to continue to pay. The exaction of interest upon such a debt is the worst form of usury imaginable.

During the Middle Ages, men and women were sometimes "immured" as a form of punishment for the worst sorts of crimes. They were forced to stand in a given spot, and a brick wall was then built all around them. Once the last brick was laid in place, it was not long before they would die of suffocation—or, if the wall was not airtight, of thirst and starvation. Prisons, however, were unknown, except for certain relatively small institutions that were used for the incarceration of suspects and criminals prior to their trials and executions. In ancient times, prisons were used on occasion, as we can see in the Biblical story of Joseph, but those occasions seem to have been quite rare. Our ancestors generally executed criminals, mutilated them, or lashed them and sent them home. They sometimes sent them off to exile or enslaved them. According to the Talmud, in ancient Israel, when a man was convicted of a noncapital crime, he was fined or flogged if the law called for that kind of punishment. Otherwise, he was sold into slavery for a period not to exceed six years. During that six-year period, he was permitted to engage in any occupation that was suitable to his station in life prior to his conviction. If he were a physician, for example, he might continue to practice medicine. If he were a skilled laborer, he would continue to do the kind of work that he was trained to do, and all of his earnings would go to the family of the person who had been harmed by his violation of the law. No one, however, could ever be sent to prison, or stripped of his dignity as a human being. In some Scandinavian countries, men convicted of criminal offenses are permitted to return to their families and to their jobs, unless they are deemed to be so dangerous to themselves or to others that they *must* be institutionalized, but a portion of their earnings is turned over to the victims of their crimes. Thus, the offender is not required to "pay his debt to society" by being deprived of rights or liberties. Instead, he must literally pay the debt he owes to the person whose rights he violated. He must compensate him for the harm he has done. Compensation is not punishment, though the two bear some resemblances to one another. If one is prepared to give up punishment altogether, for some crimes at least, then some form of enforced compensation would seem to be a reasonable substitute. It is certainly less damaging to the offender and his family, and thus to society, in the long run, than the prison system with all its manifest evils. And it has the further advantage that those who are hurt most by the criminal's behavior—his victims and their families—are compensated, to some extent at least, for the losses they have suffered. The criminal whose life is wasted away in prison can contribute nothing to the alleviation of the suffering of his victims. Instead, suffering is added to suffering with no evident advantage to society, which not only loses a potentially productive member, but must provide for all his needs in an expensive custodial institution, and then suffer from his further offenses once he is released. It is difficult to conceive of a form of punishment that has more disadvantages—socially, economically, and morally—than the imprisonment of men who might otherwise be doing useful work.

Because of the failure of the prison system to rehabilitate or reform those are consigned to it, some former advocates of liberal policies, including that of issuing indeterminate sentences so that inmates who are presumably rehabilitated might be released, however long or short a time they have served behind bars, have recently become disenchanted with the old system and have adopted a more strictly retributive approach to the penal system. They have concluded that far from being merciful, the indeterminate sentence may actually be cruel to the prisoner and unfair to society as well. It is cruel to the prisoner because he has no idea when he might be released and is under constant strain, knowing that his every action—even trivial offenses against the prison disciplinary system—may cost him additional years behind bars. It is unfair to society because too many prisoners who were thought to be ready for release have committed new crimes soon after they regained their freedom. In addition, these advocates conclude that it is unjust to subject a person who has committed a relatively minor crime to the possibility of an indefinite stay in prison, whereas a major offender may be released because he is adjudged (rightly or wrongly) to be "ready" for release. They have consequently concluded that sentences should be fixed by law and that judicial discretion should be strictly limited within specific ranges. Each potential offender would then know, or be presumed to know, what a given offense might "cost" him. And each person sent to prison would know in advance when he might expect to be released, having "done his time" and "paid his debt to society." As far as possible, penalties would be proportionate to the severity of the crime. Habitual offenders could be locked up for much longer periods, both as a retributive measure and as a deterrent, on the theory that the threat of very long confinement might be sufficient to deter at least some potential offenders from committing the crimes that they have been prone to commit; and in addition, confinement in such cases would serve to incapacitate the offenders from committing future crimes, thus offering the public the protection that it expects to receive from its government.

8

The Death Penalty

Though the Ten Commandments are often quoted as saying, "Thou shalt not kill," that passage is more correctly translated, "Thou shalt not commit murder." It is all too easy to gloss over the important distinctions entailed in these words, but in life, the distinctions will remain, whether or not we choose to acknowledge them.

It is said that life is sacred, that no decision is more momentous than the decision to take a man's life. Some people insist that no man ever has the right to take any other man's life, no matter what the provocations or the circumstances. Others allege that there are occasions when homicide is justifiable.

Some say that no war is ever justified and that the taking of human life in war is always morally wrong. Others maintain that in a struggle for national survival, or even for national honor, it is permissible, and perhaps even noble, to take the lives of enemy combatants.

Some say that the police have a right, and perhaps even a duty, to take the life of a felon who is fleeing or resisting arrest, and that any citizen has the right to take the life of another who is threatening him with a deadly weapon; others deny that anyone ever has the right to take the life of another human being, even under such extreme circumstances.

Some say that there are some offenses for which the death penalty is appropriate. Others argue that for the state to take the life of any of its citizens, even those who have been convicted of the worst offenses against their fellow citizens and against society (such as rape, kidnapping, treason, and murder), is uncivilized and unjustifiable.

If *all* deliberate taking of human life is morally wrong, then no meaningful distinction may be drawn between killing and murder as those terms are applied to human beings.* If one is to be consistent and uphold the strong position, then it would seem that one would be obliged to oppose not only capital punishment and war but also killing in self-defense, abortion, and euthanasia.

In addition to the moral argument that all taking of human life is tantamount to murder (which seems highly suspect on the face of it), a number of arguments have been put forth by those who oppose capital punishment. The most important of them may be reduced to the following.

1. Capital punishment cannot be considered a reformative measure. Statistically, there is no evidence that it has a significant deterrent effect. Therefore, it must be a retributive measure, stemming from primitive and uncivilized impulses for revenge.

2. A glance at the figures on executions carried out shows quite clearly that the poor and the underprivileged are executed far more often than the rich and that black citizens suffer the death penalty far out of proportion to their numbers in the general population. It is apparent, therefore, that the death penalty is a form of repression used against the poor and the black by the rich and the powerful.

3. All too often have innocent men been sentenced to death. Human life is too sacred to be taken when there is even the slightest possibility that justice has not been done. If a man accused and convicted of a serious crime is subjected to any other form of punishment, the penalty is not irrevocable. He can be released from prison if an error is found and compensated for the time he has lost. But there is no way to call a man back from the grave if he has been executed for a crime he has not committed.

4. The use of the death penalty diminishes the value that is placed upon human life. When the state takes the lives of its citizens, there is an inevitable pandering to the desire of some people for the sensational. The spectacle of the deliberate snuffing out of a human life, with all the bizarre ceremony

---

* It may be possible for those who oppose all deliberate taking of human life to preserve the distinction between manslaughter, accidental homicide, and murder as a means of apportioning blame, responsibility, guilt, or punishment to those who have been involved in the killing of a human being.

that accompanies it, is hideous and revolting to anyone who possesses civilized sensibilities; it is degrading to the state itself; and it exercises a corrupting influence upon those who follow it through the detailed reports that inevitably follow. Far from exercising a salutary influence upon the population, capital punishment can be maleficent, arousing perverse and vicious dispositions in the hearts of men. Inmates of prisons where executions take place, knowing the men who sit in death row, are *more* likely, rather than less, to commit murder if they return to a life of crime upon their release, for, having seen the torment of the condemned, they are not likely to suffer arrest lightly. And those who are mentally unstable have been known to emulate the crimes of men who have become notorious because of their long trials and the wide publicity that is accorded them.

5. Juries and judges in both trial courts and appellate courts are likely to strain the evidence and the law to acquit those accused of capital offenses, so repugnant is capital punishment to the moral feelings of men today. Juries may acquit even in the face of clear evidence that the accused is guilty of a capital crime. Justice is thus perverted by the existence of the death penalty. And the years of delay during the long appeal process subject the victim to unconscionable torments.

These, then, are the principal arguments raised by those who favor abolition of capital punishment. There is much to commend them to any humane person who has genuine reverence for human life. But the arguments seem to be unsound.

DETERRENCE

It is true, of course, that capital punishment is not a reformative measure. It is not true, however, that anyone has demonstrated that it does not have a deterrent effect. There is no clear proof that it *does* have such an effect, but one must not confuse the lack of proof for the proposition that capital punishment *does* deter with proof of the proposition that it *does not*. Thus far, the evidence is completely inconclusive.

It is sometimes argued that the rates of murder committed in adjacent states where one has and the other does not have the death penalty are quite comparable, thus demonstrating that the death penalty makes no difference. Indeed, some states that still have the death penalty save significantly *higher* crime rates and *higher* incidence of murder than others that have abolished the death penalty. However, such statistics prove nothing. Even those who believe that the death penalty is a deterrent acknowledge that other factors enter into the crime rate, including economic, political, social, and psychological conditions. Furthermore, murderers are not always fully aware of the latest legal developments in the state in which they happen to commit their crimes. The long-term effects of many centuries of capital punishment very likely continue to influence the conduct of many persons. A believer in the deterrent effect of the death penalty need not suppose that there are hundreds of potential murderers who are straining at the bit, waiting for the death penalty to be abolished so that they can commit their crimes without fear of being executed.

Even after the death penalty has been abolished, the deterrent effect is likely to linger on for quite some time. It is impossible to determine when the fear of the death penalty ceases to be effective. If there is a significant decline in the homicide rate after the abolition of the death penalty, it does not necessarily follow that the abolition of the penalty was the cause of the decline in homocides. Consider, for example, the following facts: In England, the ten-year average murder rate fell from 4.1 to 3.3 per million from 1910 to 1939, a period during which England not only had the death penalty, but used it. Suppose the death penalty had been abolished in 1910, and suppose further that this had resulted in 100 more murders than were actually committed during that period. There would still have been a decline in the murder rate from 4.1 to 3.5 per million. This would have led critics of the death penalty to the erroneous conclusion that the abolition of capital punishment had been followed by a decrease in the murder rate, and would seem to have lent support to their contention that there is no connection between the death penalty and the crime rate.[1]

A number of recent studies have attempted to demonstrate that the death penalty *does* deter potential killers from committing crimes that they might otherwise have committed.[2] However, these studies have been severely criticized for their treatment of the statistical evidence, just as earlier studies purporting to prove that the death penalty was *not* a deterrent were criticized for their treatment of the statistics.[3]

Opponents of the deterrent theory typically compare the homicide rates of states that have retained the death penalty with those of states that have abolished it. Others compare the homicide rates before and after abolition or restoration of the death penalty in a given state. And still others compare the homicide rates just before and just after highly publicized executions. A more refined approach has been to compare adjacent states, because one of the chief criticisms of a broader approach is the likelihood of wide geographical disparities among the states and corresponding ethnographic differences that might account for varying homicide rates. By comparing California, which had the death penalty, with its neighboring state, Oregon, which had abolished it, or Arkansas with Missouri, or New York with Pennsylvania, it was thought that some acceptable conclusions might be found. Most of these studies came up with the rather surprising result that in most cases, where the death penalty had been abolished, the homicide rate was lower than it was where it had been retained. States that have abolished the death penalty have experienced no significant increase in the homicide rate. Reintroduction of the death penalty has been followed by no significant decrease in the level of homicides. And abolition of the death penalty has sometimes been followed by a *decrease* in the homicide rate. Moreover, studies have revealed that there was no significant change in homicide rates following highly publicized executions. As a result, many criminologists and sociologists have concluded that "the death penalty has no discernible effect as a deterrent to murder." [4]

But these studies have serious defects. Among them is the fact that the figures used to measure the homicide rate are supplied by the Federal Bureau of Investigation, which does not distinguish between various forms of homicide, such as first- and second-degree murder and manslaughter. Moreover, states do not define these terms in precisely the same way. And the manner in which the criminal justice system operates in the United States (with opportunities for plea bargaining, the acceptance of lesser charges, and so on) makes it difficult to make the fine distinctions that are required for meaningful studies. Furthermore, the studies tend to ignore the relationship between the number of *actual* executions and the murder rate. If a state retains the death penalty on its books but never executes anyone, it cannot meaningfully be regarded as a retentionist state. In addition, the death penalty may operate to deter crime, not only directly through the fear of maximum punishment that it instills in potential murderers, but indirectly, by reinforcing the social condemnation of the crime, by instilling in people the feeling that murder is an awful and repulsive thing to do. Such factors as these are not readily amenable to statistical analysis.

Finally, there has been a tendency for people to point to the large numbers of prisoners on death row. "You see," they say, "here is all the evidence you need. If the death penalty were a deterrent, how does it happen that these people were not deterred?" This, of course, is no argument at all, because no advocate of any penalty for any offense has ever suggested, so far as is known, that it would be effective in deterring 100% of the potential offenders. What is important is not how many were *not* deterred, but how many *were*—and this cannot be determined by counting the number of persons convicted of homicide or by counting the number of victims of homicide. It can only be determined, if at all, by a very sophisticated study of persons who have *never* committed homicide. The crucial question is not how many persons have committed murder, but how many have not, and why they have not. This suggests that just as the fear of being fined and losing one's license deters most (but not all) potential speeders and reckless drivers, so the fear of capital punishment may deter some (though not all) potential murderers and kidnappers. The death penalty may be the *only* penalty that might possibly deter some forms of criminal behavior.

It is astounding that people can seriously argue that the fear of death is never sufficient to deter would-be murderers or kidnappers. Everyone has experienced the temptation to commit some offense or other, and everyone has at some time overcome that temptation. Although many factors enter into that decision, one of the crucial ones is frequently the fear of some penalty. The harsher the penalty, the greater the fear and the more effective its deterrent effect. It is difficult to understand how people who experience the deterrent effect of relatively trivial penalties such as those attached to traffic offenses can seriously advocate the view that death is no deterrent at all. The fear of death has been powerful enough to dissuade thousands of persons from flying. It has helped to deter thousands more (though not everyone) from smoking, despite the pleasure they derive from tobacco, and in the face of the agonizing discomforts of withdrawal. The fear of cancer or heart attacks has deterred millions of persons from eating sweets and impelled them to undergo the discomfort of special diets and the inconvenience of rigorous exercise programs. If people act on the long-term fear of death, when death is only a remote possibility, in such areas as these, why is it unreasonable to suppose that some of them, at least, might be impelled to take appropriate precautions against the possibility of being executed—one of which might be refraining from committing capital crimes?

The reluctance of social scientists to acknowledge the likelihood of the death penalty's having a deterrent effect becomes even more difficult to comprehend if we consider what we know of criminal behavior. We know that criminals will go to great lengths to avoid punishment. When faced with certain death, as when they are confronted by several policemen with drawn revolvers, most, though not all, will give up rather than attempt to escape. Given a chance to escape, however, most will, rather than stand trial and be subjected to whatever penalties are prescribed. They generally go to great lengths to avoid detection, arrest, and conviction. It would appear, then, that they are aware of the penalties assigned to the crimes they commit and are as anxious as most other persons to avoid suffering those penalties.

Most interesting of all, however, is the attitude of the criminal world toward the death penalty. It appears, at least in some circles, to be a highly respected method of enforcement. There is evidence that those associated with the major movements in organized crime employ capital punishment as a means of enforcing their own rules. The Mafia has a graduated scale of penalties, but the gravest offenses against the organization or its members merit the death penalty. Those who breach the gang's covenants, who "squeal to the cops," who attempt to sever their relations with the gang, who fail to pay their debts, who attempt to move into the territory of another gang—such persons are likely to find that a "contract" is out on them. In other words, those who are in the top echelons of organized crime believe in the efficacy of the death penalty as a deterrent. They also believe that the death penalty's power as a deterrent depends upon swift and certain enforcement. They act upon that belief.

This is not to suggest that a civilized community ought to model itself after its most barbarous members. If we use the death penalty, it is not because we want to descend to the level of criminal bosses. The point is that if we must choose between the well-intentioned efforts of sociologists to juggle statistics to prove that the death penalty is not a deterrent, and the insights provided by the practices of major criminal organizations, which reveal that they act upon the assumption that capital punishment is a deterrent, it is reasonable to conclude that the Mafia, and not the sociologists, have common sense on their side.

From 1930 through 1978, nearly a half century, there was no year in which the number of executions in the United States reached 200. The number gradually dwindled from 83 in 1952 to 15 in 1964, 7 in 1965, 1 in 1966, and 2 in 1967. There were no executions during the years 1968 to 1976, and there was one in 1977. During most of that period, the homicide rate hovered around 5 per 100,000 population. In 1963, it reached its lowest point since the measure was first taken, 4.5, and then began a swift rise during each of the following years. By 1970 it reached 7.8, an all-time high, and moved steadily upward from then on. From 1960, when there were 56 executions, to 1970, when there were none, the number of homicide victims rose from 8,464 to 16,484. From then on, the figures run as follows: [5]

Year	Homicide Victims	Rate per 100,000
1971	17,800	8.5
1972	18,700	8.9
1973	19,600	9.4
1974	20,700	9.8
1975	20,500	9.6

A good case could be made for the proposition that no statistical study of deterrence based upon the American experience is likely to yield meaningful results, because neither the absolute number of executions nor the ratio of executions to murders has ever been high enough to have a significant impact. The United States has not during the past 50 years, at least, tried in any significant way to deter murder or other major crimes by use of the death penalty. This is not to say that there were no other factors operating to deter persons from committing murder. A life in prison is not a matter to be ignored as one weighs the possible costs of committing a homicide. The consequences for oneself and one's loved ones as one seeks to avoid detection, arrest, and conviction, and the possibility of long-term detention as well as the shame for all concerned undoubtedly have some effect. Whether they have as great an effect as the possibility of being executed is a question that has not yet been definitely answered. But if even one out of a hundred murders could be deterred by the execution of those who are guilty of murder, not only the potential victims would be saved, but also the potential murderers. If 1% of the homicides committed in the United States in 1975 could have been deterred, 205 people would have been spared. Such figures cannot be ignored.

If part, at least, of the purpose of punishment is deterrence, then it is evident that certain major crimes cannot possibly be deterred by any other penalty. The revolutionary who contemplates blowing up a school bus as a means of terrorizing the population is not likely to be deterred by the threat of life imprisonment, for he believes that even if he is caught, he will be released and be given a hero's welcome by his fellow revolutionaries when the revolution succeeds. Similarly, the potential traitor in wartime will not be deterred from betraying his country by the fear of life imprisonment, for he believes that when his country is "liberated" by the enemy, his imprisonment will be brought to an end. The same must be true of criminals who are already serving life sentences in prison. The threat of yet another lengthy sentence is meaningless and can therefore have no effect at all upon the lifer who contemplates doing in his cellmate or the guard on duty in his cell block. If anything at all will deter such men from the crimes they are contemplating, nothing less than the death penalty will do. Even in those jurisdictions where the death penalty has been abolished for most other crimes, these crimes often continue to be punishable by death.

One might argue that men bent on murder or revolution will not be deterred by any penalty, no matter how severe. But with the exception of those who are insane (who are not included in this discussion, because they are not punishable) and those fanatics who would welcome martyrdom, men generally tend to weigh costs or the risks of acts that they contemplate. When the costs or the risks are too high, they usually do not do them. As the costs go down, the temptation to perform the act is more often translated into action. Thus, when the penalty for speeding is $5, people are more likely to violate the law than they are if the penalty is $50. When potential speeders realize that they are more likely to be caught, they are more likely to keep to the legal speed limit. It is next to impossible to reduce the pleasures or the imagined advantage that people might derive from performing acts that the law forbids. However, the law is able to increase both the cost of performing such acts and the risks entailed by them. By increasing the penalties attached to behavior that they are particularly anxious to deter, legislators can assure, to a higher degree, that fewer people will indulge in the forbidden behavior.

If human life is sacred, as opponents of the death penalty say, and if the threat of capital punishment will avert some murders or acts of treason, then capital punishment ought to be retained; for at the cost of some lives, many more may be saved—the lives of those who might otherwise have been the victims of capital crimes, and (what is sometimes overlooked) the lives, or at least the liberties, of those who would have committed such crimes if they had not been deterred by the threat of the death penalty. If one has genuine reverence for human life, one must be at least as concerned for the lives of those who are the innocent victims of murderous assaults as one is for those who are convicted of having committed murder. And this may entail taking the lives of those who have demonstrated their lack of control where other human lives are concerned. The assailant is often seen as an object of pity, as an innocent victim of circumstances beyond his control. But compassion for the assailant should not be permitted to misguide us into disregard for his victim. Such misplaced anxiety over the fate of the attacker has gone so far that in some schools, for example, the victims of assaults are blamed for their misfortunes. The president of one of the nation's largest teachers' unions has said:

> Victims of assaults (teachers and students) are reluctant to report assaults and to press charges because of the all-too-prevalent strategem of shifting blame from the assailant to the victim himself. A pupil-victim who has been mugged and had several dollars taken from him may be accused of having "invited" the attack by carrying too much money with him. Teacher victims may be accused of having "provoked" assault by demanding, for example, that a student return to his classroom rather than "cut" class and loiter in the cafeteria. The assailants soon learn that they can continue in their actions with virtual impunity because the innocent victims, instead of receiving official support, are themselves denounced when they ask for help.

Because the accused can call upon a host of legal experts to protect him from prosecution and punishment, whereas the victim is left to his own devices, "the assailant goes free. The teacher or student victim if he is lucky, can transfer to another school in order to be spared the anguish of being assaulted by the same person again." [6]

This grossly unjust situation in the public schools of one city (though it is certainly not confined to that school system or to that city) is merely a reflection, in microcosm, of attitudes that have come to dominate the thinking of many people. One of the fundamental purposes of the state is the protection of its citizens from bodily harm. If any legal or political system loses its capacity to protect its citizens from such harm, it has lost most of its reason for being, and any claim it may have upon the allegiance of its citizens becomes very tenuous. Ordinary men and women should not have to arm themselves against attacks by lawless persons who roam the streets. School-children and teachers should not have to go to school dressed in armor to protect themselves from brutal assaults that might be directed against them by undisciplined or vicious students who roam the halls. Pity and compassion for the assailant, and recognition of the miserable conditions in which he may (or may not) have been brought up, are no justification for permitting him to return to the streets or to the school to repeat his crimes and to injure other innocent persons. Neither the judges nor officers of the school administration can plead that *their* backgrounds make it impossible for them to treat offenders other than they do. If they are unable to carry out their mandate to protect the public, they should resign from their posts.

RETRIBUTION

In his opinion for the majority in *Gregg* v. *Georgia*, upholding the death penalty as constitutionally permissible, Justice Stewart observed that capital punishment "is an expression of society's moral outrage at particularly offensive conduct," and that even though this function may be unappealing to many, "it is essential in an ordered society that asks its citizens to rely on legal processes rather than self-help to vindicate their wrongs." Without orderly means of imposing penalties upon offenders proportionate to what the aggrieved parties feel is deserved, society runs the risk of anarchy, vigilante justice, and lynch law. Even if retribution is not the dominant objective of the criminal law, it is neither forbidden by the Constitution nor inconsistent with respect for the dignity of men, he said. Indeed, he went on, capital punishment "may be the appropriate sanction in extreme cases [as] an expression of the community's belief that certain crimes are themselves so grievous an affront to humanity that the only adequate response may be the penalty of death." As Lord Justice Denning told the British Royal Commission on Capital Punishment, "some crimes are so outrageous that society insists on adequate punishment, because the wrong-doer deserves it, irrespective of whether it is a deterrent or not."

In a report on "vicious youth gangs" in Detroit, the *New York Times* quoted a black resident as saying, "If I know who steals or breaks into my home, I'm going to get my gun. I'm going to hunt him. They can lock me up, but that's the only thing left. The police, they're not doing the job." [7] Following another report on violent juvenile crime, a reader wrote to the *Times,* "Sudden death for a young man who does not want to surrender his wallet is cruel and unusual punishment. Why not let the punishment fit the crime, even if we have to amend the Constitution? The bleeding-heart mentality has caused too much bloodshed." [8] These sentiments, expressing outrage at the government's failure to bring such crimes under control and to provide citizens with the protection that is a government's principal responsibility, are clearly shared by a very large percentage of the American people. Under some theories of government, when people agreed to lay down their rights to self-help, transferring them to their common sovereign, the sovereign assumed the duty to see that justice was done. Governments assumed the prerogative of punishing wrongdoers to prevent blood feuds from developing and spreading and to bring some order to the fixing of guilt and the exacting of retribution, which otherwise would have been done informally and summarily. As public frustration grows, as more and more innocent persons feel that they are direct or indirect victims of vicious criminals, and as more people become convinced that their demand for retribution will not be met by those they had authorized to exact the appropriate penalties from wrongdoers, the danger of vigilante justice grows ever greater.

The threat of lawlessness from the victims of crime is perhaps not a sufficient reason to justify the imposition of the penalty of death upon those who are lawless. But it is not clear that the critics of retributivism have a monopoly on truth. Their assertion that it is wrong to seek retribution appears to rest upon an intuition that is not shared by a large number of people. Few opponents of the death penalty are prepared to deny that the execution of Adolf Eichmann or the hangings of the Nazi war criminals at Nuremberg were morally wrong. With a few exceptions, most of them concede that some crimes are so monstrous as to justify a penalty of death. But once that concession has been made, the principle has been established that the death penalty may, at least in some circumstances, be justified, and it remains only to decide what crimes are of such great enormity as to deserve it. Many of the people who reject the death penalty for the likes of Eichmann claim that death is too good for them. They say that it is more appropriate to make them suffer by having to live for many years in detention—perhaps like Rudolf Hess, who has been imprisoned for three decades, most of them all alone, in Spandau Prison—so that they might think about their crimes. This is an interesting switch, for the very people who advocate keeping such criminals alive so as to increase their suffering reject capital punishment in other contexts because it causes so much suffering and is therefore a "cruel and unusual punishment."

If the deliberate killing of an innocent person is wrong, and if we lack certainty about the deterrent effects of the death penalty, is it not reasonable to take a chance in favor of saving some innocent lives by executing some guilty persons?

In his dissent in *Gregg* v. *Georgia*, Justice Marshall said that "it simply defies belief to suggest that the death penalty is necessary to prevent the American people from taking the law into their hands." He went on to assert that Lord Denning's contention that some crimes are so outrageous as to deserve the death penalty, regardless of its deterrent effects, is at odds with the Eighth Amendment. "The mere fact that the community demands the murderer's life for the evil he has done," he said, "cannot sustain the death penalty," for

> the Eighth Amendment demands more than that a challenged punishment be acceptable to contemporary society. To be sustained under the Eighth Amendment, the death penalty must [comport] with the basic concept of human dignity at the core of the Amendment; the objective in imposing it must be [consistent] with our respect for the dignity of [other] men. Under these standards, the taking of life "because the wrongdoer deserves it" surely must fail, for such a punishment has as its very basis the total denial of the wrongdoer's dignity and worth. The death penalty, unnecessary to promote the goal of deterrence or to further any legitimate notion of retribution, is an excessive penalty forbidden by the Eighth and Fourteenth Amendments.[9]

But retributive justice does not deny the wrongdoer's worth and dignity. It assumes it, and makes no sense at all unless the wrongdoer is regarded as a human being capable of making his own decisions, acting upon his own volition, and deserving moral praise or blame for what he does. The death penalty is the ultimate condemnation, morally and legally, of a person who has, through his actions, demonstrated his utter contempt for human worth and dignity and for the most fundamental rules of human society. It is precisely because of a nation's belief in the dignity and worth of those who live under the protection of its laws and because of its adherence to the principle that human life is sacred that it may choose to employ the death penalty against those who have demonstrated their disregard of those principles.

SOME ARGUMENTS AGAINST CAPITAL PUNISHMENT

Some of the major arguments against capital punishment were reiterated by members of the United States Supreme Court in the opinions they wrote in *Furman* v. *Georgia,* the 1972 decision that temporarily abolished capital punishment in this country. Among them are the following:

1. The poor and the underprivileged are executed far more often than the rich, and blacks suffer the death penalty far out of proportion to their numbers in the general population.
2. Juries have been arbitrary, capricious, and discriminatory in their selection of prisoners who have been condemned to death.
3. Even if the death penalty were a deterrent to crime, it has ceased to be effective in our society because the time that elapses between the crime and the execution is often measured in years, and may be as long as a decade or more.
4. The death penalty is cruel in that it inflicts an inordinate amount of anguish and psychological torture upon the prisoner who waits in the death cell, it strips him of human dignity and of the most basic and elementary human rights, and it is irrevocable.

Each of these points will be taken up in turn:

THE DISPROPORTION OF BLACKS AND THE POOR *
There is no doubt that the poor and blacks are executed far more often than their numbers in the population would appear to warrant. From 1930 to the end of 1970, 2,066 blacks and 1,751 white persons were executed in the United States, though in the total population black citizens were outnumbered by whites in a ratio of eight to one. This fact constituted the sole ground upon which Justices Douglas, Stewart, and White—three of the five Justices who voted with the majority in *Furman*—rendered their decisions.

Some of them reiterated what had been written in earlier cases: that the Constitution's provision against cruel and unusual punishment does not apply to the death penalty as such. In *Trop* v. *Dulles,* for example, Chief

---

* Reprinted from Burton M. Leiser, "In Defense of Capital Punishment," *Barrister*, vol. 1, no. 4 (Fall, 1974), pp. 10ff.

Justice Warren was joined by Justices Black, Douglas, and Whittaker in writing that "the death penalty . . . cannot be said to violate the constitutional concept of cruelty." [10] And Justice Black had observed in 1971 that the Eighth Amendment "cannot be read to outlaw capital punishment."

Were it not for the fact that the death penalty is imposed upon blacks and the poor in such disproportionate numbers, these three Justices, at least, might have been on the other side. Unfortunately, their reasoning leaves much to be desired.

If such fallacious logic were consistently carried forward, it would be necessary also to outlaw imprisonment and fines, for even the most cursory study will reveal that the black and the poor and the disadvantaged constitute the vast majority of the populations of virtually every jail and penitentiary in the nation. If the test for cruel and unusual punishment is to be the extent to which a given penalty is imposed upon a representative sample of the population, then it is unlikely that *any* penalty will stand the test.

If there is a reasonable suspicion that our penal code, or any part of it, is being applied unjustly to a given segment of our population, then the solution is surely not to abolish the penal system or any given penalty. The appropriate solution would be to reform the system that imposed the sentences in a discriminatory way.

An adequate remedy is at hand for *any* person who believes that he has been a victim of discrimination at the hands of a jury, regardless of the penalty that is imposed upon him. He may appeal the verdict, and if the courts find that his appeal has any merit, they can order a new trial. In the cases decided in *Furman,* no proof of jury bias was offered.

It may be appropriate to observe that blacks and the poor are no longer systematically excluded from trial juries, and that more and more defendants, black and white, rich and poor—including former Presidential assistants— are having their cases heard by juries composed of significant numbers of various minority groups.

Nor should one forget that certain kinds of criminal behavior—particularly those types that carry the heaviest penalties—may have been committed by members of certain minority groups out of all proportion to their number in the total population. If this is the case—and there is some reason to believe that it is—then it would be well to discover the causes of this phenomenon and to try to root them out. However, when black citizens, the poor, and the dispossessed are the most frequent *victims* of these very crimes, it is unjust and immoral to deprive them of any protection that the penal system is able to provide.

And if serious crimes are in fact committed more often by members of certain groups, then no one should be at all surprised to find that members of those groups are hailed before the bar of justice, are found guilty of the crimes they have committed, and are sentenced appropriately. Under such circumstances, it would be as perverse for the courts to hold that juries were discriminating against these groups as it would be for an Israeli court to hold that because a disproportionate number of Arabs had been found guilty of terrorism, Israeli juries were discriminating against a minority group.

THE ALLEGED CAPRICIOUSNESS OF JURIES

The charge by some of the Justices that American juries are capricious in their application of the death penalty is certainly shocking. The conclusion they draw from this supposed fact is more shocking still. For by some strange and unknown rule of logic, they conclude that because juries are arbitrary and discriminatory, the death penalty should be abolished.

Prior to 1833, the death penalty was mandatory and juries had no discretion whatever to set the penalty in capital cases. During the nineteenth century, humanitarians and abolitionists succeeded in having the law changed in one state after the other so that juries might be given the opportunity to save from the gallows some persons who had been convicted of what would otherwise have been capital crimes.

One result of this reform was a diminution in "jury nullification," the tendency of juries to acquit defendants when they believed the death penalty was unwarranted. Now the Supreme Court tells us that this humanitarian reform has led to a state of affairs in which juries are actually exercising the discretion that was given them and are refusing to send some murderers, rapists, and kidnappers to their deaths. If they were more consistent, and were condemning more men and women to the electric chair and the gas chamber, these Justices would evidently have concluded that the death penalty was not a cruel and unusual punishment. But because they have exercised the prerogative of mercy that the legislatures conferred upon them, their judgments are called "wanton," "capricious," and "freakish" by an Associate Justice of the Supreme Court, who concludes that the death sentences that they do impose are "cruel and unusual in the same way that being struck by lightning is cruel and unusual."

The paradoxical conclusion with which we are left is this: if the system were more inflexible and if more people were executed, the death penalty would not be cruel and unusual punishment. It is as reasonable to decree that the death penalty should be mandatory as it is that it should be abolished, and some members of the Court have drawn precisely that conclusion.

Unfortunately, however, neither solution helps much, for the culprit is not really the death penalty, but the jury. Whether the death penalty is abolished or made mandatory, we are still left with "wanton, capricious, freakish" juries who may lack the power to impose the death sentence, but continue to have the power to find guilt or innocence. The problem is not resolved; it is merely pushed back a step.

LOSS OF EFFECTIVENESS BECAUSE OF LONG DELAYS

This is a little like arguing that because the little bit of food a starving community is receiving isn't doing them much good we might as well not send them any at all. Just as the solution to that problem is to get the railroads to move the grain to the famished residents more rapidly, the solution the Court ignored would be to give capital cases top priority on court calendars so that they might be tried expeditiously and so that appeals might be heard and decisions rendered as soon after conviction and sentencing as possible.

THE INHUMANITY OF THE DEATH PENALTY

In a decision written by Justice Reed and concurred in by Chief Justice Vinson and Justices Black and Jackson, the Court once declared that "the cruelty against which the Constitution protects a convicted man is cruelty inherent in the method of punishment, not the necessary suffering involved in any method employed to extinguish life humanely." [12] No one would attempt to deny the suffering and the anguish that must be the lot of the condemned man. It is appropriate to observe, however, that he had the opportunity to avoid it but chose instead to risk the danger for some other benefit that seemed to him to render the chance worthwhile. His suffering is very real, but so was the suffering of his victims, and so will be the suffering of the victims of those others who might choose to commit similar crimes if they feel that they can do so with relative impunity.

THE CRUELTY AND IRREVOCABILITY
OF CAPITAL PUNISHMENT

It cannot be denied that the prospect of dying, knowing the precise hour of one's death, is one of the most dreadful things that can happen to a man. Enough accounts of near-executions have been published by those who suffered through them that the anguish of that experience cannot be disregarded. It is precisely that prospect that makes the death penalty such an awesome one and provides whatever deterrent effect it might have.

It must be remembered that the infliction of pain and suffering is not always morally wrong. We have already observed that in some circumstances it is not morally improper to kill another human being, and may even be morally obligatory, as in war, in defense of others, or in self-defense. Every punishment entails some deprivation and some suffering. The more severe the penalty, the greater the deprivation and the suffering. No advocate of the death penalty can deny that any person forced to undergo it must also undergo dreadful suffering. The question is, can the suffering of the criminal awaiting his execution be justified by the benefits to the society he has injured and by the requirements of justice? Those who believe that capital punishment is acceptable answer this question in the affirmative.

The death penalty, however, need not be accompanied by excessive cruelty. The person who has been sentenced to die has not also been sentenced to unnecessary torment or to a slow and painful death, at least not in any modern state. The customary methods of execution are swift and, one may assume, relatively painless. But occasionally the job is bungled. The noose is not properly adjusted, the electrical current is not sufficient to cause unconsciousness, or the marksmen miss their target. Such cases are rare, but they have occurred. Some states have been considering the use of powerful drugs instead of the traditional methods. The injection of a drug would involve minimal discomfort, would cause swift loss of consciousness, and would result in death in a very short time and under carefully controlled conditions. Some critics have objected that such a method would be even more dehumanizing than hanging, shooting, electrocution, or the gas chamber, but it is not at all clear why this should be so.

The death penalty is irrevocable. Although it is true that years spent in prison can never be returned to a man who was wrongly convicted, he at least has the opportunity of starting over; with the compensation he ought to receive from those who wrongfully deprived him of those years, he should be able to enjoy whatever remains to him. But a person who has been executed cannot be brought back if he is later found to have been innocent of the crime for which he was convicted. Such mistakes cannot be rectified. Mistakes have occurred. Innocent men have been executed. Those who support the death penalty must be prepared to live with the fact that the policy they advocate may result in the state's deliberately snuffing out the lives of persons who will later be found to have committed no crime. We all must consider whether that likelihood can be tolerated in order to achieve the benefits that proponents of capital punishment believe will flow from the execution of persons who are dangerous to others and who have committed crimes so grave as to warrant the most severe punishment.

THE CONSTITUTIONAL ISSUE

CASE 10. THE HITCHHIKING MURDERERS

The case upon which the United States Supreme Court decided the death penalty issue is fairly simple. Tony Gregg and Floyd Allen, while hitchhiking in Florida, were picked up by Fred Simmons and Bob Moore. Another hitchhiker, Dennis Weaver, was picked up later and left at Atlanta. At a rest stop a short distance from Atlanta, Simmons and Moore briefly left the car. Gregg told Allen that he intended to rob them, and as Simmons and Moore came up an embankment toward the car, Gregg fired three shots at them and they tumbled into a ditch. He then fired a shot into the head of each of them at close range, took their valuables, and drove away with Allen. After learning about the shootings, Weaver informed the police and gave them a description of Gregg and Allen and of the car they were driving. After they were picked up, Allen recounted the events as they have been described, and Gregg admitted that Allen's account was accurate. Gregg later denied he had ever admitted that Allen was telling the truth and insisted that he had killed Simmons and Moore in self-defense after they had attacked him with a pipe and a knife. The jury found Gregg guilty of two counts of armed robbery and two counts of murder. After the verdict was in, the same jury set the penalty. Neither the prosecutor nor the defense attorney offered new evidence, but both of them made lengthy arguments dealing with the propriety of capital punishment under the circumstances and the weight of evidence of the defendant's guilt. The judge instructed the jury that it could recommend either a death sentence or life imprisonment on each count, that aggravating and mitigating circumstances could be considered, and that the death penalty was authorized only if at least one of the following aggravating circumstances was found beyond a reasonable doubt to exist:

> That the offense of murder was committed while the offender was engaged in the commission of two other capital felonies, the armed robbery of [Simmons and Moore].
> That the offender committed the offense of murder for the purpose of receiving money and the automobile.
> That the offense of murder was outrageously and wantonly vile, horrible, and inhuman, . . . [involving] the depravity of [the] mind of the defendant.

The jury found that the first and second of these circumstances did exist and returned death verdicts on each count.

The Georgia Supreme Court affirmed the verdicts and the death sentences for murder after concluding that in view of the nature of the crime and the defendant the sentences had not resulted from prejudice or any other arbitrary factor and were not excessive or disproportionate. However, the court vacated the death penalty for armed robbery on the ground that it had seldom been imposed in Georgia for that offense, as well as on other grounds.

The Georgia system was hedged about with numerous protections for the defendant. During the separate hearing for setting the penalty, no evidence that had not been made known to the defendant prior to his trial is admissible, but the defendant has substantial latitude as to the kinds of evidence he may introduce. Except in cases of treason or aircraft hijacking, the jury must find beyond a reasonable doubt one of 10 specific aggravating circumstances before it may impose the death sentence. Among these aggravating circumstances are the following:

Committing murder, rape, armed robbery, or kidnapping while engaged in another capital felony or in the commission of burglary or arson.

Committing one of those offenses after having been convicted of a capital felony, or committing murder after having compiled a "substantial history of serious assaultive criminal convictions."

Committing a capital crime while knowingly creating a great risk of death to more than one person in a public place.

Committing murder for financial gain, or for payment, or hiring another to do so.

Committing a capital crime in a manner that was "outrageously or wantonly vile, horrible or inhuman in that it involved torture, depravity of mind, or an aggravated battery to the victim."

Committing murder against certain public officials, or after escaping from a peace officer or a place of lawful confinement, or in order to avoid, prevent, or interfere with a lawful arrest.

The Georgia Supreme Court automatically provides an expedited direct review of the appropriateness of the death penalty in every case in order to determine, among other things, whether the death sentence was imposed "under the influence of passion, prejudice, or any other arbitrary factor," whether the evidence supports the jury's finding that there were aggravating circumstances, and whether the death sentence is excessive or disproportionate to the penalty imposed in similar circumstances.

Gregg's appeal to the Supreme Court of the United States contended that the aggravating circumstance that authorizes the death penalty if the murder was "outrageously vile, horrible, or inhuman" is so broad that capital punishment could be imposed in any murder case. But the Court disagreed, noting that the Georgia Supreme Court had upheld only one death sentence in a case in which that factor was the only one—and that was a "horrifying torture-murder." In response to an objection to the instruction concerning endangerment to more than one person, the Court noted that the only case in which that provision had been upheld was one in which a man had stood up in a church and fired a gun indiscriminately into the congregation. The Court noted that the Georgia Supreme Court had reversed death sentences it considered to be unusual or atypical in that state.

The system adopted by the State of Georgia succeeded in avoiding the defects of those systems that were overturned by the *Furman* decision, for it provided "a check against the random or arbitrary imposition of the death penalty" and substantially eliminated the possibility that a person would be sentenced to death by an aberrant jury. "No longer can a jury wantonly and freakishly impose the death sentence; it is always circumscribed by the legislative guidelines" and held in check by the review of the State Supreme Court. For this reason, and for others that will now be considered, the Court upheld the death sentence that had been imposed upon Tony Gregg and opened the way for other States to reinstitute capital punishment by setting up similar procedures.

CRUEL AND UNUSUAL PUNISHMENT

The Eighth Amendment, which proscribed cruel and unusual punishments, was not intended to outlaw capital punishment as such. This is particularly evident if one considers that the Fifth Amendment, written and adopted at the same time, provides that "no person shall be held to answer for a capital . . . crime, unless on a presentment or indictment of a Grand Jury," and that no person "shall be deprived of life, liberty, or property, without due process of law." It is evident, then, that with a grand jury indictment, and with due process, a person may be deprived of his life, just as he may be deprived of his liberty or property. The cruel and unusual punishments that were banned by the Eighth Amendment were those that involved torture or a lingering death and those that were disproportionate to the offenses being punished. Later Courts have found, on the same basic principle, that *any* punishment for the mere status of being a drug addict is cruel and unusual, just as a single day in prison would be a cruel and unusual punishment for the "crime" of having a common cold.

The Court found that although the Eighth Amendment was dynamic, evolving over the years as public moral perceptions changed, capital punishment was not cruel and unusual as that term stands in the Constitution. As the liberal Chief Justice Earl Warren had once said, "the death penalty has been employed throughout our history, and, in a day when it is still widely accepted, it cannot be said to violate the constitutional concept of cruelty." Earlier Courts had found that that concept implied "something inhuman and barbarous, something more than the mere extinguishment of life," and that the suffering necessarily involved in any execution was not banned by the Eighth Amendment, though a cruel form of execution was. The Court noted that at least 35 state legislatures had enacted new statutes after *Furman*, providing for the death penalty, as had the Congress. It noted also that the people of California had amended their constitution, by referendum, so as to negate a decision by that state's highest court banning capital punishment. Juries, too, are a measure of public morality, and in March, 1976, more than 460 persons were subject to death sentences.

Arguing that the traditional justifications for capital punishment (deterrence and retribution) were sufficiently well founded, despite the reservations that some people have about them, to continue to play a role in penal policy, the Court concluded that the death penalty is not unreasonable, that it is consistent with contemporary moral standards, and that it is not a cruel and unusual punishment as that term is used in the Constitution. In view of the safeguards erected around defendants accused of capital offenses in Georgia and other states, the Court concluded that previous reservations about the death penalty being imposed in an arbitrary and capricious manner no longer applied and that it could therefore be imposed whenever similar safeguards existed.

In 1977, Gary Gilmore, a convicted murderer, repudiated the efforts of his mother and his attorney to appeal his conviction and to win stays of execution for him. He was convinced that he deserved to die because he had committed the crimes of which he had been convicted. Last-minute efforts to save him failed, and he was executed by a firing squad, the first person to die under court order in the United States in 10 years.

THE LIMITS OF CAPITAL PUNISHMENT

The death penalty has historically been employed for such diverse offenses as murder, espionage, treason, kidnapping, rape, arson, robbery, burglary, and theft. Except for the most serious crimes, it is now agreed that lesser penalties are sufficient.

The distinction between first- and second-degree murder do not permit fine lines to be drawn between (for example) murder for hire and the killing of a husband by his jealous wife. Most murders committed in the United States are of a domestic nature—spouses or other close relatives becoming involved in angry scenes that end in homicide. Such crimes, usually committed in the heat of a momentary passion, seem inappropriate for the supreme penalty. Although they are premeditated in the legal sense (for it takes no more than an instant for a person to form the intent that is necessary for the legal test to be satisfied), there seems to be a great difference between such crimes and those committed out of a desire for personal gain or for political motives, between a crime committed in an instant of overwrought emotion and one carefully charted and planned in advance. It is reasonable, therefore, to suggest that the vast majority of murders not be regarded as capital crimes, because the penalty may be disproportionate to the crime committed and because people caught up in such momentarily overwhelming passions are not likely to be deterred by thoughts of the possible consequences of their actions.

Only the most heinous offenses against the state and against individual persons seem to deserve the ultimate penalty. If the claim that life is sacred has any meaning at all, it must be that no man may deliberately cause another to lose his life without some compelling justification.

Such a justification appears to exist when individuals or groups employ wanton violence against others in order to achieve their ends, whatever those ends might be. However appealing the cause, however noble the motives, the deliberate, systematic destruction of innocent human beings is one of the gravest crimes any person can commit and may justify the imposition of the harshest available penalty, consistent with principles of humanity, decency, and compassion. Some penalties, such as prolonged torture, may in fact be worse than death, but civilized societies reject them as being too barbarous, too brutal, and too dehumanizing to those who must carry them out.

Perpetrators of such crimes as genocide (the deliberate extermination of entire peoples, racial, religious, or ethnic groups) clearly deserve a penalty no less severe than death. Those who perpetrate major war crimes, crimes against peace, or crimes against humanity, deliberately and without justification plunging nations into violent conflicts that entail widespread bloodshed or causing needless suffering on a vast scale, deserve nothing less than the penalty of death.

Because of the reckless manner in which they endanger the lives of innocent citizens and their clear intention to take human lives on a massive scale in order to achieve their ends, terrorists should be subject to the death penalty—particularly because no other penalty is likely to serve as a deterrent to potential terrorists.

Major crimes against the peace, security, and integrity of the state constitute particularly heinous offenses, for they shake the very foundations upon which civilization rests and endanger the lives, the liberties, and the fundamental rights of all the people who depend upon the state for protection. Treason, espionage, and sabotage, particularly during times of great danger (as in time of war), ought to be punishable by death.

Murder for personal gain and murder committed in the course of the commission of a felony that is being committed for personal gain or out of a reckless disregard for the lives or fundamental rights and interests of potential victims ought to be punishable by death.

Murder committed by a person who is serving a life sentence ought to be punishable by death, both because of the enormity of the crime and because no other penalty is likely to deter such crimes.

Any murder that is committed in a particularly vile, wanton, or malicious way ought to be punishable by death.

One of the principal justifications for the state's existence is the protection it offers those who come under its jurisdiction against violations of their fundamental rights. Those who are entrusted with the responsibility for carrying out the duties of administering the state's functions, enforcing its laws, and seeing that justice is done carry an onerous burden and are particularly likely to become the targets of hostile, malicious, or rebellious individuals or groups. Their special vulnerability entitles them to special protection. Hence, any person guilty of murdering a policeman, a fireman, a judge, a governor, a president, a lawmaker, or any other person holding a comparable position while that person is carrying out his official duties or because of the office he holds has struck at the very heart of government and thus at the foundations upon which the state and civilized society depend. The gravity of such a crime warrants imposition of the death penalty.

Because the threat of death is inherent in every act of kidnapping and airline hijacking—for without such a threat the holding of a hostage would not have the terrorizing effect the perpetrator desires in order to achieve his aim of extorting money or political concessions from those to whom his threats are delivered—those who perpetrate such crimes may appropriately be subject to capital punishment.

But those who commit homicide in a momentary fit of anger or passion, in contrast to those who carefully plan acts as well as those who commit homicide under excusing or mitigating circumstances, may either be fully excused or given some lesser penalty.

From the fact that some persons who bring about the deaths of fellow humans do so under conditions that just and humane men would consider sufficient to justify either complete exculpation or penalties less than death, it does not follow that all of them do. If guilt is clearly established beyond a reasonable doubt under circumstances that guarantee a reasonable opportunity for the defendant to confront his accusers, to cross-examine witnesses, to present his case with the assistance of professional counsel, and in general to enjoy the benefits of due process of law; if in addition he has been given the protection of laws that prevent the use of torture to extract confessions and is provided immunity against self-incrimination; if those who are authorized to pass judgment find there were no excusing or mitigating circumstances; if he is found to have committed a wanton, brutal, callous murder or some other crime that is subversive of the very foundations of an ordered society; and if, finally, the representatives of the people, exercising the people's sovereign authority, have prescribed death as the penalty for that crime; then the judge and jury are fully justified in imposing that penalty, and the proper authorities are justified in carrying it out.

Part Three
Truth, Fraud, and Business Ethics

At the beginning of the Republic, Cephalus, a wealthy old man, expressing a widely held opinion of the time, defined right conduct or justice as telling the truth, not deceiving anyone, and paying one's debts.* Socrates promptly demonstrated that this would not suffice as a definition of these difficult terms and that there were cases in which telling the truth, not engaging in deception, and paying one's debt would be the wrong thing to do.

When the question of whether one ought to tell the truth or not arises, there are three possible answers: (1) one is obliged to tell the truth, (2) one may (that is, one has the right) to tell the truth, and (3) one is obliged not to tell the truth.

Moral rights and duties must generally be distinguished from legal rights and duties, though there is often a concurrence between what one is legally permitted or obligated to do and what one is morally permitted or obligated to do. However, there are cases in which the law remains silent on matters that some moral thinkers consider to be clear and evident. In still other cases the law seems to come into conflict with what morality requires. These latter cases are most difficult, sometimes providing the grounds for civil disobedience or even rebellion.

It is not sufficient, either, to say merely that in a given case one is obliged to tell the truth, for, among other things, there is a problem of quantity. A salesman may speak nothing but the truth, but fail to mention certain important facts about his product. His silence may be enough to mislead his client into believing what is in fact not true about the product. Similarly,

* Plato, Republic, Book I, Chapter 1.

259

certain statements, though true, may give rise to false inferences because of the context in which they are uttered. What principles might, or ought, to govern such situations?

Further, what is meant by an obligation not to tell the truth? Aside from the obvious moral puzzles inherent in such a statement, there are certain ambiguities that must not be overlooked. There is a world of difference, for example, between not telling the truth and lying. One may not tell the truth about a certain subject by evading the issue, by discussing something else, by making misleading (but not false) statements about it, or by remaining silent.

There are all kinds of false statements and a multitude of circumstances in which false statements may be made that have a great bearing on the propriety of making them. A mother relating the story of the three bears to her young child is uttering a number of statements that are not "true" in one very important sense of the word, but no one would seriously maintain that she had been lying to her child. An actor on a stage may do his best to deceive his audience into believing that a certain stage prop is the skull of Yorick, but few men are purist enough to suggest that such deception is immoral. Nearly everyone would concede that there is a significant difference between a "white lie" and a con artist's attempt to defraud a widow out of her life's savings. If a neighbor asks for directions to the parade route so that he can see the president, there is no reason not to tell him the truth, but if a madman asks for directions to the parade route so that he can assassinate the president, there is every reason to mislead him. The moral issues affecting a doctor's decision as to whether to tell his patient that she is suffering from an inoperable, malignant tumor are exceedingly complex. If the patient asks what the doctor has discovered in his examination, should he conceal the truth by evading the question? Suppose the patient asks directly whether everything is normal. Is the doctor under a moral obligation to tell her the truth? Are there circumstances that would justify his evading the question—thus arousing suspicions in the patient's mind—or would lying to his patient be justified under some circumstances? What, if anything, justifies the lies and deceptions practiced by spies in wartime? Aside from the purely moral issues involved in all these questions, what role, if any, should society play in regulating these practices? Under what circumstances should moral wrongs be transformed into legal wrongs? For example, on the basis of the ancient warning caveat emptor ("let the buyer beware"), many manufacturers, salesmen, and advertisers have made false and misleading statements about their products, in some cases causing serious harm to their customers, to say nothing of financial losses. Bankers and moneylenders by a variety of devices have concealed the true rates of interest that they have charged for the loans they made to borrowers. Is the state justified in forcing them to reveal the truth plainly, even though it may cause them to lose business and possibly even contribute to a serious slowdown in the economy?

Truth may be a divine attribute and the way to freedom, peace, and justice; it may be the sovereign good of human nature, as Bacon put it; and it may be greater and mightier than all things, as a Hebrew poet wrote some 2,000 years ago. But there are other values as well, and they sometimes come into conflict with those represented by the general principle that people ought only to speak the truth; these values may require that in the real world people sometimes have the right, and sometimes perhaps even the obligation, to refrain from speaking truthfully, or even to say what they know to be false. On the other hand, if speaking the truth is of such great value, perhaps it should be reinforced by legislation, in some areas, so that those who are occasionally led astray by the rewards that may be gathered by serving at some other god's altar may be encouraged to remain faithful and true.

In the search for profits, the businessman may be tempted not only to stretch the truth, but also to engage in other practices that he might find shocking if they were done by others in other contexts. Executives of major corporations have recently been found guilty of bribery, of the corruption of public servants, of the short-weighting and deliberate adulteration and contamination of grain that was being shipped abroad under government programs to assist underdeveloped countries, of forming unlawful conspiracies to fix prices and to destroy competition—the most essential ingredient in a free market economy—and of many other offenses. Just as President Nixon and some of his close advisers believed that anything they did was right so long as it contributed to what they believed were the best interests of the United States, so many business leaders appear to believe that anything they do is right so long as it contributes to the corporation's profits. Socrates may well have been right when he said that no one deliberately does what is wrong. The existence of so much wrongdoing might then be explained by the false beliefs so many people have concerning what forms of behavior are wrong. Some people may be morally blind. Others may either be deceived as to the facts or delude themselves into believing that their acts can somehow be morally justified. Their failure to discern the proper relationships between their personal and corporate interests on the one hand, and those of the nation as a whole or their customers on the other, may result from a special "corporate mentality," which subordinates all other interests to those of the corporation. It may also flow from a misguided belief in the proposition that moral standards are purely relative, that no norms are universally binding.

People, of course, differ in their moral judgments, and different cultures evidently have different norms. But neither fact is sufficient to justify the conclusion that no moral norms are universally binding—applicable, that is, even to those who do not recognize or accept them as such. Further inquiry into ethical relativism is more suited to a book on ethical theory or metaethics. But in the chapter on competition and corporate responsibility, the reader will discover a number of principles which seem to be essential to *any ethical system that would include business within its scope. Examples of the deliberate and methodical violation of those principles are also provided. In the light of those examples, the reader is invited to consider whether any culture or society could long endure if it failed to enforce those principles, or others like them, and whether the acceptance of actions committed in violation of those principles would be more likely, in the long run, to promote or to thwart human happiness.*

9

Truth in the Marketplace: Advertisers, Salesmen, and Swindlers

The advertising industry and those that are allied with it, including general merchandising and salesmanship, have been subjected to severe criticism in recent decades because of widespread and flagrant abuses, most of them having to do with fraud and deception. So much advertising is offensive and obtrusive, so much of it is in poor taste, and so much publicity has been given to the "hidden persuaders," the "motivational researchers," and the Madison Avenue "men in the grey flannel suits" that it is easy to lose perspective and assume that the advertiser is a callous huckster concerned only with selling his product and earning his commissions, and not at all bothered with ordinary standards of taste, decency, or morality. Yet there can be no doubt that the advertiser sometimes performs a valuable service, not only for those who employ him, but for the general public as well.

CASE 11. AN ADMAN'S CONFESSION

One day when I was young in advertising I slipped a piece of paper into my typewriter and wrote an advertisement for a life insurance company. It was addressed to young husbands and fathers. One of the coupons received in reply came from a traveler in Rio de Janeiro, whose home was in New Jersey. He was thirty-eight years old, married, and the father of three children. He wanted information on a policy that, in case of his death, would guarantee his family an income of $3,000 a year.

On the man's return to New Jersey, the policy was written and the first payment made. A few days later he went to his dentist to have a wisdom tooth extracted. Somehow the cavity became infected, the infection spread and he died.

That incident made a deep impression on me. Many times in the intervening years I have been reminded that somewhere in New Jersey there are a mother and three children, now grown up, who, without the slightest suspicion of my existence, have had their whole lives changed by the fact that one day I put together some words that were printed in a magazine, and read in a faraway country by their husband and father, who was influenced to do what I suggested.*, 1

Advertisements perform a vital function in almost any society, for they help to bring buyers and sellers together. Even Plato, idealist and anti-materialist that he was, accorded the merchant a place in his ideal state, for it was obvious that under the most primitive, Spartan conditions, division of labor was still essential. If everyone was to do his own job well, people had to be relieved of the irksome tasks of producing everything for themselves and of grubbing aimlessly for the necessities of life. The merchants who brought their wares to early marketplaces relieved people of the need to wander about finding each of the many items they needed. The invention of a central location for shopping was probably as important to the growth of civilization as was the invention of the wheel, though it seems to have been overlooked by historians. The success of a market or of a merchant must have depended from earliest times on some form of advertisement—that is, of some means of attracting shoppers to the merchant's place of business, of "turning him toward" the merchant, as the Latin origin of the word indicates. Peddlers who hawked their wares through ancient streets were croaking out ads of a kind, and those who invented tunes or chanted "Cockles and mussels, alive alive-o" were performing the first singing commercials.

More important, perhaps, is the fact that certain goods and services cannot be made available at all without appropriate advertising. If it is morally right for women, under some circumstances, to seek abortions, then it is also morally right to inform them of the availability of safe abortions. If the decimation of fur-bearing animals is wrong, then it is right for the public to be informed of the availability of artificial furs. The advertisement by a domestic manufacturer of products whose purchase can contribute to a drop in unemployment and a rise in the standard of living is at least offering po-

---

* The importance of advertising to the economy and its contributions to the public welfare must not be overlooked in any balanced discussion of the subject. Whether the methods advertisers employ are ethical is another matter. The author of this "confession" advocates honesty in his profession, but admits that he frequently suppresses the truth.

tential buyers information without which they would not be able to make informed, independent moral decisions as to purchases they are thinking of making.* When there is no advertising, people may be unaware of the availability of services that may decisively enhance the quality of their lives. Many poor persons, for example, would be far better off if they could be professionally advised of their legal rights as tenants, consumers, and employees and assisted in writing contracts, wills, and other documents. Legal advertisements could help make them aware of the availability of such advice.[2]

Some professional organizations have banned all forms of advertising, presumably because the practice is "unbecoming" to professional persons, but more realistically because it is likely to lead to price competition. The American Bar Association (ABA) has argued that competitive advertising would "encourage extravagant, artful, self-laudatory brashness in seeking business and thus could mislead the layman. . . . It would inevitably produce unrealistic expectations . . . and bring about distrust of the law and lawyers."[3] Pharmacists contend that advertising would force them to cut down on professional services and would reduce their image to that of mere retailers.[4] Physicians insist that ads by members of their profession would be confusing, however truthful they might be, because patients are incapable of understanding fee information; such ads should be banned, they say, because people would select doctors on the basis of cost rather than quality of professional care.[5] The courts have held that these contentions are based upon the assumption that people are ignorant, that they must be protected from exploitation by knowledgeable professionals, and that the professionals are not to be trusted. As the court in the ABA case put it, the ABA is assuming that "the public will not be able to accurately evaluate its [the advertising's] content, for either they are intellectually incapable of understanding the complexities of legal services or they will fall prey to every huckster with a promise, law license, and a law book." If the public is so likely to fall prey to hucksters, the court said, that is all the more reason for giving it more rather than less information. In the pharmacy case, the court concluded that an alternative to the "highly paternalistic approach" of the professionals was "to assume that this information is not in itself harmful, that people will perceive their own best interests if only they are well enough informed, and that the best means to that end is to open the channels of communication rather than to close them."

In short, the utility of advertisements rests upon the fact that potentially valuable information is passed from one person to another. The right of the advertiser to hawk his wares is parallel to the consumer's right to hear the advertiser's message. Although such communication may not be deserving of the broad protection that John Stuart Mill and the authors of the United

---

* This does not address the question of the desirability of preferential purchases of domestic over foreign goods. It only points out that important moral questions are involved and that ads can help the consumer make more informed decisions.

States Constitution have conferred upon other forms of speech and artistic presentations, similar considerations justify granting advertisers relatively broad rights—rights which have recently gained some degree of recognition in American courts.[6]

On the other hand, some kinds of advertisements are immoral on their face, for they promote personally or socially harmful products or services. From the point of view of an antiabortionist, an advertisement informing pregnant women of the availability of abortions is immoral. The advertisement of cock fights, dog fights, or other cruel exhibitions, or of slave auctions (when slavery was legal), insofar as they encourage, aid, and abet wrongful behavior, are wrong. If racism and sexism are immoral, then help-wanted ads that specify racial, religious, or sexual preferences or exclusions are immoral.*

THE SOPHISTS AND MODERN ADVERTISING

The business of advertising is persuasion. Most advertisements are placed in the interests of commerce, their business being to persuade potential customers to buy some product or service. But some advertising is used for other than commercial purposes: to gain votes for a political candidate, for example, or for a bond issue, or for some other political proposition. Some are directed toward persuading people to change their personal habits, not to engage in certain practices, or to lend their support to some charitable cause. Examples would be advertising campaigns conducted by associations dedicated to discouraging smoking or drug abuse, and fund-raising campaigns of the Red Feather or United Fund agencies.

Because the fundamental aim of advertising is persuasion, it is natural that all the devices and techniques of persuasion should be employed by advertisers to achieve their aim. Because of the tremendous financial stake that business has in advertising, it is not surprising that great efforts have gone into perfecting the art, to developing new techniques, and to finding out just what factors motivate people to do one thing or another, so that advertisers may exploit that knowledge in order to motivate persons to do what they want them to do. This has given rise to the charge that advertisers "manipulate" the public, that they wield an unconscionable amount of power over the general populace, and that they are capable of molding people to their will. Phrased in this way, these charges are grossly exaggerated. But

---

* Some periodicals continue to carry help-wanted advertising that is discriminatory, despite the fact that it is contrary to American public policy. The *Chronicle of Higher Education,* for example, publishes notices of academic vacancies in certain Arab universities that obviously indicate Jewish applicants will not be accepted. The managing editor of the *Chronicle* has explained that because such discrimination is not contrary to the law of the states that place the ads, the ads do not violate any American law, and will therefore continue.

advertisers admit, and even boast, that they are able to create desires in people for products and services that they had never wanted before and that they can motivate them to change their life-styles, to some extent at least, to conform with the desires of their clients. One may argue that this may be very good and that from the skills of the advertising profession much of America's prosperity has been derived. If people had not been motivated to purchase automobiles and vacuum cleaners, great industries would never have been born, and millions of people would not be employed as they are today. In the case of the automobile, to the extent that advertising has contributed to the growth of the industry, it has helped to make America and the rest of the world what they are today and has done its part to change a whole way of life. Whether this is good or evil is not altogether clear, but its existence is indisputable. To the extent that advertisers have persuaded people to buy soap, it may be argued, they have contributed to the cleanliness of the American people and therefore to their high standards of hygiene and health. Anyone who has visited the Middle East, where vast numbers of people have never been reached by the salesmen of Procter and Gamble and Lever Brothers, and where governments are spending vast sums of money to introduce habits of personal hygiene to the populace, can appreciate the positive achievements of both the advertising and the soap and detergent industries.

But one may argue, too, that these "benefits" are mitigated by serious disadvantages, and in spite of the good that has derived from advertising, the evil that has resulted from it may be enough to cause grave reservations about the practitioners of the art. Because of false, deceptive, and misleading advertising, millions of people have been bilked out of vast sums of money. They have been inveigled into enrolling in "plans" and "schools" that promised to give them great benefits, when in fact the "plans" were ineffective, the "schools" did not employ teachers, and the benefits were totally illusory. They have been persuaded, by false promises of swift cures for the illnesses and ailments that afflicted them, to buy nostrums and remedies that were ineffective and on occasion damaging or even deadly. They have been bilked into purchasing merchandise, or land, or burial plots, or services that were either worthless or nonexistent. They have been conned into paying outrageously inflated prices for products that provided no benefit to anyone but their makers.

The art of persuasion was highly developed in ancient Greece by a group of men who came to be known as Sophists. The Sophists' greatest critic was Plato, who devoted many of his dialogues to excoriating them for their verbal trickery and for their unscientific attitudes. The Sophists claimed to be teachers, and some of them were in fact paid large sums of money by wealthy Greeks who hired them to teach their sons the art of persuasion, which they called rhetoric, on the theory that it was the key to a successful career. The Sophists claimed—correctly, no doubt—that their art gave men power over others that they could not readily achieve in any other way. In one of Plato's dialogues, a supporter of sophism argues that if he were pitted against a physician in a contest over a public health measure that came before the senate, he would be able to persuade the senators to vote in accordance with his views, whereas the physician would be helpless.

Plato, in inquiring into the nature of this art of persuasion, has Gorgias, a Sophist, explain to Socrates that rhetoric is the art of persuasion that is used in law courts and at public gatherings, and deals with justice and injustice. This is not very far from the claim that might be made by a modern public relations firm that attempts to influence legislation on behalf of a major industry. Socrates points out that there is a difference between belief and knowledge; for there can be no false knowledge, whereas people can have false beliefs as well as true beliefs. With this distinction in mind, he suggests that there must be two kinds of persuasion—one that produces belief (whether true or not) and the other that produces knowledge. And Gorgias, the Sophist, concedes that rhetoric is concerned only with producing beliefs in its subjects and is not concerned to give them scientific certainty or even reasoned arguments for such beliefs as they may have. He concedes also that the rhetorician (or—in modern terms—the advertising man or the public relations expert) is interested only in producing the desired belief, but does not particularly care whether the beliefs he propagates are true or false. To Socrates this is tantamount to an admission that rhetoricians are not *teachers* or *instructors* of men in any true sense. Instead they are merely manipulators of men. Though they may deal with law courts and assemblies over matters in which right and wrong, justice and injustice are at stake, they are not teachers of what is right and what is wrong, or of what is just and what is unjust. They may attempt to influence men on questions of public policy having to do with medicine, architecture, commerce, and engineering, but their efforts—though they may be more persuasive, in one sense, because of their knowledge of the techniques of persuasion—cannot be compared to those of experts in those fields, who may be less accomplished as public speakers and who may not be familiar with the gimmicks of the public relations man but who are able to bring their expert knowledge on the *subject* to bear in the discussion. When the Sophist is more persuasive than the doctor in a question where public health is at stake, it is a case of the ignorant being more persuasive with the ignorant public than the expert is able to be. The Sophist does not have to know the facts that are relevant to the issue, for he has devices that enable him to convince the public (that is, those who do not have knowledge about the subject themselves) that he knows more about the subject than those who really *do* know the facts. He merely *seems* to know, even when he knows nothing.

Socrates presented an intriguing analysis that is worth pondering. He distinguished between genuine arts and fraudulent ones.[7] A genuine art is a technique for achieving some genuine benefit to humanity, whereas a fraudulent art (which ought not, properly speaking, to be called an art at all) is a technique that masquerades in the form of an art, that makes a pretext of conferring a benefit upon those who apply to its practitioners, but that actually does them no good at all and may even cause considerable damage to them.

As examples of genuine arts, Socrates offers gymnastics and medicine, both of which are concerned with the health of the body. The gymnastics teacher prescribes a regimen of exercise, diet, work, and rest that is designed to preserve the body's health, and the medical doctor prescribes a similar regimen, in addition to such drugs and other treatments as he may deem necessary, to restore health to a person who has lost it. Both of these people are genuinely concerned for the health of the persons who consult them, and both of them base their prescriptions upon scientific knowledge that they have gained about the body and about what is necessary for good health.

As opposed to the gymnastic teacher and the medical doctor, there are the makeup artists and the confectioners. (In modern terms, the former would be called beauticians, cosmetic salesmen and manufacturers, girdle and brassiere manufacturers, and fashion designers, and the latter would be called gourmet chefs, convenience-food packers, bakers, candy makers, and so on.) These people are not interested in the true well-being of those who consult them or purchase their products. Their principal concern is that their customers should derive *pleasure* from their services and products, regardless of whether it is to their real benefit or not. The use of these means, Socrates says, is deceitful, for to the extent that they succeed, they merely cover up the truth and offer a false sense of security and well-being.

The Sophists of those days, like some of the image makers of today, imagined that they wielded much power, for, as they put it, they were able to cause men to be put to death, to be sent off into exile, and to lose their fortunes. They did these things without regard to the rightness or the justice of their actions.

Socrates asked whether it was worse to do injustice or to be the victim of injustice, and concluded, for his own part, that it was bad to be the victim of injustice, but that it was far worse to be the perpetrator of injustice. For in his view the unjust man was doomed to be wretched and unhappy. Injustice, as he saw it, was a psychological disease, a disorder of the mind that consisted of the individual's inability to control his emotions and desires. A rational person whose personality was not afflicted with the disease of injustice would know that the pleasures of the moment are detrimental to himself in the long run, and, though he might be sorely tempted to give in to his desires for them, he would control his impulses in order to maintain both his physical and his psychological health. Similarly, greed, avarice, and anger can lead a man to perform acts that will harm others; but from Socrates' point of view, the harm that the tyrant does to himself is far greater than any hurt that he can inflict upon his victims. For every time that he gives in to an impulse to hurt another man, he gives rein to an irrational part of his personality, he permits it to overcome his own instincts for self-preservation (like the man who becomes addicted to tobacco when he knows how damaging smoking may be to his health in the long run), and he brings himself ever closer to the time when those baser instincts will take complete control of him. When that time comes, Socrates said, they will destroy him as a human being as surely as anarchy and revolution will destroy a state. Real power, then, is not the power that one wields over other men—the power to expropriate their money, to send them off into exile, or to put them to death—but power over one's own desires, impulses, and emotions. Self-control is the sign of a well-ordered personality, of a healthy and sound man; and the self-controlled man does what is fitting and right to other men, and behaves toward them in accordance with the principles of justice. Such a person, Socrates maintained, is happy, whereas the person who lacks self-control and lets his irrational impulses rule his behavior toward others, prompting him to behave unjustly, is unhappy and wretched, however much outward appearances may deceive us into thinking otherwise. And the truly just man, he concluded, is not interested in persuading his fellow citizens to enjoy themselves at the expense of their physical or their psychological well-being. He tries, as far as possible, to fulfill the principal task of a citizen: to bend all his efforts toward persuading his fellow citizens to improve themselves, to become the masters of themselves, to behave rationally rather than impulsively, and to behave justly toward one another.[8]

The Sophist, then, and (one may suppose) his modern counterpart, the stereotype of the advertising man, may be characterized as one who attempts to wield power over other men for selfish ends; who devotes himself to the pseudoart, or the fraudulent art, of rhetoric, whereby he attempts to inculcate beliefs in other men without regard to the truth of those beliefs, and who furthers the ends of such other fraudulent arts as makeup and confectionary, playing upon the desires of other men rather than trying to improve them. To the extent that this characterization is true, it would follow, in Plato's scheme, that these men are unjust and that they are therefore not acting in their own best interests, though they may imagine that the financial profits that they earn are indicative of the extent to which they are acting in their own best interests.

In spite of the strong arguments that Plato offers in support of his point of view, it cannot be accepted uncritically. Certain assumptions that Plato makes run counter to common sense and have not been satisfactorily established by other means.

His attempt to prove that the unjust man is worse off than the just man seems more a wish that one would like to see fulfilled than a true picture of reality. Too often one sees those who have lived by nefarious practices waxing rich, respected in their communities, and—to all appearances, at least —smug and happy with themselves and their families while honest and conscientious men and women groan under their burdens and live with a broken spirit and even with broken health. That the perpetrator of injustice *should* be more wretched than his victim is devoutly to be desired, perhaps, but it is not a fact of life.

Plato's "fraudulent arts" may not be the unmitigated evils that he paints them as being. There may be some virtue in pleasure seeking, in enjoying the pleasure of the moment and not thinking always of the long-range consequences of every action. The skills of the confectioner do give much pleasure to people, and the skills of the beautician, the corset maker, and the cosmetic manufacturers may be valuable *precisely because* they make the unshapely shapely, the unseemly seemly, and the ugly beautiful, if only for a time. Can it be said unequivocally that man ought never improve upon nature, especially when nature has not been overly generous? A woman who has lost her hair because of a childhood illness can hardly be blamed for wearing a wig, and the suggestion that the wigmaker is guilty of helping her to perpetrate a fraud is extraordinarily narrow and shortsighted. Perhaps changes in style and fashion are a conceit artificially nurtured by Sophists and their followers, but they do give a great deal of pleasure to many people, including not only the vain people who change with every breeze of fashion, but those who enjoy looking at them as well.

Finally, it is not always possible to explain all the reasons for every move to each individual who ought to make it. Time does not always permit all the facts and the reasons to be presented and digested, and not everyone is prepared to grapple with all of the arguments that might be presented on every side of every issue. There are excellent reasons for the use of soap, and some that may not be so excellent. There may also be good reasons for not using soap. Many arguments might be marshalled in favor of the use of one brand of soap as against the use of some other. But it scarcely seems worth anyone's while to get all of those facts and arguments together and to weigh them in order to make a reasoned judgment on the matter. It is not so momentous as to justify much expenditure of time or energy, unless one happens to live in a place where large numbers of people are endangered because of lack of proper hygienic practices. On the other hand, if one has to decide whether to submit to an electroshock treatment, or whether a certain dam should be constructed, it might be worthwhile to get as much information as possible on the matter before doing so, in order to be sure that a proper judgment is being made.

The Sophist and his modern counterpart, the advertising man, may have their place, then. The art of persuasion, as opposed to the art of teaching, is not evil in itself. Only the perverse uses of that art are evil, those practices that make use of lies and deceptions in order to persuade people to do what the advertisers or their clients know they ought not to do. This is the aspect of advertising to which we now turn.

CAVEAT EMPTOR

The ancient maxim *Caveat emptor* ("Let the buyer beware") was coined, no doubt, because merchants in those days were known for their sharp practices. The meaning of the maxim might have been, "Buyer, be careful, for those from whom you make your purchases are not always truthful. They do not always represent their products as honestly as they might. They have a reputation for charging more than a product is worth. They sometimes sell you one thing and then, in the dark recesses of their stalls, wrap another for delivery to you. Be careful, then, lest you be cheated." This *might* have been the meaning of the maxim at one time. Later, though, it is evident that it acquired a wholly new meaning. It was raised from the status of a *warning* based on general knowledge of certain unsavory practices engaged in by some merchants to that of a *principle:* "In any commercial transaction, if there is a dispute between buyer and seller, the burden of proof shall be upon the buyer. If he has any complaints or reservations about his purchase, let him make them before he signs the sales agreement or takes delivery of the merchandise, for once the sale is consummated, the purchase is completed, and the officials of the state are obliged to enforce its provisions, whether the customer is satisfied or not."

In all the centuries that men have been selling things to one another, many devices have been perfected for making things appear to be what they are not, and for wording sales pitches and sales contracts so that they seem to say what they do not say—always to the advantage of the seller, for he is the one who writes the agreement or buys pads of printed forms that have been written by his attorneys to afford him the greatest possible protection against any action that might be brought against him by a disgruntled customer. The customer is presented a printed form and is asked to sign it. He seldom reads it, and if he does read it he does not understand all of its implications, and he hardly ever takes it to his own attorney for advice. If he does and his attorney advises him not to sign it because of possible trouble later on, he is confronted with the choice of complying with the dealer's terms or not having the product that he wants to buy. In almost all cases, then, customers make their purchases on the *seller's* terms, and not on those that would be in their own best interests. In addition, the law has been heavily weighted in the seller's favor, for until quite recently, the consumer had no advocate to argue for him before the legislatures, there was no organized consumer lobby, and very little publicity was given to any but the most flagrant abuses. Manufacturers and retail associations, on the other hand, sent well-paid lobbyists to work on their behalf at the legislative level, and assured themselves of legislative courtesies by contributing heavily to the election campaigns of those who were sympathetic to their goals.

CASE 12. THE TELEVISION SET

Mrs. Amanda Jones was a poor black woman who lived with her three children in a small rented house in a Midwestern town. She worked as a sorter in a cannery, standing on her feet for eight hours every day. For years she saved a portion of every week's earnings so that her boys could go to college some day.

One day, attracted by an ad in a local newspaper, she went to a discount store to purchase a color television set on very easy terms—$20 down and $20 per month. A few days later the set was delivered, and she and her children sat down to enjoy their new possession. Three weeks later, the set caught fire because of an overheated transformer. When Mrs. Jones called the store the following morning, she was given a long runaround. At last, the manager explained that the store was not responsible for any defect in the merchandise. It was covered by a warranty, he explained, and would be repaired by the manufacturer. The nearest authorized repair station was 300 miles away. Mrs. Jones paid a mover to pack her set and deliver it to the service outlet, and then to return it to her. The service outlet, after examining the set, concluded that it was not authorized to replace the set, but made the necessary repairs. It returned the set to Mrs. Jones at her expense, and enclosed a bill for $125 for the labor, because under the warranty, which Mrs. Jones had not read carefully, only defective parts were covered. By this time, Mrs. Jones had paid nearly $600 for her television set, though she had used it for less than three weeks.

When it was reinstalled, she noticed that human figures had a sickly green cast to them. No amount of dial-twisting and adjusting helped. The set was hopelessly out of adjustment. In anger and frustration, she complained again to the manager of the store from which she had purchased the set and threatened to make no further installment payments unless he repaired the set. (The interest on these installment payments, incidentally, added another $90 to the cost of her set, a fact that she did not fully appreciate because she had never sat down to figure it out.) The manager assured her that he had no responsibility for her problems, that that was for her and the manufacturer to work out, and that she was fully responsible for continued payment of her debt to his firm.

When Mrs. Jones tried her set once more, the green picture faded and the sound went out. She wrote an angry letter to the store and to the manufacturer, and tore up the next bill that came to remind her of the monthly installment that was due. After several reminders from the store, she received a letter from the attorney of a collection agency, informing her that her account had been turned over to him and that if she did not pay the full amount due, she would have to go to court.

Mrs. Jones was only too happy to learn that she would go to court for she felt that at last justice might be done. But to her sorrow, she found that the judge would not listen to her complaints about the set; the only question before him was whether she had failed to make payments in accordance with her contract. Because she admitted that she had failed to make the necessary payments, she was required, under terms of the contract, to make full payment of the entire amount due, plus a 10% "service charge," plus court costs and the fees of the finance company's attorneys, as well as her own attorney's fee. Because she could not possibly pay this amount in one lump sum, the judge imposed a garnishment on her wages. Her employer, assuming she must be a "deadbeat," informed her that she was no longer needed. As a result of her continuing inability to pay the judgment, the court ordered the sheriff to seize everything she had that was of any value, except those items that she needed to exist, and to sell them at public auction. At last, the savings account in which she had deposited her sons' future tuition was attached, more than $1,000 was withdrawn from it to pay all the expenses she had incurred, and Mrs. Jones and her children were left with nothing.

Case 12 actually happened and illustrates only a few of the practices engaged in by businesses when the merchandise they sell is defective. Efforts to correct these abuses are often countered by new methods that effectively leave the consumer in the same vulnerable position he had been in prior to the enactment of the legal remedy.

An example of this is the "specious cash sale," a gimmick that was developed by New York merchandisers when the state legisature passed laws designed to protect people like Mrs. Jones from some of the abuses just described.

In the state of New York legislation was passed a few years ago placing some of the responsibility for defective merchandise on the retailer who sold it. In some cases the customer who purchased the item on the installment plan would be permitted to withhold payment until he was given satisfaction for any claims he may have had about defects in the merchandise he had purchased. In order to get around this, merchants assigned the debts to finance companies and banks, who would then collect, regardless of any claims that might be made against the original seller. In 1970 a new law gave the consumer the right to file claims against the bank or finance company in an installment transaction when the dealer failed to make good on any legitimate complaints that the purchaser might have. As a result, these financial institutions refused to deal with retailers who acquired a reputation for being unscrupulous.

The boycotted dealers had to find a way to continue their practices so that they could stay in business and at the same time protect themselves and the finance companies against their customers' complaints. The solution consisted of the "specious cash sale." The retailer, after making the sale, sent his customer to a finance company that lent him the money for the sale. The customer than returned to the merchant and made a "cash" purchase.

Now if the merchant cheated his customer, overcharged him, or refused to replace defective merchandise, the customer was without recourse. He had already paid the merchant for the merchandise and the finance company had lent him the money in a separate transaction. Both the dealer and the finance company were thus in the clear.

In 1971, because of pressure from a million-member consumer lobby and labor unions, the state legislature closed the loophole for some purchases, but not for all. Under the new legislation, when the finance-company personnel are related to the dealer, when the dealer and the finance company are under common control, or when the dealer prepares the forms for paying the loan, the buyer will have the right to redress against the finance company as well as against the dealer.

Four out of five states still adhere to the old doctrine, which gives the finance company or bank that buys an installment contract from a dealer complete immunity against any complaint that the purchaser may have against the dealer. In opposing proposed rulings by the Federal Trade Commission that would do away with these practices, the American Industrial Bankers Association asserted that their practices were "time honored and recognized" and "practiced in the marketplace for many, many years." Consumer groups, on the other hand, have alleged that many cases of consumer fraud would have been impossible were it not for the doctrine that permits such transfers of indebtedness to take place without a corresponding assumption of responsibility for the original sale.[9]

Because there are so many kinds of fraud and deception in business practices, it is impossible to discuss them all here. A few of the more common types, however, will serve to indicate how varied these practices are and how difficult the moral and legal issues involved may be.

It should be noted that not all practices fall under the category of truth telling. In some of the instances to be discussed, it may be argued that no falsehood has been uttered and that the moral issue of truth telling does not arise. If the moral issue of truth telling must be confined within the rigid limits set by the distinction between "stating what is true" and "stating what is false," the discussion that follows clearly goes beyond those limits. But the moral issues surrounding truth telling are actually more subtle than that distinction allows, for the two alternatives set forth—stating what is true and stating what is false—are not exhaustive. In real human discourse there are other possibilities, including telling the truth in a misleading way; not saying anything that is false, but not providing all the information that is needed to make an informed decision; and using various devices to make things seem to be what they are not, without saying anything in words at all. In short, "stating what is true" and "stating what is false" are contraries. "Telling the truth" and "not telling the truth" are contradictories, whose meaning is not exhausted by the contraries just mentioned. Part of the complexity of the problem is bound up with the extremely complicated meanings of these phrases.

THE CONFUSION OF NEEDS AND DESIRES

At a recent conference on business ethics, the founder and president of a high-technology, multinational corporation explained that a corporation is "a group of persons whose purpose is to provide goods and services to those who need them." This is surely a most commendable goal toward which to bend one's efforts. He then went on to explain that *needs* are whatever the public will buy in the marketplace. Now if people need whatever they buy, then a corporation is merely fulfilling its purpose if it sells those goods and services to them. And any corporation that helps a person acquire what he or she needs would be doing what anyone ought morally to do, for it is *prima facie* right for one person to strive to meet the needs of another whenever he can reasonably do so. But people don't always need what they buy. From the fact that a person buys a given item, it does not necessarily follow that he *needs* that item, though it is reasonable to conclude that he *wants* or *desires* it. Men walking down Broadway may be seduced into purchasing the services of a prostitute or a supply of heroin or cocaine. Although they *desire* those goods or services when they pay for them, they can be said to *need* them only in the most extended sense of that word. In that same extended sense, purchasers of slaves in the eighteenth century needed the slaves they purchased. Few people today would argue that the slave traders performed a valuable or morally commendable service. There also are corporations that fail to meet the most elementary standards of morality, though they cater to their customers' desires (or create those desires) and sell them products and services.

People need far more than such elementary necessities of life as food, drink, clothing, and shelter. An inventor developed a plastic tube that can be implanted in the leg of a person whose circulation has been obstructed to serve as an artificial blood vessel, thus saving the leg from being amputated. Persons afflicted by grave circulatory disorders *need* that product, and the inventor performed a valuable service by making it available to them. Like the insurance ad that induced a young man to purchase a policy just a few days before his untimely death, thus assuring his widow and small children of a modest income, an advertisement about such a product would help to reduce the amount of suffering in the world and add to the sum of human happiness. By any utilitarian standard, it would be moral.

Suppose, however (contrary to the facts), that the manufacturer of the artificial blood vessel decided to increase his profits by selling his product to people who did not need it. An appropriate strategy might be to direct a well-organized advertising campaign to the medical profession to persuade physicians that circulatory bypasses ought to be employed in many conditions that are presently treated by chemical means. By offering large research grants to university professors interested in pursuing projects related to circulatory disorders, the manufacturer might succeed in commissioning a number of studies that could be cited in ads in support of his product. By offering entering medical students new instruments with his company's logo, and by sending them small gifts throughout their careers, he would attempt to build loyalty to his firm among those most likely to use or prescribe his products. Finally, if salesmen drop subtle hints about the financial advantages the physician would enjoy if he were to perform circulatory bypass surgery more often, an unscrupulous manufacturer might attempt to sell his product at the expense of persons who don't need it and would be subjected to unnecessary surgery.

Such an advertising campaign and sales tactics would be immoral, for they would contribute to the corruption of scientific researchers and the medical profession and contribute to public cynicism about the reliability of science and medicine and the trustworthiness of the academic community. If successful, such tactics would subject numerous patients to needless and potentially dangerous surgery with the expense, suffering, and possible loss of life that that entails. In earlier times, when people had a simpler way of judging one another's motivations, those responsible would have been called *greedy*.

Testimony at hearings before a United States Senate subcommittee revealed that such unscrupulous practices are not uncommon among pharmaceutical firms.[10] The case described illustrates the contrast between advertising that fulfills the conditions of morality (that it be truthful and honest, and that it contribute to human happiness and diminish human suffering) and that which does not (for it is untruthful, deceitful, corrupting, and damaging to innocent persons). However, the advertiser's motives are not especially important, for in general, motives have little, if anything, to do with the moral quality of acts. The term *greed*, for example, is not especially helpful, for it contains a moral condemnation. Only *after* a moral judgment has been rendered would one be able to determine whether he was greedy. The inventor of the artificial blood vessel readily conceded that he was motivated by a desire to make a profit. The profit motive does not render the invention and the marketing of such a life-saving device immoral or amoral. One's motive is not a sufficient determinant of the moral quality of one's act. One must be judged on the act and not on psychological attitudes. Because products cannot perform their intended function without being marketed and advertised, there can be no doubt of the moral desirability of advertising them, however much the manufacturer may be motivated by the desire for profit. After all, that desire is not evil in itself. Greed is an unrestrained desire for money, regardless of the harm its acquisition may do to others, and is condemned for that reason. It should not be confused with the desire for profit.

FALSE CLAIMS OF NEED

Part of the American scheme of things seems to be the creation of needs, the introduction of a conviction into the minds of people that they ought to have something that they had never needed before, often because it had never existed before. Not only Americans, but people the world over today feel that certain items that would have been regarded as luxuries by their grandparents—or even by themselves a few years ago—are necessities today. Yesterday's luxury has become today's necessity. Electric refrigerators, hair driers, canned foods, soup mixes, and instant potatoes are considered by many to be necessities, though the "need" for some of them has been created. The automobile is probably the most outstanding example of a product whose increasing use has in fact created a genuine need for itself by driving all the competition—not only the horse, but passenger railroads and commuter bus services—out of business. Cosmetics of all kinds are generally regarded by American women as being quite necessary, though women in other countries, including some very advanced nations, feel no particular compulsion about using them, and some American women are now beginning to question the necessity of using them as well. The need for razor blades was created some years ago by clever advertising by the Gillette Company, which convinced men that they were "cleaner" and more attractive if they were "clean-shaven" than if they wore beards or long sideburns. Many members of a new generation have not only called these premises into question, but have acted upon the assumption that it is not necessary to shave in order to be attractive.

Vaginal deodorants are another example of a created need. Full-page advertisements in women's magazines and on television are designed to convince women of the need for these deodorants and of the effectiveness of particular brands.

Many gynecologists are opposed to the use of douches because they tend to remove certain bacteria from the vagina that produce a mild acid that protects it against inflammation and infection. Women who douche, it has been observed, have a higher incidence of vaginal infection than women who do not.

The natural odor of vaginal secretions is not widely regarded as offensive, but is considered by some experts on sex to be highly attractive.[11] Offensive odors originate, for the most part, only when disease is present or when foreign matter (including stale perspiration) has been allowed to accumulate. Any artificial attempt to cover natural odors may cause unnecessary delay in consulting a physician in the event of disease that would first be noticed by an abnormal odor. And, when the offensive odor is caused by perspiration, frequent bathing or the application of talcum powder is a good remedy. One of the dangers associated with deodorant sprays is the possibility of sensitive reactions which can be quite troublesome.

Such preparations are totally unnecessary and may be harmful. But a demand is created for them by extensive advertising campaigns designed to market products that would never have been missed if they had not been produced. In this respect they do not differ at all from many products that we now use regularly without ever wondering whether we really need them, or ought to use them, at all.

One may suppose that nothing false has been stated in these advertisements. But lying behind each of them there is a suppressed premise—one that the reader is expected to supply for herself—namely, the assumption that women need vaginal deodorants. But this suppressed premise is false.

The executive vice president of the American Advertising Federation, Jonah Gitlitz, objected to legislation that would require warning signs on poisonous products on the ground that such warnings are "opposed to the whole concept of advertising." "We are opposed to the whole concept of warnings in advertising," he said, "because our primary purpose is to sell. If we do inform, it is only in order to sell." [12]

The principle that the merchant should inform his customer only when it will help him to sell his product, and its corollary—that the customer should not be informed of anything that might deter him from making a purchase, even when such information may be vitally important to him—are just a step from the swindler's principle—that the customer may be told anything, whether it is true or false, so long as he is persuaded to buy.

The swindler's principle operates in much the same way as that of the respectable advertising man. He too is interested in persuading his customer that the latter has a need for a product or service that the swindler is prepared to sell him, even though he knows that the customer does *not* need it, even when he knows that the customer's well-being may be seriously compromised by his purchase. But the principle that the sale must be made, whatever moral principles must be bent, prevails. A few examples may be instructive.

In the 1930s complaints began to pour in to Better Business Bureaus and the Federal Trade Commission (FTC) about the Holland Furnace Company, a firm that had some 500 offices throughout the United States and employed more than 5,000 persons. Salesmen, misrepresenting themselves as "furnace engineers" and "safety inspectors," gained entry to their victims' homes, dismantled their furnaces, and condemned them as hazardous. They then refused to reassemble them, on the ground that they did not want to be "accessories to murder." Using scare tactics, claiming that the furnaces they "inspected" were emitting carbon monoxide and other dangerous gases, they created, in the homeowners' minds, a need for a new furnace—and proceeded to sell their own product at a handsome profit. They sold one elderly woman nine new furnaces in six years for a total of $18,000. The FTC finally forced the company to close in 1965, but in the meantime, it had done some $30 million worth of business per year for many years.

Similar frauds have been perpetrated by home repair men who climb onto the roof, knock some bricks from the chimney, and persuade the homeowner that he must replace his chimney—at highly inflated prices—or suffer serious consequences. And some automobile repair shops and transmission dealers have been accused in a number of states of declaring that perfectly good transmissions were "burned up" or "shot" and needed replacement or rebuilding at enormous cost.[13] Again, the gimmick is to create a "need" for something when in fact there is no need at all. That is, to persuade the consumer that he ought to buy something that he really ought *not* to buy; to persuade him that it is in his best interests to pay a large sum of money for a given product or service when in fact it is highly detrimental for him to do so, and he gains no benefit whatever from his purchase.

FALSE CLAIMS OF EFFECTIVENESS

An ad in a magazine directed at the teen-age market carries a picture of a young girl whose tears are streaming down her cheeks. "Cry Baby!" the ad proclaims.

> That's right, cry if you like. Or giggle. You can even pout. Some things you can do just because you're a woman. And, also because you're a woman, you lose iron every month. The question is, are you putting that iron back? You may be among the 2 out of 3 American women who don't get enough iron from the food they eat to meet their recommended iron intake. . . . But One-A-Day Brand Multiple Vitamins Plus Iron does. . . . One-A-Day Plus Iron. One of the things you should know about, because you're a woman.

Two claims, at least, are made or implied by this advertisement. The first is that most American women do not get enough iron in their diets to make up for the "deficiency" that results from menstruation. The second is that One-A-Day tablets will fill the gap. As for the first claim, the American Medical Association pointed out long ago that "the average diet of Americans is rich in iron." This statement was made during the AMA's campaign against Ironized Yeast, which also claimed to offer beneficial results from the Vitamin B that was included in its compound. The AMA showed that Vitamin B was found in sufficient quantities in the average American diet to require no special supplement.[14] Now, if there is no significant lack of iron in the average person's diet (and this includes the average woman), there is no deficiency for One-A-Day tablets to fill. To be sure, some Americans do suffer from a lack of certain vitamins and minerals because they do not have an adequate diet. But the answer to this is not for them to take One-A-Day pills, but to eat more nutritious food.

Prior to 1922, Listerine had been advertised as "the best antiseptic for both internal and external use." It was recommended for treating gonorrhea and for "filling the cavity, during ovariotomy." During the years that followed, it was also touted as a safe antiseptic that would ward off cold germs and sore throat, and guard its users against pneumonia. Mothers were urged to rinse their hands in Listerine before touching their babies, and, after prayers, to "send those youngsters of yours into the bathroom for a good-night gargle with Listerine." During the Depression the promoters of Listerine warned those who had jobs to hold on to them. To do that it was necessary to "fight colds as never before. Use Listerine."[15] Gerald B. Lambert, a member of the family that manufactured the product, told how

Listerine came to be advertised as a mouthwash. He was deeply in debt, and, needing some cash to bail himself out, he decided to move into the family business. In discussing the advertising of the mixture, his brother asked whether it might be good for bad breath. Lambert was shocked at the suggestion that "bad breath" be used in advertising a respectable product. In the discussion that followed, the word *halitosis,* which had been found in a clipping from the British medical journal *Lancet,* was used. The word was unfamiliar to everyone at the meeting, but immediately struck Lambert as a suitable term to use in a new advertising campaign. The campaign caught on, Lambert paid off his debt, and in eight years made $25 million for his company.[16]

Now, how effective is Listerine for the ailments it claimed to cure? The AMA pointed out that the manufacturers of these antiseptics exaggerated the germ-killing powers of their products, that they did not tell of the hazardous germs that were not affected by Listerine, and that they failed to mention that the ability of a compound to kill germs in a test tube or on a glass plate in the laboratory is no indication of its capability of killing them in the mouth, the teeth, the gums, or the throat, let alone in other parts of the body.[17]

A recent case that is merely an echo of similar cases that go back many years is that in which the Federal Trade Commission ordered the ITT Continental Baking Company to stop promoting Profile bread as being less fattening than ordinary bread because it had fewer calories per slice. The advertisers neglected to mention that Profile bread had fewer calories per slice because it was sliced thinner, and that the difference between Profile and other bread slices was 58 as opposed to 63 calories, a rather insignificant amount. In addition, it had been claimed that people could lose weight by eating two slices of Profile before every meal. This was so, the FTC held, only if the consumer ate a lighter meal; and Profile bread had no special virtue, in this respect, over any other brand of bread.[18]

A similar misrepresentation was discovered in ads sponsored by the General Foods Corporation, claiming that two Toast 'ems Pop-Ups contained at least as many nutrients as a breakfast of two eggs, two slices of bacon, and two slices of toast. In a commercial showing a child mulling over such a breakfast, a voice told parents whose children were unhappy at breakfast that "two hot Toast 'ems provide 100 per cent of the minimum daily requirements of vitamins and iron. . . . As long as you know that—let them think it's just a big cookie." General Foods signed a consent order prohibiting it from making false nutritional claims for Toast 'ems or any other consumer food product.[19]

These are only a few of the better-known nationally advertised products that do not do what they claim to do. The reader is no doubt familiar with the claims made by quacks and fakers of all kinds who promise relief from a multitude of ailments through the purchase and use of their nostrums, devices, and treatments. Many people who have not found relief through normal medical channels for such diseases as arthritis, rheumatism, and cancer are prone to take the attitude that they have nothing to lose if they try these cures, particularly when virtually every "doctor" who represents such a nostrum can produce a multitude of written and living testimonials to his success. Such "doctors," whose degrees are seldom medical degrees and are often purchased from mail-order houses or from unknown and unrecognized institutions, never mention their failures, and are unwilling to submit their patients or their treatments to scientifically controlled tests.

One of the most celebrated cases of medical quackery is that of Harry M. Hoxsey, who operated cancer "clinics" for more than a third of a century. He claimed to have received the secret formula for the cure of cancer from his father, but did not disclose the fact that both his parents had died of cancer. He managed to persuade the Taylorville, Illinois, Chamber of Commerce that his "practice" would be good for local business, and thus his advertising directed inquirers to write to the Taylorville Chamber of Commerce. Before long, patients began to come, and some of them died not long after Hoxsey applied his secret paste. One doctor examined such a patient two days before his death and found "necrosis of not only the soft tissue of his face, but a complete destruction of the malar bone. This man died of hemorrhage at the hospital." Analysis at the laboratories of the AMA revealed that the paste Hoxsey used was an escharotic, a corrosive chemical mixture, whose chief active ingredient was arsenic. It ate away the flesh without distinguishing between healthy and cancerous tissue, and sometimes destroyed the blood vessels, causing death through hemorrhage. Hoxsey also prescribed certain medicines that were to be taken internally—one of them consisting of water, potassium iodide (an expectorant), cascara sagrada (a laxative), sugar syrup, prickly ash, buckthorn, alfalfa, and red clover blossoms.

Throughout his long career Hoxsey was arrested and convicted on charges of practicing medicine without a license. He sued numerous people for libel. And he was under constant attack by the AMA and various organs of the government. Pharmacologists and members of the American College of Physicians testified at his various trials to the effect that there was no remedy for cancer among the ingredients that Hoxsey used. Despite countless setbacks in court after court, Hoxsey managed to come back. It is estimated that in 1954, he treated more than 8,000 patients and grossed more than $1.5 million. In 1956 the Food and Drug Administration (FDA) issued a warning to the public, stating that his methods were worthless and that it was "imminently dangerous to rely on [his treatments] in neglect of competent and rational treatment." This warning was distributed to the press and was contained in a "Public Beware" poster that was sent to 46,000 post offices and postal substations throughout the nation. Finally, by late 1960 the Hoxsey treatment had disappeared. In 1966 the American Cancer Society issued a catalogue of *Unproven Methods of Cancer Treatment* available to the public, containing more than 25 major promotions available to Americans who feared they had the disease. After years of battling Hoxsey, the FDA succeeded, in spite of an expenditure of a quarter of a million dollars, in stopping only Hoxsey. Others took over where he left off.[20]

When a false claim of effectiveness is made, it is claimed that a product (treatment, remedy, or whatever) does X, when in fact that product does not do X. This is true of all false claims of effectiveness. But if a product does not do X, it does not follow that it does nothing else. Some products may do nothing; they may give the consumer no benefit, but at the same time do him no harm, other than the financial loss that he has suffered by buying the product. But some products may have *harmful* effects that are ignored in the promotional literature or advertisements that prompt people to buy them. Listerine may be harmless, though it will not prevent colds. Hoxsey's pastes and many other preparations were (and are) harmful. Clearly, though the promoters of both Listerine and Hoxsey's treatments are guilty of false and misleading advertising, there is a further element of guilt in Hoxsey's kind of operation.

Still, the abuses go on, by some of the most respected firms in the food and drug line. In one recent year, the Food and Drug Administration seized shipments of Peritrate SA, a drug prescribed for the massive chest pain of the heart condition known as angina pectoris (Warner-Chilcott Laboratories); Serax, a tranquillizer (Wyeth Laboratories); Lincocin, an antibiotic (Upjohn); Lasix, a diuretic (Hoechst Pharmaceuticals); and Indoklon, an alternative to electroshock in some cases of depression (Ohio Chemical and Surgical Equipment Company)—all for false and deceptive promotion directed to the medical profession. Ayerst Laboratories was required by the FDA to send a "corrective letter" to some 280,000 doctors, retracting a claim that Atromid-S had a "beneficial effect" on heart disease, and the FDA ruled that Searle, Mead-Johnson, and Syntex had sent literature to physicians that misleadingly minimized the hazards of their birth control pills (Ovulen-21, Oracon, Norquen, and Norinyl-1).[21]

Unfortunately, moral suasion is not enough. Many persons, whatever their line of work, are not sufficiently resistant to the temptation to profit at the expense of others, and they are not touched by the moral arguments that might be brought to bear against their practices. One of the state's principal functions is the protection of its citizens against harm that might be done to them by others, even when they are unwitting collaborators in doing harm to themselves. It is the government's duty to require all hazardous substances to be labeled as such, so that everyone can see for himself what dangers he might expose himself to by ingesting them. It is no infringement on the citizen's freedom for the government to require of manufacturers of poisons that they clearly label their products with a warning that everyone may recognize. And the government is not interfering unreasonably with drug manufacturers when it demands that they print only scientifically verifiable facts in the literature that they distribute to the physicians who may be prescribing those products for their patients' use. Nor is it an unconscionable denial of freedom for the government to prevent persons who claim to cure diseases from practicing upon others unless they can offer some proof that the "cures" they offer are efficacious. For the government's right to protect its citizens against physical assault has never been questioned, and the purveyors of false and misleading information about harmful substances are as surely guilty of assault (if not in the legal sense, then at least in the moral sense) as they would have been had they poured their poisons into their victims' morning coffee. To argue that because the consumer has a choice and does not have to buy the product or use it, he is responsible for whatever happens to him, is like arguing that the poison victim had the choice of not drinking his coffee, and that by lifting the cup to his lips, he absolved the poisoner of all responsibility. The law has long maintained that a person who harms another is responsible for the harm that he does, even if he did so at the victim's request and with his active assistance. When a man is seeking relief from pain or illness and in that search relies upon the statements and claims made by drug salesmen, he is certainly entitled to no less protection than is offered to one who is determined to commit suicide.

THE PROMOTION OF DANGEROUS PRODUCTS

Any person who urges another to purchase and use a product or service assumes a responsibility toward him. The advertiser is not merely an innocent middleman who conveys a message from one person to another. He helps to create the message, using all the specialized skills of his art to persuade the potential consumer to act favorably upon his appeal. He shares in the rewards of successful advertising campaigns. He therefore assumes a responsibility for the product he induces the customer to purchase. In particular, if the product is dangerous or harmful, the advertiser who has persuaded the consumer to use it shares responsibility with the manufacturer for·any harm that may result. This responsibility ought to be enforced by law, both with penal sanctions when the harm is particularly great and with appropriate remedies in tort. It is in any case a moral responsibility, for were it not for the advertiser's intervention, the consumer might never have suffered the damage done to him by the product he purchased.

By the same token, the advertiser has a right to feel, as Bruce Barton did, that he has contributed to the well-being of those who have been well served by the products and services he has helped to market. For every potential moral wrong that a person might commit, there must be an equivalent moral good that he might perform.

Those advertising agencies who have worked with the American Cancer Society to produce messages that have helped to persuade people to give up smoking or to refrain from becoming smokers have performed an important public service. Any utilitarian assessment of their performance would almost surely conclude that they had contributed to human happiness and significantly reduced the amount of pain and suffering in the world. Other advertising campaigns have assisted humanitarian organizations to raise funds for their operations and to further their causes. The government has employed advertising to discourage harmful behavior and to encourage beneficial activities. For example, during World War II, numerous ads reminded workers of the dangers inherent in talking about matters that might have helped the enemy and discouraged absenteeism at a time when the nation needed a steady supply of war matériel to carry its war effort to a successful conclusion. Similarly, advertising campaigns mounted by heavily overpopulated nations have had some effect in encouraging their citizens to employ contraceptive devices so as to bring population growth down to a manageable level. The agencies that have helped to mount such campaigns can justly take pride in their work, for it is reasonable to believe that they have contributed to the sum of human happiness through their efforts.

On the other hand, some products that are heavily advertised are known —or ought to be known by those who market them—to be dangerous and capable of inflicting grave injuries upon those who use them. For example, Ultra Sheen Permanent Creme Relaxer is an emulsion used by consumers and professional beauticians to straighten curly hair. Ads represented it as "gentle" and "easy" to use. A woman in a television commercial for the product said that it "goes on cool while it really relaxes my hair. And the Conditioner and Hair Dress protects against moisture, so my hair doesn't go back." But the FTC found that Ultra Sheen's active ingredient was sodium hydroxide—lye—which straightens hair "by breaking down the cells of the hair shaft. . . . In some instances, [it] makes it brittle and causes partial or total hair loss." Moreover, the FTC found that it was neither cool nor gentle, but is "a primary skin irritant. It is caustic to skin and breaks down the cells which form the epidermis. Ultra Sheen relaxer in some instances causes skin and scalp irritation and burns, which may produce scars and permanent follicle damage. It also causes eye irritation and may impair vision." Because direct contact with eyes, scalp or skin could cause irritation or injury, the FTC found that the product was not easy to use, contrary to the claims expressed in the ads. The FTC accordingly ordered the respondents to warn their customers of the product's dangers, to inform them of the presence of lye in it, to stop misrepresenting it, and to give clear instructions as to procedures to be followed in the event of injury to the customer.[22]

The law has for a long time recognized the duty a manufacturer owes to the purchaser of his product, particularly when the product is inherently dangerous. This duty has gradually been extended to others involved in the distribution and marketing of inherently dangerous products, so that persons and firms who retail automobiles, firearms, explosives, and poisons (for example) can be held liable in tort for damage caused by products that result from defects or negligence in the way they are labeled or handled.[23] At the very least, one would expect a warning to appear on the label of any product whose use might result in serious physical injury. The advertising and mass marketing of products that are prone to cause grave injury is a questionable practice.

This is not to say that dangerous products, including poisons, should not be sold. In the fifth chapter of *On Liberty,* John Stuart Mill argued that people ought to be permitted to purchase poisons, but that merchants who sold such substances were under a moral obligation (which should be a legal obligation as well) to label such substances clearly so that those who purchase them will know what they are buying. Mill's label rule should be extended to advertisements, because the decision to purchase a product is often made soon after an advertisement is seen. The product's hazards should be prominently displayed in advertisements so that the potential consumer may know what he or she is buying before the purchase is made.

THE AUDIENCE TO WHICH THE AD IS DIRECTED

Certain advertisements are improper, not so much because of the products they promote but because of the audiences to which they are directed. Some audiences, such as small children, are especially vulnerable because they are generally incapable of making rational judgments or distinguishing fact from fancy. Others may be in a particularly hazardous occupation, and should therefore not be exposed to advertisements designed to prey upon human weaknesses or to be influenced in their decision making by considerations that are irrelevant to the purposes for which those decisions are being made or are not founded upon a purely objective assessment of the relevant facts.

In morals and in law, the peculiar vulnerability of children has long been recognized. Children have rightly been regarded as especially entitled to measures designed to protect them against exploitation and harm perpetrated by persons who were either unscrupulous or insensitive to their need for special treatment. It is difficult to determine whether advertisers who direct their messages to children are deliberately taking advantage of the special vulnerability of those for whom their ads are designed, or merely attempting to sell their products to the persons for whom they are intended. If they are not aware that young children are often unable to distinguish reality from fantasy, however, they have a moral obligation to study the question and to discover the facts, because their actions may properly be considered an exercise of power over persons who do not have the means to resist.[24]

The moral propriety of marketing dangerous products becomes even more questionable when the advertisements are aimed at children, for the likelihood that children will misuse the products or misunderstand their proper functions is far greater than the likelihood that adults will do so. The advertising of guns in Boy Scout magazines that circulate to boys from the age of 12 is of particularly dubious moral propriety. Although the possession of guns by adolescents is not unlawful, there may be a distinction between what is permitted by law and what ought morally to be done or encouraged. It is easy enough to think of products and services that might not be prohibited by law but should nevertheless be barred from the advertising columns of magazines directed to children and adolescents.

A particularly blatant abuse of the advertiser's power to influence young minds so as to boost the sales of a product without regard to the potential harm that might be inflicted upon those for whom the product was intended was resolved by an FTC consent order prohibiting the Hudson Pharmaceutical Corporation from directing its advertising for "Spiderman" and other children's vitamins to child audiences. The Corporation's television and comic book advertisements, directed at children under the age of 12, used Spiderman, a cartoon hero who possesses spectacular agility and near-supernatural strength. The FTC found that the advertising in question tended "to blur for children the distinction between program content and advertising and to take advantage of the trust relationship developed between children and the program character." The ads led the children to believe that the product "has qualities and characteristics it does not have" and tended "to induce children to take excessive amounts of vitamin supplements which cause injury to their health." [25] The FTC found that Spiderman Vitamins with iron are a deadly poison when ingested in large amounts by children. In 1973, vitamins and mineral supplements accounted for more than 5,000 cases of poisoning among children under five years of age, an incidence exceeded only by aspirin, soaps and detergents, and plants (other than mushrooms and toadstools). [26]

Advertising consists of far more than the commercials that appear on television and the displays that are published in newspapers and magazines. Many firms prepare the potential market for their products long before the market is ready to start buying. Drug companies, for example, distribute medical instruments and other valuable items to medical students almost as soon as they enter medical school. This is done under the guise of supporting medical education. There is no need, however, for pharmaceutical manufacturers to support medical education in this fashion, by supplying students with expensive instruments engraved with their logos. Outright grants to the medical schools, which might then be used to purchase the same instruments *without* the advertising, would place the companies above suspicion. The practice continues throughout a physician's career, with free samples of drugs and various other gifts that clearly identify the company from which they come. Unlike scientific articles in journals reporting the efficacy of various drugs for particular purposes, such gifts are designed to impress the physician (or the budding physician) with a specific brand name to build his loyalty to a particular company. This is subversive of the medical profession and an unethical practice.

Large advertisers also "buy" university professors and other researchers who supply them with materials and opinions to "substantiate" their claims. A recent study by Representative Benjamin S. Rosenthal and the Center for Science in the Public Interest, entitled "Feeding at the Company Trough," revealed that significant numbers of university professors of nutrition have established remunerative connections with the food and drug industries. "Unfortunately," the study says, "many professors have developed extensive ties with the same industries of which they are asked to be objective analysts. . . . Developing ties to industry causes one to overlook problems, rationalize faults, and defend policies." Despite conclusions by many respected experts in dentistry and nutrition that a diet rich in sucrose is hazardous to a person's health, one university professor who has ties with Kellogg, Nabisco, Carnation, the Cereal Institute, and the Sugar Association insists that people can double their sugar intake without risk to their health. A report prepared at Harvard University under a grant from Kellogg concluded that presweetened cereals have no adverse effect on tooth decay, but did not reveal Kellogg's financial involvement in the study.[27] Whether or not the researchers in these cases have been corrupted, their financial involvement with the companies whose products their studies have supported represents a potential for corruption.

Advertisers should not pitch their appeals to children who are under the age of reason and discretion, should not bestow gifts upon persons whose professional judgment might thereby be distorted, and should not reveal to researchers their sponsorship of studies into questions that might affect public acceptance of their products so that objectivity may be maintained and both scholars and sponsors might remain above suspicion of corruption.

MISLEADING STATEMENTS OR CONTEXTS

Campbell Soup Company sponsored a television commercial that showed a thick creamy mixture that the announcer suggested was Campbell's vegetable soup. Federal investigators discovered that the bowl shown in the commercial had been filled with marbles to make it appear thicker than it really was and to make it seem to contain more vegetables than it did. Max Factor promoted a wave-setting lotion, Natural Wave, by showing how a drinking straw soaked in the lotion curled up. The FTC pointed out, however, that it did not logically follow that human hair would react as drinking straws did. The implication left in the viewer's mind, therefore, was false, because, in fact, straight hair did not curl after being soaked in Natural Wave. Such visual trickery is quite common in television commercials, in newspaper and magazine advertisements, in direct mail advertisements, and on package labels.

Misleading statements are also very common. Some agencies have advertised for talented men and women, and especially for children, who would be given an "excellent chance" of being put to work doing television commercials "at no fee." The agencies seldom placed anyone, and, though they charged no fees, they sent their clients to photographers who charged them substantial fees for taking their publicity pictures, or referred them to a firm that took "screen tests," also for lots of money. The photographers were always closely allied with the agencies, and the latter always shared a very healthy proportion of the fees charged.[28]

In none of these cases could one say that false statements were made. Strictly speaking, the advertisers were not guilty of lying to the public, if *lying* is defined as the deliberate utterance of an untrue statement. For, taken literally, none of the statements made in these advertisements is untrue. But the messages of the ads are misleading. Because of the pictorial matter in them, the reader or viewer makes inferences that are false, and the advertiser juxtaposes those pictures with the narrative in such a way that false inferences *will* be made. It is through those false inferences that he expects to earn enough money to pay for the ad and to have something left over for himself.

The land promoter who sends a glossy pamphlet advertising his "retirement city" in Arizona may not make a single false statement in the entire pamphlet. But by filling it with beautiful color photographs of swimming pools, golf links, and lush vegetation, none of which exists within 100 miles of the land he is selling, he leads his prospects to believe that certain features exist within that area which do *not* exist. Thus, without uttering or printing a single false statement, he is able to lead his prospects to believe what he knows is not true.

CONCEALMENT OF THE TRUTH

Merchants and producers have many ways of concealing truth from the customers—not by lying to them, but simply by not telling them facts that are relevant to the question of whether they ought to purchase a particular product or whether they are receiving full value for their money. An example that occurred a few years ago involved ham. Major packers, including Swift, Armour, and others, were selling ham that was advertised as being particularly juicy. The consumer was not told, however, that the hams were specially salted and that hypodermic syringes were used to inject large quantities of water into them. The "juice" was nothing but water that evaporated during cooking, leaving a ham some 40% smaller than the one that had been put into the oven. The housewife purchasing such a ham had no advance warning that she was purchasing water for the price of ham, unless she knew that the words *artificial ham* that were printed in small letters on the seal of the package meant that that was the case. Even that small warning was added only because of pressure brought to bear against the packers by the FTC. And there was no publicity to arouse the consumer to the special meaning of the term *artificial ham*.[29]

Probably the most common deception of this sort is price deception, the technique some high-pressure salesmen use to sell their goods by grossly inflating their prices to two, three, and even four times their real worth. Again, there may be no "untruth" in what they say, but they conceal the important fact that the same product, or one nearly identical to it, can be purchased for far less at a department or appliance store. It is not the business of salesmen and businessmen to send their clients to their competitors, but it is certainly unethical for them to fail to tell their customers that they are not getting full value for their money.

A burglar or a thief may be heavily fined or sent to jail for many months for stealing a relatively small amount of money or valuables from a single person. But a salesman who cheats hundreds of people out of equal sums of money that total, in the aggregate, hundreds of thousands of dollars, is immune to prosecution, and may, in fact, be one of the community's most respected citizens. If Armour and Swift and other large corporations can bilk their customers out of enormous sums of money and do it with impunity, why, one might ask, should the petty thief be subjected to such severe penalties?

THE DUTY TO TELL THE WHOLE TRUTH

The advertising agency is hired by a firm to sell that firm's products. By signing a contract, it undertakes an obligation to do its utmost to fulfill that goal. Acceptance of that charge does not, however, relieve employees of the agency of their duties as citizens or as human beings. Their immediate goal as advertising men may be to obtain accounts and to keep them by increasing the customer's sales, but that goal should never be achieved at the expense of harm to unsuspecting persons. The duty not to direct advertising to children is related to this moral obligation, as is the duty to label hazardous substances with clear and unmistakable warnings. Such moral obligations may not be enforced by the law. Persons who are concerned with doing what is right need not set the limits of their conduct at the bounds delineated by the law, for the law does not always conform with standards of moral right. To be more specific, if the law permits an advertiser to refrain from mentioning a particular hazard that his product poses to his customer, it does not follow that he has a moral right to withhold that information from them. If the law provides no sanctions against deceptive advertising, an ethical advertiser will nevertheless not engage in willful deception of those who place their trust in him.

In a broad view of advertising, the small leaflets that are enclosed in the boxes in which drugs are packed may be regarded as advertisements of a sort. They contain technical information for the doctor's reference and are designed to prevent improper use of the drug. But they are also designed to influence physicians to use drugs for certain medical conditions, and may therefore be regarded as at least partially intended to serve as marketing devices.

A recent study revealed that certain drugs are advertised and packaged in Latin America in ways that the FDA would condemn (or has condemned) as unacceptable in the United States. Winstrol, a synthetic derivative of testosterone, is considered too toxic in the United States for all but the narrowest use. The AMA warns that such drugs "should not be used to stimulate growth in children who are small but otherwise normal and healthy." But in Latin America, Winstrol is widely promoted as an appetite stimulant for underweight children. A spokesman from the Winthrop Drug Company complained that the advertising was quoted out of context and that the company complied with the laws and medical practices of each country in which it did business.

Another Winthrop product, Commel (dipyrone), is a pain killer that may cause fatal blood diseases and may not be sold in the United States as a routine treatment for pain, arthritis, or fever. According to the AMA, the "only justifiable use [of dipyrone] is as a last resort to reduce fever when safer measures have failed." But a packet of the drug purchased in Brazil recommends that the drug be used for "migraine headaches, neuralgia, muscular or articular rheumatism, hepatic and renal colic, pain and fever which usually accompany grippe, angina, otitis, and sinusitis, toothache, and pain after dental extractions." The company's comments about the matter were as evasive as they were about Winstrol.

E. R. Squibb & Sons' Raudixin, which is occasionally used in this country to treat high blood pressure, was found to induce such deep depressions that hospitalization was often necessary, and suicide sometimes followed. But in Brazil, the package insert says it is the "ideal medicine for the treatment of emotional disturbances such as states of tension and anxiety, and in states characterized by nervousness, irritability, excitability and insomnia. . . . Raudixin is the drug of choice in daily practice." A company spokesman acknowledged that the insert had been written 20 years ago, conceded that the insert had not been rewritten in 20 years, but insisted that it complied with Brazilian drug regulations.

The aim of drug companies' ads, and even of their package inserts, is not so much to inform physicians of the uses and potential hazards of their products as to persuade them to prescribe them. When forced to do so by government regulations, they will write truthful and informative inserts, but when government regulations are lax, they will subject the public to needless hazards and rationalize their conduct by claiming that they are doing nothing unlawful. This not only is morally unacceptable but should be legally proscribed. Those who believe in minimal government interference in private affairs would prefer to see governmental regulations of all industries, including the drug industry, reduced as much as possible. But so long as an industry behaves irresponsibly and endangers the lives and health of the persons it is supposed to serve, the public has no alternative but to rely upon government for protection.

THE FORM OF THE ADVERTISEMENT

The ethical advertiser is obligated to assume some responsibility for the product he advertises. He should design his advertising campaign in such a way that it does not prey upon the gullible, the young, and the innocent. He should refrain from corrupting professional judgments about matters that may gravely affect important human interests. And he should assume some responsibility for the form of the advertisements he creates to be certain that they do not deliberately deceive, leave false impressions, or commit fraud. Truth telling, after all, is a fundamental moral rule. Although one may not agree with Kant's insistence that one never has the right to lie, whatever the circumstances, it is nevertheless true that the liar and the cheat corrupt language and destroy confidence. In their zeal for short-term profit, some companies encourage movements for government control over themselves and their competitors so that the weak and powerless may be protected against those who would exploit them. Freedom is threatened by those who assume the right to pervert the truth for their own narrow ends. Unfortunately, advertisers have devoted much of their skill to the artful presentation of half-truths and lies, to deception of the eye and of the mind, to the creation of illusions and false expectations. These skills have proven themselves in the marketplace. False promises and clever doubletalk have been effective selling tools since the itinerant patent medicine peddler hawked his merchandise from the back of his wagon with the promise that it would cure everything from warts to cirrhosis of the liver. False promises, lies, and other deceptions can make money for those who use them and can help to drive honest competitors out of business. Even if the truth does ultimately emerge, it may come too late for the honest but bankrupt merchant. One immoral practice breeds another. Lies beget lies. The honest man who sees himself being pushed to the precipice of financial ruin may turn in self-defense to dishonest practices that he would otherwise abhor. The corrupt advertiser provides an excuse for every other advertiser to engage in corrupt practices: "Everyone else is doing it."

Some firms advertise a product as if it were on sale at a reduced price when, in fact, the product never sold at the so-called regular price. A paint manufacturer, for example, advertised: "Buy 1 gallon for $6.98 and get a second gallon free." But it *never* sold its paint at $6.98 per gallon.

Encyclopedia salesmen sometimes misrepresent themselves as agents for school boards or as public opinion pollsters. They offer "free" sets of encyclopedias, allegedly as a public relations "service," but ask for a small monthly charge for a ten-year research service that will presumably guarantee the worried customer's children their places in medical school or law school.

Record clubs and book clubs falsely advertise "free" books which are not free at all but are consideration for a binding contract to purchase a number of books at a supposedly reduced price which, after postage and handling charges are added, is often higher than the retail price of the same books. The "club" members are customers and the "clubs" are profit-making businesses.

Insurance companies and other firms use photographs or drawings of impressive buildings in their ads and on their stationery to suggest that they are large, long-established firms, even though they may occupy no more than a single office. One firm recently hung its own sign on a large, modern municipal government building and filmed its commercials in front of the disguised structure, leaving the impression that its own offices were housed there.

Small-size type may be used to obscure limitations on insurance coverage, and bold type may emphasize irrelevant facts, such as coverage that is common to all policies of a given class.

Misleading words and phrases—particularly those having special technical meanings that are unfamiliar to the uninitiated—are used to create false impressions in the minds of laymen. Ordinary language may be used in such a way as to suggest to the uninitiated that certain conditions apply when they do not apply at all. For example, an ad saying, "This policy will pay your hospital and surgical bills" suggests (though it does not literally say) that *all* of the hospital and surgical bills of the insured will be paid; and "This policy will replace your income" suggests that *all* of the insured's income will be replaced if he becomes disabled—when, in fact, only a small portion of his bills or his income will be paid or replaced.

Some companies don't hesitate to make inconsistent claims for competing products that they manufacture or distribute. The Sterling Drug Company, for example, distributes Bayer aspirin in the United States and also manufactures Vanquish. In 1970, the company was simultaneously running ads that made the following claims:

For Bayer: "Aspirin is already the strongest pain reliever you can buy." Combining Bayer with other drugs or buffering it would not improve it. "No one has ever found a way to improve on Bayer Aspirin, because Bayer Aspirin is 100% Aspirin. None is faster or more effective than Bayer Aspirin. Even WE can't improve it though we keep trying."

For Vanquish: It has "a unique way" of relieving headache "with extra strength and gentle buffers. . . . It's the only leading pain reliever you can buy that does."

Thus, Sterling Drug is both unable and able to produce a pain reliever that is more effective than Bayer. Buffering doesn't and does add to the strength or gentleness of aspirin.[30]

Another device is the half-truth which becomes an outright lie because it creates a completely false impression. Excedrin, for example, ran an ad reporting that a "major hospital study" showed that "it took more than twice as many aspirin tablets to give the same pain relief as two Excedrin." But the ad failed to point out that the Excedrin tablets contained twice as much aspirin as plain aspirin tablets and that another study had demonstrated that Excedrin had caused more intestinal upset than two brands of aspirin when given in equal doses.[31]

Although most of these examples have been derived from studies of the drug industry, that industry has no monopoly on deceptive advertising practices. Similar examples can be cited from industries as diverse as automobiles, lumber, oil, household cleaning products, and real estate. Unscrupulous and deceptive practices in many industries have caused severe financial losses to unsuspecting individuals. Even when the individual's loss is relatively small, collectively the damage may amount to hundreds of millions of dollars. With these financial losses there are inevitably other costs that are more difficult to assess, not the least of which is the emotional damage, the anger, and the resentment that must follow when the loss represents a major portion of an individual's earnings or savings. Some of this undoubtedly spills over into resentment against a system that permits what the victims perceive to be grave injustices against themselves and the classes or groups to which they belong. Advertising alone cannot be held responsible for any social dislocations that might result from such resentments, but the advertising industry cannot wholly escape responsibility for its contributions to the sense of injustice that prevails in so many quarters today.

PROMOTION OR SUPPORT OF INDECENT OR IMMORAL CAUSES OR PRACTICES

A free society cannot legally forbid everything that is morally wrong. But advertising sponsors and agencies for print and broadcast media can and should exercise restraint to reduce tasteless and insulting advertising.

Similar considerations might lead some people to conclude that other ads are not only tasteless but subversive of public morals. Some ads are also demeaning and exploitative of women.

Ads that are exploitative or that insult minority groups or other classes of persons ought to be avoided because they needlessly hurt those whose image is thus denigrated and because they reinforce stereotypes and prejudices that have no basis in fact and have historically been responsible for grave injustices and serious personal and social injuries. Examples of such exploitation abound, not only in the magazines sold in adult book stores, but in respected journals.

A FINAL WORD ON ADVERTISING

Advertising has an important and constructive role to play in the life of the nation. It is not true that all advertising men are unscrupulous or that all businessmen are concerned only with selling, no matter what the cost to their customers. Nor is it true that advertisements are necessarily misleading or fraudulent.

David Ogilvy, one of the most successful advertising executives in the United States, is the creator of such successful advertising images as Schweppes's Commander Whitehead and Hathaway Shirt's man with the eye patch.[32] In his discussion of techniques for building a successful advertising campaign, he says,

> *Give the Facts.* Very few advertisements contain enough factual information to sell the product. There is a ludicrous tradition among copywriters that consumers aren't interested in facts. Nothing could be farther from the truth. Study the copy in the Sears, Roebuck catalogue; it sells a billion dollars' worth of merchandise every year by giving *facts*. In my Rolls-Royce advertisements I gave nothing but facts. No adjectives, no "gracious living."
>
> The consumer isn't a moron; she is your wife. You insult her intelligence if you assume that a mere slogan and a few vapid adjectives will persuade her to buy anything. She wants all the information you can give her.[33]

And he adds the following bit of advice that bears directly on our subject:

> You wouldn't tell lies to your own wife. Don't tell them to mine. Do as you would be done by.
>
> If you tell lies about a product, you will be found out—either by the Government, which will prosecute you, or by the consumer, who will punish you by not buying your product a second time.
>
> Good products can be sold by *honest* advertising. If you don't think the product is good, you have no business to be advertising it. If you tell lies, or weasel, you do your client a disservice, you increase your load of guilt, and you fan the flames of public resentment against the whole business of advertising.[34]

In short, Ogilvy believes that aside from any ethical reasons that might be advanced for factual, informative, and truthful advertising, it is in the best interests of both the advertising man and his client—from a purely practical point of view—to adhere to these principles, for they keep the attorney general and the FTC away from the door, and in the long run, they are more successful in the marketplace. He claims that the "combative-persuasive" type of advertising that so many people have condemned for its lack of taste is not nearly as profitable as informative advertising.

He argues also that advertising is a force for sustaining standards of quality and service. The advertisement contains a promise that must be fulfilled if the customer is to be satisfied. The public will eventually turn against any advertiser who fails to keep the promises he has made in his public pronouncements. Ogilvy tells of firms that have warned their employees to maintain the standards of service that have been described in their advertising, and of others that have warned that they would move their accounts to other agencies if their commercials were ever cited by government agencies for dishonesty. The fear of exposure by government agencies and consumer groups in the public press and the adverse publicity that would result are enough to deter some firms from engaging in deceptive advertising.

As for the charge that advertisers create needs or desires for things that people might well do without, this is what Ogilvy has to say:

> Does advertising make people want to buy products they don't need? If you don't think people need deodorants, you are at liberty to criticize advertising for having persuaded 87 per cent of American women and 66 per cent of American men to use them. If you don't think people need beer, you are right to criticize advertising for having persuaded 58 per cent of the adult population to drink it. If you disapprove of social mobility, creature comforts, and foreign travel, you are right to blame advertising for encouraging such wickedness. If you dislike affluent society, you are right to blame advertising for inciting the masses to pursue it.
>
> If you are this kind of Puritan, I cannot reason with you. I can only call you a psychic masochist. Like Archbishop Leighton, I pray, "Deliver me, O Lord, from the errors of wise men, yea, and of good men."
>
> Dear old John Burns, the father of the Labor movement in England, used to say that the tragedy of the working class was the poverty of their desires. I make no apology for inciting the working class to desire less Spartan lives.[35]

There is certainly some truth in what Ogilvy says, but on some points there may be valid disagreement. First, he gives the advertisers more credit than may be their due when he asserts that they have persuaded 58% of the adult population to drink beer. It is not at all unlikely that some people would be drinking beer even if it were never advertised. The drinking of beer far antedates the modern advertising industry and may be traced to causes other than the efforts of copywriters. Also, the desires for social mobility, creature comforts, and foreign travel are all exploited by advertisers to sell their products, but advertisers did not invent them or create them. The critics of advertising do not believe that social mobility, creature comforts, and foreign travel are wicked, and to say that they do is to evade the issue. The issue is not the advertiser's *encouragement* of these desires, but his *exploitation* of them. Unlike beer, social mobility, and foreign travel, there was never a demand for deodorants until the advertisers created it. They did so, not to create a better society, but to make money. Those who object to the exploitation of normal human desires by persons and corporations intent on making money at a great cost to their customers and by utilizing methods that conceal or distort the facts are not psychic masochists nor are they Puritans. They are people who are outraged by what they consider to be the unconscionable methods utilized by some businesses to increase their profits at the expense of people who can often ill afford to be exploited.

Some 2,000 years ago there was a debate between the scholars of two great academies as to whether it was proper to praise the beauty of an ugly bride. According to one faction, the principle that one should refrain from uttering any falsehood required that the honest man refrain from praising the ugly bride. The other group, however, insisted that principles of kindness should prevail and that even if one had to lie, one was obliged to add to the newlyweds' happiness rather than to detract from it. They went on to say that in a matter of far less moment to a man than his marriage, the principle of kindness should take precedence, so that if a person had made a bad bargain at the market, one should not rub it in by telling him so.[36] If they were here to participate in a discussion on the issue presently under consideration, it is not hard to imagine what they might say:

> Thousands of men and women are too poor to afford foreign travel, or large and flashy automobiles, or Hathaway shirts, or expensive liquors, or costly cosmetics. What useful purpose is served by dangling these luxuries before their eyes? To some, perhaps, the enticing display of such luxuries may serve as an incentive, spurring them on to greater achievement so that they too may enjoy what their more affluent neighbors take for granted. But to many, and perhaps to most, the display may arouse feelings of frustration, anger, and hurt. "Why," they may ask, "are we unable to have all of these things, when so many others do? Why can we not give our children what those ads show other people giving their children? Why can we not share the happiness that is depicted here?" Before a man is married, it might be appropriate to point out some of his fiancée's faults; but at the wedding, when it's obviously too late, it's unkind to dwell on them. For those who cannot afford the luxuries —and they are luxuries, whatever Ogilvy may say—offered in advertisements that are often directed *specifically at them*, it is cruel to hurt them by offering them what they cannot buy, or to seduce them with false promises of happiness or prestige or success into neglecting their primary obligations in order to seek the fantasy world portrayed in advertisements.

This is not to say that all advertising is bad; but even when the message is not distorted, those who use the mass media to disseminate it should do so with some sense of social and public responsibility. It is far worse, though, when the message is distorted. And even David Ogilvy, for all his insistence on honesty in advertising, admits that he is "continuously guilty of *suppressio veri* [the suppression of the truth]. Surely it is asking too much to expect the advertiser to describe the shortcomings of his product? One must be forgiven for putting one's best foot forward." [37] So the consumer is *not* to be told all the relevant information; he is *not* to be given all the facts that would be of assistance in making a reasonable decision about a given purchase. In particular, he will *not* be told about the weaknesses of a product, about its shock hazards, for example, if it is an electrical appliance; about the danger it poses to the consumer's health if it is a cleaning fluid; about the danger it poses to his life if it is an automobile tire that is not built to sustain the heavy loads of today's automobile at turnpike speeds; or, if one carries the doctrine to its final conclusion, about the possibly harmful side effects of a new drug that is advertised to the medical profession. Telling the truth combined with *"suppressio veri"* is *not* telling the truth. It is *not* asking too much of the advertiser to reveal such facts when they are known to him, and he should *not* be forgiven for "putting his best foot forward" at his customer's expense. Ogilvy admits, too, that he sometimes tells the truth about the products he advertises in such a way that it seems to the reader that his product is different, in those respects, from similar products, whereas Ogilvy knows that all other products of the same kind possess the same features. All aspirin is the same, for example, whether it is stamped *Bayer* and sells for $1.95 per hundred or whether it is an unadvertised brand of U.S.P. aspirin that sells for 35 cents per hundred. But the advertiser will try to convince you that what is true of Bayer aspirin is not true of the other product. This is unfair to the consumer, whether he is rich or poor; but it is particularly unfair to the poor consumer, who could use in other ways the money he spends paying for Bayer's advertising.

Advertising has an important role to fill in our society. It is not likely to disappear. But it is not always carried on in the most ethical manner. Its supporters tend to exaggerate the benefits that have flowed from it, and they are not at all shy about boasting about its effectiveness in their trade meetings and in their efforts to win new business. But they often shrug off any suggestion that their efforts may have harmful effects upon some segments of society by denying that they are all *that* effective. They cannot have it both ways. If advertising is as effective as its practitioners claim it to be, then it possesses enormous potential for harm as well as for good. Because many, though not all, advertisers are concerned primarily about selling their products and only secondarily, if at all, about telling the truth, it is reasonable to suggest that some government regulation be exercised over this industry, and in particular, that advertisers—both producers and agencies— be held liable for harm or damage that results to consumers from misleading or false claims in advertisements, and that they be required to make good any financial loss that consumers may suffer as a result of reliance upon any misleading advertisement, whether the advertisement was "fraudulent" in the criminal sense or not. If laws were passed, both on the federal level and at the state or provincial level, making agencies and producers responsible for restitution of damages suffered by customers who relied upon their "messages," there would be a great incentive for those concerned to confine their claims to those that could be substantiated and to resort to fewer misleading gimmicks. Though such legislation would not eliminate all abuses, it would go a long way toward assuring the public that the advertising messages to which it was exposed respected the truth.

10

Competition and Corporate Responsibility

Competition is a relationship in which at least two persons actively strive against one another to achieve some objective, endeavoring thereby to deny it to the other.

True competition usually exists only when it is not possible for all the competitors to achieve the goal—for example, when there is not enough of a given commodity to go around. Thus, people standing in their backyards on a cool summer morning are not competing with one another for air, for there is enough for all; but the ranchers of Arizona are competing with the industries of California for water, because the limited supply of water in that part of North America is not sufficient to meet the needs or desires of all.

Moreover, competition usually consists of a relationship in which each of the competitors can react against the actions of the others so as to achieve the goal that each of them is seeking. Thus, in a boxing match, each of the boxers feints, jabs, and punches in response to his opponent's actions, and in a race, each runner keeps an eye on the others and attempts to adjust his speed to theirs. In business, if one competitor cuts his prices or increases his advertising expenditures, others will usually follow suit or try some other technique to maintain or increase their share of the market.

Although these are characteristics of many types of competition, the term is sufficiently open-ended to admit of many exceptions and variations. However, it seems clear that in any form of competition, the goal toward which the players are striving must be one that is in some sense in limited supply, one that at least some of the competitors will not succeed in achieving. If an instructor, for example, is willing to give all his students A's whenever they work up to a standard that he has set, then the students are actually

298

not competing against one another for the A's in that course. They may, of course, be competing against one another for admission to medical school, and thus each of them may be striving mightily to earn an A in the course. But there is a difference between striving to reach a goal that all can reach with sufficient effort and certain minimal abilities and striving to reach a goal that it will then be impossible for all or some others to reach. When the instructor limits the number of A's in his course, as he might by imposing a rule that the class will be graded on a curve, then the students are truly competing against one another, for the performance of each determines not only what grade he will receive but also, to some degree, those of the other students in the class.

The competitive situation is usually one in which each of the competitors can react against the actions taken by the others as the competition proceeds, but there are situations in which this is not necessarily true. Boxers naturally respond to the actions of their opponents. But runners who participate in early heats of a 400-meter relay are unable to respond to the actions of those who run in later heats, though they are in competition with them for the trophy until the last heat has been run. Similarly, a businessman who submits a sealed bid for a large contract is in competition with all others who are submitting bids for the same contract but is unable to respond to their bids even when the competitor's bid is opened first. It is possible, in a sense, to compete against a person who has retired or is deceased—as when one attempts to break a record set many years before.

Finally, although competitive situations are usually at least triadic (two persons and a goal or objective), it is possible to think of situations in which a given individual competes against himself. For example, a jogger who has succeeded in running five miles in 50 minutes may strive at a later date to run the same distance in 45 minutes. Here, the objective is nothing more than an improved performance. The jogger is in a sense competing against himself at an earlier time. If one concedes that a person at two different times is not one and the same person, then competition remains triadic in all conceivable cases.

Competition is in itself neither good nor evil. It is simply—to use a term often employed by philosophers—a *brute fact* having no intrinsic value or disvalue. The term is as aptly applied to the struggle for survival among the lower animals as it is to such human activities as the running of businesses and races. Two male elks staking out their territories and locking antlers over a female are engaged in a primtive form of competition, as are two large fish chasing after the same small one with the intention of devouring it. From the little fish's point of view, the competitive spirit demonstrated by the big fish is not especially healthy, unless neither of them succeeds in making a meal of the little fish. Among humans, it sometimes seems that competition is valued for its own sake, or at least that nothing mediates between competitions of certain types and the intrinsically good pleasures to which they give rise. Even when no prize is awarded to the winner of a game, winners and losers alike seem to feel that the enterprise was useful, for the struggle to win is a pleasurable and valuable activity.

Some forms of competition have beneficial results on the whole; others may tend to result in serious disvalues to individuals or to societies. It is necessary, then, to focus upon specific types of competition and to attempt to determine what ethical or moral norms might appropriately be applied to them. A general observation, however, should be made in regard to business ethics. Some businessmen contend that their only concern should be the so-called bottom line, the profit or loss the business has earned or suffered as a result of its officers' policies, management's efficiency, government regulations, and other factors. Every businessman must be concerned about the bottom line, but that cannot—from a moral point of view—be his *only* concern. Some policies that have proved themselves over the years to work by the bottom-line criterion—that is, policies that tend to produce greater profits than any known alternatives—may nevertheless be morally wrong and should therefore be avoided by decent, honest, ethical businessmen. That view is vigorously opposed by Milton Friedman, who insists that "there is one and only one social responsibility of business—to use its resources and engage in activities designed to increase its profits so long as it stays within the rules of the game, which is to say, engages in open and free competition, without deception or fraud." He argues that the businessman ought to pursue his own interest, assuming with Adam Smith that he might thereby more effectively promote the good of society than if he deliberately attempted to do so. The doctrine that corporate officials have any social responsibility "other than to make as much money for their stockholders as possible," he says, is "fundamentally subversive." [1]

It is impossible here to enter upon a detailed analysis of Friedman's arguments in support of this thesis. It is possible, however, to observe that the existence of corporations is sanctioned by the states in which they do business. They are given special rights and privileges—often including especially low tax rates—because the people of the state, acting through their legislators, recognize the value of permitting their fellow citizens to do business through corporate organizations. In short, the corporation is permitted to exist only because it is widely believed that it can make an important contribution to the well-being of the people. This means not only the people who own shares of the corporation's stock, but also its employees, its customers, and all the other people who are affected, directly or indirectly, by its activities. If a corporation is permitted to do business in a community, that community has the right to expect not only that the corporation will pay its fair share of taxes and that its operations will redound to the benefit of its shareholders if it is successful, but also that it will not harm the community in which it is situated and that it might contribute something to the well-being of those who reside within it.

No corporation is exempt from the principles of fairness and decency that apply to all human affairs; nor is a corporation's management exempt from the principles of justice and morality that apply to all other citizens or, for that matter, to all other human beings. Although Friedman may have some justification for his belief that businesses should not contribute to charitable causes, his broader statement on the total lack of social responsibility on the part of corporate officials is supported by no arguments whatever. It totally overlooks the fact that business is a social creation, not merely the creation of those who invest in it. And it ignores the fact that businesses are run by human beings who have social responsibilities which they cannot shed when they close their office doors behind them. If the president of a corporation participates in schemes to bribe government officials, to exclude members of religious minorities from employment, to sell inferior products at inflated prices, and to compromise the security of the United States by entering into secret agreements with foreign powers, all in the name of profits, and is innocent of any moral wrongdoing—then ex-President Nixon and the Watergate conspirators were surely guilty of no wrongdoing when they engaged in bribery, wiretapping, lying, and assorted dirty tricks in the name of national security.

UNFAIR COMPETITION

Unfair competition is distinguished from immoral competitive practices in the following way: *Unfair competition* has to do primarily with the relationship between the businessman and his business associates. *Immoral competitive practices* relate to the consequences of the businessman's actions upon the consumer or upon society as a whole, rather than upon his business associates. That is not to suggest that unfair competition is moral or that every business practice that harms a customer or the public is necessarily immoral.

Unfair competition means *predatory competition*, the marketing of a product by a powerful firm in such a way as to drive another, weaker firm out of business or to force it to sell out. An illustration is provided by the Continental and Ward Baking Companies' tactics as described in a report written by the late Senator Estes Kefauver, who presided over the Senate's subcommittee on Antitrust and Monopoly from 1957 to 1963.[2] Those companies informed a small, independent baker that they were interested in purchasing his operation, offered him a low price, and warned him that they had the power to force him to sell. As proof, they could offer numerous instances in which they had moved into an independent's territory, sold bread at five cents a loaf, and waited until the independent had run out of money and the will—or the ability—to fight. In some instances, according to the Kefauver report, Continental worked in tandem with union officials who harassed the small baker or bought off employees. In one case, at least, employees purchased their routes from their employer, the small baker, on the pretext that they wanted to become independent businessmen, and then sold the routes to Continental. Trucks then delivered Continental's products rather than those of the independent baker who had served the market for years. In addition to underselling the independent, Continental displaced his products from the grocers' shelves by foisting huge quantities of its own products on the retailer with the promise that it would accept returns of any unsold products—a practice the independent could not afford to maintain. The big baker was able to absorb the losses in a territory it was intent on monopolizing, for it would continue to make profits in other areas, but the small baker had nothing but his one operation. Once he folded, Continental raised its prices and cancelled the special deals it had given the retailers. Continental has been convicted of violating federal statutes forbidding such practices many times through the years, and has been assessed millions of dollars in penalties in suits brought by competitors who were threatened or were in fact driven out of business by Continental's predatory tactics. In *Utah Pie Co.* v. *Continental Baking Co.*, 396 F.2d 161 (10th Cir. 1968), the court found that Continental had deliberately undersold its competition in order to drive them out of business, despite the fact that it sustained huge losses by selling its products at such low prices. In *Safeway Stores, Inc.* v. *Federal Trade Commission*, 366 F.2d 975 (9th Cir. 1966), Continental was a codefendant and was ordered to cease and desist its practice of conspiring to destroy its competition on the west coast. And in *Continental Baking Co.* v. *Old Homestead Bread Co.*, 476 F.2d 97 (10th Cir. 1973), Continental was assessed more than $3 million in triple damages and attorneys' fees after it succeeded in driving a major Denver baker out of business. On the business day following the competitor's shutdown, Continental raised its prices and abolished its discounts.

Other forms of unfair competition include the misrepresentation of a competitor's goods or prices, defamation of his character, harassment of his salesmen or other employees, intimidation of his customers, the organization of boycotts against his products, theft of his trade secrets, and many others.

The operator of a giant corporation might argue, as did many supermarket chains when they moved into communities and displaced the small grocers who had made their livelihoods among their neighbors for many years, that the small operators were inefficient and that the people demanded the lower prices and the convenience that only a supermarket could offer. It's the survival of the fittest, they might say; if the small operator can't take the competition, he ought to get out. A strict *laissez-faire* approach might well insist that the small manufacturer or storekeeper who cannot compete on equal terms with a large firm has no choice but to fold and that that is nothing but the operation of the marketplace. There have recently been numerous examples of the same principle in operation—most notably in the pocket calculator industry, which saw the swift rise and fall of many firms, some of which have disappeared entirely. This industry also illustrates some of the benefits that result from competition: lower prices for the consumer, improved products, inventiveness, new jobs, and convenience. If the inventor of the chip that is the heart of the calculator had been able to withhold it from the market, the public would still be paying $300 for simple arithmetical calculators, and the makers of slide rules would still be selling their products. The demise of the slide rule was not the result of predatory competition but of the invention of a superior product. There is a moral difference between the unfair competitive practices of a large baking company and the inventiveness of a large instrument company.

IMMORAL COMPETITIVE PRACTICES

An immoral competitive practice is any action by a manufacturer, distributor, or any other segment of the business community that is designed to give it a competitive edge over its rivals in a given market and is at the same time likely to cause grave harm to workers, shippers, consumers, or the environment, or involves a violation of any of the fundamental moral norms that should govern human relationships, such as the duty to speak truthfully and the duty not to cause unnecessary suffering to one's fellow men.

In this connection, it should be remembered that what is legal is not necessarily right. Persons responsible for corporate policies and actions ought (morally) not only to act within the constraints of the law, but also to avoid overstepping the bounds of what is morally right. Acts that do overstep those bounds cannot be justified on the ground that they contribute to profits.

There is ample evidence that competition lowers prices, encourages the introduction, production, and wide distribution of valuable goods and services, contributes to a higher standard of living, and has many other beneficial effects. It would follow that in the absence of powerful evidence to the contrary, any movement that discourages competition or encourages monopoly or other forms of restraint of trade has at least a presumption against it—a defeasible presumption, but one that in any case should govern individual, corporate, and governmental decision making.

Philosophers occasionally refer to statements that are *preanalytically true*. By this they mean that prior to any detailed philosophical analysis, they would appear to any intelligent observer to be true. They are the sorts of statements that seem to need no special justification, for anyone with common sense would agree that they are true. The following text offers a number of statements of that sort, which appear to be preanalytically true. These statements are accompanied by actual cases which represent violations of the moral principle enunciated. Each of these principles is related to the quest for competitive advantage.

1. When any person has it within his power to alleviate human suffering and pain, he has a duty to do so. A person who creates or produces a device that has the capacity to alleviate pain and suffering has the right to derive a reasonable profit from his efforts, but he does not have the right to exploit the helplessness or dependence of those who need his products in order to enrich himself unreasonably at their expense. Where there is a monopoly —that is, no competitive market—the temptation to engage in such exploitation is great but ought to be resisted on moral grounds.

Some years ago, Rohm and Haas had all rights to methyl methacrylate, a plastic used in the industrial field for airplane windshields and also for the making of dentures. When it was sold for industrial uses, it brought about 85 cents per pound, but when it was sold for dental purposes, precisely the same compound was marketed at $45 per pound. When some denture manufacturers discovered this price disparity, they started to buy the industrial plastic. The chemical company decided that that was bootlegging and determined to put a stop to it. One of the tactics proposed was the addition of an ingredient, such as lead or arsenic, that would not compromise the industrial plastic's uses but would make it unacceptable to the Food and Drug Administration. Such a program would have been impossible if there had been meaningful competition in the field, but there was none. More importantly however, it was attempting to prevent its own product from competing against *the same product* in a different package by making it unfit for one of its important uses, strictly in order to maintain an unfair and higher price.[3]

2. In competing for a larger segment of the market or for greater profits, it is morally wrong, even when it is not legally wrong, to lie or to engage in deliberate deception of potential customers, especially if life or health may be at stake, but also when they are not.

The Richardson-Merrell Pharmaceutical Corporation developed and marketed an anticholesterol drug, MER/29 (triparanol) in the early 1960s with a large promotional and advertising effort. Among the claims it made for the drug was that it was "virtually nontoxic and remarkably free from side effects even on prolonged clinical use." During its first year, the drug contributed $7 million to the company's gross sales. One vice-president said that MER/29 was "the biggest and most important drug in Merrell history," and vowed to defend it at every step against accusations that there were serious side effects. The company was aware of side effects, which had developed in laboratory tests that the company concealed from the FDA. In response to FDA inquiries, the company said that there had been no blood changes in its tests of the drug on rats or monkeys, when, in fact, most of the animals had developed cataracts and severe hair loss. Only after the FDA raided the company's premises and seized its records did the company withdraw the drug from the market. In the meantime, there had been numerous reports of cataracts developing in persons treated with the drug.

During the first year (while Richardson-Merrell realized that $7 million in sales), 490 persons developed cataracts from the drug's use.[4]

3. The knowledge that there is a grave danger to human life or health from the marketing of a given product should nullify any competitive concerns and be sufficient to justify withdrawing the product from the market.

The case just cited is an example of the violation of this principle as well, but another in a different field might be of interest. Florida and Texas oranges compete against California oranges for a share of the market but frequently remain green after they are ripe. Customers tend to think that green oranges are not ripe and do not buy them. In order to entice people to purchase their product, citrus growers in the south bathe their oranges in a dye. For some time they used Red 32, which was known to be toxic to animals. Dogs fed the equivalent of one third of an aspirin tablet of the dye rapidly developed diarrhea, and it was fatal to rats at a level equal to 1% of their diet. The industry fought all attempts to ban use of the dye.[5]

4. The temptation to squelch innovation, invention, and progress in order to preserve one's competitive position in the market or to prevent a loss of business should be resisted. Economic freedom cannot exist when powerful industries can prevent the development or marketing of new products from taking place.

Some utility concerns were offended by a display of fluorescent tubes at the 1939 World's Fair in New York, for it violated an understanding that the utilities had reached with the electrical supply industry at a meeting some time earlier. As one executive wrote, "I would think [the display] violated the fundamental concept of the lamp department that advances in the lighting art should not be at the expense of wattage." [6] In other words, a conspiracy had been formed, the object of which was to prevent interested persons from learning about the energy-saving possibilities of fluorescent lighting, because such lighting would tend to reduce the profits of the electric utilities if it were widely used. The display was removed.

5. The duties corporate officers owe to the principles of democracy and liberty transcend any they might owe to the companies for which they work. Any agreement or relationship with another firm, however profitable it might be, should be superseded by these higher values. No competitive position should be preserved at the expense of compromising the fundamental values upon which civilized society depends.

Under provisions of a secret agreement between Bausch and Lomb Optical Company of Rochester, New York, and Carl Zeiss of Germany, Zeiss agreed not to invade the American market with its binoculars (thus protecting Bausch and Lomb against a serious competitive threat) and to abandon plans to build a factory in the United States. In return, Zeiss acquired one fifth of Bausch & Lomb's stock and representation on its board of directors, and Bausch & Lomb agreed to buy glass for military optical instruments exclusively from Zeiss. As a result of these arrangements, the

United States had virtually no capacity to supply its own needs for optical instruments when World War I broke out, and great efforts were required to bring the nation to self-sufficiency in optical glass and military optical instruments.

After World War I, the two companies reached other agreements concerning royalties and other commercial matters. At the same time, the American firm helped Zeiss overcome the restrictions placed upon German firms by the Versailles Treaty, which prohibited the manufacture of military hardware.

Bausch and Lomb regularly supplied Zeiss with information about American military procurements after Hitler's rise to power: the number and types of rangefinders, bombsights, and periscopes, comprehensive economic reports, and other information requested by Zeiss. It was, of course, understood that the German company would keep all of this information in the strictest confidence.

A week after Hitler's invasion of Czechoslovakia, Zeiss demanded "a precise statement of those patents of ours which you use in your manufacturing processes, designating at the same time those instruments in whose manufacture these patents are used, also indicating the turnover you have had in these instruments during the past two business years, and the volume of orders which you have at present on hand for such instruments." Bausch & Lomb complied, and added information on orders for future delivery. At the same time, Bausch and Lomb was refusing to fill orders from Britain and France on the ground that if they were not ready for war, war would be put off that much longer. Patent infringement suits were used as a threat to frighten potential competitors away from bidding on major government contracts, leaving the field entirely to Bausch & Lomb, which used its monopoly position as a means of extorting unreasonably high prices out of the armed forces for the equipment they purchased.[7]

6. In the interests of a free market and political freedom, any company that has the capacity to compete against another without doing so in a predatory fashion ought to do so.

Despite the claims of American industrialists, the United States is a far cry from a true free enterprise system. Those who have the ability to enter into competition with the giants of the industries in which they participate seldom do so. The steel industry, which is presently in serious trouble as a result of competition from foreign producers, has not known any real competition for many years. As late as 1963, the president of the National Steel Corporation testified at the Kefauver hearings that he would not undersell United States Steel even if his costs were lower because of greater efficiency. The president of Bethlehem Steel refused to acknowledge that it could ever make sense to give the consumer a break by reducing prices below those of his competitors. Kefauver noted that the steel companies follow U.S. Steel's prices "down to the third decimal." The president of Springport Steel Products testified that after trying for months to find some way to reduce his costs and being frustrated at every turn by American steel manufacturers, he finally turned to foreign producers.[8] Kefauver observed that "foreign steel producers have been vigorously competing on a price basis for the same business; the American companies, by failing to bestir themselves, have lost out. Indeed, not only have they lost out abroad; they have watched with growing alarm the inroads of foreign firms in their own backyards." [9] Fourteen years later, Kefauver's worst fears were realized as thousands of workers were laid off and major steel plants were shut down, allegedly because of foreign competition.[10] Meaningful competition within the United States, among the steel producers, might have prevented the economic catastrophe and the massive unemployment that resulted.

True competition must mean competition not only among manufacturers and products but also among workers. Many Americans have assumed without further examination that wages should never be reduced and that the government should enforce a minimum wage for all workers. It appears now that this assumption and the policies it has brought in its wake have resulted in such undesirable effects as the unemployment of millions of workers and the inability of American industry to sell its products to its own people, let alone to the citizens of other nations that are able to produce equivalent products with lower prices. If American workers will not compete against one another in a free wage market, then—unless the United States is prepared to cut itself off from all foreign competition, and therefore from all foreign trade, by erecting tariff barriers—they must compete against foreign workers. Such competition is indirect but no less meaningful.

There is always a powerful incentive for businesses to destroy their competition or to seize special advantages for themselves to enlarge their share of the market and to enhance the chances of increasing their net income. The predatory tactics of Continental Baking constitute one approach. Another, employed more broadly in recent years, is the acquisition of other firms. It is almost impossible to open the *Wall Street Journal* without noticing one or more items regarding attempts by large corporations to take over smaller ones. In some instances, such takeovers are initiated precisely to destroy meaningful competition. In one of the greatest acquisitions of this sort, the treasurer of E. I. du Pont de Nemours & Company urged his company's finance committee to purchase controlling interests of the General Motors Corporation on the ground it would "undoubtedly secure for us the entire Fabrikoid, Pyralin [celluloid], paint and varnish business of those companies, which is a substantial factor." [11] By acquiring General Motors' stock, du Pont was able to guarantee that GM would purchase certain essential products from it rather than from its competitors in the same field. Du Pont thus assured itself and its stockholders of a continuing and growing market, free of any possible competitive threat.

Such actions are inconsistent with the ideal of a free market, for they tend to destroy the market. To argue that companies should be free to enter into such deals or agreements is much like arguing that in a truly free society, the people should have the right to vote for candidates who promise them that if they are elected there will never be another election. Thomas Hobbes, the most authoritarian of political philosophers, insisted that no one can claim, on the grounds of political liberty, the right to sell himself into slavery, a condition in which he would have no liberty at all. Although it might seem to be paradoxical, it is nevertheless true that one of the conditions of freedom, political or economic, is a refusal to permit men to perform acts that make genuine liberty impossible. It is always preferable, however, for men to examine their policies carefully, to try as accurately as possible to foresee the likely consequences of those policies not only for themselves and those they represent, but for all persons who are likely to be affected by them, and then to assess the harm as well as the good that might result from such policies. If they are willing to forego personal or corporate advantage in the name of higher moral principles—the "social responsibility" that Friedman insists businessmen do not have—then the chances of both political and economic freedom being enhanced are far greater than if they take the narrower path of self-interest. When there is no freedom, there can be no genuine competition. When competition has been destroyed, so has freedom.

Part Four

The Frontiers
of Law and Morals

In a sense, all of the problems discussed thus far lie at the frontiers of law and morals, for conflicting claims and competing interests have led to unceasing conflict between those who demand greater freedom from the restrictive power of the law and those who believe that the law ought to protect them against unwarranted intrusions into their lives, unjustifiable harms committed by others against them, or unwanted and potentially dangerous deterioration in the natural or moral environment. Even so well-established a liberty as freedom of the press, enshrined in the Bill of Rights and in other great national and international declarations, is under attack by those who question its value or interpret it as permitting the exclusion of those forms of literature of which they disapprove. But in all of these areas, the law has had settled doctrines for many centuries. Though some changes in detail were made from time to time, the fact that the law should take a stand on these issues is well established and has a long history. To the extent that problems presently exist, they consist more in reforming old and possibly outdated doctrines than in the introduction of radically new ones.

But in some areas, the law has no settled doctrines. These areas are not necessarily new, because men may have been concerned about them and been discussing them at least since Plato's day. Such novelty as there is consists in the fact that people are now talking about the institution of laws to deal with them.

Civil rights were extended to slaves, former slaves, and the descendants of slaves by the Thirteenth, Fourteenth, and Fifteenth Amendments to the United States Constitution and by Congressional and state legislation fol-

lowing the Civil War. In practice, however, those rights remained a dead letter, at least in some places. Women did not win the right to vote until 1920. Discrimination against blacks, women, and members of various racial, religious, and ethnic groups in education, employment, housing, and other areas has continued to exist in law (de jure); *and even when it lacked official sanction, it continued, either openly or covertly* (de facto). *New legislation and new attitudes have gradually replaced the old, but the effects of centuries of accumulated abuse continue to haunt the nation. Attempts to rectify the wrongs of the past have been blocked, not only by diehard traditionalists and bigots, but also by the long-lasting effects of grave and widespread injustices. In order to hasten the equitable distribution and enjoyment of the benefits and opportunities of an affluent and open society, numerous programs, known collectively as affirmative action programs, have been developed, principally by administrative agencies. But these programs have run into unexpected opposition from some of the very persons who were most vocal in their support of the civil rights movements of the past several decades. The constitutionality of these programs will be decided by the courts. Their wisdom and their moral implications are matters of controversy.*

Civil disobedience is by definition a violation of the law, but it is a violation committed as an act of conscience or as an act of protest against the law itself, and therefore, in the eyes of many people, it constitutes a form of expression that ought to be accorded special privileges, as were freedom of speech and freedom of the press two centuries ago. Here law and morality clash, as it were, on the battlefield of a man's conscience. Consider such a man, whose intention is not to destroy the legal system as such or to harm any person, but merely to change a given law or a particular part of the system so as to make the whole more just and equitable than it is. Should such a person be subjected to the same penalties as those who might have violated the law out of purely selfish motives, or, indeed, should he be punished at all?

In another area—international relations—the law is still in its infancy. It is still quite primitive, lacking many of the powers and the attributes that are sometimes assumed to be essential to the existence of a genuine legal system. As a result, despite repeated efforts to reach a sufficient consensus in the world community to outlaw terrorism on an international level, every such effort has failed. Often such failures are based on the theory that one man's terrorist is another's freedom fighter. But this rather lame excuse makes no contribution whatever to the solution of one of the world's most grievous problems and offers no consolation to the victims or potential victims of the guns and bombs that are so freely employed by terrorists throughout the free world. It is perhaps worth noting that terrorism as such is almost completely unknown in those regions that are ruled by totalitarian regimes. How, then, can persons and governments committed to the principles of liberty and to rule under law respond to attacks by terrorist organiza-

tions, when there seems to be no law to which they can appeal in formulating their policy decisions? Can individuals or states morally revert to the principles of self-help—those principles sometimes known as the law of the jungle which some political philosophers believe society and civilization were designed to abolish—in order to preserve their most vital interests?

In these areas law and morals meet in a manner that we have not encountered thus far, for in some cases, what morality seems to require, the law opposes, whereas in others, what morality requires, the law until recently —and perhaps even to this day—has totally overlooked.

How, then, can the principles of criminal punishment be squared with the requirements of morality, with the demands of those who want to live in a free society, and with the realities of the law in these frontier areas where law and morals meet, clash, and conflict? And what, if anything, is being done, or ought to be done, to bridge the gap between law and morals in these difficult areas? We turn now to a consideration of these issues.

11

Affirmative Action and Reverse Discrimination

RACIAL AND SEXUAL DISCRIMINATION

The record of the mistreatment of blacks in the United States is so well known that it is unnecessary to review it in any detail. It is sufficient to recall some of the major aspects of black life over the past three centuries.

The ancestors of most present-day black Americans were transported to the shores of this continent in the holds of slave ships after being purchased from man-hunters or African chiefs, or captured by shipowners. The ships were in many instances specially designed so as to hold the maximum number of slaves with no regard to their comfort, their safety, or their health.

The captives were often chained together in prone positions, unable to rise or move about even for elementary human needs. Those who survived the journey were treated like cattle, brought to markets where they were sold at auction to the highest bidders. Once sold, they became the personal property of their owners, who had the right to do with them as they pleased. In some cases they were treated with a modicum of civility, but there was no limit to the cruelties that could be inflicted upon them by sadistic owners or foremen. They were deprived of any opportunity to learn to read or write. Children were separated from their mothers, and husbands from their wives, by market conditions or personal whims.

After more than two centuries, official slavery was brought to an end, but many of the abuses continued. In many of the states of the Union, blacks were denied such elementary rights of citizenship as the right to vote, usually through such devices as poll taxes and literacy tests. Lacking political power, they were unable to use the ballot box to right the wrongs done to them by the politicians who ran the system that continued to oppress them. Their children were denied the benefits of a meaningful education by being sent to segregated schools that were often poorly equipped and poorly staffed. In rural areas, their poverty was so desperate that many children dropped out of school because they had no shoes. When they did go, they were often so hungry that they were unable to attend to their studies. In urban areas, they were crowded into ghettoes that lacked decent sanitation, adequate garbage pickup, proper housing, and many of the other amenities of American city life.

When they sought honest labor, they found that virtually all but the most menial tasks were reserved for others. The unions closed their ranks against blacks, owners and managers would not hire them, and because of the inferior educational opportunities that were available to them, they were prevented from entering most professions, with the exception of the clergy and teaching. Even when they managed, through exceptional perseverance, to make it through a professional school, they were usually subjected to still further discrimination. Black lawyers, for example, were barred from membership in the American Bar Association, and finally formed their own guild. When they did find work, they were denied benefits equal to those of whites: their wages were usually lower, they were effectively prevented from rising beyond certain levels in an organization, and they were made to understand that they were expected to remain in a subservient position and to give at least an outward show of subservience.

Even in the entertainment world, where some blacks rose to considerable prominence, the system of discrimination and exclusion operated, not only to their detriment but to that of all who might have enjoyed witnessing the fulfillment of their talents. With a few exceptions, when a dramatic production included a black character, whites in blackface filled the roles. On the stage, screen, radio, and in the early days of television, blacks were almost always portrayed as stereotypes, as fat "mammies," as ignorant, superstitious, and obsequious men, and as funny, easily frightened children. Black performers spoke with a peculiar accent and a sing-song intonation, and most of them were obliged to utter absurd malapropisms. Few serious black actors were able to find parts. For black musicians, employment was denied in the great musical companies, such as symphony orchestras, the Metropolitan Opera, and others. Some who won international recognition were prevented by narrow-minded bigots from displaying their artistry in their native land. The great contralto, Marion Anderson, was not permitted to appear at Constitution Hall in Washington, D.C. Even when permitted to appear on stage, black artists were often subjected to humiliating conditions.

In some parts of the country, segregation and discrimination pervaded every aspect of life. Buses and railroad cars were segregated. Restaurants and cafeterias either excluded blacks altogether or provided separate and inferior accommodations for them. Blacks were not permitted to use bathrooms that were designated for whites only or to drink from water fountains that were reserved for whites. Hotels and motels that would accept black patrons were so scarce in some parts of the country that a black family might have to drive for hundreds of miles to find a place to retire for the night. Public libraries, swimming pools, and parks were closed to blacks. Many hospitals turned away black patients, and ambulances called to the scene of accidents returned to their bases without treating the victims if they discovered that the patients were black.

In 1954, the United States Supreme Court issued the first in a series of decisions designed to bring this system to an end. It concluded that blacks, as all Americans, are entitled to the equal protection of the laws; that whatever public funds provide for white Americans must also be provided to blacks; and that public schools that are segregated are inherently unequal. It therefore ordered the racial integration of public schools in those areas where they had been segregated. It placed no specific time limits on the process, but ordered that it be accomplished "with all deliberate speed." [1]

Segregationists employed every conceivable means to avoid and defer implementation of this decision: they closed public schools and provided tuition grants to white children who attended private schools. Special plans were devised that permitted children to transfer from integrated schools back to segregated ones. White children were given "freedom of choice" to stay out of integrated schools. And in extreme cases, officials and citizens resorted to physical obstruction and violence in order to prevent integration of educational facilities. [2]

The courts and successive national administrations have vigorously attempted to break down the old barriers that blocked blacks and members of other minority groups, as well as women, from enjoying the full advantages of American citizenship and equal rights under the law. Although considerable progress has taken place in each of the areas mentioned here, as well as in others, grave problems continue to exist. An overwhelming proportion of blacks and other minorities live in slums and overcrowded ghettoes, are afflicted with poor health and poverty, are unable to find employment in the better-paying, high-prestige jobs, are undereducated and therefore unable to qualify for graduate and professional programs that provide the key to a better living, and are surrounded by such negative formative influences as prostitution, drug-pushing, gambling, alcoholism, and violent crimes, as well as an extraordinarily high rate of family breakdown.

Although the problems of women are different in many respects from those of blacks, they are comparable at least insofar as educational and job opportunities are concerned. They too have been subject to discrimination. They have been denied access to certain schools and either discouraged or rejected when they have attempted to gain admittance to programs or jobs that had traditionally been thought to be the proper preserve of men only. It was assumed either that they were innately inferior or that there were pressing social justifications for denying them access to those positions. When sheer dogged determination won particular individuals the positions that were normally denied to blacks or to women, the latter found the financial and other rewards that came with such positions were significantly less for them than they were for white males.

In 1964, Congress passed a Civil Rights Act, and in subsequent years, other congressional enactments and numerous court decisions broadened the scope of protections afforded to members of minority groups and to women in many areas: housing, public accommodations, voting rights, employment, and educational opportunities, to mention only a few. In each of the congressional acts, it was stressed that there should be no discrimination or segregation based upon a person's race, color, sex, religion, or national origin. They were designed precisely to overcome the evil effects of such discrimination and to fulfill an ideal enunciated by Justice Harlan in his dissent in *Plessy* v. *Ferguson*.[3] In arguing against the majority's decision that sustained a Louisiana statute providing for "separate but equal accommodations" for white and black railway passengers, Justice Harlan insisted that such statutes were based upon the assumption that "colored citizens are so inferior and degraded that they cannot be allowed to sit in public coaches occupied by white citizens." He continued:

> The arbitrary separation of citizens, on the basis of race, . . . is a badge of servitude wholly inconsistent with the civil freedom and the equality before the law established by the Constitution. It cannot be justified upon any legal grounds. . . . The thin disguise of "equal" accommodations for passengers in railroad coaches will not mislead anyone, nor atone for the wrong this day done.[4]

He insisted that "our Constitution is color-blind," but it took nearly three quarters of a century for Congress and the Courts to agree and to adopt his reading of the Constitution.

Since the late 1960s, a new element has been added to the search for equal treatment of members of groups that were subjected to various forms of discrimination in the past. In the race for jobs, for admission to the professions, for economic security, they were so far behind, so severely handicapped, that if they were ever to catch up, they would have to be given some special assistance. Moreover, many persons believed that like those who have been wrongfully injured, they deserved to be compensated for the hurts and injustices of the past and that those who have benefited from those injustices should somehow be expected to pay, or at least to give up a portion of the advantages they have enjoyed as a result of those injustices.

Suppose Ina Plunkett had been repeatedly passed over for responsible positions for which she was eminently qualified. For no reason other than the fact that she was a woman, her employer failed to promote her or to give her raises commensurate with her ability or her performance. After years of such discriminatory treatment, she compared her salary with that of Darwin Spoonhaltz, a male colleague who entered the company at the same time, whose abilities were no greater than hers, and whose contributions were in no way superior to those that she had made or could have made if she had not been unfairly discriminated against. She discovered that her salary of $10,000 was only a third of his. Her employer, under pressure from the government to treat female employees equally, decided to make amends. He would no longer treat Ina differently. He would recognize her abilities for what they were, give her appropriate promotions, and increase her salary by the same percentage as Darwin. If he promoted her to a higher rank and immediately raised her salary to $15,000, and if Ina and Darwin received equal (percentage) increments of 6% each year thereafter, at the end of ten years her salary would be in the neighborhood of $35,000, but Darwin's would still be twice as high. Thus, besides suffering the indignity of years of labor at an inferior job and the financial loss that that entailed, Ina would find that with "equal" treatment, she would never be able to catch up. Even if she were willing to let bygones be bygones, giving up any claim to compensation for the losses she unjustly suffered in the past, it would seem that there ought to be some remedy for the future—that she should not be expected to remain indefinitely behind those who had unfair advantages to begin with. Surely she has a right to be brought up to the starting line so that she can run a fair race—namely, an immediate raise to $30,000, so that she and Darwin are at least on an equal footing.

If her employer were to balk at that or be unable to pay such a high salary to two employees, Ina might suggest that her salary increments be accelerated to twice the level of those of her male colleague. Even then, if she started at half of Darwin's salary, it would take her 13 years to come up to an equal salary and, in the meantime, she would have suffered still greater comparative losses, namely, the sum of all the money she would have made during those 13 years if she had not been discriminated against.

But suppose that even that is unsatisfactory, for her employer cannot afford to keep both Darwin and Ina on the payroll at such high levels. Ina might suggest that Darwin relinquish the position he has held for so long at her expense. Now that her rights are at last being recognized, it seems only fair, she might argue, that he should now exchange positions with her, permitting her to enjoy the prestige and income of the higher position and him to assume some of the burdens that she bore for so many years. If not for the unfair treatment to which she was subjected, after all, Darwin might never have occupied his position.

On the other hand, it is not so easy to conclude that Darwin should suffer now because of injustices perpetrated against Ina by someone else in the past. To be sure, Darwin has been the beneficiary of those injustices; but he was merely an innocent bystander, doing his job and never doing anything to harm Ina. Indeed, Darwin may have been in the forefront of the movement to win equal rights for oppressed women. To insist that he now give up his position and his income, despite his years of dedicated service, so as to compensate someone whom he never harmed, seems grossly unjust. This might be even clearer if we suppose that Darwin has just retired and that Ina demands that he give up his home and a portion of his retirement fund so that she might enjoy what she might have had if she had not been subjected to unfair treatment by her employer. The ancient legal principle that no one ought to be held liable for damages caused to another through no fault of his own, based upon an identical moral principle, appears to be both sound and appropriate in this context.

What of the employer? Ina might be entitled to compensation by him, for it would seem that he was the original perpetrator of the injustice that caused her so much suffering. He might claim that he too was a victim, that he unwittingly went along with a system that imposed standards and practices that he accepted as the ordinary way of doing business. "How," he might ask, "can I be expected to anticipate the changing fashions in morals and law? How can I be held liable to make up for wrongs done in the past that did not seem wrong at the time, but were instead universally accepted practices? Isn't it similar to an *ex post facto* law? That is, aren't you imposing a nearly impossible burden upon me, demanding of me that I anticipate the shifts of public opinion and legislative and judicial pronouncements, and penalizing me when my guesses turn out to be incorrect? If I, or any businessman, had to compensate every worker and every customer for 'wrongs' that were not regarded as wrong, either in law or in morals, at the time they were committed, we would all soon be driven out of business. None of us could survive, and everyone—our customers, our employees, our suppliers, and our communities—all of us would suffer irreparable harm. No, whereas I am prepared to acknowledge the propriety of giving every woman and every black equal treatment today, and whereas I now recognize that what we all did before we were sensitized to the injustice of our practices was morally wrong, I cannot concede that we ought now to be held liable for the damages done to the victims of those injustices. That damage was done is undeniable. That innocent persons have suffered needlessly and wrongfully is beyond question. But I strongly deny that I or any of my colleagues, as businessmen, should be held personally liable for those wrongs. We too were victims of the society in which we live and of its imperfections. To destroy us and the institutions to which we have devoted our lives so as to compensate the victims of our society's imperfections would solve nothing and would perpetrate yet another wrong."

It is obvious that someone is going to suffer a serious loss. Ina has already suffered grievous damage. She is seeking some form of redress. Although Darwin benefited from Ina's loss, there is little justification for the supposition that he caused or was responsible for that loss, and therefore it would seem to be unreasonable to demand that he make it up to her. The employer, too, has a plausible claim. In fact, if every person rejected or subjected to discriminatory treatment during the days when that was permitted came back now to demand reparations, few businesses would survive the flood of claims. The damage to them and the communities that depend upon them would be so great as to be incalculable.

Like many similar problems that communities have had to face in the past, this one is not amenable to a fully satisfactory solution. Whatever is done, the end result will be that someone will have suffered some damage, and some residue of injustice will remain. In the nineteenth century, when the well-being of the nation seemed to require the expansion and development of industry, the victims of industrial accidents had to pay for their own losses, for the protection of industry rather than the protection of individual human beings was regarded as a more important social goal. Not until fairly recently were the losses spread throughout society by a system of workmen's compensation and insurance programs designed to protect workers against work-related injuries. Similarly, in order to protect employers against endless claims, it may be necessary for victims of past discriminatory actions to suffer the losses, or for some of those losses to be borne by society at large.

It may be more constructive to look beyond the question of reparations for past wrongs toward the solution of present ills and the prevention of future injuries to innocent persons.

AFFIRMATIVE ACTION PROGRAMS

The term *affirmative action* is ambiguous. It applies to numerous programs, some of them uncontroversial and others troublesome and divisive. The general aim of all affirmative action programs is to raise the level of those groups that have suffered from discrimination in the past to a position of proportional equality in education, housing, employment, and other areas with those who have previously been relatively free from the disadvantages imposed by discriminatory policies. If a given firm has less than 1% black or women employees when blacks constitute 10% of the general population and women more than 50%, this is at least *prima facie* evidence that some form of discrimination must have been in operation in the past. In order to be quite certain that blacks and women (to use only two of several groups for which affirmative action programs have been developed) are given appropriate opportunities to compete on an equal basis for those positions that are available and to take their rightful place in society, employers have been encouraged to make special efforts to recruit members of those groups. Whereas in the past an informal network might have been used to recruit potential junior executives, for example, with present executives contacting friends and associates for recommendations of potential candidates, under affirmative action programs, employers are urged to place advertisements and notices in journals that are likely to be read by all of those who are qualified to fill the positions and to solicit applications from institutions that are known to have large numbers of minority students. If the available pool of blacks or women suffers from educational deficiencies, an affirmative action program might offer them special remedial courses or training that would enable them to compete with other applicants on an equal basis. Such programs have generated little, if any, controversy.

But there is another form of affirmative action program. If a given employer has what affirmative action workers regard as an underrepresentation of blacks or women, that employer may be expected to set a numerical goal, a timetable to reach a certain optimum balance of blacks and whites, males and females. This may be implemented in a number of different ways, one of which is the exclusive hiring or placement of persons belonging to one or more of the groups, previously discriminated against or the establishment of numerical ratios (the word *quota* is studiously avoided), which provide for the placement of a high proportion of blacks, women, or members of other minority groups, at least over a period of some years, until what is regarded as an appropriate balance is achieved. Such programs have brought about considerable controversy and have resulted in a number of legal actions. The remainder of this chapter will focus upon this type of affirmative action and the arguments over its moral as well as its legal propriety.

The most important cases in the affirmative action area both concern university admissions policies. The first one, *DeFunis* v. *Odegaard*, was brought by a white male who believed that he was unfairly discriminated against by the University of Washington Law School; the other, *Bakke* v. *Regents of University of California*, by a white male student who believed that the admissions committee of the Medical School of the University of California at Davis had unfairly discriminated against him. Both of these students contended that the affirmative action policies of the professional schools to which they sought admission unjustly and unconstitutionally deprived them of the equal protection of the law by admitting less-qualified blacks and members of other favored (but previously less favored) minority groups to the schools while keeping them out. Both of them claimed that these policies constituted a form of racial discrimination—this time discrimination against white males—that was forbidden by the Constitution and contrary to the principles of justice and equality upon which the United States was founded.

The essential facts of each of these cases may be summarized briefly:

CASE 13. DeFUNIS v. ODEGAARD [5]

Marco DeFunis applied for admission to the University of Washington Law School and was rejected. The school had received some 1,600 applications for 150 places in the first-year class. He brought suit against the university, asking that the court order the university to admit him and pay him damages of not less than $50,000. The superior court, which heard the case, dismissed his application for damages but ruled that the university had discriminated against him in violation of the equal protection of the laws guaranteed by the Fourteenth Amendment to the United States Constitution. It thereupon ordered him admitted. The university appealed to the Supreme Court of the State of Washington, which reversed the lower court's decision. A further appeal to the United States Supreme Court was accepted for hearing, but by the time the Court rendered a verdict, DeFunis was in his last quarter. Because any decision the Court might render would not have made any further difference to DeFunis' legal education, the Court rendered no decision, declaring the case to be moot. However, in an unusual move, Justice Douglas delivered a detailed dissent in which he examined many of the most important issues in the case.

Applicants for admission to the law school are required to have earned an undergraduate degree and taken the Law School Admission Test (LSAT). Under its affirmative action program, the law school gave each student the option of indicating on his application his dominant ethnic origin. Other evidence, including letters of recommendation, was also used in the admissions process.

Applicants were generally divided into three groups, based upon a mathematical formula that yielded a number called the Predicted First-Year Average (PFYA). The PFYA was arrived at by combining the applicant's grade-point average during his junior and senior years with his LSAT score (or his average LSAT score if he took it more than once) and his writing test score component (or the average if it was taken more than once). Based on experience of previous years, the admissions committee decided that the most promising candidates in the year DeFunis applied would be those whose PFYA was over 77. The full committee reviewed and decided upon applicants with PFYAs over 77 as they came in. Those with averages below 74.5 were reviewed by the committee chairman and either rejected by him or held for a later review by the full committee. However, all files of minority applicants (namely, black Americans, Chicano Americans, American

Indians, and Philippine Americans), were considered by the full committee, regardless of the individual applicant's PFYA. (When asked
by the court why Asian-Americans were not included in the minority
classification, the committee chairman explained that a significant
number could be admitted on the same basis as general applicants.)
Applicants whose PFYA fell between 74.5 and 76.99 were held for
review until after all the applications had arrived and were lumped
with those whose PFYAs were above 77 but had not been admitted
and those whose PFYAs were below 74.5 and were being held for
further consideration. DeFunis' PFYA was 76.23.

Each file was then assigned to an individual committee member, who
was to review it and report to the full committee. Such assignments
were on a random basis. However, the files of black applicants were
assigned to a professor who had worked with minority students and a
second-year black law student, and the files of other minority students
were reviewed by an associate dean.

This policy evolved as a result of a conviction on the part of the
university administration that an open door to admissions of minority
students was not sufficient and that more affirmative steps toward full
integration were required. The law school was concerned to improve
representation of minority groups in its classes and in the legal profession. It was believed that if minority students were held to the same
standards as whites, the number admitted would be quite minimal.
Therefore, minority applicants were not compared with white applicants and were admitted with PFYAs lower than those of any white
students. The committee accepted those believed qualified to do the
work required by the study of law, based upon information in the
files that went beyond the PFYA. DeFunis was rejected. Of those who
were admitted, 74 had lower PFYAs than DeFunis, including 36 minority applicants and 22 who were returning from military service and
were also given special consideration.

The trial court found that some minority students' PFYAs were so
low that if they had been white, their applications would have been
summarily denied.

The Supreme Court of the State of Washington divided the issue
into three separate questions:

1. Can race ever be considered as a factor in the admissions policy of
   a state law school, or is the consideration of race an inherent violation
   of the equal protection of the laws guaranteed by the Constitution?
2. If race is not inherently unconstitutional, how can one distinguish
   permissible from impermissible racial classifications?
3. Once an appropriate standard for racial classification has been established, does the admissions policy of the University of Washington Law School meet it?

In responding to the first question, the court concluded that only "invidious" racial classifications are banned by the Constitution, namely, those that stigmatize a racial group as inferior. The law school's policy was not invidious, because it was designed to bring the races together, not to separate them. Where there had been a long pattern of racial discrimination in public schools, for example, it would be impossible to achieve meaningful integration without taking notice of the racial composition of the student bodies.

As for the second question, the court held that only invidious forms of racial classification are impermissible; but when persons stigmatized by racial classifications are being benefited, the action is benign, and therefore permissible.

The state has a compelling interest in promoting integration in public education, the court said, and, in this case, in eliminating racial imbalance within public legal education. Moreover, minorities "must enjoy equal representation within our legal system," but that is impossible unless there are minority lawyers, prosecutors, judges, and public officials. The court concluded, therefore, that correcting the racial imbalance in the law school was essential and that the method chosen by the law school was appropriate as the only feasible plan that promises realistically to work now.

On the further question of the methods appropriate to selection of law students, the court rejected the assumption that such "objective" measures as the LSAT or the PFYA either were or should have been the sole determinative factors. There is the possibility that grades and "objective" examinations are culturally biased, so as to discriminate against persons who are not raised in middle-class American homes, with standard English as their first and primary language. Moreover, it may well be that blacks and members of other minority groups, underrepresented as they are in law school and the legal profession, might make greater contributions to both than white persons who happen to have higher PFYAs.

Finally, the court responded to DeFunis' contention that some black applicants might have been less deprived educationally, financially, and culturally than some white applicants by stating that even an affluent minority applicant might have been subjected to psychological harm through discrimination, that the essential goal was to increase the number of minority persons in the profession, and that the applicant's race rather than the level of his deprivation could be employed as a criterion for determining his suitability for admission.

Two of the Justices on the state of Washington Supreme Court registered dissents. Chief Justice Hale explained his reasons as follows:

> Racial bigotry, prejudice and intolerance will never be ended by exalting the political rights of one group or class over that of another. The circle of inequality cannot be broken by shifting the inequities from one

> man to his neighbor. To aggrandize the first will, to the extent of the
> aggrandizement, diminish the latter. There is no remedy at law except to
> abolish all class distinctions heretofore existing in law. For that reason,
> the constitutions are, and ever ought to be, color blind. Now the
> court says it would hold the constitutions color conscious that they may
> stay color blind. I do not see how they can be both color blind
> and color conscious at the same time toward the same persons and
> on the same issues, so I dissent.

In short, Justice Hale concluded that in order to fulfill the admirable
objective of enrolling more minority students, the university employed
a racial criterion that unjustly discriminated, on racial grounds, against
DeFunis and other white applicants. Not only white Americans, but
Asian Americans and members of other ethnic groups that were not
included in the preferred list were similarly deprived of "such preferences or indulgences."

He vigorously objected to the committee's assumptions that "all of
the accepted minority students were of a lower economic status" and
were more "culturally deprived" than DeFunis and other white applicants, assumptions that he said were "derived from no real evidence
whatever." He reviewed the procedures employed by the admissions
committee, observing that some of the committee's members were
first- and second-year students who were placed on the committee for
no other reason than that they had placed their names on a sign-up
sheet that had been posted by the Student Bar Association. One of
these student members was doing so poorly in his courses that he
admitted he "barely made it to the second year." Each of these students
was given 70 files and had the power to reject any of them and to
recommend favorable action on others. Each of them eliminated 50 or
60 files. Reviewing a random sample of student files, Justice Hale
concluded that students were admitted in an arbitrary and capricious
manner having little to do with their academic qualifications and that
some were admitted for no other reason than their participation in
community action projects and their racial or ethnic background.

Justice Hale found such action incompatible with the Fourteenth
Amendment. DeFunis, he said, was ousted from the list of acceptable
students solely because others were given preferred treatment based
upon their racial and ethnic origin.

He distinguished mandatory bussing cases, in which children were
bussed from one neighborhood to another in order to integrate public
schools, from this case by noting that no child was deprived of his
education by being bussed to school, whereas DeFunis was deprived
of his opportunity to attend law school. In the one case, the effect was
to provide an integrated and therefore (at least theoretically) a superior education for all; in the other, qualified applicants were deprived
of seats they might otherwise have occupied, not because of a lack of

qualifications, but because of racial origin, because other persons were given preference in an unequal contest.

Justice Douglas of the United States Supreme Court noted that by determining in advance that 15% to 20% of the places in the entering class would be set aside for minority applicants, the university reduced the total number of places for which DeFunis could compete, solely because of his race. He was critical of the objectivity and neutrality of the LSAT and indicated that he had grave reservations about the approach of the admissions committee at the University of Washington Law School. He rejected the argument that racial discrimination such as that practiced by the admissions committee could be justified by any "compelling" state interest. On such grounds, he said, large quotas of blacks or browns could be added to the bar by waiving the examinations required of other groups so that it could be better racially balanced. But that would not do, he said, for

> the Equal Protection Clause commands the elimination of racial barriers, not their creation in order to satisfy our theory as to how society ought to be organized. The purpose of the University of Washington cannot be to produce Black lawyers for Blacks, Polish lawyers for Poles, Jewish lawyers for Jews, Irish lawyers for the Irish. It should produce good lawyers for Americans. . . .

He went on to make a very important point concerning possibly negative effects upon the very people the system was designed to benefit:

> A segregated admissions process creates suggestions of stigma and caste no less than a segregated classroom, and in the end it may produce that result despite its contrary intentions. One other assumption must be clearly disapproved, that Blacks or Browns cannot make it on their individual merit. That is a stamp of inferiority that a State is not permitted to place on any lawyer. . . . All races can compete fairly at all professional levels. So far as race is concerned, any state-sponsored preference to one race over another in that competition is in my view "invidious" and violative of the Equal Protection Clause.

In the end, Justice Douglas concluded that he was unable, on the record, to determine whether DeFunis was discriminated against because of his race or whether the Law School's admissions procedures violated the Equal Protection Clause. But the principles upon which he would have made his judgment are quite clear.

CASE 14. BAKKE v. REGENTS OF THE UNIVERSITY OF CALIFORNIA [6]

The *Bakke* case is quite similar in its broad outlines to the *DeFunis* case. Allan Bakke applied for admission to the Medical School at the University of California at Davis, which had set aside a number of

places in its first-year class for minority students. In this respect, the
Bakke case differs from *DeFunis*, for in *DeFunis* there was no specific
quota. In 1973, the application form inquired whether a student desired
to be considered by a special committee that passed upon the applications of persons from economically and educationally disadvantaged
backgrounds, but the following year, the applicant was asked whether
he described himself or herself as a "White/Caucasian" or a member
of some other identifiable racial or ethnic group, and whether he
wished to be considered an applicant from a minority group. The
groups specifically listed included "Black/Afro-American, American Indian, Mexican/American or Chicano, Oriental/Asian-American, Puerto
Rican (Mainland), Puerto Rican (Commonwealth), Cuban," or
"Other."

As in the *DeFunis* case, some applicants—those whose college grade
point averages (GPA) were below 2.5—were summarily rejected.
Higher averages did not guarantee admission, but some from the
higher group were selected for interviews. A combination of GPA,
scores on the Medical College Admission Test (MCAT), and a judgment by the interviewer and members of the admissions committee on
the applicant's potential contributions to the medical profession, based
upon his motivation, character, and other factors, was used to produce
a numerical rating, called a *benchmark*.

A student who sought to enter under the special admission committee
was not automatically disqualified if his GPA was below 2.5. In fact,
some minority students whose GPAs were below 2.5 were admitted,
including some who were as low as 2.11. Bakke's GPA was 3.51. In the
four areas of the MCAT, his scores were 96, 94, 97, and 72 (in percentile). He applied for admission twice, and his benchmark scores
were 468 out of a possible 500 the first year and 549 out of a possible
600 the second year. He was neither admitted nor placed on an alter-
nate list either year. The mean MCAT scores of those admitted under
the minority admissions program were below the 50th percentile in all
four areas, and the benchmark scores of some students who were
admitted under that program were 20 to 30 points below Bakke's.

The trial court found that Bakke was a victim of invidious racial
discrimination, and the Supreme Court of the State of California upheld that decision, holding that "at least some applicants were denied
admission to the medical school solely because they were not members
of a minority race." The California Supreme Court noted that the commendable goal of integration of the medical school and the training
of physicians of diverse ethnic and racial origins need not be set back
by its decision. Nor did the court believe that rigid adherence to such
numerical scores as GPAs and MCATs was either necessary or desirable. Other methods for achieving the same goals exist, methods that
would not involve racial discrimination against white persons. For

example, the school could expand its services, and thus admit more students. It could admit disadvantaged students of all races, so long as it applied an objective standard not determined by race. It could aggressively identify and recruit disadvantaged students of all races and provide remedial schooling for them.

As for the need for providing more physicians to the black community, the court agreed that it was a pressing need, but it noted that there was no assurance that the black students who were admitted to the medical school would in fact choose to practice in the poverty-stricken black ghettoes of the state or, for that matter, that white physicians would not. It suggested, too, that other methods not involving racial discrimination might meet the need, such as the selection of applicants of whatever race who have demonstrated their concern for the disadvantaged minorities in the past and declared that practice in that community is their primary professional goal, the institution of academic and clinical courses directed to the medical needs of minorities, and emphasis on the training of general practitioners to serve the basic needs of the poor.

In a dissent, Justice Tobriner argued that the racial classifications employed by the medical school were not invidious and were "worlds apart" from those employed by segregated public school systems and other systems that imposed inferior treatment upon minorities. On the contrary, he said, it is intended to *prevent* the exclusion of any racial group from participation in the medical school; and it does *not* stigmatize any racial group as inferior, but gives "realistic recognition to the continuing effects resulting from several centuries of discriminatory treatment." "Our society," he said, "cannot be completely colorblind in the short term if we are to have a color-blind society in the long term."

He defended the lower GPA cutoff for minority students on the ground that their different cultural background combined with greater economic needs that often required them to hold jobs during their undergraduate years compelled the conclusion that their GPAs might not be fully reliable as indicators of their potential for success in the medical profession. Moreover, the "arbitrary" 2.5 cutoff point did not mean that students whose GPAs were lower were necessarily unqualified. Taking the applicant's racial background into consideration was essential if the admissions committee was to assess his qualifications objectively, for some, at least, of the numerical measures might have been culturally biased against minorities.

In responding to the charge that it is illegitimate to produce black doctors for blacks, Justice Tobriner said:

> This simplistic characterization of the special admission process surely
> does a grave disservice to the medical school. The medical school has
> by no means undertaken to train black doctors to treat blacks, or
> to train chicano doctors simply to treat chicanos; a minority doctor's

medical degree is not, of course, a license only to treat minorities. In my
view, however, it was neither unreasonable nor improper for the
medical school to conclude that at least one of the reasons for the
deplorable lack of effective medical services in minority communities is
the shortage of minority physicians, and to determine that an increase
of disadvantaged minority doctors might play at least some role in
improving the situation.

And he went on to note that the majority had no problem with the
medical school's offering preferential admissions to applicants from
northern California, where there was a shortage of physicians, and did
not suggest such alternative programs as government subsidies for
physicians who chose to practice in that area. "Since the medical
school's interest in increasing medical services in disadvantaged minority communities is surely no less valid than its interest in overcoming
the shortage of doctors in rural, less populated areas, I do not see how
we can uphold the preferential admission of rural applicants, but strike
down such preference to applicants from urban minority communities."

As for the charge that the 16 places "reserved" for the special
admission program constituted a "quota," Justice Tobriner argued that
if there were a predetermined limit on the number of disadvantaged
minorities who would be accepted regardless of how they compared
with other applicants, "the 'quota' would pose very grave, probably
fatal, constitutional questions." But if they merely represented the
university's determination to admit more than a token representation
of such groups in order to achieve the many benefits of integration,
"the specific numerical goal becomes more defensible," particularly
because California's minority population is in the neighborhood of
25% of the total, and only fully qualified applicants were admitted
in any case.

The majority's suggestion that racially "neutral" means of integrating
the school might have been available was nothing more than a "retreat
into obfuscating terminology," he said, for in any case, the principal
objective of the program would be to achieve "a racially and ethnically
integrated, rather than an economically diverse, student body." Using
racially neutral criteria to achieve that objective "cannot honestly be
described as a 'nonracial' decision." The suggestion that an increase in
the size and number of medical schools would accomplish that end "is
a cruel hoax," he said, because there is no evidence that the financial
commitment necessary to expand medical education will be forthcoming in the foreseeable future. He concluded:

> Two centuries of slavery and racial discrimination have left our nation
> an awful legacy, a largely separated society in which wealth, educational
> resources, employment opportunities—indeed all of society's benefits—
> remain largely the preserve of the white-Anglo majority. Until recently,

most attempts to overcome the effects of this heritage of racial discrimination have proven unavailing. In the past decade, however, the implementation of numerous "affirmative action" programs, much like the program challenged in this case, have resulted in at least some degree of integration in many of our institutions. . . . It is anomalous that the Fourteenth Amendment that served as the basis for the requirement that elementary and secondary schools could be *compelled* to integrate, should now be turned around to *forbid* graduate schools from voluntarily seeking that very objective.

On June 28, 1978, the United States Supreme Court rendered its decision on the *Bakke* case. The justices were divided 4–4 on the principal issues in the case, with Justice Powell providing the decisive vote, siding with one group on one issue and with the other on the second issue. The Court thus found that the special admissions program under which Allan Bakke was denied admission to the medical school of the University of California at Davis was unlawful and directed that Bakke be admitted. It also found that colleges and universities *could* consider race as one factor in the admissions process.

On the critical issues, Justice Powell, speaking for the Court, found that the assignment of 16 special admissions seats to minority applicants meant that white applicants could compete for 84 seats while minority applicants could compete for 100. Whether such a limitation was called a quota or a goal, he said, it was clearly "a line drawn on the basis of race and ethnic status." But he went on to declare that the "guarantee of equal protection cannot mean one thing when applied to one individual and something else when applied to a person of another color. If both are not accorded the same protection, then it is not equal." On the ground that racial and ethnic distinctions of any sort are inherently suspect, he concluded that this distinction called "for the most exacting judicial examination." He rejected the suggestion that discrimination against members of the white "majority" is not suspect if its purpose is characterized as benign.

> It is far too late to argue that the guarantee of equal protection to *all* persons permits the recognition of special wards entitled to a degree of protection greater than that accorded others. . . . The concepts of "majority" and "minority" necessarily reflect temporary arrangements and political judgments. . . . The white "majority" itself is composed of various minority groups, most of which can lay claim to a history of prior discrimination at the hands of the state and private individuals. Not all of these groups can receive preferential treatment and corresponding judicial tolerance of distinction drawn in terms of race and nationality, for then the only "majority" left would be a new minority of White Anglo-Saxon Protestants. There is no principled basis for deciding which groups would merit "heightened judicial solicitude" and which would not.

Justice Powell than went on to quote with approval a comment by Alexander Bickel on the question of reverse discrimination:

> The lesson of the great decisions of the Supreme Court and the lesson of contemporary history have been the same for at least a generation: discrimination on the basis of race is illegal, immoral, unconstitutional, inherently wrong, and destructive of democratic society. Now this is to be unlearned and we are told that this is not a matter of fundamental principle but only a matter of whose ox is gored. Those for whom racial equality was demanded are to be more equal than others. Having found support in the Constitution for equality, they now claim support for inequality under the same Constitution.

Justice Powell then responded to each of the four objectives of the Davis program:

1. *Reducing the historic deficit of traditionally disfavored minorities in medical schools and the medical profession.* The Court found that this amounted to preference for no reason other than race or ethnic origin and was therefore unlawful discrimination.

2. *Countering the effects of societal discrimination.* The Davis plan attempts to aid persons who are perceived to be members of relatively victimized groups at the expense of other innocent persons. But the university is not in a position to assess the extent of the injury in any given case or to manage the program in such a way as to assure the least possible harm to other innocent persons who are competing for the benefits it has to offer. Moreover, the remedying of such wrongs has previously been left to the legislatures, who are answerable to the people and in a better position to assess the problems than the administration of a medical school. In short, the faculty of the medical school had no right to impose special disadvantages upon people like Allan Bakke in order to remedy the disadvantages they felt certain other individuals had suffered—disadvantages that Bakke had nothing to do with creating.

3. *Increasing the number of physicians who will practice in communities currently underserved.* As the lower court had concluded, the university was incapable of demonstrating that its program would fulfill this goal or that it could not be fulfilled in some other way that would not involve discrimination against white males.

4. *Obtaining the educational benefits that flow from an ethnically diverse student body.* This is a commendable goal, and the university should generally have the authority to determine who will be admitted to its ranks. But the protection of individual rights is also of great importance, and where these are violated by the program, the program must fall. Moreover, ethnic diversity alone is not a reasonable goal for a university to strive for. The Davis program "would hinder rather than further attainment of genuine diversity."

By making use of an explicit racial classification, excluding members of certain racial groups from the competition for a given number of seats, however strong their qualifications might have been, the Davis program violated the rights of Bakke and others like him, and the program was therefore found to be unconstitutional.

However, the Court also concluded that the consideration of race as one factor in an admissions program may well serve a legitimate state interest, and that an admissions program that permitted race to be counted in an applicant's favor (as other admissions programs permitted geographic origin, athletic prowess, and other factors to be counted in the applicant's favor), while not excluding *any* applicant from competing for a place merely because of his race, was permissible.

It is impossible to summarize the lengthy opinions of the justices on both sides of these issues in the space available here. The conclusion reached by the Court in the *Bakke* case is not likely to resolve the deep underlying issues. It is not at all clear how a university (or a business) is supposed to avoid discriminating against members of certain racial or ethnic groups while granting members of other racial or ethnic groups preferred treatment (counting their racial or ethnic background as a "plus") when important benefits are being distributed. The narrow margin by which the Court reached its decision indicates that further litigation is inevitable and that many years may pass before a definitive decision is reached on affirmative action programs.

The judges whose decisions have been reviewed in the summaries of the *DeFunis* and *Bakke* cases have given most of the major arguments, philosophical and legal, in favor of and in opposition to affirmative action programs that entail quotas or goals. But there are others, to which we shall now turn.

THE QUESTION OF MERIT

A crucial assumption made by opponents of affirmative action quotas or goals may be formulated as follows: Persons applying for admission to medical school or law school, or being considered for a position or for promotion or tenure at a university, or for any position entailing certain special skills or abilities should be given those positions or other benefits on the basis of merit rather than on any such extraneous criterion as race, previous disadvantages, and the like.

Professor Richard Wasserstrom has argued against this assumption, at least insofar as university positions are concerned, on two grounds. The first is that those who deserve to be admitted to or employed by a university are not necessarily those who are most qualified. And the second is that the presence of minority persons is beneficial to the university in that it helps to further its most fundamental goals.[7]

Although being the most qualified person for a given position might count toward determining whether one deserves to have that position, Wasserstrom argues that it is not the sole test for making such a determination. Suppose a city had only a single tennis court. Would it follow that only the two best tennis players ought to be permitted to use it, or should those who happen to get there first, or those who enjoy playing the most, or those who are the worst and need the most practice, or those who have the chance to play least frequently get to use the court? Here, at least, the connection between ability and desert is tenuous at best.

As for students, Wasserstrom argues that they were not responsible for any native intelligence they might have, for their home environment, their parents' socioeconomic position, or the quality of the schools they attended. Because such factors contribute to a student's ability and qualifications, it does not make much sense to claim that anyone deserves them. "And because they do not deserve their abilities, they do not in any strong sense deserve to be admitted because of their abilities." To be sure, certain minimal qualifications are essential, for without them, the applicant could not benefit from his participation. But this establishes only that qualifications are relevant, not that they are decisive. In the same way, membership in a minority group may be a relevant but not a decisive consideration.

Wasserstrom's second argument rests upon the assumption that students and faculty members of different backgrounds are likely to have different points of view and different perceptions on many important matters and that their presence therefore increases the likelihood that "important truths, which would otherwise have gone undiscovered, will be discovered." Race and sex are such fundamental features of experience in our culture that women and members of minority groups are likely to perceive the world and to define problems differently from the way in which white, middle-class males are inclined to do. Women, for example, have contributed enormously to the sensitization of our society to problems faced by women who are confronted with the question of seeking an abortion and to the trauma suffered by a woman who has been raped. And blacks have helped to expose the self-serving and often unquestioned assumptions made by white persons about the black experience and the way many social institutions impinge upon the less affluent members of our society. Thus, because they are able to bring a special perspective to the search for truth and knowledge, which is the central business of the university, their membership in the class of women or racial or ethnic minorities ought to give them a special claim to participation in it, regardless of more technical qualifications.

Elsewhere,[8] Wasserstrom argues that if our society is in fact racially oppressive, and if we are committed to the proposition that a person's race should be as irrelevant as the color of his eyes (a position that Wasserstrom calls the "assimilationist ideal"), then, he says, the chief and perhaps the only question is whether affirmative action programs are well suited to bringing about the end desired. Although racial quotas may exacerbate prejudice and hostility, the redistribution of wealth and positions of power and authority to blacks brought about by such quotas, as well as the creation of role models that such redistribution would entail, might negate or even overcome any negative effects of affirmative action programs.

Wasserstrom contends that the pernicious racial quotas of the past are different from those involved in affirmative action programs. The former were "part of a larger social universe which systematically maintained an unwarranted and unjust scheme which concentrated power, authority, and goods in the hands of white male individuals, . . . [and] restricted the capacities, autonomy, and happiness of those who were the less-favored members of the society." Affirmative action quotas, however, do not seek "either to perpetuate an unjust society or to realize a corrupt ideal," and are therefore "commendable and right."

Judith Jarvis Thomson argued for what she calls "preferential hiring" in public institutions of higher learning on the ground that the members of a community equally own the community. Therefore, each member has a right to an equal chance at, or an equal share in, any benefit the community has to offer, including university jobs.[9] To be sure, qualifications are relevant, for students—who may be regarded as the university's customers—have a right to competent instruction. But if a person has been wronged, it is just that he be compensated for the wrong done to him. And although some may object that young women and blacks may not personally have been the victims of discrimination, and young white men may never personally have engaged in such acts of discrimination, Thomson insists that such objections are "quite wrong-headed." For today's blacks and women still suffer such consequences of downgrading as lack of self-confidence and self-respect, among other things. Just as a healthy, unscarred, middle-class veteran may be preferred over a poor, struggling, scarred nonveteran, so may a well-off black be preferred over a poor, struggling white man. There is nothing un-just about a white male who has had a particularly hard time losing out under affirmative action, according to Thomson, unless it can be shown that giving preference to those who have had a hard life ought to take priority over preference for blacks and women.

Finally, she argues that young white males are not being asked to make amends, for none of them is being asked to give up a job that is his. The job is the community's. "Of course the white male is asked to give up his equal chance at the job," Thomson says. "But that is not something he pays to the black or woman by way of making amends; it is something the community takes away from him in order that *it* may make amends." If there were some way for blacks and women to be compensated without harming young white males, she would favor it. But jobs are the best and most suitable form of compensation, because they restore the full member-ship in the community of which blacks and women were previously deprived, and are the only way to give them the self-respect that they lost. Besides, if white men have to pay the costs, this may merely even the scales, because so many of them have been the direct beneficiaries of policies that previously excluded or degraded women and blacks. If some way could be devised to let tenured professors share the burden, she would favor it; but failing that, she is ready to impose the burden upon new graduates.

Still another analogy was suggested by Charles Lawrence III,[10] who recalled that when he rode the school bus, the children followed a rule that they would board the bus in the order in which they had arrived at the bus stop. He surmises that the rule was probably adopted in order to keep the big kids from bullying the little ones so as to get onto the bus first. After years of this, the group decided to change the rule, with the smallest children getting on first, because the bus had become crowded and too many small children had to go without seats. One boy, Jimmy, who had made an extra effort to get to the bus stop first ever since he was very small, became angry, for he believed that the new rule was cheating him out of his rightfully earned spot. He couldn't help it if he was now one of the bigger kids. Why should his size be used against him? But Lawrence concludes that the new rule seemed to be just what was needed: "It didn't really hurt us big kids to stand during the ride to school. Besides, Jimmy had been sitting for a long time."

Now let us examine some of these arguments.

As every student of elementary logic knows, arguments by analogy are notoriously misleading and can be extremely weak. Although much may be learned from them, they must be approached with great caution. The bus analogy is a particularly weak one, though it has great emotional appeal. Jimmy would suffer no serious loss, even if he didn't get to sit on the bus, for the bus would still deliver him to the school building. Bakke, DeFunis, and others like them, however, would suffer grave losses as a result of affirmative action; for under that system, they aren't even permitted to get onto the bus or into the school building.

Wasserstrom's tennis court example is equally misleading, and so are the assumptions behind the analogy. Such public facilities are generally regarded as being for the use of any member of the public who desires to make use of them. The question of desert simply does not arise. When the facilities are in limited supply and the demand is great, some rules must be established so as to distribute the benefits fairly, and those rules may be based on first-come-first-served, rigid time limits, or numerous other formulas, all designed to ensure that every person has reasonable access to them. If one person or group of persons has greater need for the facility than another, some accommodation might be worked out so that his need will be met. But no one "deserves" to use a public tennis court, park, library, or swimming pool more than anyone else. That is to say, everyone has an equal right to use such facilities. When special requirements are established to determine the *order* in which people may use them, then whoever has met the requirements (such as by being first in line) *has a right* to use the facility *at that time,* not because he deserves to do so, but because he has met the requirements established by the rule. Some requirements are fair, and others are unfair. An example of an unfair rule is one that prohibits black persons or white ones from using the facility at all, just because of their skin color. Such a requirement is unfair because no plausible reason can be given for excluding certain racial groups from the benefits of public facilities that are open to all others.

Tennis courts differ significantly from medical schools. Medical schools are not and cannot be open to everyone in the way that tennis courts can be. There are excellent reasons for limiting access to medical schools: it takes several years to complete a medical education, the number of instructors is limited, the heavy financial outlay makes it impossible to provide more than a relatively small amount of laboratory space and equipment, and even if people could stand in line and wait for a class to graduate, some would be too old to benefit from a medical education before their turn came. Although a medical education confers undoubted benefits upon those who are fortunate enough to have one, its purpose is not so much to confer those benefits upon future physicians as it is to provide medical care to the people of the state. It makes sense, then, *not* to employ a "first-in-line" rule for admission to a medical school, but to seek instead to permit those who seem most likely to fulfill the objectives of the school to enter it and to enjoy the use of its faculty and facilities.

A great deal of controversy has centered around the use of the LSAT, the MCAT, and other means of predicting the likely success of law students, medical students, and others. It has been alleged that these examinations are "culturally biased," tending to favor persons from white, middle-class backgrounds as against those from other racial, ethnic, or economic backgrounds. Such arguments might have some relevance to the use of standardized tests designed to measure "intelligence," but it is hard to see how they can have *any* relevance where tests for admission to graduate or professional schools are concerned. If a child who has just entered the United States from Vietnam is given a test in standard English to measure his intelligence, someone ought to question the intelligence of the person administering the test. Obviously, the test cannot do what it is designed to do if the child does not know the language of the test. The intellectual capacities of children from black ghettoes and from chicano or other backgrounds may not be accurately measured by tests that use standard English or are based upon information that children raised in white middle-class homes, but not children raised in homes of different socio-economic status, commonly possess. But the LSAT, the MCAT, and other standardized tests are not designed to test intelligence. They are designed, among other things, to test a student's ability to read and use standard English, his knowledge of materials and subjects that are likely to be important to him as he progresses through law school or medical school, and, in general, to determine whether he is likely or not likely to succeed in mastering the materials that will be presented to him in his professional training. In these cases, it is perfectly appropriate to test a student's knowledge of standard English, and it is absurd to complain that the tests are culturally biased. A law student is expected to read an enormous quantity of materials, all of which are written in more or less standard English. Perhaps the judges and law professors who have written the decisions upon which our legal system is based are culturally biased, but the fact is that the language in which they have written is the language that law students must be able to read. If this is cultural bias, it is also a fact of life with which law students will have to learn to live. By the same token, it is a fact that Albert Camus and Jean-Paul Sartre wrote in French, and Plato and Aristotle in Greek, and medieval Christians in Latin. A student who wants to study French philosophy on the graduate level must know how to read French; one who wants to specialize in ancient Greek philosophy must be able to demonstrate his knowledge of ancient Greek; and one who wants to make a scholarly study of medieval Christianity must know Latin. These are not unreasonable requirements imposed upon students in order to perpetuate racial, ethnic, or sexual biases. They are reasonable requirements imposed *by the subject matter* upon *anyone* who wants to study those subjects, regardless of his racial or ethnic background.

Moreover, there must come a day of reckoning for any person who aspires to become a professional. Affirmative action advocates have argued that that day should be postponed from the traditional time, namely, the time when admission to graduate or professional school is decided, to some later time. But the very arguments they use to justify reducing the weight accorded to admissions tests or eliminating them from consideration can be employed at later phases in the process as well. If blacks or other minority lawyers or doctors are needed in the community, and if that is a reason for permitting members of those groups to be admitted with test scores lower than those of white applicants, then on the same basis, the standards employed by professors in those fields to determine who will pass and who will fail courses, who will be permitted to continue and who will be dropped from the rolls, should be lowered for blacks and members of other disadvantaged minority groups. And finally, on the same grounds, the examinations for admission to the bar [11] or for a license to practice medicine should be less rigorous for those persons than they are for white males, because otherwise, the former may be barred from entering their chosen professions after many years of preparation.

At some point, however, the standards will not be amenable to tampering on racial or ethnic grounds. The lawyer or the physician who has somehow managed to surmount all of the hurdles without becoming fully qualified to practice his profession will one day have a client or a patient in a possible life or death situation. Professional competence and skill will determine the outcome. The question is whether it is fair to the client or the patient to wait until the trial or the surgery before putting the aspiring lawyer or surgeon to the final test of competence. Or should the professional judgment of those who know the field best be permitted to weed out incompetents *before* they inflict great harm upon others.

In New York City, an examination that every prospective teacher was expected to pass was attacked on the ground that it was culturally biased because so many black and Hispanic teachers were failing. Albert Shanker, president of the American Federation of Teachers, asked whether it was inappropriate to expect teachers to have mastered the rudiments of the English language at the ninth-grade level. To subject unwitting children to incompetent teachers is a grave offense against those children. Some parents are so angry about the schools' failure to educate their children that they are bringing the schools into court. Incompetency cannot be excused on the ground that it was perpetrated in order to enable more black and Hispanic teachers to enter the system.

Wasserstrom is right when he concludes that academic qualifications are relevant but not decisive. Admissions committees are within their rights to consider such imponderables as personality traits, emotional maturity, and social responsibility before determining a candidate's suitability for a given slot. Such characteristics are part of a person's qualifications. An immature, irresponsible person may justifiably be rejected on those grounds alone, however qualified he might be academically. Just as a prior record of social service might be regarded as evidence in a candidate's favor, so a prior record of convictions for criminal behavior might be sufficient to justify rejecting him. The summary rejection of persons convicted of violent crimes is not discrimination against persons with criminal records any more than the rejection of applicants whose GPAs are under 1.5 is discrimination against people incapable of doing satisfactory academic work.

A person who is rejected because he either lacks certain skills or characteristics that are essential to the position for which he has applied, or has less of them than other applicants is not a subject of discrimination. But one who is rejected because of his skin color or because his parents or grandparents came from one part of the world rather than some other is the victim of invidious discrimination, however well-intentioned it may be. For it is based upon a criterion that is totally unrelated to the task he is expected to perform and has nothing to do with qualifications to perform that task. Both DeFunis and Bakke were rejected because of their skin color and were therefore victims of invidious discrimination, despite the benevolent intentions of the officials of the schools to which they applied. Wasserstrom's point is correct but beside the point. Academic qualifications alone are not decisive. Other considerations, such as character, are also relevant and may in some cases be decisive. However excellent an accountant might be with figures, if he has a record of embezzlement, it would be reasonable to disqualify him for service as an accountant for a bank. But unless it can be shown that being black (or brown, or some other color) has something to do with one's chances of success, it ought to be as thoroughly disregarded as the color of one's eyes.

Equally defective is Wasserstrom's attempt to defend affirmative action programs on the ground that women, blacks, and members of other minorities can make some special contribution to the search for truth. Even if one assumes that people with special backgrounds can provide special insights into the subject matter of a given discipline, it does not follow that women, blacks, or persons of Hispanic origin are unique in this regard. The descendants of coal miners, dirt farmers, steel workers, salmon fishermen, carnival workers, and street walkers might all be able to make unusual contributions to the perceptions of academics. So might the children of men and women who fled from Communist oppression and survivors of Nazi concentration camps, but there is no cry for the admission of members of such groups under affirmative action programs. Such persons are likely to be *excluded* under affirmative programs as presently administered, and their potential contributions lost.

Moreover, the special insights that members of particular ethnic or cultural groups might possess are not particularly relevant except in very limited areas. But neither Wasserstrom nor anyone else has suggested that affirmative action programs at universities be confined to those fields in the social sciences and humanities that might benefit from the presence of persons of varied cultural backgrounds. It is as important, in the eyes of affirmative action advocates, that black mathematicians, Chicano microbiologists, and female astronomers be added to the faculty (even if they have no interest whatever in social issues) as it is that they be added to departments of philosophy and sociology. Nor has anyone yet suggested that individual blacks or women be tested or interviewed in order to determine whether they do in fact have the special insights that members of their groups are alleged to have, and are willing and able to share them with the rest of the academic (or medical or legal) community.

All of this leads to the conclusion that the "special insight" theory is merely an attempt to make sense of a policy that needs justification but has not yet been satisfactorily rationalized. Compassionate men and women, troubled by the under-representation of certain minority groups in various professions, and by the history of discrimination against them, are grasping at straws in order to right the wrongs of the past without compromising their principles. Unfortunately, it does not work. Affirmative action quotas are as pernicious as were the quotas of the past.

Thomson's comparison of blacks and women to veterans is as weak as the other analogies that have been drawn.[12] Veterans are given preference not because of their injuries, but because of their service to their country. It is for that reason that uninjured veterans also receive preferential treatment. But if blacks or women are to be given such treatment because of past injustices, then so should anyone who has been the victim of similar injustices, and those blacks or women who have not been so victimized should not receive preferential treatment. The mistake lies in assuming that it is the *group* that has been injured and thus deserves to be compensated, rather than the *individual*. Furthermore, even if the group is somehow deemed to be deserving of compensation, it is difficult to see why those who are blessed with ability or marketability should be the most immediate recipients of such benefits as are distributed. If the principle upon which affirmative action is based is compensatory justice, then all of those who have been injured by the injustices of the past, and only they, should receive compensation; but preferential hiring policies and preferential admissions policies arbitrarily discriminate against some of those victims and in favor of others.

Under any system of compensatory justice, those who have committed the wrongs should bear the burden of compensation, and not those who are innocent of any wrongdoing. If the "system" is at fault, society as a whole should bear the burden, and not professors, or graduate students, or the members of any other profession or occupation.

THE CONSEQUENCES OF
AFFIRMATIVE ACTION PROGRAMS

In the New York City borough of Queens, some non-Hispanic parents claim that they are Puerto Rican so as to assure their children the opportunity to be assigned to particularly desirable schools. In Los Angeles, teachers who want to avoid being transferred to other schools to achieve mandatory quotas claim to be members of minority groups. Under a plan to "verify the forebears of teachers who want to change their ethnicity," such teachers "may be forced to prove what nationality their grandparents were" and to "face a panel of persons of the ethnic background they claim to be." And in Boston, teachers are required to take a daily racial census of their students, leading to more race consciousness in the Boston public schools than ever before.[13]

In New York City, teachers were lined up in front of two boxes, one for whites and the other for members of selected minority groups, to pick assignments for the year under terms of an order from the federal Office of Civil Rights.[14] Senator Daniel Patrick Moynihan denounced the action from the floor of the United States Senate as a "debasement of the principle of civil rights" and a mindless violation of the most fundamental principles of the United States Constitution. He compared them to the practice of apartheid in South Africa and Nazi racial measures during the 1930s and the 1940s. "Such practices," he said, "evoke one image in our lifetimes above all others: the sorting out of human beings for the death camps of Hitler's Germany." He concluded by reminding the federal Administration that "Congress has not enacted Nuremberg laws," and warned the Executive Branch to "think again before enforcing them."

There was a great hue and cry after Moynihan made his statement. There was much outrage and resentment and there were denials that affirmative action programs even remotely resembled the Nuremberg racial laws. Affirmative action quotas and the New York City teacher assignment program are benign, defenders said, for they are not intended to harm anyone, but are designed to achieve racial justice rather than injustice.

Meg Greenfield described an incident in which her nine-year-old niece innocently explained that neither she nor her younger brother could attend a special art class at their school because they were white, but their good friend Robin could because he was "part minority," namely, half-Indian. Greenfield later discovered that the children's school district "provides elaborate listings of different racial *fractions* and *mixtures* which qualify some children for certain programs and disqualify others from taking advantage of them," a "fairly widespread practice," as she learned. She conceded the good intentions behind such programs and the desirability of achieving full integration—a goal that could not be achieved without realistically taking account of the racial composition of our institutions. But she remained troubled:

> The real issue is what we are doing to the values and perspectives of small children throughout the country. By our brazen, clinical insistence on a Nuremberg-like analysis of each child's racial and ethnic background—is he half this or only a quarter that?—we are giving the young to believe that these distinctions are the proper stuff of official decisions. We are distorting their understanding of the system in which we live—and we are doing so in a very fundamental, antidemocratic way.

After recalling the civil rights battles of Selma, Alabama and Philadelphia, Mississippi, she went on to suggest that it would be extremely difficult to explain to children today what those battles were all about, because

> they simply assume—how could they not?—that it is acceptable for the folks who run things to send one person here and another there strictly because of the color of his skin. They think the half-Indianness of their friend down the street is good and sufficient reason for the authorities to decree that he be treated differently.

Ms. Greenfield found that that was not so benign and that it was not at all self-evident that that price ought to be paid in order to right old racial wrongs.[15]

SOME CONSTITUTIONAL CONSIDERATIONS

Some people have argued that the equal protection and due process clauses of the Fourteenth Amendment must be read in their proper historical context. The Thirteenth, Fourteenth, and Fifteenth Amendments were adopted together in order to free the black slaves and to assure them equality and justice under the laws of the United States identical with that accorded to whites and other free men. They conclude, therefore, that the Fourteenth Amendment has special applicability to blacks and that white persons are either not entitled to equal protection, or at least less entitled to it than blacks are. This strange reading of the Constitution has been raised so often that it must be answered, even though it is not, strictly speaking, a philosophical question.

The Thirteenth Amendment provides that "Neither slavery nor involuntary servitude, except as punishment for crime whereof the party shall have been duly convicted, shall exist within the United States or any places subject to their jurisdiction," and goes on to empower Congress to pass legislation necessary to enforce this provision. Although its immediate purpose was to free the black slaves of the South, it was so broadly worded as to apply to the enslavement of *any* person, whatever his race or ethnic origin. And the courts have consistently interpreted the Amendment in this way. As early as 1873, the Supreme Court concluded that even though Negro slavery was in the mind of Congress when it proposed the Amendment, "if Mexican peonage or the Chinese coolie labor system shall develop slavery of the Mexican or Chinese race within our territory, this amendment may safely be trusted to make it void." [16]

The courts have also held that the "badges and incidents of slavery," that is, the special disabilities that were imposed upon persons as a result of their being slaves, were abolished by these amendments at the same time as slavery was abolished. Thus, former slaves immediately acquired the right to own and dispose of property and to sue, to inherit, and so on. But the Amendments apply equally to all persons living within the territory of the United States. Therefore, no person can constitutionally be deprived of those fundamental rights on racial grounds. In 1968, the Court held that herding blacks into ghettoes and reducing their ability to buy property by means of racially discriminatory practices is "a relic of slavery," and ruled that the Thirteenth Amendment conferred upon Congress the power to extend to black citizens "the freedom to buy whatever a white man can buy, the right to live wherever a white man can live." [17] If the imposition of special disabilities on racial grounds is forbidden by the Thirteenth Amendment as one of the badges and incidents of slavery, and if the Thirteenth Amendment includes within its scope every person residing within the territory of the United States, then the imposition of racially discriminatory disabilities upon white persons—including Marco DeFunis and Allan Bakke—constitutes a violation of their fundamental rights. And this violation is not just a technical legal violation. It is fundamentally a *moral* violation—a violation of the fundamental moral principle upon which those Amendments were based—the principle that all persons are entitled to equal treatment before the law, that no person can rightly be subjected to special disabilities because of the color of his skin. Those affirmative action programs that entail the use of "goals" or quotas violate this fundamental principle. They are discriminatory and divisive. They are destructive of democracy and equality. They open the way once again to the racial quotas—including quotas of zero—that prevailed in many areas before the great civil rights battles of the middle of the twentieth century. The motives of those who support such programs, the long-run objectives they hope to achieve, the compassion from which they spring—all of these cannot alter the fact that they are fundamentally misguided. Even those who are supposed to benefit most directly from them —the minority physicians and lawyers who will eventually emerge from medical schools and law schools—are likely to be known as "affirmative action doctors and lawyers" and bear the stigma, whether it is deserved or not, of having been admitted to their professions despite their poor preparation.

ALTERNATIVES

This subject may not be left on such a negative note. The problem outlined at the beginning of this chapter still exists. Goals and quotas are misguided attempts to solve that problem. Happily, other approaches do exist, and some of them have great promise of contributing to a solution of the problem.

Temple University's law school has a special admissions program that seeks out applicants who have an outstanding record of performance and an exceptional aptitude for the study and practice of law that may not be reflected in their LSAT scores. This program is open to working men and women and their children, regardless of ethnic, racial, social, or religious heritage.

Under this special admissions program, high academic achievement is essential. Women constitute 36% of the total student body, as opposed to 2% twelve years ago. Among those admitted are a Hungarian refugee whose family was in a Nazi concentration camp, a young man of Italian ancestry who worked in a gas station 40 hours per week from age 12 through college, an American Indian who was raised on a reservation, policemen, black women, black veterans who were wounded in Vietnam, a white woman teacher who helped establish an alternative school for culturally deprived children, a Japanese-American who was raised in a World War II detention camp, and many more.[18] Similar programs could be developed and implemented elsewhere. They are not open to the objection that they are racially or ethnically discriminatory; nor could students admitted under them later be stigmatized as being unqualified. On the contrary, they are highly qualified. Their special circumstances are taken into account, not the color of their skin, their last names, or their mothers' maiden names.

Opportunities might be expanded by building additional schools or admitting larger classes. More importantly, work must go forward to improve educational oportunities and the conditions necessary for acquiring a decent education for all. Such conditions include better housing, better health and dental care, better nutrition, and other social programs, some of which have been implemented on a limited scale, but must be expanded and improved if they are to fulfill the promise of those who brought them into existence.

The most serious problem facing many applicants to professional schools, regardless of race, is financial. A massive infusion of scholarship aid and long-term, low-interest loans would greatly alleviate this problem and make it possible for many talented students to reach their full potential—a possibility that today is often beyond their reach because of financial burdens.

In employment, one of the most serious problems has arisen during times of retrenchment or massive layoffs. The seniority system, won at great cost over many years by labor unions, is being destroyed by the demand that the principle of "last hired, first fired" be abandoned in favor of an affirmative action principle; under the old formula, many staffs would revert, during times of financial hardship, to being practically all white and all male. In 1977, the St. Paul, Minnesota, school board laid off 281 white teachers because of declining enrollments. Only white teachers were laid off because of demands by recently hired minority teachers that the gains they had finally made not be vitiated by adherence to the old seniority system.[19] But this approach is discriminatory, shackling white employees with a burden of past discrimination that they did not create or administer.[20] Other solutions exist, including payless work days, payless holidays, and budget cuts in other areas. There could also be reduced work weeks, or possibly across-the-board salary cuts, with a gradual reduction of staff by attrition, if income did not permit the maintenance of both present salaries and full staff without massive layoffs. If there must be layoffs, perhaps the risks might be spread around, by drawing lots or by stipulating that a certain percentage of older employees as well as some newer ones would have to assume the burden. And there might also be a stipulation that those who are laid off because of financial exigency would have priority to be rehired as new positions become available.

Whether these or other methods be adopted to solve the problem of the under-representation of minorities and women in colleges, universities, professions, and elsewhere, *no* policy should be adopted if it makes sex or race a criterion for acceptance. Such criteria are inherently sexist or racist, however well-intentioned their proponents may be. It is important to remember that individuals, not groups or classes of persons, are admitted to professional schools or accepted for employment, and that individuals, not groups or classes of persons, are rejected.

Each applicant should be considered on his merits, not on his complexion. People should be admitted or hired, not because they "deserve" to be, but because they have been found, in a fair and open competition, to be the best-qualified person for the position, or—if there are no special qualifications or if many individuals are equally well qualified—some neutral method, such as drawing lots, should be employed to assure that the selection is made fairly and without racial or sexual bias. Every person deserves to be judged fairly, on his or her merits, and not on such irrelevant criteria as race, sex, or ethnicity. Every person has a right *not to be rejected* merely because of such irrelevant criteria. This right is the essence of the Fourteenth Amendment, of the notion of equality before the law, and of the concepts of fairness and justice.

12

Civil Disobedience

THE DILEMMA OF THE UNJUST LAW

Socrates was convicted of a capital crime, the "crime" of atheism and corrupting the morals of the youth, by the court at Athens. Waiting in his death cell a day or two before his scheduled execution, he was visited by his friend Crito, who had bribed the jailer. Crito explained that he had arranged for Socrates to escape from prison and to be spirited to Thessaly, where he would be safe. But Socrates refused to go, arguing that he had devoted all his life to teaching the importance of doing justice and respecting the laws of the state. It would be rank hypocrisy for him to violate his principles at this time, when the laws had been turned against his private interests.

He constructed an imaginary dialogue between himself and the laws of Athens. As he was preparing for his escape, the laws came to him and said, "By trying to escape, Socrates, what will you effect but the destruction of us, the laws, and the whole state? Do you imagine that a state whose laws are disregarded and subverted by private individuals, and whose court decisions are of no force, can survive?" [1]

Socrates replied that he had been injured by the state, for his case had been judged unjustly. But the laws replied, "Was that our agreement, or was it that you would abide by the state's judgments, whatever they might be?" They went on to explain that they could be compared to Socrates' parents, for his earthly father and mother had brought Socrates into this world with the sanction of the laws, and it was through them and with their protection that he was sheltered, nurtured, and educated. Just as Socrates would not have had the right to retaliate if his father had treated him badly, so did he lack the right to strike back at the laws when he fared badly at their hands.

> "If we try to destroy you," they asked, "because we think it just, will you in return do what you can to destroy us, the laws, and your country, and claim that you are acting justly when you do so? . . . Your country is worthier, more to be revered, more sacred, and held in higher honor by both gods and men of understanding than your father and your mother and all your other ancestors. . . . You should therefore respect it, submit to it, and approach it more submissively when it is angry with you than you would your own father. And you should either acquiesce in what it decrees or persuade it to excuse you. And if it sends you to war, where you might be wounded or be killed, or if it decrees that you must endure flogging or imprisonment, then you should obey in silence. That is just." [2]

After giving Socrates all the benefits that they could make available to him, the laws left him free to take his goods and leave for some other place, or to remain. "But if a man remains here, after seeing how we dispense justice and how we govern the state in other matters, he has entered into a tacit agreement that he will do whatever we decree."

Socrates believed, then, that by remaining in the community, he made a kind of tacit agreement to abide by its laws and that that agreement was binding even when it worked to his own disadvantage. For no agreement is meaningful if it can be broken at the whim of one of the parties to it whenever he sees that it is not in his best interests to abide by its provisions. If all men could repudiate their contracts so easily, no one would ever rely upon the solemn undertakings of anyone else and there would soon be no agreements at all. If every man took it upon himself to decide which laws to obey and which to disregard, there would soon be no laws at all—and thus, each man who breaks the law is contributing to the destruction of the entire legal system. Because each man owes a debt of gratitude to the system for all that it has given him and because each man has the duty to be loyal to the state, disobedience is an act of injustice, disloyalty, ingratitude, and impiety. [3]

But only a short time before, at his trial, Socrates had declared that in his teaching, in his conversations with young and old, he was innocent of corrupting the youth and spreading false doctrines about the gods (though that was the charge against him), and he went on to say, "Whether you are persuaded by Anytus [my accuser] or not, whether you acquit me or not, I shall not change my way of life, no, not if I have to die for it many times." [4]

In spite of his deep commitment to the laws, then, even Socrates seems to have felt that there were some things that he would not concede to the law or to the community. He might have to pay a price, and the price demanded might be very heavy (his life), but he would pay the price rather than give in to a demand that he felt was unjust, or, as he put it, that was contrary to the command that had been given to him by the god.

These two positions taken by Socrates—the one a powerful defense of the view that the law must be obeyed, regardless of the personal consequences to the individual citizen, and the other a resolute refusal to obey an unjust or impious law—represent the two horns of the dilemma upon which many conscientious persons have been impaled when confronted with the vexing and sometimes cruelly painful predicament of being required to act in accordance with a law that they consider to be unjust. The Hebrew midwives who deliberately disobeyed Pharaoh's express command were the earliest civil disobedients on record. They did not put the newborn babies to death, though Pharoah had ordered them to do so, because "they feared God." [5] There was, in their eyes, a law higher than that of Pharaoh—the law of God. The threat of punishment did not deter them from disobeying Pharaoh's law when it came into direct conflict with the law of God. From then until the very latest periods covered by the Hebrew Bible, acts of civil disobedience (such as Mordecai's refusal to prostrate himself before Haman, an act that eventually led to the deposition of a tyrannical ruler, according to the Biblical account) abound, and always they are justified by an appeal to a law higher than that of the state.

Aristotle observed that in order to avoid the destruction of the state, it was vital for its governors to "guard vigilantly against any lawlessness, especially its pettiest forms. For lawlessness in the form of petty crimes creeps in unnoticed, [and ultimately destroys the fabric of the state] just as small expenditures, repeated over and over again, gradually consume an entire fortune." [6] But later thinkers, including John Locke, held that because (in their view) the authority of the state ultimately derives from the people, the people have the right to disobey laws that they consider to be unjust. "If I find a law requires me to do what I think it is wrong to do," Locke wrote, "I ought to disobey it." "If the magistrate should enjoin anything by his authority that appears unlawful to the conscience of a private person," he went on, "such a private person is to abstain from the action that he judges unlawful." But he adds that "he is to undergo the punishment which it is not unlawful for him to bear. For the private judgment of any person concerning a law enacted in political matters, for the public good, does not take away the obligation of that law, nor deserve a dispensation." The civil disobedient, then, is not obliged to abide by those laws that go against his conscience, but at the same time he must be prepared to suffer the punishment prescribed by law for his breach of the statue in question. [7]

Thomas Hobbes was a strong opponent of even the slightest violation of the law, for in his view the law is all that stands between civilization and savagery. Without the law, he said, the life of man would be "solitary, poor, nasty, brutish, and short." But even Hobbes conceded that there were occasions when one would be justified in violating the commands of the law, for he maintained that certain rights were inalienable—that is, they could not be transferred to anyone, not even to the sovereign—for it was for the securing of those rights that men entered into civil society in the first place. If those rights are threatened, then the social contract that brought men together into the state is broken, and the original "state of nature," in which every man has a right to all things, returns. These fundamental, inalienable rights are, according to Hobbes, the right to life, the right to liberty, and the right to such things as make life worth living. He would have disagreed, then, with Socrates, in the latter's refusal to escape from his death cell with Crito, for in Hobbes's view, Socrates would have had a perfect right to do everything necessary to preserve his life, even though it might have been forbidden by the law, because his contract with the state came to an end the moment the state threatened to take his life from him.

It appears, then, that philosophers have perennially been disturbed by the dilemma posed by Socrates' seemingly incompatible positions on the day of his trial and in the death cell. How can one justify conscientious disobedience of laws that one considers to be unjust and still maintain a government of laws, in which right is determined not by each individual serving as legislator, judge, and jury in his own case, but by relatively impersonal organs that attempt to distribute justice to everyone alike?

THE HIGHER-LAW APPROACH: THE DIVINE-LAW VERSION

The midwives and Mordecai had a solution that has appealed to many people in later ages: there is a higher law, God's law, that transcends any merely human command, no matter how exalted the human legislator may be. When man-made law comes into conflict with the eternal law of God, then the law of God must take precedence. So far as ordinary legislation is concerned (that is, laws dealing with damages, contracts, marriage, the regulation of traffic, commerce, and the like), the "higher-law" advocate can argue that he has no quarrel with any of it and that his disobedience is therefore not directed toward the destruction or overthrow of the state. But when a particular law, such as a law requiring the slaughter of innocent babies or one that violates the deepest religious convictions of a people, is enacted and enforced, he contends that he may rightly refuse to abide by that law's provisions, for its force is nullified by the superior law decreed by God.

For the divine-law theory to work, or to be convincing to skeptics, the latter must have some access to the revelation in which God's laws are set forth. Unfortunately, there is much disagreement, even among believers, over the exact content of the divine revelation; and even those who agree on its contents are frequently at odds over its applicability or its precise meaning. Because no authoritative body exists with the power to render decisions on such matters, it would seem that everyone is left very much to his own devices when it comes to determining the nature of God's law. There are not only divisions among Christians, Jews, Moslems, and adherents of other faiths, but even among the adherents of any given faith there are often sharp divisions on the answers to be given to these questions. And then, of course, there are those who deny that there is any divine law, because they are not convinced that there is a deity, or because the deity whose existence they affirm is not the kind of being who would dictate legal precepts to earthly creatures.

THE HIGHER-LAW APPROACH:
THE NATURAL-LAW VERSION

Partly because of such difficulties as these, the "natural-law" theory has developed. Divine revelation may not be accessible to everyone, the natural-law theorists say, but the laws of nature, especially the laws of human nature, are knowable to anyone who will but take the time and make the effort to inquire into them. One of the earliest formulations of the natural-law theory is that of Cicero:

> True law is right reason in agreement with Nature; it is of universal application, unchanging and everlasting; it summons to duty by its commands, and averts from wrong-doing by its prohibitions. And it does not lay its commands or prohibitions upon good men in vain, though neither have an effect on the wicked. It is a sin to try to alter this law, nor is it allowable to attempt to repeal any part of it, and it is impossible to abolish it entirely. We cannot be freed from its obligations by Senate or People, and *we need not look outside ourselves for an expounder or interpreter of it.* And there will not be different laws at Rome and at Athens, or different laws now and in the future, but one eternal and unchangeable law will be valid for all nations and for all times, and there will be one master and one ruler, that is, God, over us all, for He is the author of this law, its promulgator, and its enforcing judge.[8]

The source of the law of nature, then, is God, but it must not be forgotten that for Cicero, the Stoic, God and nature were one and the same. The author and promulgator of the law of nature, then, is nature itself, which is unchanging in its laws. These laws are manifested in each man's own mind, through the exercise of his reason, which is constructed in accordance with the very laws of nature that govern the structure of all the universe. All any man need do, if he is in doubt as to what is required of him by the dictates of the law of nature, is look inside himself, consult his own inner (psychological, rational, moral?) nature, and he will find the answer. Everyone, provided he is endowed with the capacity to reason, is able to perform the necessary operations, for as Cicero put it:

> Those creatures who have received the gift of reason from Nature have also received right reason, and therefore they have also received the gift of Law, which is right reason applied to command and prohibition. And if they have received law, they have received Justice also. Now all men have received reason; therefore, all men have received justice.[9]

In keeping with this tradition, Gratian decreed that natural law is so superior to man-made law that any practice, whether it is merely customary or has actually been committed to writing in the constitution of a state, "if it contradicts natural law, must be considered null and void."[10] And still later, St. Thomas Aquinas wrote:

> Rational creatures are subject to divine Providence in a very special way; being themselves made participators in Providence itself, in that they control their own actions and the actions of others. So they have a certain share in the divine reason itself, deriving therefrom a natural inclination to such actions and ends as are fitting. This participation in the Eternal law by rational creatures is called the Natural law. . . . The light of natural reason, by which we discern good from evil, and which is the Natural law, [is] nothing else than the impression of the divine light in us.[11]

And on the question of civil disobedience (or perhaps even outright rebellion), he went on to say:

> If a human law is at variance in any particular with the Natural law, it is no longer legal, but rather a corruption of law. . . . Man is bound to obey secular rulers to the extent that the order of justice requires. For this reason if such rulers have no just title to power, but have usurped it, or if they command things to be done which are unjust, their subjects are not obliged to obey them, except perhaps in certain special cases, when it is a matter of
> · avoiding scandal or some particular danger.[12]

Later still, during the great revolutions that changed the entire political climate of the Western world during the last decades of the eighteenth century, similar appeals were voiced by Jefferson and the other authors of the Declaration of Independence, who proclaimed that certain "truths" are "self-evident," namely, "that all men are created equal, that they are endowed by their Creator with certain unalienable Rights, that among these are Life, Liberty and the pursuit of Happiness." Among these self-evident truths were the propositions that governments derive their just powers from the consent of the governed in order to secure those rights, and that when any government "becomes destructive" of those ends, "it is the Right of the People to alter or to abolish it [the government]." Similarly, the French Declaration of the Rights of Man set forth the "natural, inalienable and sacred Rights of Man," which are "simple and indisputable principles"—in phraseology different, but in meaning almost identical to the "self-evident truths" of the American Declaration of Independence.

These sentiments have been used to justify revolutions, but the principles behind acts of civil disobedience should be very similar, if not identical. According to the natural-law theorist, or the one who believes in the doctrine of natural rights, the principles of justice and rights are self-evident to any rational person who is exercising his rational faculties. Any law that is inconsistent with these principles is no law at all and is not binding upon anyone, least of all upon anyone who recognizes the fact that it is contrary to the laws of nature or to the natural rights of man.

This is not the place for either a comprehensive history of the natural-law theory or a detailed critique of it. But a few crucial points may be considered:

1. In the last analysis many of the weaknesses of the divine-law theory have been inherited by the natural-law theory. The epistemological problem is particularly difficult: How is one to know when a given "law" enacted by a human legislature is or is not in conformity with the natural law? One must first know what the natural law is or says or requires. But though the natural-law theorists maintain that its principles are "self-evident" to all "rational" persons, it seems that there is considerable dispute, both about their content and about their application in specific cases. Unless one assumes, for example, that George III was irrational (as he might in fact have been), it is obvious that in the days of the American Revolution there was at least one person to whom the "truths" enunciated in the Declaration of Independence were *not* self-evident; and there were thousands of loyalists, both in other parts of the British Empire and in the American colonies, who were *not* convinced of the propriety of applying those principles, assuming that they accepted them as the American revolutionaries did.

2. Every natural-law theory seems to recognize the importance of preserving the state and positive or statutory law. No natural-law theory attempts to justify the destruction of a state unless that state is ruthless and tyrannical, and every such theory hedges the occasions upon which its adherents may engage in civil disobedience very carefully—largely on the ground that (as Aristotle put it) petty crimes multiplied can spell the ruination of a society. When, and under what specific circumstances, is one justified in taking the law into one's own hands? Even supposing that a given law is unjust, is the moral or social gain to be achieved by disobeying it worth the risk of undermining all lawful authority that may be entailed in civil disobedience?

3. Again, can an organized society function, or dispense *even-handed justice*, if its citizens take it upon themselves to decide what laws they will and will not obey? Can a meaningful legal system exist in a place where citizens assume the mantle of righteousness and then do as they please, regardless of the legalities of the matter? If the supporters of school integration can violate those laws that they consider to be unjust in order to further

their cause, is there any principle that could prevent the Ku Klux Klans or the middle-class racists from acting upon the "truths" that are "self-evident" to *them* and violating other laws that are repugnant to *their* sense of justice? For every Martin Luther King who engages in civil disobedience in support of *his* convictions about justice, there is likely to be a George Wallace who will stand in the schoolhouse door, in defiance of the law, to further *his* version of the just society.

We have seen in this century how thin is the veneer of civilization, how easily it can be stripped away, and how ugly the savage beast that lurks below can be. Where the law of the jungle reigns—that is, where there is no civil law at all—there is likely to be terror, death, and decay. The law of nature, if there is one, not only must prescribe which laws are unjust, and therefore need not be obeyed *if considered in isolation, in abstract terms,* but also must provide guidelines for the practical judgment that any man who contemplates an unlawful act must make, as to whether *that particular act, in that particular place and at that particular time,* is one that he ought or ought not to perform. Unfortunately, no theory of natural law, and no book on natural law provides such concrete guidelines for real cases.

MARTIN LUTHER KING ON CIVIL DISOBEDIENCE

The most prominent recent advocate of a natural-law theory of civil disobedience was Martin Luther King, Jr. In his "Letter from a Birmingham Jail," Dr. King defended the demonstrations that ultimately led to his conviction—a conviction that was later upheld by the United States Supreme Court—on trespassing charges on the ground that "direct action" is sometimes the only way to get negotiations started. "Non-violent direct action," he wrote, "seeks to create such a crisis and establish such creative tension that a community that has constantly refused to negotiate is forced to confront the issue. It seeks so to dramatize the issue that it can no longer be ignored."

In addition to these utilitarian or political objectives, however, he contended that the laws that he had "violated" were unjust and that unjust laws are no laws at all. An unjust law, he said, is a man-made rule that is out of harmony with the moral law, the law of God, or the natural law, one that "distorts the soul and damages the personality," and relegates persons to the status of things. Further, laws that are imposed by a majority upon a minority, though they do not apply to the majority itself, are unjust and inconsistent with the divine law or the law of nature. More particularly is this the case when the minority had no part in enacting the law, because it lacked the right to vote.

Such laws, then, according to Dr. King, may be violated, but only after careful determination of the facts, after attempts to negotiate the removal of the injustices, and after "self-purification." In engaging in civil disobedience the violator breaks the unjust law "openly, lovingly," and is prepared to accept the penalty, thus expressing the very highest respect for law. To a large degree these principles follow those laid down by Thoreau in his essay "Civil Disobedience." They have formed the guidelines for much recent discussion of civil disobedience, and may be summarized as follows: *One who engages in civil disobedience violates a law (1) which he believes to be unjust or immoral; (2) in order to bring about a change in the social order; (3) in such a way as to inflict no harm or bodily injury upon any other person (that is, nonviolently); (4) openly and publicly; and (5) with a willingness to pay the penalty, if that should be necessary.*

These conditions distinguish civil disobedience from ordinary lawlessness, for the common criminal typically (1) admits that the laws he breaks are not unjust or immoral; (2) is not interested in changing the social order, but in satisfying his own needs or desires; (3) is often (though not always) unconcerned about any harm that may come to others as a result of his criminal behavior, particularly if they stand in his way; (4) does his deed clandestinely, attempting as far as possible to avoid detection; and (5) is anxious to avoid being caught and to escape punishment.

Though Dr. King's definition may serve as a set of general guidelines for some purposes, its elements are not as clear or as precise as they might be, and they are certainly not the only guidelines or criteria that have been set forth by supporters of one form or another of civil disobedience. Nor has everyone been prepared to accept Dr. King's views as constituting a sufficient justification for disobedient behavior. We shall first go through this list, analyzing some of the implications of each point and noting some other views along the way; then we shall take up certain other suggestions that have been made by students, advocates, and critics of civil disobedience.

CIVIL DISOBEDIENCE AND THE IMMORALITY OF THE LAW

All commentators on civil disobedience agree that every genuine act of civil disobedience *must have broken the law*. But they differ on certain important details regarding the state of mind of the law violator and the ultimate fate of the law itself. Must he be convinced that the law is *unconstitutional*, for example (which is not identical with its being unjust or immoral, unless one is prepared to say the Constitution recognizes only those laws that are both just and moral), or is it sufficient that he is convinced that the law he has violated is unjust or immoral *even though* it may be constitutional? Must the law turn out, in the end, to *be* unconstitutional, or is this *not* a necessary condition for civil disobedience?

The main point is that the law must have been broken: "However vehement, radical, or extraordinary is one's protest," Carl Cohen has written, "if he does not break the law he has not been disobedient. The violation of some law of the body politic is a universal and necessary feature of [civilly disobedient] conduct." [13]

According to a second view, civil disobedience occurs only when the protestor is convinced that the law against which he is protesting will be, or at least has a strong chance of being, nullified by appeal to higher authorities, such as the federal courts or the Supreme Court. "Civil disobedience must take place under an arguable claim of right," one recent commentator has said. He adds that if he can "satisfy the court that higher positive law arguably justifies his conduct or arguably condemns the action his government demands of him, then he is entitled to special treatment as a civil disobedient." [14]

A third opinion holds that the distinction between an act of civil disobedience and merely criminal behavior is finally settled by the courts. If, after all appeals have been exhausted, the defendant's conviction is upheld, then he is a criminal offender and not a true civil disobedient; but if his conviction is reversed, and the law against which he was directing his protest is declared unconstitutional or otherwise nullified, then his act was an act of civil disobedience rather than one of criminal misbehavior. [15]

Civil disobedience may be defined, then, in several different ways, each of which involves a different set of necessary conditions. These may be summarized as follows:

(A) Civil disobedience is behavior that violates a criminal law that the violator believes to be unjust or immoral, though he may believe it to be a valid law within the system of which it is a part.
(B) Civil disobedience is behavior that violates a criminal law that the protester believes to be invalid.
(C) Civil disobedience is behavior that violates a criminal law that is later declared invalid by the courts.

CIVIL DISOBEDIENCE OF PROTEST AND OF PERSONAL INTEGRITY

The civil disobedient, unlike the revolutionary, generally has considerable respect for government and for law, and is not interested in the overthrow of the entire system, but in the modification of certain of its parts. However, he may not even be particularly concerned about that. He may merely be concerned to avoid doing what the law commands on the ground that obedience to that particular law would be immoral. Aside from self-interest, which is the usual motive of criminal behavior, there are three other motives for the kinds of illegal behavior that presently concern us:

1. Overthrow of the government. *(Revolution.)*
2. Modification or reform of the system. *(Civil disobedience of protest.)*
3. Refusal to participate in immoral activity. *(Civil disobedience of personal integrity.)*

Though the Hebrew midwives may have been dissatisfied with Pharaoh's government, there is no evidence either that they were interested in overthrowing it or in bringing about reforms in its administration or in its laws. The evidence before us justifies the conclusion that they were civil disobedients of personal integrity, that they disobeyed the law because to obey it would have required of them an act that they could not do in good conscience. Many such acts come to the attention of the public from time to time. The Amish who refuse to send their children to public schools are attempting neither to overthrow the government nor to reform the educational systems of the states in which they reside. They merely want to be left free to educate their children in accordance with their own beliefs. During the Vietnam War, many American draft evaders, who fled to Canada or to other hospitable countries in order to escape from the draft and from criminal prosecution for their refusal to serve in their country's armed forces, did so in order to avoid fighting in what they considered to be an immoral war or to avoid what they considered immoral in itself—fighting in a war. Some of them, to be sure, wanted their actions to be understood back home as a protest against their government or against the war it was waging in Indochina. But many of them, knowing that their personal actions would have little effect on American foreign policy, fled from their country in order to preserve their personal integrity—to avoid being forced to do what they considered to be immoral.

By contrast, those who engage in civil disobedience of protest do so with the intention of changing the laws or the policies of their government. They choose, therefore, to make their actions as public and dramatic as possible. The illegal sit-ins, lie-ins, and pray-ins that took place at the height of the civil rights drive in the late 1950s and the early 1960s; the illegal marches and parades and demonstrations; the encouragement of public burning of draft cards at mass rallies by people like Dr. Benjamin Spock, who was not himself subject to the draft; the obstruction of traffic in New York, Washington, and other cities as a means of protesting racism or the war; all of these are examples of the disobedience of protest. Their purpose was to change public policy, though they might also have been (in part) designed to encourage or to consist partially of civil disobedience of personal integrity. (Obviously *both* of these forms of civil disobedience may sometimes be present in one and the same action.) An act of *indirect* civil disobedience * is *necessarily* an act of civil disobedience of protest, for it is, strictly,

---

* The distinction between direct and indirect civil disobedience is explained in the next section.

speaking, the violation of a law that the disobedient recognizes to be moral and just, in order to dramatize a protest against some other injustice.

THE CIVIL DISOBEDIENT AND PUNISHMENT

Like Socrates before him, Martin Luther King insisted that one who engages in civil disobedience must be prepared to accept the penalty. But whenever King was convicted of a criminal offense as a result of one of his demonstrations, he carried his appeal to the highest court in the land in an attempt to have the conviction reversed and to have the laws that he violated, or the laws against which he was protesting, overturned. It would seem, then, that in practice his position was not simply that one should be prepared to accept the penalties set by the courts (though that seems to be the implication of his position), but as a willingness to accept punishment *after all legal means of avoiding it have been exhausted.* These two positions may be summarized as follows:

(P₁) The civil disobedient must accept the punishment that the courts mete out to him. (Socrates)

(P₂) The civil disobedient may appeal to the higher courts for elimination of the penalty and nullification of the law that had been violated. (Martin Luther King)

But these are not the only views on this subject. There are at least two others.

According to some commentators, a violation "committed under a claim of legal right with the intention of seeking redress in the courts . . . can hardly be termed civil disobedience," because "a principle crucial to the philosophy of civil disobedience [is this:] that the violation of pernicious laws is justified by the fact that these laws themselves violate a higher law, which may be called moral law, natural law, or divine law. . . . But if the appeal of the law violator is not simply to moral law, but to positive articulated law such as the Constitution of the United States, it is not civil disobedience we are dealing with, but something else." [16] And Sidney Hook, who is clearly sympathetic to some forms of civil disobedience, wrote:

> An action launched in violation of a local law or ordinance, and undertaken to test it, on the ground that the law itself violates state or federal law, or launched in violation of state law in the sincerely held belief that the state law outrages the Constitution, the supreme law of the land, is not civilly disobedient. . . . [Actions] become civilly disobedient when they are in deliberate violation of laws that have been sustained by the highest legislative and judicial bodies of the nation, e.g., income tax laws, conscription laws, laws forbidding segregation in education, and discrimination in public accommodations and employment. [17]

In short, the advocates of this point of view hold that:

(P₃) The civil disobedient is one who does not appeal to the higher courts and does not rely upon a belief in his ultimate vindication by superior authorities, but appeals only to moral, natural, or divine law for justification of his actions.

Finally, there are those who maintain that if a person believes that the law he has violated is immoral or unjust, he need not acquiesce in any penalty that the courts may impose for such violation. If the law is unjust, they argue, then a penalty for its violation is also unjust; and if one is justified in disobeying unjust laws, one must be equally justified in avoiding punishment for such disobedience. This is the position that Daniel Berrigan finally adopted after his conviction for the destruction of draft records, when he fled from the FBI and spent a number of months eluding the authorities. A fourth position on the question of punishment therefore is:

(P₄) The civil disobedient may try to avoid punishment altogether, on the ground that punishment for violation of an unjust law is itself unjust (Berrigan).

A careful comparison of the three positions labeled (A), (B) and (C) in the section on Civil Disobedience and the Immorality of the Law with the four positions on punishment, (P₁), (P₂), (P₃), and (P₄), reveals that some of the latter are incompatible with some of the former. Thus, for example, position (P₃)—that the civil disobedient may not appeal to the courts for mitigation of his punishment or for nullification of the law under which he is being punished—is incompatible with both (B) and (C); for (B) permits the civil disobedient to appeal to the courts to invalidate the law against which he is protesting, and (C) makes it *impossible* for a person to be a civil disobedient *unless* the law under which he was convicted is later declared to be invalid by the courts. [Incidentally, position (P₃) may be identical with that of Socrates, position (P₁).]

Position (P₂), on the other hand—that is, Martin Luther King's view that the civil disobedient may appeal to the courts for mitigation of the penalty and invalidation of the objectionable law—is compatible with position (C), but only in the very strangest sort of way. For if (C) were correct, it would follow that one would never know whether a given violation of the law had in fact been an act of civil disobedience until all the appeals had been heard and the final judgment had been rendered. (C), in fact, leaves it to the courts to determine whether a particular law violation was an act of civil disobedience; and if the courts do not decide in favor of the protestor's view that the law against which the protest was directed was invalid, thus upholding his conviction, then it would turn out that his act had not been an act of civil disobedience at all.

Now it is true that there is no law on the books that defines civil disobedience or that provides either special penalties or special considerations for persons who engage in civil disobedience. When a person engages in an act of civil disobedience, he breaks a law that must legally be presumed to be valid at that time. The law itself may be a trespass law, a school-prayer law, a segregation law, a law forbidding indecent exposure, or any of a thousand others. The violation is a violation of one of those laws, not of any specific law forbidding civil disobedience. And for all the violator knows at the time he commits his violation (no matter what he may believe or hope), the law he breaks may well be upheld by the courts. Ordinary usage does not permit us to accept (C) as a definition of "civil disobedience" because in ordinary language, an act is an act of civil disobedience at the time of its performance, and the determination of whether it is or not does not have to wait upon the final determination of the courts. Indeed, Martin Luther King wrote his defense of civil disobedience after his conviction had been upheld by the Supreme Court, and no one was heard to complain that his act was not really civilly disobedient because his conviction was upheld by the highest court in the land and he was forced to serve out his jail sentence. No such complaint was heard because no one made the purely linguistic mistake of supposing that position (C) accurately reflects the ordinary way in which "civil disobedience" is used. Acceptance of (C) would entail that all persons who practiced civil disobedience would be innocent of committing any offense against the law, whereas anyone who attempted to commit an act of civil disobedience and was convicted (and whose conviction was subsequently upheld on appeal) would have committed an offense against the law, but would have failed to commit an act of civil disobedience, though he had every intention of doing so. These conclusions are paradoxical because (C) does not accurately reflect current usage of the term *civil disobedience*.

DIRECT AND INDIRECT CIVIL DISOBEDIENCE

Part of the reason for error that advocates of (C) have made may be a result of a rather elementary confusion between two kinds of civil disobedience. For the sake of simplicity, these may be called *direct* civil disobedience and *indirect* civil disobedience. Direct civil disobedience consists of an act that violates the very law that one is protesting against. Examples would be sit-ins at segregated lunch counters or refusal to register for the draft when one believes that the draft laws are immoral. Indirect civil disobedience consists of an act that violates a law that *may, standing alone, be completely innocuous*, as a means of protesting against *some other law* that one considers to be morally objectionable. Examples of indirect civil disobedience would be Thoreau's refusal to pay taxes as a means of dramatizing his objections to the fugitive slave law and the Mexican War, sit-ins in government offices (violating the laws of trespass) in order to protest against the Vietnam War or discriminatory practices, and the burning of draft records as a protest against the Vietnam War or the alleged napalming of innocent civilians.[18] Notice the difference between the two kinds of sit-ins. The sit-in that was part of an act of direct civil disobedience was itself forbidden by the law that was being protested against: a law forbidding black citizens to sit at lunch counters. The sit-in that was part of an act of indirect civil disobedience did not itself violate the laws that were being protested (such as the Vietnam War or discriminatory housing regulations), but were merely violative of trespass laws, which even the disobedients would agree are perfectly legitimate.

In view of this distinction, it would seem that (B) will not do either, for (B)—which defines civil disobedience as behavior that violates a criminal law which the protestor believes to be invalid—leaves no room for indirect civil disobedience. We are left, therefore, with (A) as a definition of civil disobedience—not a complete definition, of course, but a statement of one necessary condition of civil disobedience—that every act of civil disobedience must violate some law.

Socrates' views on punishment (P_1), and those of Sidney Hook and others (P_3) demand too much and are clearly not true to modern usage of the term. It is unreasonable to suppose that a person who disobeys a law because it goes against his conscience should passively submit to whatever punishment the state may have set for such violations, without so much as making an effort to defend himself in the courts. In the American scheme of things, there is often no way to test the constitutionality of a law that one finds repugnant to one's conscience without first violating the law, submitting to arrest, and taking the risk of being convicted. Some people have insisted that the true civil disobedient will gladly plead guilty to the charges that are laid against him and meekly rely upon the mercy of the court. Those who say that a man cannot attempt to escape punishment through appeals to the courts are evidently attempting to make a moral point of some kind, but they are certainly not making a logical point; for there is nothing in the meaning of *civil disobedience* that renders the statement "That civil disobedient escaped punishment by appealing to the courts," contradictory or nonsensical, as it would have to do if (P_1) or (P_3) were logically true.

As a moral claim, there may be something to them, from at least some moral points of view. One may have greater admiration for a man who lays his life or his liberty on the line, as Socrates and Thoreau did, accepting his punishment—not meekly, but courageously. Thoreau's famous statement to Emerson when the latter visited him in prison and asked him why he was there still rings with authenticity and deep conviction. "Why," he asked, "are you *outside*?" Prison is the right place for a man when other men are being imprisoned unjustly, he wrote. A great advocate of nonviolent resistance, Mohandas K. Gandhi, once wrote that he who commits civil disobedience must "cheerfully suffer imprisonment." Not all civil disobedients are interested in martyrdom, and there is some doubt as to whether martyrdom is either necessary or desirable from a tactical point of view. Many acts of civil disobedience are undertaken not only because the conscience of the disobedient is offended by the law that he considers to be unjust, but also because he wants to introduce some *change* into the way things are done in his society. If there is no alternative, circumstances undoubtedly exist in which it is morally right to violate the law, even though one knows full well that the consequence will be loss of liberty or even death itself. But human life and human liberty are far too precious to be given up lightly, particularly when there is a moral alternative. There is nothing morally reprehensible in a person's bending every effort, after he has committed an act of civil disobedience, to have the law that he found morally unacceptable overturned by the courts and thus save himself from the consequences of an unreversed criminal conviction. Far from being morally reprehensible, such a course of action is commendable; for there is another virtue: that of concern for one's fellow men. The civil disobedient who violates the law because he firmly believes that what the law requires of him is unjust or immoral, and then accepts the law's penalties for his illegal behavior, may be behaving morally. But if, though it is possible for him to contest the conviction and possibly to overturn the law, he chooses instead the path of martyrdom, he may be considered righteous, holy and saintly, but there is a clear sense in which what he has done is not moral—or at least not the *most* moral thing that he might have done. For by contesting his conviction *not* in order to save himself from the painful consequences of his illegal behavior, but in order to save *others* from being faced with the awful choice that he had to make, and to save his society from the evil consequences of the bad law that he believes is in its midst, he may not earn the title of martyr, but he will have done his best to bring greater good and greater happiness to his fellow men. This may be what saintliness is all about.

We turn now to the last of the four theories of punishment for civil disobedients, that of Daniel Berrigan, who maintains that one need not accept the penalty for an act of civil disobedience when the penalty itself is for disobeying an unjust law or is part of an unjust system.

CIVIL DISOBEDIENCE AND REVOLUTION

Daniel Berrigan is not a civil disobedient, but a revolutionary. Revolutionaries also break laws, of course, but their purpose is quite different from that of the civil disobedient. The civil disobedient, though he may violate the provisions of one or a few laws, nevertheless accepts the validity and the authority of the system as a whole. His purpose is *reform* of some parts of the system, not the overthrow of the system itself. As Martin Luther King put it, the civil disobedient breaks the unjust law "openly and lovingly," and accepts the penalty if he cannot convince the authorities that he should not be punished; he thus expresses his high regard for the law and for the system, and his willingness to suffer personal deprivation if the system itself does not recognize his claim. But Daniel Berrigan, in contrast, has openly stated that his aims went far beyond the mere reform of certain aspects of the system. After his trial, he wrote, "By such action as ours . . . the law itself is being subjected to the scrutiny of revolutionary times. The law is being judged, and the judgment is a harsh one. The law is less and less useful for the living, less and less the servant of men, less and less expressive of that social passion which . . . brought the law into corporate being." And still later, he wrote,

> But suddenly, for all of us, the American scene was no longer a good scene. It was, in fact, an immoral scene. . . . Ours was a scene that moral men could not continue to approve if they were to deserve the name of men. The American scene, in its crucial relationships—the law, the state, the Church, other societies, our own families—*was placed in mortal question.* . . . Catonsville, rightly understood, was a profound "No" aimed not merely at a federal law that protects human hunting licenses. *Our act was aimed,* as our statement tried to make clear, *at every major presumption underlying American life today.* Our act was in the strictest sense a conspiracy; that is to say we had agreed together to attack the working assumptions of American life. Our act was a denial that American institutions were presently functioning in a way that good men would approve or sanction. *We were denying that the law,* medicine, education, and systems of social welfare . . . *were serving the people.* . . . *And in attacking the American assumption, we were beyond any doubt attacking the law and its practitioners.* . . . *We were attacking the assumption that American law, in its present form, can represent us, mediate our sense of justice, judge our actions, punish us.*[19]

These confessions go far beyond those of any civil disobedient, as that term is used here. They are not the words of one who is concerned to preserve the legal and social system while reforming those parts of it that he finds unpalatable. Berrigan's words are those of one who is totally disillusioned with the system, who categorically denies that American law "represents" him, who refuses, both in word and in deed, to accept the law's verdict as to the illegality of his action, and who repudiates "every major assumption underlying American life today." By thus placing himself outside the law, or above it, as some people might want to have it—in spite of the fact that he claims to have moral motivations for doing so—he has gone beyond civil disobedience and entered the ranks of revolutionaries.

Daniel Berrigan aside, however, what may be said for the view that the *civil disobedient* need not acquiesce in his own punishment for violations of laws that he considers to be immoral or unjust? If it is granted that not everyone need be a Socrates, and that considerations of justice and morality do not require of every civil disobedient that he passively accept the verdict of the lowest court on his case, perhaps we may go one step further and concede that some civil disobedients may properly evade punishment altogether.

CRITIQUE OF THE SOCRATIC AND ARISTOTELIAN THEORY

Those who insist, as Socrates and Aristotle did, that every illegal act tends to lead to the destruction of society and the undermining of the law's authority seem to have assumed that every illegal act tends to bring others in its wake. Although this may occur, it need not occur. There does seem to be some tendency for some persons who read about acts of civil disobedience to imitate the illegal behavior that they have read about, or to do their own illegal thing. The massive protests of the 1950s were followed by an escalating and spreading wave of protests in the 1960s that moved from nonviolent demonstrations to violent confrontations and riots. But no cause–effect relationship has been demonstrated to exist between the earlier demonstrations and the later riots. Though it would not be surprising to find that the former contributed, in some measure, to the latter, there is no doubt that other forces were at work, including the Vietnam War, the slow pace of integration, a rising new pride on the part of black citizens in the very qualities that had previously been a source of shame and degradation to them, growing discontent over poverty and slum conditions in a society that was generally affluent, a new awareness on the part of college students of the role that they could play in their own education and a pervasive feeling that they should have more personal autonomy and more influence on local and national policies, and many others. In short, if one person, or a group of persons, violates a given statute out of deep moral convictions, it does not necessarily follow, either logically or from any known social law, that other persons will follow suit, that the particular law against which the protest was directed will fall into general disuse, that all or many citizens will take it upon themselves to disobey other laws not closely related to the one in question, or—in general—that society will disintegrate, that the law will be held in contempt by large numbers of persons, and that there will be a general breakdown of law and order.

Therefore, if some civil disobedients (particularly those who have disobeyed because of personal integrity rather than out of a desire to protest) choose to flee rather than to face the courts, the dire predictions of Socrates and Aristotle about the destruction of the entire legal system will not necessarily come true. Many young men, convinced that their participation in what they considered to be an immoral war would be grossly immoral and convinced also that they might spend their time more profitably, for themselves and for mankind, in Canada than behind bars at home, fled from their country with a good conscience and did very little harm, either to the social order of their nation or to any of its citizens. By studying medicine at the University of Toronto or law at McGill University, they believed they were likely to do a greater service to mankind than by doing laundry at Leavenworth Penitentiary. Though the actions that followed upon such judgments were clearly in violation of the law, it is difficult to defend the view that they were morally wrong—particularly when, looking back upon the entire affair, the resisters' judgment about the morality of the war has come to be shared by so many who were at one time the war's most vigorous defenders.

RESPONSIBILITY OF OTHERS FOR CIVIL DISOBEDIENCE

Every man has a *prima facie* duty to obey the law, and when he chooses to disobey, for whatever reason, the burden of proof is upon him. If he feels that his disobedient act was justifiable, it is up to him to prove that it was. But we must not forget that not only the citizen is involved in an act of disobedience. The law, as well as the citizen, is involved. The fault may not be that of the citizen as much as that of the law that he has disobeyed, or those who administer it. When, in a democracy, the organs of government become so remote from the people that the latter feel that they have no direct means of communicating with those who set the policies that govern their lives, they may be driven, for lack of any other means, to disobey the laws, *merely in order to bring their grievances to the attention of the public at large and of the responsible officials.* Martin Luther King tried to meet with the mayor of Montgomery but was rebuffed, until the bus boycott had achieved so much national publicity that the city's image was badly affected, and business was so seriously hurt that white merchants exercised enough pressure to bring about the changes that were demanded. Albert Bigelow tells how he appeared at the White House gate with petitions bearing 27,000 signatures in hopes of delivering them to the president; even the president's secretary, whose duty it is to handle such matters, refused to see him. After repeated phone calls, he was finally told to leave them with the policeman at the gate. He refused to do so, and later wrote, "It seems terrible to me that Americans can no longer speak to or be seen by their government. Has it become their master, not their servant? Can it not listen to their humble and reasonable pleas?" He concluded, finally, that "the experience has strengthened in me the conviction that we must, at whatever cost, find ways to make our witness and protest heard." That was to be "direct action," for without it, he said, "ordinary citizens lack the power any longer to be seen or heard by their government." [20]

Tens of thousands of young men went into exile, became fugitives from justice, and suffered all the hardships that inevitably accompany such a status rather than serve their country as the government believed they should: by fighting in what they believed was an ignoble war. That so many thousands of them would have been either cowards or traitors is an assumption that defies belief. Indeed, the sincerity of their purpose was in many instances repeated anew when they refused to accept the terms of what they regarded as an ignoble amnesty offered shortly after the war ended by President Gerald Ford. Rather than admit that they were guilty in any sense at all, or serve a relatively short term at some public service occupation in penance for their alleged wrongdoing, they chose to remain in exile, with all the hardships and disabilities that that involved for many of them. They believed that they had done no wrong, but their acts were designed to bring an end to what they regarded as an unjust war, and were in the interests of both their fellow countrymen and of the people against whom the United States was fighting. They were particularly concerned not to leave the impression that they were repentant or that they were interested in taking advantage of an amnesty or a pardon, for in their view, they had committed no offense that the authorities should forget and the government had no right to "pardon" them when they had done no wrong. Thousands of Americans remain in exile, some because they have established roots where they are, many because they have been unwilling to accept offers that appear to compromise their principles or leave the impression that they admit their culpability when in fact they do not.

When black men and women are given the promise of equal rights and opportunities for themselves and their children and see that such progress as is made barely touches their own children; when they are told to be patient, and watch their own children growing up into a world which seems to them to be little different from the one in which they themselves grew up, so far as meaningful opportunity for advancement is concerned; when they feel that the officers of the law do not treat them fairly or justly and that the laws are often stacked against their interests; and when, finally, the black community is expected to send its sons to another country where they may spill their blood for *its* freedom, while they feel that the extent of their own freedom at home is not all that it should be, it is almost inevitable that some contempt for the law and for legal processes will set in, not only in the black community, but in the white community as well. It is inevitable, too, that some laws will be broken in order to bring the focus of the nation's attention to those of its domestic problems that some of its citizens believe cannot wait any longer.

Some of the responsibility for civil disobedience rests upon the leaders of the government, on leaders of local governments, and on members of the community at large who have failed to exercise their responsibilities to correct the wrongs that have crept into the nation's legal and social structure. There is no penalty for irresponsible, insensitive, or inept political figures, and no stigma attaches to the indifferent citizen who fails to use his voice, his pen, and his vote to change the conditions that finally provoke morally outraged persons into illegal acts. But though the latter bear the brunt of the sanctions of the law, the former must bear their fair share of the moral responsibility for what has happened.

SHOULD THE CIVIL DISOBEDIENT ACCEPT PUNISHMENT?

If law and order is threatened by the civil disobedient, then it is threatened at least as much by the policies that lead to civil disobedience and by the indifference, callousness, or ineptness of those—including the ordinary voter—who fail to rectify the legal and social wrongs that lead to disrespect for the law. One who has violated such a law, not as protest but as an expression of moral outrage at the thought of obeying it, need not acquiesce passively in any punishment that may be forthcoming. To become an exile if there is a country willing to take him in, or to become a fugitive from justice, subject to arrest and prosecution at any time, is not a particularly cheerful prospect. One would be ill advised to engage in civil disobedience for kicks, as some people have done, for the consequences are very grave indeed.

One who engages in the civil disobedience of protest, however, is in a very different sort of situation, so far as the acceptance of punishment is concerned. His purpose is not merely to avoid doing what he considers to be immoral, but to focus public attention upon the law that forces him and others to make such a choice, and through his action to bring about a change in public attitudes and public policies. Because this is his goal, he must do whatever he can (within moral limits, of course, because by hypothesis he is a person of high moral standards) to further it, and he must avoid doing anything that will interfere with it or that will have the opposite effect.

Ordinarily, he must present himself for arrest and abide by the rulings of the courts, for if he makes a fugitive of himself, he loses several points in the battle:

1. He loses the publicity that often attends acts of courageous and open disobedience of the law, of inviting arrest, and of submitting to it when it comes.*
2. He loses the dramatic effect and the publicity of a trial, in which (presumably) the issues with which he is concerned will be brought out.
3. He loses a considerable degree of credibility for himself and his cause, for by "copping out," it begins to appear that he is more concerned for his personal welfare than for justice and morality.
4. He loses his opportunity to test in the courts the validity of the law against which he is directing his protest.

HOW SHOULD THE STATE
TREAT THE CIVIL DISOBEDIENT?

So far we have considered the question of punishment only from the side of the disobedient—whether he should submit to being punished or bend his efforts to avoiding punishment. We have seen that persons who engage in the civil disobedience of personal integrity may attempt to avoid

---

* There are exceptions to this. The draft evaders and others who became fugitives received more publicity than they might have if they had submitted to arrest and prosecution.

punishment, particularly if they feel that their being punished will serve no useful purpose and if they feel that they may do more good outside of jail than inside. Those who ran the underground railroad that was designed to spirit slaves through the northern states and into Canada, where they would be secure against their former masters' attempts to have them returned under the Fugitive Slave Act, would have been foolish if they had submitted to punishment, for then their effort would have been doomed to failure and countless fugitives would have been returned to slavery.[21]

Now let us consider the problem of punishment from the side of the state. Should the government punish those who have engaged in acts of civil disobedience, and if it does, should such punishment be heavier or lighter than that which would be imposed upon an offender against the same law who had not engaged in civil disobedience?

The reader will recall the various theories of punishment that were discussed previously—the theories of reform, deterrence, and retribution. So far as retribution is concerned (as that term was used in the chapter on punishment), there is no doubt that the civil disobedient should be punished for his illegal behavior, for his breaking of the rules deserves to be treated like anyone else's, though his motives (namely, to urge the other players to change the rules of the game) differ somewhat from those of the more conventional rule violator.

Reform and deterrence raise special problems that will not be discussed in detail here.[22] A few major points that have been made by others may be noted, however.

Anyone who engages in an act of civil disobedience is guilty of breaking a law deliberately, openly, with complete and admitted knowledge of the nature of his act. It may be argued that such flagrant and open violations of the law should be discouraged, for they set a very bad example for others who may not be aware of the civil disobedient's noble intentions. There is a sense in which the civil disobedient's crime is even worse than a similar act performed by a more conventional criminal, for the disobedient performs his act with the precise intention of violating the law.

On the other hand, there scarcely seems to be any reason to reform the civil disobedient. Reformatory measures are intended, after all, to inculcate in the criminal a respect for law and a feeling of moral and legal propriety that he lacked, in some measure, before. The civil disobedient, however, *is* morally concerned and *is* committed to respect for the law. His offense has come about precisely *because* of his moral concerns and his basic respect for the law, for it is his belief that the law is generally a positive force for good that brings him to contest those provisions that he feels have deleterious effects upon society and to lay his life and his freedom on the line in order to bring about what he considers to be a more just and equitable society.

It should be observed also that civil disobedients seldom harm other persons in the course of their actions. Their offenses are not wrong in themselves, as injuries to persons or property, breaches of official duty, or outrages against public decency and good morals would be if they were done willfully or corruptly. Acts of civil disobedience are usually offenses only because they are defined as such by the law, as, for example, a black sitting in at a segregated lunch counter. It may be argued that such offenses, in general, should not be punished as severely as offenses that result in personal injury or injury to property.

Still other reasons for treating civil disobedients with a certain modicum of tolerance are the fact that their behavior is a kind of outlet for what might become violent, revolutionary sentiments if it were suppressed, and the further fact that such behavior enables groups of citizens who had not entered directly into the decision-making processes of the society to play an active role in such processes and to influence the outcome of discussions on major issues in both foreign and domestic affairs. Finally, the civil disobedient often acts out of a sense of social responsibility and moral principle that ought to be encouraged, with the hope that with the passage of time he might "mellow through forbearance." Or, as another commentator has observed, "To assert that the most dangerous man in our society is the one of strong moral conviction and courage is an unhappy admission about the nature of our society. It is one that we should not be in a hurry to make." Although the civil disobedient may be more likely to proselytize others than the common offender, more stubborn and less likely to yield to the threat of mild punishment, it may be wiser to deal leniently with him until the social dangers of his acts become immediate and apparent.

THE COURTS AND CIVIL DISOBEDIENCE

RECENT COURT DECISIONS

As a general principle, the views mentioned in the last paragraph of the preceding section may have some merit, but it is worth noting that in actual practice civil disobedients are *not* being treated particularly leniently in the courts and that the law, as presently constituted, does *not* recognize some of the claims made by civil disobedients for their tactics. A few examples may be helpful.

Some disobedients maintain that the First Amendment to the United States Constitution gives them unlimited rights of free speech and that some actions, which are intended to communicate ideas, constitute a kind of "symbolic speech," which should fall under the protection of the First Amendment. The courts have not upheld either of these contentions, and as a result, many protesters who had expected to be vindicated in their appeals to higher courts have instead been sent to prison for their efforts.

DIRECT ACTION AS A KIND OF SPEECH

A notable example is a case in which a group chose to hold a religious meeting in a public park, in violation of an ordinance requiring a license for such meetings. The group appealed to the Supreme Court, assuming that the Constitutional guarantees of free speech and freedom of religion would protect them from such a restriction on their activities. Speaking for the Court, Justice Reed said:

> The principles of the First Amendment are not to be treated as a promise that everyone with opinions or beliefs to express may gather around him at any public place and at any time a group for discussion or instruction. It is a *non sequitur* to say that the First Amendment rights may not be regulated because they hold a preferred position in the hierarchy of the constitutional guarantees of the incidents of freedom. This Court . . . has indicated approval of reasonable nondiscriminatory regulation by governmental authority that preserves peace, order, and tranquillity without deprivation of the First Amendment guarantees of free speech, press and exercise of religion.
>
> The valid requirements of license are for the good of the applicants [i.e., the group that held the illegal meeting] and the public. . . . Delay is unfortunate, but the expense and annoyance of litigation is a price citizens must pay for life in an orderly society where the rights of the First Amendment have a real and abiding meaning. . . .[23]

In a later case (1965), Cox, a leader of a peaceful courthouse picket line, exhorted his followers to try to eat in segregated restaurants and lunch counters. He was convicted, and on appeal the Supreme Court reversed the conviction, but with grave reservations:

> We emphatically reject the notion urged by appellant [Cox] that the First and Fourteenth Amendments afford the same kind of freedom to those who would communicate ideas by conduct such as patrolling, marching, and picketing on streets and highways, as these amendments afford to those who communicate ideas by pure speech.[24]

Justice Goldberg, a liberal who was undoubtedly sympathetic to the aims of the demonstrators, added:

> The fact that by their lights appellant and the two thousand students were seeking justice and not its obstruction is as irrelevant as would be the motives of [a] mob. . . . Louisiana . . . has the right to construe its statute to prevent parading and picketing from unduly influencing the administration of justice . . . regardless of whether the motives of the demonstrators are good or bad.
>
> . . . Nothing we have said here . . . is to be interpreted as sanctioning riotous conduct in any form or demonstrations, however peaceful in their conduct or commendable their motives, which conflict with properly drawn statutes and ordinances designed to promote law and order, protect the community against disorder, regulate traffic, safeguard legitimate interest in

private and public property, or protect the administration of justice and other essential governmental functions.

Liberty can only be exercised in a system of law which safeguards order. We reaffirm the repeated holdings of this Court that our constitutional command of free speech and assembly is basic and fundamental and encompasses peaceful social protest, so important to the preservation of the freedoms treasured in a democratic society. We also reaffirm the repeated decisions of this Court that there is no place for violence in a democratic society dedicated to liberty under law, and that the right of peaceful protest does not mean that everyone with opinions or beliefs to express may do so at any time and at any place. There is a proper time and place for even the most peaceful protest and a plain duty and responsibility on the part of all citizens to obey all valid laws and regulations.[25]

The following year (1966), a number of persons appealed to the Supreme Court against a conviction for trespass on the grounds of a county jail where they were protesting the arrest of fellow students and segregation. The late Justice Black, who had a well-deserved reputation for being one of the staunchest supporters of the First Amendment's guarantees of freedom of speech and freedom of the press, took a hard line against the defendants in this case and later fell from grace in some liberal circles. Whether his stance in this case and subsequent ones represented a genuine change in his position is dubious, for the question is not one of prior censorship, but of the place and circumstances in which the defendants attempted to exercise their right of free speech. This is what Justice Black wrote on that occasion.

The First and Fourteenth Amendments, I think, take away from government, state and federal, all power to restrict freedom of speech, press, and assembly *where people have a right to be for such purposes.* This does not mean, however, that these amendments also grant a constitutional right to engage in the conduct of picketing or patrolling, whether on publicly owned streets or on privately owned property. . . . Picketing, though it may be utilized to communicate ideas, is not speech, and therefore is not of itself protected by the First Amendment.

He went on to explain:

There is no merit to the petitioners' argument that they had a constitutional right to stay on the property . . . because this "area chosen for the peaceful civil rights demonstration was not only 'reasonable' but also particularly appropriate. . . ." Such an argument has as its major unarticulate premise the assumption that people who want to propagandize protests or views have a constitutional right to do so whenever and however and wherever they please. That concept of constitutional law was vigorously and forthrightly rejected in two of the cases petitioners rely on [including the Cox case]. We reject it again.[26]

It should be noted that Justices Douglas, Warren, Brennan, and Fortas dissented in this case, finding that the jail was a logical place to hold the protest. Justice Black, in another case, observed:

The crowd moved by noble ideals today can become the mob ruled by hate and passion and greed and violence tomorrow. If we ever doubted that, we know it now. The peaceful songs of love can become as stirring and provocative as the Marseillaise did in the days when a noble revolution gave way to rule by successive mobs until chaos sets in.[27]

Nicholas W. Puner has suggested that the hard line taken by the courts in recent years, as opposed to the more lenient interpretations of the laws as applied to civil disobedients at the beginning of the movement for equal rights for blacks, may be the result of a combination of factors. In the beginning, acts of civil disobedience were localized phenomena, they were relatively harmless (except for the acts of reprisal that they provoked), and great social wrongs were being challenged by them. Now, he says, with the Black Power movement, a succession of violent summers, considerable progress toward fulfillment of the aims of the original civil rights movement, and the spread of unlawful protests to the point where they are an everyday occurrence all across the nation, the courts (and others) feel that it is time to proceed at a more measured and mannerly pace. "To be lenient," Puner says, "is to help kindle the fire next time." [28]

In 1967 the Court held that the burning of a draft card, though it may have been intended as a kind of communication, was not a constitutionally protected form of communication, for it could not be construed to be a form of speech. It held that the law against the mutilation or destruction of draft cards is constitutional, for the card serves a number of legitimate administrative purposes.[29]

It is evident, then, that the Supreme Court—and along with it, the lower courts—is taking an increasingly hard line on civil disobedience and that any person contemplating an act of civil disobedience should be prepared to pay the price exacted by the law for the particular violation involved. And though a theoretical case can be made for the view that certain kinds of action, though they may be nonverbal, are nevertheless forms of communication that may be used to convey ideas in striking and dramatic form, the courts do not seem disposed at this time to grant to such modes of communication the same immunities as are taken for granted in more formal, verbal means of imparting ideas and opinions.

THE THEATER OF PROTEST

In recent years dissidents have developed a kind of "theater" approach, which they have used not only in the streets, but in the courts as well. Through a variety of dramatic techniques they have attempted to create an atmosphere in which what they consider to be the absurdity, the injustice, or the evil qualities of certain institutions will be made manifest. The most widely reported instance of this technique was the trial of the Chicago Seven (the so-called Chicago Conspiracy Trial), in which four defendants in particular—David Dellinger, Rennie Davis, Thomas Hayden, and Abbie Hoffman—repeatedly disrupted the court's proceedings by shouts, obscenities, and a variety of dramatic performances, including the staging of a birthday party, complete with cake, in the midst of the trial. The judge, whose conduct was not always a model of judicial restraint, sentenced these four defendants and two of their attorneys to lengthy prison terms—subsequently overturned on largely technical grounds—for contempt of court. The defendants were deliberately attempting to draw public attention to their trial and to *keep* it in the forefront of the nation's news by their antics. Though some lawyers are noted for their penchant of playing to the galleries (including not only the juries, but the audiences in the courtroom and the readers of the daily press), defendants in criminal trials have never put on such a sustained performance. Never before had the civil disobedience of protest been directed against the courts themselves. There is some question whether this can, in fact, be called civil disobedience, or whether it ought rather to be considered a form of revolutionary activity, as defined earlier. For by attacking the courts, the protesters were interfering with the only means society has of dispensing justice, and may, therefore, have been attacking one of the pillars of government and of society itself. Actions that disrupt the operations of the courts or of other agencies of the government, or that attempt to use them to heap scorn, ridicule, and contempt upon the processes of government, are of a very different order from lunch-counter sit-ins, bus boycotts, and even the burning of draft cards. They are directed not at specific laws or practices, but at the very foundations of government itself. The disruption of business at a lunch counter may be hard on those who wish to eat there and on the owner and employees of the business, but disruption of the government's agencies is an attack upon the entire system, and may do great damage to all who live under it.

THE CIVIL DISOBEDIENT AND NONVIOLENCE

Martin Luther King, Mohandas K. Gandhi, Henry David Thoreau, and others have advocated nonviolence both as a tactic and as a guiding principle. They and others have adhered rigorously to the principle of nonviolence. Martin Luther King explained the rationale behind the principle in his speech accepting the Nobel Prize in 1964: "We adopt the means of nonviolence because our end is a community at peace with itself." [30] He recognized the dangers of violence begetting violence. A movement conceived in violence, or furthered by violence, risks the near certainty of retaliatory violence that could reverberate for generations.

Is nonviolence essential to civil disobedience? Is it an ethical principle, a religious principle, or a tactic—a strategy that may be used by some civil disobedients because it works better than violence does?

A great many commentators consider nonviolence to be essential to civil disobedience and refuse to call any violent act one of civil disobedience. They make much of the fact that it is *civil* disobedience—a violation of the law that is *civilized* and restrained. As one has put it, "In order to qualify as an act of civil disobedience, a crime must have been committed without expectation of working undue harm on anyone. . . . No act of violence to the person can ever qualify as civil disobedience."[31] And another, contrasting civil disobedience with "all forms of violence, intentional and otherwise," says that "civil disobedience is disobedience which is 'passive,' 'nonviolent,' 'courteous,' 'not uncivil.' "[32]

But instances of civil disobedience that are violent may exist. Or one can imagine situations in which one would be justified in engaging in an act that would be both violent and civilly disobedient. One may not ordinarily *approve* of violent actions, even when there may be strong justification or excuse for them; and for one who is engaged in the civil disobedience of protest, violence may be counterproductive. But it is impossible without further analysis or question begging to assert categorically that all civil disobedience must (logically) be nonviolent.

For example, suppose a member of the illegal underground railroad (pronounced illegal by the highest court in the land, by the way) is escorting a fugitive slave to the Canadian border. As he approaches a crossing he is met by two men—slave hunters—who have been dispatched to bring fugitive slaves back to their masters. They are armed with court papers giving them the right to carry out their mission. There is no way to escape from them but to fight them. He is faced with the choice of sticking to his nonviolent principles and permitting the fugitive who has been entrusted to his care to be returned to slavery or of using force to overpower the slave hunters, thus ensuring the escape of the slave. A man who chooses, in such circumstances as these, to use force to secure freedom for a man who will otherwise be returned to slavery is a civil disobedient. Though he has not engaged in civil disobedience of protest, he is nevertheless a civil disobedient of personal integrity. He has refused to acquiesce in the process of what he considers an immoral or unjust law; and in order to achieve his aim—what he considers to be a highly moral aim—he finds that he must not only disobey the court order and violate the fugitive slave act, but that he must also assault those who would carry out its provisions. This is not revolutionary, though it is clearly closer to being revolutionary than the mere disregard of the fugitive slave act would be, for the disobedient continues to respect most of the laws of the land and to live as a law-abiding citizen in every respect but this. But where this particular issue is concerned, he finds that mere passive resistance is sometimes not enough. The issues are too fundamental in his eyes to permit even considerations of nonviolence to deter him from fulfilling his mission.

It is not difficult to think of other cases—not cases in Nazi Germany, for under such conditions the rules are very different, but cases that might occur in a democratic but imperfect society. Suppose, for example, that a man has been sent to a mental hospital by some avaricious relatives who intend to use his confinement as a means to take his business interests away from him. Suppose, further, that he is about to be subjected to a form of treatment that will seriously damage his mental capacities and his memory for the rest of his life. Suppose, finally, that because of the way in which the laws of the state have been framed, his confinement is technically legal, and the courts refuse to interfere with the professional practices of physicians. Would one not be justified, under such circumstances, in securing the release of that patient, by force, if necessary, before he was subjected to the treatment that had been prepared for him? And wouldn't such forcible violation of the law be an instance of the civil disobedience of personal integrity? * Some protesters have gone farther in their tactics than the disciples of nonviolence would have done. They have paraded and picketed in such a way as to make it impossible for persons who wanted to enter or to leave certain buildings to do so—even, on occasion, interposing their bodies so as to constitute a threat of violence or to make violence inevitable if movement into or out of the building was to be effected. They have forcibly interfered with the movements of troop trains and with the operations of construction machinery at sites where racial discrimination was evident. They have thrown rotten vegetables and bags of human excrement at police and at politicians whose views they disapproved. It is difficult to say just when such actions cease to be those of the civil disobedient (the last-named scarcely seem to be civil!) and become those of the hooligan, the anarchist, or the nihilist. Much depends upon the *goals* toward which their actions are aimed and the *total effect* of those actions. The danger that any person who uses force or violence runs—if his aim is to protest against an unjust law or practice—is that he may end up committing a seriously unjust or immoral act himself, in his protest, and that in so doing he will harm the very cause for which he presumably broke the law. As for him who violates the law as a matter of personal integrity, he too runs the risk, once he permits himself to become the judge of when he may use force or violence, of committing an offense far worse than the one that he might have committed had he obeyed the law in the first place.

NONVIOLENCE AS A TACTIC

Nevertheless, it cannot be denied that the most notable civil disobedients have been nonviolent themselves and have counseled their followers to be nonviolent as well. For some (as for Martin Luther King), nonviolence was a religious principle. For others (as for some pacifists) it more closely resembles an ethical principle. But for all—including Gandhi, Martin Luther

---

* It could be converted into a protest against the state's laws and the hospital's practices as well, but this is not relevant to the purposes of the present discussion.

King, and the other leaders of great protest movements—it is a tactic, one that has proved its worth, in some situations, at least, and its power to effect radical changes in the social order. Martin Luther King drew on history to justify his espousal of the nonviolent tactic. The nonviolence of early Christians, he said, shook the mighty Roman Empire. In his view, the foundation for the freeing of the American colonies was laid in the nonviolent resistance of some of the colonists. And Gandhi, through his nonviolent tactics, was able to liberate his country from the British Empire.

For King nonviolence was not merely an ethical and religious principle, but a valuable technique for winning his battles. To be sure, it was a moral principle. "Moral force," he wrote, "has as much strength and virtue as the capacity to return a physical blow. . . . To refrain from hitting back requires more will and bravery than the automatic reflexes of defense." But far more important was its utilitarian justification. Its use enabled the movement to attract thousands of followers from every walk of life who would have been repelled by the use of violence; nonviolence "paralyzed and confused the power structures against which it was directed" and focused the attention of the world upon the events that were taking place; it had enormous psychological impact upon those who participated in the nonviolent direct action movement, raising their self-esteem, giving them dignity, and healing their internal wounds. Louis E. Lomax put the point very well: "Dr. King," he said, "is quite serious about nonviolence; he actually believes that the man who turns the other cheek will win the battle, or if he happens to lose the battle his children will win the war." "As a disciple of nonviolence," he wrote, "Martin Luther King is able to involve thousands of American white people in the Negro's struggle. I have watched white people react to King close up and, without exception, they are caught up by his addiction to nonviolent protest." [33] (Obviously these words were written long ago—in 1962, to be exact—before the great reaction, the "white backlash," had set in.)

It is likely that violence would have brought a reaction that might have set the cause for which he was fighting back by 100 years. (Indeed, there is some reason to believe that the violence of the late 1960s and early 1970s had a serious negative effect upon the willingness of Americans to integrate their towns, their schools, and their clubs, and that it contributed to the development of a new and not altogether flattering stereotype of the black American in the eyes of his white neighbor.) It would have alienated the clergy, the professionals, the intellectuals, and thousands of ordinary citizens who would not have been so ready to sing "Black and White Together" if the movement had been associated with violence. It would have made it impossible for the movement to collect the funds it so desperately needed for bail, for attorneys, for supplies, and for many other necessities—as CORE, SNCC, and other organizations discovered when their leaders began to advocate and participate in violent demonstrations. The credibility of those who claimed that the struggle was a moral one, for a moral cause, by persons of high moral integrity, would have been compromised. And the likelihood of success, against the vastly superior physical force available to those who opposed the movement, was very small indeed.

Nonviolence, then, is not logically necessary for civil disobedience, and it is possible to conceive of circumstances in which violence might be both necessary and justified as an element in civilly disobedient acts.* Nonviolence may be a moral principle or a religious principle. However that may be, it is a very important element in the tactics of civilly disobedient protest.

SUMMARY AND CONCLUSION

The analysis that has been undertaken in this chapter necessitates the rejection of much of the definition of civil disobedience set forth early on (that of Martin Luther King), at least under certain circumstances. The reader will recall that Dr. King maintained that a civil disobedient was one who violated a law (1) that he believed to be unjust or immoral, (2) in order to bring about a change in the social order, (3) in such a way as to inflict no harm or bodily injury upon any other person, (4) openly and publicly, and (5) with a willingness to pay the penalty. Dr. King was not alone, of course, in adhering to these criteria. Many others have followed him in asserting that all or most of these conditions must be met if any violation of the law is to count as an act of civil disobedience.

Such efforts may be exercises in "persuasive definition," that is, attempts to persuade the general public to adopt a given definition of civil disobedience as the only one that it will recognize as legitimate, thus relegating all other forms of illegal behavior to some other category—lawlessness, perhaps, or defiance of the law. For most people *civil disobedience* has fairly positive connotations. A civil disobedient is generally regarded as a high-minded individual—misguided perhaps, but courageous and principled, idealistic and deeply committed. One who is lawless, however, is thought of as evil, vicious, potentially dangerous, unprincipled, lacking in concern for others, self-serving, a discredit to the community. And one who is deviant refuses to obey the law because he is sick, or because he is immature and irresponsible. He too can be dangerous and a menace to society. If this definition, then, and others like it, is an attempt to persuade people to regard only such unlawful behavior as falls within its scope as morally justified and as the kind of behavior that some people, at least, may engage in with clear consciences—and even *ought* to engage in under certain circumstances —then it is a well-meaning effort, but misguided. For not only does it do

---

* If certain purists insist that such acts are uncivil and are therefore not instances of civil disobedience, I would not make an issue over it; I would merely suggest that there is another class of unlawful acts that *is* accompanied by violence and that can be justified on moral grounds. Let them call it what they will.

violence to the language, but it eliminates from the scope of morally justi-fiable unlawful acts some that may very well be justifiable, and by doing so, renders the job of some kinds of "civil disobedients" much more difficult, because it makes them seem to be mere lawbreakers.

Of course, the error may be one of insufficient analysis, or of special pleading. However that may be, it should be easier now to distinguish a number of different kinds of unlawful behavior from one another and to discuss each of them with some degree of discrimination.

Civil disobedience certainly always involves the violation of a law, though the law violated may—or may not—later be found to be invalid by the courts. The civil disobedient may himself carry the appeals through the courts to have the offending law overturned.

It is a necessary condition of all civilly disobedient behavior that the violator believe firmly either that it would be morally wrong for him to obey the law in question or that the unlawful act in which he is engaging will tend to promote the cause of justice in his society.

It is necessary, in this connection, to remember the distinction between direct and indirect disobedience, and that between disobedience of protest and disobedience of personal integrity. Though there are a number of per-mutations and combinations of these various forms of disobedience, civil disobedience of personal integrity must (as defined here) always be an act of direct civil disobedience.

This distinction enables us to draw a number of further conclusions that might otherwise have been tangled in a morass of confusion. Thus, we con-clude that one who engages in protest civil disobedience does so in order to bring about a change in the social order; but there are clear cases of civil disobedience of personal integrity where that is not the intention at all. For similar reasons acts of protest will be most effective if they are conducted in the open, but civil disobedience of personal integrity may be carried out in secret and still achieve the desired aim, or even be more advantageous— both to the individual and to society in the long run.

Though nonviolence is an excellent tactic, and though nonviolence is *generally* to be preferred (morally) to violence and the use of force, violence may occasionally be necessary to achieve the desired goals and be justified on moral grounds. Some civilly disobedient acts may be violent. But in civil disobedience of protest, violence almost always backfires and may do more harm to the cause for which the protesters are struggling than good.

In protest civil disobedience, the acceptance of punishment is important for the credibility of the movement. But one who engages in the civil dis-obedience of personal integrity *need not* (morally) accept punishment for violating what he considers to be an unjust law. However, his failure to turn himself in contributes to the undermining of society's legal foundations.

And this brings us back to the dilemma posed at the beginning of this discussion. How can one defy the law—even what one is convinced is an unjust law—and not contribute to the breakdown of one of society's most vital institutions? Obviously, this is not a question that is easily answered. It is not necessary, though, to appeal to such thoroughly questionable theories as the natural-law theory or the divine-law theory to find a justification for disobeying some laws. In spite of what Hobbes has said about the absolute obligation that every man is under to obey the laws at all times and under all conditions (with the exception of those that threaten his three inalienable rights), man may *not always* be duty-bound to obey *any* rule. For the most part, and under most circumstances, one should obey the law, just as one should—for the most part and under most circumstances—tell the truth, keep one's promises, show gratitude to one's benefactors, keep confidences and secrets, and not kill other human beings. But it is not difficult to think of occasions when any of these rules might properly be violated, because there are values other than truth telling, promise keeping, obedience to the law, and the rest. When Daniel Ellsberg handed 47 volumes of secret government documents with which he had been entrusted to the *New York Times,* he violated the law, he betrayed government secrets, he violated the trust that had been placed in him, and he violated the oath that he had taken when he first went to work for the government. But he concluded that all of this was insignificant by comparison with the benefits that might flow from public disclosure of those documents. Those benefits, he believed, far outweighed the harm that might come from his action and justified the strong risk he took of spending a good many years in prison. It is such moral judgments as these that persons contemplating civil disobedience must make.

The security apparatus of the United States government did not disintegrate because of Ellsberg's example. Nor has general lawlessness ensued from the civil protests of the recent past—though there has been a significant increase in the overall crime rate, which can be attributed to other social factors. None of the dire consequences that Socrates and Aristotle predicted might occur if men engaged in civil disobedience has occurred following the massive movements of recent decades, nor does it seem likely that they will. Men and women who are willing to take the risks inherent in civil disobedience are very rare, and the cost is far higher than most people are prepared to pay. When their conduct is such that their moral message is conveyed unequivocally and unmistakably, it cannot serve as an example, much less an excuse, for unlawful conduct for selfish ends.

There are excellent reasons for obedience to the law, though there are times when it is not wrong to break the law. No easy rules exist to guide conscientious persons as they attempt to make the hard choices that sometimes become necessary. Some people, who allow themselves to be governed by expediency and narrow self-interest when they face inconvenient traffic laws or costly income tax regulations, wax indignant when their neighbors violate laws on religious or moral grounds. At such times they are likely to appeal to something like Hobbes' condemnation of lawlessness and his dire predictions of the onset of a terrifying and destructive state of nature. However dreadful anarchy may be, it can be no worse than a legal system administered by a tyrant and created or revised by his followers. In any case, it is more likely to be brought into being from acts whose motives are like those of the petty traffic offender or the income tax cheat than from those of men and women who act under the inspiration of such people as Mahatma Gandhi, Martin Luther King, Jr., and Daniel Ellsberg.

13

Terrorism, Guerrilla Warfare, and International Morality *

DEFINING TERRORISM

Terrorism is any organized set of acts of violence designed to create an atmosphere of despair or fear, to shake the faith of ordinary citizens in their government and its representatives, to destroy the structure of authority which normally stands for security, or to reinforce and perpetuate a governmental regime whose popular support is shaky. It is a policy of seemingly senseless, irrational, and arbitrary murder, assassination, sabotage, subversion, robbery, and other forms of violence, all committed with dedicated indifference to existing legal and moral codes or with claims to special exemption from conventional social norms. The policies of terrorists are pursued with the conviction that the death and suffering of innocent persons who have little or no direct connection with the causes to which the terrorists are dedicated are fully justified by whatever success terrorists may enjoy in achieving their political ends.[1]

EXAMPLES OF NONTERRORISTIC VIOLENCE
It is as important to know what is *excluded* by this definition as it is to know what is included. A few illustrations of nonterroristic, revolutionary types of activity may be helpful:

* An earlier version of this chapter was published in Volume XII of the *Stanford Journal of International Studies,* copyright 1977 by the Board of Trustees of the Leland Stanford Junior University. All rights reserved.

Sean MacBride spent more than 20 years in the Irish Republican Army, serving for a time as commander-in-chief. In a recent interview, he explained that things being done by terrorists today, including the members of the I.R.A., "would not have been dreamt of in the I.R.A. I knew twenty or thirty years ago. . . . It used to be the rule, always, that you had to take precautions not to injure innocents or civilians. In any actions we took, ambushes or military actions, it was always the rule that we had to protect people from the effects of our battles. Very often, areas were cleared beforehand." [2] During that period, the I.R.A. directed its attacks against persons who provided the British with information regarding the Republicans and their activities. Michael Collins, another former commander-in-chief of the I.R.A., wrote that the organization conducted the conflict, as far as possible, in accordance with the rules of war. "Only the armed forces and the spies and criminal agents of the British government were attacked." [3]

In 1931, during the British Mandate over Palestine, a number of Jewish activists, dissatisfied with the purely defensive posture of other organizations, banded together to form the Irgun Zvai Leumi (National Military Organization), which eventually carried out reprisal raids against Arab terrorists in 1937 and assisted in smuggling thousands of Jews into Palestine during the Nazi era and the immediate post-World War II period. The Irgun was roundly criticized by the Jewish Agency and other organizations for its activities, but with a few major exceptions,[4] its targets were *not* civilians, but military personnel and installations. The attacks were aimed at crippling British military capabilities and acquiring arms and ammunition that were vital for future operations. In reaction against arrests, deportations, floggings, and hangings by the British, the Irgun flogged British officers and took military hostages, some of whom were hanged in retaliation for the hanging of Jewish guerrillas. A wing of the King David Hotel in Jerusalem, which served as headquarters of the British colonial government, was blown up. According to Menahem Begin, one of the Irgun's leaders and later Prime Minister of Israel, members of the Irgun took great risks in order to warn civilians away from areas that were to be attacked. He maintains that they had a strong sense of honor and propriety that would never have permitted them to engage in the kinds of tactics that have become commonplace in recent years. Their targets were strictly military, he says, or officials of the "enemy" government, never civilians. Occasionally, innocent civilians got in the way and were unavoidably injured or killed. Every such incident, according to Begin, was an occasion for deep regret and was regarded as one of the unfortunate byproducts of war. In contrast, he points out that civilians are precisely the targets most sought after by the P.L.O. and other Arab terrorists.[5]

A nineteenth-century example of a violent revolutionary group is the Narodnaya Volya in Russia. Selective assassination was one of its principal techniques, with the chief targets being police officials, policymakers, and government officials who were known for their brutality or their advocacy of repressive policies. Their ultimate target was the Czar, whom they assassinated in 1881. But they argued that they had no alternative, because the regime had closed all possible avenues of peaceful reform. Their leaders promised that if they saw signs of even the "possibility of an honest government," they would abandon terrorism.[6] Following the assassination of President Garfield, one of them wrote:

> In a land where the citizens are free to express their ideas, and where the will of the people does not merely make the law but appoints the person who is to carry the law into effect . . . political assassination is the manifestation of a despotic tendency identical with that to whose destruction in Russia we have devoted ourselves.[7]

As they saw it, their function as terrorists was to "liquidat[e] the worst government officials," to defend themselves against espionage, and to punish "the most outstanding acts of violence and despotism that the government and the administration commit."[8] When a bomb set in the dining room of the Winter Palace failed to go off when the Czar was having dinner, but killed eleven soldiers and wounded 56 more, the Executive Committee of Narodnaya Volya said:

> It is with great sorrow that we mourn the deaths of the unfortunate soldiers of the Imperial Guard. . . . But so long as the army remains the bastion of the imperial despotism . . . such tragic clashes are inevitable.[9]

It is possible to contend that the American Revolution was marked by terrorism, for some of the revolutionaries smeared their adversaries with tar and feathers, and in some instances, lynched them. However, it is clear that most of the actions of the American revolutionaries were directed against British forces. The Sons of Liberty, who are alleged to have been the most violent of the lot, seem to have been a rather unruly mob rather than a well-organized gang of terrorists. Even they vented their fury against British officials, on the whole, rather than against civilians who were not directly involved in the formulation or carrying out of British policy. To be sure, their actions were violent. But violence is not identical with terrorism and violent acts may not be terroristic.[10]

Not one of the organizations described here fits the definition of *terrorist* offered at the outset of this chapter. MacBride, Collins, and the early I.R.A. directed their fire at British officials "in accordance with the rules of war."[11] The Irgun went out of its way to avoid hitting civilian targets. The Russian revolutionaries of the nineteenth century engaged in assassination attempts, but these attempts were specifically directed at the tyrannical Czar, his police chiefs and agents. Special care was taken to avoid harming innocent bystanders, even when they were members of the royal family.[12] The most violent of the American revolutionaries attacked the king's militia and others who were considered to be spies, but not civilians who were not participating in the war. Civilians were not the targets of *any* of these groups. Their goals of overthrowing a repressive government and replacing it with one more responsive to their own views might have been identical with those of some terrorist organizations.

If some of these organizations were occasionally guilty of unjustifiable attacks upon civilians, it can at least be said of them that such attacks were not a part of their policies. When they did occur they were aberrations, excesses that were usually deplored by supporters of the causes for which those organizations were fighting and often even by members of the organizations themselves. These moral lapses, if they are that, are comparable to the excesses in which military forces conducting a lawful war sometimes indulge during the heat of battle or in the first flush of victory.

COMMON USAGE AND THE DEFINITION OF TERRORISM

Because deliberate and systematic attacks upon civilians were neither among the policies of the organizations described nor employed by them as normal tactics, such groups cannot be regarded as having engaged in terrorism as that term is defined here, though they (traditionally) have been regarded as terrorists, and their acts of assassination and sabotage have been considered, by themselves and their critics, to be acts of terrorism. Although these groups and individuals engaged in assassination, murder, bombing, and kidnapping, they focused their attacks upon their enemies, upon those whom they regarded as being cruel, despotic, tyrannical rulers, and their officers, agents, and spies. Occasionally, innocent persons might have been hurt by their operations, but such deaths and injuries were inadvertent and were usually a source of regret, even of sorrow, to those responsible. Whatever the law might say, a moral case can certainly be made in defense of such actions. It would be very difficult indeed to dream up an argument that would justify condemnation of the attempts to assassinate Hitler, for example, or the successful assassinations of a variety of other tyrants and their henchmen. When democratic processes for social change either do not exist or are unworkable, and when the people are in fact deprived of their fundamental human rights by a repressive regime, then violent and bloody rebellion may be the only way to achieve what are essentially moral ends. A discussion of the just-war concept would lead us too far afield,[13] but it is not inappropriate to observe, without further elaboration, that there is at least some good reason to believe that there *are* just wars, and by the same token, that there are just rebellions, just revolutions, and just struggles for national liberation. But the justice of such campaigns must depend upon the justice of both the ends sought and the means employed to reach those ends. The employment of means that result in disproportionate suffering or involve the deliberate infliction of grave injuries upon innocent persons may be sufficient to justify moral condemnation of the perpetrators of such acts despite the justice of their cause.

From a moral point of view, then, there are at least two significantly different forms of behavior that have traditionally been labelled as acts of terrorism. The victimization of defenseless, innocent persons is quite a different matter from the assassination of political and military leaders. Although both types of behavior have been called terroristic in common usage, the denotation of the term as it is employed in such uncritical ways is far too broad and imprecise to be of any use where finer distinctions must be made.

For the sake of precision and clarity, let it be stipulated that the word *terrorism* and its derivatives shall be employed only with reference to persons and organizations whose activities and policies fit the definition laid down at the beginning of this chapter. Other terms may then be reserved for other types of activity that may resemble terrorism to a greater or lesser degree.

EXAMPLES OF TERRORISTIC ACTS

In contrast to the revolutionary activities that have commonly been defined as terroristic, the following examples illustrate the precise meaning of terrorism.

A fairly typical attack by the Mau Mau in Kenya during the uprising in 1953 took the lives of 84 black Kenyans. The attackers also mutilated 31 others and burned a large number of huts. The black Kenyans who were murdered and mutilated were not government functionaries.[14] Later, hundreds of Kikuyu tribesmen were burned alive, and pregnant women and children were butchered.[15]

Friday, July 21, 1972, has become known as Bloody Friday in Ireland, for on that day the Provisional I.R.A. set off nineteen bombs in Belfast at one of the busiest hours of the afternoon. The first bomb went off at the Smithfield bus station, crowded with women and young children. Two bombs were in railway stations, another at a ferry terminal. Others exploded in shopping centers and other busy places. Nine persons were killed and 130 injured, including 77 women and girls, and 53 men and boys. It has been said that it was the heaviest attack on Belfast since the blitz in 1941.[16] Ten days later, three large bombs hidden in stolen cars went off, killing six and injuring 30. Among those killed were a nine-year-old girl and a mother of eight children.[17] In 1974, I.R.A. members blew up more cars, but this time in the center of London. Similar attacks continued through 1975, with bombings of tourist attractions, pubs, restaurants, and hotels. One of the worst incidents occurred in November, 1974, when a Birmingham pub was bombed, killing 21 and injuring 120.

In 1970 the F.L.Q., a terrorist group dedicated to the separation of the Province of Quebec from Canada, kidnapped James Cross, a British diplomat, and Pierre LaPorte, a prominent member of the Quebec National Assembly (the Provincial parliament). On the promise of safe conduct from Prime Minister Pierre Trudeau, the group holding Cross released him and left the country, but the gang holding LaPorte shot him and stuffed his body into the trunk of a car.[18]

The Palestinian terrorists, united under the banner of the Palestine Liberation Organization some years ago, provide the most extensive catalogue of terrorist operations in this decade. In 1970, the Popular Front for the Liberation of Palestine (P.F.L.P.) took credit for blowing up a Swiss aircraft bound for Israel, killing 47 passengers and crew, including 11 Israelis, justifying the attack on the ground that the 11 Israelis were allegedly "senior officials." [19]

On May 30, 1972, the P.F.L.P. raided Lod airport, using members of a Japanese terrorist organization to carry out the operation. Upon arriving at the airport, the terrorists brought their machine guns out of the cases in which they had been concealed, and proceeded to shoot indiscriminately into the crowds in the terminal. Twenty-seven persons—mostly Puerto Rican Christian tourists on a religious pilgrimage to the Holy Land—were killed and 71 wounded. "The killers," an editorial writer for *The Economist* (London) said, "were not bargaining for anything. There was virtually no connection between their physical targets and the object of their political disapproval. They were just squirting bullets to produce generalized terror." [20] Similarly, 32 passengers in a Pan American aircraft were murdered at Fiumicino Airport in December, 1973, when terrorists tossed grenades into the cabin.[21]

In April, 1974, the P.F.L.P. took credit for killing eight Israeli civilians, eight children, and two soldiers at Qiryat Shemona, a village whose population consists mostly of Jewish refugees from Arab lands, in northern Israel. A few days later, at Maalot, in the same general area, another band of terrorists from the same organization took a group of schoolchildren hostage, eventually killing 21 children and wounding 74 others.[22] Black September also murdered 11 members of Israel's Olympic team in Munich, in September, 1972.[23]

In March, 1973, eight Palestinian terrorists broke into the Saudi Arabian embassy in Khartoum and seized a number of hostages, including the American ambassador to Sudan, the U.S. Deputy Chief of Mission, and the Belgian Chargé. Many of the diplomats escaped while the terrorists were issuing their demands that various persons in Israel and Jordan, as well as members of the Baader-Meinhoff gang in West Germany, be released from the prisons in which they were being held. Upon the failure of negotiations, they murdered the three diplomats.[24]

At various times, letter bombs have been sent to persons, some of whom seem to have been selected at random, and time bombs have been set to go off while in the post office, their targets evidently being random postal employees.

Other hijackings, machine-gunnings, and bombings of aircraft are too numerous to mention, but special attention should be directed to the cold-blooded murder of a West German banker who was on a British DC-10 that had been hijacked from Dubai to Tunisia in 1974.[25]

This incomplete catalogue of some of the types of operations engaged in by terrorists should be sufficient to illustrate the distinctions between them and the revolutionary groups whose activities were listed before. The chief distinction lies in the randomness in the selection of victims. Revolutionaries concentrated their attacks upon members of the ruling power, whereas the terrorists have no compunctions about destroying innocent bystanders who lack even remote connections with the regimes against which they are battling.

TERRORISTS AND GUERRILLAS

Terrorists have become accustomed to claiming that they are engaged in guerrilla warfare. It is true that there are some resemblances between terrorists and guerrillas, but guerrillas do not behave like terrorists. To put the matter more accurately, by carefully distinguishing terrorism from the activities of certain revolutionary groups we are enabled to draw a useful distinction between guerrilla warfare and terrorism. Some of the groups that have engaged in guerrilla warfare have also engaged in terrorism, and others have not.

Guerrilla warfare is characterized by small-scale, unconventional, limited actions carried out by irregular forces *against regular military forces, their supply lines, and communications.* This has been the meaning of the term since its first use by the Spanish and Portuguese *guerrilleros* who joined the Duke of Wellington's forces during their Iberian campaigns against the French, blocking roads, intercepting couriers and convoys, and waging various forms of warfare against them. American colonists formed guerrilla bands to fight the redcoats during the Revolution. During the American Civil War, guerrillas under the command of John Mosby harassed the Union Army in Virginia. During World War II, guerrilla groups, sometimes called partisans, devoted themselves to the destruction of German communications, blowing up trains and trucks, and killing an estimated 250,000 German soldiers.[26]

Mao Tse-Tung was particularly emphatic about the necessity for the guerrilla to be able to survive for long periods of time behind the enemy's lines. The prevailing belief that this was impossible, he said, "reveals lack of comprehension of the relationship that should exist between the people and the troops. The former may be likened to water and the latter to the fish who inhabit it. How may it be said that these two cannot exist together? It is only undisciplined troops who make the people their enemies and who, like the fish out of its native element, cannot live." [27] Maltreatment of the people leads to precisely what Mao believed the guerrilla had to avoid at all costs: popular resistance. In fact, one of the tactics Mao used in winning the war was treating captured soldiers with consideration, and caring for those wounded who fell into his hands. "If we fail in these respects, we strengthen the solidarity of our enemy." [28] Similarly, General George Grivas, leader of the E.O.K.A. (National Organization of Cypriot Fighters), in defending his tactics against the British during his struggle to win the independence of Cyprus, indirectly made the same point:

> The British, who arm their commandos with knives and instruct them to kill . . . from the rear—protested vigorously when such tactics were applied to themselves. It may be argued that these things are only permissible in war. This is nonsense. I was fighting a war in Cyprus against the British, and if they did not recognize the fact from the start they were forced to at the end. *The truth is that our form of war,* in which a few hundred fell in four years, *was more selective than most,* and I speak as one who has seen battle-fields covered with dead. *We did not strike, like the bomber, at random. We shot only British servicemen* who would have killed us if they could have fired first, *and civilians who were traitors or intelligence agents.* To shoot down your enemies in the street may be unprecedented, but I was looking for results, not precedents. [29]

It has been suggested that terrorism is one of the tactics of guerrilla warfare. But on closer analysis, it turns out that the terrorism to which reference is made consists of assassinations of military and political leaders, sneak attacks on military installations, and other actions designed to weaken and destroy the morale of the enemy. This is different from the indiscriminate killing of civilians that is the hallmark of terrorism as defined herein. Guerrilla warfare has certain fairly well-defined characteristics. Despite the fact that some of those characteristics are shared in common with present-day terrorists, others are not and should be perceived as essential differences between them. To broaden the meaning of *every* term that refers to irregular armed forces so that it will encompass both those who fight honorably against the armies of enemy regimes and those that attempt to overthrow them by attacks on the weak and the defenseless is to debase and cheapen our language, to obscure thought, to render clear analysis and meaningful moral judgment impossible. The word *guerrilla* should be reserved for those irregular forces that operate against regular military machines and against those who are actively collaborating with the enemy during wartime (spies, saboteurs, and informers). The word *terrorist,* however, applies to persons and groups engaged in irregular activities that are directed against civilians and other nonmilitary targets.

OFFICIAL TERRORISM

Nothing in the definition of terrorism precludes the possibility of a government being regarded as a terroristic regime. Indeed, certain periods of history have been rightly dubbed "reigns of terror," for the principal characters who played official roles in them were terrorists and employed the methods of terrorism, under color of law, to achieve their political objectives.

Torquemada and the Spanish Inquisitors tortured their victims and committed judicial murder on a massive scale.

During the period between (roughly) September, 1793, and August, 1794, the French experienced a reign of terror that has seldom been equalled anywhere. The French National Convention authorized the notorious Committee of Public Safety and its agents to arrest, without warning, "any returned emigré, any relative of an emigré, any public official suspended and not reinstated, anyone who had given any sign of opposition to the Revolution or the war." [30] Nearly all nonrevolutionists were thus put in constant fear of arrest and death. After the execution of Queen Marie Antoinette, the Revolutionary Tribunal issued an average of seven death sentences per day.[31] Representatives of the Committee, possessed of almost absolute authority and charged with the responsibility of bringing the provinces into line, carried out their mission mercilessly. One man alone, who had been warned by the Committee to beware of "false and mistaken humanity," slaughtered about 550 men and women in a few weeks, working "in a sort of fever," according to his secretary. Another, objecting that trials were a waste of time, exterminated 4,000 human beings in four months. Enraged by a political and military reverse in Lyons, Robespierre ordered the demolition of the city. Hundreds of prisoners were marched in front of trenches and blown into them by cannon blasts, until nearly 2,000 had been executed.[32]

No more than the name of Hitler need be mentioned to remind one of the most insane and brutal reigns of terror in all of history. If that is insufficient, a few additional names may revive the reader's memory: Nuremberg, Lidice, The Warsaw Ghetto, Auschwitz, Bergen-Belsen, and Treblinka.

Stalin and many of the czars who preceded him as absolute monarchs of the Russian people and their neighbors used terrorist tactics to acquire sovereignty or to keep it, and sometimes simply to demonstrate the totality of their power and the inexorability of their wills.

No legal system can exist without sanctions of some kind. If a legal system is just on the whole, and if its rules are enforced with due regard to the principles of truth and justice, then the use of force by the police and the courts does not in itself constitute any form of terrorism. However, corrupt management of the government, deprivation of what the people perceive to be their fundamental rights, and the use of state power in furtherance of such deprivations comes close to being state terrorism and may easily cross the border into outright terrorism of the most frightful sort. It is exceedingly difficult to overcome terrorism cloaked in the appearance of legitimacy that is conferred by control of state institutions and the enormous power wielded by those who are able to command a nation's military machine. Those who possess that power can use it to crush almost any opposition and to inflict enormous damage upon large numbers of innocent persons.

State terror has often grown out of revolutionary terror. The very people whose revolutionary propaganda included appeals to the rights of man and rhetoric based upon the ideals of freedom, liberty, equality, and justice often continued to employ the methods that brought them to the seats of power on a wider and grander scale once they had achieved their aims, under the assumption that such methods would help them to maintain the power they had won. The French, the Russian, and the Chinese revolutions all illustrate the point. It is in fact almost impossible to find examples of men who have ridden into power on a campaign of terrorism whose regimes have later turned out to be models of liberalism. This may be a consequence of the fact that terrorist ideologies have little if anything to do with freedom. They are principally designed to provide a justification for carrying on the battle in the particularly vicious manner the terrorists have chosen to pursue, but have little to say about the society that is to emerge once the campaign has succeeded in removing the hated old regime. Terrorist rhetoric plays upon the positive emotive force of such words as "freedom" and "liberty," but their value is largely exhausted once they have produced the desired propaganda effect. A terrorist may have only the most rudimentary conception of the political and philosophical foundations of democracy and freedom and still find that the terms suit his purposes very well indeed. He may have only the vaguest notion of the kind of society he aspires to construct, but with single-minded dedication may be satisfied to concentrate upon his immediate goal, and leave more remote enterprises to a later time. His rhetoric—largely derived from Marxist sources in the contemporary world—is one of his most important weapons.

TERRORIST IDEOLOGY AND RHETORIC

Terrorists act as if *no* law applied to them, as if they were above the law. Any form of behavior, however atrocious it might be in the eyes of civilized men and women, is justified in the terrorist's mind if it succeeds in achieving the limited goal for which it was designed and thus in helping the cause along toward its long-range objectives. The Petrograd *Red Gazette*, for example, defended the Red Terror, in which thousands of persons were summarily shot and others slowly starved to death after Lenin was hit by two bullets fired at him by a Social Revolutionary terrorist:

> Sentimental fools who are afraid of shedding innocent blood should step aside! How many deaths of women and children of the working class are on the conscience of each bourgeois! No one is innocent. Each drop of Lenin's blood will cost the bourgeoisie and the Whites hundreds of dead.[33]

Karl Kautsky, one of Marxism's chief theoreticians, wondered what possible difference there might be between Bolshevik terror and Czarist terror.[34] In response, Trotsky wrote:

> Don't you understand, you saintly man? Let us explain. Tsarist terror was directed against the proletariat. The Tsarist police crushed workers who were

struggling for a socialist regime. Our Extraordinary Commissions, on the other hand, shoot landowners, capitalists, and generals, all of whom are doing their best to restore capitalism. Do you see the difference? For us Communists, it is clear enough to justify our actions.[35]

Between 1918 and 1920, this reasoning was used to justify at least 13,000 executions, and probably far more than that.[36]

In discussing revolutionary ethics, Lenin said that the Communists' morality "is entirely subordinated to . . . [and] derived from the interests of the class struggle of the proletariat. Morality is that which serves to destroy the old exploiting society and to unite all the toilers around the proletariat, which is creating a new Communist society." [37] This conviction that violence is legitimate and that politics is to be pursued with guns prepared Lenin's followers to engage in terrorism, which he sanctioned in numerous publications. He insisted that Marxists never "invented" any forms of struggle, but "merely organize[d] the tactics of strife and render[ed] them suitable for general use." More importantly, he said, "Marxism rejects all abstract thinking and doctrinaire prescriptions about types of struggle," remaining ever ready to adopt new and different methods of defense and attack as the conflict develops. "In this field," he said, "Marxism is *learning* from the practice of the masses." [38] Thus, the ultimate criteria of the morality of any particular method of attack are its effectiveness and the fact that it is being employed by Marxist fighters. Conventional moral terms and arguments were totally rejected as being irrelevant. "[I]n the name of Marxist principles, we must insist that civil war be analyzed seriously and that shopworn phrases such as anarchism, Blanquism [a particularly heinous and callous form of terrorism] and terrorism not be thrown into the debate." [39]

The rhetoric of contemporary terrorist ideologies is full of certain catch-phrases and emotionally charged terms designed to justify violent methods. One such term employed by terrorists, and often adopted by news commentators and others, is *political prisoner*, used to refer to any bomb thrower, murderer, arsonist, bank robber, kidnapper, or hijacker who cloaks his actions in political rhetoric. Terrorists expect these political prisoners to be treated as a select class of prisoner different from ordinary persons who commit the same crimes. Presumably, the fact that they espouse revolutionary doctrines while planting their bombs, setting conflagrations, and causing the deaths of innocent persons makes the authorities guilty of punishing them for exercising their rights of free speech.

In fact, "liberty" in this new language doesn't resemble the term as it is used by most other persons. The freedom to speak, write, or publish any opinion, to travel abroad without restriction, to reside where one pleases, to buy and sell almost anything, to worship in a place and in a manner of one's own choosing or to refrain from any religious practice, to join with neighbors in the furtherance of causes (within what most people consider to be reasonable legal limits)—none of this counts as "liberty" in the terrorist's new vocabulary. As he demands "liberation," he not only fails to explain what new liberties he intends to offer those whom he claims are enslaved and exploited, he also takes it upon himself to "liberate" them from their lives if they fail to join him, on the ground that they are "collaborating" with the "enemy." Those who presumably are to benefit from the terrorist's programs are not consulted; they are given no vote. No matter how small or unrepresentative of the total population the terrorist's band may be, its members presume that *their* form of paternalism is wholly justifiable and that they have a perfect right to decide for the "masses" what kind of "democracy" the latter are to live in. Like Plato's philosopher-king, the terrorist has a direct insight into the fundamental truths of politics, and therefore he need not consult with the *Lumpenproletariat* [40] who know less about what they *really* want than this self-appointed guardian of their interests.

We can gain an excellent insight into the true meaning of terrorist rhetoric if we examine the pronouncements of the various Palestinian terrorist groups.[41] The Palestinian terrorist movement as a whole is characterized as a "liberation" movement, which its leaders hail as "another historical example of a people's inevitable triumph over colonialism, racism, and oppression." [42] The existence of a small, independent, Jewish state is somehow regarded as colonialist, racist, and oppressive, but the destruction of that state and the banishment of its Jewish citizens constitutes a form of liberation and is neither racist nor oppressive. Yasir Arafat explains further:

> The United Nations charter gives all peoples the right to self-determination. Not only are we deprived of this right, but of our country itself. So every Palestinian, wherever he is, is a victim of the same injustice practiced against him. This feeling was the common motive for all Palestinians to regain their identity, their nationality, and their homeland through armed struggle. Since we are facing an enemy supported by imperialist funds and technical achievements, we have chosen long-term war as the strategy for our struggle. . . . This leads to enemy exhaustion through continuous operations, whether by attacking military and industrial targets or by destroying shipping lines wherever they are. Finally comes the stage of liberation of areas on the way to total liberation. . . .[43]

Here again, an interesting double standard is apparent: The Israelis are supported by "imperialist" funds and technology, but the Arabs, who have been given financial, political, and military aid by the Soviet Union, which is probably the world's largest and most ruthless colonial power,[44] are presumably free of any taint of trafficking with imperialists. Similarly, the "liberation" of Palestine from its Jewish occupiers by terroristic methods would presumably be consistent with the U.N. Charter's guarantee of the right to self-determination—a right which evidently applies to all the peoples of the world with the single notable exception of the Israelis.

The Palestinian National Covenant, adopted by the Palestinian National Council in Cairo in 1968, summarizes the principal positions of the Palestinian organizations involved in the conflict with Israel. Among its articles are the following:

(Article 5) The Palestinians are the Arab citizens who were living permanently in Palestine until 1947, whether they were expelled from there or remained. Whoever is born to a Palestinian Arab father after this date, within Palestine or outside it, is a Palestinian.

(Article 6) Jews who were living permanently in Palestine until the beginning of the Zionist invasion will be considered Palestinians.[45]

The differences between Jewish and Arab Palestinians are striking. Even more striking, however, is the term "Zionist invasion," which was defined in a resolution of the Congress as having begun in 1917. Evidently those Jews who arrived after 1917, the vast majority of the Jewish population of Israel, are to be regarded as aliens in the newly liberated Palestine and subject to deportation.

After declaring that *fedayeen* (terrorist) action "forms the nucelus of the popular Palestinian War of Liberation," (Article 10), and invoking Arab unity and the "sacred national aim" of "the destiny of the Arab nation," (Article 14), the Covenant continues:

(Article 15) The liberation of Palestine, from an Arab viewpoint, is a national duty to repulse the Zionist, Imperialist invasion from the great Arab homeland and to purge the Zionist presence from Palestine. . . .

The struggle of the Palestinian people to liberate Palestine is "necessitated by the requirements of self-defense," (Article 18), so that there is international legal sanction of *fedayeen* assaults upon Israel. However, since Israel is an illegal entity in the first place—the U.N. partition of 1947 and the Balfour Declaration both being null and void (Articles 19 and 20)— Israel's attempts to defend itself are nothing more than extensions of the original aggression which begot the state. In any case, there is no historical or spiritual tie between Jews and Palestine, for "Jews are not one people with an independent personality. They are rather citizens of the states to which they belong" (Article 20). Hence, Jews have no claim of any kind to Israel or any other state, for they are not a people. The Arab Palestinians, being a people, have the only legitimate claim to that territory. Finally:

(Article 22) Zionism is a political movement organically related to world imperialism and hostile to all movements of liberation and progress in the world. It is a racist and fanatical movement in its formation; aggressive, expanionist, and colonialist in its aims; and Fascist and Nazi in its means. Israel is . . . a concentration and jumping-off point for imperialism in the heart of the Arab homeland, to strike at the hopes of the Arab nation for liberation, unity and progress.

Thus the groundwork was laid for the General Assembly's resolution in November, 1975, to the effect that Zionism is a form of racism.[46] The loaded terminology in each of these paragraphs is obvious. But some of the contradictions must be emphasized. Jews who struggle for national liberation are racist tools of imperialism, whereas Arabs who want to "purge the Zionist presence" are merely fulfilling their national destiny. Jews who were born and educated in Israel of parents who were also born and educated there are not Palestinians and have no right to be there, but Arabs born in Kuwait to fathers of Palestinian ancestry who were born in Egypt *are* Palestinians and have a right to "return" to their "homeland." However, a Jew whose grandfather left Egypt for the land of Israel in 1920 is an Egyptian. (He could not be a Kuwaiti or a Saudi Arabian, of course, because Jews have never been allowed to live in those democratic republics.)

TERRORISTS AND THE LAW OF NATIONS

The law, then, does not apply to terrorists, for they have a sacred mission to perform, a mission that cannot be limited by mere considerations of lawfulness or morality. By the very nature of their conception of their mission, it is impossible for terrorists to adhere to either domestic or international codes, conventions, and usages that have been designed to maintain order, preserve life and property, minimize the horrors of war and place limits upon the conduct of fighting men. For the terrorist, such laws merely stand in his way and obstruct the path to true justice as he sees it. They were established to protect the Established Order that he is dedicated to destroying. Nevertheless, to the extent that these laws are founded upon principles of justice and decency, they offer a measure of protection for all who come under their dominion, including even those who refuse to abide by them. The nations of the world are fully entitled to demand that all persons abide by them and to employ all reasonable measures, including the imposition of sanctions, upon those who choose to place themselves outside the law.

According to Article 22 of the Hague Regulations, "the belligerents have not an unlimited right as to the means they adopt for injuring the enemy." [47] And the Geneva Conventions of 1949 specify that even if parties to the convention should denounce it, they are nevertheless bound by "the principles of the law of nations, as they result from the usages established among civilized peoples, from the laws of humanity and dictates of public conscience." [48] According to the laws of war, even noncombatant members of armed forces, to say nothing of private enemy persons showing no hostile conduct, are exempt from major applications of force, since they are not taking part in the armed conflict itself and since the purpose of violence is so to disable combatants that they can no longer participate in the fighting. [49] Private enemy persons who do not take part in the fighting "may not be directly attacked and killed or wounded." [50] The Geneva Convention of 1949 specifies that the murder, mutilation, cruel treatment, and torture of prisoners is forbidden, and that the taking of hostages is outlawed. [51] Although no terrorist group has signed these conventions or treaties, the treaties do represent the conscience of civilized humanity.

The utter contempt that present-day terrorists have for the norms of international law and morality is demonstrated by the fact that they not only violate these norms, they deliberately and systematically adopt and carry out policies that are diametrically opposed to them. Not only noncombatants, but even subjects of neutral states are murdered—frequently on neutral territory. The bodies of dead victims are desecrated. Prisoners are subjected to cruel treatment, are held out as hostages, and are murdered when it serves the terrorists' purposes.[52]

Private individuals who commit hostilities, even during time of war, have been treated as war criminals.[53] And any of the acts listed here is generally regarded as a war crime, even when perpetrated during regular hostilities.[54] Because terrorists make regular use of such practices, they must be regarded as criminals, and their organizations condemned as criminal bands. The precise nature of this criminality deserves further attention at this point.

TERRORISTS: ENEMIES OF MANKIND

The term *hostes humani generis* has traditionally been reserved for pirates, who were generally private persons roving the sea in armed vessels for the purpose of seizing by force whatever ships or vessels they might choose to plunder.[55] As time went on, the term piracy was broadened to include numerous other offenses that were committed upon the high seas or from ships sailing the high seas. Terrorism is clearly not piracy in the classical sense. Neither the traditional international law of piracy nor the statutes dealing with that crime apply directly to terrorism. However, the parallels between piracy and terrorism are so striking—both as regards the offenses committed by the perpetrators of such crimes and as regards their effects upon international commerce and the peace and security of nations and their inhabitants—that many of the principles that once dealt with piracy should, today, be applied to terrorism as well.

Chief Justice Story, in *United States* v. *The Brig Malek Adhel*, explained that pirates are regarded as enemies of mankind because they commit "hostilities upon the subjects and property of any or all nations, without any regard to right or duty, or any pretense of public authority." [56] Nicholas Trott, Judge of the Vice-Admirality and Chief Justice of the Province of Carolina (1703–1729), in sentencing some defendants convicted of piracy, said of their crime:

> It is so destructive of all trade and commerce between nation and nation, that pirates are called enemies to mankind with whom no faith or oath ought to be kept; and they are termed in our law brutes and beasts of prey, and therefore it is in the interests, as well as the duty, of all governments to bring such offenders to punishment.[57]

Sir Leoline Jenkins, an admiralty judge of the seventeenth century, explained that what is called robbery on land is called piracy if it is committed upon the sea. Piracy consists of three things: A violent assault, the removal of a man's goods from his possession or person, and placing the victim in fear. In explaining what is meant by calling pirates *hostes humani generis,* he said that they were:

> Enemies, not of one nation, or of one sort of people only, but of all mankind. They are outlawed as I may say, by the laws of all nations; that is, out of the protection of all princes, and of all laws whatsoever.[58]

Robbery was not the only crime that constituted piracy. In *United States v. Pirates,* one of the defendants, John Furlong, was found guilty of "piratical murder." [59] More recently, the definition of piracy has been extended to cover "generally ruthless acts of lawlessness on the high seas by whomsoever committed." [60] According to some commentators, piracy is best defined as "any armed violence at sea which is not a lawful act of war," for although most pirates are merely "robber[s] of the vulgarest and cruelest kind," the term includes "acts done by unauthorized persons for political ends." [61]

Pirates were regarded as enemies of mankind because they acknowledged no law, because they acted as if they were a law unto themselves. As Hobbes put it, if a man refuses to submit to the decrees of those who set up civil societies, he is "left in the condition of war he was in before, wherein he might without injustice be destroyed by any man whatsoever." [62] To be sure, the system of international law is still frail and rudimentary, but there is clearly *some* sense [63] in which such a system does exist. In any event, it is the principal means adopted by the peoples of the world to assure peace among nations. One who flouts this fragile system, who transgresses against the sovereign rights of peoples and governments in their own territories or who violates the fundamental norms of international society, must stand condemned as an international outlaw and be regarded as if he had in fact declared war upon the system and upon all who owe allegiance to it and to the values it is designed to preserve.

The terrorists of the present day clearly fall into this category. They respect no international boundaries. The laws of no nation are sacred in their eyes. Flying from one country to another, spreading death and destruction, they recklessly murder young children, Olympic athletes, and innocent and unsuspecting passengers. They bomb public and private buildings without regard to the consequences of their acts. Because one of the chief purposes of terrorist actions is the achievement of maximum publicity for the deed, the more horrendous it is, the greater is the likelihood of "success."

The inviolability of diplomatic envoys, a vital principle of civilized international discourse that has been recognized and accepted since antiquity, is treated with disdain by these criminals. From Khartoum to Montreal they have assaulted, kidnapped, and murdered diplomats representing states that are presumably neutral relative to the terrorists and have little or nothing to do with the political ambitions of the "liberation" movements to which the latter belong.[64] But none of this is deemed relevant so long as they believe that they are furthering their causes.

If ever there was a justification for describing a class of persons as enemies of mankind, this must be it. If history provides any precedent, then the reaction of Thomas Jefferson to the depredations of the Barbary pirates against American vessels should provide one. The United States had been sending enormous sums of "protection" money to them. In October, 1800, the Dey of Algiers forced an American man-of-war, the *George Washington*, to haul down the American flag and raise that of Algiers. When the captain protested his being forced to pay blackmail to the sultan, the Dey replied, "You pay me tribute, by which you become my slaves. I have, therefore, a right to order you as I may think proper." [65] Jefferson concluded, "Tribute or war is the usual alternative of these Barbary pirates. Why not build a navy and decide on war?" [66] Why not indeed?

PIRACY AND TERRORISM

One might suppose that any attempt to draw an analogy between piracy and terrorism is bound to fail because pirates were principally interested in personal gain, whereas terrorists are principally interested in political change. It is certainly true that many pirates were simply brigands of the sea, comparable to ordinary robbers and murderers. But some and by all accounts the most important used their power to gain political positions and to build mighty military machines. Arouj Barbarossa, for example, started out as a private adventurer, but swiftly gathered power and influence all along the North African coast. He and his brother Khizr (also known as Kheyr-ed-din and, after Arouj's death, as Barbarossa) cultivated the political and religious leaders of Oran, Bougie, Tunis, Algiers, and other coastal towns. In the first quarter of the sixteenth century Arouj had virtually become king of Algeria and extended his rule into Tunis and Tilimsan. He took over Algiers in 1516 by taking advantage of local unrest, marching in with 5000 men, and personally strangling the ruler.[67] Khizr Barbarossa engaged in considerable political maneuvering, declaring himself the humble vassal of the Ottoman Empire, one of the super-powers of the day. By 1538 his fleet outmatched the combined naval forces of Venice, Spain, and the Pope, and a few years later he was able to take on the combined navies of all Christendom.[68]

Despite numerous attempts by Britain, France, Spain, and others to exterminate the corsairs or at least bring them under control, they constituted one of the greatest threats to international commerce in the Mediterranean and on the Atlantic and were able to exact tribute from every maritime power in Europe and later in North America. Kidnappings, murders, enslavement, and plunder continued on a grand scale until France subjugated the entire area in 1820.[69]

The acts perpetrated by terrorists are as monstrous as those perpetrated by the pirates. They have precisely the same consequences upon the world community—disrupting international commerce, the free flow of goods and persons from one place to another; depriving persons of the right to move about and participate in innocent activities free of the fear that they may be put in deadly peril for no other reason than that they happen to be there when the attacker chooses to strike; hampering the free exchange of ideas by placing psychological obstacles in the way of tourists, scholars, and scientists who are deterred from attending international congresses by their fear of possible attack; and most important of all, subjecting persons to terrifying ordeals, using them as unwilling pawns in deadly political games, assaulting them, kidnapping them, and murdering them.

How then do they differ? Surely not because the terrorists are better sloganeers than the pirates used to be. Some pirates were first-rate sloganeers and would have been among the most admired terrorists in the world if they were around today. The French Captain Misson, for example, was a scholar, an idealist, founder of the Republic of Libertatia and a vicious thief and murderer. These are his words to his pirate crew:

> Since you have unanimously resolved to seize upon and defend your liberty which ambitious men had usurped, I recommend that you display a brotherly love to each other; the banishment of all private piques and grudges and a strict agreement and harmony among yourselves. In throwing off the yoke of tyranny I hope that none of you will follow the example of the tyrants, and turn your back upon justice; for when equity is trodden underfoot, misery, confusion and mutual distress naturally follow. . . .[70]

However, he pointed out, there are men who would not accept the freedom that they had so dearly won, and would brand them with the invidious name of *pirates*, thinking that it would be meritorious to destroy them. Like Yasir Arafat and George Habash, Misson declared war upon all those unjust and tyrannical persons and governments who refused to acquiesce in his demand that they supply him with whatever he chose to take.

The actions of contemporary terrorists are so similar to those of pirates that we are fully justified in seeking guidance in the laws of piracy. The arena of their activities is similar inasmuch as it cuts across international boundaries. They utilize today's equivalent of sailing vessels. Like the pirates, they take hostages for ransom, for the release of prisoners, and for various forms of blackmail. They commit their crimes with the same callous disregard for the victim and the consequences that befall others.

Moreover, international law *must* be invoked because the relative ease with which terrorists are able to move from state to state makes it impossible to appeal to domestic law in most instances. The international character of terrorist activity is well illustrated by the French airliner from Tel Aviv that was hijacked in Athens and taken to Uganda by Arab terrorists who had flown into Greece from other nations. Finally, there seems to be no other category in international law that matches the behavior of terrorists as closely as that of piracy.

THE INTERNATIONAL CONNECTION

Despite the efforts that many terrorist organizations have evidently made to coalesce into a single world conspiracy, there is little likelihood that such a coalition will be formed successfully or that it would be viable for long if it were. The internecine battles of the various groups—most notably the constituent organizations of the P.L.O.—provide the best possible evidence for this.[71] But it is obvious that the various national movements do work together, providing one another with instruction, training grounds, weapons, places of refuge, and propaganda support whenever it is needed.[72]

No more than a few examples are needed to establish the existence of the international cooperation of these groups.[73]

In December, 1973, the French arrested 13 suspected revolutionaries, including Turks, Palestinians, and an Algerian. The Turks, members of the Popular Liberation Front of Turkey, had been trained by the Arabs in revolutionary warfare. A few days later, an American woman possessing arms and ammunition was arrested at Heathrow Airport with a Moroccan who had met her, and this was followed by the arrest of a Pakistani associate. The Moroccan belonged to a group seeking the deposition of King Hassan II.[74]

In January, 1974, British intelligence disclosed that links between the I.R.A. and the Arabs had been discovered, and that the Arabs had agreed to cooperate in terrorist attacks in Britain.[75]

In France, the Breton Liberation Front has cooperated with the I.R.A. and Basque separatists.[76]

Members of the Japanese *Renyo Sikigum* terrorist organization undertook the Lod airport massacre on behalf of their Arab friends,[77] and Philippine members of the Moslem International Guerrillas seized a Greek freighter to coerce the Greek government into commuting the death sentences of some Arab terrorists who had been captured there.[78]

Palestinian groups have received aid from groups in Trieste and West Germany, including most notably the Baader-Meinhoff gang, and have in turn attempted to secure the release of the latter from the German prisons in which they have been incarcerated.[79]

The seizure of the Saudi embassy in Khartoum, engineered (according to Sudanese President Numeiry) by Yasir Arafat and the P.L.O., was intended, at least in part, to win the release of Sirhan Sirhan (Robert Kennedy's assassin), Arabs detained in Israel, and members of the Baader-Meinhoff gang.[80]

There is no proof of the existence of a worldwide conspiracy or a network of terrorist gangs that is manipulated by a central control. But there can be no doubt about the contributions made to the various groups of terrorists by certain communist powers.[81] Nor do these powers conceal their determination to "liberate" all the countries of Africa, Asia, and Latin America. Their writings have made it clear time and again that their messianic vision extends to the entire world, and that they believe that the forces of history, which must be helped along by them, are operating in such a manner as to assure the eventual conversion of the entire globe to communism.

RESPONSES TO TERRORISM

It has been suggested that international cooperation through the United Nations could produce concrete solutions to the international terrorist threat. However, the ability of the United Nations to engage in creative endeavors to deal with terrorists and generally to improve the prospects for world peace has been destroyed by the obsession of the Arab and Communist blocs with the Arab-Israel dispute and by their determination to expunge Israel from the community of nations. The paralysis of the U.N. with regard to terrorists is complete, and hence no solution can possibly come from it.

It follows that if any positive action against terrorism is to be undertaken it must begin either with unilateral acts on the part of states that are determined to deal forcefully with the issue, or with small alliances of like-minded states. Because the vital interests of states are at stake, either unilateral or joint action is fully justified.

All civilized states should consider terrorists and terrorist organizations to be implacable foes that must be eliminated as a danger to every state's very existence. They are enemies of mankind, a menace to world peace and order, and a threat to civilization.

Unilateral action may take the form of legislation forbidding the payment of ransom, the offer of safe passage, the release of so-called political prisoners, or the making of political concessions. Such legislation would discourage terrorists from attempting to employ these tactics.

Steadfast resistance to the temptation to negotiate with terrorists would help eliminate one of the chief sources of terrorist publicity, and thus deprive them of success in achieving one of their main objectives. Compassion may seem to dictate that every effort be made to save hostages, that their lives ought to be the principal consideration. However, there are limits to the lengths to which honorable governments can go in order to save their nationals from violent and lawless persons and organizations. The Italian government gave a particularly dramatic and heartrending demonstration of adherence to this principle when it refused to accede to the demands of the Red Brigades, a terrorist organization that had kidnapped Aldo Moro, a former Premier of Italy. In April, 1978, when it became clear that the government would not compromise, the terrorists murdered their hostage. Though there is always a strong likelihood that hostages will be murdered, more lives are likely to be saved if potential kidnappers and hijackers are deterred from carrying out their designs. Terrorists should be forewarned that if the lives of some hostages must be lost, no effort will be spared to bring them to justice, and that under no circumstances will they be permitted to escape with hostages. In any case, if a government does negotiate under duress, it should not feel morally bound to fulfill any conditions to which it has assented. It may act as it sees fit—in its own interest and in that of others most directly concerned—despite promises or agreements it may have made.

The highest responsibility of any government lies in the protection of its citizens' lives. The dramatic rescue by Israeli forces of Air France passengers who were being held hostage by Arab hijackers at Entebbe Airport in Uganda [82] is a striking case of a government's acting on that principle. The community of nations should explicitly recognize the right of any state to rescue its citizens in such situations, even though such rescue cannot be effected without an intrusion into the territory of a sovereign state. In the absence of such recognition, states whose citizens are in mortal peril as a result of such criminal behavior may resort to self-help to effect a rescue when other acceptable means of securing the hostages' release seem unlikely to be successful.

Joint action by states can also serve to deter terrorists. Not only the states directly concerned but all others should lawfully pursue the terrorists wherever they may flee. When appropriate treaties exist, terrorists should be extradited for prosecution in the states most directly offended by their acts. But any state may prosecute them and punish them according to its own or to international laws.

Air piracy should be treated as classical sea piracy. If a flight is international or connects with flights that are international in character, any hijacking connected with it should be punishable as an act of air piracy, regardless of the hijacker's motives.[83]

The Draft Convention on Piracy did not allow for hot pursuit of pirates into the territorial waters of an alien state if that state had prohibited such pursuit.[84] Nor could one initiate a pursuit of a pirate ship or seize it within the territorial jurisdiction of another state. In the context of contemporary air piracy, these qualifications should be rejected, despite the potentially serious consequences of pursuing terrorists into a state that is willing to grant them refuge and that prohibits such hot pursuit. Modern conditions of transport render such limitations obsolete. A jet aircraft can move in and out of national jurisdictions in a matter of minutes. In the days of galleons and sailing ships, chases might last for hours or days, and battles on the high seas were not only possible but very likely. The chances of a pirate ship's making it to a friendly harbor were no greater than those of a pursuing ship's being able to cut it off before it reached its refuge. Such considerations are meaningless today.

No state should give refuge to terrorists or permit any person under its jurisdiction to protect, conceal, or assist them in any manner whatever. Every nation should endeavor to punish all persons guilty of such acts. Any nation that shelters terrorists should be given fair warning that if it persists, it will be adjudged an international outlaw and that appropriate sanctions, ranging from partial or complete interruption of economic relations, of rail, sea, air, postal, telegraphic, radio and other means of communication, and the severance of diplomatic relations to blockade, invasion, or open warfare, will be applied, depending upon the gravity of the offense and the persistence of the offender in pursuing its policy.

Granting refuge to terrorists who are engaging in depredations against sister states is an act of war. War should be avoided wherever possible and disputes should ideally be settled peaceably rather than by force of arms, but no self-respecting power should shrink from its national and international responsibilities by not responding forcefully to acts of war that threaten its stability, its national security, its citizens' lives, and its territorial integrity. If a sister state harbors terrorists, and if all efforts should fail to bring either their depredations or that state's protection of them to an end, then punitive expeditions would be perfectly appropriate.[85]

Terrorists should be entitled to a fair trial before an impartial tribunal, humane treatment during confinement, and no cruel and inhuman punishment. But this does not preclude the possibility of their being subject to the death penalty, which is not excessive considering the nature of the crimes terrorists commit. Some argue that the death penalty would create martyrs for terrorist movements and help them on their way toward political victory. A glance at a list of terrorist incidents and the ultimate disposition of the terrorists reveals that a very large number of them are captured but are eventually released or otherwise regain their freedom.[86] Terrorism is certainly a hazardous occupation, but the odds are not all against the terrorist, particularly if he is a member of one of the larger, more militant organizations. A significant increase in the number of deaths might discourage some who might otherwise succumb to the romance of the terrorist's life.

Concern that the death penalty would merely assure the deaths of hostages because their captors would face certain death anyway is misplaced. Kamikaze-type terrorists will not be deterred by any threat. Others are likely to assume, or at least to hope, that they will be able to escape death in one way or another. Some of them, at least, would rather give up than commit suicide, just as many felons who are arrested for capital crimes give up to face a jury in preference to battling it out with the police. There is no easy way to deal with such persons. However, the death penalty may be a more effective deterrent to potential terrorists than mere imprisonment.

As Walter Laqueur recently observed, "If governments did not give in to terrorist demands, there would be no terror, or it would be very much reduced in scale. . . . [Giving in] may save a few human lives in the short run, but it is an invitation to further such acts and greater bloodshed." [87]

During the week of April 20, 1975, some anarchists seized the West German embassy in Stockholm and demanded that the Bonn government release 26 of their comrades from prison. Chancellor Schmidt steadfastly refused to bow to these demands, despite the terrorists' threat to blow up the embassy building and to kill twelve hostages. In the end, two embassy employees were killed, the ambassador and a number of other hostages were wounded, some of them seriously, one of the terrorists was killed, and the other five were jailed. Chancellor Schmidt said afterward, "The plague of international terrorism needs international cooperation," and assured the world of West Germany's full cooperation in combatting terrorism in the future. The Israeli raid on the terrorist-held Entebbe Airport in Uganda, the West German raid on a terrorist-held airliner in Mogadishu, Somalia, and the Dutch raid on a passenger train that was being held by South Moluccan terrorists all followed refusals by the governments concerned to bow to terrorist demands. They were risky operations—risky to the hostages, risky to the military men who carried out the raids, and in the long run, risky to the governments that gambled with the lives of many innocent people rather than submit to the escalating demands of the terrorists. But the alternative was even riskier: the reinforcement of terrorist organizations, inflation of their self-esteem, enhancement of their public image, and encouragement of more ambitious terrorist operations in the future. A firm stand must be taken at some point, for the only alternative is total capitulation to the terrorists and the destruction of democratic governments.

Chapter Notes

Chapter 1. Lord Devlin and the Enforcement of Morals

1. The Wolfenden Report, entitled "Report of the Committee on Homosexual Offences and Prostitution Presented to Parliament by the Secretary of State for the Home Department and the Secretary of State for Scotland by Command of Her Majesty," September 1957 (Cmmd. 247), para. 13.
2. Ibid.
3. Ibid., para. 61.
4. Ibid., para. 247.
5. Ibid., para. 257.
6. Sir Patrick Devlin, *The Enforcement of Morals* (Oxford: Oxford University Press, 1959); reprinted, with later lectures and a new introduction and explanatory notes, in *The Enforcement of Morals* (New York: Oxford University Press, 1965). All citations will be to the latter. Page 6.
7. Ibid., p. 10.
8. Ibid., p. 8.
9. Ibid., p. 15.
10. Ibid., p. 16.
11. Ibid., p. 17.
12. These last qualifications were added by Devlin in the preface to the 1965 edition, cited in note 6, in response to criticisms of this stand by Hart and others in the years following the publication of the Maccabean Lecture. Cf. p. viii.
13. Ibid., p. 17.
14. Ibid., p. 18.
15. Ibid., pp. 20 f.
16. H. L. A. Hart, *Law, Liberty, and Morality* (Stanford, Calif.: Stanford University Press, 1963), Chapter 1.
17. John Stuart Mill, *On Liberty*, Chapter 1. In Library of Liberal Arts edition, p. 13.
18. Ibid.
19. Hart, op. cit., pp. 21 f.
20. Ibid., p. 29.
21. Ibid., p. 32.
22. Ibid., p. 40.
23. Ibid., p. 51.

24. Ibid., p. 52.
25. Ibid.
26. Barbara Wootton, *Crime and the Criminal Law* (London: Stevens and Sons, 1963), p. 43.
27. Ibid., p. 44.
28. Ibid., p. 46.
29. Ibid., p. 55.
30. Cf. Sir Henry Maine, *Ancient Law* (London: Oxford University Press, 1931), Chapter 1, for a number of examples.
31. Wootton, op. cit., p. 56.
32. *Repouille* v. *United States*, 165 F. 2d 152 (1947).
33. Cf. *La. ex. Rel. Francis* v. *Resweber, Sheriff*, 329 U.S. 459 (1947), and the decision rendered by the United States Supreme Court *In re Kemmler*, 136 U.S. 447, where the Court held that the word *cruel* in the Seventh Amendment "implies . . . something inhuman and barbarous, something more than the mere extinguishing of life."
34. Cf. decision in case cited in note 33.
35. *Solesbee* v. *Balkcom*, Warden, 339 U.S. 9 (1949).
36. *Petition of Benitez*, 113 F. Supp. 105 (S.D.N.Y. 1953).
37. *Schmidt* v. *United States*, 177 F. 2d 450 (2nd Cir. N.Y. 1949).
38. *In re Edgar*, 253 F. Supp. 951 (E.D. Mich. 1966).
39. *Petition of Spak*, 164 F. Supp. 257 (E.D. Pa. 1958).
40. *In re Schmidt*, 289 N.Y.S. 2d 89 (1968).
41. *In re Labady*, 326 F. Supp. 924 (S.D.N.Y. 1971).
42. *Petition of Suey Chin*, 173 F. Supp. 510 (S.D.N.Y. 1959).
43. *Application of Brooks*, 355 P. 2d 840 (Wash. 1960).
44. *Commonwealth* v. *Elliott*, 371 Pa. 70, 89 A. 2d 782 (1952). Emphasis added.
45. Cf. Goode and Hatt, *Methods of Social Research*, 1952, p. 173. Cited in R. C. Donnelly, Joseph Goldstein, and Richard D. Schwartz, *Criminal Law* (New York: The Free Press, 1962), p. 36.
46. *U.S.* v. *Rosenberg*, 195 F. 2d 583, 608 (1952).
47. Cf. Alfred C. Kinsey, *Sexual Behavior in the Human Male* and *Sexual Behavior in the Human Female* (Philadelphia: W. B. Saunders Co., 1948 and 1953, respectively).
48. Cf., e.g., *Sexual Behavior in the Human Male*, p. 384, where Kinsey says that "the highest incidences of the homosexual, however, are in the group which most often verbalizes its disapproval of such activity."
49. I am indebted to Louis B. Schwartz's review of the first Kinsey Report in the *University of Pennsylvania Law Review*, Vol. 96 (1946), p. 916, for this example.
50. Cf. the literature cited in the bibliography for some of these critiques.
51. Cf. Plato, *The Republic*, XXXI, 557c ff.

Chapter 2. Homosexuality

1. Leviticus, 18:22, 20:13.
2. Deuteronomy, 23:18–19.
3. See Louis Ginzberg, *Legends of the Jews* (Philadelphia: Jewish Publication Society, 1911–38), Vol. 1, p. 254, and Vol. 5, p. 241, n. 175.

4. Ibid., Vol. 5, p. 173, n. 17; p. 178, n. 26; p. 182, n. 39. Cf. also the sources cited there.

5. Ibid., Vol. 6, p. 420, n. 93.

6. Romans 1:26–27.

7. I Corinthians 6:9, 10.

8. Confessions, VIII, 1–15.

9. Justinian, *Novellae*, from *Les Novelles de L'Empereur Justinian* (Metz: Lamort, 1811), No. 77.

10. Cf. *The Symposium.*

11. Cf. G. Lowes Dickinson, *The Greek View of Life* (London: Methuen, 1957).

12. See C. S. Ford and F. A. Beach, *Patterns of Sexual Behavior* (New York: Harper & Row, 1951); Ruth Benedict, "Sex in Primitive Society," *American Journal of Orthopsychiatry*, 9:570 ff.; Margaret Mead, *Growing Up in New Guinea* (New York: W. Morrow, 1930); D. J. West, *Homosexuality* (Chicago: Aldine, 1967), pp. 17 ff.

13. Cf. M. Hirschfeld, *Sexual Anomalies and Perversions* (London: Francis Aldor, 1944); H. M. Hyde, *The Trials of Oscar Wilde* (London: William Hodge, 1948); West, op. cit., pp. 26 ff.

14. Donald W. Cory, *The Homosexual in America: A Subjective Approach*, Second Edition (New York: Castle Books, 1960), p. 53

15. These practices are far more widespread than one might suppose, according to the best statistics presently available. Cf. the two Kinsey reports.

16. Cf. *State* v. *Pilcher*, 242 N.W. 2d 348 (Iowa, 1976); *Gossett* v. *State*, 242 N.W. 2d 899 (Wis., 1976); *People* v. *Mehr*, 383 N.Y.S. 2d 798 (N.Y., 1976).

17. The *Pilcher* case, cited in n. 16.

18. *Gossett* and *Mehr*, n. 16.

19. *Doe* v. *Commonwealth's Attorney for City of Richmond, Va.*, 403 F. Supp. 1199 (E.D. Va., 1975).

20. Cf. *B.* v. *B.*, 78 Misc. 2d 112, 355 N.Y.S. 2d 712 (1974), in which the husband was a transsexual—a woman who had undergone a sex-change operation to become a male. The wife brought an action for an annulment on the ground that her husband was a female, and therefore no marriage ever existed. The court ruled in the wife's favor, arguing that because the husband could not function as a male for the purpose of procreation, the couple had never entered into a valid marriage. In an earlier decision concerning *Anonymous* v. *Anonymous*, 67 Misc. 2d 982, 325 N.Y.S. 2d 712 (Sup. Ct., 1974), the same New York court had ruled that a marriage between two males was invalid, despite the fact that one of them had later undergone surgery to become a female. The courts did not discuss the possible objection that the ability to procreate is also lacking when one of the parties to a marriage is sterile, but this is not regarded as grounds for an annulment. In Minnesota, a homosexual couple applied for a marriage license, the license was denied, and the courts concluded that because procreation is one of the purposes of marriage, no license need be issued. That case was *Baker* v. *Nelson*, 191 N.W. 2d 185 (1971), appeal dismissed, 409 U.S. 810 (1972). In Kentucky, where two women applied for a marriage license, the court held in *Jones* v. *Hallahan*, 501 S. W. 2d 588 (Ky. App., 1973) that no license need be issued because they were not really proposing to be married (what they intended to do was not a marriage as the court understood that term).

21. Cf. William D. Lentz, "Marriage Rights: Homosexuals and Transsexuals," *Akron Law Review*, Vol. 8, 1975, pp. 369 ff.; Comment, "Homosexuality and the Law—A Right to be Different," *Albany Law Review*, Vol. 38, 1973, pp. 84 ff.; Comment, "The Homosexual's Legal Dilemma," *Arkansas Law Review*, Vol. 27, 1973, pp. 687 ff.

22. Cf. Army Regulation 601-210, which prohibits enlistment of homosexuals. Cf. Marcel T. Saghir and Eli Robins, *Male and Female Homosexuality: A Comprehensive Investigation* (Baltimore: Williams & Wilkins, 1973), pp. 173 ff.

23. Cf. the literature cited in bibliography for this chapter.

24. Cf. Martin Hoffman, *The Gay World* (New York: Harper & Row, 1965), p. 11 et passim; Jens Jersild, *The Normal Homosexual Male Versus the Boy Molester* (Copenhagen: Hyt Nordisk Forlag Arnold Busck, 1967), passim; Kurt Freund, *Die Homosexualität Beim Mann* (Leipzig: Hirzel Verlag, 1963), passim; K. Freund, "On the Problem of Male Homosexuality," *Review of Czechoslovak Medicine*, 11:11 ff. Gordon Westwood, surveying a sample of male homosexuals, found only three men out of a total of 127 interviewed in his study who evinced a strong preference for boys. The rest either had had no contact with underage boys or (in a total of 7% of the interviews) had had occasional sexual relations with boys fourteen or fifteen years of age. His findings were published in *A Minority* (London: Longmans, 1960). The Kinsey Institute report found that only 9% of all men convicted for homosexual offenses with adults had ever had such a relationship with a child. However, they did find that a third of them had had sexual relationships with sexually mature youths under sixteen. It should be remembered, though, that this study was confined to men convicted of homosexual misbehavior. Whether these figures would hold up for the general run of homosexual society is questionable. Any attempt to use findings in a prison population as a base for drawing inferences about any general population is naturally suspect.

25. Cf., for example, Hoffman, op. cit., Chapter 3.

26. *New York Times*, July 26, 1975, p. 19.

27. Hoffman, op. cit., p. 166.

28. Ibid., pp. 166 ff.

29. Kinsey, *Sexual Behavior in the Human Female* (Philadelphia: W. B. Saunders Co., 1953), p. 682.

30. Saghir and Robins, op. cit., p. 64.

31. C. A. Tripp, *The Homosexual Matrix* (New York: McGraw-Hill Book Company, 1975), p. 153.

32. Saghir and Robins, op. cit., pp. 224 ff.

33. L. M. Terman and Catherine C. Miles, *Sex and Personality* (New York: McGraw-Hill, 1936). Cited in West, op. cit., pp. 48 ff.

34. Cf. West, op. cit., p. 50, and the literature cited there.

35. Ibid., pp. 50 ff. and the studies cited there.

36. Sigmund Freud, *Three Essays on the Theory of Sexuality* (New York: Basic Books, 1962), p. 25.

37. Edmund Bergler, *Homosexuality: Disease or Way of Life?* (New York: Hill and Wang, 1957), p. 16.

38. Ibid., p. 17.

39. Ibid., p. 19.

40. Ibid., p. 20.

41. Ibid., pp. 31 f.
42. Ibid., pp. 28 f.
43. Ibid., p. 293.
44. Ibid.
45. Corey, op. cit., pp. xxi ff.
46. Saghir and Robins, op. cit., p. 318.
47. See Judd Marmor, "Homosexuality," in Mary S. Calderone (ed.), *Sexuality and Human Values* (New York: Association Press, 1974), pp. 31 f.
48. Cf. *Time*, Sept. 8, 1975, p. 36. *New York Times*, Dec. 16, 1973, and April 9, 1974.
49. Cf. the literature cited in Edwin M. Schur, *Crimes Without Victims* (Englewood Cliffs, N.J.: Prentice-Hall, 1965).
50. Senate Committee on Expenditures in the Executive Departments, "Employment of Homosexuals and Other Sex Perverts in Government," S. Doc. No. 241, 81st Cong. 2nd Sess. 1, 19 (1950).
51. Karl M. Bowman, "Review of Sex Legislation and Control of Sex Offenders in the United States of America," *California Sexual Deviation Research, Final Report, XX* (1954), p. 31.
52. William Blackstone, *Commentaries on the Laws of England*, Book IV, "Of Public Wrongs." Chapter XV, § 4 (Boston: Brown Press, 1912), pp. 241 ff.
53. *Kelly* v. *U.S.*, 194 F. 2d 150 (D.C. Cir. 1951), Justice Prettyman's decision.
54. Wolfenden Report, p. 53.
55. *Reynolds* v. *United States*, 98 U.S. 145 (1878), at 166.
56. *Cantwell* v. *Connecticut*, 310 U.S. 296 (1940).
57. Chief Justice Warren, in *Braunfeld* v. *Brown*, 366 U.S. 599 (1961).
58. *Reynolds* v. *United States*, 98 U.S. 145 (1878).
59. *Braunfeld* v. *Brown*, 366 U.S. 599 (1961).
60. *Prince* v. *Massachusetts*, 321 U.S. 158 (1944).
61. *Jacobson* v. *Massachusetts*, 197 U.S. 11 (1905); *Memorial Hospital* v. *Anderson*, 42 N.J. 421, cert. den. 377 U.S. 959 (1964); *Application of Georgetown College*, 377 U.S. 978 (1964); *Lawson* v. *Commonwealth*, 164 S.W. 2d 972 (Ky. 1942). Cf. *People* v. *Woody*, 61 Cal. 2d 716 (1964), on the banning of the hallucinogenic drug peyote in connection with bona fide religious ceremonies.
62. *Tinker* v. *Des Moines School District*, 393 U.S. 503 (1969).
63. *Street* v. *New York*, 394 U.S. 576 (1969).
64. See Pope Pius XI, *Casti Connubii*.
65. For a fascinating account of inversion among the lower mammals, see Chapters 2 and 3 of Tripp, op. cit. Chapter 5 contains a good review of the practices of some other cultures, including some that the reader might find most revealing.
66. Cf. *N.Y. Times Magazine*, October 10, 1971.
67. London *Times*, May 12, 1965, cited in West, op. cit., p. 100.
68. Code 1951, 22-1112 (a), Supp. VIII.
69. *Rittenour* v. *District of Columbia*, 163 A. 2d 558 (1960).
70. C. H. Rolph, "The Problem for the Police," *New Statesman* (June 25, 1960), p. 945. Cited in Edwin M. Schur, *Crimes Without Victims* (Englewood Cliffs, N.J.: Prentice-Hall, 1965), p. 80.
71. *Kelly* v. *United States*, 194 F. 2d 150 (D.C. Cir. 1951).

72. *Guarro* v. *U.S.*, 237 F. 2d 578 (D.C. Cir. 1956), quoting *McDermett* v. *U.S.*, D.C. Munic. App. 1953, 98 A. 2d 287, 290.

73. Cf. James S. Campbell et al., *Law and Order Reconsidered,* Report of the Task Force on Law and Law Enforcement to the National Commission on the Causes and Prevention of Violence (New York: Bantam Books, 1970), Chapter 23. "The Problem of 'Overcriminalization,'" esp. p. 612, and the sources cited there.

74. Report of the British Roman Catholic Advisory Committee on Prostitution and Homosexual Offences and the Existing Law, reprinted in "Homosexuality and the Law: A Catholic Memorandum," *The Dublin Review,* Vol. 230 (Summer, 1956), pp. 60 ff. Reprinted in part in Donnelly et al., *Criminal Law,* pp. 140 ff.

75. Cf. Jersild, op. cit., p. 70.

76. Cf. the literature cited in Schur, op. cit., pp. 105 ff.

77. Kenneth A. Briggs, "Homosexuals Among the Clergy," *New York Times,* January 24, 1977.

78. Roger Ricklefs, "Campaigns to Sell to Homosexual Market. . . ," *Wall Street Journal,* May 13, 1975, p. 40.

79. See the *New York Times,* February 14, 1977, p. 31; Saghir and Robins, op. cit., 163 ff. A survey revealed that one-third of the homosexuals studied had been robbed, physically assaulted, threatened, or blackmailed, and that 42% of those had had more than one such incident. Most such incidents arose out of casual pickups. Also, see *New York Times,* July 26, 1976, p. 19.

Chapter 3. Contraception and Abortion

1. *New York Times,* Dec. 28, 1976.

2. Ibid.

3. *Wall Street Journal,* Jan. 13, 1977, p. 13.

4. *Griswold* v. *Connecticut,* 381 U.S. 479 (1965).

5. Ibid., from *Poe* v. *Ullman,* 367 U.S. 497.

6. Ibid.

7. Germain Grisez, "Abortion: Ethical Arguments," excerpts from *Abortion: The Myths, the Realities, and the Arguments* (New York: Corpus Books, 1970), reprinted in Richard Wasserstrom, *Today's Moral Problems* (New York: Macmillan Publishing Co., Inc., 1975), p. 102. Emphasis in original.

8. Plato, *Republic,* tr. by F. M. Cornford (Oxford: Oxford University Press, 1945), p. 461.

9. Ibid., p. 460.

10. Aristotle, *Politics,* Translation by Ernest Barker in *The Politics of Aristotle* (Oxford: Oxford University Press, 1946), 1265b.

11. Ibid., 1335b.

12. Will Durant, *The Life of Greece* (New York: Simon and Schuster, 1939), p. 81.

13. Ibid., pp. 567 f.

14. See Durant, *Caesar and Christ* (New York: Simon and Schuster, 1944), pp. 221 ff.

15. Ibid., pp. 363 f.

16. Gen. 1:27–28, 9:1; Ex. 23:26; Deut. 7:13–14; cf. Gen. 15:5, 22:17, 26:4, and elsewhere.

17. Luke 20:34–36.
18. Matthew 19:12.
19. Ibid., 22:30.
20. I Corinthians 7:33–34.
21. John T. Noonan, Jr., *Contraception: A History of Its Treatment by the Catholic Theologians and Canonists* (Cambridge, Mass.: Harvard University Press), pp. 40 ff.
22. I Corinthians 7–10.
23. Cf. the citations in Noonan, pp. 46 ff.
24. Noonan, op. cit., p. 78, quoting Lactantius. For other quotations, see ibid., pp. 76 f.
25. *Marriage and Concupiscence*, 1:15:17. Cited by Noonan, op. cit., p. 136.
26. Cf. Noonan, op. cit., pp. 162 ff.
27. Cf. e.g., Noonan, op. cit., p. 196.
28. St. Thomas Aquinas, *Summa* 2–2:154:12.
29. Noonan, op. cit., pp. 260 ff.
30. Ibid., p. 400.
31. Ibid., p. 401.
32. Aristotle, *Nicomachean Ethics*, 1175b.
33. Cf. Noonan, op. cit., pp. 292 ff.
34. Ibid., p. 308.
35. Ibid.
36. Ibid., pp. 324 ff.
37. Cf. Noonan, op. cit., pp. 315 ff.; also David M. Feldman, *Birth Control in Jewish Law* (New York: New York University Press, 1968), pp. 83 ff., and Glanville Williams, *The Sanctity of Life and the Criminal Law* (New York: Knopf, 1957), pp. 52 ff.
38. *De Fide*, § 70, cited by Williams, op. cit., p. 194.
39. Canon 747. Cf. *Ethical and Religious Directives for Catholic Hospitals* (St. Louis: 1949), p. 3.
40. *Decisiones Sanctae Sedis*, pp. 19–20. Noonan, op. cit., p. 403.
41. This reasoning, which derived from Ryan, according to Noonan, was embodied in a pastoral letter of the Archbishops and Bishops of the United States, dated September 26, 1919. Cf. Noonan, op. cit., pp. 423 ff.
42. Lambeth Conference, 1930, Resolution 15.
43. *AAS* 22.560.
44. Noonan, op. cit., p. 427.
45. Ibid., p. 428. Cf. also the other opinions cited there.
46. Cf. Noonan, op. cit., last chapters, and Williams, op. cit., Chapters 2, 5, and 6.
47. The encyclical *Humanae Vitae* is now available in many editions. It was published in full in the *New York Times* immediately after its release by the Vatican in September, 1968, and was published in an appendix to Leo Pyle, ed., *Pope & Pill* (Baltimore: Helicon Press, 1969). All references will be to section numbers and subhead titles. The present quotation is from "Conjugal Love," Section 8.
48. "Responsible Parenthood," Section 9. Also "Union and Procreation," Section 12, and "Faithfulness to God's Design," Section 13.
49. "Illicit Ways of Regulating Birth," Section 14. Emphasis added.

50. Ibid.
51. "Illicit Ways of Regulating Birth," Section 14.
52. "Grave Consequences of Methods of Artificial Birth Control," Section 17.
53. Quotation from Archbishop Cowderoy of Southwark, in an encyclical published in Pyle, op. cit., pp. 173 ff.
54. For an important collection of documents on both sides of the question, both prior to and immediately following *Humanae Vitae,* see Pyle, op. cit.
55. This doctrine goes back to Aristotle's day and is based on some obsolete physiological and psychological theories.
56. Cf. Lawrence Lader, *Abortion* (Indianapolis: Bobbs-Merrill, 1966), p. 79, and the letters quoted on p. 185, n. 9.
57. For a review of some of the legislation and court decisions, cf. Lader, op. cit., pp. 85 ff., and Williams, op. cit., pp. 156 ff. An excellent review of the development of the common law and of the law on abortion in Great Britain may be found in Bernard M. Dickens, *Abortion and the Law* (London: MacGibbon and Kee, 1966), pp. 20 ff. The status of British law at the time of the book's writing is discussed in detail on pp. 29 ff. British law is also discussed, but in less detail, by Williams, op. cit., pp. 152 ff.
58. *Foster* v. *State,* 182 Wis. 298, 196 N.W. 233 (1923), cited in Williams, op. cit., p. 157.
59. For the prayer, cf. Philip Birnbaum, *Daily Prayer Book* (New York: Hebrew Publishing Company, 1949), p. 16, or Chief Rabbi Joseph H. Hertz, *The Authorized Daily Prayer Book,* Rev. Ed. (New York: Bloch Publishing Co., 1948), p. 19. Cf. Hertz's commentary on pp. 18 f.
60. Cf. the excellent discussion in G. F. Moore, *Judaism in the First Centuries of the Christian Era,* Vol. 1 (Cambridge, Mass.: Harvard University Press, 1954), Part III, Chapter 2, esp. pp. 467 ff.
61. Maimonides, *Commentary to Mishnah, Sanhedrin* 7:4.
62. For a thorough discussion of this, see David M. Feldman, *Birth Control in Jewish Law* (New York: New York University Press, 1968), pp. 109 ff., 148 ff.
63. Leviticus 18:16. The Hebrew term *karet,* often translated "cut off," was understood by the rabbis to refer to heavenly punishment consisting of early death.
64. Cf. Feldman, op. cit., p. 151.
65. Jerusalem Talmud, Yeb. 1:1.
66. *Genesis Rabbah, Bereshit,* 17:2. Cited in C. G. Montefiore and H. Loewe, *A Rabbinic Anthology* (Philadelphia: Jewish Publishing Society, 1960), p. 507.
67. *Ruth Zuta,* ed. Buber, 4:11; in Montefiore and Loewe, op. cit., p. 511.
68. *T'shuvot Rivash,* no. 15, cited in Feldman, op. cit., pp. 41 f. This decision was later incorporated into the codes that were held to be normative from the fifteenth century to the present day.
69. Exodus 21:10 Cf. *Mekilta ad loc.,* Jerusalem Talmud *Ketubot* 5:6.
70. Babylonian Talmud, *Nedarim* 81b, *Ketubot* 61b.
71. Cf. Bailey, *Sexual Relation in Christian Thought* (New York: Harper & Row, 1959), pp. 33 ff.
72. Deuteronomy 24:5.
73. Maimonides, *Mishneh Torah, H. De'ot,* 3:1.

74. Cf. Gershom Scholem, *Major Trends in Jewish Mysticism*, Third Edition (New York: Schocken, 1954), pp. 106, 235.
75. *Sefer Hasidim*, cited in Scholem, p. 106.
76. Maimonides, *Mishneh Torah, H. Issurei Bi'ah*, 21:9.
77. Translated by Feldman, op. cit., p. 102.
78. The passage is from a *baraita* and appears a number of times in the Talmud and in the Tosefta. For a full discussion, see Feldman, op. cit., pp. 169 ff.
79. Cf. Tosephta, Yevamot, 8:2.
80. Judah Assad, quoted, among others, in Feldman, op. cit., p. 242.
81. *Resp. Hatam Sofer, E. H.*, no. 20, cited in Feldman, op. cit., p. 242.
82. *Resp. Mahaneh Hayyim*, no. 53, cited in Feldman, op. cit., p. 105.
83. Cf. Feldman, op. cit., p. 248.
84. Exodus 21:12.
85. Babylonian Talmud, *Niddah*, p. 44b.
86. Cf. *Mekilta*, an early legal midrash, ad loc.
87. See *Tosafot* to *Niddah*, pp. 44a-b, s.v. *'ihu*, and the references cited there.
88. Cf. *Mishnah, Oholot*, 7:7; *Bab. Talmud., Sanhedrin* 59a and *Tosafot* s.v. *Leka*; ibid., 72b.
89. For Abulafia, see his commentary, *Yad Ramah*, on *Sanhedrin*, 91b and 72b. Cf. the discussion in Feldman, op. cit., pp. 273 ff.
90. Decided by a rabbi of the early eighteenth century, Yehudah Ayyas. Cf. Feldman, op. cit., p. 287.
91. *Or Dagol*, no. 31. Cited in Feldman, op. cit., p. 287.
92. Ibid., pp. 293 ff.
93. For an up-to-date account of the latest thinking in rabbinical circles on contraception and abortion, see Immanuel Jakobovits, *Jewish Medical Ethics* (New York: Bloch Publishing Co., 1975), Chapters 13 and 14, especially pp. 267–275.
94. Cf. the Texas statute, Arts. 1191–1194 and 1196, cited in n. 1 of the United States Supreme Court's decision in *Roe* v. *Wade*, 410 U.S. 118 (1973) which is fairly typical. In Texas, the penalty for procuring an abortion was a fine of "not less than one hundred nor more than one thousand dollars," except when the mother's life was lost, in which case the abortionist was to be regarded as having committed murder. The statute provided for an exception for an abortion procured or attempted "by medical advice for the purpose of saving the life of the mother." Under the Georgia statute, the penalty was imprisonment for one to ten years. Each state had its own variations in both the definition of the offense and the penalties for violation of the statute. New York and several other states had liberalized their laws by the time the Supreme Court rendered its decision.
95. *Roe* v. *Wade*, p. 117.
96. *Griswold* v. *Connecticut*, 381 U.S. 479 (1965).
97. *Roe* v. *Wade*, p. 153.
98. Ibid., p. 158, n. 54.
99. Ibid., p. 161.
100. Ibid., pp. 162 f.
101. Ibid., pp. 164 f.
102. *Doe* v. *Bolton*, 410 U.S. 179 (1973).

103. *Planned Parenthood of Central Missouri* v. *Danforth,* 96 S.Ct. 2831 (1976). Unless otherwise stated, all of the decisions referred to in the following paragraphs were made in this case.

104. For citations, see United States Commission on Civil Rights, *Constitutional Aspects of the Right to Limit Childbearing* (Washington, D.C., April, 1975), pp. 20f.

105. Ibid., p. 23.

106. *Beal* v. *Doe,* 97 S.Ct. 2366 (1977) and *Maher* v. *Roe,* 97 S.Ct. 2376 (1977).

107. S.J. Res. 119 and S.J. Res. 130, 93rd Cong., First Sess. Cf. Hearings before the Subcommittee on Constitutional Amendments of the Committee on the Judiciary of the United States Senate; Ninety-Third Congress, Second Session, on S.J. Res. 119 and S.J. Res. 130, March 6, March 7, April 10, 1974 (Washington: Government Printing Office, 1974), pp. 1 f. This volume will be referred to as *Abortion Hearings.*

108. Sherri Finkbine, "The Lesser of Two Evils," in Allan F. Guttmacher, *The Case for Legalized Abortion* (Berkeley, Calif.: Diablo Press, 1967), pp. 15 ff.

109. Lader, op. cit., p. 5.

110. Jerome E. Bates and Edward S. Zawadzki, *Criminal Abortion: A Study in Medical Sociology* (Springfield, Ill.: Charles C Thomas, 1964), p. 41.

111. *Look,* July 11, 1967.

112. *Journal of the American Medical Association,* Cf. *Wall Street Journal,* Feb. 1, 1977, p. 21.

113. Statement of Senator Charles H. Percy, *Abortion Hearings,* p. 445.

114. See, for example, Thomas Hobbes, *Leviathan,* Library of Liberal Arts ed., p. 112.

115. Almost any text on embryology or human development contains these facts with more detail. One of the best sources for the layman is Chapter 1 of Germain G. Grisez's book, *Abortion: The Myths, the Realities, and the Arguments* (New York: Corpus Books, 1970).

116. Grisez, op. cit., p. 274.

117. Meade O'Boyle, M.D., "The Humanity of the Unborn Child," in *Abortion Hearings* (1974), p. 487.

118. Statement of John Cardinal Krol, *Abortion Hearings,* p. 163. Cf. also the "Testimony of the United States Catholic Conference" beginning on p. 184 in the *Hearings,* and many others throughout.

119. Ashley Montagu, *Life Before Birth* (New York: Signet Books, 1965), p. 12. Cited in Grisez, op. cit., p. 277. These arguments are all derived from Grisez's book. The critic's response is in each case Grisez's own response to the argument. My replies are thus replies to Grisez.

120. Grisez, op. cit., p. 284.

121. Richard A. McCormick, S.J., "Abortion," *America,* June 19, 1965, p. 877.

122. Cf. *New York Times,* October 17, 1970, p. 30.

123. McCormick, op. cit., p. 879.

124. Ibid.

125. Cf. ibid., p. 880, and many other articles and books for the same argument in different forms.

126. Ronald M. Green, "Abortion and Promise-Keeping," *Christianity and Crisis,* May 15, 1967, p. 110.

127. The article from which this excerpt came was a defense of liberalization, but its argument is fallacious because of its improper use of *promise*.
128. Cited in Dickens, op. cit., p. 118.
129. Judith Jarvis Thomson, "A Defense of Abortion," *Philosophy and Public Affairs*, 1:47ff (Fall, 1971). Cf. the bibliography to this chapter for references to articles that discuss Thomson's arguments.
130. Ibid., p. 57.
131. Ibid., p. 65.
132. Ibid., pp. 66, 65.

Chapter 4. **Freedom of the Press and Censorship**
1. In the Helsinki accords of 1975.
2. Cf. C. L. Sulzberger, "Who Calls the Kettle Black?" *New York Times*, March 5, 1977.
3. "Only in the West Can We Fulfill Our Art," interview with John Gruen, *New York Times*, March 23, 1975, p. D-17.
4. *New York Times*, June 28, 1977, p. 2.
5. *New York Times*, Sept. 16, 1974, p. 1.
6. Editorial, "Creativity and Communism," *Wall Street Journal*, Oct. 7, 1975.
7. *New York Times*, Dec. 12, 1975, p. 6.
8. Avtandil Rukhadze, "Not Simply Drones," January 5, 1977, Novosti Press Agency (APN).
9. Vladimir Lysenkov, " 'Soviet Dissidents': Who Needs Them?" APN, March 25, 1977.
10. Y. Volkov, "Bukovsky Trial Opens in Moscow," APN, Jan. 7, 1977.
11. Cf. Shirley Hazzard, " 'Gulag' and the Men of Peace," *New York Times Book Review*, Aug. 25, 1974, p. 35.
12. *New York Times*, May 13, 1977, p. A-26.
13. The "Charter 77 Manifesto," translated and published in the Jan. 31, 1977 issue of *The New Leader* and reprinted in the *New York Times*, Jan. 27, 1977.
14. Cf. *Freedom at Issue*, No. 42 (Sept.–Oct., 1977), for a complete list of violations, broken down by country, "The Helsinki Watch," VI, p. 16 ff.
15. For details, see Dennis L. Wilcox, "What Hope for Free Press in Africa?" *Freedom at Issue*, No. 40 (March–April, 1977), p. 10 ff.
16. *New York Times*, July 17, 1976.
17. *New York Times*, May 28, 1975, p. 1.
18. *New York Times*, October 29, 1977, p. 22.
19. Walter Schneir, "Steps by FBI to Bar Rosenberg Book from TV," *Authors Guild Bulletin*, Sept.–Oct., 1976, pp. 9 f.
20. *New York Times*, July 10, 1977. Richard Flaste, "Banning 'Bad' Books in a 'Good' Cause."
21. *New York Times*, Aug. 30, 1977, p. 1.
22. *New York Times*, Sept. 4, 1977, p. E14.
23. Ibid., Sept. 15, 1977, p. 42.
24. Ibid., Aug. 23, 1977.
25. Babatunde Jose, "Anti-Colonial Strategy Now Destructive," *IPI Report*, Aug., 1975, p. 9, cited in Wilcox, op. cit., p. 12.
26. Cf. Leonard R. Sussman, "A Fateful Year for the News Media," *Freedom at Issue*, No. 39, Jan.–Feb., 1977, pp. 2 ff.

27. Quoted in Sussman, op. cit., without further reference.
28. Shelton A. Gunaratne, "The Taming of the Press in Sri Lanka," *Journalism Monographs*, No. 39 (Lexington, Ky.: Association for Education in Journalism, 1975).
29. Printed in full, together with other documents, in the *AAUP Bulletin*, Winter, 1976, pp. 29 ff.
30. Ibid., p. 34.
31. Ibid., p. 36.
32. Ibid., p. 39.
33. These points have been developed, either directly or by elaboration, from the dissenting opinion of Kenneth J. Barnes in the Yale Report, ibid., pp. 37 ff.
34. Letter from Professor Gerard R. Wolfe, *New York Times*, Feb. 4, 1977.
35. *New York Times*, Jan. 16, 1977.
36. Citing *Chaplinsky* v. *New Hampshire*, 315 U.S. 568 (1942).
37. Ibid.
38. *Dennis* v. *the United States*, 341 U.S. 494 (1951).
39. Ibid.
40. Ibid.
41. *New York Times Co.* v. *the United States*, 403 U.S. 713 (1971).
42. Thomas Hobbes, *Leviathan*, Chapter 18. In Library of Liberal Arts Edition (Indianapolis: Bobbs-Merrill, 1958), p. 147.
43. Joshua 10:12–13.
44. Psalms 103:5.
45. Ecclesiastes 1:5.
46. For an excellent review of the principal facts about this controversy, see the article on Galileo by Giorgia D. de Santillana in the 1967 edition of *Encyclopedia Britannica*. For more details, see Will and Ariel Durant, *The Age of Reason Begins* (Vol. 7 of *The Story of Civilization*). (New York: Simon and Schuster, 1961), Chapter 22. Galileo's own writings are available in a number of translations. See also H. Butterfield, *The Origins of Modern Science* (London: G. Bell, 1957), Lane Cooper, *Aristotle, Galileo, and the Tower of Pisa* (Ithaca, N.Y.: Cornell University Press, 1935), Hermann Kesten, *Copernicus and His World* (New York: Roy, 1945), and D. W. Singer, *Giordano Bruno, His Life and Thought* (New York: Schuman, 1950).
47. John Stuart Mill, *On Liberty*, Chapter 2.
48. Alexander Meiklejohn, *Political Freedom: The Constitutional Powers of the People* (New York: Oxford University Press, 1965), p. 57.
49. *New York Times Co.* v. *United States*, 403 U.S. 713 (1971).
50. *New York Times Co.* v. *Sullivan*, 376 U.S. 254 (1964).
51. *Whitney* v. *California*, 274 U.S. 357 (1927).
52. See Justice Goldberg's concurring opinions in *New York Times Company* v. *Sullivan* (376 U.S. 255).
53. See Justice Brennan's opinion, for the Court, in the *New York Times* case cited in note 52.

Chapter 5. Obscenity and Pornography

1. *Chicago Tribune*, May 24, 1959, p. 8.
2. Judge Jacobs' opinion in *N.J.* v. *Hudson News Company and Hudson News Dealers Supply Company*, 41 N.J. 247 (1963).

3. Cited by Chief Justice Warren in his dissent in *Times Film Corp.* v. *Chicago,* 356 U.S. 43 (1961).
4. *New York Times,* Dec. 4, 1974, p. 32.
5. Cf. Pamela Hansford Johnson, *On Iniquity: Some Personal Reflections Arising Out of the Moors Murder Trial* (London: Macmillan, 1967).
6. Ernest Van den Haag, "Is Pornography a Cause of Crime?" in David Holbrook (ed.), *The Case Against Pornography* (New York: Library Press, 1973), pp. 161 ff.
7. Ibid.
8. Raymond D. Gastil, "The Moral Right of the Majority to Restrict Obscenity and Pornography through Law," *Ethics,* vol. 86 (1976), pp. 231 ff.
9. Cf. *Young* v. *American Mini Theatres, Inc.,* 427 U.S. 50 (1975), which upheld a Detroit ordinance regulating such businesses and restricting them to certain parts of the city. Cf. *New York Times* editorials on the subject (Jan. 5 and Feb. 15, 1977), and letters to the *Times* (Feb. 15, 1977).
10. *New York Times,* Feb. 15, 1977, p. 32.
11. This illustration is from Irving Kristol, "Is This What We Wanted?" in *The Case Against Pornography,* pp. 187 ff.
12. Joel Feinberg, "Harmless Immoralities and Offensive Nuisances," in N. Care and T. Trelogan, *Issues in Law and. Morality* (Cleveland: Case Western Reserve University Press, 1973).
13. *Davis* v. *Beason,* 133 U.S. 333 (1890).
14. *Trist* v. *Child,* cited in Clor, op. cit., p. 181.
15. Lord Devlin, *The Enforcement of Morals* (New York: Oxford University Press, 1965), p. 94.
16. Clor, op. cit., p. 194.
17. Ibid.
18. *Commonwealth* v. *Gordon,* 68 Pa. D. & C. 101 (1949). Among the books that were under attack was *Studs Lonigan,* to name only one.
19. Ibid.
20. *Ginzburg* v. *United States,* 383 U.S. 463 (1966).
21. *U.S.* v. *One Book Entitled "Ulysses,"* 72 F. 2d 705.
22. American Law Institute, *Model Penal Code,* sec. 251.4.
23. *Roth* v. *U.S.,* 354 U.S. 476 (1957).
24. *Jacobellis* v. *Ohio,* 378 U.S. 197.
25. *Miller v. California,* 413 U.S. 15 (1973).
26. *Paris Adult Theater I* v. *Slaton,* 413 U.S. 49 (1973).
27. *Jenkins* v. *Georgia,* 418 U.S. 153 (1974).
28. *Smith* v. *State,* 97 S.Ct. 1756 (1977).
29. Ernest Van den Haag, "Is Pornography a Cause of Crime?" in *Encounter,* Dec., 1967, p. 53. He has made the same argument in "The Case for Pornography Is the Case for Censorship and Vice Versa," *Esquire,* May, 1967, p. 135.
30. Ibid.
31. Ibid.
32. Harold Gardiner, *Catholic Viewpoint on Censorship* (Garden City, N.Y.: Doubleday, 1961), pp. 62 ff.
33. E. and P. Kronhausen, *Pornography and the Law,* Rev. Ed. (New York: Ballantine Books, 1964), p. 18.

34. George Elliott, "Against Pornography," *Harper's Magazine,* Vol. 230 (May 1965), p. 52.
35. Harry M. Clor, *Obscenity and Public Morality: Censorship in a Liberal Society* (Chicago: University of Chicago Press, 1969), Chapter 6.
36. Ibid., p. 244.
37. Ibid., p. 245.
38. *The Report of the Commission on Obscenity and Pornography* (New York: Bantam Books, 1970), p. 32.
39. Ibid., Part IV, pp. 443 ff.
40. *Smith* v. *California,* 361 U.S. 147, and elsewhere.
41. *Report* (see n. 38 above), pp. 57 ff.

Chapter 6. The Concept of Punishment

1. Cf. *Alexander* v. *Louisiana,* 405 U.S. 625 (1972); *Peters* v. *Kiff,* 407 U.S. 493 (1972); *Patton* v. *Mississippi,* 332 U.S. 463 (1947).
2. *Olmstead* v. *United States,* 277 U.S. 438, at 471, 485.
3. *Brewer* v. *Williams,* 97 S.Ct. 1232 (1977).
4. Ibid.
5. For a useful but one-sided handbook on this subject, see Oliver Rosengart, *The Rights of Suspects* (New York: Avon Books, 1974), one of a series of such handbooks published by the American Civil Liberties Union.
6. A volume that is equally one-sided, but from an opposite point of view, is Frank G. Carrington, *The Victims* (New Rochelle, N.Y.: Arlington House, 1975). Among the statistics Carrington cites are the following: Between 1960 and 1969, the United States Supreme Court reversed 60% of the federal criminal convictions that were brought before it and nearly 80% of the state convictions.
7. See *Stone* v. *Powell,* 428 U.S. 465 (1976). The case is analyzed and its historical background is discussed in Ira P. Robbins and James E. Sanders, "Judicial Integrity, the Appearance of Justice, and the Great Writ of Habeas Corpus: How To Kill Two Thirds (or More) with One *Stone*," *American Criminal Law Review* 15:63 ff. (Summer, 1977).
8. Thomas Hobbes, *Leviathan,* Part I, Chapter 13, Library of Liberal Arts ed., p. 107.
9. *Buck* v. *Bell,* 274 U.S. 200 (1926). For more recent cases along the same lines, see *In Re Cavitt,* 157 N.W.2d 171 (Neb. 1968), in which the Supreme Court of Nebraska held that a statute empowering the board of examiners of mental deficients to require the sterilization of patients in a home for the mentally deficient as a prerequisite to their release from the home was constitutional. Also *Holmes* v. *Powers,* 439 S.W.2d 579 (Ky. 1969), in which the Kentucky Court of Appeals held that a sterilization operation could not be performed upon a mentally incompetent woman because if she was actually incompetent, she could not legally consent to it. The court left open the possibility that a legally constituted committee might make such a choice for her.
10. *New York Times,* Sept. 5, 1977, p. 4.
11. Erving Goffman, *Asylums: Essays on the Social Situation of Mental Patients and Other Inmates* (Chicago: Aldine Publishing Company, 1962).

12. Johannes Andenaes, "Deterrence and Specific Offenses: Drunken Driving," *University of Chicago Law Review*, 38:537ff. (1971).

13. For an account of the Montreal riot, see Gerald Clark, "What Happens When the Police Strike," *New York Times Magazine* (Nov. 16, 1969), pp. 79 ff. Other police strikes have occurred without a noticeable rise in violence, including one that took place in New York City in the late 1960s.

14. *"Principles of Judicial Procedure,"* Chapter 3, cited in A.C. Ewing, *The Morality of Punishment*, Reprint Ed. (Montclair, N.J.: Patterson Smith, 1970), p. 54; first published in London by Kegan Paul, Trench, Trubner & Co., Ltd., in 1929.

15. Genesis 4:10–11.

16. Numbers 32:33. Cf. also Deuteronomy 21:1–9, *et passim*. Cf. also Shakespeare's portrayal of guilt in such scenes as that in which Lady Macbeth attempts to wash away the blood that she imagines stains her hands.

17. Immanuel Kant, *Philosophy of Law*, tr. by Hastie (Edinburgh: T. & T. Clark, 1887), p. 198.

18. Hastings Rashdall, *Theory of Good and Evil*, Vol. 1, pp. 287 ff., cited in Ewing, op. cit., pp. 26 f.

19. Ewing, op. cit., p. 18.

20. Ibid., p. 29.

21. These objections were culled from Ewing, ibid., pp. 37 ff.

22. Herbert Fingarette, "Punishment and Suffering," in *Proceedings and Addresses, American Philosophical Association*, 50:504ff. (Aug., 1977).

23. John Hospers, "Free Will and Psychoanalysis," *Philosophy and Phenomenological Research*, 1950; reprinted in Paul Edwards et al., *A Modern Introduction to Philosophy*, Second Ed. (New York: Free Press, 1965).

24. Sidney Gendin, "A Critique of the Theory of Criminal Rehabilitation," in Milton Goldinger, *Punishment and Human Rights* (Cambridge, Mass.: Schenkman Pub. Co., 1974), pp. 28 f.

25. *M'Naghten's Case*, 10 Clark and Finnelly 200 (1843).

26. *Durham* v. *United States*, 214 F.2d 862 (U.S. App. D.C., 1954), 45 A.L.R. 2d 1430.

27. *McDonald* v. *United States*, 312 F.2d 847 (1962).

28. Herbert Fingarette, *The Meaning of Criminal Insanity* (Berkeley: University of California Press, 1972), pp. 34 ff. The analysis that follows relies heavily upon Fingarette's extensive and detailed treatment of the subject.

29. Ibid., p. 189.

30. Ibid., p. 198.

Chapter 8. The Death Penalty

1. I am indebted to H. L. A. Hart for this point. See his book *Punishment and Responsibility: Essays in the Philosophy of Law* (New York: Oxford University Press, 1968).

2. Cf. especially Isaac Ehrlich, "The Deterrent Effect of Capital Punishment: A Question of Life and Death," *American Economic Review*, 65:397ff. (June, 1975); "Deterrence: Evidence and Inference," *Yale Law Review*, 85:209ff. (Dec. 1975); and "Participation in Illegitimate Activities: A Theoretical and Empirical Investigation," *Journal of Political Economy*, 81:521ff. (May–June, 1973). Also, James A. Yunker, "Is the Death Penalty a Deterrent to Homicide?

Some Time Series Evidence," *Journal of Behavioral Economics*, **5**:45ff (1976).

3. For a number of recent articles in this area, cf. Chapter 5 of Hugo A. Bedau and Chester M. Pierce, eds., *Capital Punishment in the United States* (New York: AMS Press, Inc., 1975). Cf. also Passell, "The Deterrent Effect of the Death Penalty: A Statistical Test," *Stanford Law Review*, **28**:61ff. (1975), and Vol. 85 (1975–76) of the *Yale Law Journal*, which contains articles critical of Ehrlich's work as well as a rejoinder by him. In addition, the opinions of Justice Marshall and Justice Brennan in the capital punishment cases contain a wealth of material. Cf. *Gregg* v. *Georgia*, 428 U.S. 153 (1976) and *Furman* v. *Georgia*, 408 U.S. 241 (1972).

4. William C. Bailey, "Murder and Capital Punishment: Some Further Evidence," in Bedau and Pierce, op. cit., p. 316.

5. Numbers of victims are rounded off to the nearest hundred. From *U.S. Statistical Abstracts*. The decline that began in 1974 continued, according to preliminary figures for 1976.

6. Albert Shanker, in his weekly column, published as an advertisement of the United Federation of Teachers in the *New York Times*.

7. *New York Times*, Aug. 18, 1976, p. 16.

8. *New York Times*, March 4, 1975.

9. *Gregg* v. *Georgia*, 428 U.S. 153, at 240–241. Ellipses and quotation marks omitted.

10. *Trop* v. *Dulles*, 356 U.S. 86 (1957), at 99.

11. *McGautha* v. *California*, 402 U.S. 183 (1970), at 226.

12. *State of Louisiana* v. *Resweber*, 329 U.S. 459 (1947), at 464.

Chapter 9. Truth in the Marketplace: Advertising, Salesmen, and Swindlers

1. Bruce Barton (a founder of Batten, Barton, Durstine and Osborne advertising agency), "Advertising: Its Contribution to the American Way of Life," *Reader's Digest*, **66**:103ff. (April, 1955).

2. *Consumers Union of United States, Inc.* v. *American Bar Association*, 427 F Supp. 506 (E.D. Va., 1976).

3. Ibid.

4. *Virginia State Board of Pharmacy* v. *Virginia Citizens Consumer Council, Inc.*, 96 S.Ct. 1817 (1976).

5. *Health Systems Agency of Northern Virginia* v. *Virginia State Board of Medicine*, 424 F. Supp. 267 (E.D. Va., 1976).

6. Cf. the cases cited in notes 2–4.

7. These are not the exact terms used in his dialogues, but they give a more accurate picture of Plato's meaning, in modern terms, than the translations that I have seen thus far. For example, W. C. Helmbold calls gymnastics and medicine *arts*, whereas makeup and cookery are called *knacks*. *Knack*, in modern English, is very far, in my opinion, from what Plato had in mind. See Helmbold's translation of Plato's *Gorgias* (Indianapolis: Bobbs-Merrill, 1952), pp. 23 ff. Compare other translations of the same passages for similarly inept renderings.

8. These doctrines can be studied best in Plato's dialogue, *The Gorgias*, though they are discussed in many other dialogues in the Platonic corpus. I would recommend particularly *The Republic*, *The Symposium*, and *The Protagoras*, in that order. Plato's assaults on the Sophists are scattered throughout his

writings. His theory of justice received many different expressions, from the early Socratic dialogues (e.g., *The Apology, The Crito,* and *The Euthyphro*) through the lengthy *Republic* to the late dialogues *The Statesman* and *The Laws.*

9. See Robert J. Cole, "New Law Bars Unscrupulous Ruse to Deprive a Debtor of Legal Rights," *New York Times,* August 19, 1971, p. 51.

10. Cf. the Hearings on Effect of Promotion of Advertising Over-the-Counter Drugs before the Subcommittee on Monopoly of the Select Committee on Small Business of the U.S. Senate (92nd Congress) beginning in 1971.

11. This point, and those below, were made by Dr. Lou Harris of the University of Toronto Medical School on a radio broadcast on the Canadian Broadcasting Company's Consumer Affairs program. See also Th. H. Van de Velde, *Ideal Marriage,* Revised Edition (New York: Random House, 1965), pp. 28 ff.

12. *Consumer Reports,* Vol. 36 (September 1971), p. 526.

13. Warren G. Magnuson and Jean Carper, *The Dark Side of the Marketplace* (Englewood Cliffs, N.J.: Prentice-Hall, 1968), Chapters 1 and 2 *et passim.*

14. See James G. Burrow, *AMA: Voice of American Medicine* (Baltimore: Johns Hopkins Press, 1963), p. 268, and Arthur J. Cramp, *Nostrums and Quackery and Pseudo-medicine* (Chicago: University of Chicago Press, 1936), Vol. III, pp. 29–31.

15. James H. Young, *The Medical Messiahs* (Princeton, N.J.: Princeton University Press, 1967), pp. 147 f.

16. See David Ogilvy, *Confessions of an Advertising Man* (New York: Atheneum, 1963), p. 86. Also Gerald B. Lambert, "How I Sold Listerine," in *The Amazing Advertising Business,* ed. by the Editors of *Fortune* (New York: Simon & Schuster, 1957), Chapter 5.

17. Young, op. cit., p. 155.

18. *Consumer Reports,* Vol. 36 (September 1971), pp. 525 f.

19. Ibid., p. 561.

20. For the full story of the Hoxsey case, see Young, op. cit., Chapter 17. This is a fully documented account, gleaned from files of the AMA, the FDA, and transcripts of court hearings, as well as from newspapers, journals, and other publications of the period.

21. Mortin Mintz, "Drugs: Deceptive Advertising," in David Sanford (ed.), *Hot War on the Consumer* (New York: Pitman, 1969), pp. 91 ff.

22. *FTC in the Matter of Johnson Products Company, Inc., and Bozell & Jacobs, Inc.,* Docket no. C-2788 (Feb. ·10, 1976).

23. Cf. John G. Fleming, *The Law of Torts,* Fourth Edition (Sydney, Australia: The Law Book Company, Ltd., 1971), pp. 452 ff.

24. Cf. *ITT Continental Baking Co., Inc., et al. Final Order to Cease and Desist, and Opinion of the Commission (Wonder Bread Case),* Dkt. 8860, Oct. 10, 1973, 3 Trade Reg. Rep. Par. 20, 464 at 20, 372 (Jan. 14, 1974), cited in *Action for Children's Television Petition before the FTC,* Oct., 1975 (hereinafter referred to as *ACT*), p. 22.

25. FTC File no. 762–3054, *Consent Order to Cease and Desist and Accompanying Complaint,* Sept. 2, 1976.

26. *ACT,* Appendix G, Tables 1 and 2.

27. *ACT News,* vol. 6 (Fall, 1976), p. 11.

28. *Consumer Reports,* **36**:560 (September 1971).

29. Cf. *Consumer Reports,* March and August, 1961; follow-up reports, April and August, 1962.

30. Select Committee Hearings, Part 1, *Analgesics* (Washington: U.S. Govt. Printing Office, 1971), p. 230.

31. Ibid.

32. The firm is Ogilvy, Benson and Mather.

33. David Ogilvy, *Confessions of an Advertising Man* (New York: Atheneum, 1963), pp. 95 f.

34. Ibid., p. 99.

35. Ibid., p. 159.

36. Babylonian Talmud, *Ketuvot,* p. 17a. The academies were those that went under the names of Shammai and Hillel, respectively. The "debate" was not comparable to the kind of oratory contest that might be staged by college debating teams. It was a serious discussion on matters of legal and moral principle.

37. Ogilvy, op. cit., pp. 158 f.

Chapter 10. Competition and Corporate Responsibility

1. Milton Friedman, *Capitalism and Freedom* (Chicago: University of Chicago Press, 1962), p. 133.

2. Estes Kefauver, *In a Few Hands: Monopoly Power in America* (New York: Pantheon Books, 1965), pp. 138 ff.

3. Wendell Berge, *Cartels: Challenge to a Free World* (Washington, D.C.: Public Affairs Press, 1944), pp. 28 ff.

4. *Toole* v. *Richardson-Merrell Inc.,* 251 Cal. App. 2d 689, 60 Cal. Rptr. 398 (Ct. of Appeals, First Dist., 1967).

5. Cf. Page Keeton and Marshall S. Shapo, *Products and the Consumer: Defective and Dangerous Products* (Mineola, N.Y.: The Foundation Press, 1970), p. 177, and the cases cited there, esp. *Flemming* v. *Florida Citrus Exchange,* 358 U.S. 153 (1958).

6. Berge, op. cit., pp. 44 ff.

7. Ibid., pp. 142 ff.

8. Ibid., pp. 116 ff.

9. Ibid., p. 116.

10. Cf. *Wall Street Journal,* Oct. 25, 1977, p. 2, "National Steel's Net Plunged 54% For 3rd Quarter: Concern Cites . . . Big Rise in Imports." James Reston, "Japan's Economic Invasion," New York *Times,* No. 25, 1977, p. 25. *Wall Street Journal,* Nov. 9, 1977, p. 2: "New Approach to Protect Steel Industry from Imports . . ."

11. *United States* v. *E. I. du Pont de Nemours & Company,* 353 U.S. 586 (1957), in which the Supreme Court ordered du Pont to divest itself of its holdings of General Motors stock and to refrain from certain other activities on the ground that du Pont had acted in restraint of trade (thus restricting free competition) by acquiring GM stock and thus procuring for itself a captive market for its paints, plastics, and synthetic fabrics.

Chapter 11. Affirmative Action and Reverse Discrimination

1. *Brown* v. *Board of Education,* 349 U.S. 294 (1955). Cf. 347 U.S. 483 (1954).

2. The reader may be interested in reviewing accounts of the integration of the

public schools of Little Rock, Arkansas, and the University of Mississippi, which entailed such violence that federal troops had to be deployed to protect the students involved.

3. *Plessy* v. *Ferguson,* 163 U.S. 537 (1896), dissenting opinion.
4. Ibid.
5. 416 U.S. 312 (1974), 507 P.2d 1169 (Wash. 1973).
6. 553 P.2d 1152 (Cal. 1976).
7. Richard Wasserstrom, "The University and the Case for Preferential Treatment," *American Philosophical Quarterly,* 13:165ff. (April, 1976).
8. Wasserstrom, "Racism and Sexism," unpublished manuscript.
9. Judith Jarvis Thomson, "Preferential Hiring," *Philosophy and Public Affairs,* 2:364ff. (Summer, 1973).
10. Epilogue, "The Bakke Case: Are Racial Quotas Defensible?" *Saturday Review* (Oct. 15, 1977), p. 16.
11. In fact, there have already been demands that the passing grades on bar exams be reduced so as to ensure the admission of larger numbers of blacks, because so many of them were failing; and at least one state (Pennsylvania) has acceded to those demands.
12. Cf. Robert Simon, "Preferential Hiring: A Reply to Judith Jarvis Thomson," *Philosophy and Public Affairs,* 3:312ff. (Spring, 1974).
13. Albert Shanker, in the *New York Times,* Oct. 9, 1977, p. E7.
14. Cf. *New York Times,* Sept. 23, 1977. Also cf. Statement by Senator Daniel Patrick Moynihan, Sept. 23, 1977 and Albert Shanker, *New York Times,* Sept. 11, 1977, p. E9.
15. Meg Greenfield, "Teaching Kids the New Discrimination," *Newsweek,* July 4, 1977.
16. *Slaughter House Cases,* 16 Wall., 83 U.S. 36 (1873).
17. *Jones* v. *Alfred H. Mayer Co.,* 392 U.S. 409 (1968).
18. Cf. John H. Bunzel, "Affirmative Action without Quotas," *Wall Street Journal* (Oct. 3, 1977), p. 24.
19. *Minneapolis Tribune,* May 22, 1977, pp. 1B, 16B.
20. Cf. *New York Times,* Jan. 29, 1975, p. 17, for a review of court decisions on this issue.

Chapter 12. **Civil Disobedience**
1. *Crito,* 50b (Library of Liberal Arts edition, p. 60).
2. Ibid., 51c (LLA ed., p. 61).
3. Ibid., 54c–d (LLA ed., p. 65).
4. *Apology,* 30b (LLA ed., p. 36).
5. Exodus, I:15ff.
6. Aristotle, *Politics,* V., viii, 1307b.
7. John Locke, A *Letter Concerning Toleration,* 2nd ed. (Indianapolis: Bobbs-Merrill, Library of Liberal Arts), p. 48.
8. *De Republica,* III, xxii, 33. Emphasis added.
9. *De Legibus,* I, xii, 33.
10. *Decretalia Gratiani,* I, viii, 2.
11. *Summa Theologica,* 1a 2ae, quae. 91, art. 2.
12. Ibid., 1a 2ae, quae. 95 and 104, 6.

13. Carl Cohen, *Civil Disobedience* (New York: Columbia University Press, 1971), p. 4.
14. Craig Colby, "Civil Disobedience: A Case for Separate Treatment"; Bernard G. Segal, and Herbert L. Packer, "Civil Rights and Civil Disobedience to Law," in Hugo Adam Bedau, ed., *Civil Disobedience: Theory and Practice* (New York: Pegasus, 1969), pp. 90 ff.
15. Nicholas W. Puner, "Civil Disobedience: An Analysis and Rationale," *New York University Law Review*, 43:651ff. (1968). Puner does not hold this view himself, but cites it and criticizes it.
16. William L. Taylor, "Civil Disobedience: Observations on the Strategies of Protest," in Bedau, op. cit., p. 99.
17. Sidney Hook, "Social Protest and Civil Disobedience," *The Humanist*, Vol. 27, 1967, reprinted in Paul Kurtz (ed.), *Moral Problems in Contemporary Society* (Englewood Cliffs, N.J.: Prentice-Hall, 1969), p. 163.
18. I am indebted to Carl Cohen's book *Civil Disobedience* for some of these illustrations.
19. Daniel Berrigan, "Conscience, the Law, and Civil Disobedience," *U.S. Catholic*, June 1969, reprinted in his book *No Bars to Manhood* (New York: Bantam Books, 1970), pp. 40 f. My emphasis throughout.
20. Albert Bigelow, "Why I am Sailing This Boat into the Bomb-Test Area," *Liberation*, February 1956, reprinted in Bedau, op. cit., pp. 146 ff.
21. Again, I am indebted to Carl Cohen for the example.
22. Cf. Cohen, op. cit., Chapter IV, for an excellent treatment of this subject.
23. 345 U.S. 405, 409 (1953).
24. 379 U.S. 536, 555 (1965).
25. 379 U.S. 559, 567, 574 (1965).
26. 379 U.S. 559, 578 (1965).
27. 383 U.S. 168 (1966).
28. Puner, op. cit., p. 697.
29. *U.S.* v. *Miller*, 386 U.S. 911 (1967).
30. *New York Times*, December 12, 1964.
31. Colby, op. cit.
32. Bedau, op. cit., introduction, p. 19.
33. Louis E. Lomas, *The Negro Revolt* (New York: New American Library, 1963), pp. 102 ff.

Chapter 13. **Terrorism, Guerrilla Warfare, and International Morality**

1. See S. Andreski, "Terror," in Julius Gould and William L. Kolb, eds., *A Dictionary of the Social Sciences* (New York: The Free Press, 1965); Paul Wilkinson, *Political Terrorism* (New York: John Wiley & Sons, 1974), pp. 11 ff.; J. Thornton, "Terror as a Weapon of Political Agitation," in Harry Eckstein, ed., *Internal War* (New York: The Free Press, 1964), pp. 73 ff.; Carl Leiden and Karl M. Schmitt, *The Politics of Violence: Revolution in the Modern World* (Englewood Cliffs, N.J.: Prentice-Hall, 1968), pp. 30 ff.; Anthony M. Burton, *Urban Terrorism: Theory, Practice, and Response* (New York: The Free Press, 1975), pp. 3 ff.; Douglas Pike, *Viet Cong: The Organization and Techniques of the National Liberation Front of South Vietnam* (Cambridge, Mass.: MIT Press, 1966), pp. 85 f.; Geoffrey Fairbairn, *Revolu-*

tionary Guerrilla Warfare: The Countryside Version (Harmondsworth, England: Penguin Books, 1974), pp. 348 ff.

2. Burnett, Interview with Sean MacBride, *Skeptic,* vol. 8 (Jan.–Feb., 1976), p. 50.

3. Dorothy Macardle, *The Irish Republic,* quoted in Stencel, "Skeptic Backgrounder—Terrorism: An Idea Whose Time Has Come," *Skeptic,* vol. 8 (Jan.–Feb., 1976), p. 50.

4. The extremist Stern Gang carried out a number of attacks on civilian and diplomatic targets, including the assassinations of Lord Moyne, British Minister of State for the Middle East (1944), and Count Folke Bernadotte, United Nations mediator (1948), as well as the infamous massacre of civilians in Deir Yassin (April 9, 1948), which has since served as a major point in Arab propaganda. See Anthony M. Burton, op. cit., pp. 158 ff.; Robert B. Asprey, *War in the Shadows: The Guerrilla in History* (Garden City, N.Y.: Doubleday, 1975), vol. 2, pp. 843 ff.; Netanel Lorch, *Edge of the Sword: Israel's War of Independence* (New York: G.P. Putnam's Sons, 1961), passim; Arthur Koestler, *Promise and Fulfilment: Palestine, 1917–1949* (London: Macmillan, 1949); Samuel Katz, *Days of Fire* (Garden City, N.Y.: Doubleday, 1968); Menachem Begin, *The Revolt: Story of the Irgun,* tr. Samuel Katz (New York: Henry Schuman, 1951).

5. Begin, op. cit., pp. 212 ff. In the attack on the King David Hotel, hotel authorities were warned on the phone that the building was about to be blown up. The French consulate, which was nearby, was also notified. In the explosion, nearly 200 persons were killed or wounded, evidently because the warnings failed to get through or because they were ignored.

6. Stencel, op. cit.

7. Ibid.

8. Roland Gaucher, *The Terrorists: From Tsarist Russia to the O.A.S.,* tr. Paula Spurlin (London: Secker & Warburg, 1968), p. 12.

9. Ibid., p. 21.

10. See Samuel Eliot Morison, *The Oxford History of the American People* (New York: Oxford University Press, 1965), pp. 186 f. Morison notes that in general "the Sons of Liberty kept the mobs well in hand, and no blood was shed anywhere."

11. Dorothy Macardle, op. cit.

12. The poet Kaliaev passed up an opportunity to assassinate the Grand Duke Sergius because other members of his family were riding in a coach with him at the time. Stencel, loc. cit. Cf. Melvin C. Wren, *The Course of Russian History,* 3rd ed. (New York: Macmillan, 1968), p. 442.

13. See Dugard, "International Terrorism and the Just War," *Stanford Journal of International Studies,* vol. 12 (1977), p. 21.

14. Robert B. Asprey, op. cit., p. 969.

15. David C. Rapoport, *Assassination and Terrorism* (Toronto: Canadian Broadcasting Corp., 1971), p. 62.

16. Richard Clutterbuck, *Protest and the Urban Guerrilla* (London: Cassell, 1973), p. 132.

17. Ibid., p. 134.

18. Gustav Morf, *Terror in Quebec: Case Studies of the FLQ* (Toronto: Clarke, Irwin & Co., 1970), pp. 164 ff.

19. Edward Weisband and Damir Roguly, "Palestinian Terrorism: Violence, Verbal Strategy, and Legitimacy," in Yonah Alexander, ed., *International Terrorism: National, Regional, and Global Perspectives* (New York: Frederick A. Praeger, 1976), p. 284.

20. Wilkinson, op. cit., p. 123.

21. Ibid.

22. Alexander, op. cit., p. 303.

23. Israel Ministry for Foreign Affairs, *Accessories to Terror* (Jerusalem, 1972), p. 46.

24. Jenkins, "International Terrorism: A New Mode of Conflict," in David Carlton, ed., *International Terrorism* (New York: John Wiley & Sons, 1975), p. 35.

25. *New York Times*, Nov. 24, 1974, p. 1.

26. Robert B. Asprey, op. cit., passim.

27. Ibid., pp. 391 f.

28. Ibid.

29. George Grivas, *The Memoirs of General Grivas*, ed. Charles Foley (New York: Frederick A. Praeger, 1965).

30. Will and Ariel Durant, *The Age of Napoleon* (New York: Simon and Schuster, 1975), p. 65.

31. Ibid., p. 66.

32. Ibid., p. 70.

33. Gaucher, op. cit., p. 113.

34. Ibid.

35. Ibid., p. 115.

36. Ibid.

37. V. I. Lenin, *Collected Works*, vol. 17, p. 321; cited in Fairbairn, p. 72.

38. Fairbairn, op. cit., p. 73.

39. See Franklin M. Osanka, *Modern Guerrilla Warfare* (New York: The Free Press, 1962), p. 75.

40. In Marxist writings, the *Lumpenproletariat* are degraded and contemptible members of the working class, inferior to other members of their class.

41. But cf. Guttmann, "The Palestinian Myth," *Commentary*, vol. 60 (Oct., 1975), p. 43.

42. See J. Bowyer Bell, *Transnational Terror* (Washington, D.C.: American Enterprise Institute for Public Policy Research, Hoover Institution Studies, 1975), p. 57.

43. Jay Mallin, ed., *Terror and Urban Guerrillas: A Study of Tactics and Documents* (Coral Gables, Fla.: University of Miami Press, 1971), p. 47.

44. This is illustrated most notably by the suppression of the Hungarian uprising of 1956 and the invasion of Czechoslovakia in 1968, as well as the continued occupation of Lithuania, Latvia, Estonia, the Ukraine, and other once-free nations of Eastern Europe.

45. Harkabi, "The Palestinian National Covenant," in Michael Curtis et al., eds., *The Palestinians: People, History, Politics* (New Brunswick, N.J.: Transaction Books, 1975). The *Covenant* is reprinted in full with a commentary.

46. The interesting shift of Soviet propaganda from the early post-war period, when it strongly supported Israel, to more recent years when it has pushed the "Zionism is racism" line, is documented in Baruch A. Hazan, *Soviet*

Propaganda: A Case Study of the Middle East Conflict (Jerusalem: Keter Publishing House of Jerusalem Ltd., 1976).

47. But cf. Lassa Oppenheim, *International Law,* H. Lauterpacht, ed., 7th Ed. (London: Longmans, 1952), Vol. II, p. 336.
48. Ibid., p. 337.
49. Ibid., p. 338.
50. Ibid., p. 346.
51. Ibid., p. 370.
52. For example, the murder of Pierre LaPorte by the F.L.Q. and the German airline passenger by the P.F.L.P.
53. Oppenheim, op. cit., p. 266.
54. But cf. ibid., p. 567, n. 1.
55. Cf. 61 Am. Jur. 2d 429.
56. 2 How. 210 (1844), at 232.
57. 15 Howell's State Trials 1286 (1718), cited in Joseph W. Bingham, "Piracy," in *Research in International Law* (Cambridge: Harvard Law School, 1932), p. 804.
58. *United States* v. *The Pirates,* 18 U.S. (5 Wheat.) 174 (1820).
59. Ibid., at 184.
60. Lassa Oppenheim, *International Law: A Treatise,* 8th Edition, ed. by H. Lauterpacht (London: Longmans, 1955), vol. I, p. 614.
61. T. J. Lawrence, *The Principles of International Law,* cited in Bingham, op. cit., p. 773. See also Bingham, pp. 777 and 792.
62. Thomas Hobbes, *Leviathan* (New York: Library of Liberal Arts, 1958), p. 146.
63. It is rather difficult to define precisely what that sense may be, but scholars of international law have been trying. For one such attempt, see Burton M. Leiser, *Custom, Law, and Morality: Conflict and Continuity in Social Behavior* (Garden City, N.Y.: Doubleday, 1969), pp. 99 ff.
64. See Kilner, ed., *Arab Report and Record* no. 3 (March, 1973), p. 117.
65. Thomas A. Bailey, *A Diplomatic History of the American People,* 4th ed. (New York: Appleton-Century-Crofts, 1950), p. 92.
66. T. Harry Williams et al., *A History of the United States* (New York: Alfred A. Knopf, 1959), p. 248. Actually the process took years. In 1805 the United States concluded a favorable treaty with Tripoli, but still had to pay $60,000 to ransom American prisoners. Finally, in 1816 Algiers, Tunis and Tripoli were forced to pay for losses to American shipping.
67. Philip Gosse, *The History of Piracy* (London: Longmans, 1932), p. 15.
68. Ibid.
69. Ibid., p. 69, n. 1.
70. Hamilton Cochran, *Freebooters of the Red Sea: Pirates, Politicians, and Pieces of Eight* (Indianapolis: Bobbs-Merrill, 1965), p. 89.
71. But cf. A. Yaniv, *P.L.O.: A Profile* (Jerusalem: Israel Universities Study Group for Middle Eastern Affairs, 1974), p. 7; Waxman, "Varieties of Palestinian Nationalism," in Curtis, op. cit.; Porat, "The Palestinian-Arab Nationalist Movement," in Curtis, op. cit.; Neyer, "The Emergence of Yasser Arafat," in Curtis, op. cit.; Anabtawi, "The Palestinians and the 1973 Middle East War," in Middle East Information Series no. 15 (1973–74), pp. 40 ff.
72. Cf. Bell, op. cit., pp. 72 ff.
73. Cf. Bell, ibid.; Clutterbuck, op. cit., p. 165; and Weisband, op. cit., pp. 115 ff.

74. Bell, op. cit., p. 72.
75. Ibid.
76. Ibid.
77. Ibid.
78. Ibid., p. 73.
79. Ibid.
80. Ibid.
81. But cf. Fairbairn, op. cit.; Asprey, op. cit.; Weisband, op. cit.; Colebrook, "Israel—with Terrorists," *Commentary*, vol. 35 (July 1974), pp. 35 ff.; and Romaniecki, "The Soviet Union and International Terrorism," *Soviet Studies*, vol. 26 (1974), pp. 417 ff.
82. See *New York Times*, June 28, 1976–July 6, 1976, for a running account of the incident. The story has been told in more detail by William Stevenson, *Ninety Minutes at Entebbe* (New York: Bantam Books, 1976).
83. "The pirate of tradition attacked on or from the sea. Certainly today, however, one should not deem the possibility of similar attacks in or from the air as too slight or too remote for consideration in drafting a convention on jurisdiction over piratical acts. With rapid advance in the arts of flying and air-sailing, it may not be long before bands of malefactors, who now confine their efforts to land, will find it profitable to engage in depredations in or from the air beyond territorial jurisdiction. Indeed, there even may occur thus a re-crudescence of large scale piracy." Bingham, op. cit., p. 809.
84. Ibid., p. 744.
85. In his comment on Article 7 of the Draft Convention on Piracy, Bingham observes that although there is considerable disagreement, some writers "argue that the pursuit is legal even against the protest of the littoral state." Ibid., p. 833.
86. *The Treatment of Arab Terrorists* (Jerusalem: Israel Information Center, 1975).
87. Laqueur, "The Futility of Terrorism," *Harper's Magazine*, vol. 252 (March, 1976), p. 105.

Selected Bibliography

The following list is not intended to be complete, though it contains many of the most recent works on the topics covered. It is intended, rather, as a guide for the interested student who may wish to delve further into any of the topics discussed here. Many important books and articles have been omitted because of lack of space, but by referring to books listed in this bibliography, the student will be able to trace the literature through footnotes and more specialized bibliographies.

Chapter 1. **Lord Devlin and the Enforcement of Morals**

ARMOUR, LESLIE. "The Concept of Crime." *Philosophy in Context,* 2 (1973), 23 ff.

CONWAY, DAVID A. "Law, Liberty, and Indecency." *Philosophy,* 49 (1974), 135 ff.

DEVLIN, SIR PATRICK. *The Enforcement of Morals.* Oxford: Oxford University Press, 1964.

DONNELLY, RICHARD C., et al. *Criminal Law.* New York: The Free Press, 1962.

DYBILOWSKI, J. C. "Lord Devlin's Morality and Its Enforcement." *Proceedings of the Aristotelian Society,* 75 (1974–75), 89 ff.

FLETCHER, JOSEPH F. *Morals and Medicine.* Princeton, N.J.: Princeton University Press, 1954.

FUCHS, JOSEF. *Natural Law,* trans. by Helmut Reckter and John A. Dowling. New York: Sheed and Ward, 1965.

GASTIL, RAYMOND. "Societal Limits on Majority Rights." *Journal of Social Philosophy,* 7 (1976), 8 ff.

HART, H. L. A. *Law, Liberty, and Morality.* Stanford, Calif.: Stanford University Press, 1963.

MARITAIN, JACQUES. *Man and the State.* Chicago: University of Chicago Press, 1951.

PACKARD, VANCE. *The Sexual Wilderness.* New York: David McKay, 1968.

PACKER, HERBERT L. *The Limits of the Criminal Sanction.* Stanford, Calif.: Stanford University Press, 1968.

PIKE, JAMES A. *You and the New Morality.* New York: Harper & Row, 1967.

ST. JOHN-STEVAS, NORMAN. *Life, Death and the Law.* Bloomington, Ind.: Indiana University Press, 1961.

SCHUR, EDWIN M. *Crimes Without Victims.* Englewood Cliffs, N.J.: Prentice-Hall, 1965.

TAYLOR, PAUL W., ed. *Problems in Moral Philosophy: An Introduction to Ethics*, Belmont, Calif.: Dickenson, 1967.

THIELICKE, HELMUT. *The Ethics of Sex*, trans. John W. Doberstein. New York: Harper & Row, 1964.

WHITELEY, C. H. and W. M. *Sex and Morals*. New York: Basic Books, 1967.

WILLIAMS, GLANVILLE. *The Sanctity of Life and Criminal Law*. New York: Knopf, 1957.

WISDOM, JOHN. *Logic and Sexual Morality*. Baltimore: Penguin, 1965.

WOOTTON, BARBARA. *Crime and the Criminal Law*. London: Stevens and Sons, 1963.

Chapter 2. Homosexuality

ALLEN, CLIFFORD. *Textbook of Psychosexual Disorders*, 2nd ed. New York: Oxford University Press, 1969.

ALTMAN, DENNIS. *The Homosexual: Oppression and Liberation*. New York: Outerbridge and Dienstfrey, 1971.

ANONYMOUS. "Homosexuality and the Law—A Right to Be Different." *Albany Law Review*, 38 (1973), 84 ff.

ANONYMOUS. "The Homosexual's Legal Dilemma." *Arkansas Law Review*, 27 (1973), 687 ff.

BAILEY, D. SHERWIN. *Homosexuality and the Western Christian Tradition*. New York: Longmans, Green, 1955.

BENSON, R. O. D. *In Defense of Homosexuality, Male and Female*. New York: Julian Press, 1965.

BERGLER, E. *Homosexuality: Disease or Way of Life?* New York: Hill and Wang, 1957.

BIEBER, IRVING, et al. *Homosexuality: A Psychoanalytic Study*. New York: Basic Books, 1962.

BRECHER, EDWARD M. *The Sex Researchers*. Boston: Little, Brown, 1969.

BRITISH COUNCIL OF CHURCHES. *Sex and Morality*. London: SCM Press, 1966.

CAPRIO, FRANK S., and DONALD R. BRENNER. *Sexual Behavior: Psycho-Legal Aspects*. New York: Citadel, 1961.

COCHRAN, W. G., et al. *Statistical Problems of the Kinsey Report*. Westport, Conn.: Greenwood Press, 1954.

COMMITTEE ON HOMOSEXUAL OFFENSES AND PROSTITUTION. *The Wolfenden Report*. New York: Stein and Day, 1963.

CORY, D. W. *The Homosexual in America*, 2nd ed. Pasadena, Calif.: Castle Press, 1960.

CORY, D. W., and J. P. LeROY. *The Homosexual and His Society: A View from Within*. New York: Citadel, 1963.

DeRIVER, J. PAUL. *Crime and the Sexual Psychopath*. Springfield, Ill.: Charles C Thomas, 1958.

ELLIS, ALBERT. *Homosexuality; Its Causes and Cure*. New York: Lyle Stuart, 1965.

ELLIS, ALBERT, and RALPH BRANCALE. *The Psychology of Sex Offenders*. Springfield, Ill.: Charles C Thomas, 1956.

FISHER, PETER. *The Gay Mystique: The Myth and Reality of Male Homosexuality*. New York: Stein and Day, 1972.

FLUGEL, J. C. *Man, Morals and Society.* New York: International Universities Press, 1948.

GEBHARD, PAUL H., et al. *Sex Offenders.* New York: Harper & Row, 1965.

GEDDES, D. P., ed. *An Analysis of the Kinsey Reports on Sexual Behavior in the Human Male and Female.* New York: New American Library, 1962.

GIBBENS, TREVOR C. N., and JOYCE PRINCE. *Child Victims of Sex Offences.* London: ISTD, 1963.

HIRSCHFELD, MAGNUS. *Sexual Anomalies and Perversions.* London: Encyclopaedic Press, 1966.

HOFFMAN, MARTIN. *The Gay World: Male Homosexuality and the Social Creation of Evil.* New York: Basic Books, 1968.

HYDE, H. M. *The Trials of Oscar Wilde.* London: William Hodge, 1948.

JERSILD, JENS. *The Normal Homosexual Male Versus the Boy Molester.* Copenhagen: Nyt Nordisk Forlag Arnold Busck, 1967.

LENTZ, WILLIAM B. "Marriage Rights: Homosexuals and Transsexuals." *Akron Law Review,* 8 (1975), 369 ff.

MARMOR, JUDD. "Homosexuality," in Mary S. Calderone (ed.), *Sexuality and Human Values.* New York: Association Press, 1974.

MARMOR, JUDD, ed. *Sexual Inversion: The Multiple Roots of Homosexuality.* New York: Basic Books, 1965.

MASTERS, R. E. L. *The Homosexual Revolution.* New York: Julian Press, 1962.

McCORD, WILLIAM, and JOAN McCORD. *Psychopathy and Delinquency.* New York: Grune and Stratton, 1956.

MOHR, J. W., et al. *Pedophilia and Exhibitionism.* Toronto: Toronto University Press, 1965.

NAGEL, THOMAS. "Sexual Perversion." *The Journal of Philosophy,* 66 (1969), 5 ff.

PARKER, WILLIAM. *Homosexuality Bibliography: Supplement, 1970–75.* Metuchen, N.J.: Scarecrow Press, 1977.

PITTENGER, NORMAN. "Homosexuality and the Christian Tradition." *Christianity and Crisis,* 34 (1974), 178 ff.

PLUMMER, D. *Queer People.* New York: Citadel, 1965.

RADZINOWICZ, L. *Sexual Offences: A Report of the Cambridge Department of Criminal Science.* London: Macmillan, 1957.

REINHARDT, JAMES M. *Sex Perversions and Sex Crimes.* Springfield, Ill.: Charles C Thomas, 1957.

RUDDICK, SARA. "On Sexual Morality," in James Rachel (ed.), *Moral Problems.* New York: Harper and Row, 1971.

SAGHIR, MARCEL T., and ELI ROBINS. *Male and Female Homosexuality.* Baltimore: Williams and Wilkins, 1973.

SCHOFIELD, MICHAEL. *Sociological Aspects of Homosexuality: A Comparative Study of Three Types of Homosexuals.* Boston: Little, Brown, 1966.

SLOVENKO, RALPH, ed. *Sexual Behavior and the Law.* Springfield, Ill.: Charles C Thomas, 1965.

STORR, ANTHONY. *Sexual Deviation.* Baltimore: Penguin, 1964.

TEAL, DONN. *The Gay Militants.* New York: Stein and Day, 1971.

TRIPP, C. *The Homosexual Matrix.* New York: McGraw-Hill, 1975.

WARREN, CAROL A. B. *Identity and Community in the Gay World.* New York: John Wiley & Sons, 1974.

WASSERSTROM, RICHARD (ed.). *Morality and the Law*. Belmont, Calif.: Wadsworth Publishing Co., 1970.

WEINBERG, MARTIN S., et al. *Homosexuality: An Annotated Bibliography*. New York: Harper and Row, 1972.

WEINBERG, MARTIN S., et al. *Male Homosexuals: Their Problems and Adaptations*. New York: Oxford University Press, 1974.

WEST, DONALD J. *The Young Offender*. Baltimore: Penguin, 1967.

———. *Homosexuality*. Chicago: Aldine, 1967.

———. *Homosexuality Re-examined*. Minneapolis: University of Minnesota Press, 1977.

WHITELEY, C. H., and W. M. WHITELEY. *Sex and Morals*. London: Batsford, 1967.

WILLIAMS, COLIN J. *Homosexuals and the Military: A Study of Less Than Honorable Discharge*. New York: Harper and Row, 1971.

Chapter 3. Contraception and Abortion

ABBOTT, WALTER M., S. J., ed. *The Documents of Vatican II*. New York: Herder and Herder, 1966.

Abortion: An Ethical Discussion. London: Church Assembly Board for Social Responsibility, 1965.

ATKINSON, GAY M. "The Morality of Abortion." *International Philosophical Quarterly*, 14 (1974), 347 ff.

BAILEY, DERRICK SHERWIN. *Sexual Relations in Christian Thought*. New York: Harper & Row, 1959.

BARR, SAMUEL J. A. *Woman's Choice*. New York: Rawson Associates, 1977.

BARRETT, DONALD N., ed. *The Problem of Population: Moral and Theological Considerations*. Notre Dame, Ind.: University of Notre Dame Press, 1964.

BATES, JEROME E., and EDWARD S. ZAWADZKI. *Criminal Abortion: A Study in Medical Sociology*. Springfield, Ill.: Charles C Thomas, 1964.

BENN, S. I. "Abortion, Infanticide, and Respect for Persons," in Feinberg, Joel (ed.), *The Problem of Abortion*. Belmont, Cal.: Wadsworth Publishing Co., 1973.

BOK, SISSELA. "Ethical Problems of Abortion." *Hastings Center Studies*, No. 2 (Jan., 1974), 33 ff.

BRANDT, R. B. "The Morality of Abortion." *The Monist*, 56 (1972), 503 ff.

BRODY, BARUCH A. "Abortion and the Law." *Journal of Philosophy*, 68 (1971).

———. "Abortion and the Sanctity of Human Life." *American Philosophical Quarterly*, 10 (1973), 133 ff.

BROMBY, DOROTHY DUNBAR. *Catholics and Birth Control, Contemporary Views on Doctrine*. New York: The Devin-Adair Company, 1965.

BURTON, RICHARD T. *Religious Doctrine and Medical Practice*. Springfield, Ill.: Charles C Thomas, 1958.

CALLAHAN, DANIEL. *Abortion: Law, Choice and Morality*. New York: Macmillan, 1970.

CALLAHAN, DANIEL, ed. *The Catholic Case for Contraception*. New York: Macmillan, 1969.

———. *The American Population Debate*. Garden City, N.Y.: Doubleday-Anchor Books, 1971.

CARRIER, L. S. "Abortion and the Right to Life." *Social Theory and Practice*, 3 (1975), 381 ff.

CHASTEEN, EDGAR R. *The Case for Compulsory Birth Control.* Englewood Cliffs, N.J.: Prentice-Hall, Inc., 1971.

CHILDRESS, JAMES. "A Response to 'Conferred Rights and the Fetus.' " *Journal of Religious Ethics,* 2 (1974), 77 ff.

CLARK, L. M. G. "Reply to Sumner on Abortion." *Canadian Journal of Philosophy,* 4 (1974), 183 ff.

COFFEY, PATRICK J. "Toward a Sound Moral Policy on Abortion." *The New Scholasticism,* 47 (1973), 105 ff.

CONNERY, JOHN R. *Abortion: The Development of the Roman Catholic Perspective.* Chicago: Loyola University Press, 1977.

COOKE, ROBERT E., et al. *The Terrible Choice: The Abortion Dilemma.* New York: Bantam, 1968.

CURRAN, CHARLES, ed. *Contraception: Authority and Dissent.* New York: Herder and Herder, 1969.

CURRAN, CHARLES E. *A New Look at Christian Morality.* Notre Dame, Ind.: Fides Publishers, 1968.

DE GEORGE, RICHARD T. "Legal Enforcement, Moral Pluralism, and Abortion." *Proceedings, Catholic Philosophical Association,* 49 (1975), 171 ff.

DENES, MAGDA. *In Necessity and Sorrow: Life and Death in an Abortion Hospital.* New York: Basic Books, 1976.

DICKENS, BERNARD H. *Abortion and the Law.* Bristol, England: MacGibbon and Kee Ltd., 1966.

DRAPER, ELIZABETH. *Birth Control in the Modern World.* Baltimore: Penguin, 1965.

DRINAN, ROBERT F. "The Morality of Abortion Laws." *The Catholic Lawyer,* 14 (1968).

DUHAMEL, JOSEPH S. *The Catholic Church and Birth Control.* New York: Paulist Press, 1963.

DUPRÉ, LOUIS. *Contraception and Catholics: A New Appraisal.* Baltimore: Helicon, 1964.

EHRLICH, PAUL R. *The Population Bomb.* New York: Ballantine, 1968.

ENGELHARDT, H. TRISTRAM, JR. "The Ontology of Abortion." *Ethics,* 84 (1974), 217 ff.

ENGLISH, JANE. "Abortion and the Concept of a Person." *Canadian Journal of Philosophy,* 5 (1975), 233 ff.

EPSTEIN, LOUIS. *Sex Laws and Customs in Judaism.* New York: Bloch, 1948.

FEINBERG, JOEL, ed. *The Problem of Abortion.* Belmont, Cal.: Wadsworth Publishing Co., 1973.

FELDMAN, DAVID M. *Birth Control in Jewish Law.* New York: New York University Press, 1968.

FINNIS, JOHN. "The Rights and Wrongs of Abortion: A Reply to Judith Thomson." *Philosophy and Public Affairs,* 2 (1973), 117 ff.

FLETCHER, JOSEPH F. "Four Indicators of Humanhood: The Enquiry Matures." *Hastings Center Report,* 4 (Dec., 1974), 4 ff.

FOOT, PHILLIPPA, "The Problem of Abortion and the Doctrine of Double Effect." *The Oxford Review,* 5 (1967).

FOST, NORMAN. "Our Curious Attitude Toward the Fetus." *Hastings Center Report,* 4 (Feb., 1974), 4 f.

FREEHOF, SOLOMON. *Recent Reform Responsa.* Cincinnati: Hebrew Union College Press, 1963.

GEBHARD, PAUL H., et al. *Pregnancy, Birth and Abortion.* New York: Harper & Row, 1958.

GERBER, R. J. "Abortion: Parameters for Decision." *Ethics,* **82** (1972), 137 ff.

GERBER, D. "Abortion: The Uptake Argument." *Ethics,* **83** (1973), 80 ff.

GOOD, FREDERICK L., and OTIS F. KELLY. *Marriage, Morals and Medical Ethics.* New York: P. J. Kennedy, 1951.

GOODRICH, J. "The Morality of Killing." *Philosophy,* **44** (1969).

GORDIS, ROBERT. *Sex and the Family in Jewish Tradition.* New York: Burning Bush Press, 1967.

GRANFIELD, DAVID. *The Abortion Decision.* Garden City, N.Y.: Doubleday, 1969.

GREEN, RONALD. "Conferred Rights and the Fetus." *Journal of Religious Ethics,* **2** (1974), 55 ff.

GRISEZ, GERMAIN G. *Abortion: The Myths, the Realities, and the Arguments.* New York: Corpus Books, 1970.

GROUP FOR THE ADVANCEMENT OF PSYCHIATRY: COMMITTEE ON PSYCHIATRY AND LAW. *The Right to Abortion: A Psychiatric View.* New York: Scribner, 1970.

GREEP, ROY O., ed. *Human Fertility and Population Problems.* Cambridge, Mass.: Schenkman, 1963.

GUTTMACHER, ALLAN F. *Babies by Choice or by Chance.* New York: Avon, 1961.

GUTTMACHER, ALLAN F., ed. *The Case for Legalized Abortions Now.* Berkeley, Calif.: Diablo Press, 1967.

HALL, ROBERT E. *Abortion in a Changing World,* Vols. I and II. New York: Columbia University Press, 1970.

HARE, R. M. "Abortion and the Golden Rule." *Philosophy and Public Affairs,* **4** (1975), 201 ff.

HARRISON, STANLEY M. "The Unwilling Dead." *Proceedings, Catholic Philosophical Association,* **46** (1972), 199 ff.

HIMES, NORMAN. *Medical History of Contraception.* Baltimore: Williams and Wilkins, 1936.

HUMBER, JAMES M. "Abortion: The Avoidable Moral Dilemma." *Journal of Value Inquiry,* **9** (1975), 282 ff.

————. "The Case Against Abortion." *The Thomist,* **39** (1975), 65 ff.

HUSER, ROGER J. *The Crime of Abortion in Common Law,* Canon Law Studies No. 162. Washington, D. C.: Catholic University of America Press, 1942.

INSTITUTE OF MEDICINE. *Legalized Abortion and the Public Health: Report of a Study.* Washington, D.C.: National Academy of Sciences, 1975.

JAGGAR, ALISON. "Abortion and a Woman's Right to Decide." *Philosophical Forum,* **5** (1973), 347 ff.

JAKOBOVITS, IMMANUEL. *Jewish Medical Ethics.* New York: Bloch, 1975.

JENKINS, ALICE. *Law for the Rich.* London: Victor Gollancz, 1961.

KAHANA, K. *The Concept of Marriage in Jewish Law.* Leiden: E. J. Brill, 1966.

KINSEY, ARTHUR C. et al. *Sexual Behavior in the Human Female.* Philadelphia: W. B. Saunders, 1953.

————. *Sexual Behavior in the Human Male.* Philadelphia: W. B. Saunders, 1948.

KOHL, MARVIN. "Abortion and the Argument from Innocence." *Inquiry,* **14** (1971).

LADER, LAURENCE. *Abortion*. Indianapolis: Bobbs-Merrill, 1966.

————. *Margaret Sanger and the Fight for Birth Control*. Garden City, N.Y.: Doubleday, 1955.

LEE, NANCY HOWELL. *The Search for an Abortionist*. Chicago: University of Chicago Press, 1969.

LINDSAY, ANNE. "On the Slippery Slope Again." *Analysis*, **35** (1974).

MARGOLIS, JOSEPH. "Abortion." *Ethics*, **84** (1973), 51 ff.

MONTAGU, ASHLEY. *Life Before Birth*. New York: New American Library, 1964.

MOORE, HAROLD F. "Abortion and the Logic of Moral Justification." *Journal of Value Inquiry*, **9** (1975), 140 ff.

MYRNA, FRANCES. "Abortion: A Philosophical Analysis." *Feminist Studies*, **1** (1972), 49 ff.

NARVESON, JAN. "Semantics, Future Generations, and the Abortion Problem." *Social Theory and Practice*, **3** (1975), 461 ff.

NEWTON, LISA. "Humans and Persons: A Reply to Tristram Englehardt." *Ethics*, **85** (1975), 332 ff.

NOONAN, JOHN T., JR. *Contraception*. Cambridge, Mass.: Harvard University Press, 1965.

————. *The Morality of Abortion: Legal and Historical Perspectives*. Cambridge, Mass.: Harvard University Press, 1970.

PERKINS, ROBERT L., ed. *Abortion: Pro and Con*. Cambridge, Mass.: Schenkman Publishing Co., 1974.

PERRY, M. J. "Abortion, the Public Morals, and the Police Power: The Ethical Function of Substantive Due Process." *UCLA Law Review*, **23** (1976), 689 ff.

PLUHAR, WERNER S. "Abortion and Simple Consciousness." *Journal of Philosophy*, **74** (1977), 159 ff.

POLE, NELSON. "To Respect Human Life." *Philosophy in Context*, **2** (1973), 16 ff.

POTTS, MALCOLM, et al. *Abortion*. Cambridge, England: Cambridge University Press, 1977.

PYLE, LEO, ed. *Pope and Pill*. Baltimore: Helicon Press, 1969.

RAMSEY, PAUL. *Deeds and Rules in Christian Ethics*. New York: Scribner, 1967.

————. *Life or Death: Ethics and Options*. Seattle: University of Washington Press, 1968.

————. "Abortion: A Review Article." *The Thomist*, **37** (1973).

ROCK, JOHN. *The Time Has Come: A Catholic Doctor's Proposal to End the Battle Over Birth Control*. New York: Knopf, 1963.

ROSEN, HAROLD, ed. *Abortion in America*. Boston: Beacon Press, 1967.

RUDINOW, JOEL. "On 'The Slippery Slope.'" *Analysis*, **34** (1974), 173 ff.

ST. JOHN-STEVAS, NORMAN. *Birth Control and Public Policy*. Santa Barbara, Calif.: Center for the Study of Democratic Institutions, 1960.

————. *The Right To Life*. New York: Holt, 1964.

SARVIS, BETTY, and HYMAN RODMAN. *The Abortion Controversy*, 2nd ed. New York: Columbia University Press, 1974.

SCHULDER, DIANE, and FLORYNCE KENNEDY. *Abortion Rap*. New York: McGraw-Hill, 1971.

SHAW, RUSSELL. *Abortion on Trial.* Dayton, Ohio: Pflaum Press, 1968.

SHER, GEORGE. "Hare, Abortion, and the Golden Rule." *Philosophy and Public Affairs,* 6 (1977), 185–90.

SHUSTER, GEORGE N. *The Problem of Population: Practical Catholic Application,* Vol. II. Notre Dame, Ind.: University of Notre Dame Press, 1964.

SMITH, DAVID T., ed. *Abortion and the Law.* Cleveland: Western Reserve University, 1967.

SOCIETY OF FRIENDS, AMERICAN FRIENDS SERVICE COMMITTEE. *Who Shall Live?* New York: Hill and Wang, 1970.

STITSKIN, LEON D. *Studies in Torah Judaism.* New York: Yeshiva University Press, 1969.

SUENENS, LEON JOSEPH CARDINAL. *Love and Control: The Contemporary Problem,* tr. by George J. Robinson. Westminster, Md.: The Newman Press, 1961.

SULLOWAY, ALVAH W. *Birth Control and Catholic Doctrine.* Boston: Beacon Press, 1959.

SUMNER, L. W. "Toward a Credible View of Abortion." *Canadian Journal of Philosophy,* 5 (1974), 163 ff.

TEO, WESLEY, D. H. "Abortion: The Husband's Constitutional Rights." *Ethics,* 85 (1975), 337 ff.

THOMSON, JUDITH JARVIS. "A Defense of Abortion." *Philosophy and Public Affairs,* 1 (1971), 47 ff.

————. "Rights and Deaths." *Philosophy and Public Affairs,* 2 (1973), 146 ff.

TOOLEY, MICHAEL. "Abortion and Infanticide." *Philosophy and Public Affairs,* 2 (1972), 37 ff.

UNITED STATES COMMISSION ON CIVIL RIGHTS. *Constitutional Aspects of the Right to Limit Childbearing.* Washington, D.C.: U.S. Government Printing Office, 1975.

UNITED STATES SENATE, HEARING BEFORE THE SUBCOMMITTEE ON CONSTITUTIONAL AMENDMENTS, 93rd Congress, Second Session on S.J. Res. 110 and S.J. Res. 130, March 6, March 7, April 10, 1974. Washington, D.C.: U.S. Govt. Printing Office, 1974.

WARREN, MARY ANNE. "On the Moral and Legal Status of Abortion." *The Monist,* 57 (1973), 43 ff.

WERNER, RICHARD. "Hare on Abortion." *Analysis,* 36 (1976), 177 ff.

WERTHEIMER, ROGER. "Understanding the Abortion Argument." *Philosophy and Public Affairs,* 1 (1971), 67 ff.

WILLIAMS, GLANVILLE. "Euthansia and Abortion." *University of Colorado Law Review,* 38 (1966).

————. *The Sanctity of Life and the Criminal Law.* New York: Knopf, 1968.

Chapter 4. Freedom of the Press and Censorship.

Chapter 5. Obscenity and Pornography

AMERICAN CIVIL LIBERTIES UNION. *Annual Reports.*

BERLIN, ISAIAH. *Four Essays on Liberty.* New York: Oxford University Press, 1970.

BERNINGHAUSEN, DAVID K. *The Flight from Reason: Essays on Intellectual Freedom in the Academy, the Press, and the Library.* Chicago: American Library Association, 1975.

BOGEN, DAVID S. "The Supreme Court's Interpretation of the Guarantee of Free Speech." *Maryland Law Review,* **35** (1976), 555 ff.

BOSLEY, KEITH, et al., ed. and tr. *Russia's Underground Poets.* New York: Praeger, 1969.

BOSMAJIAN, HAIG A. *The Language of Oppression.* Washington, D.C.: Public Affairs Press, 1974.

————. *Principles and Practice of Freedom of Speech.* Boston: Houghton Mifflin, 1971.

BOYER, PAUL S. *Purity in Print.* New York: Scribner, 1968.

BRINK, ANDRE P. "Literature and Offense." *Philosophical Papers,* **5** (1976), 53 ff.

CAPALDI, NICHOLAS, ed. *Clear and Present Danger: The Free Speech Controversy.* New York: Pegasus, 1969.

CHAFFEE, ZECHARIAH, JR. *Government and Mass Communications.* Hamden, Conn.: Shoe String Press, 1965.

CLOR, HARRY M. *Obscenity and Public Morality: Censorship in a Liberal Society.* Chicago: University of Chicago Press, 1969.

COMMAGER, HENRY S. *Freedom, Loyalty, Dissent.* New York: Oxford University Press, 1954.

COMSTOCK, ANTHONY. *Traps for the Young.* Cambridge, Mass.: Harvard University Press, 1967.

COUNTS, GEORGE S. *Education and the Foundations of Human Freedom.* Pittsburgh: University of Pittsburgh Press, 1963.

DEWHIRST, MARTIN, and ROBERT FARRELL. *The Soviet Censorship.* Metuchen, N.J.: Scarecrow Press, 1973.

DAILY, J. ELWOOD. *The Anatomy of Censorship.* New York: M. Dekker, 1973.

EDGERTON, JUDGE HENRY W. *Freedom in the Balance.* Ithaca, N.Y.: Cornell University Press, 1960.

EMERSON, THOMAS I. *The System of Freedom of Expression.* New York: Random House, 1970.

————. *Toward a General Theory of the First Amendment.* New York: Random House, 1966.

ERNST, MORRIS L., and ALAN U. SCHWARTZ. *Censorship: The Search for the Obscene.* New York: Macmillan, 1964.

GERBER, ALBERT. *Sex, Pornography, and the Law.* 2nd rev. ed. New York: Ballantine, 1964.

GILMORE, DONALD H. *Sex, Censorship, and Pornography.* San Diego: Greenleaf Classics, 1969.

GOODELL, CHARLES E. *Political Prisoners in America.* New York: Random House, 1973.

HACHTEN, WILLIAM. *The Supreme Court on Freedom of The Press: Decisions and Dissents.* Ames, Iowa: Iowa State University Press, 1968.

HAIMAN, FRANKLIN S. *Freedom of Speech.* New York: Random House, 1965.

HANEY, ROBERT W. *Comstockery in America.* Boston: Beacon Press, 1960.

HOLBROOK, DAVID, ed. *The Case Against Pornography.* LaSalle, Ill.: Library Press, 1972.

HOLLINGER, ROBERT. "Can a Scientific Theory Be Legitimately Criticized, Rejected, Condemned, or Suppressed on Ethical or Political Grounds?" *Journal of Value Inquiry,* 9 (1975), 303 ff.

HOOK, SIDNEY. *Paradoxes of Freedom.* Berkeley: University of California Press, 1962.

HOSPERS, JOHN. *Libertarianism: A New Turn in Political Philosophy.* Los Angeles: Nash Publishing Company, 1970.

HOYT, OLGA G., and EDWIN P. HOYT. *Censorship in America.* New York: Seabury Press, 1970.

HUGHES, DOUGLAS A., ed. *Perspectives in Pornography.* New York: St. Martin's Press, 1970.

JONES, H. M. "Censorship, State Secrets and Participatory Democracy." *Analysis,* 33 (1973), 143 f.

KONVITZ, MILTON R. *Expanding Liberties: Freedom's Gains in Postwar America.* New York: Viking, 1960.

KOROBEINIKOV, V. "What Is Behind the 'Freedom of Information' Concept?" *International Affairs* (Moscow), 2 (1976), 102 ff.

KURLAND, PHILIP B., ed. *Free Speech and Association: The Supreme Court and the First Amendment.* Chicago: University of Chicago Press, 1975.

LABEDZ, LEOPOLD, ed. *Solzhenitsyn: A Documentary Record,* enlarged ed. Bloomington, Ind.: Indiana University Press, 1973.

LISTON, ROBERT A. *The Right To Know: Censorship in America.* New York: F. Watts, 1973.

McCOY, RALPH E. *Freedom of the Press: An Annotated Bibliography.* Carbondale: Southern Illinois University Press, 1968.

MACDONALD, I. A. "The 'Offence Principle' As a Justification for Censorship." *Philosophical Papers,* 5 (1976), 67 ff.

McKEON, RICHARD, et al. *The Freedom To Read: Perspective and Program.* New York: R. R. Bowker, 1957.

MARCUSE, LUDWIG. *Obscene: The History of an Indignation.* New York: Fernhill House, 1965.

MARNELL, WILLIAM H. *The Right to Know: Media and the Common Good.* New York: Seabury Press, 1973.

MARX, KARL. *On Freedom of the Press and Censorship,* tr. Saul K. Padover. New York: McGraw-Hill, 1974.

MAYER, MILTON, ed. *Tradition of Freedom.* New York: Oceana, 1957.

MEIKLEJOHN, ALEXANDER. *Political Freedom: The Constitutional Powers of the People.* New York: Oxford University Press, 1965.

MEIKLEJOHN, DONALD. *Freedom and the Public: Public and Private Morality in America.* Syracuse: Syracuse University Press, 1965.

MOORE, JOHN BRUCE. "On Philosophizing about Freedom of Speech." *Southwestern Journal of Philosophy,* 6 (1975), 47 ff.

NELSON, HAROLD N., ed. *Freedom of the Press from Hamilton to the Warren Court.* Indianapolis: Bobbs-Merrill, 1966.

NEWCITY, MICHAEL A. "The Universal Copyright Convention as an Instrument of Repression: The Soviet Experiment." *Journal of International Law and Economics,* 39 (1975), 42 ff.

OBOLER, ELI M. *The Fear of the Word: Censorship and Sex.* Metuchen, N.J.: Scarecrow Press, 1974.

Obscenity Report. New York: Stein and Day, 1970.

POLANYI, MICHAEL. *Logic of Liberty.* Chicago: University of Chicago Press, 1951.

RANDALL, RICHARD S. *Censorship of the Movies: The Social and Political Control of a Mass Medium.* Madison: University of Wisconsin Press, 1968.

REMBAR, CHARLES. *The End of Obscenity.* New York: Simon and Schuster, 1970.

RUCKER, BRYCE W. *The First Freedom.* Carbondale: Southern Illinois University Press, 1971.

ST. JOHN-STEVAS, NORMAN. *Obscenity and the Law.* London: Secker and Warburg, 1956.

SCHAUER, FREDERICK F. *The Law of Obscenity.* Washington, D.C.: Bureau of National Affairs, 1976.

SCHROEDER, THEODORE A. *Free Speech Bibliography.* Philadelphia: B. Franklin, 1969.

_____. *Free Speech for Radicals.* Philadelphia: B. Franklin, 1969.

_____. *Constitutional Free Speech Defined and Defended.* New York: DaCapo Press, 1970.

SHAPIRO, MARTIN. *Freedom of Speech: The Supreme Court and Judicial Review.* Englewood Cliffs, N.J.: Prentice-Hall, 1966.

SHARP, DONALD B., ed. *Commentaries on Obscenity.* Metuchen, N.J.: Scarecrow Press, 1970.

SOMERVILLE, JOHN. "The Constitutional Rights of Communist Teachers and the Angela Davis Case." *Revolutionary World,* 9 (1974), 41 ff.

STRAUSS, LEO. *Persecution and the Art of Writing.* New York: The Free Press, 1952.

TINDER, GLENN E. *Tolerance: Toward a New Civility.* Amherst, Mass.: University of Massachusetts Press, 1976.

TUSSMAN, JOSEPH. *Government and the Mind.* New York: Oxford University Press, 1977.

UNITED STATES SENATE, COMMITTEE ON GOVERNMENT OPERATIONS, PERMANENT SUBCOMMITTEE ON INVESTIGATIONS. Negotiations and Statecraft: Hearing, Part 4. . . . *International Freedom to Write and Publish* (94th Congress, 1st Session). Washington, D.C.: U.S. Government Printing Office, 1975.

WIDMER, ELEANOR, ed. *Freedom and Culture: Literary Censorship in the Seventies.* Belmont, Calif.: Wadsworth Publishers, 1970.

WILSON, JAMES Q. "Violence, Pornography, and Social Science." *The Public Interest,* 22 (1971), 45 ff.

WOETZEL, R. K. *Philosophy of Freedom.* New York: Oceana, 1966.

WOLFSON, LEWIS W. "Whose First Amendment? The People Also Have a Right to Know about the Press." *Progressive,* 39 (Jan. 1975), 42 ff.

Chapter 6. The Concept of Punishment

ACTON, H. B., ed. *The Philosophy of Punishment.* New York: St. Martin's, 1969.

ANDENAES, JOHANNES. "Deterrence and Specific Offenses: Drunken Driving." *University of Chicago Law Review,* 38 (1971), 537 ff.

_____. *Punishment and Deterrence.* Ann Arbor: University of Michigan Press, 1974.

ARMSTRONG, K. G. "The Retributivist Hits Back." *Mind*, **70** (1961).

ATKINSON, MAX. "Interpreting Retributive Claims." *Ethics*, **85** (1974), 80 ff.

BAIER, KURT. "Is Punishment Retributive?" *Analysis*, **16** (1955).

BARNES, HARRY E. *The Repression of Crime*. Montclair, N.J.: Smith, Patterson, 1969.

BEDAU, HUGO, ed. *The Death Penalty in America*. Garden City, N.Y.: Doubleday Anchor Books, 1964.

————. *Capital Punishment in the United States*. New York: AMS Press, 1976.

BLUMBERG, ABRAHAM S. *Criminal Justice*. Chicago: Quadrangle Books, 1967.

CAHN, EDMOND N. *The Sense of Injustice: An Anthropomorphic View of Law*. New York: New York University Press, 1949.

CAHN, LENORE L., ed. *Confronting Injustice: The Edmond Cahn Reader*. Boston: Little, Brown, 1966.

CARD, CLAUDIA. "Retributive Penal Liability." *American Philosophical Quarterly Monograph*, **7** (1973), 17 ff.

CARRINGTON, FRANK G. *The Victims*. New Rochelle, N.Y.: Arlington House, 1975.

CHAMPLIN, T. S. "Punishment Without Offence." *American Philosophical Quarterly*, **13** (1976), 85 ff.

"Correcting Criminals: The Balance Shifts to Retribution. A Symposium." *Trial*, **12** (March, 1976), 12 ff.

CRESSEY, DONALD R. *Theft of the Nation: The Structure and Operations of Organized Crime in America*. New York: Harper & Row, 1969.

DERSHOWITZ, A. M. "Indeterminate Confinement: Letting the Therapy Fit the Harm." *University of Pennsylvania Law Review*, **123** (1974), 297 ff.

"Dismantling the Criminal Law System: Decriminalization and Divestment." *Wayne Law Review*, **19** (1973).

DOYLE, JAMES F. "Justice and Legal Punishment." *Philosophy*, **42** (1967).

EAST, SIR W. NORWOOD, ed. *The Roots of Crime*. London: Butterworth, 1954.

EWING, A. C. *The Morality of Punishment*. London: Routledge & Kegan Paul, 1929. Reprinted ed. Montclair, N.J.: Patterson Smith, 1970.

EZORSKY, GERTRUDE (ed.). *Philosophical Perspectives on Punishment*. Albany: State University of New York Press, 1972.

FEINBERG, JOEL. "Noncomparative Justice." *Philosophical Review*, **83** (1974), 297 ff.

FINGARETTE, HERBERT. "Addiction and Criminal Responsibility." *Yale Law Journal*, **84** (1975), 413 ff.

————. "Punishment and Suffering." *Proceedings and Addresses, American Philosophical Association*, **50** (1977), 504 ff.

FLEW, ANTONY. "The Justification of Punishment." *Philosophy*, **29** (1954).

FREUND, PAUL A. *On Law and Justice*. Cranbury, N.J.: A. S. Barnes, 1968.

GERBER, RUDOLPH J. and PATRICK D. MCANANY, eds. *Contemporary Punishment: Views, Explanations and Justifications*. Notre Dame, Ind.: University of Notre Dame Press, 1972.

GIBBS, JACK P. *Crime, Punishment, and Deterrence*. New York: Elsevier, 1975.

HART, H. L. A. *Punishment and Responsibility: Essays in the Philosophy of Law*. New York: Oxford University Press, 1968.

HARWARD, DONALD W. "The Bitter Pill of Punishment: Retribution." *Journal of Value Inquiry*, **10** (1976), 199 ff.

HIBBERT, CHRISTOPHER. *The Roots of Evil*. Boston: Little, Brown, 1963.

HONDERICH, T., ed. *Punishment: The Supposed Justifications*. New York: Harcourt Brace Jovanovich, 1970.

HOULGATE, LAURENCE D. "Excuses and the Criminal Law." *Southern Journal of Philosophy*, **13** (1975), 187 ff.

KIDDER, JOEL. "Requital and Criminal Justice." *International Philosophical Quarterly*, **15** (1975), 255 ff.

KLEINIG, JOHN. *Punishment and Desert*. The Hague: Martinus Nijhoff, 1973.

LADENSON, ROBERT F. "Does the Deterrence Theory of Punishment Exist?" *Philosophical Research Archives*, **2**, No. 1090 (1976).

LYONS, DAVID B. "Rights Against Humanity." *Philosophical Review*, **85** (1976), 208 ff.

LYONS, WILLIAM. "Deterrence Theory and Punishment of the Innocent." *Ethics*, **84** (1974), 346 ff.

McCLINTOCK, FREDERICK H. *Crimes of Violence*. New York: St. Martin's Press, Inc., 1963.

MABBOTT, J. D. "Punishment." *Mind*, **58** (1939).

MADDEN, EDWARD H., et al. *Philosophical Perspectives on Punishment*. Springfield, Ill.: Charles C Thomas, 1968.

MARGOLIS, JOSEPH. "Punishment." *Social Theory and Practice*, **2** (1973), 347 ff.

MENNINGER, KARL. *The Crime of Punishment*. New York: Viking, 1968.

_____. *The Vital Balance*. New York: Viking, 1963.

MESSICK, HANS. *The Silent Syndicate*. New York: Macmillan, 1967.

MIDDENDORFF, WOLF. *The Effectiveness of Punishment*. New York: F. B. Rothman, 1968.

MOBERLY, WALTER H. *The Ethics of Punishment*. Hamden, Conn.: Shoe String Press, 1968.

MORRIS, NORVAL. *The Habitual Criminal*. Cambridge, Mass.: Harvard University Press, 1951.

MORRIS, HERBERT. *On Guilt and Innocence: Essays in Legal Philosophy and Moral Pathology*. Berkeley: University of California Press, 1976.

MUELLER, S. O. W. *Crime, Law, and the Scholars*. Seattle: University of Washington Press, 1969.

MUNDLE, C. W. K. "Punishment and Desert." *Philosophical Quarterly*, **4** (1954).

NARVESON, JAN. "Three Analysis Retributivists." *Analysis*, **34** (1974), 185 ff.

OPTON, E. M., JR. "Psychiatric Violence Against Prisoners; When Therapy Is Punishment." *Mississippi Law Journal*, **45** (1974), 605 ff.

OSTERMAN, ROBERT. *A Report in Depth on Crime in America*. Silver Spring, Md.: *The National Observer*, 1966.

PARENT, W. A. "The Whole Life View of Criminal Desert." *Ethics*, **86** (1976), 350 ff.

PINCOFFS, EDMUND L. *The Rationale of Legal Punishment*. New York: Humanities Press, 1966.

POUPKO, CHANA K. "Political Ideas Underlying the Utilitarian Approach to Punishment." *Philosophy Today*, **18** (1974), 285 ff.

_____. "The Religious Basis of the Retributive Approach to Punishment." *The Thomist*, 39 (1975), 528 ff.

QUINNEY, RICHARD. *The Social Reality of Crime*. Boston: Little, Brown, 1970.

QUINTON, ANTHONY M. "On Punishment." *Analysis*, 14 (1954).

RAAB, FRANCIS V. "A Moralist Looks at the Durham and M'Naghton Rules." *Minnesota Law Review*, 46 (1961).

RAWLS, JOHN. "Two Concepts of Rules." *Philosophical Review*, 64 (1955).

RAY, ISAAC. *A Treatise on the Medical Jurisprudence of Insanity*, Winfred Overholser, ed. Cambridge, Mass.: Harvard University Press, 1962.

ROBBINS, IRA P., and JAMES E. SANDERS. "Judicial Integrity, the Appearance of Justice, and the Great Writ of Habeas Corpus: How to Kill Two Birds (Or More) with One *Stone*." *American Criminal Law Review*, 15 (1977), 63 ff.

ROSENGART, OLIVER. *The Rights of Suspects*. New York: Avon Books, 1974.

ROSS, ALF. *On Guilt, Responsibility, and Punishment*. Berkeley: University of California Press, 1975.

SCHEDLER, GEORGE. "On Telishing the Guilty." *Ethics*, 86 (1976), 256 ff.

SHAW, GEORGE BERNARD. *The Crime of Punishment*. New York: Citadel Press, 1961.

SZASZ, THOMAS. *Psychiatric Justice*. New York: Macmillan, 1965.

TARDE, GABRIEL. *Penal Philosophy*, trans. by R. Howell. Montclair, N.J.: Smith, Peterson, 1968.

TEICHMAN, JENNY. "Punishment and Remorse." *Philosophy*, 48 (1973), 335 ff.

THOMPSON, D. "The Means of Dealing with Criminals." *Philosophy of the Social Sciences*, 5 (1975), 1 ff.

VAN DEN HAAG, ERNEST. *Punishing Criminals: Concerning a Very Old and Painful Question*. New York: Basic Books, 1975.

VON HIRSCH, ANDREW. *Doing Justice: The Choice of Punishments*. Report of the Committee for the Study of Incarceration. New York: McGraw-Hill, 1976.

_____. "Giving Criminals Their Just Deserts." *Civil Liberties Review*, 3 (April–May, 1976), 23 ff.

WAGNER, PAUL A. and KEN WOODS. "Reason and the Criminal Rehabilitation Process." *Journal of Thought*, 12 (1977), 20 ff.

WASSERSTROM, RICHARD. "H. L. A. Hart and the Doctrines of Mens Rea and Criminal Responsibility." *Chicago Law Review*, 35 (1967), 92 ff.

WENNBERG, ROBERT N. "Act Utilitarianism, Deterrence, and the Punishment of the Innocent." *The Personalist*, 56 (1975), 178 ff.

WERTHAM, FREDERIC. *A Sign for Cain*. New York: Macmillan, 1966.

WERTHEIMER, ALAN. "Should Punishment Fit the Crime?" *Social Theory and Practice*, 3 (1975), 403 ff.

WILLIAMS, GLANVILLE L. *The Mental Element in Crime*. London: Oxford University Press, 1965.

WITTMAN, DONALD. "Punishment as Retribution." *Theory and Decision*, 4 (1974), 209 ff.

WOLFGANG, MARVIN E. *Crime and Race*. New York: Institute of Human Relations Press, 1964.

WOOTTON, BARBARA et al. *Social Science and Social Pathology*. New York: Macmillan, 1959.

ZIMRING, FRANKLIN E. et al. *Deterrence: The Legal Threat in Crime Control*. Chicago: University of Chicago Press, 1973.

Chapter 7. **Imprisonment**

CONRAD, JOHN. *Crime and Its Correction.* Berkeley: University of California Press, 1965.

DRESSLER, DAVID. *Practice and Theory of Probation and Parole.* New York: Columbia University Press, 1969.

EDWARDS, GEORGE. *The Police on the Urban Frontier.* New York: Institute of Human Relations Press, 1968.

FISHMAN, JOSEPH F. *Crucibles of Crime: The Shocking Story of the American Jail.* Montclair, N.J.: Smith, Patterson, 1969.

GIALLOMBARIO, ROSE. *Society of Women: A Study of a Women's Prison.* New York: John Wiley & Sons, 1966.

GLUECK, SHELDON. *Crime and Correction.* Cambridge, Mass.: Kraus Reprint Corporation, 1952.

GOLDFARB, RONALD. *Ransom: A Critique of the American Bail System.* New York: Harper & Row, 1965.

HAWKINS, GORDON. *The Prison: Policy and Practice.* Chicago: University of Chicago Press, 1976.

JOHNSON, ELMER HUBERT. *Crime, Correction and Society,* rev. edition. Homewood, Ill.: Dorsey, 1968.

KLARE, H. J. *Changing Concepts of Crime and Its Treatment.* New York: Pergamon, 1966.

LEOPOLD, NATHAN F. *Life Plus 99 Years.* Garden City, N.Y.: Doubleday, 1958.

LINDNER, ROBERT M. *Stone Walls and Men.* New York: Odyssey Press, 1946.

McGRATH, W. T., ed. *Crime and Its Treatment in Canada.* New York: St. Martin's, 1965.

MORRIS, NORVAL. *The Future of Imprisonment.* Chicago: University of Chicago Press, 1974.

_____. "The Future of Imprisonment: Toward a Punitive Philosophy." *Michigan Law Review,* **72** (1974), 1161 ff.

MORRIS, PAULINE. *Prisoners and Their Families.* London: George Allen and Unwin, 1965.

RIVELLO, J. ROBERTA. "The Prison As a Surd Community: A Solution." *Aitia,* **4** (1976), 21 ff.

SHERIZEN, SANFORD. *A Bibliography of Imprisonment and Its Alternatives: Selected Current European and North American Sources.* Monticello, Ill.: Council of Planning Librarians, 1975.

SOMMER, ROBERT. *The End of Imprisonment.* New York: Oxford University Press, 1976.

STILLMAN, PETER. "Prisons and Punishment." *Journal of Social Philosophy,* **5** (1974), 11 ff.

THOMAS, D. A. *Principles of Sentencing.* New York: Heineman, 1970.

VON HIRSCH, ANDREW. *Doing Justice: The Choice of Punishments.* Report of the Committee for the Study of Incarceration. New York: Hill and Wang, 1976.

WALKER, NIGEL. *Sentencing in a Rational Society.* New York: Basic Books, 1970.

WILKINS, LESLIE T. *Evaluation of Penal Measures.* New York: Random House, 1969.

Chapter 8. The Death Penalty

BEDAU, HUGO A., ed. *Capital Punishment in the United States*. New York: AMS Press, 1976.

————. *The Death Penalty in America*, rev. ed. Garden City, N.Y.: Doubleday, 1965.

————. "Deterrence and the Death Penalty: A Reconsideration." *Journal of Criminal Law, Criminology, and Police Science*, 62 (1971), 539 ff.

————. "The Right to Die by Firing Squad." *Hastings Center Report*, 7 (Feb. 1977), 5 ff.

BLACK, CHARLES LUND. *Capital Punishment: The Inevitability of Caprice and Mistake*. New York: Norton, 1974.

CHAUNCEY, ROBERT. "Deterrence: Certainty, Severity, and Skyjacking." *Criminology*, 12 (1975), 447 ff.

CHRISTOPH, JAMES B. *Capital Punishment and British Politics*. Chicago: University of Chicago Press, 1962.

CONWAY, DAVID A. "Capital Punishment and Deterrence: Some Considerations in Dialogue Form." *Philosophy and Public Affairs*, 3 (1974), 431 ff.

FOX, K. O. "Capital Punishment and Terrorist Murder: The Continuing Debate [Great Britain]." *Army Quarterly and Defense Journal*, 106 (1976), 189 ff.

GARDINER, GERALD. *Capital Punishment as a Deterrent*. London: Gollancz, 1956.

GOWERS, SIR ERNEST. *A Life for a Life*. London: Chatto and Windus, 1956.

HALE, LESLIE. *Hanged in Error*. Baltimore: Penguin, 1961.

JOYCE, J. A. *Capital Punishment: A World View*. New York: Thomas Nelson & Sons, 1961.

KOESTLER, ARTHUR. *Reflections on Hanging*. New York: Macmillan, 1957.

KOESTLER, ARTHUR, and C. H. RALPH. *Hanged by the Neck*. Baltimore: Penguin, 1961.

LONG, THOMAS A. "Capital Punishment: 'Cruel and Unusual'?" *Ethics*, 83 (1973), 214 ff.

PASSELL, PETER. "The Deterrent Effect of the Death Penalty: A Statistical Test." *Stanford Law Review*, 28 (1975), 61 ff.

POTTER, JOHN D. *The Art of Hanging*. New York: A. S. Barnes, 1969.

The Royal Commission on Capital Punishment 1949–1953 Report. (Cmd. 8932.)

SATRE, THOMAS W. "The Irrationality of Capital Punishment." *Southwest Journal of Philosophy*, 6 (1975), 75 ff.

SCHEDLER, GEORGE. "Capital Punishment and Its Deterrent Effect." *Social Theory and Practice*, 4 (1976), 47 ff.

SELLIN, J. T., ed. *Capital Punishment*. New York: Harper & Row, 1967.

SELLIN, THOMAS. *The Death Penalty*. Philadelphia: American Law Institute, 1959.

"Statistical Evidence on the Deterrent Effect of Capital Punishment," *Yale Law Journal*, 85 (1975), 164–227. (Three articles, tables, and charts.)

WELLING, B. and L. A. HIPFNER. "Cruel and Unusual? Capital Punishment in Canada." *University of Toronto Law Journal*, 26 (1976), 55 ff.

WOLFE, BURTON H. *Pileup on Death Row*. Garden City, N. Y.: Doubleday, 1973.

YUNKER, JAMES A. "Is the Death Penalty a Deterrent to Homicide? Some Time Series Evidence." *Journal of Behavioral Economics,* 5 (1976), 45 ff.

ZEISEL, H. "Deterrent Effect of the Death Penalty: Facts v. Faiths." *Supreme Court Review* (1976), 317 ff.

The Ehrlich Deterrence Debate

BAILEY, WILLIAM C. and RONALD W. SMITH. "Punishment: Its Severity and Certainty." *Journal of Criminal Law, Criminology, and Police Science,* 65 (1974), 530 ff.

BALDUS, DAVID C. and JAMES W. L. COLE. "A Comparison of the Work of Thorsten Sellin and Isaac Ehrlich on the Deterrent Effect of Capital Punishment." *Yale Law Journal,* 85 (1975), 170 ff.

BECKER, GAY S. "Crime and Punishment: An Economic Approach." *Journal of Political Economy,* 76 (1968), 169 ff.

BOWERS, WILLIAM J. and GLENN L. PIERCE. "The Illusion of Deterrence in Isaac Ehrlich's Research on Capital Punishment." *Yale Law Journal,* 85 (1975), 187 ff.

EHRLICH, ISAAC. "Participation in Illegitimate Activities: A Theoretical and Empirical Investigation." *Journal of Political Economy,* 81 (1973), 521 ff.

_____. "The Deterrent Effect of Capital Punishment: A Question of Life and Death." *American Economic Review,* 65 (1975), 397 ff.

_____. "Deterrence: Evidence and Inference." *Yale Law Journal,* 85 (1975), 209 ff.

GIBBS, JACK D. "Crime, Punishment and Deterrence." *Social Science Quarterly,* 48 (1971), 515 ff.

PHILLIPS, LLAD and HAROLD L. VOTEY, JR. "An Economic Analysis of the Deterrent Effect of Law Enforcement on Criminal Activity." *Journal of Criminal Law, Criminology, and Police Science,* 63 (1972), 330 ff.

VAN DEN HAAG, ERNEST. "On Deterrence and the Death Penalty." *Journal of Criminal Law, Criminology and Police Science,* 60 (1969).

Chapter 9. Truth in the Marketplace: Advertising, Salesmen, and Swindlers

ALEXANDER, G. J. *Honesty and Competition.* Syracuse, N.Y.: Syracuse University Press, 1967.

BACKMAN, JULES. *Advertising and Competition.* New York: New York University Press, 1967.

BARRIE, GORDON J., and AUDREY L. DEAMOND. *The Consumer, Society and the Law,* rev. ed. London: MacGibbon and Kee, Ltd., 1966.

BAUER, R. A., and S. A. GREYSER. *Advertising in America: The Consumer View.* Boston: Harvard University, Graduate School of Business Administration, 1967.

BERTON, PIERRE. *The Big Sell.* New York: Knopf, 1963.

BURROW, JAMES G. *AMA: Voice of American Medicine.* Baltimore: The Johns Hopkins Press, 1963.

BUZZI, GIANCARLO. *Advertising: Its Cultural and Political Effects,* trans. by B. David Garmize, Minneapolis: University of Minnesota Press, 1968.

CONE, FAIRFAX M. *With All Its Faults: A Candid Account of Forty Years in Advertising.* Boston: Little, Brown, 1969.

Cox, Edward F. *The Nader Report on the Federal Trade Commission.* New York: Richard W. Baron, 1969.

Cramp, Arthur J. *Nostrums and Quackery and Pseudo-Medicine.* Chicago: University of Chicago Press, 1936.

Freedom of Information Conference, University of Missouri. *Freedom of Information in the Market Place.* Fulton, Mo.: Avid Bell Press, 1967.

Geller, Max A. *Advertising at the Crossroads.* New York: Ronald Press, 1952.

Gentry, Curt. *The Vulnerable Americans.* Garden City, N.Y.: Doubleday, 1966.

Gould, Leslie. *The Manipulators.* New York: David McKay, 1966.

Hancock, Ralph, and Henry Chafetz. *The Compleat Swindler.* New York: Macmillan, 1968.

Hutchinson, R. A. *The Gospel According to Madison Avenue.* New York: Bruce, 1969.

McClellan, Grant S., ed. *The Consuming Public.* New York: H. W. Wilson, 1968.

Magnuson, W. G., and Jean Carper. *Dark Side of the Marketplace: The Plight of the American Consumer.* Englewood Cliffs, N.J.: Prentice-Hall, 1968.

Margolius, Sidney. *Innocent Consumer vs. the Exploiters.* New York: Simon and Shuster, 1967.

Marshall, M. L. *F.T.C. and Deceptive Advertising.* Freedom of Information Center Report No. 183. Columbia: University of Missouri School of Journalism, 1967.

Masters, Dexter L. *The Intelligent Buyer and the Telltale Seller.* New York: Knopf, 1966.

Mintz, Morton. *By Prescription Only,* 2nd ed. Boston: Beacon Press, 1967.

Ogilvy, David. *Confessions of an Advertising Man.* New York: Atheneum, 1963.

Oppenheim, S. C. *Cases on Federal Anti-Trust Laws.* St. Paul, Minn.: West, 1968.

Packard, Vance. *Hidden Persuaders.* New York: David McKay, 1957.

_____. *Status Seekers.* New York: David McKay, 1959.

Rivers, William L., and W. L. Schramm. *Responsibility in Mass Communication,* rev. ed. New York: Harper & Row, 1969.

Sanford, David, ed. *Hot War on the Consumer.* New York: Pitman, 1969.

Sargent, W. W. *The Battle for the Mind.* Garden City, N.Y.: Doubleday, 1957.

Tyler, Poyntz, ed. *Advertising in America.* New York: H. W. Wilson, 1959.

Young, James Harvey. *The Medical Messiahs: A Social History of Health Quackery in Twentieth Century America.* Princeton, N.J.: Princeton University Press, 1967.

Chapter 10. Competition and Corporate Responsibility

Berge, Wendell. *Cartels: Challenge to a Free World.* Washington, D.C.: Public Affairs Press, 1944.

Bunting, John R. *The Hidden Face of Free Enterprise: The Strange Economics of the American Businessman.* New York: McGraw-Hill, 1964.

FRIEDMAN, MILTON. *Capitalism and Freedom*. Chicago: University of Chicago Press, 1962.

HARLAN, H. C., ed. *Readings in Economics and Politics*. New York: Oxford University Press, 1961.

HAVENGA, J. J. D. *Retailing: Competition and Trade Practices*. Leiden, Holland: A. W. Sijthoff, 1973.

HAYEK, F. A. *The Constitution of Liberty*. Chicago: University of Chicago Press, 1960.

HUNTER, ALEX, ed. *Monopoly and Competition*. New York: Penguin, 1969.

KEETON, PAGE and MARSHALL S. SHAPO. *Products and the Consumer: Defective and Dangerous Products*. Mineola, N.Y.: Foundation Press, 1970.

KEFAUVER, ESTES. *In a Few Hands: Monopoly Power in America*. New York: Pantheon Books, 1963.

KINTER, EARL W. *An Antitrust Primer*. New York: Macmillan, 1964.

MASSEL, MARK S. *Competition and Monopoly: Legal and Economic Issues*. Washington, D.C.: The Brookings Institution, 1962.

MUELLER, WILLARD F. *A Primer on Monopoly and Competition*. New York: Random House, 1970.

SHEPERD, WILLIAM G. *Market Power and Economic Welfare: An Introduction*. New York: Random House, 1970.

STERN, LOUIS W. and JOHN R. GRABNER, JR. *Competition in the Marketplace*. Glenview, Ill.: Scott, Foresman & Co., 1970.

THEOBALD, ROBERT. *Free Men and Free Markets*. New York: Clarkson N. Potter, 1963.

Chapter 11. Affirmative Action and Reverse Discrimination

BAYLES, MICHAEL D. "Compensatory Reverse Discrimination in Hiring." *Social Theory and Practice*, 2 (1973), 301 ff.

_____. "Reparations to Wronged Groups." *Analysis*, 33 (1973), 182 ff.

BLACK, VIRGINIA. "The Erosion of Legal Principles in the Creation of Legal Principles." *Ethics*, 84 (1974), 93 ff.

BLACKSTONE, WILLIAM T. "Compensatory Justice and Affirmative Action." *Proceedings of the Catholic Philosophical Association*, 49 (1975), 218 ff.

_____. "Reverse Discrimination and Compensatory Justice." *Social Theory and Practice*, 3 (1975), 253 ff.

_____ and ROBERT D. HESLEP, eds. *Social Justice and Preferential Treatment: Women and Racial Minorities in Education and Business*. Athens, Georgia: University of Georgia Press, 1977.

BURKE, ARMAND. "Another View of Reverse Discrimination." *Philosophical Exchange*, 1 (1975), 17 ff.

COWAN, J. L. "Inverse Discrimination." *Analysis*, 33.

CRANDALL, JOHN C. "Affirmative Action: Goals and Consequences." *Philosophical Exchange*, 1 (1974), 21 f.

EZORSKY, GERTRUDE. "It's Mine." *Philosophy and Public Affairs*, 3 (1974), 321 ff.

FEINBERG, JOEL. "Noncomparative Justice." *Philosophical Review*, 83 (1974), 297 ff.

FRIED, MARLENE G. "In Defense of Preferential Hiring." *Philosophical Forum*, 5 (1973), 309 ff.

GLAZER, NATHAN. *Affirmative Discrimination: Ethnic Inequality and Public Policy.* New York: Basic Books, 1975.

GOLDMAN, ALAN H. "Affirmative Action." *Philosophy and Public Affairs,* 5 (1976), 178 ff.

————. "Limits to the Justifications of Reverse Discrimination." *Social Theory and Practice,* 3 (1975), 289 ff.

GOLIGHTLY, CORNELIUS L. "Justice and 'Discrimination For' in Higher Education." *Philosophical Exchange,* 1 (1974), 5 ff.

GOVIER, TRUDY. "Woman's Place." *Philosophy,* 49 (1974), 303 ff.

GROSS, BARRY R. "Is Turnabout Fair Play?" *Journal of Critical Analysis,* 5 (1975), 126 ff.

————, ed. *Reverse Discrimination.* Buffalo: Prometheus Books, 1977.

HARE, ROBERT P. *Affirmative Action in Higher Education: A Selected and Annotated Bibliography.* Monticello, Ill.: Council of Planning Librarians, 1977.

LUCAS, J. R. "Because You Are a Woman." *Philosophy,* 48 (1971), 161 ff.

MARTIN, MICHAEL. "Pedagogical Arguments for Preferential Hiring and Tenuring of Women Teachers in the University." *Philosophical Forum,* 5 (1973), 325 ff.

McGARY, HOWARD, JR. "Reparations and 'Inverse Discrimination.'" *Dialogue,* 17 (1974), 8 ff.

MELDEN, A. I., ed. *Human Rights.* Belmont, Calif.: Wadsworth, 1970.

MILL, JOHN STUART. *The Subjection of Women.* London: Longmans, 1869.

NAGEL, THOMAS. "Equal Treatment and Compensatory Discrimination." *Philosophy and Public Affairs,* 2 (1973), 348 ff.

NEWTON, LISA H. "Reverse Discrimination As Unjustified." *Ethics,* 83 (1973), 308 ff.

NICKEL, JAMES W. "Classification by Race in Compensatory Programs." *Ethics,* 84 (1974), 146 ff.

————. "Discrimination and Morally Relevant Characteristics." *Analysis,* 32 (1972).

————. "Should Reparations Be to Individuals or to Groups?" *Analysis,* 34 (1974), 154 ff.

NUNN, WILLIAM A. III. "Reverse Discrimination." *Analysis,* 34 (1974), 151 ff.

SHER, GEORGE. "Justifying Reverse Discrimination in Employment." *Philosophy and Public Affairs,* 4 (1975), 159 ff.

SHINER, ROGER A. "Individuals, Groups, and Inverse Discrimination." *Analysis,* 33 (1973), 185 ff.

SIMON, ROBERT. "Preferential Hiring: A Reply to Judith Jarvis Thomson." *Philosophy and Public Affairs,* 3 (1974), 312 ff.

TAYLOR, PAUL W. "Reverse Discrimination and Compensatory Justice." *Analysis,* 33 (1973), 177 ff.

THALBERG, IRVING. "Justification of Institutional Racism." *Philosophical Forum,* 3 (1972), 243 ff.

————. "Reverse Discrimination and the Future." *Philosophical Forum,* 5 (1973), 294 ff.

THOMSON, JUDITH JARVIS. "Preferential Hiring." *Philosophy and Public Affairs,* 2 (1973), 364 ff.

VETTERLING, MARY. "Some Common Sense Notes on Preferential Hiring." *Philosophical Forum,* 5 (1973), 320 ff.

WASSERSTROM, RICHARD. "The University and the Case for Preferential Treatment." *Philosophical Quarterly,* 13 (1976), 165 ff.

Chapter 12. Civil Disobedience

AMERICAN ACADEMY OF POLITICAL AND SOCIAL SCIENCE. *Protest in the Sixties.* Philadelphia: American Academy of Political and Social Sciences, 1969.

BEDAU, HUGO A., ed. *Civil Disobedience: Theory and Practice.* New York: Pegasus, 1969.

BELL, INGE P. *CORE and the Strategy of Non-violence.* New York: Random House, 1968.

BERRIGAN, DANIEL. *No Bars to Manhood.* New York: Bantam, 1970.

BICKEL, ALEXANDER M. *The Morality of Consent.* New Haven: Yale University Press, 1975.

BROWN, STUART M., JR. "Civil Disobedience." *Journal of Philosophy,* 58 (1961).

CHILDRESS, JAMES F. "Nonviolent Resistance: Trust and Risk Taking." *Journal of Religion and Ethics,* 1 (1973), 87 ff.

COHEN, CARL. *Civil Disobedience.* New York: Columbia University Press, 1971.

————. "Civil Disobedience and the Law." *Rutgers Law Review,* 21 (1966).

COHEN, MARSHALL. "Civil Disobedience in a Constitutional Democracy." *The Massachusetts Review,* 10 (1969).

COX, ARCHIBALD, et al. *Civil Rights, the Constitution and the Courts.* Cambridge, Mass.: Harvard University Press, 1967.

CROCKENBERG, VINCENT. "Civil Disobedience As Public Education: The Case For Daniel Ellsberg." *Journal of Thought,* 9 (1974), 104 ff.

CROZIER, BRIAN. *A Theory of Conflict.* New York: Scribners, 1974.

DWORKIN, RONALD. "A Theory of Civil Disobedience," in Milton Munitz et al. (eds.), *Ethics and Social Disobedience.* New York: New York University Press, 1968.

ERIKSON, ERIK H. *Gandhi's Truth.* New York: Norton, 1969.

FARRELL, DANIEL M. "Paying the Penalty: Justifiable Civil Disobedience and the Problem of Punishment." *Philosophy and Public Affairs,* 6 (1977), 165 ff.

FINN, JAMES. *Protest: Pacifism and Politics; Some Passionate Views on War and Nonviolence.* New York: Random House, 1968.

GANDHI, M. K. *Gandhi on Non-Violence.* New York: New Directions, 1966.

HAKSAR, VINIT. "Coercive Proposals (Rawls and Gandhi)." *Political Theory,* 4 (1976), 65 ff.

HARE, A. P., and H. H. BLUMBERG, eds. *Non-Violent Direct Action.* New York: World, 1968.

HASKINS, JAMES. *Resistance: Profiles in Nonviolence.* Garden City, N.Y.: Doubleday, 1970.

HEIMLER, EUGENE. *Resistance Against Tyranny.* New York: Praeger, 1967.

HERSHBERGER, GUY F. *War, Peace, and Nonresistance,* 3rd rev. ed. Herald Press, 1959.

HOOK, SIDNEY. "Social Protest and Civil Disobedience," in Paul Kurtz (ed.), *Moral Problems in Contemporary Society.* Englewood Cliffs, N.J.: Prentice-Hall, 1968.

————. "In Defense of Terminological Sobriety: A Reply to Professor Kellner." *Journal of Politics*, **37** (1975).

HUGHES, GRAHAM. "Civil Disobedience and the Political-Question Doctrine." *New York University Law Review*, **43** (1968).

JAMES, GENE G. "The Orthodox Theory of Civil Disobedience." *Social Theory and Practice*, **2** (1973), 475 ff.

————. "Socrates on Civil Disobedience and Rebellion." *Southern Journal of Philosophy*, **11** (1973), 119 ff.

KADISH, MORTIMER R. and SANFORD R. KADISH. *Discretion to Disobey: A Study of Lawful Departures from Legal Rules*. Stanford: Stanford University Press, 1973.

KAPLAN, MORTON A. *Dissent and the State in Peace and War*. New York: Dunellen, 1970.

KELLNER, MENACHEM MARC. "Democracy and Civil Disobedience." *Journal of Politics*, **37** (1975), 899 ff.

KELLY, DEREK A. "Conditions for Legal Obligation." *Southwestern Journal of Philosophy*, **4** (1973), 43 ff.

KENTON, MORRIS. "The Morality of Civil Disobedience." *Texas Law Review*, **43** (1965).

KING, MARTIN LUTHER, JR. *Why We Can't Wait*. New York: New American Library, 1964.

KURTZ, PAUL, ed. *Moral Problems in Contemporary Society*. Englewood Cliffs, N.J.: Prentice-Hall, 1969.

LENS, SIDNEY, ed. *Non-Violence in America*. Indianapolis: Bobbs-Merrill, 1966.

LENS, SIDNEY. *Radicalism in America*. New York: Macmillan, 1969.

LOMAX, LOUIS E. *The Negro Revolt*. New York: New American Library, 1963.

LYND, STAUGHTON, ed. *Nonviolence in America: A Documentary History*. Indianapolis: Bobbs-Merrill, 1966.

MADDEN, EDWARD H. *Civil Disobedience and Moral Law in Nineteenth-Century American Philosophy*. Seattle: University of Washington Press, 1970.

MILLER, W. R. *Nonviolence: A Christian Interpretation*. New York: Schocken, 1966.

Monist, The. "Legal Obligation and Civil Disobedience." **54**, No. 4 (Oct. 1970).

MORISON, SAMUEL ELIOT, et al. *Dissent in Three American Wars*. Cambridge, Mass.: Harvard University Press, 1970.

MORREALL, JOHN. "The Justifiability of Violent Civil Disobedience." *Canadian Journal of Philosophy*, **6** (1976), 35 ff.

MURPHY, JEFFRIE, ed. *Civil Disobedience and Violence*. Belmont, Cal.: Wadsworth Publishing Co., 1971.

PENNOCK, ROLAND J. and JOHN W. CHAPMAN, eds. *Political and Legal Obligation* (Nomos XII). New York: Atherton Press, 1970.

PITKIN, HANNAH. "Obligation and Consent." *American Political Science Review*, **5** (1969), 990 ff.

ROBERTS, ADAM, ed. *Civilian Resistance as a National Defence Non-Violent Action Against Aggression*. Baltimore: Penguin Books, 1967.

SCHWARZ, ROBERT. "Disobeying the Law: A Critique of a Critique." *Journal of Social Philosophy,* **4** (1973), 11 ff.

SHUMAN, SAMUEL I., ed. *Law and Disorder: The Legitimation of Direct Action as an Instrument of Social Policy.* Detroit: Wayne State University Press, 1971.

SIBLEY, M. O. *The Obligation to Disobey.* New York: Council on Religion and International Affairs.

SINGER, PETER. *Democracy and Disobedience.* Oxford: Clarendon Press, 1973.

STEVENS, FRANKLIN. *If This Be Treason.* New York: P. H. Wyden, 1970.

STEVICK, D. B. *Civil Disobedience and the Christian.* New York: Seabury, 1969.

STRINGFELLOW, WILLIAM. *Dissenter in a Great Society: A Christian View of America in Crisis.* Nashville: Abingdon Press, 1967.

_____. *My People Is the Enemy: An Autobiographical Polemic.* Garden City, N.Y.: Doubleday, 1966.

THALBERG, IRVING. "Philosophical Problems of Civil Disobedience." *Scientia,* **101** (1966).

THOMAS, NORMAN M. *Great Dissenters.* New York: Norton, 1970.

TOLSTOI, LEO N. *Tolstoy's Writings on Civil Disobedience and Nonviolence.* New York: Bergman Publishers, 1967.

WASKOW, A. *From Race Riot to Sit-in: 1919 and the 1960s.* Garden City, N.Y.: Doubleday, 1966.

U.S. NATIONAL ADVISORY COMMISSION ON CIVIL DISORDERS. *Report.* New York: Bantam, 1968.

U.S. NATIONAL COMMISSION ON THE CAUSES AND PREVENTION OF VIOLENCE. *Rights in Conflict: The Walker Report to The National Commission on the Causes and Prevention of Violence.* New York: Bantam, 1968.

U.S. NATIONAL COMMISSION ON THE CAUSES AND PREVENTION OF VIOLENCE. *To Establish Justice, To Insure Domestic Tranquility: The Final Report of the National Commission on the Causes and Prevention of Violence.* New York: Bantam, 1970.

VAN EIKEMA HOMMES, H. J. "The Limits of the Legal Competence of the State." *Philosophia Reformata,* **41** (1976), 9 ff.

VEYSEY, LAWRENCE R. *Law and Resistance: American Attitudes Toward Authority.* New York: Harper & Row, 1970.

WALZER, MICHAEL L. *Obligations.* Cambridge, Mass.: Harvard University Press, 1970.

_____. "The Obligation to Disobey." *Ethics,* **77** (1967).

WASSERSTROM, RICHARD A. "The Obligation to Obey the Law." *U.C.L.A. Law Review,* **10** (1963).

WEINGARTNER, RUDOLF H. "Justifying Civil Disobedience." *Columbia Forum,* **9** (1966).

WILHOIT, FRANCIS M. *The Politics of Massive Resistance.* New York: Braziller, 1973.

WITTNER, LAWRENCE S. *Rebels Against War.* New York: Columbia University Press, 1969.

WOOZLEY, A. D. "Civil Disobedience and Punishment." *Ethics,* **86** (1976), 323 ff.

ZAHN, G. C. *War, Conscience and Dissent.* New York: Hawthorne, 1967.

ZASHIN, ELIOT M. *Civil Disobedience and Democracy.* New York: Free Press, 1972.

ZINN, HOWARD. *Disobedience and Democracy: Nine Fallacies on Law and Order.* New York: Random House, 1968.

ZWIEBACH, BURTON. *Civility and Disobedience.* New York: Columbia University Press, 1975.

Chapter 13. Terrorism, Guerrilla Warfare, and International Morality

ASPREY, ROBERT B. *War in the Shadows: The Guerrilla in History.* Garden City, N.Y.: Doubleday, 1975.

BEGIN, MENACHEM. *The Revolt: Story of the Irgun,* tr. Samuel Katz. New York: Henry Schuman, 1951. Rev. ed., New York: Nash, 1977.

BELL, J. BOWYER. *Transnational Terror.* Washington, D.C.: American Enterprise Institute for Public Policy Research, Hoover Institution Studies, 1975.

BINGHAM, JOSEPH W. *Piracy.* Cambridge, Mass.: Harvard Law School, 1932.

BURTON, ANTHONY M. *Urban Terrorism: Theory, Practice, and Response.* New York: The Free Press, 1975.

CARLTON, DAVID, ed. *International Terrorism.* New York: John Wiley & Sons, 1975.

COCHRAN, HAMILTON. *Freebooters of the Red Sea: Pirates, Politicians and Pieces of Eight.* Indianapolis: Bobbs-Merrill, 1965.

CURTIS, MICHAEL, et al., eds. *The Palestinians: People, History, Politics.* New Brunswick, N.J.: Transaction Books, 1975.

FAIRBAIRN, GEOFFREY. *Revolutionary Guerrilla Warfare: The Countryside Version.* Harmondsworth, England: Penguin Books, 1974.

GAUCHER, ROLAND. *The Terrorists: From Tsarist Russia to the O.A.S.,* tr. Paula Spurlin. London: Secker & Warburg, 1968.

GOSSE, PHILIP. *The History of Piracy.* London: Longmans, 1932.

KATZ, SAMUEL. *Days of Fire.* Garden City, N.Y.: Doubleday, 1968.

LAQUEUR, WALTER. "The Futility of Terrorism." *Harper's,* **99** (March 1976), 99 ff.

LEIDEN, CARL and KARL M. SCHMITT. *The Politics of Violence: Revolution in the Modern World.* Englewood Cliffs, N.J.: Prentice-Hall, 1968.

MALLIN, JAY, ed. *Terror and Urban Guerrillas: A Study of Tactics and Documents.* Coral Gables, Fla.: University of Miami Press, 1971.

MORF, GUSTAVE. *Terror in Quebec: Case Studies of the FLQ.* Toronto: Clarke, Irwin & Co., 1970.

OSANKA, FRANKLIN M. *Modern Guerrilla Warfare.* New York: The Free Press, 1962.

PIKE, DOUGLAS. *Viet Cong: The Organization and Techniques of the National Liberation Front of South Vietnam.* Cambridge, Mass.: MIT Press, 1966.

STATE OF ISRAEL, MINISTRY FOR FOREIGN AFFAIRS. *Accessories to Terror.* Jerusalem, 1972.

RAPAPORT, DAVID C. *Assassination and Terrorism.* Toronto: Canadian Broadcasting Corp., 1971.

STEVENSON, WILLIAM. *Ninety Minutes at Entebbe.* New York: Bantam, 1976.

WEISBAND, EDWARD and DAMIR ROGULY. "Palestinian Terrorism: Violence, Verbal Strategy, and Legitimacy," in YONAH ALEXANDER, ed., *International Terrorism: National, Regional, and Global Perspectives.* New York: Praeger, 1976.

WILKINSON, PAUL. *Political Terrorism.* New York: John Wiley & Sons, 1974.

YANIV, ALEXANDER. *P.L.O.: A Profile.* Jerusalem: Israel Universities Study Group for Middle Eastern Affairs, 1974.

Index

Major topics are indicated by SMALL CAPITALS. Within a given topic, pages that contain major discussions of the topic are indicated by **boldface** type.

abnormal, equated with *unnatural,* 55
abnormal growth, as term to apply to aborted fetus, 104
ABORTION, 11, 14, 54, **74ff.**, 237, 265, 330; and acorn analogy, 111f.; advertising of, 263; and church doctrine, 81ff.; and consent of husband or parents of mother, 101; and danger to health of existing child, 97; and discrimination against poor or blacks, 121; and fear of governmental abuses, 120; and genocide, 115; and hereditary diseases, 106f.; and infanticide, 112f., 115; and Medicaid, 102, 122; and Nazi tyranny, 115; and promiscuity, 118f.; and racial purification programs, 112; and the right of privacy, 99ff.; and the blueprint analogy, 112; and the Hitler argument, 114ff.; and the "tacit promise" argument, 119f.; and the United States Supreme Court, 90, 98ff., arguments for liberal laws, 120ff.; by quack doctors, 105; compulsory, 120, 172; history of, **79ff.**; in ancient Greece and Rome, 79ff.; Jewish doctrine on, 91ff.; modern developments, 86ff.; philosophical arguments against 107ff.; psychological effects of, 121; right to, distinct from right to kill fetus, 124f.; socialization argument,

112; therapeutic, 88, 97; to save mother's life, 197; violates fetus's right to life, 108
abstinence, as a means of contraception, 88
Abulafia, Meir, 97
accused, rights of, 192ff.
act utilitarianism, 212
admissions tests, culturally biased, 321ff.
adultery, 12ff., 30, 80, 83
ADVERTISING, 5, 155, **262ff.**; and children, **285ff.**; and half-truths, 292; and indecent or immoral causes or practices, 293; and particular audiences, **285ff.**; and personal hygiene, 266; and public service, 284; and sophistry, **265ff.**; misleading, **287ff.**; of abortion clinics, 102, 263; of dangerous products, 283ff.; of immoral or unlawful activities, 265; of poisons, 285; professional, 264
AFFIRMATIVE ACTION, **311ff.**; aims of, 317; and American Indians, 340; and Asian Americans, 322; and compensatory justice, 337; and criteria for minority classification, 321, 337f.; and culturally deprived students, 322; and desert, 332; and ethnic diversity, 328; and Italian Americans, 340; and merit, **329ff.**; and need, 332; and

447

Bentham, Jeremy, 211
Bergen-Belsen, 383
Bergler, Dr. Edmund, 41ff.
Bernardine, 83
Bernadotte, Count Folke, 418, n. 4
Berrigan, Daniel, 354, 357f.
bestiality, 161
Bethlehem Steel Corp., 306
Better Business Bureaus, 278
Bhutto, Ali, 75
Bible, 81f.; on homosexuality, 30ff.; and retribution, 214
Bickel, Alexander, 328
Bigelow, Albert, 360
Bill of Rights, 77. *See also* United States Constitution, 1st to 10th Amendments
birth control. *See* contraception
Bjorklund, Lasse, 208f.
Black September, 380
Black, Justice Hugo, 50, 147, 148, 166, 182, 184, 197, 250, 366
Blackmun, Justice Harry, 98, 142
blacks, and affirmative action, **311ff.**; and jury service, 195; and slavery, 339; and the death penalty, 237, 247ff.; discrimination against, 1ff., 51, 310ff.
Blackstone, William, 47
blanquism, 385
blood transfusions, compulsory, 50f.
Bloody Friday, 379
Blue Laws. *See* Sunday closing laws
Boccaccio, Giovanni, 157
bodily organs, "natural" uses of, 55f.
Bok, Judge Curtis, 165f.
Bolshevik terror, 384
book clubs, 292
boycotts, 302
Boy Scouts, 286
Boyle's Law, 53
Brandeis, Justice Louis Dembitz, 148, 197, 199
Brennan, Justice William Joseph, Jr., 169, 171, 172, 174, 366
Breton Liberation Front, 393
Bruno, Giordano, 157
Buckley Amendment, 102
Bukovsky, Vladimir, 128

bullfighting, 160
Burger, Chief Justice Warren E., 170, 197, 199
Burns, John, 295
bus boycotts, 368
business ethics, 3, 5, 300. *See also* advertising, competition
Butler, Samuel, 220
Butz, Earl, 138f.

Caldwell, Erskine, 157, 186
Calvin, John, 143
Campbell Soup Co., 287
Camus, Albert, 334
Canada, maximum security prisons in, 231
cancer "clinics," 281
cannibalism, 51
"Canons" of Gregory, 83
capital punishment. *See* death penalty
"Carmen," 158
"*Casti connubii*," 87
Catholic Church. *See* Roman Catholic Church *and under names of various popes and saints*
caveat emptor, 260, **270ff.**
celluloid, 307
CENSORSHIP, **125ff.**; and assumption of infallibility, 149; and "classics," 182; and littered-town-square argument, 183; and national news agencies, 130f.; and offensive displays, 161f.; and public morality, 163; and Roman Catholic Church, 126; and standards of reasonable avoidability, 161; and zoning laws, 160; case against, **181ff.**; chilling effect of, 186; clear and present danger test, 185; deterrent effect of, 163; educative effect of, 164; evil consequences of, **144ff.**; in Brazil, 128; in colleges and universities, 135ff.; in Eastern Europe, 126ff.; in Montreal, 130; in the Third World, 126, 133ff.; in the United States, 131ff.; in the Union of South Africa, 126; of artistic expression, **126ff.**; of films, 157.; of racist materials, 182f.

National Rifle Association, 132
national security and corporate responsibility, 301
National Security Agency, 131
National Steel Corporation, 306
NATURAL LAW, **346ff.**, 374; and homosexuality, **52ff.**
Natural Wave, 287
naturalization and sexual morals, 19
natural and *unnatural* as normative terms, 58f.
natural, various senses of, 52ff.
nature, interference with, not evil, 54
nature, meanings of, distinguished, 52ff.
nature, descriptive laws of, **52ff.**; prescriptive laws of, **52ff.**
Nazi concentration camps, 340
Nazi Germany, 49, 114ff., 138f., 158, 246; concentration camps, 340; racial measures, 337
needs, creation of, 276; distinguished from desires, 274ff.; false claims of, 276
Nero, 31
Netherlands, terrorism in the, 397
New York City, power failure, 211
New York Times, 132, 141, 148, 374
Nixon, Pres. Richard, 132, 261, 301
Noah, 30, 81
nonviolence, **368ff.**; as a tactic, 370ff.
Noonan, John T., 82ff.
Norquen, 282
Norinyl-1, 282
nudity, public, 161, 165
Nuremberg laws, 337; trials, 383
obligations. *See* duty

OBSCENITY, **156ff.**; and artistic distance, 175; and the average man, 168; and brutality, 176; and death, 176; and dehumanization, 159, 176; and impersonal lust, 176; and juvenile delinquency, 179; and masturbation, 179; and misleading advertising, 173; and public safety, 171; and Roman Catholic Church, 174; and sense of disgust and outrage, 164f.; and sense of privacy, 175; and sex crimes, 179;

as patently offensive, 167; as "sexual impurity," 165; community standards of, 167f., 171; definitions of, **164ff.**; dominant effect test, 169; effects of, **178ff.**; extrinsic qualities of, 172; Hicklin test of, 168f.; indefinable, 166, 186; intention of, 173; intrinsic qualities of, 172; literature, compared to, 173; no objective criteria of, 168; public displays of, 187; redeeming social value test, 167; unsolicited advertisements of, 187
Occam's Razor, 117
Oedipus, 214
Office of Civil Rights. *See under* United States
official terrorism, 382
Ogilvy, David, 294, 296
Ohio Chemical and Surgical Equipment Co., 282
Olympics, Munich, 380
On Liberty, 144ff., 285
Onan, 81, 91f., 94
One-a-Day Plus Iron, 279
optical glass, 306
Oracon, 282
oranges, coloring of, 305
Origen, 82, 85
original sin, 85f., 91, 94, 97
Oswald, Lee Harvey, 183f.
Ottoman Empire, 391
overpopulation, 74ff.
Ovulen-21, 282
Ovid, 157

pain and suffering, alleviation of, 304
pain for its own sake, 215
pain killers, 290
Pakistan, 75
Palestine Liberation Organization (PLO), **376ff.**, **393ff.**
Palestine National Council, 386
Palestinian National Covenant, **386ff.**
Palestinian terrorists, 380, **386ff.**
Parchman Prison, conjugal visits, 231
parole, 5
Panov, Valery and Galina, 127
parricide, 83